Instructor's Manual and Complete Solutions

General, Organic, and Biological

Chemistry

Structures of Life

Karen C. Timberlake

Professor Emeritus, Los Angeles Valley College

Benjamin Cummings

San Francisco • Boston • New York
Capetown • Hong Kong • London • Madrid • Mexico City
Montreal • Munich • Paris • Singapore • Sydney • Tokyo • Toronto

Acquisitions Editor: Maureen Kennedy
Project Editor: Claudia Herman
Managing Editor: Joan Marsh
Cover Designer: Tony Asaro
Cover Photographs: John Bagley, Richard Tauber
Cover Illustration: Blakeley Kim
Manufacturing Coordinator: Vivian McDougal
Marketing Manager: Christy Lawrence

ISBN 0-8053-3562-5

Benjamin
Cummings

1 2 3 4 5 6 7 8 9 10–DPC–05 04 03 02 01

www.aw.com/bc

To the Chemistry Instructor

Welcome to *General, Organic, and Biological Chemistry: Structures of Life*. This Instructor's Manual is designed to accompany the textbook, the Laboratory Manual, and the Study Guide. In each of these books I have connected the ideas of chemistry to the student's personal experiences in the real world by incorporating everyday relationships to chemistry into the text, the end of chapter problems, and the laboratory exercises.

In the first part of each chapter of this Instructor's Manual, I highlight chapter topics and give suggestions for demonstrations, activities, and laboratory experiments that can be used to illustrate the concepts. The *Laboratory Manual for General, Organic, and Biological Chemistry: Structures of Life* stresses safety information for working in a chemistry laboratory and is accompanied by a safety quiz and safety pledge. Safety may be further emphasized by showing the safety video available with the adoption of the text. Since many students are in a chemistry laboratory for the first time, I include a description of laboratory skills that may be demonstrated by the instructor before students begin a new experiment. This may be useful for a new teacher or a laboratory instructor, or it may serve as a guide for a teaching assistant who may be grading the laboratory reports. Included in each chapter is a complete set of answers and solutions for the questions and problems in the text. The solutions for the odd-numbered problems also appear in the Study Guide.

Karen C. Timberlake

The following resources are available to instructors who are qualified adopters of the text.

Instructor's Manual and Complete Solutions for *General, Organic, and Biological Chemistry: Structures of Life* and *Organic and Biological Chemistry: Structures of Life.* Highlights chapter topics and includes suggestions for the laboratory. Includes goals, demonstrations and teaching strategies, and suggested experiments for each chapter in the text. Also includes answers and solution for all problems in the text.

Report Pages with Answers to All Lab Exercises: ChemPlace Companion Website. The online Instructor's Manual for the Lab Exercises includes completed report pages and answers to all the experiments and problems in *Laboratory Manual for General, Organic, and Biological Chemistry: Structures of Life* and *Laboratory Manual for Organic and Biological Chemistry: Structures of Life.*

Test Bank by Lynn Carlson, University of Wisconsin, Parkside. Contains more than 2000 questions, including multiple choice, matching, and short answer. The Test Bank is also available in TestGen-EQ software for Windows and Macintosh, which allows instructors to scramble questions, add new questions, and select questions based on level of difficulty.

Tranparency Acetates. A set of 300 full-color transparency acetates and 50 transparency masters with problems provides key figures, tables, and illustrations from *General, Organic, and Biological Chemistry: Structures of Life* and *Organic and Biological Chemistry: Structures of Life.*

Benjamin Cummings Digital Library CD-ROM for *General, Organic, and Biological Chemistry: Structures of Life* and *Organic and Biological Chemistry: Structures of Life.* This easy-to-search CD-ROM includes every figure and table from the text. The images can be exported into PowerPoint presentations, other presentation tools, and web sites.

Laboratory Manual for General, Organic, and Biological Chemistry: Structures of Life **and** *Laboratory Manual for Organic and Biological Chemistry: Structures of Life*. The experiments in the Laboratory Manuals are coordinated with the sequence of topics in the text. Students are introduced immediately to lab safety, lab equipment, and basic laboratory skills. Students carry out laboratory investigations, develop the skills of manipulating lab equipment, gather and report data, solve problems, calculate, and draw conclusions. For each experiment, there is a discussion of the topics, pre-lab questions, report pages, and questions that relate the experimental results to the corresponding topics.

Special Edition of the Chemistry Place for *General, Organic, and Biological Chemistry: Structures of Life* **and** *Organic and Biological Chemistry: Structures of Life*. **www.chemplace.com/college** This web site, tailored specifically to *General, Organic, and Biological Chemistry: Structures of Life*, offers comprehensive and interactive teaching and learning resources for chemistry. Features include tutorials, simulations, practice quizzes, web links, career resources, and an interactive periodic table. The online syllabus manager allows instructors to post class notes and assignments on the Web. Packaged with every new copy of the book

Study Guide with Selected Solutions for General, Organic, and Biological Chemistry: Structures of Life **and** *Study Guide with Selected Solutions for Organic and Biological Chemistry: Structures of Life*. The Study Guides review the basic concepts, provide learning drills, and give practice tests, all with answers. At the end of each chapter in the Study Guides, there is a practice exam that students may group together to make a comprehensive exam. All the sections in the Study Guides are keyed to the learning goals in the text for easy cross-referencing. By utilizing the practice tests, students can identify areas of difficulty and review the material again. Also contains complete solutions to odd-numbered problems in the text.

The Chemistry Tutor Center
www.aw.com/tutorcenter
Provides one-to-one tutoring by phone, fax, email, and/or the Internet during evening hours and weekends. Qualified college instructors answer questions and provide instruction regarding examples, exercises, and other content from the text.

Contents

Study Goals
Chapter Outline with Health and Environment Notes
Demonstrations and Classroom Activities
Suggestions for Experiments
Laboratory Skills to Demonstrate
Answers and Solutions to Text Problems

Measurements

This chapter is crucial to the development of problem solving for the rest of the text. Students review math and learn to do calculations while working everyday examples of problems in health and medicine using metric units. Students confront their fear of word problems by learning a system for analyzing and solving work problems. Scientific notations, accuracy and precision and the use of a calculator are now included in the chapter. It is a chapter that is well worth taking some time on.

Study Goals
- Learn the base units and abbreviations for the metric (SI) system.
- Distinguish between measured numbers and exact numbers.
- Determine the number of significant figures in a measurement.
- Use prefixes to change base units to larger or smaller units.
- Form conversion factors from units in an equality
- Use metric units, U.S. units, percent and density as conversion factors.
- In problem solving, convert the initial unit of a measurement to another unit.
- Round off a calculator answer to report an answer with the correct number of significant figures.
- Calculate temperature values in degrees Celsius and Kelvins.

Chapter Outline

1.1 **Units of Measurement**
    Explore Your World: Units Listed on Labels
1.2 **Scientific Notation**
1.3 **Measured and Exact Numbers**
1.4 **Significant Figures**
    Explore Your World: Temperature Scales on Thermometers
1.5 **Significant Figures in Calculations**
    Career Focus: Phlebotomist
1.6 **SI and Metric Prefixes**
1.7 **Problem Solving Using Conversion Factors**
    Explore Your World: SI and Metric Equalities on Product Labels
1.8 **Density**
    Explore Your World: Sink or Float?
    Health Note: Determination of Percentage of Body Fat
    Health Note: Specific Gravity of Urine
1.9 **Temperature**
    Health Note: Variation in Body Temperature

Chapter Summary and Demonstrations

1. Measurement and Significant Figures

Measurements in the U.S. and metric systems are compared. Consideration of real-life situations and health-related examples and at home explore activities introduce or elaborate the discussion. The student is taught to recognize and count significant figures in measurements and calculations.

Demonstration: To demonstrate differences in measuring by different observers, I pass out several sheets of paper along with metric rulers and ask the students to measure the width and the length and to calculate the area. I list some of the responses, which are in centimeters, inches or without units, some with two significant figures, and some with three. The last digit is often different. Since all of the measurements are done with the same size sheets of paper, we discuss measurements, differences in observing measuring tools, estimations, significant figures, units, and the importance of specifying units. Finally, we look at the calculation of area using their measurements and talk about the need to use significant figures when reporting calculator answers. I also take some time here to discuss calculator operations.

2. Counting Numbers, Percent and Conversion Factors

Equalities and conversion factors are carefully explained through many examples. Problem solving utilizes dimensional analysis to convert between U.S. and metric units. The emphasis on metric units, significant figures and numerical problem-solving exercises prepares the student for problem solving throughout the text.

Demonstration: To begin our study of numbers from measurement and exact numbers, I use the following kind of grid on a transparency, but expand for the number of lecture teams. I bring in bags of small M&Ms and give one to each team. They are asked to predict the number of yellow, green, brown M&Ms. You may want to add red, green, and tan. Each group could do this outside of class and bring in their results. Then they open the bag and determine the actual amounts. They calculate % and the grams per M&M (using the mass written on the package), and write their results on the transparency. We compare predictions and actual, discuss a counting number and a measured number (mass of the package contents and grams/M&M) and what to do with significant figures. This is an exercise remembered by all the students and helps to allay the fear of working with numbers in chemistry.

M and M's Statistics

Team	# MM's predict/actual	# yellow predict/actual	# brown predict/actual	% yellow	% brown	pkg mass	grams M&M
1							
2							
3							
4							

3. Density
Density is defined and used as a conversion factor.

Demonstration: I introduce density by dropping an ice cube into a beaker containing water and into one containing isopropyl alcohol. This discrepant event (ice cube sinking in the alcohol) leads to questions about the densities of the substances and the liquids and the reason one substance sinks or floats in another. Discussion follows on what adjustments are made in density to make hot air balloons rise, and divers descend or ascend.

4. Temperature
Temperature is defined and the scales used for measuring temperature are described.

Demonstration: To develop the idea of temperature units, I have students imagine that we have some unmarked thermometers that need temperature scales. We determine reference systems for a Fahrenheit scale, and then for a metric scale and mark a line for the freezing points and another line for the boiling point. Then we talk about how many units of temperature must be placed between the freezing and boiling lines. Compare the size of the °F with a °C. Use the zero points and the degree conversion factor to set up an equation that converts between °F and °C. This gives students a practical approach to the temperature equation. Then, I use everyday temperature examples to convert between the two temperature scales. Finally, we add the Kelvin scale to the group of thermometers with a similar approach to freezing and boiling points. Another equation is derived by again comparing the Celsius and Kelvin scales.

Laboratory Suggestions

The suggested experiments are from the Laboratory Manual 1e that accompanies General, Organic, and Biological Chemistry: Structures of Life.

Working Safely in the Lab

The laboratory work in the preface may be used to increase the awareness of practicing laboratory safety and waste disposal. Students learn the safety rules for working with chemicals and participating in a safe manner when carrying out laboratory procedures. The lab includes a safety quiz and a commitment to lab safety to be signed by each student. Students learn to identify common laboratory equipment. A quiz on identifying equipment and a check-in list is included.

A. Preparing for Laboratory Work
B. Handling Chemicals Safely
C. Heating Chemicals Safely
D. Waste Disposal
E. Safety Quiz
F. Laboratory Equipment A Visual Guide to Laboratory Equipment
   List of Equipment for Student Lockers

Laboratory Skills to Demonstrate
Proper attention to safe behavior in the lab
Using a sample drawer in the laboratory, describe and identify some typical laboratory equipment.

Lab 1 Measurement and Significant Figures

Students measure length, mass, and volumes of liquids and record values with units.
A. Measuring Length
B. Measuring Volume
C. Measuring Mass

Laboratory Skills to Demonstrate
Describe the units on a metric stick.
Use of a laboratory balance
Give examples of measured and exact numbers.
Reading a graduated cylinder
Writing numbers in scientific notation

Lab 2 Conversion Factors in Calculations

From length measurements, areas are calculated and the volume of a solid is determined. Volume displacement of a matching object compares two methods of volume determination. Measurements in metric and U.S. systems are used to produce metric-U.S. conversion factors for length and volume. Students determine the mass of objects on a balance and determine conversion factors using mass percent. Food products are used to derive a conversion factor for g/lb and lb/kg. Temperature conversions are done between Fahrenheit, Kelvin, and Celsius. The counting of significant figures in measured numbers and their effect on calculated answers is defined and studied. Students learn to round off calculator answer to the correct number of significant figures.

A. Rounding Off
B. Significant Figures in Calculations
C. Conversion Factors for Length
D. Conversion Factors for Volume
E. Conversion Factors for Mass
F. Percent by Mass
G. Converting Temperature

Laboratory Skills to Demonstrate

Describe the units on a metric stick.
Use of a laboratory balance
Give examples of measured and exact numbers.
Reading a graduated cylinder
Techniques of measurement using a balance, meter stick, and graduated cylinders.
Review common operations on a calculator.
Give examples of counting significant figures and using them in calculations.
Review the formulas for calculating area and volume of solids.
Demonstrate rounding off numbers.

Lab 3   Density and Specific Gravity

The mass and volume of a liquid and a solid are used to calculate density. Specific gravity for the liquids are determined using a hydrometer and compared to the value obtained earlier. The relationship between mass and volume of a liquid is graphed. The student is taught to prepare a data table, label axes with units of measurement, apply equal intervals, and to plot the data points on a graph.
A. Density of A Solid
B. Density of a Liquid
C. Specific Gravity
D. Graphing Mass and Volume

Laboratory Skills to Demonstrate

Calculations of density and specific gravity
Reading a hydrometer
Preparation of a graph

Answers and Solutions to Text Problems

Note: In some of the following solutions, the calculator display is shown in square brackets, [ ] followed by the correct answer rounded to the proper number of significant figures indicated by an arrow →. The correct units will be attached.

1.1 A student in the United States would use pounds, feet and inches, gallons, and °F, while a student in France would use kilograms, meters, liters, and °C to measure weight (mass), length, volume, and temperature, respectively.

1.2 Without units it is difficult to guess what someone is talking about. For example, replace my selection of the unit *miles* with *minutes* in part a of this problem and you may be less impressed with your friend's workout.
   a. I rode my bicycle for 15 *miles* today.   **b.** My dog weighs 45 *kilograms*.
   c. It is hot today. It is 40°C.   **d.** I lost 3.5 *pounds* last week.

1.3 Lengths in the metric system are in meters. The American system utilizes inches, feet, yards, and miles.

1.4 Units of milligrams, grams, kilograms, and metric tons are often used in mass measurements in the metric system. The American system utilizes ounces, pounds, and tons.

1.5 **a.** meters (used to measure length)   **b.** grams (mass)   **c.** milliliters (volume)
   d. meters (length)   **e.** Celsius degrees (temperature)

1.6 **a.** liter (used to measure volume)   **b.** meter (length)   **c.** kilogram (mass)
   d. gram (mass)   **e.** Kelvin (temperature)

1.7 **a.** 5.5×10^4 m   **b.** 4.8×10^2 g   **c.** 5×10^{-6} cm   **d.** 1.4×10^{-4} s

1.8 **a.** 1.8×10^8 g   **b.** 6×10^{-5} m   **c.** 7.5×10^5 g   **d.** 1.5×10^{-1} m

1.9 **a** 7.2×10^3 **b.** 3.2×10^{-2} **c.** 1×10^4 **d.** 6.8×10^{-2}

1.10 **a.** 5.5×10^{-9} **b.** 3.4×10^2 **c.** 5×10^{-8} **d.** 4×10^{-10}

1.11 **a.** 12 000   **b.** 0.0825   **c.** 4 000 000

1.13 **a.** The *estimated digit* is the last digit reported in a measurement. In 8.6 m, the 6 in the first decimal (tenths) place was estimated and has some uncertainty.
   b. The *estimated digit* is the 5 in the second decimal (hundredths) place.
   c. The *estimated digit* would be the 0 in the first decimal (tenths) place.

1.14 **a.** The 4 in the second decimal (hundredths) place
   b. The 7 in the third decimal (thousandths) place.
   c. The 8 in the first decimal (tenths) place.

1.15 Because the number of chairs was determined by counting; no measurements were involved.
1.16 It is part of a definition; one week consists of seven days.

1.17 Measured numbers are obtained using some kind of measuring tool. Exact numbers are numbers obtained by counting or from a definition in the metric or the American measuring system.
   a. measured   **b.** exact   **c.** exact   **d.** measured

1.18 **a.** exact   **b.** measured   **c.** measured   **d.** measured

1.19 **a.** not significant   **b.** significant   **c.** significant
   d. significant   **e.** not significant

1.20   **a.** no   **b.** yes   **c.** yes   **d.** yes   **e.** no

1.21   **a.** five   **b.** two   **c.** two   **d.** three   **e.** four   **f.** three

1.22   **a.** four   **b.** six   **c.** three   **d.** three   **e.** three   **f.** two

1.23   **a.** 5.0×10^3 L   **b.** 3.0×10^4 g   **c.** 1.0×10^5 m

1.24   **a.** 5.10×10^6 **b.** 2.60×10^3 **c.** 4.00×10^4

1.25   Calculators carry out mathematical computations and display answers without any regard to significant figures. Our task is to round the calculator's answer to the number of significant figures allowed by the precision of the original data.

1.26   The whole number would not reflect the precision (significant figures) allowed by the original data without the additional zero.

1.27   In multiplication and/or division, the answer must contain the same number of significant figures as the measurement with the smallest number of significant figures.

1.28   In addition and/or subtraction, the answer must be rounded so that it includes only unquestionable digits. For example: $54.7 + 49.521 = [\,104.221\,] \rightarrow$ (rounds to) 104.2.

1.29   **a.** 1.85   **b.** 184   **c.** 0.00474   **d.** 8810   **e.** 1.83

1.30   **a.** 1.9   **b.** 180   **c.** 0.0047   **d.** 8800   **e.** 1.8

1.31   **a.** $45.7 \times 0.034 \quad [\,1.5538\,] \rightarrow$ (which rounds to) 1.6

      b. $0.00278 \times 5 = [\,0.0139\,] \rightarrow 0.01$

      c. $\dfrac{34.56}{1.25} = [\,27.648\,] \rightarrow 27.6$

      d. $\dfrac{(0.2465)(25)}{1.78} = [\,3.462078652\,] \rightarrow 3.5$

1.32   **a.** $400 \times 185 = [\,74000\,] \rightarrow$ (which rounds to) 7×10^4

      b. $\dfrac{2.40}{(4)(125)} = [\,0.0048\,] \rightarrow 0.005$

      c. $0.825 \times 3.6 \times 5.1 = [\,15.147\,] \rightarrow 15$

      d. $\dfrac{3.5 \times 0.261}{8.24 \times 20.0} = [\,0.005543082\,] \rightarrow 0.0055$

1.33   **a.** $45.48 \text{ cm} + 8.057 \text{ cm} = [\,53.537\,] \rightarrow$ (which rounds to) 53.54 cm

      b. $23.45 \text{ g} + 104.1 \text{ g} + 0.025 \text{ g} = [\,127.575\,] \rightarrow 127.6$ g

      c. $145.675 \text{ mL} - 24.2 \text{ mL} = [\,121.475\,] \rightarrow 121.5$ mL

      d. $1.08 \text{ L} - 0.585 \text{ L} = [\,0.495\,] \rightarrow 0.50$ L

1.34   **a.** $5.08 \text{ g} + 25.1 \text{ g} = [\,30.18\,] \rightarrow$ (which rounds to) 30.2 g

      b. $85.66 \text{ cm} + 104.10 \text{ cm} + 0.025 \text{ cm} = [\,189.785\,] \rightarrow 189.79$ cm

      c. $24.568 \text{ mL} - 14.25 \text{ mL} = [\,10.318\,] \rightarrow 10.32$ mL

      d. $0.2654 \text{ L} - 0.2585 \text{ L} = [\,0.0069\,] \rightarrow 0.0069$ L

1.35 A decimal system is more convenient when conversion factors are needed, (multiply or divide by factors of ten), and if used world–wide, it would make trade (and vacationing) simpler. However, for industry to re–tool and for those unfamiliar with the metric system, a change could be both expensive and frustrating.

1.36 One *cent* is one hundredth of a dollar, and one *dime* is one tenth of a dollar.

1.37 The km/hr markings indicate how many kilometers (how much distance) will be traversed in one hour's time if the speed is held constant. The mph markings indicate the same distance traversed but measured in miles during the one hour of travel.

1.38 $\dfrac{80 \text{ km}}{\text{hr}} \times \dfrac{1000 \text{ m}}{\text{km}} \times \dfrac{39.4 \text{ in.}}{1 \text{ mi.}} \times \dfrac{1 \text{ ft}}{12 \text{ in.}} \times \dfrac{1 \text{ mi.}}{5280 \text{ ft}} = [\,49.74747475\,] \rightarrow 50$ mph

You are <u>not</u> exceeding the 55 mph speed limit if your speedometer reads 80 kph.

1.39 Because the prefix *kilo* means one thousand times, a *kilo*gram is equal to 1000 grams.

1.40 Because the prefix *centi* means one hundredth, a *centi*meter is one hundredth of a meter.

1.41 **a.** mg **b.** dL **c.** km **d.** kg **e.** μL

1.42 **a.** centimeter **b.** kilogram **c.** deciliter **d.** millimeter **e.** microgram

1.43 **a.** 0.01 **b.** 1000 **c.** 0.001 **d.** 0.1 **e.** 1 000 000

1.44 **a.** 1.0 decigram **b.** 1 microgram **c.** 1 kilogram
      d. 1 centigram **e.** 1 milligram

1.45 **a.** 100 cm **b.** 1000 m **c.** 0.001 m **d.** 1000 mL

1.46 **a.** 1 kg = 1000 g **b.** 1 mL = 0.001 L **c.** 1 g = 0.001 kg **d.** 1 g = 1000 mg

1.47 **a.** kilogram **b.** milliliter **c.** km **d.** kL

1.48 **a.** mg **b.** millimeter **c.** μm

1.49 Because a conversion factor is unchanged when inverted; $\dfrac{1 \text{ m}}{100 \text{ cm}}$ and $\dfrac{100 \text{ cm}}{1 \text{ m}}$

1.50 Verify that the units cancel when the conversion factors are applied.

1.51 1 kg = 1000 g

1.52 1 m = 100 cm

1.53 **a.** 1 yd = 3 ft $\qquad \dfrac{1 \text{ yd}}{3 \text{ ft}}$ and $\dfrac{3 \text{ ft}}{1 \text{ yd}}$

      b. 1 mi. = 5280 ft $\qquad \dfrac{1 \text{ mi}}{5280 \text{ ft}}$ and $\dfrac{5280 \text{ ft}}{1 \text{ mi}}$

      c. 1 min = 60 s $\qquad \dfrac{1 \text{ min}}{60 \text{ s}}$ and $\dfrac{60 \text{ s}}{1 \text{ min}}$

      d. 1 gal = 27 mi. $\qquad \dfrac{1 \text{ gal}}{27 \text{ mi.}}$ and $\dfrac{27 \text{ mi.}}{1 \text{ gal}}$

1.54 **a.** 1 gal = 4 qt $\qquad \dfrac{1 \text{ gal}}{4 \text{ qt}}$ and $\dfrac{4 \text{ qt}}{1 \text{ gal}}$

      b. 1 lb = \$ 1.29 $\qquad \dfrac{1 \text{ lb}}{\$1.29}$ and $\dfrac{\$1.29}{1 \text{ lb}}$

      c. 1 week = 7 days $\qquad \dfrac{1 \text{ week}}{7 \text{ days}}$ and $\dfrac{7 \text{ days}}{1 \text{ week}}$

      d. \$1 = 4 quarters $\qquad \dfrac{\$1}{4 \text{ quarters}}$ and $\dfrac{4 \text{ quarters}}{\$1}$

1.55 Learning the relationships between the metric prefixes will help you write the following equalties and their resulting conversion factors.

  a. 1 m = 100 cm $\dfrac{1\ m}{100\ cm}$ and $\dfrac{100\ cm}{1\ m}$

  b. 1 g = 1000 mg $\dfrac{1\ g}{1000\ mg}$ and $\dfrac{1000\ mg}{1\ g}$

  c. 1 L = 1000 mL $\dfrac{1\ L}{1000\ mL}$ and $\dfrac{1000\ mL}{1\ L}$

  d. 1 dL = 100 mL $\dfrac{1\ dL}{100\ mL}$ and $\dfrac{100\ mL}{1\ dL}$

1.56 **a.** 1 in. = 2.54 cm $\dfrac{1\ in.}{2.54\ cm}$ and $\dfrac{2.54\ cm}{1\ in.}$

  b. 1 kg = 2.20 lb $\dfrac{1\ kg}{2.20\ lb}$ and $\dfrac{2.20\ lb}{1\ kg}$

  c. 1 lb = 454 g $\dfrac{1\ lb}{454\ g}$ and $\dfrac{454\ g}{1\ lb}$

  d. 1 qt = 946 mL $\dfrac{1\ qt}{946\ mL}$ and $\dfrac{946\ mL}{1\ qt}$

1.57 When using a conversion factor you are trying to cancel existing units and arrive at a new (desired) unit. The conversion factor must be setup properly so the unit cancellation (numerator to denominator) can be accomplished.

1.58 The new (desired) unit should be in the numerator of the conversion factor.

1.59 **a.** 24 f̶t̶ $\times$ $\dfrac{1\ yd}{3\ f̶t̶}$ = [8] $\rightarrow$ (which needs a significant zero) 8.0 yd

  b. 15 m̶i̶n̶ $\times$ $\dfrac{60\ s}{1\ m̶i̶n̶}$ = [900] $\rightarrow$ 9.0×10^2 s

  c. 3.5 q̶t̶ $\times$ $\dfrac{1\ gal}{4\ q̶t̶}$ = [0.875] $\rightarrow$ 0.88 gal

1.60 **a.** 2.6 o̶z̶ $\times$ $\dfrac{1\ lb}{16\ o̶z̶}$ = [0.1625] $\rightarrow$ (which rounds to) 0.16 lb

  b. 2.4 m̶i̶.̶ $\times$ $\dfrac{5280\ ft}{1\ m̶i̶.̶}$ = [12672] $\rightarrow$ 13 000 ft

  c. \$3.50 $\times$ $\dfrac{4\ q̶u̶a̶r̶t̶e̶r̶s̶}{\$1}$ $\times$ $\dfrac{1\ game}{1\ q̶u̶a̶r̶t̶e̶r̶}$ = [14] $\rightarrow$ 14.0 games

1.61 **a.** 175 c̶m̶ $\times$ $\dfrac{1\ m}{100\ c̶m̶}$ = 1.75 m

  b. 5500 m̶L̶ $\times$ $\dfrac{1\ L}{1000\ m̶L̶}$ = 5.5 L

  c. 0.0055 k̶g̶ $\times$ $\dfrac{1000\ g}{1\ k̶g̶}$ = 5.5 g

1.62 **a.** 800 m̶g̶ $\times$ $\dfrac{1\ g}{1000\ m̶g̶}$ = 0.8 g

  b. 0.85 d̶L̶ $\times$ $\dfrac{100\ mL}{1\ d̶L̶}$ = 85 mL

  c. 2840 m̶g̶ $\times$ $\dfrac{1\ g}{1000\ m̶g̶}$ = 2.84 g

1.63 **a.** Unit plan: qt $\longrightarrow$ mL

  0.750 q̶t̶ $\times$ $\dfrac{946\ mL}{1\ q̶t̶}$ = [709.5] $\rightarrow$ (which rounds to) 710. mL

b. Unit plan: lb ⟶ kg

$$165 \text{ lb} \times \frac{1 \text{ kg}}{2.20 \text{ lb}} = [\,75\,] \rightarrow 75.0 \text{ kg}$$

c. Unit plan: in. ⟶ cm ⟶ mm

$$19.5 \text{ in.} \times \frac{2.54 \text{ cm}}{1 \text{ in.}} \times \frac{10 \text{ mm}}{1 \text{ cm}} = [\,495.3\,] \rightarrow 495 \text{ mm}$$

d. Unit plan: weeks ⟶ lb ⟶ kg

$$6 \text{ weeks} \times \frac{3.5 \text{ lb}}{1 \text{ week}} \times \frac{1 \text{ kg}}{2.20 \text{ lb}} = [\,9.545454545\,] \rightarrow 9.5 \text{ kg}$$

1.64 **a.** $4.0 \text{ oz} \times \dfrac{1 \text{ lb}}{16 \text{ oz}} \times \dfrac{454 \text{ g}}{1 \text{ lb}} = [\,113.5\,] \rightarrow 110 \text{ g}$

b. $5.0 \text{ pt} \times \dfrac{1 \text{ qt}}{2 \text{ pt}} \times \dfrac{946 \text{ mL}}{1 \text{ qt}} = [\,2365\,] \rightarrow 2400 \text{ mL}$

c. $560 \text{ mm} \times \dfrac{1 \text{ cm}}{10 \text{ mm}} \times \dfrac{1 \text{ in.}}{2.54 \text{ cm}} \times \dfrac{1 \text{ ft}}{12 \text{ in.}} = [\,1.837270341\,] \rightarrow 1.8 \text{ ft}$

d. $4.0 \text{ hrs} \times \dfrac{2.0 \text{ in.}}{1 \text{ hr}} \times \dfrac{2.54 \text{ cm}}{1 \text{ in.}} = [\,20.32\,] \rightarrow 20. \text{ cm}$

1.65 **a.** Unit plan: L ⟶ qt ⟶ gal

$$250 \text{ L} \times \frac{1.06 \text{ qt}}{1 \text{ L}} \times \frac{1 \text{ gal}}{4 \text{ qt}} = [\,66.25\,] \rightarrow 66 \text{ gal}$$

b. Unit plan: g ⟶ mg ⟶ tablet

$$0.024 \text{ g} \times \frac{1000 \text{ mg}}{1 \text{ g}} \times \frac{1 \text{ tablet}}{8 \text{ mg}} = [\,3\,] \rightarrow 3.0 \text{ tablets (add significant zero)}$$

c. Unit plan: lb ⟶ g ⟶ kg ⟶ mg ampicillin

$$34 \text{ lb body weight} \times \frac{454 \text{ g}}{1 \text{ lb}} \times \frac{1 \text{ kg}}{1000 \text{ g}} \times \frac{115 \text{ mg ampicillin}}{1 \text{ kg body weight}} = [\,1775.14\,] \rightarrow 1.8 \times 10^3 \text{ mg}$$

1.66 **a.** $1 \text{ day} \times \dfrac{24 \text{ hr}}{1 \text{ day}} \times \dfrac{1.0 \text{ g tetracycline}}{6 \text{ hr}} \times \dfrac{1000 \text{ mg}}{1 \text{ g}} \times \dfrac{1 \text{ tablet}}{500 \text{ mg}} = [\,8\,] \rightarrow 8.0 \text{ tablets}$

b. $425 \text{ mg} \times \dfrac{1 \text{ kg body wt}}{5.00 \text{ mg}} \times \dfrac{2.20 \text{ lb}}{1 \text{ kg}} = [\,187\,] \rightarrow 187 \text{ lb}$

c. $325 \text{ mg} \times \dfrac{1 \text{ g}}{1000 \text{ mg}} \times \dfrac{1 \text{ mL}}{0.50 \text{ g}} = [\,0.65\,] \rightarrow 0.65 \text{ mL}$

1.67 **a.** $325 \text{ g crust} \times \dfrac{46.7 \text{ g oxygen}}{100.0 \text{ g crust}} = [\,151.775\,] \rightarrow 152 \text{ g oxygen}$

b. $1.25 \text{ g crust} \times \dfrac{2.1 \text{ g magnesium}}{100.0 \text{ g crust}} = [\,0.02625\,] \rightarrow 0.026 \text{ g magnesium}$

1.68 **a.** $5.0 \text{ g hydrogen} \times \dfrac{100.0 \text{ g water}}{11.2 \text{ g hydrogen}} \times \dfrac{1 \text{ kg}}{1000 \text{ g}} = [\,0.044642857\,] \rightarrow 0.045 \text{ kg water}$

b. $2.25 \text{ kg oxygen} \times \dfrac{100 \text{ kg water}}{88.8 \text{ kg oxygen}} \times \dfrac{1000 \text{ g water}}{1 \text{ kg water}} = [\,2533.783784\,] \rightarrow 2530 \text{ g}$

1.69 Because aluminum has a density of 2.70 g/mL, silver has a density of 10.5 g/mL, and lead has a density of 11.3 g/mL, we can identify the unknown metal by calculating its density as follows:

$$\frac{217 \text{ g metal}}{19.2 \text{ mL metal}} = [\,11.30208333\,] \rightarrow 11.3 \text{ g/mL} \quad (1 \text{ mL} = 1 \text{ cm}^3)$$

Thus, the metal is lead.

1.70 The volume of a cube, 2.0 cm on each edge, is calculated as follows:

$(2.0 \text{ cm})^3 \times 1 \text{ mL}/1 \text{ cm}^3 = [\,8\,] \rightarrow 8.0 \text{ mL}$

(Both cubes have the same volume, but their masses differ.) A cube will displace its volume when submerged in water, so the final volume reading in each graduated cylinder is:

40.0 mL water + 8.0 mL metal = 48.0 mL total volume

1.71 Density is the mass of a substance divided by its volume. The densities of solids and liquids are usually stated in g/ml or g/cm³.

$$\text{Density} = \frac{\text{mass (grams)}}{\text{Volume (mL)}}$$

    a. $\dfrac{24.0 \text{ g}}{20.0 \text{ mL}} = [\,1.2\,] \rightarrow 1.20 \text{ g/mL}$

    b. $\dfrac{1.65 \text{ lb}}{170 \text{ mL}} \times \dfrac{454 \text{ g}}{1 \text{ lb}} = [\,4.406470588\,] \rightarrow 4.4 \text{ g/mL}$

    c. volume of gem volume: 34.5 mL total − 20.0 mL water = 14.5 mL

    density of gem: $\dfrac{45.0 \text{ g}}{14.5 \text{ mL}} = [\,3.103448276\,] \rightarrow 3.10 \text{ g/mL}$

1.72 **a.** 3.85 g/3.00 mL = [1.283333333] → 1.28 g/mL
    b. 155 g/125 mL = [1.24] → 1.24 g/mL
    c. 5.025 g/5.00 mL = [1.005] → 1.01 g/mL

1.73 **a.** $150 \text{ mL} \times \dfrac{1.4 \text{ g}}{1 \text{ mL}} = [\,210\,] \rightarrow 210 \text{ g}$

    b. $0.500 \text{ L} \times \dfrac{1000 \text{ mL}}{1 \text{ L}} \times \dfrac{1.15 \text{ g}}{1 \text{ mL}} = [\,575\,] \rightarrow 575 \text{ g}$

    c. Unit plan: mL $\longrightarrow$ g $\longrightarrow$ lb $\rightarrow$ oz

    $225 \text{ mL} \times \dfrac{7.8 \text{ g}}{1 \text{ mL}} \times \dfrac{1 \text{ lb}}{454 \text{ g}} \times \dfrac{16 \text{ oz}}{1 \text{ lb}} = [\,61.85022026\,] \rightarrow 62 \text{ oz}$

1.74 **a.** 35.6 g × 1 mL/10.5 g = [3.39047619] → 3.39 mL silver metal
    18.0 mL water + 3.39 mL silver = 21.4 mL total volume
    b. 8.3 g × 1 mL/13.6 g = [0.610294117] → 0.61 mL mercury metal
    c. $35 \text{ gal} \times \dfrac{4 \text{ qt}}{1 \text{ gal}} \times \dfrac{946 \text{ mL}}{1 \text{ qt}} \times \dfrac{1.0 \text{ g}}{1 \text{ mL}} \times \dfrac{1 \text{ lb}}{454 \text{ g}} = [\,291.7180617\,] \rightarrow 290 \text{ lb}$

1.75 **a.** $\dfrac{1.030 \text{ g/mL}}{1.000 \text{ g/mL (H}_2\text{O)}} = 1.030$

    b. $\dfrac{45.0 \text{ g}}{40.0 \text{ mL}} = [\,1.125\,] \rightarrow \dfrac{1.13 \text{ g/mL}}{1.000 \text{ g/mL (H}_2\text{O)}} = 1.13$

    c. 0.85 (oil sp. gr.) × 1.000 g/mL (H₂O density) = 0.85 g/mL (oil density)

1.76   **a.** 1.20 (sp gr) $\times$ 1.000 g/mL (H_2O density) = 1.20 g/mL (density of solution)
       500 ~~mL solution~~ $\times$ 1.20 g /1 ~~mL~~ = [600] $\rightarrow$ 600 g solution

   b. 0.850 (sp. gr) $\times$ 1.000 g/mL (H_2O density) = 0.850 g/mL

       325 ~~g solution~~ $\times$ $\dfrac{1\ mL}{0.850\ \text{~~g solution~~}}$ = [382.3529412] $\rightarrow$ 382 mL solution

   c. 0.86 (sp. gr. of butter) $\times$ $\dfrac{1.000\ g\ (H_2O\ \text{density})}{1\ mL}$ = 0.86 g/mL (density of butter)

       2.15 ~~L butter~~ $\times$ $\dfrac{1000\ \text{~~mL~~}}{1\ \text{~~L~~}}$ $\times$ $\dfrac{0.86\ g\ butter}{1\ \text{~~mL butter~~}}$ = [1849] $\rightarrow$ 1800 g butter

1.77   The Fahrenheit temperature scale is still used in the United States. A normal body temperature is 98.6°F on this scale. To convert her temperature to the equivalent reading on the Celsius scale, the following calculation must be performed:
$\dfrac{(99.8°F - 32)}{1.8}$ = 37.7°C   (32 is exact)
Because a normal body temperature is 37.0 on the Celsius scale, her temperature of 37.7°C would be a mild fever.

1.78   Because Mexico uses the Celsius temperature scale, he is accustomed to setting the oven's temperature in Celsius degrees. I would advise him that ovens in the United States are calibrated in Fahrenheit degrees and that we would need to determine the equivalent of 175°C on the Fahrenheit scale, as follows:
       1.8 (175°C) + 32 = 347°F

   We would then set the oven to 350°F and watch the cooking time carefully.

1.79   **a.** 1.8 (37.0°C) + 32 = 66.6 + 32 = 98.6°F
   b. $\dfrac{(65.3°F - 32)}{1.8}$ = $\dfrac{33.3}{1.8}$ = 18.5°C (1.8 is exact)
   c. −27°C + 273 = 246 K
   d. 62°C + 273 = 335 K
   e. $\dfrac{(114°F - 32)}{1.8}$ = $\dfrac{82}{1.8}$ = 46°C
   f. $\dfrac{(72°F - 32)}{1.8}$ = $\dfrac{40.}{1.8}$ = 22°C; 22°C + 273 = 295 K

1.80   **a.** 1.8 (25°C) + 32 = 45 + 32 = 77°F
   b. 1.8 (155°C) + 32 = 279 + 32 = 311°F
   c. $\dfrac{-25°F - 32}{1.8}$ = $\dfrac{-57}{1.8}$ = −32°C
   d. 224 K − 273 = −49°C
   e. 545 K − 273 = 295°C
   f. 875 K − 273 = 602°C;   1.8 (602°C) + 32 = 1080 + 32 = 1110°F

1.81   **a.** $\dfrac{(106°F - 32)}{1.8}$ = $\dfrac{74}{1.8}$ = 41°C
   b. $\dfrac{(103°F - 32)}{1.8}$ = $\dfrac{71}{1.8}$ = 39°C
   No, there is no need to phone the doctor. The child's temperature is less than 40.0°C.

1.82   **a.** $\dfrac{145°F - 32}{1.8}$ $= \dfrac{113}{1.8}$ $= 62.8°C$ (1.8 is exact)

   b. $1.8\,(20.6°C) + 32$ $= 37.1 + 32$ $= 69.1°F$ (32 is exact)

1.83   This problem requires several conversion factors. Let's take a look first at a possible unit plan. When you write out the unit plan, be sure you know a conversion factor you can use for each step.

ft $\longrightarrow$ in. $\longrightarrow$ cm $\longrightarrow$ m $\longrightarrow$ min

7500 ft $\times$ $\dfrac{12 \text{ in.}}{1 \text{ ft}}$ $\times$ $\dfrac{2.54 \text{ cm}}{1 \text{ in.}}$ $\times$ $\dfrac{1 \text{ m}}{100 \text{ cm}}$ $\times$ $\dfrac{1 \text{ min}}{55.0 \text{ m}}$ $= [\,41.56363636\,] \to 42$ min

1.84   **a.** 22 kg salmon + 5.5 kg crab + 3.48 kg oysters = $[\,30.98\,] \to$ 31 kg seafood

   b. 22 kg salmon $\times$ $\dfrac{2.20 \text{ lb}}{1 \text{ kg}}$ $= [\,48.4\,] \to$ 48 lb salmon

   5.5 kg crab $\times$ $\dfrac{2.20 \text{ lb}}{1 \text{ kg}}$ $= [\,12.1\,] \to$ 12 lb crab

   3.48 kg oysters $\times$ $\dfrac{2.20 \text{ lb}}{1 \text{ kg}}$ $= [\,7.656\,] \to$ 7.66 lb oysters

   48 lb salmon + 12 lb crab + 7.66 lb oysters $= [\,67.66\,] \to$ 68 lb seafood (total)

1.85 $\dfrac{14 \text{ francs}}{1 \text{ kg}}$ $\times$ $\dfrac{1 \$}{7.5 \text{ francs}}$ $\times$ $\dfrac{1 \text{ kg}}{2.20 \text{ lb}}$ $= [\,0.8484848\,] \to \$0.85/\text{lb}$

1.86   0.45 lb $\times$ $\dfrac{1 \text{ kg}}{2.20 \text{ lb}}$ $\times$ $\dfrac{125 \text{ pesos}}{1 \text{ kg}}$ $\times$ $\dfrac{\$1}{7.5 \text{ pesos}}$ $= [\,3.409090909\,] \to \$3.4$

1.87   4.0 lb $\times$ $\dfrac{454 \text{ g}}{1 \text{ lb}}$ $\times$ $\dfrac{1 \text{ onion}}{115 \text{ g}}$ $= [\,15.79130435\,] \to$ 16 onions

1.88 $1420 $\times$ $\dfrac{1 \text{ lb}}{\$1.75}$ $\times$ $\dfrac{1 \text{ kg}}{2.20 \text{ lb}}$ $= [\,368.8311688\,] \to 4 \times 10^2$ kg

1.89   **a.** 8.0 oz $\times$ $\dfrac{6 \text{ crackers}}{0.50 \text{ oz}}$ $= [\,96\,] \to$ 96 crackers

   b. 10 crackers x $\dfrac{1 \text{ serving}}{6 \text{ crackers}}$ x $\dfrac{4 \text{ g fat}}{1 \text{ serving}}$ x $\dfrac{1 \text{ lb}}{454 \text{ g}}$ x $\dfrac{16 \text{ oz}}{1 \text{ lb}}$ $= [\,0.234948605\,] \to$ 0.2 oz fat

   c. 50 boxes x $\dfrac{8.0 \text{ oz}}{1 \text{ box}}$ x $\dfrac{1 \text{ serving}}{0.50 \text{ oz}}$ x $\dfrac{140 \text{ mg sodium}}{1 \text{ serving}}$ x $\dfrac{1 \text{ g}}{1000 \text{ mg}}$ $= [\,112\,] \to$ 110 g sodium

1.90   75,000 mL $\times$ $\dfrac{1 \text{ qt}}{946 \text{ mL}}$ $\times$ $\dfrac{1 \text{ gal}}{4 \text{ qt}}$ $= [\,19.82029598\,]$ 20. gal

1.91   **b.** 10 days $\times$ $\dfrac{4 \text{ tablets}}{1 \text{ day}}$ $\times$ $\dfrac{250 \text{ mg amoxycillin}}{1 \text{ tablet}}$ $\times$ $\dfrac{1 \text{ g}}{1000 \text{ mg}}$ $\times$ $\dfrac{1 \text{ lb}}{454 \text{ g}}$ $\times$ $\dfrac{16 \text{ oz}}{1 \text{ lb}}$

   $= [\,0.352422907\,] \to$ 0.35 oz amoxycillin

1.92   8.0 oz burger $\times$ $\dfrac{15.0 \text{ oz protein}}{100.0 \text{ oz burger}}$ $\times$ $\dfrac{1 \text{ lb}}{16 \text{ oz}}$ $\times$ $\dfrac{454 \text{ g}}{1 \text{ lb}}$ $= [\,34.05\,] \to$ 34 g protein

Yes, the hamburger contains 34 g of protein, which is ten grams more than she is allowed. To Stay within her diet, Celeste could only have a 5.6 oz burger, as shown by the following calculation:

$24 \text{ g protein} \times \dfrac{1 \text{ lb}}{454 \text{ g}} \times \dfrac{16 \text{ oz}}{1 \text{ lb}} \times \dfrac{100.0 \text{ oz burger}}{15.0 \text{ oz protein}} = [\,5.63876652\,] \rightarrow 5.6 \text{ oz burger}$

This one burger would use her entire day's allowance of protein!

1.93 This problem has two units. Convert g to mg, and convert L in the denominator to dL.

$\dfrac{1.85 \text{ g}}{1 \text{ L}} \times \dfrac{1000 \text{ mg}}{1 \text{ g}} \times \dfrac{1 \text{ L}}{10 \text{ dL}} = 185 \text{ mg/dL}$

1.94 442.5 mL total − 325.2 mL water = 117.3 mL object

$\dfrac{3.15 \text{ oz object}}{117.3 \text{ mL object}} \times \dfrac{1 \text{ lb}}{16 \text{ oz}} \times \dfrac{454 \text{ g}}{1 \text{ lb}} = [\,0.761988491\,] \rightarrow 0.762 \text{ g/mL}$

1.95 The difference between the initial volume of the water and its volume with the lead object will give us the volume of the lead object.

285 mL total − 215 mL water = 70. mL lead

Using the density of lead, we can convert mL to the mass in grams of the lead object.

$70. \text{ mL lead} \times \dfrac{11.3 \text{ g lead}}{1 \text{ mL lead}} = [\,791\,] \rightarrow 790 \text{ g lead}$

1.96 $15.0 \text{ g iron} \times \dfrac{1 \text{ cc iron}}{7.86 \text{ g iron}} \times \dfrac{1 \text{ mL}}{1 \text{ cc}} = [\,1.908396947\,] \rightarrow 1.91 \text{ mL iron}$

$20.0 \text{ g lead} \times \dfrac{1 \text{ cc lead}}{11.3 \text{ g lead}} \times \dfrac{1 \text{ mL}}{1 \text{ cc}} = [\,1.769911504\,] \rightarrow 1.77 \text{ mL lead}$

155 mL water + 1.91 mL iron + 1.77 mL lead = [158.68] → 159 mL total volume

1.97 Unit plan: L gas ⟶ mL gas ⟶ g gas ⟶ g oil ⟶ mL oil ⟶ cm³ oil

$1.00 \text{ L gas} \times \dfrac{1000 \text{ mL gas}}{1 \text{ L gas}} \times \dfrac{0.66 \text{ g gas}}{1 \text{ mL gas}} \times \dfrac{1 \text{ g oil}}{1 \text{ g gas}} \times \dfrac{1 \text{ mL oil}}{0.92 \text{ g oil}} \times \dfrac{1 \text{ cm}^3}{1 \text{ mL}}$
$= [\,717.3913043\,] \rightarrow 720 \text{ cm}^3 \text{ oil}$

1.98 0.79 (sp. gr alcohol) × 1.000g/mL (density water) = 0.79 g/mL (density alcohol)

$1.50 \text{ kg alcohol} \times \dfrac{1000 \text{ g}}{1 \text{ kg}} \times \dfrac{1 \text{ mL alcohol}}{0.79 \text{ g alcohol}} \times \dfrac{1 \text{ qt}}{946 \text{ mL}} = [\,2.007118581\,] \rightarrow 2.0 \text{ qt alcohol}$

1.99 $175 \text{ lb body weight} \times \dfrac{1 \text{ kg}}{2.20 \text{ lb}} \times \dfrac{55 \text{ kg water}}{100. \text{ kg body weight}} = [\,43.75\,] \rightarrow 44 \text{ kg water}$

1.100 $65 \text{ kg body weight} \times \dfrac{2.20 \text{ lb}}{1 \text{ kg}} \times \dfrac{55 \text{ lb water}}{100. \text{ lb body weight}} = [\,78.65\,] \rightarrow 79 \text{ lb water}$

1.101 a. $45 \text{ kg body weight} \times \dfrac{3.0 \text{ kg fat}}{100.0 \text{ kg body weight}} = [\,1.35\,] \rightarrow 1.4 \text{ kg fat}$

b. $3.0 \text{ L fat} \times \dfrac{1000 \text{ mL}}{1 \text{ L}} \times \dfrac{0.94 \text{ g fat}}{1 \text{ mL fat}} \times \dfrac{1 \text{ lb}}{454 \text{ g}} = [\,6.211453744\,] \rightarrow 6.2 \text{ lb fat}$

1.102   50.0 kg (in air) − 2.0 kg (in water) = 48.0 kg water displaced

    a. 48.0 ~~kg water~~ × $\dfrac{1000\ \text{g}}{1\ \text{kg}}$ × $\dfrac{1\ \text{mL water}}{1.00\ \text{g water}}$ × $\dfrac{1\ \text{L}}{1000\ \text{mL}}$ = [48] → 48.0 L water

    b. The person's volume is equal to the volume of water that has been displaced, 48.0 L.

    c. $\dfrac{50.0\ \text{kg person}}{48\ \text{L person}}$ × $\dfrac{1\ \text{L}}{1000\ \text{mL}}$ × $\dfrac{1000\ \text{g}}{1\ \text{kg}}$ = [1.041666667]   1.04 g/mL person

1.103   **a.** 1.012 (urine's sp. gr.) × 1.000g/mL (H_2O's density) = 1.012 g/mL (urine's density)

    b. 1.022 (urine's sp. gr.) × 1.000g/mL (H_2O's density) = 1.022 g/mL (urine's density)

    5.00 ~~mL urine~~ × $\dfrac{1.022\ \text{g urine}}{1\ \text{mL urine}}$ = [5.11] → 5.11 g urine

1.104 $\dfrac{10.31\ \text{g urine}}{10.0\ \text{mL urine}}$ × $\dfrac{1\ \text{mL } H_2O}{1\ \text{g } H_2O}$ = [1.031] → 1.03 (urine specific gravity)

This sample of urine is in the high end of the normal range.

Atoms and Elements

Study Goals

- Write the name of an element from its symbol or its period and group number.
- Classify an element as a metal or nonmetal.
- Describe the three important particles in the atom, their location, charges, and relative masses.
- Describe Rutherford's gold-foil experiment and how it led to the current model of the atom.
- Use atomic number and mass number of an atom to determine the number of protons, neutrons, and electrons in the atom.
- Understand the relationship of isotopes to the atomic mass of an element on the periodic table.
- Write the electron configurations for elements in the periodic table.
- Explain the relationship between electron arrangement, group number and periodic law.

Chapter Outline

2.1 Elements and Symbols
  Health Note: Elements Essential to Health
  Health Note: Latin Names for Elements in Clinical Usage
  Explore Your World: Origins of Element Names
  Explore Your World: Physical Properties of Aluminum
2.2 The Periodic Table
  Health Note: Some Important Trace Elements in the Body
  Career Focus: Optician
2.3 The Atom
  Explore Your World: Repulsion and Attraction
2.4 Atomic Number and Mass Number
2.5 Isotopes and Atomic Mass
2.6 Electron Energy Levels
  Explore Your World: Light Released from Candy
  Environmental Note: Biological Reactions to UV Light
2.7 Subshells and Orbitals
2.8 Electron Configurations

Chapter Summary and Demonstrations

1. Elements and Atoms

The elements and their corresponding symbols are described for commonly occurring element and elements prevalent in biological systems. The atom is discussed in terms of protons, neutrons and electrons. The subatomic particles of the atom are described and related to atomic number and atomic mass. Examples of isotopes of an element and their contribution to the weighted average atomic mass of an element are discussed.

Demonstration: Tear up a piece of paper into smaller and smaller pieces. Ask students how many times they need to do this to get to atoms. Have a student with a brush handy run the brush (or comb) through their hair and place it near the bits of paper. Discuss the idea of electron attractions. Placing the comb (charged) near a thin stream of water will cause the stream to bend. If you have a cathode ray tube, show the bending of the ray by a magnet.

2. Periodic Table and Electron Arrangement

The elements on the periodic chart are classified by their group and period, and as metals or nonmetals. The chemical behavior of an element is related to its electron arrangement.

Demonstration: Heating a small amount of different chloride salts produces energy changes in the visible range with striking flame colors.

$BaCl_2$	yellowish-green	$LiCl_2$	red
$CaCl_2$	red-orange	KCl	pinkish-purple (brief)
$CuCl_2$	blue-green	$SrCl_2$	red

Discuss the source of the color and lead into a discussion of energy levels and the arrangement of electrons in atoms.

Laboratory Suggestions

Lab 4 Atomic Structure

Students match the symbols and names of elements. A set of elements is observed and their physical properties are recorded. Elements are categorized as metals or nonmetals and their location on the periodic chart determined. The subatomic particles in a set of isotopes are determined and compared to the atomic number and the mass number.

A. Physical Properties of Elements
B. Periodic Table
C. Subatomic Particles
D. Isotopes

Laboratory Skills to Demonstrate
   Review subatomic particles.
   Review the relationship between atomic number of protons, mass number and protons and neutrons.

Lab 5 Electronic Configuration and Periodic Properties

A graph of atomic numbers 1-20 are plotted against their atomic diameters. Students observe the trend in atomic diameters across a period and the similar trend in the next period. Flame tests of Group 1 and 2 elements are recorded and used to identify an unknown element. Students practice writing electron configurations.

A. Flame Tests
B. Drawing Models of Atoms
C. Graphing a Periodic Property: Atomic Radius

Laboratory Skills to Demonstrate
   Demonstrate the loop on a flame test wire and the formation of a film on the loop.
   Write the electron configurations.

Answers and Solutions to Text Problems

2.1 **a.** Cu   **b.** Si   **c.** K   **d.** N
    e. Fe   **f.** Ba   **g.** Pb   **h.** Sr

2.2 **a.** O   **b.** Li   **c.** S   **d.** Al
    e. H   **f.** Ne   **g.** Sn   **h.** Au

2.3 **a.** carbon   **b.** chlorine   **c.** iodine   **d.** mercury
    e. fluorine   **f.** argon   **g.** zinc   **h.** nickel

2.4 **a.** helium   **b.** phosphorus   **c.** sodium   **d.** magnesium
    e. calcium   **f.** bromine   **g.** cadmium   **h.** silicon

2.5 **a.** sodium and chlorine
    b. calcium, sulfur, and oxygen
    c. carbon, hydrogen, chlorine, nitrogen, and oxygen
    d. calcium, carbon, and oxygen

2.6 **a.** hydrogen and oxygen
    b. sodium, hydrogen, carbon, and oxygen
    c. sodium, oxygen, and hydrogen
    d. carbon, hydrogen, and oxygen

2.7 **a.** Period 2   **b.** Group 8A (18)   **c.** Group 1A (1)   **d.** Period 2

2.8 **a.** Group 1A (1)   **b.** Period 2   **c.** Group 8A (18)   **d.** Group 7A (17)

2.9 **a.** alkaline earth   **b.** transition element   **c.** noble gas
    d. alkali metal   **e.** halogen

2.10 **a.** noble gas   **b.** alkaline earth metal   **c.** transition element
    d. halogen   **e.** alkaline earth metal

2.11 **a.** C   **b.** He   **c.** Na   **d.** Ca   **e.** Al

2.12 **a.** Be   **b.** P   **c.** Kr   **d.** I   **e.** Ge

2.13 On the periodic table, metals are elements located to the left of the heavy zigzag line, while the nonmetals are elements to the right.
    a. metal   **b.** nonmetal   **c.** metal   **d.** nonmetal
    e. nonmetal   **f.** nonmetal   **g.** metal   **h.** metal

2.14 **a.** metal   **b.** metal   **c.** nonmetal   **d.** metal
    e. nonmetal   **f.** nonmetal   **g.** nonmetal   **h.** metal

2.15 **a.** electron   **b.** proton   **c.** electron   **d.** neutron

2.16 **a.** neutron   **b.** proton and neutron   **c.** electron   **d.** electron

2.17 The two most massive subatomic particles, protons and neutrons, are located in a very small region of the atom, which is called the nucleus.

2.18 Because protons are present in the nucleus of every element and protons are the positively charged subatomic particles.

2.19   Selection b (a proton and an electron) is the only one with a pair of particles having opposite charges.

2.20   Selections a (two protons) and c (two electrons) are pairs of particles having the same charge.

2.21   Because the hair strands repel one another, there must be like electrical charges on each strand.

2.22   Because the clothes cling to each other, there must be opposite electrical charges on the clothing.

2.23   **a.** atomic number   **b.** both   **c.** mass number   **d.** atomic number

2.24   **a.** number of protons and electrons, if a neutral atom
           b. number of particles (protons plus neutrons) in the nucleus
           c. number of neutrons
           d. nothing useful

2.25   **a.** lithium, Li   **b.** fluorine, F   **c.** calcium, Ca   **d.** zinc, Zn
           e. neon, Ne   **f.** silicon, Si   **g.** iodine, I   **h.** Oxygen, O

2.26   **a.** hydrogen, H   **b.** sodium, Na   **c.** potassium, K   **d.** iron, Fe
           e. bromine, Br   **f.** silver, Ag   **g.** phosphorus, P   **h.** helium, He

2.27   **a.** 12   **b.** 30   **c.** 53   **d.** 19

2.28   **a.** 6   **b.** 9   **c.** 20   **d.** 16

2.29

Name of Element	Symbol	Atomic Number	Mass Number	Number of Protons	Number of Neutrons	Number of Electrons
Aluminum	Al	13	27	13	14	13
Magnesium	Mg	12	24	12	12	12
Potassium	K	19	39	19	20	19
Sulfur	S	16	31	16	15	16
Iron	Fe	26	56	26	30	26

2.30

Name of Element	Symbol	Atomic Number	Mass Number	Number of Protons	Number of Neutrons	Number of Electrons
Nitrogen	N	7	15	7	8	7
Calcium	Ca	20	42	20	22	20
Strontium	Sr.	38	88	38	50	38
Silicon	Si	14	30	14	16	14
Barium	Ba	56	138	56	82	56

2.31   **a.** Since the atomic number of aluminum is 13, every Al atom has 13 protons. An atom of aluminum with a mass number 27 and an atomic number 13 has 14 neutrons.
           27 – 13 = 14 n   Therefore, 13 protons, 14 neutrons, 13 electrons
           b. 24 protons, 28 neutrons, 24 electrons
           c. 16 protons, 18 neutrons, 16 electrons
           d. 26 protons, 30 neutrons, 26 electrons

2.32   **a.** 1 proton, 1 neutron, 1 electron
           b. 7 protons, 7 neutrons, 7 electrons
           c. 14 protons, 12 neutrons, 14 electrons
           d. 30 protons, 40 neutrons, 30 electrons

2.33 a. $^{31}_{15}P$ b. $^{80}_{35}Br$ c. $^{27}_{13}Al$ d. $^{35}_{17}Cl$

2.34 a. $^{18}_{8}O$ b. $^{9}_{4}Be$ c. $^{56}_{26}Fe$ d. $^{24}_{11}Na$

2.35 a. $^{32}_{16}S$ $^{33}_{16}S$ $^{34}_{16}S$ $^{36}_{16}S$

b. They all have the same atomic number, (the same number of protons and electrons).
c. They have different numbers of neutrons, which is reflected in their mass numbers.
d. The atomic mass of sulfur on the periodic table is the average atomic mass of all the naturally occurring isotopic masses.

2.37 To calculate the average atomic mass of an element, I would need the actual mass and the percent abundance of each naturally occurring isotope.

2.38 a. $^{84}_{38}Sr$ $^{86}_{38}Sr$ $^{87}_{38}Sr$ $^{88}_{38}Sr$

b. They all have the same atomic number, (the same number of protons and electrons).
c. They have different numbers of neutrons, which is reflected in their mass numbers.
d. The atomic mass of strontium on the periodic table is the weighted average of all the naturally occurring isotopic masses.

2.39 69 (60.1/100) = 41.5   71 (39.9/100) = 28.3 thus 41.5 + 28.3 = 69.8 amu (average mass)

2.40 84 (0.0056) = 0.47   86 (0.0986) = 8.48   87 (0.0700) = 6.09   88 (0.8258) = 72.7
total = 0.47 + 8.48 + 6.09 + 72.7 = 87.7

2.41 The electrons surrounding a nucleus have specific energies. Electrons with similar energies will be found grouped together within a specific energy level.

2.42 The first energy level is filled with two electrons. The second energy level can hold a maximum of eight electrons. Because we are only considering the first twenty elements, the third energy level will have eight electrons present and the fourth energy level will have only two electrons in it.

2.43 a. 8   b. 5   c. 8   d. 0   e. 8

2.44 a. zero   b. six   c. five   d. eight   e. zero

2.45 a. 2, 4   b. 2, 8, 8   c. 2, 8, 6   d. 2, 8, 4   e. 2, 8, 3   f. 2, 5

2.46 a. 2, 8, 5   b. 2, 8   c. 2, 6   d. 2, 8, 8   e. 2, 8, 3   f. 2, 8, 4

2.47 a. Li   b. Mg   c. H   d. Cl   e. O

2.48 a. N   b. S   c. C   d. Ar   e. Al

2.49 a. gain   b. emit

2.50 a. X-rays have higher energies than microwaves and radio waves.
b. We shield ourselves from unnecessary exposure to x-rays because our tissues are damaged by high energies.

2.51 a. boron: 2, 3   aluminum: 2, 8, 3   b. Three   c. Group 3A (3)

2.52 a. fluorine: 2, 7   chlorine: 2, 8, 7   b. Seven   c. Group 7

2.53 a. 2 e⁻, Group 2A (2)   b. 7 e⁻, Group 7A (17)   c. 6 e⁻, Group 6A (16)
d. 5 e⁻, Group 5 A (5)   e. 2 e⁻, Group 2A (2)   f. 7 e⁻, Group 7A (17)

2.54 **a.** 1 e⁻, Group 1A (1) **b.** 4 e⁻, Group 4A (4) **c.** 8 e⁻, Group 8A (18)
d. 8 e⁻, Group 8A (18) **e.** 4 e⁻, Group 4A (4) **f.** 1 e⁻, Group 1A (1)

2.55 Mg, Ca, and Sr have similar properties because they are members of the same group (family) in the periodic table. Chemical properties are related to the number of electrons in the outermost occupied energy level, and these three elements all have two electrons in their outermost shell.

2.56 Bromine and iodine (you could also have selected fluorine or astatine) would exhibit physical and chemical properties similar to chlorine.

2.57 An *s* subshell holds up to 2 electrons, a *p* subshell up to 6 electrons, a *d* subshell up to 10 electrons, and an *f* subshell up to 14 electrons. An orbital holds up to two electrons. There is one orbital in an s subshell, 3 orbitals in a *p* subshell, 5 orbitals in a *d* subshell, and 7 orbitals in a *f* subshell.
   a. 2 electrons (orbital)   **b.** 6 electrons   **c.** 10 (*s* + *p*)   **d.** 2 electrons

2.58 **a.** 2 electrons   **b.** 2 electrons   **c.** 18 (*s* + *p* + d)   **d.** 2 electrons

2.59 **a.** $1s^2 2s^2 2p^6 3s^2$ **b.** $1s^2 2s^2 2p^6 3s^2 3p^3$ **c.** $1s^2 2s^2 2p^6 3s^2 3p^6$
   d. $1s^2 2s^2 2p^6 3s^2 3p^4$ **e.** $1s^2 2s^2 2p^6 3s^2 3p^5$ **f.** $1s^2 2s^2 2p^6 3s^2 3p^6 4s^2 3d^{10}$
   g. $1s^2 2s^2 2p^6 3s^2 3p^6 4s^2 3d^{10} 4p^6 5s^2$ **h.** $1s^2 2s^2 2p^6 3s^2 3p^6 4s^2 3d^{10} 4p^6 5s^2 4d^{10} 5p^5$

2.60 **a.** $1s^2 2s^2 2p^6 3s^2 3p^6 4s^1$ **b.** $1s^2 2s^2 2p^6 3s^1$ **c.** $1s^2 2s^2$ **d.** $1s^2 2s^2 2p^3$
   e. $1s^2 2s^2 2p^2$ **f.** $1s^2 2s^2 2p^6 3s^2 3p^6 4s^2$ **g.** $1s^2 2s^2 2p^6 3s^2 3p^6 4s^2 3d^5$
   h. $1s^2 2s^2 2p^6 3s^2 3p^6 4s^2 3d^{10} 4p^6 5s^2 4d^{10} 5p^6 6s^2$

2.61 **a.** hydrogen (H)   **b.** nitrogen (N)   **c.** sodium (Na)
   d. neon (Ne)   **e.** silicon (Si)   **f.** bromine (Br)

2.62 **a.** carbon (C)   **b.** lithium (Li)   **c.** sulfur (S)
   d. calcium (Ca)   **e.** sulfur (S)   **f.** strontium (Sr)

2.63 Any element with a two-letter symbol has the first letter capitalized and the second letter in lower case. CO would indicate a compound made of the two elements carbon and oxygen.

2.64 **a.** Incorrect. The symbol for copper is Cu   **b.** Incorrect. The symbol for silicon is Si.
   c. Correct as written   **d.** Incorrect. The symbol for fluorine is F.
   e. Incorrect. The symbol for potassium is K   **f.** Correct as written
   g. Correct as written   **h.** Incorrect. The symbol for lead is Pb.

2.65 **a.** Mg, magnesium   **b.** Br, bromine   **c.** Al, aluminum **d.** O, oxygen

2.66 **a.** Group 1, period 4   **b.** Group 5, period 3   **c.** Group 4, period 2   **d.** Group 8, period 8

2.67 **a.** The proton is a *positive* particle.   **b.** Electrons are found *outside of the nucleus*.
   c. The nucleus is the *smallest* part of the atom.   **d.** The *electron* has a negative charge.
   e. Most of the mass of the atom is due to its *protons and neutrons*.

2.68 **a.** 1 proton, 1 neutron   **b.** 17 protons, 20 neutrons
   c. 48 protons, 58 neutrons   **d.** 83 protons, 126 neutrons

2.69 **a.** 26 protons, 30 neutrons, 26 electrons

   b. $^{51}_{26}\text{Fe}$ **c.** $^{51}_{24}\text{Cr}$

2.70 No. The atomic mass is the weighted average of the eight naturally occurring isotopic masses.

2.71 **a.** Atoms are the smallest particles of an element that retain the properties of that element. Isotopes are atoms of an element with a specific mass number (specific number of neutrons).

b. The atomic number indicates the number of protons found in the nucleus of an atom. (It is also equal to the number of electrons present in a neutral atom.) The mass number indicates the total number of particles (protons plus neutrons) present in the nucleus of a particular atom.

2.72 **a.** An elemental symbol is the unique one- or two-letter shorthand notation used for each element found on the periodic table. An atomic symbol specifies a single isotope of an element.

b. The atomic number indicates the number of protons found in the nucleus of an atom. (It is also equal to the number of electrons present in a neutral atom.) Atomic mass is the actual mass of a particular isotope of an element.

2.73 **a.** $^{16}_{8}X$ $^{17}_{8}X$ $^{18}_{8}X$ All have 8 protons

b. $^{16}_{8}X$ $^{17}_{8}X$ $^{18}_{8}X$ All are isotopes of oxygen

c. $^{16}_{8}X$ $^{16}_{9}X$ Mass number of 16

   $^{18}_{10}X$ $^{18}_{8}X$ Mass number of 18

d. $^{16}_{8}X$ $^{18}_{10}X$ Both have 8 neutrons

2.74 **a.** $^{64}_{30}Zn$ $^{66}_{30}Zn$ $^{67}_{30}Zn$ $^{68}_{30}Zn$ $^{70}_{30}Zn$

b. All of these isotopes contain 30 protons and 30 electrons. Zinc-64 contains 34 neutrons, Zinc-66 contains 36 neutrons, Zinc-67 contains 37 neutrons, Zinc-68 contains 38 neutrons, and Zinc-70 contains 40 neutrons.

2.75 Portion of mass due to copper-63:   (63 amu $\times$ 0.692) = 43.6 amu
Portion of mass due to copper-65:   (65 amu $\times$ 0.308) = 20.0 amu
Adding these numbers yields the weighted average atomic mass for copper:
   43.5 + 20.0 = 63.6 amu

2.76 Portion of mass due to Magnesium-24:   (24 amu $\times$ 0.790) = [18.96] $\rightarrow$ 19.0 amu
Portion of mass due to Magnesium-25:   (25 amu $\times$ 0.100) = [2.5] $\rightarrow$ 2.50 amu
Portion of mass due to Magnesium-26:   (26 amu $\times$ 0.110) = [2.86] $\rightarrow$ 2.86 amu
Adding the numbers gives the weighted average atomic mass of magnesium:
   19.0 + 2.50 + 2.86 = 24.4 amu

2.77 $1 \text{ in.} \times \dfrac{2.54 \text{ cm}}{1 \text{ in.}} \times \dfrac{1 \text{ atom}}{3.14 \times 10^{-8} \text{ cm}} = 8.09 \times 10^{7}$ atoms

2.78 $2.00 \text{ cc} \times \dfrac{11.3 \text{ g}}{1 \text{ cc}} \times \dfrac{1 \text{ atom}}{3.4 \times 10^{-22} \text{ g}} = 6.6 \times 10^{22}$ atoms

2.79 Any two of the following in each part are correct responses:
a. helium, beryllium, magnesium, calcium, strontium, barium, and radium
b. oxygen, sulfur, selenium, tellurium, and polonium
c. neon, argon, krypton, xenon, and radon
d. boron, aluminum, gallium, indium, and thallium

2.80 **a**. Atomic mass is the actual mass of a particular isotope of an element. The average atomic mass is the weighted average of all naturally occurring isotopic masses.

b. Atoms are the smallest particles of an element that retain the properties of that element. A nucleus is the very small region within an atom which contains all of that atom's protons and neutrons.

2.81 Any two of the following in each part are correct responses:
a. fluorine, chlorine, bromine, iodine, and astatine
b. helium, neon, argon, krypton, xenon, and radon
c. lithium, sodium, potassium, rubidium, cesium, and francium
d. beryllium, magnesium, calcium, strontium, barium, and radium

2.82 **a**. metal   **b**. metal   **c**. metal   **d**. nonmetal
e. metal   **f**. nonmetal   **g**. metal   **h**. metal

2.83 **a**. 3   **b**. 3   **c**. 10   **d**. 2

2.85 **a**. Ga, gallium   **b**. C, carbon   **c**. Rb, rubidium
d. Ti, titanium   **e**. Kr, krypton

2.86 **a**. phosphorus   **b**. sulfur   **c**. indium
d. gallium   **e**. radium   **f**. potassium

2.87 **a**. $1s^2\, 2s^2\, 2p^6\, 3s^2\, 3p^6\, 4s^2\, 3d^{10}\, 4p^3$ or [Ar] $4s^2\, 3d^{10}\, 4p^3$
b. $1s^2\, 2s^2 2p^6\, 3s^2\, 3p^6\, 4s^2\, 3d^{10}\, 4p^6\, 5s^1$ or [Kr] $5s^1$
c. $1s^2\, 2s^2\, 2p^6\, 3s^2\, 3p^6\, 4s^2\, 3d^{10}\, 4p^6\, 5s^2\, 4d^{10}\, 5p^6\, 6s^2$ or [Xe] $6s^2$
d. $1s^2\, 2s^2\, 2p^6\, 3s^2\, 3p^2$ or [Ne] $3s^2\, 3p^2$
e. $1s^2\, 2s^2\, 2p^6\, 3s^2\, 3p^6\, 4s^2\, 3d^{10}\, 4p^5$ or [Ar] $4s^2\, 3d^{10}\, 4p^5$

2.88 **a**. F, fluorine   **b**. Al, aluminum   **c**. Fe, iron
d. Ar, argon   **e**. Cd, cadmium   **f**. Cs, cesium

Nuclear Radiation

Study Goals

- Identify the types of radiation as alpha particles, beta particles or gamma radiation.
- Describe the methods required for proper shielding for each type of radiation.
- Write an equation for an atom that undergoes radioactive decay.
- Identify some radioisotopes used in nuclear medicine.
- Calculate the amount of radioisotope that remains after a given number of half-lives.
- Describe nuclear fission and fusion.

Chapter Outline

3.1 Natural Radioactivity
   Health Note: Biological Effects of Radiation
   Explore Your World: Dental X rays

3.2 Nuclear Equations
   Health Note: Radon in Our Homes
   Explore Your World: Smoke Detectors
   Health Note: Beta Emitters in Medicine

3.3 Producing Radioactive Isotopes

3.4 Radiation Detection and Measurement
   Health Note: Radiation and Food

3.5 Half-Life of a Radioisotope
   Explore Your World: Modeling Half-Lives
   Environmental Note: Dating Ancient Objects

3.6 Medical Applications Using Radioactivity
   Health Note: Radiation Doses in Diagnostic and Therapeutic Procedures
   Health Note: Other Imaging Methods

3.7 Nuclear Fission and Fusion

Chapter Summary and Demonstrations

1. Radiation

Radiation is defined and the types of radiation are explained. The damaging effects of ionizing radiation and radiation protection are discussed. Nuclear equations are written and balanced for alpha, beta and gamma emitters. Several diagrams highlight the presentation.

Demonstration: Use a Geiger-Müller tube to determine a background count. Some students do not realize that some radiation is present naturally. Measure the counts per minutes for an alpha source. Use various shielding materials such as paper, cloth, cardboard, or lead sheets to determine the effect of shielding. Move the source along a meter stick taking one-minute counts at several distances up to 100 cm away. Plot the data and show that twice the distance from a source will result in 1/4 the radiation.

abnormal compared to normal conditions. Scans may sometimes be obtained from a local hospital, radiologist, or nuclear medicine units. Many of us may now have personal scans we can share.

3. Half-life

The half-lives of short- and long-lived radioisotopes including carbon-14 are explained and used to calculate the time of decay for radioisotopes. The process of transmutation, fission and fusion completes the chapter.

Demonstration: I illustrate half-life by handing out graph paper and sticks of licorice. The students measure the length of the licorice and mark it on the graph. Place units of length on the vertical axis and time on the horizontal axis. Each minute, the students break the licorice in half, eat the other half (if they wish), and measure the remaining half. (You may change time intervals to two or three or five minutes.) The remaining piece of licorice becomes shorter and shorter until they cannot halve it anymore. Connecting the data points gives a curve that is analogous to a half-life curve. They can see that most of the licorice disappears in the first few half-lives.

Laboratory Suggestions

Lab 6 Nuclear Radiation

The instructor uses a Geiger-Müeller detection tube to measure the radiation of several radioactive sources. After determining background count, the effects of shielding materials, distance from the source, and time are determined.

A. Background Count
B. Radiation from Radioactive Sources
C. Effect of Shielding, Time and Distance

Laboratory Skills to Demonstrate

Use of the Geiger-Müeller tube
Measurement of background count
Determine the effect of shielding materials, distance, and time on radiation
Complete a nuclear equation

Answers and Solutions to Text Problems

3.1   a. An α-particle and a helium nucleus both contain 2 protons and 2 neutrons. However, an α-particle has no electrons and carries a 2+ charge. Alpha particles are emitted from unstable nuclei during radioactive decay.

    b. α, $^4_2$He

3.2   a. A β-particle and an electron each carry a negative charge. When a neutron in the nucleus of an unstable atom breaks apart, it generates a proton and ejects a β-particle.

    b. β^-, $^{\ 0}_{-1}$e

3.3   a. $^{39}_{19}$K, $^{40}_{19}$K, $^{41}_{19}$K

    b. Each isotope has 19 protons and 19 electrons, but they differ in the number of neutrons present. Potassium-39 has 20 neutrons, potassium-40 has 21 neutrons, and potassium-41 has 22 neutrons.

3.4 **a.** $^{125}_{53}\text{I}$, $^{127}_{53}\text{I}$, $^{130}_{53}\text{I}$

b. Each isotope has 53 protons and 53 electrons, but they differ in the number of neutrons present. Iodine-125 has 72 neutrons; iodine-127 has 74 neutrons, and iodine-130 has 77 neutrons.

3.5

Medical Use	Nuclear Symbol	Mass Number	Number of Protons	Number of Neutrons
Heart imaging	$^{201}_{81}\text{Tl}$	201	81	120
Radiation therapy	$^{60}_{27}\text{Co}$	60	27	33
Abdominal scan	$^{67}_{31}\text{Ga}$	67	31	36
Hyperthyroidism	$^{131}_{53}\text{I}$	131	53	78
Leukemia treatment	$^{32}_{15}\text{P}$	32	15	17

3.6

Medical Use	Nuclear Symbol	Mass Number	Number of Protons	Number of Neutrons
Cancer treatment	$^{60}_{27}\text{Co}$	60	27	33
Brain scan	$^{99}_{43}\text{Tc}$	99	43	56
Blood flow	$^{141}_{58}\text{Ce}$	141	58	83
Bone scan	$^{85}_{38}\text{Sr}$	85	38	47
Lung function	$^{133}_{54}\text{Xe}$	133	54	79

3.7 **a.** α, $^{4}_{2}\text{He}$ **b.** $^{1}_{0}\text{n}$ **c.** β, $^{0}_{-1}\text{e}$ **d.** $^{15}_{7}\text{N}$ **e.** $^{125}_{53}\text{I}$

3.8 **a.** $^{1}_{1}\text{H}$ **b.** γ **c.** $^{0}_{-1}\text{e}$ **d.** $^{131}_{56}\text{Ba}$ **e.** $^{60}_{27}\text{Co}$

3.9 **a.** β (or e^-)   **b.** α (or He)   **c.** n   **d.** Na   **e.** C

3.10 **a.** proton   **b.** phosphorus-32   **c.** γ **d.** iron-59   **e.** strontium-85

3.11 **a.** Because β-particles move faster than α-particles, they can penetrate further into tissue.

b. Ionizing radiation breaks bonds and forms reactive species that cause undesirable reactions in the cells.

c. X-ray technicians leave the room to increase their distance from the radiation source. A thick wall or one that contains lead also shields them.

d. Wearing gloves shields the skin from α and β radiation.

3.12   **a.** Keep your distance from the radioactive source, wear protective clothing, and keep exposure time to a minimum.

b. Because cancer cells are rapidly dividing, they are more susceptible to ionizing radiation.

c. A lead apron protects the remainder of a patient's body from radiation while the x-rays are emitted.

d. The thick walls help to shield people in the radiology office from radiation emitted in the procedure rooms.

3.13   The mass number of the radioactive atom is reduced by 4 when an alpha particle is emitted. The unknown product will have an atomic number that is 2 less than the atomic number of the radioactive atom.

a. $^{208}_{84}\text{Po} \rightarrow {}^{204}_{82}\text{Pb} + {}^{4}_{2}\text{He}$ b. $^{232}_{90}\text{Th} \rightarrow {}^{228}_{88}\text{Ra} + {}^{4}_{2}\text{He}$

c. $^{251}_{102}\text{No} \rightarrow {}^{247}_{100}\text{Fm} + {}^{4}_{2}\text{He}$ d. $^{220}_{86}\text{Rn} \rightarrow {}^{216}_{84}\text{Po} + {}^{4}_{2}\text{He}$

3.14   a. $^{243}_{96}\text{Cm} \rightarrow {}^{239}_{94}\text{Pu} + {}^{4}_{2}\text{He}$

b. $^{252}_{99}\text{Es} \rightarrow {}^{248}_{97}\text{Bk} + {}^{4}_{2}\text{He}$

c. $^{251}_{98}\text{Cf} \rightarrow {}^{247}_{96}\text{Cm} + {}^{4}_{2}\text{He}$

d. $^{261}_{107}\text{Bh} \rightarrow {}^{257}_{105}\text{Db} + {}^{4}_{2}\text{He}$

3.15   a. $^{25}_{11}\text{Na} \rightarrow {}^{25}_{12}\text{Mg} + {}^{0}_{-1}\text{e}$ b. $^{20}_{8}\text{O} \rightarrow {}^{20}_{9}\text{F} + {}^{0}_{-1}\text{e}$

c. $^{92}_{38}\text{Sr} \rightarrow {}^{92}_{39}\text{Y} + {}^{0}_{-1}\text{e}$ d. $^{42}_{19}\text{K} \rightarrow {}^{42}_{20}\text{Ca} + {}^{0}_{-1}\text{e}$

3.16   a. $^{42}_{19}\text{K} \rightarrow {}^{42}_{20}\text{Ca} + {}^{0}_{-1}\text{e}$

b. $^{59}_{26}\text{Fe} \rightarrow {}^{59}_{27}\text{Co} + {}^{0}_{-1}\text{e}$

c. $^{60}_{26}\text{Fe} \rightarrow {}^{60}_{27}\text{Co} + {}^{0}_{-1}\text{e}$

d. $^{141}_{56}\text{Ba} \rightarrow {}^{141}_{57}\text{La} + {}^{0}_{-1}\text{e}$

3.17   a. $^{28}_{13}\text{Al} \rightarrow {}? + {}^{0}_{-1}\text{e}$ $? = {}^{28}_{14}\text{Si}$

b. $? \rightarrow {}^{86}_{36}\text{Kr} + {}^{1}_{0}\text{n}$ $? = {}^{87}_{36}\text{Kr}$

c. $^{66}_{29}\text{Cu} \rightarrow {}^{66}_{30}\text{Zn} + {}?$ $? = {}^{0}_{-1}\text{e}$

d. $? \rightarrow {}^{4}_{2}\text{He} + {}^{234}_{90}\text{Th}$ $? = {}^{238}_{92}\text{U}$

3.18   a. $^{11}_{6}\text{C} \rightarrow {}^{7}_{4}\text{Be} + {}?$ $? = {}^{4}_{2}\text{He}$

b. $^{35}_{16}\text{S} \rightarrow$? $+ \, ^{0}_{-1}\text{e}$? $= \, ^{35}_{17}\text{Cl}$

c. ? $\rightarrow$ $^{90}_{39}\text{Y} + \, ^{0}_{-1}\text{e}$? $= \, ^{90}_{38}\text{Sr}$

d. $^{210}_{83}\text{Bi} \rightarrow$? $+ \, ^{4}_{2}\text{He}$? $= \, ^{206}_{81}\text{Tl}$

3.19   **a.** $^{9}_{4}\text{Be} + \, ^{1}_{0}\text{n} \rightarrow$?   ? $= \, ^{10}_{4}\text{Be}$

      b. $^{32}_{16}\text{S} + \,$? $\rightarrow \, ^{32}_{15}\text{P}$? $= \, ^{0}_{-1}\text{e}$

      c. ? $+ \, ^{1}_{0}\text{n} \rightarrow \, ^{24}_{11}\text{Na} + \, ^{4}_{2}\text{He}$? $= \, ^{27}_{13}\text{Al}$

      d. To balance the mass numbers, the unknown product must have a mass of 1. Balancing the number of protons gives an atomic number of 1. The unknown product is a proton.
$^{27}_{13}\text{Al} + \, ^{4}_{2}\text{He} \rightarrow \, ^{30}_{14}\text{Si} + \,$?   ? $= \, ^{1}_{1}\text{H}$

3.20   **a.** $^{40}_{18}\text{Ar} + \,$? $\rightarrow \, ^{43}_{19}\text{K} + \, ^{1}_{1}\text{H}$? $= \, ^{4}_{2}\text{He}$

      b. $^{238}_{92}\text{U} + \, ^{1}_{0}\text{n} \rightarrow$?   ? $= \, ^{239}_{92}\text{U}$

      c. ? $+ \, ^{1}_{0}\text{n} \rightarrow \, ^{14}_{6}\text{C} + \, ^{1}_{1}\text{H}$? $= \, ^{14}_{7}\text{N}$

      d. $^{4}_{2}\text{He} + \, ^{14}_{7}\text{N} \rightarrow$? $+ \, ^{1}_{1}\text{H}$? $= \, ^{17}_{8}\text{O}$

3.21   **a.** When radiation enters the Geiger counter, it ionizes a gas in the detection tube. The ions created in the tube move toward an electrode of opposite charge (recall that opposite electrical charges attract one another). This flow of charge produces an electric current, which is detected by the instrument.
      b. The becquerel (Bq), is the SI unit for activity. The curie (Ci), is the original unit for activity of radioactive samples.
      c. The SI unit for absorbed dose is the gray (Gy). The rad (radiation absorbed dose) is a unit of radiation absorbed per gram of sample. It is the older unit.
      d. A kilogray is 1000 gray, which is also equivalent to 100 000 rads.

3.22   **a.** Background radiation is the radiation emitted as naturally occurring radioisotopes undergo normal decay processes.
      b. The rem (radiation equivalent in humans) is the older unit used when measuring the biological effect of radiation. The SI unit for such measurements is the sievert (Sv).
      c. The millicurie (1/1000 of a Curie) is abbreviated mCi; mrem represents the millirem (which is 1/1000 of a rem).
      d. Because the different species (α, β, etc) produce different degrees of biological damage, a factor must be applied to reflect the severity of the damage.

3.23   **a.** $3.0 \, \cancel{\text{Ci}} \times \dfrac{3.7 \times 10^{10} \, \cancel{\text{dis/s}}}{1 \, \cancel{\text{Ci}}} \times 20. \, \cancel{\text{s}} = 2.2 \times 10^{12}$ disintegrations

      b. $70.0 \, \cancel{\text{kg}} \times \dfrac{4.20 \, \mu\text{Ci}}{1 \, \cancel{\text{kg}}} = 294 \, \mu\text{Ci}$

3.24   **a.** $50.0 \, \cancel{\text{kg}} \times \dfrac{20 \, \cancel{\mu\text{Ci}}}{1 \, \cancel{\text{kg}}} \times \dfrac{1 \, \text{mCi}}{1000 \, \cancel{\mu\text{Ci}}} = 1 \, \text{mCi}$

      b. $50 \, \cancel{\text{mrad}} \times \dfrac{1 \, \cancel{\text{rad}}}{1000 \, \cancel{\text{mrad}}} \times \dfrac{1 \, \text{Gy}}{100 \, \cancel{\text{rad}}} = 5 \times 10^{-4} \, \text{Gy}$

27

$$50 \text{ mrad} \times \frac{1 \text{ rad}}{1000 \text{ mrad}} \times \frac{1 \text{ rem}}{1 \text{ rad}} \times \frac{1000 \text{ mrem}}{1 \text{ rem}} = 50 \text{ mrem}$$

c. $50 \text{ mrad} \times \frac{1 \text{ rad}}{1000 \text{ mrad}} \times \frac{20 \text{ rem}}{1 \text{ rad}} \times \frac{1000 \text{ mrem}}{1 \text{ rem}} = 1000 \text{ mrem}$

Because alpha particles cause 20 times more biological damage, there are 20 times more mrem from the alpha radiation exposure than the chest x-ray!

3.25   While flying a plane, a pilot is exposed to higher levels of background radiation because there is less atmosphere to act as a shield against cosmic radiation.

3.26   Some symptoms of radiation sickness are: nausea, vomiting, fatigue, a reduced white blood cell count, loss of hair, and infection.

3.27   Half-life is the time required for one-half of a radioactive sample to decay.

3.28   Radioisotopes with short half-lives release much of their radiation soon after they are administered to a patient. Therefore, smaller amounts can be used and still provide sufficient radiation for detection. Because the radioisotopes decay quickly, they are rapidly cleared from the body.

3.29   a. After one half-life, one-half of the sample would be radioactive: $80.0 \text{ mg} \times \_ = 40.0 \text{ mg}$

b. After two half-lives, one-fourth of the sample would still be radioactive

$80.0 \text{ mg} \times \_ \times \_ = 80.0 \text{ mg} \times 1/4 = 20.0 \text{ mg}$

c. $18 \text{ hr} \times \frac{1 \text{ half-life}}{6.0 \text{ hr}} = 3.0 \text{ half-lives}$

$80.0 \text{ mg} \times \_ \times \_ \times \_ = 80.0 \text{ mg} \times 1/8 = 10.0 \text{ mg}$

d. $24 \text{ hr} \times \frac{1 \text{ half-life}}{6.0 \text{ hr}} = 4.0 \text{ half-lives}$

$80.0 \text{ mg} \times \_ \times \_ \times \_ \times \_ = 80.0 \text{ mg} \times 1/16 = 5.00 \text{ mg}$

3.30 $2 \_ \text{days} \times \frac{24 \text{ hr}}{1 \text{ day}} \times \frac{1 \text{ half-life}}{15 \text{ hr}} = 4.0 \text{ half-lives}$

$12 \text{ mCi} \times \_ \times \_ \times \_ \times \_ = 12 \text{ mCi} \times 1/16 = 0.75 \text{ mCi}$

3.31   The radiation level in a radioactive sample is cut in half with each passing half-life. To answer the question we must first determine the number of half-lives.
$\_ = \_ \times \_ = 2 \text{ half-lives}$

Because each half-life is 64 days, it will take 128 days for the radiation level of strontium-85 to fall to one fourth of its original value. 2 half-lives $\times$ 64 days/half-life = 128 days

To determine the amount of time for the strontium-85 to drop to one-eight its original activity, we calculate the number of half-lives. $1/8 = \_ \times \_ \times \_ = 3 \text{ half-lives}$

Because each half-life is 64 days, it will take 192 days for the radiation level of strontium-85 to fall to one eighth of its original value.   3 half-lives $\times$ 64 days/half-life = 192 days

3.32 Because 5 _ hours pass between 8 AM and 1:30 PM some of the Fluorine-18 will have decayed. To determine how the amount of remaining radioisotope, we must determine the number of half-lives that have transpired.

$$5\_ \cancel{\text{hrs}} \times \frac{60\ \cancel{\text{min}}}{1\ \cancel{\text{hr}}} \times \frac{1\ \text{half-life}}{110\ \cancel{\text{min}}} = 3.0\ \text{half-lives}$$

$$100\ \text{mg} \times \_ \times \_ \times \_ = 100\ \text{mg} \times 1/8 = [12.5] \rightarrow 10\ \text{mg}$$

3.33 a. Because the elements calcium and phosphorus are part of bone, any calcium and/or phosphorus atom, regardless of isotope, will be carried to and become part of the bony structures in the body. Once there, the radiation emitted by the radioisotope can be used for diagnosis or treatment of bone diseases.

b. Strontium is chemically similar to calcium, so it too will be carried to the bones. Once in the bone, the radiation emitted can destroy healthy bone and bony structures.

3.34 a. Because gamma radiation causes less biological damage than alpha or beta, it is preferred for diagnostic imaging.

b. Because Phosphorus is a component of bone, all atoms of Phosphorus will be transported to and incorporated into the skeleton. Once there, the radiation emitted due to the decay of radioactive isotopes will destroy some of the bone marrow cells. This reduces the production of red blood cells.

3.35 $4.0\ \cancel{\text{mL}} \times \dfrac{45\ \mu\text{Ci}}{1\ \cancel{\text{mL}}} = 180\ \mu\text{Ci}$

3.36 $3.0\ \cancel{\text{mCi}} \times \dfrac{1\ \text{mL}}{2.0\ \cancel{\text{mCi}}} = 1.5\ \text{mL}$

3.37 Nuclear fission is the splitting of a large atom into smaller fragments with a simultaneous release of large amounts of energy.

3.38 In a commonly observed process, after a Uranium nucleus is bombarded with a neutron, it breaks apart generating a large amount of energy, forming two daughter products, and releasing three neutrons. Each of these three neutrons bombards another Uranium nucleus. Each bombardment reaction generates energy, creates daughter products, and releases three additional neutrons. The chain reaction occurs because each bombardment process produces enough neutrons to initiate three additional reactions!

3.39 $^{235}_{92}\text{U} + ^{1}_{0}\text{n} \rightarrow ^{131}_{50}\text{Sn} + ? + 2\,^{1}_{0}\text{n}$? = $^{103}_{42}\text{Mo}$

3.40 $^{235}_{92}\text{U} + ^{1}_{0}\text{n} \rightarrow ^{94}_{38}\text{Sr} + ^{139}_{54}\text{Xe} + 3\,^{1}_{0}\text{n} + \text{energy}$

3.41   **a.** fission   **b.** fusion   **c.** fission   **d.** fusion

3.42   **a.** fusion   **b.** fusion   **c.** fusion   **d.** fusion and fission

3.43 Both carbon-12 and carbon-14 contain 6 protons and 6 electrons, but there are only 6 neutrons in a carbon-12 nucleus while a carbon-14 nucleus has 8. Carbon-12 is a stable isotope, but carbon-14 is radioactive and will emit radiation.

3.44   **a.** Boron-10   5 protons, 5 neutrons, and 5 electrons
      b. Zinc-72   30 protons, 42 neutrons, and 30 electrons
      c. Iron-59   26 protons, 33 neutrons, and 26 electrons
      d. Gold-198   79 protons, 119 neutrons, and 79 electrons

3.45 **a**. Alpha (α) and beta (β) radiation consist of particles emitted from an unstable nucleus, while gamma (γ) rays are radiation emitted as pure energy.

b. Alpha radiation is abbreviated as α, $^4_2\alpha$, and ^4_2He. Beta radiation is abbreviated as β, β^-, $^0_{-1}\beta$, and $^0_{-1}\text{e}$. Gamma radiation is abbreviated as γ and $^0_0\gamma$.

c. Alpha particles cannot penetrate skin, beta particles penetrate 4 to 5 mm into body tissue, and gamma radiation easily passes through body tissues.

d. Lightweight clothing or a piece of paper will shield against alpha particles, heavy clothing and gloves shield against beat particles, thick concrete and lead will shield against gamma rays.

3.46 The lead apron protects the remainder of a your body from radiation while the x-rays are emitted. The technician leaves the room to increase the distance to the radiation source and for the shielding provided by a thick wall (or one that contains a lead lining).

3.47 **a**. $^{225}_{90}\text{Th} \rightarrow {}^{221}_{88}\text{Ra} + {}^4_2\text{He}$ **b**. $^{210}_{83}\text{Bi} \rightarrow {}^{206}_{81}\text{Tl} + {}^4_2\text{He}$

c. $^{137}_{55}\text{Cs} \rightarrow {}^{137}_{56}\text{Ba} + {}^0_{-1}\text{e}$ **d**. $^{126}_{50}\text{Sn} \rightarrow {}^{126}_{51}\text{Sb} + {}^0_{-1}\text{e}$

3.48 **a**. $^{40}_{19}\text{K} \rightarrow {}^{40}_{20}\text{Ca} + {}^0_{-1}\text{e}$

b. $^{35}_{16}\text{S} \rightarrow {}^{35}_{17}\text{Cl} + {}^0_{-1}\text{e}$

c. $^{190}_{78}\text{Pt} \rightarrow {}^{186}_{76}\text{Os} + {}^4_2\text{He}$

d. $^{210}_{88}\text{Ra} \rightarrow {}^{206}_{86}\text{Rn} + {}^4_2\text{He}$

3.49 **a**. $^{14}_7\text{N} + {}^4_2\text{He} \rightarrow ? + {}^1_1\text{H}$ $? = {}^{17}_8\text{O}$

b. $^{27}_{13}\text{Al} + {}^4_2\text{He} \rightarrow {}^{30}_{14}\text{Si} + ?$ $? = {}^1_1\text{H}$

c. $^{235}_{92}\text{U} + {}^1_0\text{n} \rightarrow {}^{90}_{38}\text{Sr} + 3\,{}^1_0\text{n} + ?$ $? = {}^{143}_{54}\text{Xe}$

3.50 **a**. $^{59}_{27}\text{Co} + ? \rightarrow {}^{56}_{25}\text{Mn} + {}^4_2\text{He}$ $? = {}^1_0\text{n}$

b. $? \rightarrow {}^{14}_7\text{N} + {}^0_{-1}\text{e}$ $? = {}^{14}_6\text{C}$

c. $^{76}_{36}\text{Kr} + {}^0_{-1}\text{e} \rightarrow ?$ $? = {}^{76}_{35}\text{Br}$

3.51 **a**. $^{16}_8\text{O} + {}^{16}_8\text{O} \rightarrow {}^4_2\text{He} + ?$ $? = {}^{28}_{14}\text{Si}$

b. $^{249}_{98}\text{Cf} + {}^{18}_8\text{O} \rightarrow ? + 4\,{}^1_0\text{n}$ $? = {}^{263}_{106}\text{Sg}$

c. $^{222}_{86}\text{Rn} \rightarrow {}^4_2\text{He} + ?$ $? = {}^{218}_{84}\text{Po}$

Then the polonium-218 decays as follows:

$$^{218}_{84}\text{Po} \rightarrow {}^4_2\text{He} + ? \qquad ? = {}^{214}_{82}\text{Pb}$$

3.52 **a.** $^{210}_{84}\text{Po} \rightarrow {}^{4}_{2}\text{He} + ?$ $? = {}^{206}_{82}\text{Pb}$

b. $^{211}_{83}\text{Bi} \rightarrow {}^{4}_{2}\text{He} + ?$ $? = {}^{207}_{81}\text{Tl}$

and now the Thallium-207 decays as follows:

$$^{207}_{81}\text{Tl} \rightarrow {}^{0}_{-1}\text{e} + ? \qquad\qquad ? = {}^{207}_{82}\text{Pb}$$

3.53 Half of a radioactive sample decays with each half-life:

_ lives   (1)   (2)

1.2 g $\longrightarrow$ 0.60 g $\longrightarrow$ 0.30 g

Therefore, the amount of phosphorus-32 will drop to 0.30 g in two half-lives, which is 28 days. One half-life is 14 days.   28 days/2 half-lives = 14 days/half-life

3.54 Half of a radioactive sample decays with the passing of each half-life, as shown:
0.4 g $\times$ _ = 0.2 g

A single half-life does not yield the appropriate number of grams of Iodine-123, so additional calculations must be performed, (rounding to the correct number of significant digits after all divisions are completed), as shown: 0.2 $\times$ _ = 0.1 g

This amount agrees with the amount of Iodine-123 that remains after 26.2 hours have passed. Therefore, two half-lives must have transpired during this time, yielding the half-life for Iodine-123, as shown: 26.2 hours/2 half-lives = 13.1 hours/half-life

3.55 **a.** $^{131}_{53}\text{I} \longrightarrow {}^{0}_{-1}\text{e} + {}^{131}_{47}\text{Xe}$

b. First we must determine the number of half-lives.
40 ~~days~~ $\times$ $\dfrac{1\ \text{half-life}}{8.0\ \text{days}}$ = 5.0 half-lives

Now we can calculate the number of grams of Iodine-131 remaining:
2.0 g $\times$ (_ $\times$ _ $\times$ _ $\times$ _ $\times$ _) = 12.0 g $\times$ 1/32 = 0.375 g

c. One-half of a radioactive sample decays with each half-life:
_ lives (1)   (2)   (3)   (4)
48 g $\longrightarrow$ 24 g $\longrightarrow$ 12 g $\longrightarrow$ 6.0 g $\longrightarrow$ 3.0 g

When 3.0 g remain, four half-lives must have passed. Because each half-life is 8.0 days, we can calculate the number of days that the sample required to decay to 3.0 g.
4 ~~half-lives~~ $\times$ $\dfrac{8.0\ \text{days}}{1\ \text{half-life}}$ = 32 days

3.56 **a.** $^{137}_{55}\text{Cs} \longrightarrow {}^{0}_{-1}\text{e} + {}^{137}_{56}\text{Ba}$

b. First we must determine how many half-lives have transpired:
90 ~~yrs~~ $\times$ $\dfrac{1\ \text{half-life}}{30\ \text{yrs}}$ = 3 half-lives
Now we can calculate the number of grams of cesium-137 remaining:
16 g $\times$ $1/(2)^3$ = 16 g $\times$ 1/8 = 2.0 g

c. Half of a radioactive sample decays with the passing of each half-life, as shown:

28 g × _ = 14 g

A single half-life does not yield the appropriate number of grams of cesium-137, so additional calculations must be performed, as shown, (rounding to the proper number of significant figures after all divisions are completed):

14 × _ = 7,   7 × _ = 3.5 g

This final amount agrees with the amount of Cesium-137 that remains. Therefore, 3 half-lives must have passed. To calculate the number of years that have transpired we use cesium-137's half-life combined with the number of half-lives:

3 half-lives × $\dfrac{30 \text{ yrs}}{1 \text{ half-life}}$ = 90 yrs

3.57 First, calculate the number of half-lives that have passed since the nurse was exposed:

36 hrs × $\dfrac{1 \text{ half-life}}{12 \text{ hrs}}$ = 3.0 half-lives

Because the activity of a radioactive sample is cut in half with each half-life, the activity must have been double its present value prior to each half-life. For 3.0 half-lives, we need to double the value 3 times.

2.0 µCi × (2 × 2 × 2) = 16 µCi

3.58 Assuming that the activity of Carbon-12 in present day wood is equal to the activity of Carbon-12 when the ancient tree was chopped down to create the artifact, we must calculate how many half-lives must pass for the activity to fall to 10 counts per minute (cpm). Half of a radioactive sample decays with the passing of each half-life, as shown:

40 cpm × _ = 20 cpm

A single half-life does not yield the proper activity, so an additional calculation must be performed, as shown, (rounding to the proper number of significant figures after all divisions are completed):

20 × _ = 10 cpm

Therefore, 2 half-lives have passed. To calculate the number of years that has passed (the approximate age of the wood), we use Carbon-12's half-life combined with the number of half-lives:

2 half-lives × $\dfrac{5730 \text{ yrs}}{1 \text{ half-life}}$ = 1.15×10^4 yrs

3.59 First, calculate the number of half-lives:

24 hrs × $\dfrac{1 \text{ half-life}}{6.0 \text{ hrs}}$ = 4.0 half-lives

And now calculate the amount of Technetium-99^m that remains after 4 half-lives have passed:

120 mg × (_ × _ × _ × _) = 120 mg × 1/16 = 7.5 mg

3.60 For the activity to drop to 500 Bq from 4000 Bq, three half-lives must have passed, as the following calculation shows:

4000 Bq × (_ × _ × _) = 4000 Bq × 1/8 = 500 Bq

Combining the number of half-lives with Oxygen-15's half-life will yield the time that must transpire, as shown:

3 half-lives × $\dfrac{124 \text{ sec}}{1 \text{ half-life}}$ × $\dfrac{1 \text{ min}}{60 \text{ sec}}$ = 6.20 mins

3.61   Because a technician is near a radiation source frequently, the technician's exposure to radiation levels must be carefully monitored. A film badge detects the amount of radiation exposure. The badge is checked periodically to make sure that a technician has not received more than the maximum permissible radiation dose.

3.62   With the proper lab tests, exposure levels between about 25 and 100 rem can be detected because this causes a temporary decrease in the number of white blood cells. Exposure levels greater than 100 rem result in the common symptoms of radiation sickness: nausea, vomiting, and fatigue, as well as a reduction in white blood cell counts.

3.63   Irradiating foods kills bacteria that are responsible for food borne illnesses and food spoilage. As a result, shelf life of the food is extended.

3.64   **a.** Lack of understanding on the consumers' part has caused an unfavorable reaction to irradiated foods.
b. I have purchased irradiated foods due to my increased confidence in its cleanliness. Some vitamins may have been lost in the radiation process.

3.65   Nuclear fission is the splitting of a large atom into smaller fragments with a simultaneous release of large amounts of energy. Nuclear fusion occurs when two (or more) nuclei combine (fuse) to form a larger species, with a simultaneous release of large amounts of energy.

3.66   **a.** The production of more than one neutron from each uranium-235 bombardment reaction allows a chain reaction to occur.
b. The control rods are made from materials that absorb neutrons. By carefully positioning the control rods in the vicinity of the fuel rods, excess neutrons (emitted from the bombardment of the uranium-235 fuel) are absorbed. Thus subsequent Uranium-235 bombardment reactions are moderated.

3.67   Fusion reactions naturally occur in stars, such as our sun.

3.68   Although the conditions for fusion reactions are difficult to achieve, the effort is worthwhile because energy can be produced without the formation of radioactive wastes.

Compounds and Their Bonds

4

Study Goals

- Write an electron dot formula for an atom of a representative element.
- Use the octet rule to determine the ionic charge of ions for representative elements.
- Use charge balance to write an ionic formula.
- Draw the electron dot structure for covalent compounds.
- Write the correct names for ionic and covalent compounds.
- Use electronegativity values to identify polar and nonpolar covalent bonds.
- Write ionic formulas and names of compound with polyatomic ions.
- Use VSEPR theory to determine the shape and bond angles of a molecule.
- Identify a covalent compound as polar or nonpolar.

Chapter Outline

4.1 Valence Electrons
4.2 Ions and the Octet Rule
   Health Note: Some Uses for Noble Gases
   Health Note: Some Important Ions in the Body
4.3 Ionic Compounds
4.4 Naming and Writing Ionic Formulas
   Career Focus: Physical Therapy
4.5 Covalent Bonds
4.6 Naming and Writing Formulas of Covalent Compounds
4.7 Bond Polarity
4.8 Polyatomic Ions
   Health Note: Polyatomic Ions in Bone and Teeth
   Explore Your World: Names of Compounds Listed on Products
4.9 Shapes of Molecules
4.10 Polar and Nonpolar Molecules

Chapter Summary and Demonstrations

1. Valence Electrons and Ionic Compounds

The electron configurations discussed in Chapter 2 lead into the concept of valence shells. Electron dot formulas are used to represent the valence electrons. Using the noble gases as models of stable atoms, the formation of positive and negative ions and their participation in ionic bonds is discussed. Students learn the relationship between group numbers, valence electrons, and the formation of ionic and covalent compounds. Ions from transition elements with variable valences and polyatomic ions are introduced. Students learn the naming systems for binary and tertiary ionic compounds as well as covalent compounds.

Demonstration: Large paper cutouts can be used to show charge balance of positive and negative ions. I use squares for 1+, 1– ions, rectangles twice the length of the square for 2+, 2– ions and longer rectangles (3x) for 3+, 3– ions. By matching them up until the total length of the positive ions equals the total length of the negative ions, the concept of charge balance and zero overall charge can be visually illustrated. Many students find this helpful when their algebra does not suffice.

charge can be visually illustrated. Many students find this helpful when their algebra does not suffice.

2. Covalent Compounds

The bonding of electrons in covalent compounds is illustrated through the sharing of electrons in electron dot formulas. Electronegativity values are used to describe equal and unequal sharing in covalent and polar bonds. The rules for naming binary ionic and covalent compounds are given with many examples. Polyatomic ions are introduced and the way they are named in ionic compounds is explained.

Demonstration: Read the list of ingredients on some products in the kitchen and bathroom cabinet. Identify them as ionic or molecular. Try to write the corresponding formula. A chemistry handbook such as the Merck Index may be needed.

3. Shapes and Polarity of Molecules

The shapes of molecules are described using valence electrons, electron-dot structures, and valence-shell electron-pair repulsion (VSEPR). Students identify polar and nonpolar bonds and predict the shape and polarity of molecules.
The electronic and molecular shape of a molecule is determined by identifying the number of electron pairs and the number of bonded atoms.

Demonstration: Students improve their understanding of the three-dimensional shapes of molecules and polyatomic ions by participating in hands on activities. For example, students can use two, three and four balloons to demonstrate the linear, trigonal planar, and tetrahedral shapes of molecules and polyatomic ions. An instructor can demonstration with large model sets and students can used Styrofoam balls bonded with toothpicks to demonstrate how electronic shape is based on the number of electron pairs around the central atom and how the number of bonded atoms and lone pairs of electrons determines shape.

Laboratory Suggestions

Lab 7 Compounds and Their Formulas

The elements and the number of atoms in a compound formula are recorded. The physical properties of different types of compounds are described. Subscripts are written to indicate the lowest ratio of atoms in the formula. The components making up ionic and covalent compounds are identified. Students learn to identify compounds as ionic or covalent based on the combination of elements in that compound. Students predict the shapes and polarity of molecules.
A. Electron Dot Structures
B. Ionic Compounds and Formulas
C. Ionic Charges with Transition Metals
D. Ionic Compounds with Polyatomic Ions
E. Covalent (Molecular) Compounds
F. Electron Dot Structure and Molecular Shape

Answers and Solutions to Text Problems

4.1 Valence electrons are found in the outermost energy level in an atom.

4.2 Because the electrons in an atom's outer shell determine its chemical properties, the group number was chosen to equal the number of valence electrons present in representative elements.

4.3 **a.** $1s^2 2s^2 2p^3$ five valence electrons
       b. $1s^2 2s^2 2p^4$ six valence electrons
       c. $1s^2 2s^2 2p^6 3s^2 3p^6$ eight valence electrons
       d. $1s^2 2s^2 2p^6 3s^2 3p^6 4s^1$ one valence electron
       e. $1s^2 2s^2 2p^6 3s^2 3p^4$ six valence electrons

4.4 **a.** 2, 8, 1   one valence electron   **b.** 2, 8, 3   three valence electrons
       c. 2, 8, 7   seven valence electrons   **d.** 2, 8, 2   two valence electrons
       e. 2, 8, 5   five valence electrons

4.5 The number of dots is equal to the number of valence electrons as indicated by the group number.

       a. Sulfur has 6 valence electrons $:\!S\!\cdot$

       b. Nitrogen has 5 valence electrons $\cdot\!N\!\cdot$

       c. Calcium has 2 valence electrons $Ca\cdot$

       d. Sodium has 1 valence electron $Na\cdot$

       e. Potassium has 1 valence electron $K\cdot$

4.6 **a.** 4, $\cdot\!C\!\cdot$ **b.** 6, $:\!O\!\cdot$ **c.** 7, $:\!F\!\cdot$ **d.** 1, Li $\cdot$ **e.** 7, $:\!Cl\!\cdot$

4.7 **a.** M $\cdot$ **b.** $\cdot$ M $\cdot$

4.8 **a.** $\cdot$ Nm $\cdot$ **b.** $:$ Nm $\cdot$

4.9 Alkali metals are members of Group 1A, and each has one valence electron.

4.10 Halogens are members of Group 7A, and each has seven valence electrons.

4.11 **a.** If sodium atom loses its valence electron, its second energy level has a complete octet.
       b. A neon atom has the same electronic arrangement as a sodium ion.
       c. Group 1A and Group 2A elements do not have a stable octet until each has lost one or two electrons, respectively. Electrically charged ions are formed when electrons are lost, and these positively-charged ions are attracted to negatively-charged ions resulting in the formation of compounds. Group 8A (18) elements have stable octets that remain electrically neutral, and have no tendency to form compounds.

4.12   **a.** When a chlorine atom gains an electron, its valence shell achieves a complete octet.
   b. An argon atom has the same electronic arrangement as a chloride ion.
   c. Group 7 elements do not have a stable octet until each has gained an electron. Electrically charged ions are formed when electrons are gained, and these negatively-charged ions are attracted to other positively-charged ions resulting in the formation of compounds. Group 8 elements have stable octets while remaining electrically neutral, and thus have no tendency to form compounds.

4.13   **a.**

   $: \text{Ne} :$ Neon has a complete valence shell.

   b. $: \text{O} \cdot$ Oxygen does *not* have a complete valence shell.

   c. $\text{Li} \cdot$ Lithium does *not* have a complete valence shell.

   d.

   $: \text{Ar} :$ Argon has a complete valence shell.

4.14   **a.** $\text{Mg} \cdot$ Magnesium does *not* have a complete valence shell

   b. $\cdot \text{N} \cdot$ Nitrogen does *not* have a complete valence shell

   c. $\text{He}:$ Helium has a complete valence shell of two electrons.

   d. $\text{K} \cdot$ Potassium does *not* have a complete valence shell

4.15   Atoms with 1, 2 or 3 valence electrons will lose those electrons.
   a. one   **b.** two   **c.** three   **d.** one   **e.** two

4.16   **a.** one   **b.** two   **c.** three   **d.** one   **e.** three

4.17   **a.** Ne   **b.** Ne   **c.** Ar   **d.** Ne   **e.** Ne

4.18   **a.** He   **b.** Kr   **c.** Ar   **d.** Ne   **e.** Kr

4.19   **a.** lose $2e^-$ **b.** gain $3e^-$ **c.** gain $1e^-$ **d.** lose $1e^-$ **e.** lose $3e^-$

4.20   **a.** gain $2e^-$ **b.** lose $2e^-$ **c.** gain $1e^-$ **d.** lose $1e^-$ **e.** gain $3e^-$

4.21   **a.** Li^+ **b.** F^- **c.** Mg^{2+} **d.** Fe^{3+} **e.** Zn^{2+}

4.22   **a.** 8 protons, 10 electrons   **b.** 19 protons, 18 electrons
   c. 35 protons, 36 electrons   **d.** 16 protons, 18 electrons
   e. 38 protons, 36 electrons

4.23   **a.** Cl^- **b.** K^+ **c.** O^{2-} **d.** Al^{3+}

4.24   **a.** F^- **b.** Ca^{2+} **c.** Na^+ **d.** Li^+

4.25   **a.** potassium   **b.** sulfide   **c.** calcium   **d.** nitride

4.26   **a.** magnesium   **b.** barium   **c.** iodide   **d.** chloride

37

4.27 **a.** (Li and Cl)   and   **c.** (K and O) will form ionic compounds

4.28 **b.** (Mg and Cl)   and   **d.** (K and S) will form ionic compounds

4.29

a. $K \cdot + \cdot \overset{\cdot\cdot}{\underset{\cdot\cdot}{Cl}} : \rightarrow K^+ + \left[: \overset{\cdot\cdot}{\underset{\cdot\cdot}{Cl}} : \right]^- \longrightarrow KCl$

b. $\cdot Ca \cdot + \cdot \overset{\cdot\cdot}{\underset{\cdot\cdot}{Cl}} : + \cdot \overset{\cdot\cdot}{\underset{\cdot\cdot}{Cl}} : \rightarrow Ca^{2+} + 2 \left[: \overset{\cdot\cdot}{\underset{\cdot\cdot}{Cl}} : \right]^- \longrightarrow CaCl_2$

c. $Na \cdot + Na \cdot + Na \cdot + \cdot \overset{\cdot\cdot}{\underset{\cdot}{N}} \cdot \rightarrow 3 Na^+ + \left[: \overset{\cdot\cdot}{\underset{\cdot\cdot}{N}} : \right]^{3-} \longrightarrow Na_3N$

4.30

a. $\cdot Mg \cdot + \cdot \overset{\cdot\cdot}{\underset{\cdot\cdot}{S}} \cdot \rightarrow Mg^{2+} + \left[: \overset{\cdot\cdot}{\underset{\cdot\cdot}{S}} : \right]^-$

b. $\cdot Al \cdot + \cdot \overset{\cdot\cdot}{\underset{\cdot\cdot}{Cl}} : + \cdot \overset{\cdot\cdot}{\underset{\cdot\cdot}{Cl}} : + \cdot \overset{\cdot\cdot}{\underset{\cdot\cdot}{Cl}} : \rightarrow Al^{3+} + \left[: \overset{\cdot\cdot}{\underset{\cdot\cdot}{Cl}} : \right]^- + \left[: \overset{\cdot\cdot}{\underset{\cdot\cdot}{Cl}} : \right]^- + \left[: \overset{\cdot\cdot}{\underset{\cdot\cdot}{Cl}} : \right]^-$

c. $Li \cdot + Li \cdot + \cdot \overset{\cdot\cdot}{\underset{\cdot\cdot}{O}} \cdot \rightarrow Li^+ + Li^+ + \left[: \overset{\cdot\cdot}{\underset{\cdot\cdot}{O}} : \right]^{2-}$

4.31	**a.** Na_2O	**b.** $AlBr_3$	**c.** BaO	**d.** $MgCl_2$	**e.** Al_2S_3
4.32	**a.** $AlCl_3$	**b.** CaS	**c.** Li_2S	**d.** K_3N	**e.** KI
4.33	**a.** Na_2S	**b.** K_3N	**c.** AlI_3	**d.** Li_2O	
4.34	**a.** $CaCl_2$	**b.** $BaBr_2$	**c.** Na_3P	**d.** MgO	

4.35 **a.** aluminum oxide   **b.** calcium chloride   **c.** sodium oxide
d. magnesium nitride   **e.** potassium iodide

4.36 **a.** magnesium chloride   **b.** potassium phosphide
c. lithium sulfide   **d.** lithium bromide
e. magnesium oxide

4.37 The Roman numeral is used to specify the positive charge on the transition metal in the compound. It is necessary for most transition metal compounds because many transition metals can exist as more than one cation; transition metals have variable ionic charges.

4.38 Because calcium ion only has a +2 charge, (it never varies), the name calcium is sufficient to specify the ion. However, Copper ions can exist with either a +1 or a +2 charge. Thus, the Roman numeral is used to specify which Copper ion is present in the compound.

4.39 **a.** iron (II); ferrous   **b.** copper (II); cupric   **c.** zinc   **d.** lead (IV); plumbic

4.40 **a.** silver   **b.** copper (I); cuprous   **c.** iron (III); ferric   **d.** tin (II); stannous
4.41 **a.** Tin (II) chloride; stannous chloride   **b.** Iron (II) oxide; ferrous oxide

c. Copper (I) sulfide; cuprous sulfide   **d.** Copper (II) sulfide; cupric sulfide

4.42   **a.** Silver phosphide   **b.** Lead(II) sulfide; plumbous sulfide
        c. Tin(IV) oxide; stannic oxide   **d.** Gold(III) chloride; auric chloride

4.43   **a.** +3   **b.** +3   **c.** +4   **d.** +2

4.44   **a.** +2   **b.** +2   **c.** +3   **d.** +3

4.45   **a.** $MgCl_2$ **b.** Na_2S **c.** Cu_2O **d.** Zn_3P_2 **e.** AuN

4.46   **a.** Fe_2O_3 **b.** BaF_2 **c.** $SnCl_4$ **d.** Ag_2S **c.** $CuCl_2$

4.47   **a.** $:\!Br\!:\!Br\!:$ **b.** $H:H$ **c.** $H:F\!:$ **d.** $:\!F\!:\!O\!:$
                                                                       $:\!F\!:$

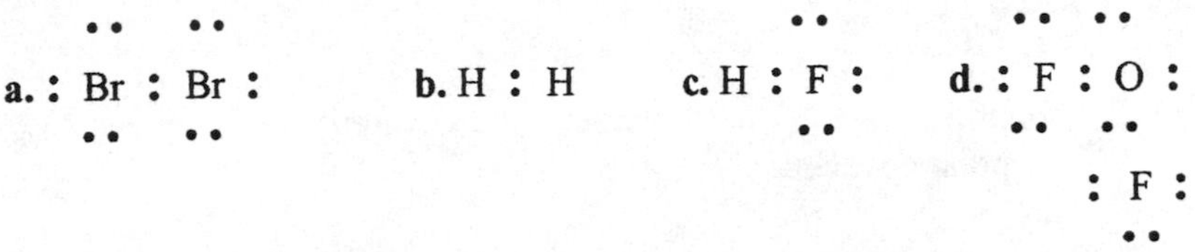

4.48   **a.** $:\!Cl\!:\!N\!:\!Cl\!:$ with $:\!Cl\!:$ above   **b.** $:\!Cl\!:\!C\!:\!Cl\!:$ with $:\!Cl\!:$ above and $:\!Cl\!:$ below

       c. $:\!Cl\!:\!Cl\!:$ **d.** $:\!F\!:\!Si\!:\!F\!:$ with $:\!F\!:$ above and $:\!F\!:$ below

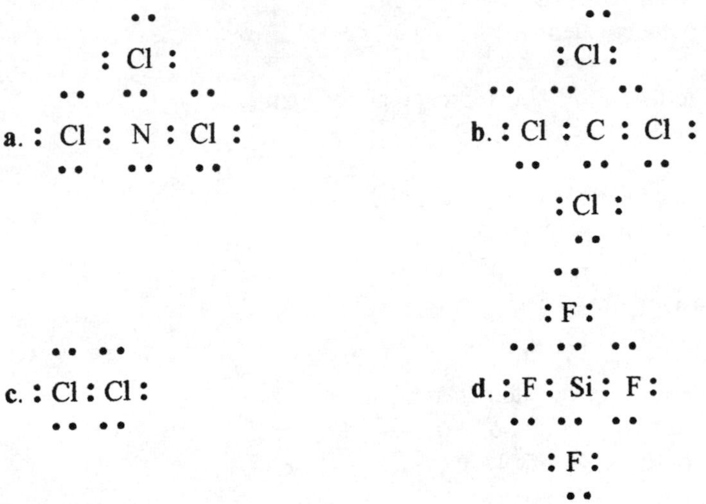

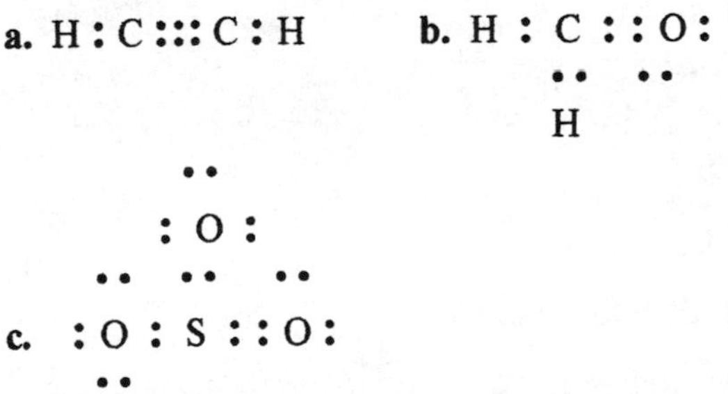

4.49   **a.** $H:C:::C:H$ **b.** $H:C::O:$ with H below

       c. $:O:S::O:$ with $:O:$ above

4.50   **a.** $H:C:::N:$ **b.** $H:C::C:H$ with H H below

       c. $H:O:N::O:$

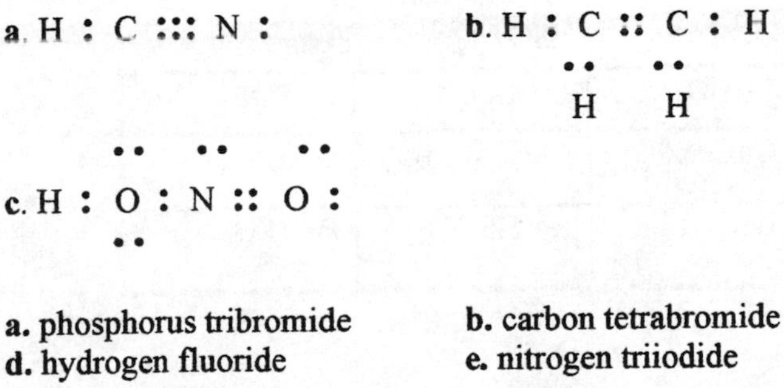

4.51   **a.** phosphorus tribromide   **b.** carbon tetrabromide   **c.** silicon dioxide
        d. hydrogen fluoride   **e.** nitrogen triiodide

4.52   **a.** carbon disulfide   **b.** diphosphorus pentoxide   **c.** dichlorine oxide
        d. phosphorus trichloride   **e.** dinitrogen tetroxide

4.53 **a.** dinitrogen trioxide   **b.** nitrogen trichloride   **c.** silicon tetrabromide
    d. phosphorus pentachloride   **e.** sulfur trioxide

4.54 **a.** silicon tetrafluoride   **b.** iodine tribromide   **c.** carbon dioxide
    d. sulfur dioxide   **e.** dinitrogen oxide

4.55 **a.** CCl_4 **b.** CO **c.** PCl_3 **d.** N_2O_4

4.56 **a.** SO_2 **b.** $SiCl_4$ **c.** IF_5 **d.** N_2O

4.57 **a.** OF_2 **b.** BF_3 **c.** N_2O_3 **d.** SF_6

4.58 **a.** SBr_2 **b.** CS_2 **c.** P_4O_6 **d.** N_2O_5

4.59 **a.** nonpolar covalent   **b.** none   **c.** nonpolar covalent
    d. ionic   **e.** polar covalent

4.60 **a.** ionic   **b.** polar covalent   **c.** ionic
    d. nonpolar covalent   **e.** polar covalent

4.61 **a.** polar covalent   **b.** ionic   **c.** polar covalent
    d. nonpolar covalent   **e.** polar covalent

4.62 **a.** ionic   **b.** nonpolar covalent   **c.** polar covalent
    d. polar covalent   **e.** polar covalent

4.63 **a.** F   **b.** F   **c.** Cl   **d.** Br   **e.** Cl

4.64 **a.** Li   **b.** Cl   **c.** O   **d.** F   **e.** Br

4.65 In a polar covalent bond, the more electronegative atom is assigned δ^-.

        $\overset{\delta^+}{}\overset{\delta^-}{}$ $\overset{\delta^+}{}\overset{\delta^-}{}$ $\overset{\delta^+}{}\overset{\delta^-}{}$ $\overset{\delta^+}{}\overset{\delta^-}{}$
    a. H—F   **b.** C—Cl   **c.** N—O   **d.** N—F

        $\overset{\delta^-}{}\overset{\delta^+}{}$ $\overset{\delta^-}{}\overset{\delta^+}{}$ $\overset{\delta^+}{}\overset{\delta^-}{}$ $\overset{\delta^+}{}\overset{\delta^-}{}$
4.66 **a.** O—H   **b.** O—S   **c.** P—Cl   **d.** S—Cl

4.67 **a.** HCO_3^- **b.** NH_4^+ **c.** PO_4^{3-} **d.** HSO_4^-

4.68 **a.** NO_2^- **b.** SO_3^{2-} **c.** OH^- **d.** PO_3^{3-}

4.69 **a.** sulfate   **b.** carbonate   **c.** phosphate   **d.** nitrate

4.70 **a.** hydroxide   **b.** hydrogen sulfite (or bisulfite)   **c.** cyanide   **d.** nitrite

4.71

	OH^-	NO_2^-	CO_3^{2-}	HSO_4^-	PO_4^{3-}
Li^+	LiOH	$LiNO_2$	Li_2CO_3	$LiHSO_4$	Li_3PO_4
Cu^{2+}	$Cu(OH)_2$	$Cu(NO_2)_2$	$CuCO_3$	$Cu(HSO_4)_2$	$Cu_3(PO_4)_2$
Ba^{2+}	$Ba(OH)_2$	$Ba(NO_2)_2$	$BaCO_3$	$Ba(HSO_4)_2$	$Ba_3(PO_4)_2$

4.72

	OH^-	NO_3^-	HCO_3^-	SO_3^{2-}	PO_4^{3-}
NH_4^+	NH_4OH	NH_4NO_3	NH_4HCO_3	$(NH_4)_2SO_3$	$(NH_4)_3PO_4$
Al^{3+}	$Al(OH)_3$	$Al(NO_3)_3$	$Al(HCO_3)_3$	$Al_2(SO_3)_3$	$AlPO_4$
Pb^{4+}	$Pb(OH)_4$	$Pb(NO_3)_4$	$Pb(HCO_3)_4$	$Pb(SO_3)_2$	$Pb_3(PO_4)_4$

4.73 **a.** CO_3^{2-}, sodium carbonate **b.** NH_4^+, ammonium chloride

c. PO_4^{3-}, lithium phosphate **d.** NO_2^-, copper (II) or cupric nitrite

e. SO_3^{2-}, iron (II) or ferrous sulfite

4.74 **a.** K $\boxed{OH}$ Potassium Hydroxide **b.** Na $\boxed{NO_3}$ Sodium Nitrate

c. Cu $\boxed{CO_3}$ Copper(II) or Cupric Carbonate

d. Na $\boxed{HCO_3}$ Sodium Bicarbonate **e.** Ba $\boxed{SO_4}$ Barium Sulfate

4.75 **a.** $Ba(OH)_2$ **b.** Na_2SO_4 **c.** $Fe(NO_3)_2$ **d.** $Zn_3(PO_4)_2$ **e.** $Fe_2(CO_3)_3$

4.76 **a.** $AlCl_3$ **b.** $(NH_4)_2O$ **c.** $Mg(HCO_3)_2$ **d.** $NaNO_2$ **e.** Cu_2SO_4

4.77 **a.** This is an ionic compound with Al^{3+} ion and the sulfate SO_4^{2-} polyatomic ion. The correct name is aluminum sulfate
b. This is an ionic compound with Ca^{2+} ion and the carbonate CO_3^{2-} polyatomic ion. The correct name is calcium carbonate
c. This is a covalent compound because it contains two nonmetals. Using prefixes, it is named dinitrogen monoxide.
d. This is an ionic compound with sodium ion Na^+ and the PO_4^{3-} polyatomic ion. The correct name is sodium phosphate
e. This ionic compound contains two polyatomic ions ammonium NH_4^+ and sulfate SO_4^{2-}. It is named ammonium sulfate
f. This is an ionic compound containing the variable metal ion Fe^{3+} and oxide ion O^{2-}. It is named using the Roman numeral as iron(III) or ferric oxide

4.78 **a.** nitrogen **b.** magnesium phosphate
c. iron(II) or ferrous sulfate **d.** magnesium sulfate
e. copper(I) or cuprous oxide **f.** tin(II) or stannous fluoride

4.79 **a.** Linear. Two groups of electrons bonded to a central atom with no lone pairs gives a linear shape to the molecule.
b. Pyramidal. Four electron pairs are arranged in a tetrahedron. The shape is pyramidal because there are three atoms and one lone pair bonded to the central atom.

4.80 **a.** Four groups of electrons bonded to a central atom with no lone pairs give a tetrahedral shape.
b. Four electron pairs are arranged as a tetrahedron with 109° angles. When only two pairs are bonded to atoms, it has a bent shape.

4.81 The four electron groups in PCl_3 have a tetrahedral arrangement, but three bonded atoms around a central atom give a pyramidal shape.

4.82 In the electron dot structure of H_2S, the central atom S has four electrons pairs arranged as a tetrahedron. Because there are two bonded atoms and two lone pairs, H_2S has a bent shape. The arrangement of electron pairs determine the angels between the pairs, whereas the number of bonded atom determines the shape of the molecule.

4.83 In the electron dot structure of BH_3, the central atom B has three bonded atoms and no lone pairs, which give BH_3 a trigonal planar shape with angles of 120°. In the molecule NH_3, the central atom N is bonded to three atoms and one lone pair. The structure of the electron groups is tetrahedral, which gives NH_3 a pyramidal shape with angles of 109°.

4.84 In CH_4 and H_2O the central atoms of C and O have four electron pairs arranged as tetrahedrons, which have 109° angles. The shapes are different because CH_4 has four bonded atoms (tetrahedral shape), whereas H_2O has two bonded atoms and two lone pairs (bent shape).

4.85 **a.** Two atoms in a molecule have a linear shape.
b. The central oxygen atom has four electron pairs with two bonded to fluorine atoms. Its shape is bent with 109° angles.
c. The central atom C has two electron groups bonded to two atoms; HCN is linear.
d. The central atom C has four electron pairs bonded to four chlorine atoms; CCl_4 has a tetrahedral shape.

4.86 **a.** tetrahedral **b.** pyramidal **c.** bent **d.** linear

4.87 To find the total valence electrons for an ion, add the total valence electrons for each atom and add the number of electrons indicated by a negative charge.
a. C (4 valence electrons) + 3 O (3 x 6 valence electrons) + charge (2 electrons) = $4e^- + 18e^- + 2e^- = 24\ e^-$ total for the electron dot structure

3 electron groups around C; trigonal planar shape

b. S (6 valence electrons) + 4 O (4 × 6 valence electrons) + charge (2 electrons) = $6e^- + 24e^- + 2e^- = 32\ e^-$ total for the electron dot structure

4 electron pairs around S; tetrahedral shape

4.88 To find the total valence electrons for an ion, add the total valence electrons for each atom and add the number of electrons indicated by a negative charge.
a. N (5 valence electrons) + 2 O (2 x 6 valence electrons) + charge (1 electron) = $5e^- + 12e^- + 1e^- = 18\ e^-$ total for the electron dot structure

3 electron groups around N; two bonded atoms and one lone pair give a bent molecular shape with 120° angles.

b. P (5 valence electrons) + 4 O (4 x 6 valence electrons) + charge (3 electrons) =
5e⁻ + 24e⁻ + 3e⁻ = 32 e⁻ total for the electron dot structure

$$
\left[\begin{array}{c} :\overset{..}{O}: \\[2pt] \overset{..}{:O}:\overset{..}{\underset{..}{P}}:\overset{..}{O}: \\[2pt] :\overset{..}{\underset{..}{O}}: \end{array} \right]^{3-}
$$

4 electron pairs around P and four bonded atoms give a tetrahedral shape

4.89 Cl₂ is a nonpolar molecule because there is a nonpolar covalent bond between Cl atoms, which have identical electronegativity values. In HCl, the bond is a polar bond, which is a dipole and makes HCl a polar molecule.

4.90 CH₄ with four equal polar bonds has four equal dipoles that cancel to give a nonpolar molecule. In CH₃Cl, the one C—Cl bond is much more polar than the C—H bonds. Therefore, the dipoles will not cancel, which makes CH₃Cl a polar molecule.

4.91 Write the symbols δ^+ and δ^- over the atoms that are in polar bonds.

                                            $\delta^+ \quad \delta^-$ $\delta^+ \quad \delta^-$

a. Cl—Cl   **b.** C—Cl   **c.** N—O

      $\delta^+ \quad \delta^-$ $\delta^+ \quad \delta^-$ $\delta^- \quad \delta^+$

d. H—O   **e.** P—F   **f.** S—H

4.92 Write the symbols δ^+ and δ^- over the atoms that are in polar bonds.

      $\delta^- \quad \delta^+$ $\delta^+ \quad \delta^-$

a. F—Cl   **b.** P—H   **c.** C—O

      $\delta^+ \quad \delta^-$ $\delta^+ \quad \delta^-$ $\delta^- \quad \delta^+$

d. S—O   **e.** N—F   **f.** O—Cl

4.93 **a.** two dipoles cancel; nonpolar   **b.** dipoles do not cancel; polar
       c. four dipoles cancel; nonpolar   **d.** three dipoles cancel; nonpolar

4.94 **a.** dipoles do not cancel; nonpolar   **b.** dipoles do not cancel; polar
       c. four dipoles cancel; nonpolar   **d.** dipoles do not cancel; polar

4.95 **a.** P   **b.** Na   **c.** Al   **d.** Si

4.96 **a.** 2,8,8   **b.** 2,8   **c.** 2,8,8   **d.** 2,8,8   **e.** 2,8,8

4.97 **a.** $1s^2\,2s^2\,2p^6$ **b.** $1s^2\,2\underline{s}^2\,2p^6$ **c.** $1s^2\,2\underline{s}^2\,2p^6$
       d. $1s^2\,2\underline{s}^2\,2p^6$ **e.** $1s^2$

4.98 **a.** Ne   **b.** Ar   **c.** Ar   **d.** Ne   **e.** Ne

4.99 **a.** Group 2A   **b.** •X•   **c.** Be

4.100 **a.** X is in Group 1; Y is in Group 6   **b.** ionic   **c.** X⁺, Y²⁻
        d. X₂Y   **e.** XCl   **f.** YCl₂

4.101 **a.** Sn⁴⁺   **b.** 50 protons, 46 electrons   **c.** SnO₂   **d.** Sn₃(PO₄)₄

4.102 Calcium, phosphate, and hydroxide ions are present in calcium hydroxyapatite.

4.103 Compounds with a metal and nonmetal are classified as ionic; two nonmetals as covalent.
    a. ionic   **b.** covalent   **c.** covalent   **d.** covalent
    e. ionic   **f.** covalent   **g.** ionic   **h.** ionic

4.104 With a filled energy level, helium is a stable, unreactive element. Hydrogen does not have a filled energy level, and it is a reactive element, (in fact it burns). Thus, helium is used to avoid potentially hazardous conditions.

4.105   **a.** iron(III) or ferric chloride   **b.** dichlorine heptoxide
    c. bromine   **d.** calcium phosphate
    e. phosphorus trichloride   **f.** aluminum carbonate
    g. lead(IV) or plumbic chloride   **h.** magnesium carbonate
    i. nitrogen dioxide   **j.** tin (II) or stannous sulfate
    k. barium nitrate   **l.** copper(II) or cupric sulfide

4.106   **a.** $SnCO_3$ **b.** Li_3P **c.** $SiCl_4$ **d.** Fe_2S_3 **e.** CO_2
    f. $CaBr_2$ **g.** Na_2CO_3 **h.** NO_2 **i.** $Al(NO_3)_3$ **j.** Cu_3N
    k. K_3PO_3 **l.** PbS_2

4.107 **a.** trigonal planar, dipoles cancel, nonpolar
    b. bent, dipoles do not cancel, polar
    c. linear, dipoles cancel, nonpolar

4.108 **a.** Tetrahedral; dipoles cancel; nonpolar
    b. Pyramid; dipoles do not cancel; polar
    c. Tetrahedral; dipoles do not cancel; polar

4.109 **a.** bent, dipoles do not cancel, polar
    b. pyramidal, dipoles do not cancel, polar
    c. trigonal planar, dipoles cancel, nonpolar

4.110 **a.** Linear; equal atoms, nonpolar
    b. Tetrahedral; dipoles cancel; nonpolar
    c. Linear; unlike atoms, polar

4.111 **a.** trigonal planar   **b.** tetrahedral   **c.** tetrahedral

4.112 **a.** trigonal planar   **b.** pyramidal   **c.** bent (120°)

Study Goals
- Describe potential and kinetic energy.
- Calculate the calories or joules lost or gained by a specific amount of a substance for a specific temperature change.
- Determine the kilocalories for food samples.
- Determine the energy lost or gained during a change of state at the melting or boiling point.
- Describe the types of forces that hold particles together in liquids and solids.
- Identify the states of matter and changes of state on heating and cooling curves.

Chapter Outline

5.1 Energy
Environmental Note: Global Warming
Career Focus: Histology Technician

5.2 Measuring Heat Energy
Explore Your World: Loss and Gain of Heat
Explore Your World: Specific Heat

5.3 Energy and Nutrition
Explore Your World: Counting Calories
Health Note: Losing and Gaining Weight
Explore Your World: Calories in One Day

5.4 States of Matter
Explore Your World: States of Matter

5.5 Attractive Forces Between Particles

5.6 Melting and Freezing

5.7 Boiling and Condensation
Health Note: Steam Burns

5.8 Heating and Cooling Curves

Chapter Summary and Demonstrations

1. Specific heat
Specific heat is discussed and the calorie and Joule are defined. The amount of heat as calories or joules is calculated from temperature change and mass of substance, usually water.

Demonstration: The connection between the high specific heat of water, the high amount of water in the body, and water's function in maintaining a narrow range of body temperature makes is a very dramatic application for the concept of specific heat. The concept can also be applied to show how the presence or absence of nearby oceans affects climates.

2. Caloric Values
A practical discussion of the caloric content of food brings the discussion into the "real world" of the student. Heat and energy is discussed as the caloric energy values of foodstuffs, and the loss and gain of weight.

Demonstration: This can be done as an at-home or in-class activity by passing out empty container that list nutritional information. Students learn to read the data by calculating the Calories for protein, fat, and carbohydrate and compare to the Calories per serving listed in the nutritional data.

3. States of Matter

The chapter closes with a discussion of the states of matter and the changes of states. These states and changes are illustrated as heating and cooling curves. Heats of fusion and vaporization are included in the calculations.

Demonstration (A): Items in the room are identified as solid, liquid, and gas. Ice and boiling water are used to show melting and boiling and the temperatures at which those processes occur is discussed. Calculations showing why a steam burn causes more damage than hot water are of interest to students. The exothermic effects of freezing are illustrated with the example that water is sprayed in orchards during freezing temperatures. The processes of raining or snowing are exothermic and warm the air. The reversible change of state in a refrigerator demonstrates how heat is removed from the inside of a refrigerator.

Demonstration(B): Obtain three petri dishes and some BBs. For a solid, make a layer in one dish of BBs. For the liquid, add BBs to cover 1/3-1/2 the surface. For the gas, place 3-4 BBs in the dish. Place the "solid" dish on an overhead projector and agitate. The BBs vibrate but can't move around much indicating some motion but no change in shape. Slant the "liquid" dish and agitate. The BBs move around more, but remain at the lower part of the dish. When you agitate the "gas" dish, the BBs have a lot of space to move in and move all the way to the edges of the dish.

Laboratory Suggestions

Lab 8 Energy and Specific Heat

Students determine the specific heat of a metal by heating the metal to boiling and placing it in a measured quantity of cool water in a Styrofoam calorimeter cup. The temperature change, mass of water, and the specific heat of water are used in the specific heat calculation. Burning a food and measuring the temperature change in water demonstrate the measurement of caloric value of food. The nutrition information on food products is used to determine caloric values of food products.

A. Specific Heat of A Metal

B. Measure the Caloric Value of a Food

C. Food Calories

Laboratory Skills to Demonstrate

Setup for heating water and need for caution when boiling water.

Setup of a Styrofoam cup as a calorimeter.

Calculate calories using mass of water and temperature change

Use caloric food values to calculate kilocalories using the nutritional data on food labels.

Lab 9 Energy and Matter

The temperature of water that is heated is recorded each minute, graphed as a heating curve, and used to identify the boiling point. The temperature change of water is measured when a sample of ice melts. Using the mass of water, temperature change and specific heat of water, the heat of fusion is calculated.

A. A Heating Curve for Water

B. Graphing a Cooling Curve

C. Energy in Changes of State

Laboratory Skills to Demonstrate

Setup for heating water and need for caution when boiling water.

Setup and use of the freezing point apparatus

Prepare graphs of heating and a cooling curves.

Answers and Solutions to Text Problems

5.1 At the top of the hill, all of the energy of the car is in the form of potential energy. As it descends down the hill, potential energy is being converted into kinetic energy. When the car reaches the bottom, all of its energy is in the form of motion (kinetic energy).

5.2 As the elevator (lift) moves to the top of the ramp, the skier's potential energy is increasing. As the skier descends down the ramp (ski jump), potential energy is being converted into kinetic energy.

5.3 **a.** potential **b.** kinetic **c.** potential **d.** potential

5.4 **a.** potential **b.** potential **c.** kinetic **d.** kinetic

5.5 **a.** Using a hair dryer converts electrical energy into heat energy, (the air is warmed).
b. Using a fan converts electrical energy into kinetic energy.
c. Burning gasoline converts chemical energy into kinetic energy as the car is propelled down the road, and heat energy as the car's components warm up.
d. Radiant energy is converted into heat energy by the solar water heater.

5.6 **a.** Electrical energy becomes radiant and heat energies when the filament glows.
b. Burning gas converts chemical energy into radiant and heat energies.
c. Electrical energy is converted into heat energy.
d. The chemical energy of the log is converted into radiant and heat energies.

5.7 Copper has the lowest specific heat of the samples and will reach the highest temperature.

5.8 The specific heat of A must be less than the specific heat of B because the amount of temperature change depends on the amount of energy supplied (or removed, if cooling), the amount of material present, and its specific heat. If the same amount of energy is applied to each substance and equal masses of A and B are used, the only variable that remains is the specific heat for each material. A substance with a low specific heat will produce a larger temperature change that a substance with a high specific heat.

5.9 **a.** $3500 \text{ cal} \times \dfrac{1 \text{ kcal}}{1000 \text{ cal}} = 3.5 \text{ kcal}$

b. $28 \text{ cal} \times \dfrac{4.18 \text{ J}}{1 \text{ cal}} = 120 \text{ J}$

c. $425 \text{ J} \times \dfrac{1 \text{ cal}}{4.18 \text{ J}} = 102 \text{ cal}$

d. $4.5 \text{ kJ} \times \dfrac{1000 \text{ J}}{1 \text{ kJ}} \times \dfrac{1 \text{ cal}}{4.18 \text{ J}} = 1100 \text{ cal}$

5.10 **a.** $8.1 \text{ kcal} \times \dfrac{1000 \text{ cal}}{1 \text{ kcal}} = 8100 \text{ cal}$

b. $325 \text{ J} \times \dfrac{1 \text{ kJ}}{1000 \text{ J}} = 0.325 \text{ kJ}$

c. $2250 \text{ cal} \times \dfrac{4.18 \text{ J}}{1 \text{ cal}} \times \dfrac{1 \text{ kJ}}{1000 \text{ J}} = 9.41 \text{ kJ}$

d. $2.50 \text{ kcal} \times \dfrac{1000 \text{ cal}}{1 \text{ kcal}} \times \dfrac{4.18 \text{ J}}{1 \text{ cal}} = 1.05 \times 10^4 \text{ J}$

5.11 **a.** $\Delta T = 25°C - 15°C = 10.°C$ $25 \text{ g} \times \dfrac{1.00 \text{ cal}}{\text{g°C}} \times 10.°C = 250 \text{ cal}$

b. $150 \text{ g} \times \dfrac{4.18 \text{ J}}{\text{g°C}} \times 75°C$ $= 47\,000 \text{ J}$

c. $10.0 \text{ g} \times \dfrac{0.39 \text{ J}}{\text{g°C}} \times 250.°C$ $= 980 \text{ J}$

d. $150 \text{ g} \times \dfrac{4.18 \text{ J}}{\text{g°C}} \times 62°C \times \dfrac{1 \text{ kJ}}{1000 \text{ J}}$ $= 39 \text{ kJ}$

e. $10.0 \text{ g Ag} \times 222°C \times \dfrac{0.24 \text{ J}}{\text{g°C}}$ $= 530 \text{ J}$

5.12 **a.** $\Delta T = 45°C - 25°C = 20.°C$ $85 \text{ g} \times \dfrac{1.00 \text{ cal}}{\text{g°C}} \times 20.°C = 1700 \text{ cal}$

b. $0.50 \text{ kg} \times \dfrac{1000 \text{ g}}{1 \text{ kg}} \times \dfrac{4.18 \text{ J}}{\text{g°C}} \times 20.°C$ $= 42\,000 \text{ J or } 4.2 \times 10^4 \text{ J}$

c. $250. \text{ g} \times \dfrac{0.19 \text{ cal}}{\text{g°C}} \times 113°C \times \dfrac{1 \text{ kcal}}{1000 \text{ cal}}$ $= 5.4 \text{ kcal}$

d. $25 \text{ g} \times \dfrac{4.18 \text{ J}}{\text{g°C}} \times 25°C$ $= 2600 \text{ J or } 2.6 \times 10^3 \text{ J}$

e. $5.0 \text{ kg} \times \dfrac{1000 \text{ g}}{1 \text{ kg}} \times \dfrac{1.00 \text{ cal}}{\text{g°C}} \times 6°C \times \dfrac{1 \text{ kcal}}{1000 \text{ cal}}$ $= 30 \text{ kcal} = 3 \times 10^1 \text{ kcal}$

5.13 **a.** Rearrange the equation $\text{cal} = \text{g} \times \Delta T \times \text{specific heat}$ for mass (g)

$$g = \frac{\text{cal}}{\Delta T \times \text{spec. heat}} = \frac{450 \text{ cal}}{(12°C)(0.031 \text{ cal/g°C})} = 1200 \text{ g}$$

b. $g = \dfrac{\text{cal}}{\Delta T \times \text{spec. heat}} = \dfrac{2500 \text{ cal}}{(28°C)(1.00 \text{ cal/g°C})} = 89 \text{ g}$

c. Rearrange the equation $\text{cal} = \text{g} \times \Delta T \times \text{specific heat}$ for specific heat

$$\text{spec. heat} = \frac{\text{cal}}{\text{g} \times \Delta T} = \frac{320 \text{ cal}}{(25 \text{ g})(102°C)} = 0.13 \text{ cal/g°C}$$

d. $\text{spec. heat} = \dfrac{\text{cal}}{\text{g} \times \Delta T} = \dfrac{1500 \text{ cal}}{(36 \text{ g})(217°C)} = 0.19 \text{ cal/g°C}$

5.14 $\text{Heat} = \text{g} \times \Delta T \times \text{sp. ht.}$
$\text{Mass (g)} = \text{heat}/(\Delta T \times \text{sp. ht.})$

a. $\Delta T = 26°C - 14°C = 12°C$

$g = \dfrac{180 \text{ cal}}{12°C \times 0.057 \text{ cal/g °C}} = 260 \text{ g}$ (2 SF)

b. $g = \dfrac{3200 \text{ cal}}{40.°C \times 1.0 \text{ cal/g °C}} = 80. \text{ g}$ (2 SF)

c. $\text{spec. heat} = \text{heat}/(\text{g} \times \Delta T)$

$= \dfrac{260 \text{ cal}}{28 \text{ g} \times 212°C} = 0.044 \text{ cal/g°C}$

d. sp. ht. = $\dfrac{2100 \text{ cal}}{45 \text{ g} \times 184°C}$ = 0.25 cal/g°C

5.15 **a.** 500. g̶ × $\dfrac{1.00 \text{ c̶a̶l̶}}{\text{g̶°C̶}}$ × 10.°C̶ × $\dfrac{1 \text{ Cal}}{1000 \text{ c̶a̶l̶}}$ = 5.0 Cal

b. 5000. g̶ × $\dfrac{1.00 \text{ c̶a̶l̶}}{\text{g̶°C̶}}$ × 42°C̶ × $\dfrac{1 \text{ Cal}}{1000 \text{ c̶a̶l̶}}$ = 210 Cal

c. 1000. g̶ × $\dfrac{1.00 \text{ c̶a̶l̶}}{\text{g̶°C̶}}$ × 25°C̶ × $\dfrac{1 \text{ Cal}}{1000 \text{ c̶a̶l̶}}$ = 25 Cal

5.16 To calculate heat, we need the mass of the water, its specific heat, and the temperature change. The only additional task is to divide the heat energy absorbed by the water, (which is equivalent to the energy released by the combustion of fuel), by the grams of octane burned, as follows:

1200 g̶ × $\dfrac{4.18 \text{ J̶}}{\text{g̶°C̶}}$ × 4°C̶ × $\dfrac{1 \text{ kJ}}{1000 \text{ J̶}}$ × $\dfrac{1}{0.50 \text{ g octane}}$ = 40 kJ/g octane

5.17 Recall that a Calorie is equivalent to a kilocalorie!
  a. Because the orange juice contains both carbohydrate and protein, two calculations will be needed.

26 g̶ ̶c̶a̶r̶b̶o̶h̶y̶d̶r̶a̶t̶e̶ × $\dfrac{4 \text{ Cal}}{\text{g̶ ̶c̶a̶r̶b̶o̶h̶y̶d̶r̶a̶t̶e̶}}$ =   100 Cal

2 g̶ ̶p̶r̶o̶t̶e̶i̶n̶ × $\dfrac{4 \text{ Cal}}{\text{g̶ ̶p̶r̶o̶t̶e̶i̶n̶}}$ =   8 Cal

Total: 100 Cal + 8 Cal = 110 Cal

  b. With only carbohydrate present, a single calculation is all that is required.

72 k̶c̶a̶l̶ × $\dfrac{1 \text{ g carbohydrate}}{4 \text{ k̶c̶a̶l̶}}$ =   18 g carbohydrate

  c. With only fat present, a single calculation is all that is required.

14 g̶ ̶f̶a̶t̶ × $\dfrac{9 \text{ Cal}}{\text{g̶ ̶f̶a̶t̶}}$ =   130 Cal

  d. Three calculations are needed:

30. g̶ ̶c̶a̶r̶b̶o̶h̶y̶d̶r̶a̶t̶e̶ × $\dfrac{4 \text{ kcal}}{\text{g̶ ̶c̶a̶r̶b̶o̶h̶y̶d̶r̶a̶t̶e̶}}$ × $\dfrac{1 \text{ Cal}}{1 \text{ k̶c̶a̶l̶}}$ =   120 Cal

15 g̶ ̶f̶a̶t̶ × $\dfrac{9 \text{ kcal}}{\text{g̶ ̶f̶a̶t̶}}$ × $\dfrac{1 \text{ Cal}}{1 \text{ k̶c̶a̶l̶}}$ =   140 Cal

5 g̶ ̶p̶r̶o̶t̶e̶i̶n̶ × $\dfrac{4 \text{ kcal}}{\text{g̶ ̶p̶r̶o̶t̶e̶i̶n̶}}$ × $\dfrac{1 \text{ Cal}}{1 \text{ k̶c̶a̶l̶}}$ =   20 Cal

Total: 120 Cal + 140 Cal + 2 0 Cal   =   280 Cal

5.18 Recall that a Calorie is equivalent to a kilocalorie. (All values are rounded to the tens place)
  a. Three calculations are needed:

6 g̶ ̶c̶a̶r̶b̶o̶h̶y̶d̶r̶a̶t̶e̶ × $\dfrac{4 \text{ kcal}}{\text{g̶ ̶c̶a̶r̶b̶o̶h̶y̶d̶r̶a̶t̶e̶}}$ = 20 kcal

16 g̶ ̶f̶a̶t̶ × $\dfrac{9 \text{ kcal}}{\text{g̶ ̶f̶a̶t̶}}$ = 140 kcal

7 g̶ ̶p̶r̶o̶t̶e̶i̶n̶ × $\dfrac{4 \text{ kcal}}{\text{g̶ ̶p̶r̶o̶t̶e̶i̶n̶}}$ = 30 kcal

Total: 20 kcal + 140 kcal + 30 kcal   = 190 kcal

  b. First, we need to calculate how many Calories are due to fat and carbohydrate:

7 g̶ ̶f̶a̶t̶ × $\dfrac{9 \text{ Calories}}{\text{g̶ ̶f̶a̶t̶}}$ = 60 Calories

9 g̶ ̶c̶a̶r̶b̶o̶h̶y̶d̶r̶a̶t̶e̶ × $\dfrac{4 \text{ Calories}}{\text{g̶ ̶c̶a̶r̶b̶o̶h̶y̶d̶r̶a̶t̶e̶}}$ = 40 Calories

Total: 60 Calories + 40 Calories = 100 Calories

Subtracting the Calories due to fat and carbohydrate from 110 Calories yields the Calories due to protein. From this information, we can calculate the mass of protein present in the soup, as follows:

110 Calories − 100 Calories = 10 Calories

10 ~~Calories~~ × $\dfrac{1 \text{ g protein}}{4 \text{ ~~Calories~~}}$ = 3 g protein

c. With just carbohydrate present, only a single calculation is required.

140 ~~Calories~~ × $\dfrac{1 \text{ g carbohydrate}}{4 \text{ ~~Calories~~}}$ = 35 g carbohydrate (sugar)

d. First, we need to calculate how many Calories are due to carbohydrate and protein:

13 ~~g carbohydrate~~ × $\dfrac{4 \text{ Calories}}{\text{g carbohydrate}}$ = 50 Calories

5 ~~g protein~~ × $\dfrac{9 \text{ Calories}}{\text{g protein}}$ = 50 Calories

Total: 50 Calories + 50 Calories = 100 Calories

Subtracting the Calories due to carbohydrate and protein from the total of 405 Calories yields the Calories due to fat. From this information, we can calculate the mass of fat present in the avocado, as follows:

405 Calories − 100 Calories = 305 (or 310) Calories

310 ~~Calories~~ × $\dfrac{1 \text{ g fat}}{9 \text{ ~~Calories~~}}$ = 34 g fat

5.19 Three calculations are needed:

9 ~~g protein~~ × $\dfrac{4 \text{ kcal}}{\text{g protein}}$ = 40 kcal

12 ~~g fat~~ × $\dfrac{9 \text{ kcal}}{\text{g fat}}$ = 110 kcal

16 ~~g carbohydrate~~ × $\dfrac{4 \text{ kcal}}{\text{g carbohydrate}}$ = 64 kcal

Total: 40 kcal + 110 kcal + 64 kcal = 210 kcal

Then 210 ~~kcal~~ × $\dfrac{4.18 \text{ kJ}}{1 \text{ ~~kcal~~}}$ = 880 kJ

5.20 Three calculations are needed:

70. ~~g carbohydrate~~ × $\dfrac{4 \text{ kcal}}{\text{g carbohydrate}}$ = 280 kcal

150 ~~g protein~~ × $\dfrac{4 \text{ kcal}}{\text{g protein}}$ = 600 kcal (5.0 x 10² kcal)

5.0 ~~g fat~~ × $\dfrac{9 \text{ kcal}}{\text{g fat}}$ = 45 kcal

Total: 280 kcal + 600 kcal + 45 kcal = 930 kcal

Then 280 ~~kcal~~ × $\dfrac{4.18 \text{ kJ}}{1 \text{ ~~kcal~~}}$ = 1200 kJ

600 ~~kcal~~ × $\dfrac{4.18 \text{ kJ}}{1 \text{ ~~kcal~~}}$ = 2500 kJ

45 ~~kcal~~ × $\dfrac{4.18 \text{ kJ}}{1 \text{ ~~kcal~~}}$ = 190 kJ

Total: 1200 kJ + 2500 kJ + 190 kJ = 3900 kJ

5.21   **a.** gas   **b.** gas   **c.** solid

5.22   **a.** liquid   **b.** gas   **c.** gas

5.23   **a.** dipole-dipole   **b.** ionic   **c.** dispersion
           d. hydrogen bond   **e.** dispersion

5.24   **a.** dipole-dipole   **b.** ionic   **c.** dipole-dipole
           d. dispersion forces   **e.** hydrogen bond

5.25   **a.** HF; hydrogen bonds are stronger than dipole-dipole interactions of HBr
           b. NaF; ionic bonds are stronger than the hydrogen bonds in HF
           c. $MgBr_2$; ionic bonds are stronger than the dipoles-dipole interactions in PBr_3
           d. C_4H_{10} has more electrons and therefore more dispersion forces than CH_4.

5.26   **a.** $MgCl_2$ **b.** H_2O **c.** NH_3 **d.** HF

5.27   Both b (liquid water freezes) and d (solid butter melts) describe processes that involve a change
           of state.

5.28   Both a (solid water sublimes) and c (solid1 nitrogen melts) describe processes that involve a
           change of state.

5.29   **a.** melting   **b.** melting   **c.** sublimation   **d.** freezing

5.30   **a.** sublimation   **b.** melting   **c.** freezing   **d.** freezing

5.31   **a.** 65 g ice × $\dfrac{80.\ cal}{1\ g\ ice}$ = 5200 cal absorbed

   b. 17.0 g ice × $\dfrac{80.\ cal}{1\ g\ ice}$ × $\dfrac{4.18\ J}{1\ cal}$ = 5700 J absorbed

   c. 225 g water × $\dfrac{80.\ cal}{1\ g\ water}$ × $\dfrac{1\ kcal}{1000\ cal}$ = 18 kcal released

   d. 50.0 g water × $\dfrac{80.\ cal}{1\ g\ water}$ × $\dfrac{4.18\ J}{1\ cal}$ × $\dfrac{1\ kJ}{1000\ J}$ = 17 kJ released

5.32   **a.** 35 g water × $\dfrac{80.\ cal}{1\ g\ water}$ = 2800 cal (released)

   b. 250 g water × $\dfrac{80.\ cal}{1\ g\ water}$ × $\dfrac{4.18\ J}{1\ cal}$ = 84 000 J or 8.4 x 10^4 J (released)

   c. 140 g ice × $\dfrac{80.\ cal}{1\ g\ ice}$ × $\dfrac{1\ kcal}{1000\ cal}$ = 11 kcal (absorbed)

   d. 5.0 kg ice × $\dfrac{1000\ g}{1\ kg}$ × $\dfrac{80.\ cal}{1\ g\ ice}$ × $\dfrac{4.18\ J}{1\ cal}$ × $\dfrac{1\ kJ}{1000\ J}$ = 1700 kJ (absorbed)

5.33   **a.** condensation   **b.** evaporation   **c.** boiling   **d.** condensation

5.34   **a.** boiling   **b.** condensation   **c.** evaporation   **d.** boiling

5.35   **a.** The liquid water in perspiration absorbs heat and changes to vapor. The heat needed for
           the change is removed from the skin.
           b. On a hot day, there are more liquid water molecules in the damp clothing that have
           sufficient energy to become water vapor. Thus, water evaporates from the clothes more
           readily on a hot day.
           c. Some water molecules evaporate but they cannot escape from the sealed bag. The high
           humidity in the bag allows some of the gaseous water to condense back to liquid, so the
           clothes will not dry.

5.36 **a.** The liquid absorbs heat from the skin to evaporate, thus the skin is chilled (numbed).

b. In a wide dish, there are more molecules at the surface from which evaporation must occur. The number of molecules with sufficient energy to evaporate and in position to evaporate is greater in the wide dish, so the water evaporates faster than it can in a tall glass.

c. The sandwich on a plate dries out faster. Any water that evaporates from the sandwich sealed in plastic wrap cannot escape, and the sandwich does not dry out.

5.37 **a.** $10.0 \text{ g water} \times \dfrac{540 \text{ cal}}{1 \text{ g water}}$ = 5400 cal absorbed

b. $50.0 \text{ g water} \times \dfrac{540 \text{ cal}}{1 \text{ g water}} \times \dfrac{4.18 \text{ J}}{1 \text{ cal}}$ = 110,000 J absorbed

c. $8.0 \text{ kg steam} \times \dfrac{1000 \text{ g}}{1 \text{ kg}} \times \dfrac{540 \text{ cal}}{1 \text{ g steam}} \times \dfrac{1 \text{ kcal}}{1000 \text{ cal}}$ = 4300 kcal released

d. $170 \text{ g steam} \times \dfrac{540 \text{ cal}}{1 \text{ g steam}} \times \dfrac{4.18 \text{ J}}{1 \text{ cal}} \times \dfrac{1 \text{ kJ}}{1000 \text{ J}}$ = 380 kJ released

5.38 **a.** $10.0 \text{ g steam} \times \dfrac{540 \text{ cal}}{1 \text{ g steam}}$ = 5 400 cal (released)

b. $75. \text{ g steam} \times \dfrac{540 \text{ cal}}{1 \text{ g steam}} \times \dfrac{4.18 \text{ J}}{1 \text{ cal}}$ = 170 000 J or $1.7 \times 10^{5.}$ J (released)

c. $44 \text{ g water} \times \dfrac{540 \text{ cal}}{1 \text{ g water}} \times \dfrac{1 \text{ kcal}}{1000 \text{ cal}}$ = 24 kcal (absorbed)

d. $5.0 \text{ kg water} \times \dfrac{1000 \text{ g}}{1 \text{ kg}} \times \dfrac{540 \text{ cal}}{1 \text{ g water}} \times \dfrac{4.18 \text{ J}}{1 \text{ cal}} \times \dfrac{1 \text{ kJ}}{1000 \text{ J}}$ = 11 000 kJ (1.1×10^4 kJ absorbed)

5.39

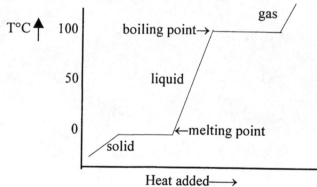

5.40

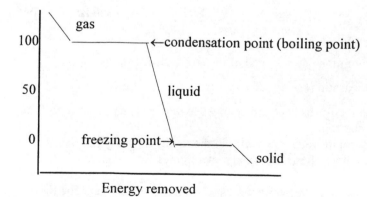

5.41 **a.** 20.0 g $\times$ $\dfrac{1.00\ cal}{g°C}$ $\times$ 57°C = 1100 cal

  b. Two calculations are needed:

  50.0 g-ice $\times$ $\dfrac{80.\ cal}{1\ g\ ice}$ = 4000 cal (2 sig figs)

  50.0 g $\times$ $\dfrac{1.00\ cal}{g°C}$ $\times$ 65°C   = 3300 cal

  Total: 4000 cal + 3300 cal   = 7300 cal

  c. Two calculations are needed:

  15 g-steam $\times$ $\dfrac{540\ cal}{1\ g\ steam}$ $\times$ $\dfrac{4.18\ J}{1\ cal}$ $\times$ $\dfrac{1\ kJ}{1000\ J}$ = 34 kJ

  15 g $\times$ $\dfrac{4.18\ J}{g°C}$ $\times$ 100.°C $\times$ $\dfrac{1\ kJ}{1000\ J}$ = 6.3 kJ

  Total: 34 kJ + 6.3 kJ   = 40. kJ

  d. Three calculations are needed:

  24 g-ice $\times$ $\dfrac{80.\ cal}{1\ g\ ice}$ $\times$ $\dfrac{1\ kcal}{1000\ cal}$ = 1.9 kcal

  24 g $\times$ $\dfrac{1.00\ cal}{g°C}$ $\times$ 100.°C $\times$ $\dfrac{1\ kcal}{1000\ cal}$ = 2.4 kcal

  24 g-water $\times$ $\dfrac{540\ cal}{1\ g\ water}$ $\times$ $\dfrac{1\ kcal}{1000\ cal}$ = 13 kcal

  Total: 1.9 kcal + 2.4 kcal + 13 kcal   = 17 kcal

5.42 **a.** Two calculations are needed:

  125 g-steam $\times$ $\dfrac{540\ cal}{1\ g\ steam}$ = 68 000 cal or 5.8 $\times$ 10^4 cal

  125 g $\times$ $\dfrac{1.00\ cal}{g°C}$ $\times$ 85°C   = 11 000 cal or 1.1 $\times$ x 10^4 cal

  Total: 68 000 cal + 11000 cal   = 79000 cal or 7.9 $\times$ 10^4 cal

  b. Two calculations are needed:

  525 g-ice $\times$ $\dfrac{80.\ cal}{1\ g\ ice}$ $\times$ $\dfrac{4.18\ J}{1\ cal}$ = 180 000 J or 1.8 $\times$ 10^5 J

  525 g $\times$ $\dfrac{4.18\ J}{g°C}$ $\times$ 15°C   = 33 000 J or 3.3 $\times$ 10^4 J

  Total: 1.8 $\times$ 10^5 J + 3.3 $\times$ 10^4 J   = 213 000 J or 2.1 $\times$ 10^5 J

  c. Three calculations are needed:

  85 g-steam $\times$ $\dfrac{540\ cal}{1\ g\ steam}$ $\times$ $\dfrac{1\ kcal}{1000\ cal}$ = 46 kcal

  85 g $\times$ $\dfrac{1.00\ cal}{g°C}$ $\times$ 100.°C $\times$ $\dfrac{1\ kcal}{1000\ cal}$ = 8.5 kcal

  85 g-water $\times$ $\dfrac{80.\ cal}{1\ g\ water}$ $\times$ $\dfrac{1\ kcal}{1000\ cal}$ = 6.8 kcal

  Total: 46 kcal + 8.5 kcal + 6.8 kcal   = 61 kcal

d. Two calculations are needed:

$$55 \text{ mL water} \times \frac{1.0 \text{ g}}{1 \text{ mL water}} \times \frac{1.00 \text{ cal}}{\text{g}°\text{C}} \times 90.°\text{C} \times \frac{1 \text{ kcal}}{1000 \text{ cal}} = 5.0 \text{ kcal}$$

$$55 \text{ mL water} \times \frac{1.0 \text{ g}}{1 \text{ mL water}} \times \frac{540 \text{ cal}}{1 \text{ g}} \times \frac{1 \text{ kcal}}{1000 \text{ cal}} = 30. \text{ kcal}$$

Total: 5.0 kcal + 30. kcal = 35 kcal

5.43   Two calculations are needed:

$$250 \text{ g ice} \times \frac{80. \text{ cal}}{1 \text{ g ice}} \times \frac{1 \text{ kcal}}{1000 \text{ cal}} = 20. \text{ kcal}$$

$$250 \text{ g} \times \frac{1.00 \text{ cal}}{\text{g}°\text{C}} \times 21°\text{C} \times \frac{1 \text{ kcal}}{1000 \text{ cal}} = 6.0 \text{ kcal}$$

Total: 20. kcal + 6.0 kcal = 26 kcal

$$26 \text{ kcal} \times \frac{4.18 \text{ kJ}}{1 \text{ kcal}} = 110 \text{ kJ}$$

5.44   Three calculations are needed:

$$115 \text{ g steam} \times \frac{540 \text{ cal}}{1 \text{ g steam}} \times \frac{1 \text{ kcal}}{1000 \text{ cal}} = 62 \text{ kcal}$$

$$115 \text{ g} \times \frac{1.00 \text{ cal}}{\text{g}°\text{C}} \times 100.°\text{C} \times \frac{1 \text{ kcal}}{1000 \text{ cal}} = 11.5 \text{ kcal}$$

$$115 \text{ g water} \times \frac{80. \text{ cal}}{1 \text{ g water}} \times \frac{1 \text{ kcal}}{1000 \text{ cal}} = 9.2 \text{ kcal}$$

Total: 62 kcal + 11.5 kcal + 9.2 kcal = 83 kcal

$$62 \text{ kcal} \times \frac{4.18 \text{ kJ}}{1 \text{ kcal}} = 260 \text{ kJ}$$

$$11.5 \text{ kcal} \times \frac{4.18 \text{ kJ}}{1 \text{ kcal}} = 48.1 \text{ kJ}$$

$$9.2 \text{ kcal} \times \frac{4.18 \text{ kJ}}{1 \text{ kcal}} = 38 \text{ kJ}$$

Total: 260 kJ + 48.1 kJ + 38 kJ = 350 kJ

5.45   From Table 5.1, we see that liquid water has a high specific heat (1.00 cal/g °C), which means that a large amount of energy is required to cause a significant temperature change. Sand, on the other hand, has a low specific heat (0.19 cal/g °C). Even a small amount of energy will cause a significant temperature change in the sand.

5.46   Because the iced tea is cold, the air surrounding the glass is also cooled as the air molecules collide with the glass. Any moisture (humidity) in the cooled air will also be cooled sufficiently to undergo a phase change from gas to liquid. The condensed water forms the droplets on the glass of iced tea.

5.47   Both water condensation (formation of rain) and deposition (formation of snow) from the gaseous moisture in the air are exothermic processes (heat is released). The heat released in either of these processes warms the surrounding air, and so the air temperature is in fact raised.

5.48   **a.** As the liquid water freezes, heat must be released into the air. The temperature in the orchard will not go below 0°C until all the water has frozen.

b. Two calculations are required:

$$5.0 \text{ kg} \times \frac{1000 \text{ g}}{1 \text{ kg}} \times \frac{1.00 \text{ cal}}{\text{g} \cdot {}^\circ\text{C}} \times 15 {}^\circ\text{C} \times \frac{1 \text{ kcal}}{1000 \text{ cal}} = 75 \text{ kcal}$$

$$5.0 \text{ kg} \times \frac{1000 \text{ g}}{1 \text{ kg}} \times \frac{80. \text{ cal}}{1 \text{ g}} \times \frac{1 \text{ kcal}}{1000 \text{ cal}} = 400 \text{ kcal} \ (4.0 \times 10^2 \text{ kcal})$$

For a total of: $75 \text{ kcal} + 4.0 \times 10^2 \text{ kcal} = 480 \text{ kcal}$

5.49 $2{,}000 \text{ Cal} \times \dfrac{1000 \text{ cal}}{1 \text{ Cal}} = 2\,000\,000 \text{ cal}$

$\text{cal} = \text{g} \times \text{specific heat} \times \Delta T$

$$\Delta T = \frac{\text{cal}}{\text{g} \times \text{spec. heat}} = \frac{2\,000\,000 \text{ cal}}{50{,}000 \text{ g} \times 1.00 \text{ cal/g} \, {}^\circ\text{C}} = 40{}^\circ\text{C}$$

Final $T = 20{}^\circ\text{C} + 40{}^\circ\text{C} = 60{}^\circ\text{C}$

5.50   The data that 18.9 kJ are released when 0.50 g of oil is burned start the calculation. The remainder of the calculation involves unit conversions.

$$\frac{18.9 \text{ kJ}}{0.50 \text{ g oil}} \times \frac{1000 \text{ J}}{1 \text{ kJ}} \times \frac{1 \text{ cal}}{4.18 \text{ J}} \times \frac{1 \text{ kcal}}{1000 \text{ cal}} = 9.0 \text{ kcal/g oil}$$

5.51   **a.** For 15% of one's total Calories (kcal) to be supplied by protein, a conversion factor of 15 kcal from protein/100 kcal total in the daily diet will be used in the calculation. Similar factors will be used for the carbohydrate (carbs) and fat calculations.

$$1200 \text{ kcal (total)} \times \frac{15 \text{ kcal (protein)}}{100 \text{ kcal (total)}} \times \frac{1 \text{ g protein}}{4 \text{ kcal (protein)}} = 45 \text{ g protein}$$

$$1200 \text{ kcal (total)} \times \frac{45 \text{ kcal (carbs)}}{100 \text{ kcal (total)}} \times \frac{1 \text{ g carbs}}{4 \text{ kcal (carbs)}} = 140 \text{ g carbohydrate}$$

$$1200 \text{ kcal (total)} \times \frac{40. \text{ kcal (fat)}}{100 \text{ kcal (total)}} \times \frac{1 \text{ g fat}}{9 \text{ kcal (fat)}} = 53 \text{ g fat}$$

b. The calculations for part b differ from part a only in the total kcal per day.

$$1900 \text{ kcal (total)} \times \frac{15 \text{ kcal (protein)}}{100 \text{ kcal (total)}} \times \frac{1 \text{ g protein}}{4 \text{ kcal (protein)}} = 71 \text{ g protein}$$

$$1900 \text{ kcal (total)} \times \frac{45 \text{ kcal (carbs)}}{100 \text{ kcal (total)}} \times \frac{1 \text{ g carbs}}{4 \text{ kcal (carbs)}} = 210 \text{ g carbohydrate}$$

$$1900 \text{ kcal (total)} \times \frac{40. \text{ kcal (fat)}}{100 \text{ kcal (total)}} \times \frac{1 \text{ g fat}}{9 \text{ kcal (fat)}} = 84 \text{ g fat}$$

c. The calculations for part c again differ only in the total kcal per day.

$$2600 \text{ kcal (total)} \times \frac{15 \text{ kcal (protein)}}{100 \text{ kcal (total)}} \times \frac{1 \text{ g protein}}{4 \text{ kcal (protein)}} = 98 \text{ g protein}$$

$$2600 \text{ kcal (total)} \times \frac{45 \text{ kcal (carbs)}}{100 \text{ kcal (total)}} \times \frac{1 \text{ g carbs}}{4 \text{ kcal (carbs)}} = 290 \text{ g carbohydrate}$$

$$2600 \text{ kcal (total)} \times \frac{40. \text{ kcal (fat)}}{100 \text{ kcal (total)}} \times \frac{1 \text{ g fat}}{9 \text{ kcal (fat)}} = 120 \text{ g fat}$$

5.52   The meal contains a total of 45 g protein, (31 g + 3 g + 11 g), a total of 49 g fat, and a total of 120 g carbohydrate. The total caloric content of the meal must be determined to answer the question.

45 ~~g protein~~   × $\dfrac{4 \text{ kcal}}{1 \text{ g protein}}$ = 180 kcal due to protein

49 ~~g fat~~   × $\dfrac{9 \text{ kcal}}{1 \text{ g fat}}$ = 440 kcal due to fat

120 ~~g carbohydrate~~ × $\dfrac{4 \text{ kcal}}{1 \text{ g carbohydrate}}$ = 480. kcal due to carbohydrate

Total: 180 kcal + 440 kcal + 480. kcal   = 1.10×10^3 kcal (1100 kcal)

Using Table 5.5, 2.0 hours are needed to "burn off" the total caloric content of the meal.

1.10×10^3 ~~kcal~~ × $\dfrac{1 \text{ hr}}{550 \text{ kcal}}$ = 2.0 hr

5.53   Because each gram of body fat contains 15% water, a person actually loses 85 grams of fat per hundred grams of body fat. (We considered 1 lb of fat as exactly 1 lb.)

1 ~~lb body fat~~ × $\dfrac{454 \text{ g}}{1 \text{ lb}}$ × $\dfrac{85 \text{ g fat}}{100 \text{ g body fat}}$ × $\dfrac{9 \text{ kcal}}{1 \text{ g fat}}$ = 3500 kcal

3500 ~~kcal~~   × $\dfrac{4.18 \text{ kJ}}{1 \text{ kcal}}$ = 15,000 kJ

5.54   This question requires three calculations to obtain the total kcal.

12 ~~g carbohydrate~~ × $\dfrac{4 \text{ kcal}}{1 \text{ g carbohydrate}}$ = 50 kcal due to carbohydrate

9 ~~g fat~~   × $\dfrac{9 \text{ kcal}}{1 \text{ g fat}}$ = 80 kcal due to fat

9 ~~g protein~~   × $\dfrac{4 \text{ kcal}}{1 \text{ g protein}}$ = 40 kcal due to protein

Total: 50 kcal + 80 kcal + 40 kcal   = 170 kcal

5.55   725 ~~g~~   × $\dfrac{4.18 \text{ J}}{\text{g }^\circ\text{C}}$ ×   28 ~~°C~~   × $\dfrac{1 \text{ kJ}}{1000 \text{ J}}$ = 85 kJ

5.56   1.5 ~~gal~~ × $\dfrac{4 \text{ qt}}{1 \text{ gal}}$ × $\dfrac{946 \text{ mL}}{1 \text{ qt}}$ × $\dfrac{0.74 \text{ g}}{1 \text{ mL}}$ × $\dfrac{11.5 \text{ kcal}}{1 \text{ g}}$ = 4.8×10^4 kcal

5.57   **a.** HF   **b.** H_2O **c.** KCl   **d.** NH_3

5.58   **a.** Dipole-dipole attractions occur between the positive end of one polar molecule and the negative end of another polar molecule.
   b. Hydrogen bonds are strong dipole-dipole bonds that occur between a partially positive hydrogen atom and one of the strongly electronegative atoms of F, O, or N.
   c. Dispersion forces occur between temporary dipoles that form within nonpolar molecules. Larger nonpolar compounds containing a greater number of electrons produce more temporary dipoles within the molecule.

5.59   In nonpolar compounds, there are no dipoles. However, they do interact by dispersion forces from temporary dipoles that result from a momentary shift of electrons. Because octane, C_8H_{18}, has more electrons than ethane, C_2H_6, octane can form larger temporary dipoles, which results in a higher melting point.

5.60   The hydrogen bonds between NH_3 molecules are stronger than the dipole-dipole bonds in PH_3 and require higher boiling point to break.

5.61 **a.** 3   **b.** 3   **c.** 4
      d. 2   **e.** 3   **f.** 1

5.62 25°C $\longrightarrow$ 0°C: 325 g $\times$ 25°C $\times \dfrac{4.18 \text{ J}}{\text{g °C}} \times \dfrac{1 \text{ kJ}}{1000 \text{ J}}$ =   34kJ

water 0°C $\longrightarrow$ ice 0°C: 325 g $\times \dfrac{80. \text{ cal}}{1 \text{ g}} \times \dfrac{4.18 \text{ J}}{1 \text{ cal}} \times \dfrac{1 \text{ kJ}}{1000 \text{ J}}$ =   110 kJ

Total: 34 kJ   110 kJ = 140 kJ

5.63 $3.00 \text{ kg} \times \dfrac{1000 \text{ g}}{1 \text{ kg}} \times \dfrac{0.028 \text{ cal}}{\text{g °C}} \times 300.°C$ = 25200 cal available to melt ice

Since 80. cal are needed to melt 1 gram of ice, we can calculate the number of grams of ice that can melt.

25200 cal $\times$ $\dfrac{1 \text{ g}}{80. \text{ cal}}$ = 320 g of ice will be melted

5.64

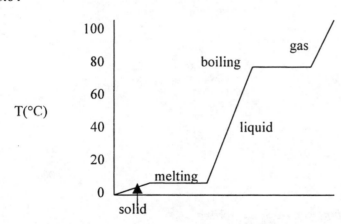

a. liquid   **b.** benzene melts   **c.** liquid
d. gas   **e.** boiling temperature of 80.1°C

5.65 First, calculate heat required to melt the ice. Second, combine the masses of melted ice and liquid water, (both of which are at 0°C), and then continue with the heating and evaporation calculations.

$50.0 \text{ g ice} \times \dfrac{80. \text{ cal}}{1 \text{ g ice}} \times \dfrac{1 \text{ kcal}}{1000 \text{ cal}}$ = 4.0 kcal are required to melt the ice

50.0 g melted ice + 50.0 g liquid water   = 100.0 g liquid water at 0°C.

$100.0 \text{ g} \times \dfrac{1.00 \text{ cal}}{\text{g °C}} \times 100.°C \times \dfrac{1 \text{ kcal}}{1000 \text{ cal}}$ = 10.0 kcal (to warm the liquid)

$100.0 \text{ g water} \times \dfrac{540 \text{ cal}}{1 \text{ g water}} \times \dfrac{1 \text{ kcal}}{1000 \text{ cal}}$ = 54 kcal (to boil the liquid)

Total: 4.0 kcal + 10.0 kcal + 54 kcal   = 68 kcal

Chemical Reactions

Study Goals

- Classify a change in matter as a chemical change or a physical change.
- Show that a balanced equation has an equal number of atoms of each element on the reactant side and the product side.
- Write a balanced equation for a chemical reaction when given the formulas of the reactants and products.
- Classify an equation as a combination, decomposition, replacement and/or combustion reaction.
- Describe the features of an oxidation-reduction reaction.
- Describe the factors that affect the rate of a reaction.
- Use the concept of reversible reactions to explain chemical equilibrium.

Chapter Outline

6.1 Chemical Changes
Explore Your World: Evidence of a Chemical Change
6.2 Chemical Equations
6.3 Balancing a Chemical Equation
6.4 Types of Reactions
Health Note: Smog and Health Concerns
6.5 Oxidation-Reduction Reactions
Explore Your World: Oxidation of Fruits and Vegetables
6.6 Energy in Chemical Reactions
Health Note: Hot Packs and Cold Packs
Explore Your World: Hotter or Colder?
Explore Your World: How Fast Can it Go?
6.7 Rate of Reaction
6.8 Chemical Equilibrium
Explore Your World: Modeling an Equilibrium System
Health Note: Oxygen, Hemoglobin, and Carbon Monoxide Poisoning
Health Note: Homeostasis: Regulation of Body Temperature

Chapter Summary and Demonstrations

1. Chemical Reactions and Equations

Examples of physical and chemical changes introduce the idea of chemical reaction. The process of writing and balancing a chemical equation is carefully explained with several sample problems. In the final sections of the chapter, mole relationships and mole conversion factors in an equation are written from the equation coefficients and used to calculate the grams or moles of a reactant or product in a reaction.

Demonstration: I use examples of an everyday process to introduce the idea of writing an equation. A cooking example: 2 slices of bread + 3 slices turkey + 1 slice tomato + 2 lettuce leaves = 1 turkey-tomato-lettuce sandwich. Any recipe could be used. A sport example: 1 can tennis balls + 2 tennis racquets + 1 net + 2 players = 1 tennis game.

2. Energy in Chemical Reactions

The heat of reaction is described as the energy difference between reactants and products. In exothermic reactions, heat is released; in endothermic, heat is absorbed. The rate of reaction is the speed at which products form and can be increase by adding more reactant, raising the temperature, or adding a catalyst.

Demonstration: Obtain some hot packs and/or cold packs at a pharmacy. Have students read the labels to determine contents. Then have them hit the packs to break the vials. Describe the results. Which solution reaction was exothermic? Which reaction was endothermic? In which pack was the energy of the reactant higher than the product?

Laboratory Suggestions

Lab 10 Chemical Reactions and Equations

Students carry out a variety of chemical reactions that demonstrate the combustion of magnesium, the reactions of zinc and $CuSO_4$ (aq), metals and acid, and double replacement reactions. Students describe the physical properties of the reactants and the products to show evidence of reaction. A balanced equation is written for each reaction and the type of reaction is determined.
A.   Magnesium and Oxygen
B.   Zinc and Copper (II) Sulfate
C.   Metals and HCl
D.   Reactions of Ionic Compounds
E.   Sodium Carbonate and HCl

Laboratory Skills to Demonstrate
Proper handling of reagent bottles and water disposal
Labeling test tubes and organizing beakers
Balancing a chemical equation.
Identifying the type of reaction

Lab 11 Reaction Rates and Equilibrium

In an *exothermic* reaction, heat is released causing the temperature of the surroundings to increase. An *endothermic* reaction absorbs heat, which causes a drop in the temperature of the surroundings. The rate or speed at which a reaction occurs depends on the *amounts of the reactants,* the *temperature,* and the presence of a *catalyst.* When a reaction begins, reactants are converted to products. As the reaction proceeds, products react to form reactants. Increasing reactants shifts a reversible reaction to products; an increase in products shifts the equilibrium to reactants.
A. Exothermic and Endothermic Reactions
B. Rates of Reactions
C. Reversible Reactions
D. Iron (III)-thiocyanate equilibrium

Laboratory Skills to Demonstrate
Describe how to write heat as a reactant or product in an equation.
Review the factors that affect the rate of a reaction.
Review the effects of temperature, reactants and products on a reversible reaction.
Relate the change in appearance of a reactant or product to a shift in equilibrium.

Answers and Solutions to Text Problems

6.1 A chemical change occurs when the atoms of the initial substances rearrange to form new substances. Chemical change is indicated by a change in properties of the reactants. For example, a rusting nail, souring milk, and a burning match are all chemical changes.
   a. physical: the shape changes, but not the substance.
   b. chemical: new substances form
   c. physical: water evaporates forming gaseous water
   d. chemical: the composition of the substances change to give new substances
   e. physical: water freezes
   f. chemical: new substances form

6.2 **a.** physical   **b.** chemical   **c.** physical
   d. chemical   **e.** chemical   **f.** physical

6.3 **a.** On the reactant side, there are two nitrogen atoms and four oxygen atoms. On the product side, there are two nitrogen atoms (2NO) and four oxygen atoms ($2NO + O_2$)
   b. On the reactant side, there are five carbon atoms (5C), two sulfur atoms ($2SO_2$), and four oxygen atoms ($2SO_2$). On the product side, there are five carbon atoms, two sulfur atoms, and four oxygen atoms
   c. On the reactant side, there are four carbon atoms, four hydrogen atoms, and ten oxygen atoms. On the product side, there are four carbon atoms, four hydrogen atoms, and ten oxygen atoms.
   d. On the reactant side, there are two nitrogen atoms, eight hydrogen atoms, and four oxygen atoms. On the product side, there are two nitrogen atoms, eight hydrogen atoms, and four oxygen atoms

6.4 **a.** On the reactant side, there are one carbon atom, four hydrogen atoms, and four oxygen atoms. On the product side, there are one carbon atom, four hydrogen atoms, and four oxygen atoms.
   b. On the reactant side, there are four phosphorus atoms, and ten oxygen atoms. On the product side, there are four phosphorus atoms, and ten oxygen atoms
   c. On the reactant side, there are ten nitrogen atoms, twelve hydrogen atoms, and six oxygen atoms. On the product side, there are ten nitrogen atoms, twelve hydrogen atoms, and six oxygen atoms.
   d. On the reactant side, there are six carbon atoms, eighteen oxygen atoms, and twelve hydrogen atoms. On the product side, there are six carbon atoms, eighteen oxygen atoms, and twelve hydrogen atoms

6.5 An equation is balanced when there are equal numbers of atoms of each element on the reactant as on the product side.
   a. not balanced   **b.** balanced   **c.** not balanced   **d.** balanced

6.6 **a.** balanced   **b.** balanced   **c.** not balanced   **d.** not balanced

6.7 **a.** There are two sodium atoms and two chlorine atoms on each side of the equation.
   b. There are three chlorine atoms, one phosphorus atom, and six hydrogen atoms on each side of the equation.
   c. There are four phosphorus atoms, sixteen oxygen atoms, and twelve hydrogen atoms on each side of the equation.

6.8 **a.** There are four nitrogen atoms and six oxygen atoms.
   b. There are two aluminum atoms, three oxygen atoms, six hydrogen atoms, and six chlorine atoms.
   c. There are five carbon atoms, twelve hydrogen atoms, and sixteen oxygen atoms.

6.9 Place coefficients in front of formulas until you make the atoms of each element equal on each side of the equation. Try starting with the formula that has subscripts.

a. $N_2 + O_2 \rightarrow 2NO$ **b.** $2HgO \rightarrow 2Hg + O_2$

c. $4Fe + 3O_2 \rightarrow 2Fe_2O_3$ **d.** $2Na + Cl_2 \rightarrow 2NaCl$

e. $2Cu_2O + O_2 \rightarrow 4CuO$

6.10 **a.** $2Al + 3Cl_2 \rightarrow 2AlCl_3$ **b.** $P_4 + 5O_2 \rightarrow P_4O_{10}$

c. $C_4H_8 + 6O_2 \rightarrow 4CO_2 + 4H_2O$ **d.** $Sb_2S_3 + 6HCl \rightarrow 2SbCl_3 + 3H_2S$

e. $Fe_2O_3 + 3C \rightarrow 2Fe + 3CO$

6.11 **a.** There are two NO_3 in the product. Balance by placing a 2 before $AgNO_3$.

        $Mg + 2AgNO_3 \rightarrow Mg(NO_3)_2 + 2Ag$

b. $CuCO_3 \rightarrow CuO + CO_2$

c. Start with the formula $Al_2(SO_4)_3$. Balance the Al by writing 2 Al and balance the SO_4^{2-} by writing $3CuSO_4 + Al + 3CuSO_4 \rightarrow 3Cu + Al_2(SO_4)_3$

d. $Pb(NO_3)_2 + 2NaCl \rightarrow PbCl_2 + 2NaNO_3$

e. $2Al + 6HCl \rightarrow 2AlCl_3 + 3H_2$

6.12 **a.** $Zn + H_2SO_4 \rightarrow ZnSO_4 + H_2$ **b.** $2Al + 3H_2SO_4 \rightarrow Al_2(SO_4)_3 + 3H_2$

c. $K_2SO_4 + BaCl_2 \rightarrow BaSO_4 + 2KCl$ **d.** $CaCO_3 \rightarrow CaO + CO_2$

e. $Al_2(SO_4)_3 + 6KOH \rightarrow 2Al(OH)_3 + 3K_2SO_4$

6.13 **a.** Decomposition. A single reactant splits into two simpler substances (elements).

b. This is a single replacement reaction. I_2 in BaI_2 is replaced by Br_2.

6.14 **a.** Two elements unite to form a compound.

b. The components in two reactants exchange places.

6.15 **a.** combination and combustion   **b.** single replacement   **c.** decomposition

d. double replacement   **e.** combustion   **f.** decomposition

g. double replacement   **h.** combination and combustion

6.16 **a.** double replacement   **b.** combination   **c.** combustion

d. double replacement   **e.** combination and combustion **f.** single replacement

g. decomposition   **h.** double replacement

6.17 **a.** Combine the reactants to form a large compound:

         $Mg + Cl_2 \rightarrow MgCl_2$

b. Split the reactant to give simpler substances:

         $2HBr \rightarrow H_2 + Br_2$

c. Replace the Zn with Mg:

         $Mg + Zn(NO_3)_2 \rightarrow Mg(NO_3)_2 + Zn$

d. Switch metals placing K^+ with NO_3^- and Pb^{2+} with S^{2-}:

         $K_2S + Pb(NO_3)_2 \rightarrow 2KNO_3 + PbS$

e. Write the products CO_2 and H_2O and balance:

         $2C_2H_6 + 7O_2 \rightarrow 4CO_2 + 6H_2O$

6.18 **a.** $Ca + S \rightarrow CaS$ **b.** $PbO_2 \rightarrow Pb + O_2$

c. $2KI + Cl_2 \rightarrow 2KCl + I_2$ **d.** $CuCl_2 + Na_2S \rightarrow CuS + 2NaCl$

e. $C_2H_4 + 3O_2 \rightarrow 2CO_2 + 2H_2O$

6.19 **a.** oxidation   **b.** reduction   **c.** oxidation   **d.** reduction

6.20   **a.** oxidation   **b.** reduction   **c.** reduction   **d.** oxidation

6.21 **a.** Zinc(Zn) is oxidized because it loses electrons to form Zn^{2+}; chlorine (Cl_2) is reduced
b. Bromide ion $(2Br^-)$ is oxidized to Br_2^0; chlorine (Cl_2) is reduced to $2\ Cl^-$ (gains electrons)
c. Oxide ion (O^{2-}) is oxidized to O_2^0 (loses electrons); lead (II) ion Pb^{2+} is reduced
d. Sn^{2+} ion is oxidized to Sn^{4+} (loses electrons); Fe^{3+} ion is reduced to Fe^{2+} (gains electrons)

6.22   **a.** Lithium is oxidized and fluorine is reduced
b. Iodide ion is oxidized and chlorine is reduced
c. Zinc is oxidized and copper (II) ion is reduced
d. Iron is oxidized and copper (II) ion is reduced

6.23 **a.** $Fe^{3+} + e^- \rightarrow Fe^{2+}$ is a reduction.   **b.** $Fe^{2+} \rightarrow Fe^{3+} + e^-$ is an oxidation.

6.24   For chlorine to become chloride ion, each chlorine atom must gain an electron:
$Cl_2 + 2e^- \rightarrow 2Cl^-$ Thus the reaction is a reduction.

6.25   Because the linoleic acid adds hydrogen, the acid has been reduced.

6.26   **a.** Because the reaction of succinic acid involves the loss of hydrogen, the acid is oxidized.
b. Because the reaction of the coenzyme FAD involves the addition of hydrogen, the coenzyme
is reduced.
c. Because an oxidation always accompanies a reduction, one would expect the reaction of
succinic acid to occur along with the FAD reaction.

d.

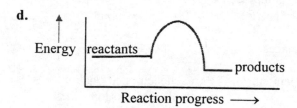

6.28   **a.** The heat of reaction is the heat energy that is given off (or used up) during a reaction as
a result of reactant(s) bonds being broken and product(s) bonds being formed.
b. In an exothermic reaction, energy is given off because the products are lower in energy than
the reactants. In an endothermic reaction, energy is absorbed in forming products with a
higher energy than the reactants.
c. Because energy is absorbed during an endothermic reaction, the products have a higher
energy than the reactants.
d.

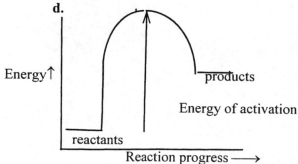

6.29   **a.** exothermic; heat loss   **b.** endothermic; heat gain
          c. exothermic; heat loss

6.30   **a.** The reaction is exothermic.   **b.** The reaction is endothermic.
          c. The reaction is endothermic.

6.31   **a.** exothermic   **b.** endothermic   **c.** exothermic

6.32   **a.** The reaction is exothermic.   **b.** The reaction is exothermic.
          c. The reaction is endothermic.

6.33   **a.** The rate of a reaction relates the speed at which reactants are transformed into products.
          b. Because more reactants will have the energy necessary to proceed to products, (the activation energy), at room temperature than at refrigerator temperatures, the rate of formation of mold will be higher at room temperature.

6.34   **a.** A catalyst provides an alternate reaction pathway with a lower activation energy, and thus more reactants will have the energy necessary to form products. This results in an increased rate of reaction.
          b. The use of pure oxygen increases the amount of reactant present, increasing the rate of oxygenation of hemoglobin in blood.

6.35   **a.** Addition of a reactant increases the reaction rate.
          b. Increasing the temperature increases the number of collisions with the energy of activation. The rate of reaction will be increased.
          c. Addition of a catalyst increases the reaction rate.
          d. Removal of reactant decreases the reaction rate.

6.36   **a.** Addition of a reactant increases the reaction rate.
          b. Lowering the temperature decreases the number of reactant molecules with the energy necessary for reaction to occur, (activation energy). The rate of reaction will be decreased.
          c. Removing reactant decreases the reaction rate.
          d. Addition of a catalyst increases the reaction rate.

6.37   In a reversible reaction, the forward reaction converts reactants to products and a reverse reaction converts products back to reactants again.

6.38   A reversible reaction reaches equilibrium when the rate of the forward reaction is equal to the rate of the reverse reaction, and the amounts of each species present remain constant.

6.39   **a.** Addition of a reactant pushes the reaction toward the product side.
          b. Addition of heat to an exothermic reaction pushes the reaction toward the reactant side.
          c. Removal of a product pulls the reaction toward the product side.
          d. Removal of a reactant pulls the reaction toward the reactant side.

6.40   **a.** Removal of a reactant pulls the reaction toward the reactant side in an attempt to re-establish equilibrium.
          b. Removing heat from an exothermic reaction pulls the reaction toward the product side in an attempt to re-establish equilibrium.
          c. Addition of a product pushes the reaction toward the reactant side in an attempt to re-establish equilibrium.
          d. Addition of a reactant pushes the reaction toward the product side in an attempt to re-establish equilibrium.

6.41 **a.** Addition of a reactant pushes the reaction toward the product side.
b. Addition of a product pushes the reaction toward the reactant side.
c. Addition of heat to an endothermic reaction pushes the reaction toward the product side.
d. Removal of heat from an endothermic reaction pulls the reaction to the reactant side.

6.42 **a.** Addition of heat to an endothermic reaction pushes the reaction toward the product side in an attempt to re-establish equilibrium.
b. Removal of heat from an endothermic reaction shifts the reaction toward the reactant side in an attempt to re-establish equilibrium.
c. Removal of CO, which is a product, shifts the reaction toward the product side in an attempt to re-establish equilibrium.
d. Addition of a reactant pushes the reaction toward the product side in an attempt to re-establish equilibrium.

6.43 As gaseous carbon dioxide escapes into the atmosphere, product is removed from the reaction system. According to LeChatelier's principle, the reaction will shift toward the product side in an attempt to re-establish equilibrium. However, the soda is open to the atmosphere and will continue to lose its carbonation.

6.44 More reactants must be consumed for the forward reaction's rate to increase. Because we obtain the reactant oxygen by breathing, our breathing rate must also increase.

6.45 **a.** $2Al + 3Cl_2 \rightarrow 2AlCl_3$ combination
b. $2Fe + 3H_2SO_4 \rightarrow Fe_2(SO_4)_3 + 3H_2$ single replacement
c. $2AgNO_3 + H_2S \rightarrow Ag_2S + 2HNO_3$ double replacement
d. $Cl_2 + 2KI \rightarrow 2KCl + I_2$ single replacement

6.46 **a.** $2NI_3 \rightarrow N_2 + 3I_2$ decomposition
b. $3Mg + N_2 \rightarrow Mg_3N_2$ combination
c. $3Na_2SO_4 + 2Al(OH)_3 \rightarrow Al_2(SO_4)_3 + 6NaOH$ double replacement
d. $2Fe + 6HCl \rightarrow 2FeCl_3 + 3H_2$ single replacement

6.47 **a.** $C_4H_8 + 6O_2 \rightarrow 4CO_2 + 4H_2O$
b. $C_5H_{12} + 8O_2 \rightarrow 5CO_2 + 6H_2O$
c. $C_6H_{12}O_6 + 6O_2 \rightarrow 6CO_2 + 6H_2O$

6.48 **a.** $2C_2H_6 + 7O_2 \rightarrow 4CO_2 + 6H_2O$
b. $2C_6H_6 + 9O_2 \rightarrow 6CO_2 + 6H_2O$
c. $2C_3H_8O_3 + 7O_2 \rightarrow 6CO_2 + 8H_2O$

6.49 **a.** $Zn^{2+} + 2e^- \rightarrow Zn$ reduction   **b.** $Al \rightarrow Al^{3+} + 3e^-$ oxidation
c. $Pb \rightarrow Pb^{2+} + 2e^-$ oxidation   **d.** $Cl_2 + 2e^- \rightarrow 2Cl^-$ reduction

6.50 **a.** $S + Cl_2 \rightarrow SCl_2$ **b.** $Cl_2 + 2NaBr \rightarrow Br_2 + 2NaCl$
c. $2Al + Fe_2O_3 \rightarrow Al_2O_3 + 2Fe$ **d.** $2CuO + C \rightarrow 2Cu + CO_2$

6.51 **a.** $S \rightarrow S^{2+} + 2e^-$ S oxidized; $Cl_2 + 2e^- \rightarrow 2Cl^-$ Cl_2 reduced
b. $Cl_2 + 2e^- \rightarrow 2Cl^-$ Cl_2 reduced; $2Br^- \rightarrow Br_2 + 2e^-$ Br^- oxidized
c. $Al \rightarrow Al^{3+} + 3e^-$ Al oxidized; $Fe^{3+} + 3e^- \rightarrow Fe$ Fe^{3+} reduced
d. $Cu^{2+} + 2e^- \rightarrow Cu$ Cu^{2+} reduced; $C \rightarrow C^{4+} + 4e^-$ C oxidized

6.52   Although gas will burn in the atmosphere, (as we have all seen in the lab and when using a gas stove), the activation energy must be provided to initiate the reaction. The energy provided by a lit match or by a spark is sufficient to initiate the combustion of gas.

6.53 $N_2(g) + 2O_2(g) + heat \rightleftharpoons 2NO_2(g)$
   a. Addition of heat will push the reaction to the right, which favors the formation of product, NO_2.
   b. Removal of N_2 will pull the reaction to the left, forming more reactants.
   c. Addition of O_2 will push the reaction to the right, forming more NO_2 product.
   d. Removal of NO_2 would pull the reaction to the right, which forms more NO_2 product.
   e. Removing heat favors the reaction to the left, which forms more reactants.

6.54   A high activation energy would be difficult to attain, except for just a few of the reactants present, and the reaction would therefore be slow.

6.55   An increase in hemoglobin molecules pushes the reaction towards the products, which provides more oxygenated hemoglobin in the blood.

6.56 $C_2H_6O + 3O_2 \longrightarrow 2CO_2 + 3H_2O$
   a. Addition of reactant(s) would increase the rate of reaction.
   b. Addition of a catalyst would also increase the rate of reaction.

Chemical Quantities

Study Goals

- Use Avogadro's number to determine the number of particles in a given number of moles.
- Determine the molar mass of a compound from its formula.
- Use the molar mass to convert between the grams of a substance and the number of moles.
- Calculate the percent composition of a compound using its formula.
- Use a mole-mole conversion factor to determine the corresponding number of moles for a reactant or a product.
- For a given mass of a substance in a reaction, use the appropriate mole factors and molar masses to calculate the mass of a reactant or a product.
- Determine the percent yield for a given amount of reactant.
- Write the equilibrium constant for an equation.

Chapter Outline

7.1 The Mole
7.2 Molar Mass
7.3 Calculations Using Molar Mass
7.4 Percent Composition and Empirical Formulas
  Explore Your World: Percent Composition of Common Substances
  Environmental Note: Chemistry of Fertilizers
  Career Focus: Clinical Laboratory Scientist
7.5 Mole Relationships in Chemical Equations
7.6 Mass Calculations for Reactions
7.7 Percent Yield
7.8 Equilibrium Constants
  Health Note: Oxygen-Hemoglobin Equilibrium and Hypoxia

Chapter Summary and Demonstrations

1. Moles and Avogadro's Number

The atomic masses of the elements are used to determine the molar masses of compounds. The mole concept is developed from common terms for collections of items such as trios, dozen and gross. One mole is introduced as a collection of a very large number of items on the atomic level such as atoms, molecules, and ions.

Demonstration: I begin the concept of moles by passing around bottles containing 1-mole quantities of elements (Zn, Cu, Al, Fe) and compounds (H_2O, NaCl, sucrose $C_{12}H_{22}O_{11}$). We discuss the idea that all the samples contain the *same* number 6.02×10^{23} of particles (atoms, molecules, or formula units).

2. Molar Mass

The mass in grams of one mole of an element or compound is called its *molar mass*. The molar mass of an element or a compound is then used as a conversion factor to change moles to grams, or grams to moles.

Demonstration: Particles and mass of a Mole Using an electronic balance in the classroom, I obtain a mole by weighing out the atomic mass in grams (atomic mass) for an elements such as copper and a compound such as $CaCO_3$. Then I return to the 1-mole samples in the bottles and we determine the molar mass of each of the substances such as 32.1 g/mole S, 18.0 g/mole H_2O or 342 g/mole sucrose. By comparing the particles in a mole, and the mass of a mole in grams, students become aware that all the molar mass of a substance contains Avogadro's number of atoms, molecules, or formula units.

3. Conservation of Mass

In a balanced equation, the total mass of the reactants is equal to that of the products. Therefore, the number of atoms of each element in the reactants is equal to the number of atoms of each element in the products.

Demonstration: Weigh a beaker containing some HCl and a surgical glove (that fits tightly over the beaker) containing some $CaCO_3$ in the fingers = mass of reactants. Place the glove on the beaker and shake the $CaCO_3$ in the HCl. A reaction occurs. With the help of the students write and balance the equation $2HCl + CaCO_3 \longrightarrow CO_2 + H_2O + CaCl_2$. Reweigh the beaker, products, and glove. There should be no change of mass because mass is conserved. By calculating the mass of the reactants and products in the equation, we note that the masses in the experiment were not the same as in the equation, but in each case mass is conserved. Sometimes, I do the experiment without attaching the glove to the beaker, which allows the CO_2 to escape. Then of course the mass values don't match.

Laboratory Suggestions

Lab 12 Moles and Chemical Formulas

The simplest formula for a compound of magnesium and oxygen is determined by measuring the mass and moles of oxygen that reacts with a specific amount of magnesium. Students heat a hydrate and measure the loss in mass to determine the amount of water and its percent in a hydrated salt. From the calculation of moles of anhydrate and water, the formula for the hydrate is written.
A. Finding the Simplest Formula
B. Formula of a Hydrate

Laboratory Skills to Demonstrate
Set up a crucible and react a magnesium ribbon with oxygen in air. The hottest part of the flames reaches the bottom of the crucible. If the flame is not adjusted properly, the magnesium does not ignite.
Use the moles of the elements in a formula to determine the subscript ratio
Calculate the % water in a hydrate.
Determine the formula of a hydrate

Answers and Solutions to Text Problems

7.1 A mole is the amount of a substance that contains 6.02×10^{23} items. For example, one mole of water contains 6.02×10^{23} molecules of water.

7.2 Avogadro's number is 6.02×10^{23}, which equals the number of items in one mole.

7.3 **a.** One mole of carbon contains 6.02×10^{23} atoms of carbon.
   b. One mole of iron contains 6.02×10^{23} atoms of iron.

$$2.0 \text{ moles Fe} \times \frac{6.02 \times 10^{23} \text{ atoms Fe}}{1 \text{ mole Fe}} = 1.2 \times 10^{24} \text{ atoms Fe}$$

   c. $0.50 \text{ moles CO}_2 \times \dfrac{6.02 \times 10^{23} \text{ molecules CO}_2}{1 \text{ mole CO}_2} = 3.0 \times 10^{23} \text{ molecules CO}_2$

7.4 **a.** $2.5 \text{ moles S} \times \dfrac{6.02 \times 10^{23} \text{ atoms S}}{1 \text{ mole S}} = 1.5 \times 10^{24} \text{ atoms S}$

   b. $0.020 \text{ mole Ag} \times \dfrac{6.02 \times 10^{23} \text{ atoms Ag}}{1 \text{ mole Ag}} = 1.2 \times 10^{22} \text{ atoms Ag}$

   c. $8.0 \text{ moles H}_2\text{O} \times \dfrac{6.02 \times 10^{23} \text{ molecules H}_2\text{O}}{1 \text{ mole H}_2\text{O}} = 4.8 \times 10^{24} \text{ molecules H}_2\text{O}$

7.5 The subscripts indicate the moles of each element in one mole of that compound.
   a. 24 moles of H

   b. $5.0 \text{ moles quinine} \times \dfrac{20 \text{ moles C atoms}}{1 \text{ mole quinine}} \times \dfrac{6.02 \times 10^{23} \text{ atoms C}}{1 \text{ mole C}} = 6.0 \times 10^{25} \text{ atoms C}$

   c. $0.020 \text{ moles quinine} \times \dfrac{2 \text{ moles N atoms}}{1 \text{ mole quinine}} \times \dfrac{6.02 \times 10^{23} \text{ atoms N}}{1 \text{ mole N atoms}} = 2.4 \times 10^{22} \text{ atoms N}$

7.6 The subscripts indicate the moles of each element in one mole of that compound.
   a. $3.0 \text{ moles Al}_2(\text{SO}_4)_3 \times \dfrac{3 \text{ moles S atoms}}{1 \text{ mole Al}_2(\text{SO}_4)_3} = 9.0 \text{ moles S}$

   b. $0.40 \text{ moles Al}_2(\text{SO}_4)_3 \times \dfrac{2 \text{ moles Al ions}}{1 \text{ mole q Al}_2(\text{SO}_4)_3} \times \dfrac{6.02 \times 10^{23} \text{ Al ions}}{1 \text{ mole Al ions}} = 4.8 \times 10^{23} \text{ Al ions}$

   c. $1.5 \text{ moles Al}_2(\text{SO}_4)_3 \times \dfrac{3 \text{ moles SO}_4 \text{ ions}}{1 \text{ mole Al}_2(\text{SO}_4)_3} \times \dfrac{6.02 \times 10^{23} \text{ SO}_4 \text{ ions}}{1 \text{ mole SO}_4 \text{ ions}} = 2.7 \times 10^{24} \text{ SO}_4^{2-} \text{ ions}$

7.7 **a.** $2.5 \text{ moles of C atoms} \times \dfrac{6.02 \times 10^{23} \text{ atoms of C}}{1 \text{ mole of C atoms}} = 1.5 \times 10^{24} \text{ atoms C}$

   b. $2.0 \text{ moles PCl}_3 \times \dfrac{3 \text{ moles Cl atoms}}{1 \text{ mole PCl}_3} \times \dfrac{6.02 \times 10^{23} \text{ atoms Cl}}{1 \text{ mole Cl atoms}} = 3.6 \times 10^{24} \text{ atoms Cl}$

   c. $5.0 \times 10^{24} \text{ atoms O} \times \dfrac{1 \text{ moles O atoms}}{6.02 \times 10^{23} \text{ atoms O}} \times \dfrac{1 \text{ mole SO}_3}{3 \text{ mole O atoms}} = 2.8 \text{ moles SO}_3$

7.8 **a.** $1.5 \text{ moles of Au atoms} \times \dfrac{6.02 \times 10^{23} \text{ atoms of Au}}{1 \text{ mole of Au atoms}} = 9.0 \times 10^{23} \text{ atoms Au}$

   b. $0.30 \text{ moles NBr}_3 \times \dfrac{3 \text{ moles Br atoms}}{1 \text{ mole NBr}_3} \times \dfrac{6.02 \times 10^{23} \text{ atoms Br}}{1 \text{ mole Br atoms}} = 5.4 \times 10^{23} \text{ atoms Br}$

c. 5.0×10^{24} ~~H atoms~~ $\times$ $\dfrac{1 \text{ mole H atoms}}{6.02 \times 10^{23} \text{ H atoms}}$ $\times$ $\dfrac{1 \text{ mole } C_2H_6O}{6 \text{ moles H atoms}}$ $= 1.4$ moles C_2H_6O

7.9 **a.** 1 mole of Na and 1 mole of Cl:
$23.0 \text{ g} + 35.5 \text{ g} = 58.5 \text{ g/mole NaCl}$

b. 2 mole of Fe and 3 moles of O:
$111.8 \text{ g} + 48.0 \text{ g} = 159.8 \text{ g/mole } Fe_2O_3$

c. 2 mole of Li and 1 mole of C and 3 moles of O:
$13.8 \text{ g} + 12.0 \text{ g} + 48.0 \text{ g} = 73.8 \text{ g/mole } Li_2CO_3$

d. 2 mole of Al and 3 moles of S and 12 moles of O:
$54.0 \text{ g} + 96.3 \text{ g} + 192.0 \text{ g} = 342.3 \text{ g/mole } Al_2(SO_4)_3$

e. 1 mole of Mg and 2 moles of O and 2 moles of H:
$24.3 \text{ g} + 32.0 \text{ g} + 2.0 \text{ g} = 58.3 \text{ g/mole } Mg(OH)_2$

f. 16 moles of C and 19 moles of H and 3 moles of N and 5 moles of O and 1 mole of S:
$192.0 \text{ g} + 19.0 \text{ g} + 42.0 \text{ g} + 80.0 \text{ g} + 32.1 \text{ g} = 365.1 \text{ g/mole } C_{16}H_{19}N_3O_5S$

7.10 **a.** 1 mole of Fe and 1 mole of S and 4 moles of O:
$55.9 \text{ g} + 32.1 \text{ g} + 64.0 \text{ g} = 152.0 \text{ g/mole } FeSO_4$

b. 2 moles of Al and 3 moles of O:
$54.0 \text{ g} + 48.0 \text{ g} = 102.0 \text{ g/mole } Al_2O_3$

c. 7 moles of C, 5 moles of H, 1 mole of N, 3 moles of O, and 1 mole S:
$84.0 \text{ g} + 5.0 \text{ g} + 14.0 \text{ g} + 48.0 \text{ g and } 32.1 = 183.1 \text{ g/mole } C_7H_5NO_3S$

d. 3 moles of C and 8 moles of H and 1 mole of O:
$36.0 \text{ g} + 8.0 \text{ g} + 16.0 \text{ g} = 60.0 \text{ g/mole } C_3H_8O$

e. 2 moles of N and 8 moles of H and 1 mole of C and 3 moles of O:
$28.0 \text{ g} + 8.0 \text{ g} + 12.0 \text{ g} + 48.0 \text{ g} = 96.0 \text{ g/mole } (NH_4)_2CO_3$

f. 1 mole of Zn and 4 moles of C and 6 moles of H and 4 moles of O:
$65.4 \text{ g} + 48.0 \text{ g} + 6.0 \text{ g} + 64.0 \text{ g} = 183.4 \text{ g/mole } Zn(C_2H_3O_2)_2$

7.11 **a.** 2.00 ~~mole Na~~ $\times$ $\dfrac{23.0 \text{ g Na}}{1 \text{ mole Na}}$ $= 46.0$ g Na

b. 2.80 ~~mole Ca~~ $\times$ $\dfrac{40.1 \text{ g Ca}}{1 \text{ mole Ca}}$ $= 112$ g Ca

c. 0.125 ~~mole Sn~~ $\times$ $\dfrac{118.7 \text{ g Sn}}{1 \text{ mole Sn}}$ $= 14.8$ g Sn

7.12 **a.** 1.50 ~~mole K~~ $\times$ $\dfrac{39.1 \text{ g K}}{1 \text{ mole K}}$ $= 58.7$ g K

b. 2.5 ~~mole C~~ $\times$ $\dfrac{12.0 \text{ g C}}{1 \text{ mole C}}$ $= 30.$ g C

c. 0.25 ~~mole P~~ $\times$ $\dfrac{31.0 \text{ g P}}{1 \text{ mole P}}$ $= 7.8$ g P

7.13   **a.** 0.500 ~~mole NaCl~~ $\times$ $\dfrac{58.5 \text{ g NaCl}}{1 \text{ ~~mole NaCl~~}}$ = 29.3 g NaCl

       b. 1.75 ~~mole Na$_2$O~~ $\times$ $\dfrac{62.0 \text{ g Na}_2\text{O}}{1 \text{ ~~mole Na}_2\text{O~~}}$ = 109 g Na$_2$O

       c. 0.225 ~~mole H$_2$O~~ $\times$ $\dfrac{18.0 \text{ g H}_2\text{O}}{1 \text{ ~~mole H}_2\text{O~~}}$ = 4.05 g H$_2$O

7.14   **a.** 2.0 ~~mole MgCl$_2$~~ $\times$ $\dfrac{95.3 \text{ g MgCl}_2}{1 \text{ ~~mole MgCl}_2\text{~~}}$ = 190 g MgCl$_2$

       b. 3.5 ~~mole C$_3$H$_8$~~ $\times$ $\dfrac{44.0 \text{ g C}_3\text{H}_8}{1 \text{ ~~mole C}_3\text{H}_8\text{~~}}$ = 150 g C$_3$H$_8$

       c. 5.00 ~~mole C$_2$H$_6$O~~ $\times$ $\dfrac{46.0 \text{ g C}_2\text{H}_6\text{O}}{1 \text{ ~~mole C}_2\text{H}_6\text{O~~}}$ = 230. g C$_2$H$_6$O   (2.30 $\times$ 10^2 g)

7.15   **a.** 0.500 ~~mole K~~ $\times$ $\dfrac{39.1 \text{ g K}}{1 \text{ ~~mole K~~}}$ = 19.6 g K

       b. 0.500 ~~mole Cl$_2$~~ $\times$ $\dfrac{71.0 \text{ g Cl}_2}{1 \text{ ~~mole Cl}_2\text{~~}}$ = 35.5 g Cl$_2$

       c. 0.500 ~~mole Na$_2$CO$_3$~~ $\times$ $\dfrac{106.0 \text{ g Na}_2\text{CO}_3}{1 \text{ ~~mole Na}_2\text{CO}_3\text{~~}}$ = 53.0 g Na$_2$CO$_3$

7.16   **a.** 2.25 ~~mole N$_2$~~ $\times$ $\dfrac{28.0 \text{ g N}_2}{1 \text{ ~~mole N}_2\text{~~}}$ = 63.0 g N$_2$

       b. 2.25 ~~mole NaBr~~ $\times$ $\dfrac{102.9 \text{ g NaBr}}{1 \text{ ~~mole NaBr~~}}$ = 232 g NaBr

       c. 2.25 ~~mole C$_6$H$_{14}$~~ $\times$ $\dfrac{86.0 \text{ g C}_6\text{H}_{14}}{1 \text{ ~~mole C}_6\text{H}_{14}\text{~~}}$ = 194 g C$_6$H$_{14}$

7.17   **a.** 5.00 ~~mole MgSO$_4$~~ $\times$ $\dfrac{120.4 \text{ g MgSO}_4}{1 \text{ ~~mole MgSO}_4\text{~~}}$ = 602 g MgSO$_4$

       b. 0.25 ~~mole CO$_2$~~ $\times$ $\dfrac{44.0 \text{ g CO}_2}{1 \text{ ~~mole CO}_2\text{~~}}$ = 11 g CO$_2$

7.18   **a.** 0.25 ~~mole C$_3$H$_6$~~ $\times$ $\dfrac{42.0 \text{ g C}_3\text{H}_6}{1 \text{ ~~mole C}_3\text{H}_6\text{~~}}$ = 11 g C$_3$H$_6$

       b. 0.025 ~~mole C$_{15}$H$_{22}$ClNO$_2$~~ $\times$ $\dfrac{283.5 \text{ g C}_{15}\text{H}_{22}\text{ClNO}_2}{1 \text{ ~~mole C}_{15}\text{H}_{22}\text{ClNO}_2\text{~~}}$ = 7.1 g C$_{15}$H$_{22}$ClNO$_2$

7.19   **a.** 50.0 ~~g Ag~~ $\times$ $\dfrac{1 \text{ mole Ag}}{107.9 \text{ ~~g Ag~~}}$ = 0.463 mole Ag

       b. 0.200 ~~g C~~ $\times$ $\dfrac{1 \text{ mole C}}{12.0 \text{ ~~g C~~}}$ = 0.0167 mole C

       c. 15.0 ~~g NH$_3$~~ $\times$ $\dfrac{1 \text{ mole NH}_3}{17.0 \text{ ~~g NH}_3\text{~~}}$ = 0.882 mole NH$_3$

       d. 75.0 ~~g SO$_2$~~ $\times$ $\dfrac{1 \text{ mole SO}_2}{64.1 \text{ ~~g SO}_2\text{~~}}$ = 1.17 mole SO$_2$

7.20 **a.** 25.0 g Ca $\times$ $\dfrac{1 \text{ mole Ca}}{40.1 \text{ g Ca}}$ = 0.623 mole Ca

b. 5.00 g S $\times$ $\dfrac{1 \text{ mole S}}{32.1 \text{ g S}}$ = 0.156 mole S

c. 40.0 g H_2O $\times$ $\dfrac{1 \text{ mole } H_2O}{18.0 \text{ g } H_2O}$ = 2.22 mole H_2O

d. 100.0 g O_2 $\times$ $\dfrac{1 \text{ mole } O_2}{32.00 \text{ g } O_2}$ = 3.125 mole O_2 (Use atomic mass to 4 sig figs)

7.21 **a.** 25.0 g CO_2 $\times$ $\dfrac{1 \text{ mole } CO_2}{44.0 \text{ g } CO_2}$ = 0.568 mole CO_2

b. 25.0 g Al(OH)$_3$ $\times$ $\dfrac{1 \text{ mole Al(OH)}_3}{78.0 \text{ g Al(OH)}_3}$ = 0.321 mole Al(OH)$_3$

c. 25.0 g $MgCl_2$ $\times$ $\dfrac{1 \text{ mole } MgCl_2}{95.3 \text{ g } MgCl_2}$ = 0.262 mole $MgCl_2$

7.22 **a.** 4.00 g NH_3 $\times$ $\dfrac{1 \text{ mole } NH_3}{17.0 \text{ g } NH_3}$ = 0.235 mole NH_3

b. 4.00 g Ca(NO$_3$)$_2$ $\times$ $\dfrac{1 \text{ mole Ca(NO}_3)_2}{164.1 \text{ g Ca(NO}_3)_2}$ = 0.0244 mole Ca(NO$_3$)$_2$

c. 4.00 g SO_3 $\times$ $\dfrac{1 \text{ mole } SO_3}{80.1 \text{ g } SO_3}$ = 0.0499 mole SO_3

7.23 480 g NaOH $\times$ $\dfrac{1 \text{ mole NaOH}}{40.0 \text{ g NaOH}}$ = 12 mole NaOH

7.24 35.0 g Au $\times$ $\dfrac{1 \text{ mole Au}}{197.0 \text{ g Au}}$ = 0.178 mole Au

7.25 **a.** 25 g S $\times$ $\dfrac{1 \text{ mole S}}{32.1 \text{ g S}}$ = 0.78 moles of S

b. 125 g SO_2 $\times$ $\dfrac{1 \text{ mole } SO_2}{64.1 \text{ g } SO_2}$ $\times$ $\dfrac{1 \text{ mole S}}{1 \text{ mole } SO_2}$ = 1.95 moles of S

c. 275 g Al_2S_3 $\times$ $\dfrac{1 \text{ mole } Al_2S_3}{150.1 \text{ g } Al_2S_3}$ $\times$ $\dfrac{3 \text{ moles S}}{1 \text{ mole } Al_2S_3}$ = 5.50 moles of S

7.26 **a.** 75 g C $\times$ $\dfrac{1 \text{ mole C}}{12.0 \text{ g C}}$ = 6.3 moles C

b. 0.25 mole C_2H_6 $\times$ $\dfrac{2 \text{ mole C}}{1 \text{ mole } C_2H_6}$ = 0.50 mole of C

c. 5.0 x 10^{24} CO_2 molecules $\times$ $\dfrac{1 \text{ mole } CO_2 \text{ molecules}}{6.02 \text{ x } 10^{23} \text{ } CO_2 \text{ molecules}}$ $\times$ $\dfrac{1 \text{ mole C atoms}}{1 \text{ mole } CO_2 \text{ molecules}}$

   = 8.3 mole C atoms

7.27 **a.** 40.0 g N $\times$ $\dfrac{1 \text{ mole N}}{14.0 \text{ g N}}$ $\times$ $\dfrac{6.02 \text{ x } 10^{23} \text{ atoms of N}}{1 \text{ mole N}}$ = 1.7×10^{24} atoms of N

b. 1.5 moles N_2O_4 $\times$ $\dfrac{2 \text{ mole N}}{1 \text{ mole } N_2O_4}$ $\times$ $\dfrac{6.02 \text{ x } 10^{23} \text{ atoms of N}}{1 \text{ mole N}}$ = 1.8×10^{24} atoms of N

c. $2.0 \text{ moles N}_2 \times \dfrac{2 \text{ mole N}}{1 \text{ mole N}_2} \times \dfrac{6.02 \times 10^{23} \text{ atoms of N}}{1 \text{ mole N}} = 2.4 \times 10^{24} \text{ atoms of N}$

7.28   **a.** $5.0 \text{ g Ag atoms} \times \dfrac{1 \text{ mole Ag atoms}}{107.9 \text{ g Ag atoms}} \times \dfrac{6.02 \times 10^{23} \text{ Ag atoms}}{1 \text{ mole Ag atoms}} = 2.8 \times 10^{22} \text{ Ag Atoms}$

b. $0.40 \text{ mole Ag}_2\text{S} \times \dfrac{6.02 \times 10^{23} \text{ Ag}_2\text{S}}{1 \text{ mole Ag}_2\text{S}} \times \dfrac{2 \text{ Ag atoms}}{1 \text{ Ag}_2\text{S}} = 4.8 \times 10^{23} \text{ Ag Atoms}$

c. $0.75 \text{ g AgCl} \times \dfrac{1 \text{ mole AgCl}}{143.4 \text{ g AgCl}} \times \dfrac{6.02 \times 10^{23} \text{ AgCl units}}{1 \text{ mole AgCl units}} \times \dfrac{1 \text{ Ag ion}}{1 \text{ AgCl unit}} = 3.2 \times 10^{21} \text{ ions}$

7.29   **a.** $\dfrac{24.3 \text{ g Mg}}{62.3 \text{ g MgF}_2} \times 100 = 39.0\% \text{ Mg}$ $\dfrac{38.0 \text{ g F}}{62.3 \text{ g MgF}_2} \times 100 = 61.0\% \text{ F}$

b. $\dfrac{40.1 \text{ g Ca}}{74.1 \text{ g Ca(OH)}_2} \times 100 = 54.1\% \text{ Ca}$ $\dfrac{32.0 \text{ g O}}{74.1 \text{ g Ca(OH)}_2} \times 100 = 43.2\% \text{ O}$

$\dfrac{2.0 \text{ g H}}{74.1 \text{ g Ca(OH)}_2} \times 100 = 2.7\% \text{ H}$

c. $\dfrac{48.0 \text{ g C}}{120.0 \text{ g C}_4\text{H}_8\text{O}_4} \times 100 = 40.0\% \text{ C}$ $\dfrac{8.0 \text{ g H}}{120.0 \text{ g C}_4\text{H}_8\text{O}_4} \times 100 = 6.7\% \text{ H}$

$\dfrac{64.0 \text{ g O}}{120.0 \text{ g C}_4\text{H}_8\text{O}_4} \times 100 = 53.3\% \text{ O}$

7.30   **a.** $\dfrac{32.1 \text{ g S}}{142.1 \text{ g Na}_2\text{SO}_4} \times 100 = 22.6\% \text{ S}$

b. $\dfrac{96.3 \text{ g S}}{150.3 \text{ g Al}_2\text{S}_3} \times 100 = 64.1\% \text{ S}$

c. $\dfrac{32.1 \text{ g S}}{80.1 \text{ g SO}_3} \times 100 = 40.1\% \text{ S}$

7.31   **a.** $3.2 \text{ g N} \times \dfrac{1 \text{ mole N}}{14.0 \text{ g N}} = 0.23 \text{ mole N}$

$1.8 \text{ g O} \times \dfrac{1 \text{ mole O}}{16.0 \text{ g O}} = 0.11 \text{ mole O}$

$0.23 \text{ mole N} \div 0.11 \text{ mole} = 2.1 \text{ moles N}$
$0.11 \text{ mole O} \div 0.11 \text{ mole} = 1.0 \text{ mole O}$ formula $= \text{N}_2\text{O}$

b. $8.0 \text{ g C} \times \dfrac{1 \text{ mole C}}{12.0 \text{ g C}} = 0.67 \text{ mole C}$

$2.0 \text{ g H} \times \dfrac{1 \text{ mole H}}{1.0 \text{ g H}} = 2.0 \text{ moles H}$

$2.0 \text{ moles H} \div 0.67 \text{ mole} = 3.0 \text{ moles H}$
$0.67 \text{ mole C} \div 0.67 \text{ mole} = 1.0 \text{ mole C}$ formula $= \text{CH}_3$

c. $1.6 \text{ g H} \times \dfrac{1 \text{ mole H}}{1.0 \text{ g H}} = 1.6 \text{ moles H}$

$22. \text{ g N} \times \dfrac{1 \text{ mole N}}{14.0 \text{ g N}} = 1.6 \text{ moles N}$

$$76 \ \cancel{g \ O} \ \times \ \frac{1 \text{ mole O}}{16.0 \ \cancel{g \ O}} = 4.8 \text{ moles O}$$

1.6 moles H ÷ 1.6 moles = 1.0 mole H
1.6 moles N ÷ 1.6 moles = 1.0 mole N
4.8 moles O ÷ 1.6 moles = 3.0 mole O   formula = HNO_3

7.32 a. $2.9 \ \cancel{g \ Ag} \ \times \ \dfrac{1 \text{ mole Ag}}{107.9 \ g \ Ag} = 0.027 \text{ mole Ag}$

$0.43 \ \cancel{g \ S} \ \times \ \dfrac{1 \text{ mole S}}{32.1 \ \cancel{g \ S}} = 0.013 \text{ mole S}$

0.027 mole Ag ÷ 0.013 mole = 2.1 moles Ag
0.013 mole S ÷ 0.013 mole = 1.0 mole S   formula = Ag_2S

b. $22 \ \cancel{g \ Na} \ \times \ \dfrac{1 \text{ mole Na}}{23.0 \ g \ Na} = 0.96 \text{ mole Na}$

$7.7 \ \cancel{g \ O} \ \times \ \dfrac{1 \text{ mole O}}{16.0 \ \cancel{g \ O}} = 0.48 \text{ moles O}$

0.96 moles Na ÷ 0.48 mole = 2.0 moles Na
0.48 mole O ÷ 0.48 mole = 1.0 mole O   formula = Na_2O

c. $19 \ \cancel{g \ Na} \ \times \ \dfrac{1 \text{ mole Na}}{23.0 \ g \ Na} = 0.83 \text{ mole Na}$

$0.83 \ \cancel{g \ H} \ \times \ \dfrac{1 \text{ mole H}}{1.0 \ \cancel{g \ H}} = 0.83 \text{ mole H}$

$27 \ \cancel{g \ S} \ \times \ \dfrac{1 \text{ mole S}}{32.1 \ \cancel{g \ S}} = 0.84 \text{ mole S}$

$53 \ \cancel{g \ O} \ \times \ \dfrac{1 \text{ mole O}}{16.0 \ \cancel{g \ O}} = 3.3 \text{ moles O}$

0.83 mole Na ÷ 0.83 moles = 1.0 mole Na
0.83 mole H ÷ 0.83 moles = 1.0 mole H
0.83 mole S ÷ 0.83 moles = 1.0 mole S
3.3 moles O ÷ 0.83 moles = 4.0 mole O   formula = $NaHSO_4$

7.33 a. Converting from % by mass to grams in a100 g sample gives 71 g K and 29 g S

$71 \ \cancel{g \ K} \ \times \ \dfrac{1 \text{ mole K}}{39.1 \ \cancel{g \ K}} = 1.8 \text{ moles K}$

$29 \ \cancel{g \ S} \ \times \ \dfrac{1 \text{ mole S}}{32.1 \ \cancel{g \ S}} = 0.90 \text{ moles S}$

1.8 moles K ÷ 0.90 mole = 2.0 moles K
0.90 mole S ÷ 0.90 mole = 1.0 mole S   formula = K_2S

b. Converting from % by mass to grams in a100 g sample gives 55 g Ga and 45 g F

$55 \ \cancel{g \ Ga} \ \times \ \dfrac{1 \text{ mole Ga}}{69.7 \ \cancel{g \ Ga}} = 0.79 \text{ mole Ga}$

$$45 \text{ g F} \times \frac{1 \text{ mole F}}{19.0 \text{ g F}} = 2.4 \text{ moles F}$$

$$0.79 \text{ mole Ga} \div 0.79 \text{ mole} = 1.0 \text{ mole Ga}$$

$$2.4 \text{ moles F} \div 0.79 \text{ mole} = 3.0 \text{ moles F} \qquad \text{formula} = GaF_3$$

c. Converting from % by mass to grams in a100 g sample gives 31 g B and 69 g O

$$31 \text{ g B} \times \frac{1 \text{ mole B}}{10.8 \text{ g B}} = 2.9 \text{ moles B}$$

$$69 \text{ g O} \times \frac{1 \text{ mole O}}{16.0 \text{ g O}} = 4.3 \text{ moles O}$$

$$2.9 \text{ mole B} \div 2.9 \text{ mole} = 1.0 \text{ mole B} \quad \times 2 = 2.0 \text{ moles B}$$

$$4.3 \text{ moles O} \div 2.9 \text{ mole} = 1.5 \text{ moles O} \times 2 = 3.0 \text{ moles O} \quad \text{formula} = B_2O_3$$

7.34 **a.** Converting from % by mass to grams in a100 g sample gives 56 g Ca and 44 g S

$$56 \text{ g Ca} \times \frac{1 \text{ mole Ca}}{40.1 \text{ g Ca}} = 1.4 \text{ moles Ca}$$

$$44 \text{ g S} \times \frac{1 \text{ mole S}}{32.1 \text{ g S}} = 1.4 \text{ moles S}$$

$$1.4 \text{ moles Ca} \div 1.4 \text{ mole} = 1.0 \text{ moles Ca}$$

$$1.4 \text{ mole S} \div 1.4 \text{ mole} = 1.0 \text{ mole S} \qquad \text{formula} = CaS$$

b. Converting from % by mass to grams in a100 g sample gives 78 g Ba and 22 g F

$$78 \text{ g Ba} \times \frac{1 \text{ mole Ba}}{137.3 \text{ g Ba}} = 0.57 \text{ mole Ba}$$

$$22 \text{ g F} \times \frac{1 \text{ mole F}}{19.0 \text{ g F}} = 1.2 \text{ moles F}$$

$$0.57 \text{ mole Ba} \div 0.57 \text{ mole} = 1.0 \text{ mole Ba}$$

$$1.2 \text{ moles F} \div 0.57 \text{ mole} = 2.1 \text{ moles F} \qquad \text{formula} = BaF_2$$

c. Converting from % by mass to grams in a100 g sample gives 76 g Zn and 24 g P

$$76 \text{ g Zn} \times \frac{1 \text{ mole Zn}}{65.4 \text{ g Zn}} = 1.2 \text{ moles Zn}$$

$$24 \text{ g P} \times \frac{1 \text{ mole P}}{31.0 \text{ g P}} = 0.77 \text{ mole P}$$

$$1.2 \text{ moles Zn} \div 0.77 \text{ mole} = 1.55 \text{ moles Zn} \times 2 = 3.1 \text{ moles Zn}$$

$$0.77 \text{ mole P} \div 0.77 \text{ mole} = 1.0 \text{ moles P} \times 2 = 2.0 \text{ moles P} \quad \text{formula} = Zn_3P_2$$

7.35 **a.** Two SO_2 molecules react with one O_2 molecule to produce two SO_3 molecules. Two moles of SO_2 react with one mole of O_2 to produce two moles of SO_3.
b. Four P atoms react with five O_2 molecules to produce two P_2O_5 molecules. Four moles of P react with five moles of O_2 to produce two moles of P_2O_5.

7.36 **a.** Two aluminum atoms react with three chlorine molecules to produce two formula units of $AlCl_3$. Two moles of Aluminum react with three moles of chlorine to produce two moles of $AlCl_3$.

b. Four HCl molecules react with one O_2 molecule to produce two Cl_2 molecules and two H_2O molecules. Four moles of HCl react with one mole of O_2 to form two moles of Cl_2 and two moles of H_2O.

7.37 **a.** Reactants: 2 moles of SO_2 plus 1 mole of $O_2 =$
2 moles (64.1 g/mole) + 1 mole (32.0 g/mole) = 160.2 g
Products: 2 moles of $SO_3 =$ 2 moles (80.1 g/mole) = 160.2 g

b. Reactants: 4 moles of P and 5 moles of $O_2 =$
4 moles (31.0 g/mole) + 5 moles (32.0 g/mole) = 284 g
Products: 2 moles of $P_2O_5 =$ 2 moles (142 g/mole) = 284 g

7.38 **a.** Reactants: 2 moles of Al and 6 moles of Cl =
54.0 g + 213 g = 267 g
Products: 2 moles of Al and 6 moles of Cl =
54.0 g + 213 g = 267 g

b. Reactant: 4 moles of H and 4 moles of Cl plus 2 moles of O =
4.0 g + 142.0 g + 32.0 g = 178.0 g
Products: 4 moles of Cl plus 4 moles of H and 2 moles of O =
142.0 g + 4.0 g + 32.0 g = 178.0 g

7.39 **a.** $\dfrac{2 \text{ mole } SO_2}{1 \text{ mole } O_2}$ and $\dfrac{1 \text{ mole } O_2}{2 \text{ mole } SO_2}$ $\qquad$ $\dfrac{2 \text{ mole } SO_2}{2 \text{ mole } SO_3}$ and $\dfrac{2 \text{ mole } SO_3}{2 \text{ mole } SO_2}$

$\dfrac{1 \text{ mole } O_2}{2 \text{ mole } SO_3}$ and $\dfrac{2 \text{ mole } SO_3}{1 \text{ mole } O_2}$

b $\dfrac{4 \text{ mole } P}{5 \text{ mole } O_2}$ and $\dfrac{5 \text{ mole } O_2}{4 \text{ mole } P}$ $\qquad$ $\dfrac{4 \text{ mole } P}{2 \text{ mole } P_2O_5}$ and $\dfrac{2 \text{ mole } P_2O_5}{4 \text{ mole } P}$

$\dfrac{5 \text{ mole } O_2}{2 \text{ mole } P_2O_5}$ and $\dfrac{2 \text{ mole } P_2O_5}{5 \text{ mole } O_2}$

7.40 **a.** $\dfrac{2 \text{ mole } Al}{3 \text{ mole } Cl_2}$ and $\dfrac{3 \text{ mole } Cl_2}{2 \text{ mole } Al}$ $\qquad$ $\dfrac{2 \text{ mole } Al}{2 \text{ mole } AlCl_3}$ and $\dfrac{2 \text{ mole } AlCl_3}{2 \text{ mole } Al}$

$\dfrac{3 \text{ mole } Cl_2}{2 \text{ mole } AlCl_3}$ and $\dfrac{2 \text{ mole } AlCl_3}{3 \text{ mole } Cl_2}$

b. $\dfrac{4 \text{ mole } HCl}{1 \text{ mole } O_2}$ and $\dfrac{1 \text{ mole } O_2}{4 \text{ mole } HCl}$ $\qquad$ $\dfrac{4 \text{ mole } HCl}{2 \text{ mole } Cl_2}$ and $\dfrac{2 \text{ mole } Cl_2}{4 \text{ mole } HCl}$

$\dfrac{4 \text{ mole } HCl}{2 \text{ mole } H_2O}$ and $\dfrac{2 \text{ mole } H_2O}{4 \text{ mole } HCl}$ $\qquad$ $\dfrac{1 \text{ mole } O_2}{2 \text{ mole } Cl_2}$ and $\dfrac{2 \text{ mole } Cl_2}{1 \text{ mole } O_2}$

$\dfrac{1 \text{ mole } O_2}{2 \text{ mole } H_2O}$ and $\dfrac{2 \text{ mole } H_2O}{1 \text{ mole } O_2}$ $\qquad$ $\dfrac{2 \text{ mole } Cl_2}{2 \text{ mole } H_2O}$ and $\dfrac{2 \text{ mole } H_2O}{2 \text{ mole } Cl_2}$

7.41 **a.** 2.0 mole H_2 $\times$ $\dfrac{1 \text{ mole } O_2}{2 \text{ mole } H_2}$ = 1.0 mole O_2

b. 5.0 mole O_2 $\times$ $\dfrac{2 \text{ mole } H_2}{1 \text{ mole } O_2}$ = 10. mole H_2

c. 2.5 mole O_2 $\times$ $\dfrac{2 \text{ mole } H_2O}{1 \text{ mole } O_2}$ = 5.0 mole H_2O

7.42 **a.** 1.0 ~~mole N$_2$~~ $\times$ $\dfrac{3 \text{ moles } H_2}{1 \text{ mole } N_2}$ = 3.0 moles H$_2$

b. 0.60 ~~mole NH$_3$~~ $\times$ $\dfrac{1 \text{ mole } N_2}{2 \text{ moles } NH_3}$ = 0.30 mole N$_2$

c. 1.4 ~~moles H$_2$~~ $\times$ $\dfrac{2 \text{ moles } NH_3}{3 \text{ mole } H_2}$ = 0.93 mole NH$_3$

7.43 **a.** 0.500 ~~mole SO$_2$~~ $\times$ $\dfrac{5 \text{ mole } C}{2 \text{ mole } SO_2}$ = 1.25 mole C

b. 1.2 ~~mole C~~ $\times$ $\dfrac{4 \text{ mole } CO}{5 \text{ mole } C}$ = 0.96 mole CO

c. 0.50 ~~mole CS$_2$~~ $\times$ $\dfrac{2 \text{ mole } SO_2}{1 \text{ mole } CS_2}$ = 1.0 mole SO$_2$

d. 2.5 ~~mole C~~ $\times$ $\dfrac{1 \text{ mole } CS_2}{5 \text{ mole } C}$ = 0.50 mole CS$_2$

7.44 **a.** 2.00 ~~mole C$_2$H$_2$~~ $\times$ $\dfrac{5 \text{ mole } O_2}{2 \text{ mole } C_2H_2}$ = 5.00 mole O$_2$

b. 3.5 ~~mole C$_2$H$_2$~~ $\times$ $\dfrac{4 \text{ mole } CO_2}{2 \text{ mole } C_2H_2}$ = 7.0 mole CO$_2$

c. 0.50 ~~mole H$_2$O~~ $\times$ $\dfrac{2 \text{ mole } C_2H_2}{2 \text{ mole } H_2O}$ = 0.50 mole C$_2$H$_2$

d. 0.100 ~~mole O$_2$~~ $\times$ $\dfrac{4 \text{ mole } CO_2}{5 \text{ mole } O_2}$ = 0.080 mole CO$_2$

7.45 **a.** 2.5 ~~mole Na~~ $\times$ $\dfrac{2 \text{ mole } Na_2O}{4 \text{ mole } Na}$ $\times$ $\dfrac{62.0 \text{ g } Na_2O}{1 \text{ mole } Na_2O}$ = 78 g Na$_2$O

b. 18.0 ~~g Na~~ $\times$ $\dfrac{1 \text{ mole } Na}{23.0 \text{ g } Na}$ $\times$ $\dfrac{1 \text{ mole } O_2}{4 \text{ mole } Na}$ $\times$ $\dfrac{32.0 \text{ g } O_2}{1 \text{ mole } O_2}$ = 6.26 g O$_2$

c. 75.0 ~~g Na$_2$O~~ $\times$ $\dfrac{1 \text{ mole } Na_2O}{62.0 \text{ g } Na_2O}$ $\times$ $\dfrac{1 \text{ mole } O_2}{2 \text{ mole } Na_2O}$ $\times$ $\dfrac{32.0 \text{ g } O_2}{1 \text{ mole } O_2}$ = 19.4 g O$_2$

7.46 **a.** 1.8 ~~mole H$_2$~~ $\times$ $\dfrac{2 \text{ mole } NH_3}{3 \text{ mole } H_2}$ $\times$ $\dfrac{17.0 \text{ g } NH_3}{1 \text{ mole } NH_3}$ = 20. g NH$_3$

b. 2.80 ~~g N$_2$~~ $\times$ $\dfrac{1 \text{ mole } N_2}{28.0 \text{ g } N_2}$ $\times$ $\dfrac{3 \text{ mole } H_2}{1 \text{ mole } N_2}$ $\times$ $\dfrac{2.0 \text{ g } H_2}{1 \text{ mole } H_2}$ = 0.60 g H$_2$

c. 12 ~~g H$_2$~~ $\times$ $\dfrac{1 \text{ mole } H_2}{2.0 \text{ g } H_2}$ $\times$ $\dfrac{2 \text{ mole } NH_3}{3 \text{ mole } H_2}$ $\times$ $\dfrac{17.0 \text{ g } NH_3}{1 \text{ mole } NH_3}$ = 68 g NH$_3$

7.47 **a.** 8.0 ~~mole NH$_3$~~ $\times$ $\dfrac{3 \text{ mole } O_2}{4 \text{ mole } NH_3}$ $\times$ $\dfrac{32.0 \text{ g } O_2}{1 \text{ mole } O_2}$ = 190 g O$_2$

b. 6.50 ~~g O$_2$~~ $\times$ $\dfrac{1 \text{ mole } O_2}{32.0 \text{ g } O_2}$ $\times$ $\dfrac{2 \text{ mole } N_2}{3 \text{ mole } O_2}$ $\times$ $\dfrac{28.0 \text{ g } N_2}{1 \text{ mole } N_2}$ = 3.79 g N$_2$

c. 34 ~~g NH$_3$~~ $\times$ $\dfrac{1 \text{ mole } NH_3}{17.0 \text{ g } NH_3}$ $\times$ $\dfrac{6 \text{ mole } H_2O}{4 \text{ mole } NH_3}$ $\times$ $\dfrac{18.0 \text{ g } H_2O}{1 \text{ mole } H_2O}$ = 54 g H$_2$O

7.48 **a.** 2.50 mole Fe$_2$O$_3$ × $\dfrac{3 \text{ mole C}}{1 \text{ mole Fe}_2\text{O}_3}$ × $\dfrac{12.0 \text{ g C}}{1 \text{ mole C}}$ = 90.0 g C

b. 36.0 g C × $\dfrac{1 \text{ mole C}}{12.0 \text{ g C}}$ × $\dfrac{3 \text{ mole CO}}{3 \text{ mole C}}$ × $\dfrac{28.0 \text{ g CO}}{1 \text{ mole CO}}$ = 84.0 g CO

c. 6.00 g Fe$_2$O$_3$ × $\dfrac{1 \text{ mole Fe}_2\text{O}_3}{159.8 \text{ g Fe}_2\text{O}_3}$ × $\dfrac{2 \text{ mole Fe}}{1 \text{ mole Fe}_2\text{O}_3}$ × $\dfrac{55.9 \text{ g Fe}}{1 \text{ mole Fe}}$ = 4.20 g Fe

7.49 **a.** 40.0 g C × $\dfrac{1 \text{ mole C}}{12.0 \text{ g C}}$ × $\dfrac{1 \text{mole CS}_2}{5 \text{ moles C}}$ × $\dfrac{76.2 \text{ g CS}_2}{1 \text{ mole CS}_2}$ = 50.8 g CS$_2$

$\dfrac{36.0 \text{ g CS}_2 \text{ (actual)}}{50.8 \text{ g CS}_2 \text{(theoretical)}}$ × 100 = 70.9%

b. 32.0 g SO$_2$ × $\dfrac{1 \text{ mole SO}_2}{64.1 \text{ g SO}_2}$ × $\dfrac{1 \text{mole CS}_2}{2 \text{ moles SO}_2}$ × $\dfrac{76.2 \text{ g CS}_2}{1 \text{ mole CS}_2}$ = 19.0 g CS$_2$

$\dfrac{12.0 \text{ g CS}_2 \text{ (actual)}}{19.0 \text{ g CS}_2 \text{(theoretical)}}$ × 100 = 63.1%

7.50 a. Theorectical yield of Fe:

65.0 g Fe$_2$O$_3$ × $\dfrac{1 \text{ mole Fe}_2\text{O}_3}{159.8 \text{ g Fe}_2\text{O}_3}$ × $\dfrac{2 \text{ mole Fe}}{1 \text{ mole Fe}_2\text{O}_3}$ × $\dfrac{55.9 \text{ g Fe}}{1 \text{ mole Fe}}$ = 45.5 Fe

Percent yield:
$\dfrac{15.0 \text{ g Fe (actual)}}{45.5 \text{ g Fe(theoretical)}}$ × 100 = 33.0 % Fe actually produced

b. Theorectical yield of CO$_2$:

75.0 g CO × $\dfrac{1 \text{ mole CO}}{28.0 \text{ g CO}}$ × $\dfrac{3 \text{ mole CO}_2}{3 \text{ moles CO}}$ × $\dfrac{44.0 \text{ g CO}_2}{1 \text{ mole CO}_2}$ = 118 g CO$_2$

Percent yield:
$\dfrac{15.0 \text{ g CO}_2 \text{ (actual)}}{118.0 \text{ g CO}_2 \text{(theoretical)}}$ × 100 = 12.7 % CO$_2$ actually produced

7.51 50.0 g Al × $\dfrac{1 \text{ mole Al}}{27.0 \text{ g Al}}$ × $\dfrac{2 \text{ moles Al}_2\text{O}_3}{4 \text{ moles Al}}$ × $\dfrac{102.0 \text{ g Al}_2\text{O}_3}{1 \text{ mole Al}_2\text{O}_3}$ = 94.4 g Al$_2$O$_3$

Use the percent yield to convert theoretical to actual:
94.4 g Al$_2$O$_3$ × $\dfrac{75.0 \text{ g Al}_2\text{O}_3}{100 \text{ g Al}_2\text{O}_3}$ = 70.8g Al$_2$O$_3$ (actual)

7.52 Theorectical yield of CO$_2$:
45.0 g C$_3$H$_8$ × $\dfrac{1 \text{ mole C}_3\text{H}_8}{44.0 \text{ g C}_3\text{H}_8}$ × $\dfrac{3 \text{ moles CO}_2}{1 \text{ moles C}_3\text{H}_8}$ × $\dfrac{44.0 \text{ g CO}_2}{1 \text{ mole CO}_2}$ = 135 g CO$_2$

Use the percent yield to convert theoretical to actual:
135 g CO$_2$ × $\dfrac{60.0 \text{ g CO}_2}{100 \text{ g CO}_2}$ = 81.0 g CO$_2$ (actual)

7.53 In the expression for K$_{eq}$ the products are divided by the reactants with each concentration raised to a power that equals the coefficient in the equation:

a. $K_{eq} = \dfrac{[CS_2][H_2]^4}{[CH_4][H_2S]^2}$ **b.** $K_{eq} = \dfrac{[N_2][O_2]}{[NO]^2}$

c. $K_{eq} = \dfrac{[CS_2][O_2]^4}{[SO_3]^2[CO_2]}$

7.54 In the expression for K_{eq} the products are divided by the reactants with each concentration raised to a power that equals the coefficient in the equation:

    a. $K_{eq} = \dfrac{[H_2][Br_2]}{[HBr]^2}$ **b.** $K_{eq} = \dfrac{[CH_3OH]}{[CO][H_2]^2}$

    c. $K_{eq} = \dfrac{[CS_2][H_2]^4}{[H_2S]^2[CH_4]}$

7.55   **a.** A large K_{eq} means that the products are favored.
       b. A small Keq means that the reactants are favored.

7.56   **a.** A small K_{eq} means that the reactants are favored.
       b. A large Keq means that the products are favored.

7.57   **a.** $\dfrac{78.2 \text{ g K}}{194.2 \text{ g K}_2\text{CrO}_4} \times 100 = 40.3\% \text{ K}$ $\dfrac{52.0\text{g Cr}}{194.2 \text{ g K}_2\text{CrO}_4} \times 100 = 26.8 \%\text{Cr}$

        $\dfrac{64.0 \text{ g O}}{194.2 \text{ g K}_2\text{CrO}_4} \times 100 = 33.7\% \text{ O}$

    b. $\dfrac{27.0 \text{ g Al}}{210.0 \text{ g Al(HCO}_3)_3} \times 100 = 12.9\% \text{ Al}$ $\dfrac{3.0\text{g H}}{210.0 \text{ g Al(HCO}_3)_3} \times 100 = 1.4 \%\text{H}$

        $\dfrac{36.0 \text{ g C}}{210.0 \text{ g Al(HCO}_3)_3} \times 100 = 17.1\% \text{ C}$ $\dfrac{144.0 \text{ g O}}{210.0 \text{ g Al(HCO}_3)_3} \times 100 = 68.6\% \text{ O}$

    c. $\dfrac{72.0 \text{ g C}}{180.0 \text{ g C}_6\text{H}_{12}\text{O}_6} \times 100 = 40.0\% \text{ C}$ $\dfrac{12.0\text{g H}}{180.0 \text{ g C}_6\text{H}_{12}\text{O}_6} \times 100 = 6.7 \%\text{H}$

        $\dfrac{96.0 \text{ g O}}{180.0 \text{ g C}_6\text{H}_{12}\text{O}_6} \times 100 = 53.3\% \text{ O}$

7.58   **a.** $\dfrac{124.0 \text{ g P}}{284 \text{ g P}_4\text{O}_{10}} \times 100 = 43.7 \% \text{ P}$

    b. $\dfrac{62.0 \text{ g P}}{134.9 \text{ g Mg}_3\text{P}_2} \times 100 = 46.0 \% \text{ P}$

    c. $\dfrac{62.0 \text{ g P}}{310.3 \text{ g Ca}_3(\text{PO}_4)_2} \times 100 = 20.0 \% \text{ P}$

7.59   **a.** $2.20 \text{ g S} \times \dfrac{1 \text{ mole S}}{32.1 \text{ g S}} = 0.0685 \text{ mole S}$

        $7.81 \text{ g F} \times \dfrac{1 \text{ mole F}}{19.0 \text{ g F}} = 0.411 \text{ mole F}$

        $0.0685 \text{ mole S} \div 0.0685 \text{ mole} = 1.00 \text{ mole S}$

        $0.411 \text{ moles F} \div 0.0685 \text{ mole} = 6.00 \text{ moles F}$ formula = SF_6

    b. $6.35 \text{ g Ag} \times \dfrac{1 \text{ mole Ag}}{107.9 \text{ g Ag}} = 0.0589 \text{ mole Ag}$

        $0.825 \text{ g N} \times \dfrac{1 \text{ mole N}}{14.0 \text{ g N}} = 0.0589 \text{ mole N}$

        $2.83 \text{ g O} \times \dfrac{1 \text{ mole O}}{16.0 \text{ g O}} = 0.177 \text{ mole O}$

        $0.0589 \text{ mole Ag} \div 0.0589 \text{ mole} = 1.00 \text{ mole Ag}$

0.0589 mole N ÷ 0.0589 mole = 1.00 mole N

0.177 moles O ÷ 0.0589 mole = 3.00 moles O formula = $AgNO_3$

c. 89.2 g̶ ̶A̶u̶ × $\dfrac{1 \text{ mole Au}}{197.0 \text{ g̶ ̶A̶u̶}}$ = 0.453 mole Au

10.9 g̶ ̶O̶ × $\dfrac{1 \text{ mole O}}{16.0 \text{ g̶ ̶O̶}}$ = 0.681 mole O

0.453 mole Au ÷ 0.453 mole = 1.00 mole Au × 2 = 2.00 moles Au

0.681 moles O ÷ 0.453 mole = 1.50 moles O × 2 = 3.00 mole O formula = Au_2O_3

7.60 **a.** 61 g̶ ̶S̶n̶ × $\dfrac{1 \text{ mole Sn}}{118.7 \text{ g̶ ̶S̶n̶}}$ = 0.51 mole Sn

39 g̶ ̶F̶ × $\dfrac{1 \text{ mole F}}{19.0 \text{ g̶ ̶F̶}}$ = 2.1 moles F

0.51 mole Sn ÷ 0.51 mole = 1.0 mole Sn

2.1 moles F ÷ 0.51 mole = 4.1 moles F formula = SnF_4

b. 25.9 g̶ ̶N̶ × $\dfrac{1 \text{ mole N}}{14.0 \text{ g̶ ̶N̶}}$ = 1.85 moles N

74.1 g̶ ̶O̶ × $\dfrac{1 \text{ mole O}}{16.0 \text{ g̶ ̶O̶}}$ = 4.63 moles O

1.85 moles N ÷ 1.85 mole = 1.00 mole N

4.63 moles O ÷ 1.85 mole = 2.50 moles O

Calculation of whole numbers

1.00 mole N × 2 = 2.00 mole N

2.50 moles O × 2 = 5.00 moles O Formula N_2O_5

c. 22.1 g̶ ̶A̶l̶ × $\dfrac{1 \text{ mole Al}}{27.0 \text{ g̶ ̶A̶l̶}}$ − 0.819 mole Al

25.4 g̶ ̶P̶ × $\dfrac{1 \text{ mole P}}{31.0 \text{ g̶ ̶P̶}}$ = 0.819 mole P

52.5 g̶ ̶O̶ × $\dfrac{1 \text{ mole O}}{16.0 \text{ g̶ ̶O̶}}$ = 3.28 moles O

0.819 mole Al ÷ 0.819 mole = 1.00 mole Al

0.819 moles P ÷ 0.819 mole = 1.00 moles O

4.00 moles O ÷ 0.819 mole = 4.00 mole O formula = $AlPO_4$

7.61 70.0 k̶g̶ ̶b̶o̶d̶y̶ ̶w̶t̶ × $\dfrac{60.0 \text{ k̶g̶ ̶H̶}_2\text{O̶}}{100 \text{ k̶g̶ ̶b̶o̶d̶y̶ ̶w̶t̶}}$ × $\dfrac{1000 \text{ g}}{1 \text{ k̶g̶}}$ × $\dfrac{1 \text{ mole H}_2\text{O}}{18.0 \text{ g̶ ̶H̶}_2\text{O̶}}$ = 2.33 × 10^3 moles H_2O

7.62 10.0 m̶L̶ ̶b̶l̶o̶o̶d̶ × $\dfrac{400. \text{ m̶g̶ ̶C̶}_2\text{H̶}_6\text{O̶}}{100 \text{ mL b̶l̶o̶o̶d̶}}$ × $\dfrac{1 \text{ g}}{1000 \text{ m̶g̶}}$ × $\dfrac{1 \text{ mole C}_2\text{H}_6\text{O}}{46.0 \text{ g̶ ̶C̶}_2\text{H̶}_6\text{O̶}}$ = 8.70 × 10^{-4} mole C_2H_6O

7.63 **a.** 124 g̶ ̶C̶₂̶H̶₆̶O̶ × $\dfrac{1 \text{ m̶o̶l̶e̶ ̶C̶}_2\text{H̶}_6\text{O̶}}{46.0 \text{ g̶ ̶C̶}_2\text{H̶}_6\text{O̶}}$ × $\dfrac{1 \text{ mole C}_6\text{H}_{12}\text{O}_6}{2 \text{ m̶o̶l̶e̶ ̶C̶}_2\text{H̶}_6\text{O̶}}$ = 1.35 mole $C_6H_{12}O_6$

b. $0.240 \text{ kg C}_6\text{H}_{12}\text{O}_6 \times \dfrac{1000 \text{ g}}{1 \text{ kg}} \times \dfrac{1 \text{ mole C}_6\text{H}_{12}\text{O}_6}{180.0 \text{ g C}_6\text{H}_{12}\text{O}_6} \times \dfrac{2 \text{ mole C}_2\text{H}_6\text{O}}{1 \text{ mole C}_6\text{H}_{12}\text{O}_6} \times \dfrac{46.0 \text{ g C}_2\text{H}_6\text{O}}{1 \text{ mole C}_2\text{H}_6\text{O}}$

$= 123 \text{ g C}_2\text{H}_6\text{O}$

7.64 **a.** $\text{C}_2\text{H}_6\text{O} + 3\text{O}_2 \rightarrow 2\text{CO}_2 + 3\text{H}_2\text{O}$

b. $4.0 \text{ mole C}_2\text{H}_6\text{O} \times \dfrac{3 \text{ mole O}_2}{1 \text{ mole C}_2\text{H}_6\text{O}} \qquad = 12 \text{ mole O}_2$

c. $88 \text{ g CO}_2 \times \dfrac{1 \text{ mole CO}_2}{44.0 \text{ g CO}_2} \times \dfrac{3 \text{ mole O}_2}{2 \text{ mole CO}_2} \times \dfrac{32.0 \text{ g O}_2}{1 \text{ mole O}_2} = 96 \text{ g O}_2$

d. $125 \text{ g C}_2\text{H}_6\text{O} \times \dfrac{1 \text{ mole C}_2\text{H}_6\text{O}}{46.0 \text{ g C}_2\text{H}_6\text{O}} \times \dfrac{2 \text{ mole CO}_2}{1 \text{ mole C}_2\text{H}_6\text{O}} \times \dfrac{44.0 \text{ g CO}_2}{1 \text{ mole CO}_2} = 239 \text{ g CO}_2$

$125 \text{ g C}_2\text{H}_6\text{O} \times \dfrac{1 \text{ mole C}_2\text{H}_6\text{O}}{46.0 \text{ g C}_2\text{H}_6\text{O}} \times \dfrac{3 \text{ mole H}_2\text{O}}{1 \text{ mole C}_2\text{H}_6\text{O}} \times \dfrac{18.0 \text{ g H}_2\text{O}}{1 \text{ mole H}_2\text{O}} = 147 \text{ g}$

7.65 $2\text{NH}_3 + 5\text{F}_2 \rightarrow \text{N}_2\text{F}_4 + 6\text{HF}$

a. $4.00 \text{ mole HF} \times \dfrac{2 \text{ mole NH}_3}{6 \text{ mole HF}} = 1.33 \text{ mole NH}_3$

$4.00 \text{ mole HF} \times \dfrac{5 \text{ mole F}_2}{6 \text{ mole HF}} = 3.33 \text{ mole F}_2$

b. $1.50 \text{ mole NH}_3 \times \dfrac{5 \text{ mole F}_2}{2 \text{ mole NH}_3} \times \dfrac{38.0 \text{ g F}_2}{1 \text{ mole F}_2} = 143 \text{ g F}_2$

c. $3.40 \text{ g NH}_3 \times \dfrac{1 \text{ mole NH}_3}{17.0 \text{ g NH}_3} \times \dfrac{1 \text{ mole N}_2\text{F}_4}{2 \text{ mole NH}_3} \times \dfrac{104.0 \text{ g N}_2\text{F}_4}{1 \text{ mole N}_2\text{F}_4} = 10.4 \text{ g N}_2\text{F}_4$

7.66 Theoretical yield

$50.0 \text{ g Fe}_2\text{O}_3 \times \dfrac{1 \text{ mole Fe}_2\text{O}_3}{159.8 \text{ g Fe}_2\text{O}_3} \times \dfrac{2 \text{ moles Fe}}{1 \text{ mole Fe}_2\text{O}_3} \times \dfrac{55.9 \text{ g Fe}}{1 \text{ mole Fe}} = 35.0 \text{ g Fe}$

Percent yield

$\dfrac{32.8 \text{ g Fe}}{35.0} \times 100 = 93.7 \text{ % Fe}$ (actual yield)

7.67 $\text{C}_2\text{H}_2(g) + 3\text{O}_2(g) \longrightarrow 2\text{CO}_2(g) + \text{H}_2\text{O}(g)$

$22.5 \text{ g C}_2\text{H}_2 \times \dfrac{1 \text{ mole C}_2\text{H}_2}{26.0 \text{ g C}_2\text{H}_2} \times \dfrac{2 \text{ moles CO}_2}{1 \text{ mole C}_2\text{H}_2} \times \dfrac{44.0 \text{ g CO}_2}{1 \text{ mole CO}_2} = 76.2 \text{ g CO}_2$ (theoretical)

$\dfrac{62.0 \text{ g (actual)}}{76.2 \text{ g (theoretical)}} \times 100 = 81.4\%$ (percent yield)

7.68 Theoretical yield would be

$30.0 \text{ g NH}_3 \times \dfrac{100.0 \text{ g NH}_3}{65.0 \text{ %}} = 46.2 \text{ g NH}_3$

$46.2 \text{ g NH}_3 \times \dfrac{1 \text{ mole NH}_3}{17.0 \text{ g NH}_3} \times \dfrac{1 \text{ mole N}_2}{2 \text{ moles NH}_3} \times \dfrac{28.0 \text{ g N}_2}{1 \text{ mole N}_2} = 38.0 \text{ g N}_2$ reacted

Gases

Study Goals

- Describe the kinetic theory of gases.
- Use the gas laws to determine the new pressure, volume or temperature of a specific amount of gas.
- Describe the relationship between the amount of a gas and its volume.
- Use the ideal gas law to calculate the unknown property.
- Use partial pressure to calculate the total pressure of a gas mixture.

Chapter Outline

8.1 Properties of Gases
  Explore Your World: Forming a Gas
8.2 Gas Pressure
  Health Note: Measuring Blood Pressure
8.3 Pressure and Volume (Boyle's Law)
  Health Note: Pressure-Volume Relationship in Breathing
  Explore Your World: Medicine Dropper "Diver"
8.4 Temperature and Volume (Charles' Law)
  Explore Your World: Temperature and Volume
8.5 Temperature and Pressure (Gay-Lussac's Law)
  Explore Your World: Vapor Pressure
8.6 The Combined Gas Law
8.7 Volume and Moles (Avogadro's Law)
8.8 The Ideal Gas Law
8.9 Partial Pressures (Dalton's Law)
  Explore Your World: Oxygen in the Air
  Health Note: Hyperbaric Chambers

Chapter Summary and Demonstrations

1. Properties of Gases

Kinetic molecular theory is used to describe the behavior of gas molecules. The physical properties of pressure, volume, temperature and moles of gas describe a gas.

Demonstration: Properties of A Gas
a. Pour a small amount of ammonia cleaner in a bowl. How close do you have to be to smell the ammonia? In 5 minutes, return to the bowl of ammonia. How close do you have to get before you can smell the ammonia?

b. Fill a glass one-quarter full of vinegar. Place a small amount of baking soda in the finger of a plastic glove. (The glove should fit tightly around the glass.) Carefully place the glove on the glass and slowly shake the baking soda into the vinegar. What happens to the glove? Explain.

2. Gas Laws

Gas laws are developed that relate two of the properties. Boyle's Law is applied to the process of ventilation in the human body. The combined gas law and Dalton's Law extend the applications of the gas laws.

Demonstration: Pressure Gradients Add a small amount of water to a soft drink can and place it on a hot place. When steam comes out, use tongs remove the soda can and immediately invert it into a large container of ice and water. The sudden influx of cold water will cause the can to collapse dramatically.

Students discuss how a soda can is "crushed" by the atmospheric pressures as the temperature of the water (vapor) inside decreases. (The decrease in temperature caused the steam inside to condense to liquid, which takes up less space and creates much less pressure. The resulting pressure gradient of the ambient atmospheric greater than inside crushes the can.)

3. Partial Pressures

Gas mixtures and partial pressures are described and used in discussions of blood gases and hyperbaric chambers

Demonstration: Partial Pressure of Oxygen in Air Materials: shallow dish, candles of different heights, food coloring, and a large beaker (400-mL) to cover candles.
a. Place a candle in the shallow dish, light it, and place a beaker (I use a 400-mL) over the lighted candle. The candle goes out. Discuss the results.

b. Place three candles of different heights in the shallow dish of water, light them, and cover them with a large beaker. The candles go out starting with the tallest one. The hot carbon dioxide rises, cools, and falls to the bottom of the system. (CO_2 is heavier than air.) Discuss the reason for staying close to the floor in the event of a fire.

c. Light the candle(s) in the dish again, add 1-2 cm water, and food coloring (optional) to the dish. Cover with the beaker. As oxygen reacts and is replaced with carbon dioxide, the carbon dioxide dissolves in the water due to its solubility. As the pressure decreases, water inside the beaker rises. The height of the water inside the beaker can be used to estimate roughly the percentage of oxygen (19%) in the air.

Demonstration: Partial Pressures A bell jar can be used to create a vacuum and demonstrate the effect of lower pressure. I place a balloon, partially inflated or a small beaker about 1/3-1/2 full of shaving cream in the bell jar. As the pressure drops, the balloon inflates, and the shaving cream expands and builds to great heights within the chamber due to the butane gas in the foam. It can be quite spectacular. The return of air into the bell jar rapidly deflates the balloon and foam.

4. Lecture Review Activity "It's A Gas "

To review the concepts in the chapter on gases, I place slips of paper containing single questions in a larger beaker. Students form teams and a student for each team tries to answer the question that is drawn. Sometimes this activity is run as a quiz and points are given. But mostly it is fun and students can assess how well they know the material. Some sample questions follow:
What are three units used for the pressure of a gas?
If pressure increase, n and T are constant, what happens to volume?
What happens to V if the T is decreased while P and n are constant?
If initial volume and pressure are 8.0 L and 800 mm Hg, what is the new volume if pressure changes to 400 mm Hg, n and T constant?
What is the total pressure exerted by a mixture of oxygen 525 mm Hg and nitrogen at 1.00 atm?

What temperature scale must be used to specify temperature in a gas law equation?

A gas has a pressure of 740 mm Hg at a temperature of 400 K. What temperature is needed to change the pressure to 1200 mm Hg?

Is the partial pressure of oxygen higher in the lungs or in active cells of the body tissue?

Is the partial pressure of carbon dioxide higher in the lungs or in active cells of the body tissue?

How many atm are in 1250 mm Hg?

What is the total pressure of a gas mixture containing 2.00 atm O_2, 1.5 atm N_2 and 3.0 atm Ne?

True or false: The pressure of a gas increase when the volume increases at constant temperature and moles.

What is the volume at STP of 32.0 g O_2?

How many moles of nitrogen gas are in 44.8 L of N_2 at STP?

Laboratory Suggestions

Lab 13 Gas Laws: Boyle's and Charles'

Data for the effect of volume change on the pressure of a gas sample are used to calculate the PV constant. Students are asked to explain Boyle's Law. P versus V is graphed to show the inverse relationship between pressure and volume.

In an application of Charles' Law, students heat a flask and invert it in water baths at different temperatures. The decrease in temperature creates a partial vacuum. The water that enters the flask is used to determine the remaining gas volume. Volume and temperature are graphed to determine the V and T relationship. The Celsius temperature at absolute zero is predicated by extrapolating the graph to zero volume.

A. Boyle's Law

B. Charles' Law

Laboratory Skills to Demonstrate

Calculation of PV constant

Graphing P versus V

Setup for water bath for heating flask

Equalization of water levels for Charles' Law while flask is inverted

Extrapolation of graph to zero volume to determine the Kelvin temperature of absolute zero

Lab 14   Partial Pressures of Oxygen, Nitrogen and Carbon Dioxide in Air

Iron filings in a moist test tube inverted in water form rust using the oxygen trapped in the tube. By measuring the loss in volume, the amount of oxygen, % oxygen, and partial pressure of oxygen are determined. The CO_2 in the atmospheric air and in expired air is measured and compared.

A. Partial Pressures of Oxygen and Nitrogen in Air

B. Carbon Dioxide in the Atmosphere

C. Carbon Dioxide in Expired Air

Laboratory Skills to Demonstrate

Reading a barometer

Care in the use of NaOH

Setup for flask and tubing for CO_2 measurement. Continuous shaking of the flask is needed to absorb all of the carbon dioxide from the expired air. Shake carefully until the level of water in the glass tubing no longer rises. Be careful not to warm the flask with your hands.

Answers and Solutions to Text Problems

8.1 **a.** Gaseous particles have greater kinetic energies at higher temperatures. Because kinetic energy is a measure of the energy of motion, the gaseous particles must be moving faster at higher temperatures than at lower values.

b. Because particles in a gas are very far apart, gases can be easily compressed without the particles bumping into neighboring gas particles. Neighboring particles are much closer together in solids and liquids, and they will "bump" into each other and repel each other if the sample is compressed.

c. Because the particles of a gas are very far apart, only a small amount of mass (due to the gas particles themselves) is found in a given volume of space.

8.2 **a.** At the higher temperature in the fire, the number of collisions against the container's walls increase because the gaseous particles have greater velocities. This increases the pressure in the can, and if that pressure exceeds what the container can endure, then the container will explode.

b. The particles of a gas move faster at higher temperatures. This causes the particles to spread farther apart, reducing the gas sample's density. The density of air in the balloon is less, which causes it to rise until its density becomes equal to the surrounding atmosphere.

c. Because there are fewer gaseous particles in a sample of air at a higher altitude, there will be fewer collisions and thus a lower pressure.

8.3 **a.** temperature   **b.** volume   **c.** amount of gas   **d.** pressure

8.4 **a.** temperature   **b.** pressure   **c.** volume   **d.** amount of gas

8.5 Some units used to describe the pressure of a gas are pounds per square inch (lb/in.^{2} which is also abbreviated as psi), atmospheres (abbreviated atm), torr, mm Hg, in. Hg, and pascals.

8.6 Statements a, d, and e describe the pressure of a gas.

8.7 **a.** $2.00 \text{ atm} \times \dfrac{760 \text{ torr}}{1 \text{ atm}} = 1520 \text{ torr}$

     b. $2.00 \text{ atm} \times \dfrac{14.7 \text{ lb/in.}^2}{1 \text{ atm}} = 29.4 \text{ lb/in.}^2$

     c. $2.00 \text{ atm} \times \dfrac{760 \text{ mm Hg}}{1 \text{ atm}} = 1520 \text{ mm Hg}$

8.8 **a.** $467 \text{ mm Hg} \times \dfrac{1 \text{ atm}}{760 \text{ mm Hg}} = 0.614 \text{ atm}$

     b. $467 \text{ mm Hg} \times \dfrac{1 \text{ torr}}{1 \text{ mm Hg}} = 467 \text{ torr}$

     c. $467 \text{ mm Hg} \times \dfrac{1 \text{ cm}}{10 \text{ mm}} \times \dfrac{1 \text{ in. Hg}}{2.54 \text{ cm}} = 18.4 \text{ in. Hg}$

8.9 The gases in the diver's lungs (and dissolved in the blood) will expand because pressure decreases as the diver ascends. Unless the diver exhales, the expanding gases could rupture the membranes in the lung tissues. In addition, the formation of gas bubbles in the bloodstream could cause "the bends."

8.10 According to Boyle's law, gases expand as the pressure is decreased. Because atmospheric pressure decreases as altitude increases, the volume of gas sealed in the bag of chips will increase at higher altitudes.

8.11 During expiration the volume (capacity) of the lungs is decreased.

8.12 A respirator inflates the lungs with air that is rich in oxygen, (and has a low concentration of carbon dioxide). This allows the blood to rid itself of the waste CO_2 from the body's cells and pick up more O_2 to be delivered to the body's cells as the blood circulates.

8.13 **a.** According to Boyle's law, for the pressure to increase while temperature and quantity of gas remains constant, the gas volume must decrease. Thus, cylinder A would represent the final volume.

b.

	Initial	**Final**
P	650 mm Hg	1.2 atm
V	220 mL	160 mL

Because $P_1V_2 = P_2V_2$, then $V_2 = P_1V_1/P_2$
$$V_2 = 220 \text{ mL} \times \frac{650 \text{ mm Hg}}{1.2 \text{ atm}} \times \frac{1 \text{ atm}}{760 \text{ mm Hg}} = 160 \text{ mL}$$

8.14 **a.** According to Boyle's law, the volume must increase when the pressure is decreased, so diagram C should represent the balloon's final volume at an increased altitude.
b. When there is no change in the pressure, there is no change in the volume. Diagram B would represent the "final" volume of the balloon.
c. With an increase in pressure there will be a decrease in volume. Thus diagram A would describe the balloon's final volume.

8.15 **a.** The pressure doubles when the volume is halved.
b. The pressure falls to one-third the initial pressure when the volume expands to three times its initial volume.
c. The pressure increases to ten times the original pressure when the volume decreases to 1/10 of its initial volume.

8.16 **a.** The volume decreases to one-third the initial volume, when pressure increases to three times its initial pressure.
b. The volume doubles when pressure falls to one-half its initial pressure.
c. The volume is 5 times greater when pressure is decreased to 1/5 its initial pressure.

8.17 From Boyle's law we know that pressure is inversely related to volume. (For example, the pressure increases when the volume decreases.)

a. Volume increases; pressure must decrease.
$$655 \text{ mm Hg} \times \frac{10.0 \text{ L}}{20.0 \text{ L}} = 328 \text{ mm Hg}$$

b. Volume decreases; pressure must increase.
$$655 \text{ mm Hg} \times \frac{10.0 \text{ L}}{2.50 \text{ L}} = 2620 \text{ mm Hg}$$

c. The mL units must be converted to L for unit cancellation in the calculation, and because the volume decreases; pressure must increase.
$$655 \text{ mm Hg} \times \frac{10.0 \text{ L}}{1500 \text{ mL}} \times \frac{1000 \text{ mL}}{1 \text{ L}} = 4400 \text{ mm Hg}$$

d. The mL units must be converted to L for unit cancellation in the calculation, and because the volume decreases; pressure must increase.
$$655 \text{ mm Hg} \times \frac{10.0 \text{ L}}{120. \text{ mL}} \times \frac{1000 \text{ mL}}{1 \text{ L}} = 55\,000 \text{ mm Hg}$$

8.18 From Boyle's Law we know that pressure is inversely related to volume.

    a. 1.20 atm   × $\dfrac{5.00 \text{ L}}{1.00 \text{ L}}$ = 6.00 atm

    b. The mL units must be converted to L for unit cancellation in the calculation.

    1.20 atm   × $\dfrac{5.00 \text{ L}}{2500 \text{ mL}}$ × $\dfrac{1000 \text{ mL}}{1 \text{ L}}$ = 2.4 atm

    c. 1.20 atm   × $\dfrac{5.00 \text{ L}}{750 \text{ mL}}$ × $\dfrac{1000 \text{ mL}}{1 \text{ L}}$ = 8.0 atm

    d. 1.20 atm   × $\dfrac{5.00 \text{ L}}{8.00 \text{ L}}$ = 0.750 atm

8.19 760 mm Hg   × $\dfrac{4.5 \text{ L}}{2.0 \text{ L}}$ = 1700 mm Hg

8.20 15.0 atm   × $\dfrac{20.0 \text{ L}}{300.0 \text{ L}}$ = 1.00 atm

8.21 From Boyle's Law we know that pressure is inversely related to volume.

    a. Pressure increases; volume must decrease.

    50.0 L   × $\dfrac{760 \text{ mm Hg}}{1500 \text{ mm Hg}}$ = 25 L

    b. The mm Hg units must be converted to atm for unit cancellation in the calculation.

    50.0 L   × $\dfrac{760 \text{ mm Hg}}{2.0 \text{ atm}}$ × $\dfrac{1 \text{ atm}}{760 \text{ mm Hg}}$ = 25 L

    c. The mm Hg units must be converted to atm for unit cancellation in the calculation.

    50.0 L   × $\dfrac{760 \text{ mm Hg}}{0.500 \text{ atm}}$ × $\dfrac{1 \text{ atm}}{760 \text{ mm Hg}}$ = 100. L

    d. The mm Hg units must be converted to torr for unit cancellation in the calculation.

    50.0 L   × $\dfrac{760 \text{ mm Hg}}{850 \text{ torr}}$ × $\dfrac{1 \text{ torr}}{1 \text{ mm Hg}}$ = 45 L

8.22 From Boyle's Law we know that pressure is inversely related to volume.

    a. 25 mL   × $\dfrac{0.80 \text{ atm}}{0.40 \text{ atm}}$ = 50. mL

    b. 25 mL   × $\dfrac{0.80 \text{ atm}}{2.00 \text{ atm}}$ = 10. mL

    c. 25 mL   × $\dfrac{0.80 \text{ atm}}{2500 \text{ mm Hg}}$ × $\dfrac{760 \text{ mm Hg}}{1 \text{ atm}}$ = 6.1 mL

    d. 25 mL   × $\dfrac{0.80 \text{ atm}}{80.0 \text{ torr}}$ × $\dfrac{760 \text{ torr}}{1 \text{ atm}}$ = 190 mL

8.23 5.0 L   × $\dfrac{5.0 \text{ atm}}{1.0 \text{ atm}}$ = 25 L

8.24 615 mL × $\dfrac{760 \text{ mm Hg}}{752 \text{ mm Hg}}$ = 620 mL

8.25 **a.** Inspiration begins when the diaphragm flattens causing the lungs to expand. The increased volume reduces the pressure in the lungs such that air flows into the lungs.

    b. Expiration occurs as the diaphragm relaxes causing a decrease in the volume of the lungs. The pressure of the air in the lungs increases and air flows out of the lungs.

c. Inspiration occurs when the pressure in the lungs is less than the pressure of the air in the atmosphere.

8.26 **a.** Expiration occurs when the diaphragm relaxes and decreases the volume of the lungs.
b. Inspiration occurs when the lungs expand.
c. Expiration occurs when the pressure in the lungs is higher than the pressure in the atmosphere.

8.27 According to Charles' law, there is a direct relationship between temperature and volume. For example, volume increases when temperature increases while the pressure and amount of gas remains constant.
a. Diagram C describes an increased volume corresponding to an increased temperature.
b. Diagram A describes a decreased volume corresponding to a decrease in temperature.
c. Diagram B shows no change in volume, which corresponds to no change in temperature.

8.28 According to Charles' law, an increase in temperature will give an increase in volume.
a. Because the gas warms, its volume must also increase.
b. Because the warm gas will cool, its volume must decrease.
c. Because the gas warms, its volume must increase.

8.29 Heating a gas in a hot air balloon increases the volume of gas, which reduces its density and allows the balloon to rise above the ground.

8.30 As the temperature decreases, the volume of the gas in the tire decreases, which makes the tire appear lower or flat in the morning.

8.31 According to Charles' law, gas volume is directly proportional Kelvin temperature when P and n are constant. In all gas law computations, temperatures must be in Kelvin units. (Temperatures in °C are converted to K by the addition of 273.)
a. When temperature decreases, volume must also decrease.

$75°C + 273 = 348 \text{ K} \quad 55°C + 273 = 328 \text{ K}$

$2500 \text{ mL} \quad \times \quad \dfrac{328 \text{ K}}{348 \text{ K}} \quad = 2400 \text{ mL}$

b. When temperature increases, volume must also increase.

$2500 \text{ mL} \quad \times \quad \dfrac{680 \text{ K}}{348 \text{ K}} \quad = 4900 \text{ mL}$

c. $-25°C + 273 = 248 \text{ K}$

$2500 \text{ mL} \quad \times \quad \dfrac{248 \text{ K}}{348 \text{ K}} \quad = 1800 \text{ mL}$

d. $2500 \text{ mL} \quad \times \quad \dfrac{240 \text{ K}}{348 \text{ K}} \quad = 1700 \text{ mL}$

8.32 According to Charles' law, a change in a gas's volume is directly proportional to the change in its Kelvin temperature. In all gas law computations, temperatures must be in Kelvin units. (Temperatures in °C are converted to K by the addition of 273.)
a. $0°C + 273 = 273 \text{ K}$

$273 \text{ K} \times \quad \dfrac{10.0 \text{ L}}{4.00 \text{ L}} = 683 \text{ K} \qquad 683 \text{ K} - 273 \quad = 410.°C$

b. $273 \text{ K} \times \quad \dfrac{1.2 \text{ L}}{4.00 \text{ L}} \quad = 82 \text{ K} \qquad 82 \text{ K} - 273 \quad = -191°C$

c. $273 \text{ K} \times \quad \dfrac{2.50 \text{ L}}{4.00 \text{ L}} \quad = 171 \text{ K} \qquad 171 \text{ K} - 273 \quad = -102°C$

d. $273 \text{ K} \times \quad \dfrac{0.0500 \text{ L}}{4.00 \text{ L}} = 3.4 \text{ K} \qquad 3.4 \text{ K} - 273 \quad = -270°C$

8.33 Because gas pressure increases with an increase in temperature, the gas pressure in an aerosol can may exceed the tolerance of can when it is heated and cause it to explode.

8.34 The pressure in a tire is lower at the typical temperatures encountered on a winter morning, but it increases as the temperature increases. If the pressure increases beyond the tire's pressure rating, then the tire may suffer a "blow-out."

8.35 When the temperature of the oxygen in the tanks increases, the pressure also increases, which may cause the tanks to explode.

8.36 According To Gay-Lussac's law, the pressure of a gas is directly related to the temperature when volume and the number of moles remain constant.

8.37 According to Gay-Lussac's law, temperature is directly related to pressure. For example, temperature increases when the pressure increases. In all gas law computations, temperatures must be in Kelvin units. (Temperatures in °C are converted to K by the addition of 273.)
   a. 155°C + 273 = 428 K   0°C + 273 = 273 K
   1200 torr   × $\dfrac{273 \text{ K}}{428 \text{ K}}$ = 770 torr

   b. 12°C + 273 = 285 K   35°C + 273 = 308 K
   1.40 atm   × $\dfrac{308 \text{ K}}{285 \text{ K}}$ = 1.51 atm

8.38 According to Gay-Lussac's law, pressure is directly related to temperature. For example, pressure increases when the temperature increases. In all gas law computations, temperatures must be in Kelvin units. (Temperatures in °C are converted to K by the addition of 273.)
   a. 0°C + 273 = 273 K
   273 K   × $\dfrac{1500 \text{ torr}}{250 \text{ torr}}$ = 1600 K

   1600 K - 273   = 1300°C

   b. (This is *not* a Gay-Lussac law problem! It is a Charles law problem, but is solved in an analogous fashion to a Gay-Lussac problem.)
          −10.°C + 273 = 263 K   37°C + 273 = 310. K

   500.0 mL   × $\dfrac{310. \text{ K}}{263 \text{ K}}$ = 589 mL

8.39 **a.** boiling point   **b.** vapor pressure
       c. atmospheric pressure   **d.** boiling point

8.40 Boiling would occur in b and c because in both of these the vapor pressure equals the atmospheric (external) pressure.

8.41 **a.** Water boils at temperatures less than 100°C because the atmospheric pressure is less than one atmosphere on a mountain. The boiling point is the temperature at which the vapor pressure of a liquid becomes equal to the external (in this case, atmospheric) pressure.
   b. The pressure inside a pressure cooker is greater than one atmosphere; therefore water boils above 100°C. Foods cook faster at higher temperatures.

8.42 **a.** The wind carries away the water vapor molecules, reducing the humidity near the damp towel.
   b. At an external pressure of 2.0 atm water will boil at 120°C.

8.43 Boyle's, Charles', and Gay-Lussac's laws are united into the combined gas law.

$$\frac{P_1 V_1}{T_1} = \frac{P_2 V_2}{T_2}$$

8.44 **a.** $V_2 = \dfrac{P_1 \times V_1 \times T_2}{P_2 \times T_1}$ **b.** $P_2 = \dfrac{P_1 \times V_1 \times T_2}{V_2 \times T_1}$

8.45 $T_1 = 25°C + 273 = 298\ K;\ V_1 = 6.50\ L;\ P_1 = 845\ mm\ Hg\ (1.11\ atm)$

a. $T_2 = 325\ K;\ V_2 = 1.85\ L$

$$1.11\ atm \times \frac{6.50\ \cancel{L}}{1.85\ \cancel{L}} \times \frac{325\ \cancel{K}}{298\ \cancel{K}} = 4.25\ atm$$

b. $T_2 = 12°C + 273 = 285\ K;\ V_2 = 2.25\ L$

$$1.11\ atm \times \frac{6.50\ \cancel{L}}{2.25\ \cancel{L}} \times \frac{285\ \cancel{K}}{298\ \cancel{K}} = 3.07\ atm$$

c. $T_2 = 47.°C + 273 = 320\ K;\ V_2 = 12.8\ L$

$$1.11\ atm \times \frac{6.50\ \cancel{L}}{12.8\ \cancel{L}} \times \frac{320\ \cancel{K}}{298\ \cancel{K}} = 0.605\ atm$$

8.46 $T_1 = 112°C + 273 = 385\ K;\ P_1 = 1.20\ atm;\ V_1 = 735\ mL$

a. $T_2 = 281\ K;\ P_2 = 658\ mm\ Hg\ (0.866\ atm)\ V_2 = ?\ mL$

$$V_2 = 735\ mL \times \frac{1.20\ \cancel{atm}}{0.866\ \cancel{atm}} \times \frac{281\ \cancel{K}}{385\ \cancel{K}} = 743\ mL$$

b. $T_2 = 75°C + 273 = 348\ K;\ P_2 = 0.55\ atm\ V_2 = ?\ mL$

$$V_2 = 735\ mL \times \frac{1.20\ \cancel{atm}}{0.55\ \cancel{atm}} \times \frac{348\ \cancel{K}}{385\ \cancel{K}} = 1450\ mL$$

c. $T_2 = -15°C + 273 = 258\ K;\ P_2 = 15.4\ atm\ V_2 = ?mL$

$$V_2 = 735\ mL \times \frac{1.20\ \cancel{atm}}{15.4\ \cancel{atm}} \times \frac{258\ \cancel{K}}{385\ \cancel{K}} = 3.84\ mL$$

8.48 $T_1 = 8°C + 273 = 281\ K;\ V_1 = 50.0\ mL;\ P_1 = 3.00\ atm$

$T_2 = 37°C + 273 = 310.\ K;\ V_2 = 150.0\ mL\ P_2 = ?$

$$P_2 = 3.00\ atm \times \frac{50.0\ \cancel{mL}}{150.0\ \cancel{mL}} \times \frac{310.\ \cancel{K}}{281\ \cancel{K}} = 1.10\ atm$$

8.49 Addition of more air molecules to a tire or basketball will increase its volume.

8.50 Air molecules are escaping from the balloon, (it is deflating), as it flies around the room.

8.51 According to Avogadro's law, a change in a gas's volume is directly proportional to the change in the number of moles of gas.

a. $8.00\ L \times \dfrac{2.00\ \cancel{mole}}{4.00\ \cancel{mole}} = 4.00\ L$

b. $25.0\ \cancel{g\ neon} \times \dfrac{1\ mole\ neon}{20.2\ \cancel{g\ neon}} = 1.24\ mole\ Ne\ added$

$$1.50 \text{ mole } + 1.24 \text{ mole } = 2.74 \text{mole}$$

$$8.00 \text{ L} \quad \times \quad \frac{2.74 \text{ mole}}{1.50 \text{ mole}} \quad = \quad 14.6 \text{ L}$$

c. $1.50 \text{ mole } + 3.50 \text{ mole } = 5.00 \text{ mole}$

$$8.00 \text{ L} \quad \times \quad \frac{5.00 \text{ mole}}{1.50 \text{ mole}} \quad = \quad 26.7 \text{ L}$$

8.52 **a.** $4.80 \text{ g } O_2 \quad \times \quad \dfrac{1 \text{ mole } O_2}{32.0 \text{ g } O_2} = 0.150 \text{ mole } O_2$ New moles $= 0.650 \text{ mole } O_2$

$15.0 \text{ L} \quad \times \quad \dfrac{0.650 \text{ mole } O_2}{0.150 \text{ mole } O_2} = 65.0 \text{ L}$

b. $0.150 \text{ mole } \times \dfrac{10.0 \text{ L}}{15.0 \text{ L}} = 0.100 \text{ mole } O_2$ remain;

$0.150 \text{ mole } O_2 - 0.100 \text{ mole } O_2 = 0.050 \text{ mole } O_2$ removed

c. $4.00 \text{ g He } \times \dfrac{1 \text{ mole He}}{4.00 \text{ g He}} = 1.00 \text{ mole He}$ New moles $= 1.15$ moles of gases

$15.0 \text{ L} \quad \times \quad \dfrac{1.15 \text{ moles gas}}{0.15 \text{ mole } O_2} = 115 \text{ L}$

8.53 At STP, the molar volume of any gas is 22.4 L per mole.

a. $44.8 \text{ L} \quad \times \quad \dfrac{1 \text{ mole } O_2}{22.4 \text{ L}} = 2.00 \text{ mole } O_2$

b. $4.00 \text{ L} \quad \times \quad \dfrac{1 \text{ mole } CO_2}{22.4 \text{ L}} = 0.179 \text{ mole } CO_2$

c. $6.40 \text{ g } O_2 \quad \times \quad \dfrac{1 \text{ mole } O_2}{32.0 \text{ g } O_2} \times \dfrac{22.4 \text{ L}}{1 \text{ mole } O_2} = 4.48 \text{ L}$

d. $50.0 \text{ g Ne} \quad \times \quad \dfrac{1 \text{ mole Ne}}{20.2 \text{ g Ne}} \times \dfrac{22.4 \text{ L}}{1 \text{ mole Ne}} \times \dfrac{1000 \text{ mL}}{1 \text{ L}} = 55\,400 \text{ mL}$

8.54 At STP, the molar volume of any gas is 22.4 L per mole.

a. $2.5 \text{ mole } N_2 \quad \times \quad \dfrac{22.4 \text{ L}}{1 \text{ mole } N_2} = 56 \text{ L } N_2$

b. $0.420 \text{ mole He} \times \dfrac{22.4 \text{ L}}{1 \text{ mole He}} \times \dfrac{1000 \text{ mL}}{1 \text{ L}} = 9410 \text{ mL}$

c. $11.2 \text{ L} \quad \times \dfrac{1 \text{ mole Ne}}{22.4 \text{ L}} \times \dfrac{20.2 \text{ g Ne}}{1 \text{ mole Ne}} = 10.1 \text{ g Ne}$

d. $1600 \text{ mL} \times \dfrac{1 \text{ L}}{1000 \text{ mL}} \times \dfrac{1 \text{ mole } H_2}{22.4 \text{ L}} = 0.071 \text{ mole } H_2$

8.55 $P = \dfrac{nRT}{V} = \dfrac{(2.00 \text{ moles})(0.0821 \text{ L} \cdot \text{atm})(300 \text{ K})}{(10.0 \text{ L})(\text{mole} \cdot \text{K})} = 4.93 \text{ atm}$

8.56 $PV = nRT$

$V = \dfrac{nRT}{P} \quad \dfrac{(4.0 \text{ moles})(0.0821 \text{ L} \cdot \text{atm})(291 \text{ K})}{(1.40 \text{ atm})(\text{mole} \cdot \text{K})} = 68 \text{ L}$

8.57 $\quad n = \dfrac{PV}{RT} = \dfrac{(845 \text{ mm Hg})(20.0 \text{ L})}{(62.4 \frac{\text{L·mm Hg}}{\text{mole·K}})(295 \text{K})} \times \dfrac{32.0 \text{ g O}_2}{1 \text{ mole O}_2} = 29.4 \text{ g O}_2$

8.58 $\quad 10.0 \text{ g Kr} \quad \times \quad \dfrac{1 \text{ mole Kr}}{83.8 \text{ g Kr}} = 0.119 \text{ mole Kr}$

$\quad V = \dfrac{nRT}{P} \quad \dfrac{(0.119 \text{ mole})(62.4 \text{ L·mm Hg})(298 \text{ K})}{(575 \text{ mm Hg})(\text{mole·K})} = 3850 \text{ mL}$

8.59 $\quad n = 25.0 \text{ g N}_2 \quad \times \quad \dfrac{1 \text{ mole N}_2}{28.0 \text{ g}} = 0.893 \text{ mole}$

$\quad T = \dfrac{PV}{nR} \quad \dfrac{(630 \text{ mm Hg})(50.0 \text{ L})}{(0.893)(62.4 \frac{\text{L·mm Hg}}{\text{mole·K}})} = 565 \text{ K} \ (= 292°\text{C})$

8.60 $\quad n = 0.226 \text{ g CO}_2 \times 1 \text{ mole CO}_2 / 44.0 \text{ g} = 0.0.00514 \text{ mole}$

$\quad T = \dfrac{PV}{nR} \quad \dfrac{(455 \text{ mm Hg})(0.525 \text{ L})}{(0.00514 \text{ mole})(62.4 \frac{\text{L·mm Hg}}{\text{mole·K}})} = 745 \text{ K} -273 = 472 \text{ °C}$

8.61 Each gas particle in a gas mixture exerts a pressure as it strikes the walls of the container. The total gas pressure for any gaseous sample is thus a sum of all of the individual pressures. When the portion of the pressure due to a particular type of gaseous particle is discussed, it is only part of the total. Accordingly, these "portions" are referred to as "partial" pressures.

8.62 Because the helium and oxygen "particles" in the sample must have the same average kinetic energies, each particle will exert the same average pressure against the container's walls. For the partial pressures for each of these gases to be same, there must be equal numbers of these two types of gaseous particles.

8.63 To obtain the total pressure in a gaseous mixture, add up all of the partial pressures (provided each carries the same pressure unit).

$P_{\text{total}} \quad = P_{\text{Nitrogen}} + P_{\text{Oxygen}} + P_{\text{Helium}}$
$\qquad\qquad = 425 \text{ torr} + 115 \text{ torr} + 225 \text{ torr} = 765 \text{ torr}$

8.64 To obtain the total pressure in a gaseous mixture, add up all of the partial pressures, (provided each carries the same pressure unit).

$P_{\text{total}} \quad = P_{\text{Argon}} + P_{\text{Neon}} + P_{\text{Nitrogen}}$
$\qquad\qquad = 415 \text{ mm Hg} + 75 \text{ mm Hg} + 125 \text{ mm Hg} = 615 \text{ mm Hg}$
$\quad 615 \text{ mm Hg} \quad \times \quad \dfrac{1 \text{ atm}}{760 \text{ mm Hg}} = 0.809 \text{ atm}$

8.65 Because the total pressure in a gaseous mixture is the sum of the partial pressures (provided each carries the same pressure unit), addition and subtraction is used to obtain the "missing" partial pressure.

$P_{\text{Nitrogen}} = P_{\text{total}} - (P_{\text{Oxygen}} + P_{\text{Helium}})$
$\qquad\qquad = 925 \text{ torr} \quad - (425 \text{ torr} + 75 \text{ torr}) = 425 \text{ torr}$

8.66 Because the total pressure in a gaseous mixture is the sum of the partial pressures, (provided each carries the same pressure unit), addition and subtraction is used to obtain the "missing" partial pressure.

$P_{\text{Helium}} \quad = P_{\text{total}} - P_{\text{Mixture of oxygen, Nitrogen, and Neon}}$
$\qquad\qquad = 1.50 \text{ atm} - 1.20 \text{ atm} = 0.30 \text{ atm}$

8.67 **a.** If oxygen cannot readily cross from the lungs into the bloodstream, then the partial pressure of oxygen will be lower in the blood of an emphysema patient.

b. An increase in the partial pressure of oxygen in the air supplied to the lungs will result in an increase in the partial pressure of oxygen in the bloodstream (addition of reactant causes the formation of more product). Because an emphysema patient has a lower partial pressure of oxygen in the blood, the use of a portable oxygen tank helps to bring the oxygenation of the patient's blood to a more desirable level.

8.68 **a.** When ventilation is difficult, the body's cells are consuming oxygen, but the blood is not being replenished with oxygen in the lungs. Thus, the partial pressure of oxygen in the bloodstream of a person who cannot ventilate properly would be lower than normal. In a similar fashion, the partial pressure of carbon dioxide in the bloodstream would be higher than normal as the cells produce CO_2 but it is not eliminated at the lungs.

b. More gases will pass through the lungs and into the blood when higher gas pressure is introduced by a ventilator. Conversely, more gases will pass out of the blood and into the lungs when a lower gas pressure is introduced into the lungs. Because the air mixture has a higher partial pressure of oxygen than the blood, oxygen would enter the bloodstream. Similarly, the air mixture has a lower partial pressure of carbon dioxide than the blood, and CO_2 would be expelled.

8.69 Gas particles move faster at higher temperatures. This causes the force that each particle exerts against the wall to increase. Pressure is the sum of these forces. Thus, pressure increases with an increase in temperature at constant volume.

8.70 The pressure above the liquid inside the straw is less than the pressure above the liquid elsewhere. The liquid will rise up the straw because it is being pushed harder elsewhere than it is in the straw.

8.71 **a.** The volume of the chest and lungs will decrease when compressed during the Heimlich maneuver.

b. A decrease in volume causes the pressure to increase. A piece of food would be dislodged with a sufficiently high pressure.

8.72 **a.** 650 ~~mm Hg total~~ $\times$ $\dfrac{21 \text{ mm Hg O}_2}{100. \text{ ~~mm Hg total~~}}$ = 140 mm Hg

b. 100 ~~mm Hg O₂~~ $\times$ $\dfrac{100. \text{ mm Hg total}}{21 \text{ ~~mm Hg O}_2~~}$ = 476 mm Hg

8.73 Recall that all temperatures *must* be in kelvins in computations involving gas laws!

150 ~~lbs/in.~~^{2} $\times$ $\dfrac{348 \text{ ~~K~~}}{298 \text{ ~~K~~}}$ $\times$ $\dfrac{1 \text{ atm}}{14.7 \text{ ~~lbs/in.~~}^2}$ = 12 atm

8.74 Remember to convert temperatures to Kelvin units and to use pressure conversion factors for unit cancellation!

750 L $\times$ $\dfrac{380 \text{ ~~torr~~}}{0.20 \text{ ~~atm~~}}$ $\times$ $\dfrac{1 \text{ ~~atm~~}}{760 \text{ ~~torr~~}}$ $\times$ $\dfrac{228 \text{ ~~K~~}}{281 \text{ ~~K~~}}$ = 1500 L

8.75 Remember to use Kelvin temperature units in the calculation and convert to Celsius degrees after completing the calculation!

400. K $\times$ $\dfrac{0.25 \text{ ~~atm~~}}{2.00 \text{ ~~atm~~}}$ = 50. K 50. K − 273 = −223°C

8.76 **a.** $P_{\text{Nitrogen}} = P_{\text{total}} + VP_{\text{water}}$
  $= 745 \text{ mm Hg} - 32 \text{ mm Hg} = 713 \text{ mm Hg}$

b. $T_1 = 30.°C + 273 = 303 \text{ K};$ $P_1 = 713 \text{ mm Hg};$ $V_1 = 250 \text{ mL}$
  $T_2 = 0°C + 273 = 273 \text{ K};$ $P_2 = 760 \text{ mm Hg}$ $\underline{V_2} = ? \text{ mL}$

$V_2 = V_1 \times P_1/P_2 \times T_2/T_1$

$= 250 \text{ mL} \times \dfrac{713 \text{ mm Hg}}{760 \text{ mm Hg}} \times \dfrac{273 \text{ K}}{303 \text{ K}} = 210 \text{ mL}$

8.77 The partial pressure of each gas is proportional to the number of particles of each type of gas that is present. Thus, a ratio of partial pressure to total pressure is equal to the ratio of moles of that gas to the total number of moles of gases that are present:
$P_{\text{Helium}}/P_{\text{total}} = n_{\text{Helium}}/n_{\text{total}}$

Solving the equation for the partial pressure of helium yields:
$P_{\text{Helium}} = 2400 \text{ torr} \times \dfrac{2.0 \text{ mole}}{8.0 \text{ mole}} = 600 \text{ torr}$ (or 6.0×10^2 torr to show two sig figs)

And for oxygen:
$P_{\text{Oxygen}} = 2400 \text{ torr} \times \dfrac{6.0 \text{ mole}}{8.0 \text{ mole}} = 1800 \text{torr}$

8.78 Because the total pressure is to be reported in mm Hg, the atm and torr units (for argon and nitrogen, respectively) must be converted to mm Hg, as follows:

$0.25 \text{ atm} \times \dfrac{760 \text{ mm Hg}}{1 \text{ atm}} = 190 \text{ mm Hg}$

$360 \text{ torr} \times \dfrac{1 \text{ mm Hg}}{1 \text{ torr}} = 360 \text{ mm Hg}$

and $P_{\text{total}} = P_{\text{Argon}} + P_{\text{Helium}} + P_{\text{Nitrogen}}$
  $= 190 \text{ mm Hg} + 350 \text{ mm Hg} + 360 \text{ mm Hg} = 900 \text{ mm Hg}$ (9.0×10^2 mm Hg

8.79 Because the partial pressure of nitrogen is to be reported in torr, the atm and mm Hg units (for oxygen and argon, respectively) must be converted to torr, as follows:

$0.60 \text{ atm} \times \dfrac{760 \text{ torr}}{1 \text{ atm}} = 460 \text{ torr}$

$425 \text{ mm Hg} \times \dfrac{1 \text{ torr}}{1 \text{ mm Hg}} = 425 \text{ torr}$

and $P_{\text{Nitrogen}} = P_{\text{total}} - (P_{\text{Oxygen}} + P_{\text{Argon}})$
  $= 1250 \text{ torr} - (460 \text{ torr} + 425 \text{ torr}) = 370 \text{ torr}$

8.80 Because we need the answer in mm Hg we must include a pressure unit conversion factor for oxygen.
$P_{\text{oxygen}} = 0.450 \text{ atm} \times \dfrac{760 \text{ mm Hg}}{1 \text{ atm}} = 342 \text{ mm Hg}$

$255 \text{ torr} \times \dfrac{1 \text{ mm Hg}}{1 \text{ torr}} = 255 \text{ mm Hg}$

Total pressure $= 255 \text{ mm Hg} + 342 \text{ mm Hg} = 597 \text{ mm Hg}$
If the initial volume is 1 V, the final volume is ½ V or 0.500 V. (Temperature remains constant).
  $P_2 = 597 \text{ mm Hg} \times \dfrac{1 \text{ }V}{0.500 \text{ }V} = 1190 \text{ mm Hg}$

8.81 $D = \dfrac{\text{mass}}{\text{volume}} = \dfrac{32.0 \text{ g O}_2}{1 \text{ mole}} \times \dfrac{1 \text{ mole}}{22.4 \text{ L (STP)}} = 1.43 \text{ g/L}$

8.82 When a balloon is filled with helium and placed to a hot light, the helium will expand. If the expansion is greater than what the balloon's material can stretch to accommodate, it will rupture.

8.83 **a.** The partial pressure of oxygen in the lungs is greater than what is present in blood in the alveoli.
   b. Arterial blood picks up oxygen in the lungs and delivers oxygen to the body tissues. Arterial blood has a higher partial pressure of oxygen than venous blood.
   c. Because carbon dioxide is generated in body tissues, the partial pressure of CO_2 will be greater in the tissues than in arterial blood.
   d. The venous blood is returning to the lungs from body tissues. Venous blood, which has a higher partial pressure of carbon dioxide than the lungs, transports the excess CO_2 to the lungs to be exhaled.

8.84 **a.** The oxygen will diffuse from the lungs into the blood in the alveoli.
   b. The oxygen in arterial blood will diffuse into venous blood.
   c. The carbon dioxide will diffuse from the tissues into the arterial blood.
   d. The carbon dioxide in venous blood will diffuse into the lungs.

8.85 The mole-mole conversion factor is obtained from the reaction and used to convert to moles of gas, and the STP molar volume conversion factor is used to convert moles of gas into liters of gas, as shown below:

$$2.00 \text{ mole } CaCO_3 \times \frac{1 \text{ mole } CO_2}{1 \text{ mole } CaCO_3} \times \frac{22.4 \text{ L}}{1 \text{ mole } CO_2} = 44.8 \text{ L } CO_2$$

8.86 **a.** $16.00 \text{ g } O_2 \times \dfrac{1 \text{ mole } O_2}{32.0 \text{ g}} = 0.500 \text{ mole } O_2$

$$V = \frac{nRT}{P} = \frac{(0.500 \text{ mole})(0.0821 \text{ L}\cdot\text{atm})(400.\text{ K})}{(0.800 \text{ atm})(\text{mole}\cdot\text{K})} = 20.5 \text{ L}$$

Alternatively, the volume at STP can be calculated for new conditions.
AT STP, the volume of 0.500 mole O_2 is

$$0.500 \text{ mole } O_2 \times \frac{22.4 \text{ L}}{1 \text{ mole } O_2} = 11.2 \text{ L}$$

Solving for the final volume at 0.800 atm and 400.K

$$11.2 \text{ L} \times \frac{400.\text{ K}}{273 \text{ K}} \times \frac{1.00 \text{ atm}}{0.800 \text{ atm}} = 20.5 \text{ L}$$

   b. $16.00 \text{ g } O_2 \times \dfrac{1 \text{ mole } O_2}{32.0 \text{ g } O_2} \times \dfrac{2 \text{ moles } H_2O}{1 \text{ mole } O_2} = 1.00 \text{ mole } H_2O$

   c. $V = \dfrac{nRT}{P} = \dfrac{(1.00 \text{ mole})(62.4 \text{ L}\cdot\text{mm Hg})(388 \text{ K})}{(760 \text{ mm Hg})(\text{mole}\cdot\text{K})} = 31.9 \text{ L}$

Alternatively, 1.00 mole H_2O has a volume of 22.4 L at STP, which can be used to calculate the volume at the new conditions when only the temperature changes.

$$22.4 \text{ L} \times \frac{388 \text{ K}}{273 \text{ K}} = 31.8 \text{ L}$$

8.87 $8.0 \text{ g } Mg \times \dfrac{1 \text{ mole } Mg}{24.3 \text{ g } Mg} \times \dfrac{1 \text{ mole } O_2}{2 \text{ moles } Mg} \times \dfrac{22.4 \text{ L } O_2 \text{ (STP)}}{1 \text{ mole } O_2} = 3.7 \text{ L } O_2$

8.88 $n(N_2) = \dfrac{PV}{RT} = \dfrac{(840 \text{ mm Hg})(2.0 \text{ L})}{(62.4 \frac{\text{L} \cdot \text{mm Hg}}{\text{mole} \cdot \text{K}})(297 \text{K})} \times \dfrac{2 \text{ moles NO}_2}{1 \text{ mole N}_2} \times \dfrac{46.0 \text{ g NO}_2}{1 \text{ mole NO}_2} = 8.3 \text{ g NO}_2$

8.89 $n = \dfrac{PV}{RT} = \dfrac{(1.2 \text{ atm})(35.0 \text{ L})}{(0.0821 \frac{\text{L} \cdot \text{atm}}{\text{mole} \cdot \text{K}})(278 \text{K})} \times \dfrac{6.02 \times 10^{23} \text{ molecules}}{1 \text{ mole CO}_2} = 1.1 \times 10^{24} \text{ CO}_2 \text{ molecules}$

8.90 $50.0 \text{ g N}_2 \times \dfrac{1 \text{ mole N}_2}{28.0 \text{ g N}_2} = 1.79 \text{ moles N}_2$

$\dfrac{P = nRT}{V} = \dfrac{(1.79 \text{ moles N}_2)(0.0821 \text{ L} \cdot \text{atm})(298 \text{ K})}{(15.0 \text{ L})(\text{mole} \cdot \text{K})} = 2.92 \text{ atm}$

8.91 $n = \dfrac{PV}{RT} = \dfrac{(2500 \text{ mm Hg})(2.00 \text{ L})}{(62.4 \frac{\text{L} \cdot \text{mm Hg}}{\text{Mole} \cdot \text{K}})(291 \text{K})} \times \dfrac{16.0 \text{ g CH}_4}{1 \text{ mole CH}_4} = 4.4 \text{ g CH}_4$

8.92 $4.0 \times 19^{22} \text{ O}_2 \text{ molecules} \times \dfrac{1 \text{ mole O}_2}{6.02 \times 10^{23} \text{ molecules}} = 0.066 \text{ mole O}_2$

$V = \dfrac{nRT}{P} = \dfrac{(0.066 \text{ mole})(62.4 \text{ L} \cdot \text{mm Hg})(278 \text{ K})}{(845 \text{ mm Hg})(\text{mole} \cdot \text{K})} = 1.4 \text{ L} \times \dfrac{1000 \text{ mL}}{1 \text{ L}} = 1400 \text{ mL}$

8.93 $425 \text{ mL} \times \dfrac{745 \text{ mm Hg}}{0.115 \text{ atm}} \times \dfrac{1 \text{ atm}}{760 \text{ mm Hg}} \times \dfrac{178 \text{ K}}{297 \text{ K}} = 2170 \text{ mL}$

8.94 $225 \text{ mL} \times \dfrac{1 \text{ L}}{1000 \text{ mL}} \times \dfrac{1 \text{ mole gas}}{22.4 \text{ L (STP)}} = 0.0100 \text{ moles of gas}$

molar mass = g/mole = 1.15 g gas/ 0.0100 mole gas = 115 g/mole

Using ideal gas law:
PV = nRT   PV = (g/MM) RT   MM = $\dfrac{\text{gRT}}{\text{PV}}$

$\text{MM} = \dfrac{(1.15 \text{ g})(0.0821 \text{ L} \cdot \text{mm Hg})(273 \text{K})}{(1.0 \text{ atm})(0.225 \text{ L})(\text{mole} \cdot \text{K})} = 115 \text{ g/mole}$

8.95 1 torr = 1 mm Hg   molar mass = g of gas/moles of gas

$n = \dfrac{PV}{RT} = \dfrac{(748 \text{ torr})(0.941)}{(62.4 \frac{\text{L} \cdot \text{mm Hg}}{\text{mole} \cdot \text{K}})(293 \text{K})} = 0.0385 \text{ mole}$

molar mass = $\dfrac{1.62 \text{ g}}{0.0385 \text{ mole}} = 42.1 \text{ g/mole}$

8.96 $762 \text{ mL} \times \dfrac{1 \text{ L}}{1000 \text{ mL}} \times \dfrac{1 \text{ mole gas}}{22.4 \text{ L (STP)}} = 0.0340 \text{ moles of gas}$

molar mass = g/mole = 1.02 g gas/ 0.0340 mole gas = 30. g/mole

Using ideal gas law:
PV = nRT   PV = (g/MM) *RT*   MM = $\dfrac{gRT}{PV}$

$$MM = \frac{(1.02 \text{ g})(0.0821 \text{ L·mm Hg})(273\text{K})}{(1.0 \text{ atm}) (0.762 \text{ L})(\text{mole ·K})} = 30. \text{ g/mole}$$

Because CH_3 has a molar mass of 15, there must be two CH_3 units, which gives a molecular formula of C_2H_6.

8.97 $25.0 \text{ g Zn} \times \dfrac{1 \text{ mole Zn}}{65.4 \text{ g Zn}} \times \dfrac{1 \text{ mole } H_2}{1 \text{ mole Zn}} \times \dfrac{22.4 \text{ L } H_2 \text{ (STP)}}{1 \text{ mole } H_2} = 8.56 \text{ L of } H_2 \text{ (g) STP}$

8.98 $12.0 \text{ g Mg} \times \dfrac{1 \text{ mole Mg}}{24.3 \text{ g Mg}} \times \dfrac{1 \text{ mole } H_2}{1 \text{ mole Mg}} = 0.494 \text{ mole } H_2$

$$V = \frac{nRT}{P} = \frac{(0.494 \text{ mole})(0.0821 \text{ L ·atm})(297 \text{ K})}{(1.10 \text{ atm })(\text{mole ·K})} = 11.0 \text{ L}$$

8.99 a. $2.5 \times 10^{23} \text{ molecules } NO_2 \times \dfrac{1 \text{ mole } NO_2}{6.02 \times 10^{23} \text{ molecules}} \times \dfrac{7 \text{ mole } O_2}{4 \text{ moles } NO_2} \times \dfrac{22.4 \text{ L } O_2 \text{ (STP)}}{1 \text{ mole } O_2}$

$= 16 \text{ L } O_2 \text{ (g)}$

b. Moles $(NH_3) = \dfrac{PV}{RT} = \dfrac{(725 \text{ mm Hg})(5.00 \text{ L})}{(62.4 \text{ L ·mm Hg})(648\text{K})} \times \dfrac{4 \text{ moles } NH_3}{6 \text{ moles } H_2O} \times \dfrac{17.0 \text{ g } NH_3}{1 \text{ mole } NH_3}$

$\phantom{\text{Moles } (NH_3) =} \overline{} \text{mole ·K}$

$= 1.02 \text{ g } NH_3 \text{ (g)}$

8.100 $1.00 \text{ g } CO_2 \times \dfrac{1 \text{ mole } CO_2}{44.0 \text{ g } CO_2} = 0.0227 \text{ mole } CO_2$

$$P = \frac{nRT}{V} = \frac{(0.0227 \text{ moles } CO_2) (62.4 \text{ L·mm Hg})(297 \text{ K})}{(4.6 \text{ L}) (\text{mole ·K})} = 91 \text{ mm Hg}$$

8.101 $5.4 \text{ g Al} \times \dfrac{1 \text{ mole Al}}{27.0 \text{ g Al}} \times \dfrac{3 \text{ mole } O_2}{4 \text{ mole Al}} \times \dfrac{22.4 \text{ L } O_2 \text{ (STP)}}{1 \text{ mole } H_2} = 3.4 \text{ L } O_2 \text{ (g)}$

Study Goals

- Describe hydrogen bonding in water.
- Identify the solute and solvent in a solution
- Describe electrolytes in a solution.
- Define solubility and determine whether a salt will dissolve in water.
- Calculate the percent concentrations and molarity of a solution
- Distinguish between a solution, a colloid, and a suspension.
- Describe the behavior of a red blood cell in hypotonic, isotonic, and hypertonic solutions.

Chapter Outline

9.1 Properties of Water
  Health Note: Water in the Body
  Explore Your World: Surface Tension
  Explore Your World: Surfactants
9.2 Solutions
  Explore Your World: Like Dissolves Like
9.3 Electrolytes and Nonelectrolytes
9.4 Equivalents
  Health Note: Electrolytes in Body Fluids
9.5 Solubility
  Explore Your World: Preparing Solutions
  Explore Your World: Rock Candy: A Saturated Solution
  Health Note: Gout: A Problem of Saturation in Body Fluids
  Health Note: Kidney Stones Are Insoluble Salts
9.6 Percent Concentration
9.7 Molarity
9.8 Colloids and Suspensions
  Explore Your World: Tyndall Effect
  Health Note: Colloids and Solutions in the Body
9.9 Osmosis and Dialysis
  Explore Your World: Everyday Osmosis
  Health Note: Dialysis by the Kidneys and the Artificial Kidney

Chapter Summary and Demonstrations

1. Water and Solutions

Solutions are systems containing solutes and solvents.

Demonstration: To show the formation of a solution, I place a small crystal of $KMnO_4$ in beakers containing hot and cold water. Immediately there is a distinct difference in the movement of solute in the hot compared to the cold water. One can also test the effect of stirring a solution, or the final color if more solute is added.

2. Surface Tension

The importance of hydrogen bonding by water as a solvent leads to a discussion of surface tension.

Demonstration:
a. The surface tension of water can be illustrated by dropping pennies, sideways, one at a time, into a glass filled to the rim with water. I have students predict how many pennies I will be able to add before a drop of water spills over. Often, 20-30 pennies can be added before water spills over. A large dome of water can be observed as the result of the surface tension of water.

b. Fill a small bowl about 2/3 full with water. Float a needle or a paper clip on the surface of the water. Touch a bar of soap to the edge of the water surface. What happens to the surface tension of the water? Why? Repeat the experiment using a drop of liquid soap. Repeat the experiment using pepper flakes on the top of the water.

3. Electrolytes

The concept of electrolytes leads into a discussion of equivalents. Equivalents are defined and used to give the normal ranges for electrolytes in the body.

Demonstration: Various IV solutions are illustrated as examples of the electrolytes in the body and the concentrations as expressed in milliequivalents per liter.

4. Solubility

The solubility rules for salts are used to predict their solubility in water and the formation of a precipitate when two salt solutions are mixed. Gout is discussed as an example of uric acid saturation in the body fluids.

Demonstration (A): Solubility Rules A clear spot plate (plastic or glass) is handy to use on the overhead projects. A blank transparency sheet beneath the spot plate protects against spills. The formation of precipitates using solubility rules can be demonstrates by mixing drops of various soluble salts. Students can predict the formation of a precipitate or not, and then test the result. Equations are written as the reactions occur.

Demonstration (B): Saturated Solutions Sugar can be added to cold and hot water to show the formation of a saturated and unsaturated solution. Cooling the hot water and sugar solution will reform some sugar as solubility is reached.
   A supersaturated solution of sodium thiosulfate • $5H_2O$ can be prepared by heating and carefully cooling. I bring the flask containing the solution to class and seed it with one crystal. The beautiful crystals fill the container and it warms considerably during the exothermic process.

5.   Concentrations of Solutions

Concentrations of solutions are expressed in terms of mass-mass percent, mass-volume percent, and volume-volume percent concentration. Molarity is defined as the number of moles of solute in one liter of solution.

Demonstration: I weigh out a sample of a solute and some water, mix them, and form a solution. We weigh the solution and determine its volume. Then we express the concentration of the solution in terms of mass/mass %, mass/volume %, and molarity. A similar demo can be done to obtain a volume/volume % using 5 mL of water and 5 mL of acetone or ethanol. This is also good for showing that final volume is not necessarily the sum of the individual volumes.

6. Osmosis

Osmotic pressure is described and the transport mechanisms of diffusion, osmosis, and dialysis are related to the types of solutions, and concentrations gradients. The effects of isotonic, hypertonic, and hypotonic solutions are described for red blood cells. The special example of hemodialysis illustrates a medical use of the dialysis principle.

Demonstration (A): Obtain *unused* dialysis systems (membranes and coils) from a dialysis center in a nearby hospital. Students can observe the tubing and its various arrangements in which it acts as a semipermeable membrane replacing the action of the kidneys.

Demonstration (B): Placing a sucrose solution in a thistle tube and covering the end with an osmotic membrane such as cellophane can show the concept of osmosis. The tube is suspended in water. After marking the initial level of solution, students can observe its rise in the tube. I have done a similar demonstration by placing a piece of glass tubing in a stopper, which was inserted into a hollowed-out section of a carrot. The carrot was filled with sucrose solution, and suspended in a beaker of water. The carrot acts as an osmotic membrane.

Laboratory Suggestions

Lab 15 Solutions, Electrolytes, and Concentration

Students determine if a solute is soluble in polar and a nonpolar solvent. A conductivity apparatus is placed in various kinds of solutions and students identify when the solutions contain electrolytes or nonelectrolytes. Equations for the formation of those solutions are written. Students interpret the labels on various intravenous solutions, calculate the equivalents for cations and anions, and determine that the net charge is zero.

       After measuring the volume and mass of a salt solution, it is evaporated to dryness and the mass of the solute found. Calculations of the mass/mass percent, mass/volume percent, and molar concentration are calculated for a NaCl solution.

A. Polarity of Solutes and Solvents
B. Electrolytes and Conductivity
C. Electrolytes in Body Fluids
D. Concentration of a Sodium Chloride Solution

Laboratory Skills to Demonstrate
    Proper handling of iodine crystals
    Use and disposal of cyclohexane
    Observation of solution formation
    Safety and observation of the conductivity apparatus
    Read the label on an IV bag.
    Measure the volume and mass of a salt solution.
    Setup for evaporating a solution in an evaporating dish.
    Calculations of the mass/mass percent, mass/volume percent, and molarity concentrations of the solution.

Lab 16   Soluble and Insoluble Salts

Students distinguish between an unsaturated and saturated solution. The solubility of KNO_3 is determined at various temperatures and a solubility curve constructed. Water samples are tested for water hardness. Some water treatment techniques are used to illustrate water purification.

A. Soluble and Insoluble Salts
B. Solubility of KNO_3
C. Testing the Hardness of Water
D. Purification of Water

Laboratory Skills to Demonstrate

Identification of an insoluble salt
Determination of the temperature at which crystals form to indicate a saturated KNO_3 solution
Calculating the solubility of KNO_3 at various temperatures

Lab 17   Testing for Cations and Anions

Identification tests for cations and anions give the positive test results. An unknown containing one cation and one anion is tested to determine the identification of the salt. The correct formula and name are written for the unknown salt.

A. Tests for Positive Ions (Cations)
B. Tests for Negative Ions (Anions)
C. Writing the Formulas of Your Unknown Salt
D. Testing Consumer Products for Ions

Laboratory Skills to Demonstrate

How to run a reaction in a test tube
How to interpret the presence or absence of ions as a result of a chemical reaction
Give examples of possible ionic formulas for unknown salts

Lab 18   Solutions, Colloids and Suspensions

The positive tests for chloride, glucose, and starch are observed. Those results are used to identify the colloids and suspensions during filtration; and colloids and solutions during dialysis.

A. Identification Tests
B. Dialysis
C. Filtration

Laboratory Skills to Demonstrate

Interpretation of results of a positive iodine test for starch, and Benedict's test for glucose
Caution about the staining of the skin by $AgNO_3$
Illustrate the folding of filter paper for a funnel
Preparation of a dialysis bag

Answers and Solutions to Text Problems

9.1 **a.**

In a water molecule, the oxygen has a partial negative charge and the hydrogens have partial positive charges.

b.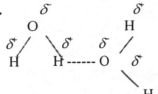

9.2 **a.** The surface tension of the tightly packed water molecules at the surface is sufficient to support the weight of small bugs.
b. A surfactant is a compound that disrupts the hydrogen bonds that contribute to surface tension.

9.3 The component present in the smaller amount is the solute; the larger amount is the solvent.
a. Sodium chloride, solute; water, solvent
b. Water, solute; ethanol, solvent
c. Oxygen, solute; nitrogen, solvent

9.4 The component present in the smaller amount is the solute; the larger amount is the solvent.
a. Silver, solvent; mercury, solute
b. Water, solvent; sugar, solute
c. Iodine, solute; alcohol, solvent

9.5 **a.** Potassium chloride, an ionic solute would be soluble in water (a polar solvent).
b. Iodine, a nonpolar solute would be soluble in carbon tetrachloride (a nonpolar solvent).
c. Sugar, a polar solute would be soluble in water, which is a polar solvent.
d. Gasoline, a nonpolar solute, would be soluble in carbon tetrachloride, which is a nonpolar solvent.

9.6 **a.** Vegetable oil, a nonpolar substance should be soluble in hexane, (a nonpolar substance)
b. Benzene, a nonpolar substance should be soluble in hexane
c. Lithium nitrate, an ionic substance is soluble in water, (a polar, solvent)
d. Sodium sulfate, an ionic substance is soluble in water, (a polar solvent)

9.7 The K^+ and I^- ions at the surface of the solid are pulled into solution by the polar water molecules where the hydration process surrounds separate ions with water molecules.

9.8 The Li^+ and Br^- ions at the surface of the crystal are pulled apart as the polar water molecules begin to surround each ion in the hydration process. The ions in solution are hydrated.

9.9 The molar mass of $Na_2SO_4 \cdot 10\ H_2O$ is 322. The % water is calculated as
$$\frac{180}{322} \times 100 = 55.9\ \%$$

9.10 $MgSO_4 \cdot 7H_2O$

$$\% \ H_2O = \frac{\text{mass of } 7 \ H_2O}{\text{molar mass } MgSO_4 \cdot 7H_2O} \times 100 = \frac{126 \ g}{246.4 \ g} \times 100 = 51.1 \ \% \ H_2O$$

9.11 The salt KF dissociates into ions when it dissolves in water. The weak acid HF exists as mostly molecules along with some ions when it dissolves in water.

9.12 NaOH completely dissociates into ions when it is dissolved in water. As CH_3OH dissolves in water it remains molecular.

9.13 Strong electrolytes dissociate into ions.

9.14 **a.** $LiBr \longrightarrow Li^+ + Br^-$ **b.** $NaNO_3 \longrightarrow Na^+ + NO_3^-$
c. $FeCl_3 \longrightarrow Fe^{3+} + 3 \ Cl^-$ **d.** $Mg(NO_3)_2 \longrightarrow Mg^{2+} + 2 \ NO_3^-$

9.15 **a.** In solution, a weak electrolyte exists mostly as molecules with a few ions.
b. Sodium bromide is a strong electrolyte and forms ions in solution.
c. A nonelectrolyte does not dissociate and forms only molecules in solution.

9.16 **a.** $Na_2SO_4(s) \longrightarrow 2Na^+(aq) + SO_4^{2-}(aq)$
Sodium sulfate is a strong electrolyte in solution, and exists only as ions in solution.

b. $C_2H_5OH(l) \longrightarrow C_2H_5OH(aq)$ molecules only
A nonelectrolyte exists only as molecules in solution.

c. $HCN(aq) \rightleftharpoons H^+(aq) + CN^-(aq)$ mostly molecules, some ions
A weak electrolyte exists as both molecules and some ions in solution.

9.17 **a.** Strong electrolyte because only ions are present in the K_2SO_4 solution.
b. Weak electrolyte because both ions and molecules are present in the NH_4OH solution.
c. Nonelectrolyte because only molecules are present in the $C_6H_{12}O_6$ solution

9.18 **a.** a nonelectrolyte   **b.** a strong electrolyte   **c.** a weak electrolyte

9.19 **a.** $1 \ \text{mole} \ K^+ \times \dfrac{1 \ Eq}{1 \ \text{mole} \ K^+} = 1 \ \text{equivalent} \ K^+$

b. $2 \ \text{moles} \ OH^- \times \dfrac{1 \ Eq}{1 \ \text{mole} \ OH^-} = 2 \ \text{equivalents}$

c. $1 \ \text{mole} \ Ca^{2+} \times \dfrac{2 \ Eq}{1 \ \text{mole} \ Ca^{2+}} = 2 \ \text{equivalents}$

d. $3 \ \text{moles} \ CO_3^{2-} \times \dfrac{2 \ Eq}{1 \ \text{mole} \ CO_3^{2-}} = 6 \ \text{equivalents}$

9.20 **a.** 1 mole Mg^{2+} = 2 equivalents   **b.** 0.5 mole H^+ = 0.5 equivalent
c. 4 moles Cl^- = 4 equivalents   **d.** 2 moles Fe^{3+} = 6 equivalents

9.21 **a.** $25.0 \ g \ Cl^- \times \dfrac{1 \ \text{mole} \ Cl^-}{35.5 \ g \ Cl^-} \times \dfrac{1 \ Eq}{1 \ \text{mole} \ Cl^-} = 0.704 \ \text{Equiv}$

b. $15.0 \ g \ Fe^{3+} \times \dfrac{1 \ \text{mole} \ Fe^{3+}}{55.9 \ g \ Fe^{3+}} \times \dfrac{3 \ Eq}{1 \ \text{mole} \ Fe^{3+}} = 0.805 \ \text{Equiv}$

c. $4.0 \ g \ Ca^{2+} \times \dfrac{1 \ \text{mole} \ Ca^{2+}}{40.1 \ g \ Ca^{2+}} \times \dfrac{2 \ Eq}{1 \ \text{mole} \ Ca^{2+}} = 0.20 \ \text{Equiv}$

d. $1.0 \ g \ H^+ \times \dfrac{1 \ \text{mole} \ H^+}{1.0 \ g \ H^+} \times \dfrac{1 \ Eq}{1 \ \text{mole} \ H^+} = 1.0 \ \text{Equiv}$

9.22   **a.** $10.0 \; \text{g Na}^+ \; \times \; \dfrac{1 \; \text{mole Na}^+}{23.0 \; \text{g Na}^+} \; \times \; \dfrac{1 \; \text{equivalent}}{1 \; \text{mole Na}^+} \; = 0.435 \; \text{equivalent}$

   b. $8.0 \; \text{g OH}^- \; \times \; \dfrac{1 \; \text{mole OH}^-}{17.0 \; \text{g OH}^-} \; \times \; \dfrac{1 \; \text{equivalent}}{1 \; \text{mole OH}^-} \; = 0.47 \; \text{equivalent}$

   c. $20.0 \; \text{g Mg}^{2+} \; \times \; \dfrac{1 \; \text{mole Mg}^{2+}}{24.3 \; \text{g Mg}^{2+}} \; \times \; \dfrac{2 \; \text{equivalents}}{1 \; \text{mole Mg}^{2+}} \; = 1.65 \; \text{equivalents}$

   d. $4.0 \; \text{g Al}^{3+} \; \times \; \dfrac{1 \; \text{mole Al}^{3+}}{27.0 \; \text{g Al}^{3+}} \; \times \; \dfrac{3 \; \text{equivalents}}{1 \; \text{mole Al}^{3+}} \; = 0.44 \; \text{equivalent}$

9.23 $5.0 \; \text{L} \; \times \; \dfrac{3.0 \; \text{mEq}}{1 \; \text{L}} \; \times \; \dfrac{1 \; \text{Eq}}{1000 \; \text{mEq}} \; \times \; \dfrac{1 \; \text{mole Mg}^{2+}}{2 \; \text{Eq}} \; \times \; \dfrac{24.3 \; \text{g Mg}^{2+}}{1 \; \text{mole Mg}^{2+}} \; = 0.18 \; \text{g Mg}^{2+}$

9.24 $5.0 \; \text{L} \; \times \; \dfrac{110.0 \; \text{mEq}}{1 \; \text{L}} \; \times \; \dfrac{1 \; \text{Eq}}{1000 \; \text{mEq}} \; \times \; \dfrac{1 \; \text{mole Cl}^-}{1 \; \text{Eq}} \; \times \; \dfrac{35.5 \; \text{g Cl}^-}{1 \; \text{mole Cl}^-} \; = 20. \; \text{g Cl}^-$

9.25 $1.0 \; \text{L} \; \times \; \dfrac{154 \; \text{mEq}}{1 \; \text{L}} \; \times \; \dfrac{1 \; \text{Eq}}{1000 \; \text{mEq}} \; \times \; \dfrac{1 \; \text{mole Na}^+}{1 \; \text{Eq}} \; \times \; \dfrac{23.0 \; \text{g Na}^+}{1 \; \text{mole Na}^+} \; = 3.5 \; \text{g Na}^+$

   $1.0 \; \text{L} \; \times \; \dfrac{154 \; \text{mEq}}{1 \; \text{L}} \; \times \; \dfrac{1 \; \text{Eq}}{1000 \; \text{mEq}} \; \times \; \dfrac{1 \; \text{mole Cl}^-}{1 \; \text{Eq}} \; \times \; \dfrac{35.5 \; \text{g Cl}^-}{1 \; \text{mole Cl}^-} \; = 5.5 \; \text{g Cl}^-$

9.26 $1.5 \; \text{L} \; \times \; \dfrac{40. \; \text{mEq}}{1 \; \text{L}} \; \times \; \dfrac{1 \; \text{Eq}}{1000 \; \text{mEq}} \; \times \; \dfrac{1 \; \text{mole K}^+}{1 \; \text{Eq}} \; \times \; \dfrac{39.1 \; \text{g K}^+}{1 \; \text{mole K}^+} \; = 2.3 \; \text{g K}^+$

   $1.5 \; \text{L} \; \times \; \dfrac{40. \; \text{mEq}}{1 \; \text{L}} \; \times \; \dfrac{1 \; \text{Eq}}{1000 \; \text{mEq}} \; \times \; \dfrac{1 \; \text{mole Cl}^-}{1 \; \text{Eq}} \; \times \; \dfrac{35.5 \; \text{g Cl}^-}{1 \; \text{mole Cl}^-} \; = 2.1 \; \text{g Cl}^-$

9.27   The total equivalents of anions must be equal to the equivalents of cations in any solution.
mEq of anions = 40. mEq Cl^-/L + 15 mEq HPO_4^{2-} /L = 55 mEq/L
mEq Na^+ = mEq anions = 55 mEq Na^+ /L

9.28   The total equivalents of cations must be equal to the equivalents of anions in any solution.
147 mEq Na^+/ L + 4 mEq K^+/ L + 4 mEq Ca^{2+}/L = 155 mEq/L cations = 155 mEq Cl^- /L

9.29   **a.** The solution must be saturated because no additional solute dissolves.
   b. The solution was unsaturated because the sugar cube dissolves.

9.30   **a.** The solution was unsaturated because the salt dissolves.
   b. The solution must be saturated because undissolved solute remains on the bottom of the glass.

9.31   **a.** It is unsaturated because 34.0 g KCl is the maximum that dissolves in 100 g H_2O at 20°C.
   b. Adding 11.0 g $NaNO_3$ to 25 g H_2O is the same as 44.0 g $NaNO_3$ in 100 g H_2O. At 20°C, 88.0 g $NaNO_3$ can dissolve so the solution is unsaturated.
   c. Adding 400.0 g sugar to 125 g H_2O is 320 g in 100 g H_2O. At 20°C, only 203.9 g sugar can dissolve, which is less than 320 g. The sugar solution is saturated and excess sugar is present.

9.32   **a.** At 50°C, 42.6 g of KCl are soluble in 100 g of H_2O, which means that 21.3 g KCl are soluble in 50 g H_2O. Therefore add 25.0 g of KCl to 50 g of exceeds the solubility and gives a saturated solution.
   b. Adding 150.0 g of $NaNO_3$ to 75 g of H_2O is the same ratio as 200.0 g of $NaNO_3$ in 100 g H_2O. This solution is saturated because 200.0 g $NaNO_3$ exceeds the solubility of 114.0 g that can dissolve in 100 g water at 50°C.
   c. At 50°C, 260.4 g of sugar can dissolve in 100 g H_2O. Adding 80.0 g of sugar to 25 g H_2O is the same ratio as 320 g sugar in 100 g H_2O. This exceed the solubility, which means that the solution is saturated.

9.33   **a.** $\dfrac{34.0 \text{ g KCl}}{100 \text{ g } H_2O} \times 200 \text{ g } H_2O = 68.0 \text{ g of KCl}$ (This will dissolve at 20°C)

At 20°C 68.0 g KCl can dissolve in 200 g H2O.

    b. Since 80.0 g of KCl dissolves at 50°C and 68.0 g is in solution at 20°C, the mass of solid is 80.0g – 68.0g = 12.0 g KCl.

9.34   **a.** The solubility at 20°C of 88.0 g $NaNO_3$ in 100 g H_2O is the same ratio as 66.0 g $NaNO_3$ in 75 g H_2O. Thus, 66.0 g of the $NaNO_3$ remain in solution at 20°C.

    b. Because 66.0 g $NaNO_3$ remain in solution, 14.0 g $NaNO_3$ (80.0 g – 66.0 g) precipitated out of the solution as it cooled.

9.35   **a.** In general, the solubility of solid ionic solutes increases as temperature is increased.

    b. The solubility of a gaseous solute (CO_2) decreases as the temperature is increased.

    c. The solubility of a gaseous solute is lowered as temperature increases. When the can of warm soda is opened, more CO_2 is released producing more spray.

9.36   **a.** The solubility of CO_2 gas, which makes the soda "fizz", decreases as the temperature increases. When the can of warm soda is opened, CO_2 is released more rapidly than from a can that is still at cooler refrigerator temperatures.

    b. Any gas, (such as Cl_2), is less soluble as the cool tap water warms to room temperature.

    c. A soluble solid solute such as sugar is less soluble at cooler temperatures (iced coffee) than at warmer temperatures (hot coffee).

9.37   **a.** soluble: Rule 1: Li^+ salts are soluble.

    b. insoluble: Rule 2: the Cl^- salt containing Ag^+ is insoluble.

    c. insoluble: Rule 4: salts containing CO_3^{2-} are usually insoluble.

    d. soluble: Rule 1: salts containing K^+ ions are soluble.

    e. soluble: Rule 1: salts containing NO_3^- ions are soluble.

9.38   **a.** insoluble   Rule 4: salts containing S^{2-} are usually insoluble.

    b. soluble   Rule 1: salts containing Na^+ are soluble.

    c. soluble   Rule 1: salts containing Na^+ are soluble.

    d. insoluble   Rule 4: salts containing O^{2-} are usually insoluble.

    e. insoluble   Rule 3: $CaSO_4$ is an insoluble sulfate

9.39   **a.** No solid forms; rule 1 states that a salt containing K^+ and Na^+ is soluble.

    b. Solid silver sulfide forms: $2 AgNO_3 + K_2S \rightarrow 2 KNO_3 + Ag_2S(s)$

    c. Solid calcium sulfate forms: $CaCl_2 + Na_2SO_4 \rightarrow 2 NaCl + CaSO_4(s)$

9.40   **a.** Solid silver phosphate will form:

$$Na_3PO_4 + 3AgNO_3 \rightarrow 3NaNO_3 + Ag_3PO_4(s)$$

    b. No solid should form because rule 1 states that a salt containing K^+ or Na^+ is soluble.

    c. Solid lead(II) carbonate will form:

$$Pb(NO_3)_2 + Na_2CO_3 \rightarrow 2 NaNO_3 + PbCO_3(s)$$

9.41   A 5% (m/m) glucose solution contains 5 g glucose in 100 g of solution (5 g glucose + 95 g water), while a 5% (m/v) glucose solution contains 5 g glucose in 100 mL solution.

9.42   A 10 %(v/v) methyl alcohol solution contains 10 mL of methyl alcohol in 100 mL of solution, whereas a 10% (m/m) methyl alcohol solution contains 10 g methyl alcohol in 100 grams of solution (10 g methyl alcohol + 90 g water).

9.43 **a.** $\dfrac{25 \text{ g of KCl}}{150 \text{ g solution}}$ $\times$ 100 $= 17 \% \text{ (m/m)}$

b. $\dfrac{8.0 \text{ g CaCl}_2}{80. \text{g solution}}$ $\times$ 100 $= 10. \% \text{ (m/m)}$

c. $\dfrac{12 \text{ g sugar}}{225 \text{ g solution}}$ $\times$ 100 $= 5.3 \% \text{ (m/m)}$

9.44 **a.** $\dfrac{75 \text{ g NaOH}}{325 \text{ g solution}}$ $\times$ 100 $= 23.1\% \text{ (m/m) NaOH}$

b. 2.0 g KOH + 20.0 g H_2O = 22.0 g solution

$\dfrac{2.0 \text{ g KOH}}{22.0 \text{ g solution}}$ $\times$ 100 $= 9.1 \% \text{ (m/m) KCl}$

c. $\dfrac{48.5 \text{ g Na}_2\text{CO}_3}{250.0 \text{ g solution}}$ $\times$ 100 $= 19.4 \% \text{ (m/m) Na}_2\text{CO}_3$

9.45 **a.** $\dfrac{75 \text{ g Na}_2\text{SO}_4}{250 \text{ mL solution}}$ $\times$ 100 $= 30. \% \text{(m/v)}$

b. $\dfrac{0.50 \text{ g KI}}{15.0 \text{ mL solution}}$ $\times$ 100 $= 3.3 \% \text{ (m/v)}$

c. $\dfrac{39 \text{ g sucrose}}{355 \text{ mL solution}}$ $\times$ 100 $= 11 \% \text{ (m/v)}$

9.46 $\dfrac{\text{mass (in grams) solute}}{\text{volume (in mL) solution}}$ $\times$ 100 $= \% \text{ mass/volume}$

a. $\dfrac{2.50 \text{ g KCl}}{50.0 \text{ mL solution}}$ $\times$ 100 $= 5.0 \% \text{ (m/v) KCl}$

b. $\dfrac{7.5 \text{ g casein}}{120 \text{ mL solution}}$ $\times$ 100 $= 6.3 \% \text{ (m/v) casein}$

c. $\dfrac{0.78 \text{ g LiBr}}{24 \text{ mL solution}}$ $\times$ 100 $= 3.3 \% \text{ (m/v) LiBr}$

9.47 **a.** 50.0 ~~mL solution~~ $\times$ $\dfrac{5.0 \text{ g KCl}}{100 \text{ mL solution}}$ = 2.5 g KCl

b. 1250 ~~mL solution~~ $\times$ $\dfrac{4.0 \text{ g NH}_4\text{Cl}}{100 \text{ mL solution}}$ = 50. g NH_4Cl

c. 250 ~~mL solution~~ $\times$ $\dfrac{10.0 \text{ mL acetic acid}}{100 \text{ mL solution}}$ = 25 mL acetic acid

9.48 **a.** 150 ~~mL solution~~ $\times$ $\dfrac{40.0 \text{ g LiNO}_3}{100 \text{ mL solution}}$ = 60. g $LiNO_3$

b. 450 ~~mL solution~~ $\times$ $\dfrac{2.0 \text{ g KCl}}{100 \text{ mL solution}}$ = 9.0 g KCl

c. 225 ~~mL solution~~ $\times$ $\dfrac{15 \text{ mL isopropyl alcohol}}{100 \text{ mL solution}}$ = 34 mL isopropyl alcohol

9.49   355 ~~mL solution~~ $\times$ $\dfrac{22.5 \text{ mL alcohol}}{100 \text{ mL solution}}$ = 79.9 mL alcohol

9.50   750 ~~mL solution~~ $\times$ $\dfrac{11 \text{ mL alcohol}}{100 \text{ mL solution}}$ = 83 mL alcohol

9.51   **a.** 1 ~~hr~~ $\times$ $\dfrac{100 \text{ mL solution}}{1 \text{ hr}}$ $\times$ $\dfrac{20 \text{ g mannitol}}{100 \text{ mL solution}}$ = 20 g mannitol

　　　b. 15 ~~hr~~ $\times$ $\dfrac{100 \text{ mL solution}}{1 \text{ hr}}$ $\times$ $\dfrac{20 \text{ g mannitol}}{100 \text{ mL solution}}$ = 300 g mannitol

9.52   **a.** 250 ~~mL solution~~ $\times$ $\dfrac{4.0 \text{ g amino acid}}{100 \text{ mL solution}}$ = 10. g amino acids

　　　b. 24 ~~hr~~ $\times$ $\dfrac{250 \text{ mL solution}}{12 \text{ hr}}$ $\times$ $\dfrac{4.0 \text{ g amino acid}}{100 \text{ mL solution}}$ = 20. g amino acids

9.53   **a.** 10.0 ~~g HCl~~ $\times$ $\dfrac{100 \text{ g solution}}{4.0 \text{ g HCl}}$ = 250 g solution

　　　b. 5.0 ~~g LiNO₃~~ $\times$ $\dfrac{100 \text{ mL solution}}{25 \text{ g LiNO}_3}$ = 20. mL solution

　　　c. 40.0 ~~g KOH~~ $\times$ $\dfrac{100 \text{ mL solution}}{10.0 \text{ g KOH}}$ = 400. mL solution

　　　d. 2.0 ~~mL acetic acid~~ $\times$ $\dfrac{100 \text{ mL solution}}{10.0 \text{ mL acetic acid}}$ = 20. mL solution

9.54   **a.** 7.50 ~~g NaCl~~ $\times$ $\dfrac{100 \text{ mL solution}}{2.0 \text{ g NaCl}}$ = 380 mL solution

　　　b. 4.0 ~~g NaOH~~ $\times$ $\dfrac{100 \text{ mL solution}}{25 \text{ g NaOH}}$ = 16 mL solution

　　　c. 20.0 ~~g KBr~~ $\times$ $\dfrac{100 \text{ mL solution}}{8.0 \text{ g KBr}}$ = 250 mL solution

9.55   100 ~~g glucose~~ $\times$ $\dfrac{100 \text{ mL solution}}{5 \text{ g glucose}}$ $\times$ $\dfrac{1 \text{ L}}{1000 \text{ mL}}$ = 2 L solution

9.56   2.0 ~~g NaCl~~ $\times$ $\dfrac{100 \text{ mL solution}}{0.90 \text{ g NaCl}}$ = 220 mL solution

9.57   Molarity = moles of solute/L of solution
　　　a. $\dfrac{2.0 \text{ mole glucose}}{4.0 \text{ L solution}}$ = 0.50 M glucose
　　　b. $\dfrac{0.10 \text{ mole NaCl}}{0.0400 \text{ L solution}}$ = 2.5 M NaCl
　　　c. $\dfrac{4.0 \text{ g KOH}}{2.0 \text{ L solution}}$ $\times$ $\dfrac{1 \text{ mole KOH}}{56.1 \text{ g KOH}}$ = 0.036 M KOH

9.58   molarity = moles of solute/L of solution
　　　a. $\dfrac{0.50 \text{ mole glucose}}{0.200 \text{ L solution}}$ = 2.5 M Glucose

　　　b. $\dfrac{0.35 \text{ mole LiBr}}{0.35 \text{ L solution}}$ = 1.0 M LiBr

c. $\dfrac{36.5 \text{ g HCl}}{1.0 \text{ L solution}} \times \dfrac{1 \text{ mole HCl}}{36.5 \text{ g HCl}} = 1.0 \text{ M HCl}$

9.59 **a.** $1.0 \text{ L solution} \times \dfrac{3.0 \text{ mole NaCl}}{1 \text{ L solution}} = 3.0 \text{ mole NaCl}$

b. $0.40 \text{ L solution} \times \dfrac{1.0 \text{ mole KBr}}{1 \text{ L solution}} = 0.40 \text{ mole KBr}$

c. $0.25 \text{ L solution} \times \dfrac{4.0 \text{ mole NaCl}}{1 \text{ L solution}} = 1.0 \text{ mole NaCl}$

9.60 **a.** $5.0 \text{ L solution} \times \dfrac{2.0 \text{ mole CaCl}_2}{1 \text{ L solution}} = 10. \text{ mole CaCl}_2$

b. $4.0 \text{ L solution} \times \dfrac{0.10 \text{ mole NaOH}}{1 \text{ L solution}} = 0.40 \text{ mole NaOH}$

c. $0.025 \text{ L solution} \times \dfrac{1.0 \text{ mole KBr}}{1 \text{ L solution}} = 0.025 \text{ mole KBr}$

9.61 **a.** $2.0 \text{ L} \times \dfrac{1.5 \text{ mole NaOH}}{1 \text{ L}} \times \dfrac{40.0 \text{ g NaOH}}{1 \text{ mole NaOH}} = 120 \text{ g NaOH}$

b. $4.0 \text{ L} \times \dfrac{0.20 \text{ mole KCl}}{1 \text{ L}} \times \dfrac{74.6 \text{ g KCl}}{1 \text{ mole KCl}} = 60. \text{ g KCl}$

c. $25 \text{ mL} \times \dfrac{1 \text{ L}}{1000 \text{ mL}} \times \dfrac{1.0 \text{ mole NaCl}}{1 \text{ L}} \times \dfrac{58.5 \text{ g NaCl}}{1 \text{ mole NaCl}} = 1.5 \text{ g NaCl}$

9.62 **a.** $2.0 \text{ L solution} \times \dfrac{6.0 \text{ mole NaOH}}{1 \text{ L solution}} \times \dfrac{40.0 \text{ g NaOH}}{1 \text{ mole NaOH}} = 480 \text{ g NaOH}$

b. $5.0 \text{ L solution} \times \dfrac{0.10 \text{ mole CaCl}_2}{1 \text{ L solution}} \times \dfrac{111.1 \text{ g CaCl}_2}{1 \text{ mole CaCl}_2} = 56 \text{ g CaCl}_2$

c. $1.5 \text{ L solution} \times \dfrac{2.0 \text{ mole NaCl}}{1 \text{ L solution}} \times \dfrac{58.5 \text{ g NaCl}}{1 \text{ mole NaCl}} = 180 \text{ g NaCl}$

9.63 **a.** $3.0 \text{ moles NaOH} \times \dfrac{1 \text{ L}}{2 \text{ moles NaOH}} = 1.5 \text{ L NaOH}$

b. $15 \text{ moles NaCl} \times \dfrac{1 \text{ L}}{1.5 \text{ moles NaCl}} = 10. \text{ L NaCl}$

c. $16 \text{ g NaOH} \times \dfrac{1 \text{ moles NaOH}}{40.0 \text{ g NaOH}} \times \dfrac{1 \text{ L}}{6.0 \text{ moles NaOH}} = 0.067 \text{ L NaOH}$

9.64 **a.** $0.100 \text{ mole KCl} \times \dfrac{1 \text{ L solution}}{4.0 \text{ mole KCl}} = 0.025 \text{ L solution}$

b. $125 \text{ g NaOH} \times \dfrac{1 \text{ mole NaOH}}{40.0 \text{ g NaOH}} \times \dfrac{1 \text{ L solution}}{1.0 \text{ mole NaOH}} = 3.13 \text{ L solution}$

c. $5.0 \text{ mole HCl} \times \dfrac{1 \text{ L solution}}{6.0 \text{ mole HCl}} = 0.83 \text{ L solution}$

9.65 **a.** A solution cannot be separated by a semipermeable membrane.
b. A colloid will scatter light (Tyndall effect).
c. A suspension settles as time passes.

9.66   **a.** A colloid cannot pass through semipermeable membranes but passes through filter paper.
       b. A solution will not scatter light.
       c. A suspension contains large solute particles.

9.67   An emulsion is a colloid that occurs when a liquid solute is dispersed in a liquid or solid.

9.68   An aerosol contains either a solid or a liquid solute dispersed in a gaseous solution.

9.69   **a.** Water in the soil diffuses through the plant's root membranes to dilute the solutions in these cells. Because the cells above these root-cells contain more concentrated solutions than the root-cells, water moves up from the roots to dilute the more concentrated cell solutions.
       b. The pickling (brine) solution contains more solutes and less solvent than the pickle's cells. Thus, solvent flows out of the cells of the cucumber and into the brine solution, and the cucumber shrivels and becomes a pickle.

9.70   **a.** Seawater contains higher concentrations of solutes than our body's cells. Thus, water will flow out of our cells, causing dehydration.
       b. Salt will draw moisture out of foods, due to osmotic pressure. Because the microorganisms which cause our foods to spoil require moisture, they cannot survive under the dry conditions found in salted foods.

9.71   **a.** The 10% (m/v) starch solution has a higher osmotic pressure than pure water.
       b. The water will initially flow into the starch solution to dilute solute concentration.
       c. The volume of the starch solution will increase due to inflow of water.

9.72   **a.** The 2% (m/v) albumin solution has a higher osmotic pressure than the 0.1% (m/v) albumin solution.
       b. Because there is a higher concentration of solvent in the 0.1% albumin solution than in the 2% solution, water will flow out of the 0.1% albumin solution into the 2% solution.
       c. Water will flow into the 2% (m/v) albumin solution, which will increase in volume.

9.73   Water flows out of the solution with the higher solvent concentration (which corresponds to a lower solute concentration) to the solution with a lower solvent concentration (which corresponds to a higher solute concentration).
       a. Water flows into compartment B, which contains the 10% (m/v) glucose solution.
       b. Water flows into compartment B, which contains the 8% (m/v) albumin solution.
       c. Water flows into compartment B, which contains the 10% (m/v) NaCl solution.

9.74   Water will flow from a region of higher solvent concentration, (which corresponds to a lower solute concentration), to a region of lower solvent concentration, (which corresponds to a higher solute concentration).
       a. Water will flow into compartment A, which contains the 20% (m/v) glucose solution.
       b. Water will flow into compartment A, which contains the 10% (m/v) albumin solution.
       c. Water will flow into compartment B, which contains the 5% (m/v) NaCl solution.

9.75   A red blood cell has osmotic pressure of a 5 % (m/v) glucose solution or a 0.9 % (m/v) NaCl solution. In a hypotonic solution (lower osmotic pressure), solvent flows from the hypotonic into the red blood cell. When a red blood cell is placed in a hypertonic solution (higher osmotic pressure), solvent (water) flows from the red blood cell to the hypertonic solution. Isotonic solutions have the same osmotic pressure and a red blood cell in an isotonic solution will not change volume because the flow of solvent into and out of the cell is equal.
       a. Distilled water is a hypotonic solution when compared to a red blood cell's contents.
       b. A 1% (m/v) glucose solution is a hypotonic solution.
       c. A 0.9% (m/v) NaCl solution is isotonic with a red blood cell's contents.
       d. A 5% (m/v) glucose solution is an isotonic solution.

9.76   Hemolysis will occur when a red blood cell is placed in a hypotonic solution. Crenation occurs when a red blood cell is placed into a hypertonic solution. No change will occur when a red blood cell is placed into an isotonic solution.
   a. Hemolysis will occur because a 1% (m/v) glucose solution is a hypotonic solution.
   b. Crenation occurs because 2% (m/v) NaCl is a hypertonic solution.
   c. Crenation occurs because 5% (m/v) NaCl is hypertonic.
   d. Hemolysis occurs because 0.1% (m/v) NaCl is hypotonic.

9.77   Colloids cannot pass through the semipermeable dialysis membrane; water and solutions freely pass through semipermeable membranes.
   a.   Sodium and chloride ions will both pass through the membrane into the distilled water.
   b.   The amino acid alanine can pass through a dialysis membrane, the colloid starch will not.
   c.   Sodium and chloride ions will both be present in the water surrounding the dialysis bag; the colloid starch will not.
   d.   Urea will diffuse through the dialysis bag into the water.

9.78   Neither colloids nor suspensions can pass through the semipermeable dialysis membrane; water and solutions freely pass through semipermeable membranes.
   a. Potassium, chloride ions, and glucose molecules will all pass through the semipermeable membrane into the distilled water.
   b. Only water is present outside the dialysis bag because albumin cannot pass through the membrane.
   c. Potassium, chloride ions, and glucose molecules will all pass through the semipermeable membrane into the distilled water. The albumin, which is a colloid, will remain inside the dialyzing bag.
   d. Sodium, chloride ions, and urea molecules will all pass through the semipermeable membrane into the distilled water.

9.79   The moles of ions in an ionic compound is used to calculate the osmolarity as moles of ions/liter of solution.
   a. $NaCl(s) \longrightarrow Na^+(aq) + Cl^-(aq)$ = 2 moles ions/1 mole NaCl = 2 osmols/1 mole NaCl
   $$\frac{0.20 \; \text{mole NaCl}}{1 \; L} \times \frac{2 \; \text{osmols}}{1 \; \text{mole NaCl}} = 0.40 \; \text{osmols/L} = 0.40 \; \text{Osm NaCl}$$

   b. $CaCl_2(s) \rightarrow Ca^{2+}(aq) + 2Cl^-(aq)$ = 3 moles ions/1 mole $CaCl_2$ = 3 osmols/1 mole
   $$\frac{0.50 \; \text{mole CaCl}_2}{1 \; L} \times \frac{3 \; \text{osmols}}{1 \; \text{mole CaCl}_2} = 1.5 \; \text{osmols/L} = 1.5 \; \text{Osm CaCl}_2$$

   c. $K_3PO_4(s) \longrightarrow 3K^+(aq) + PO_4^{3-}(aq)$ = 4 moles ions/1 mole = 4 osmols/1 mole K_3PO_4
   $$\frac{0.10 \; \text{mole K}_3\text{PO}_4}{1 \; L} \times \frac{4 \; \text{osmols}}{1 \; \text{mole K}_3\text{PO}_4} = 0.40 \; \text{osmols/L} = 0.40 \; \text{Osm K}_3\text{PO}_4$$

9.80   An 0.1 M glucose dissolves as molecules and forms a 0.1 Osm solution. The NaCl in a 0.1 M solutions dissociates to give two particles in solution, which is a 0.2 Osm solution. A 0.1 M $CaCl_2$ dissociates to give three particles in solution and an 0.3 Osm solution, which has the greatest osmotic pressure of the three solutions.

9.81   Iodine is a nonpolar molecule and needs a nonpolar solvent such as hexane. Iodine does not dissolve in water because water is a polar solvent.

9.82   An increase in temperature usually increases the solubility of solids and decreases the solubility of gases in water. According to Henry's law, an increase in pressure of a gas above a liquid increases the solubility of a gas within that solution. However, a change in pressure has no effect on the solubility of solids.

9.83 ~~80.0 g NaCl~~ $\times$ $\dfrac{\text{100 g of water}}{\text{36.0 g NaCl}}$ = 222 g water

9.84 In a saturated solution of NaCl, there is an equilibrium between the amount of NaCl the dissolves and the amount of NaCl that is crystallizing back to solid. Therefore, the amount of NaCl in solution stays the same.

9.85 When solutions of $NaNO_3$ and KCl are mixed, no insoluble product forms because all the possible combinations of salts are soluble. When KCl and $Pb(NO_3)_2$ solutions are mixed, the insoluble salt $PbCl_2$ forms.

9.86 **a.** soluble   **b.** soluble   **c.** insoluble
　　　　 d. soluble   **e.** insoluble

9.87 $\dfrac{\text{15.5 g Na}_2\text{SO}_4}{\text{15.5 g Na}_2\text{SO}_4 + \text{75.5 g water}}$ $\times$ 100 = 17.0% (m/m)

9.88 750 ~~mL solution~~ $\times$ $\dfrac{\text{3.5 g K}_2\text{CO}_3}{\text{100 mL solution}}$ = 26 g K_2CO_3

9.89 **a.** 24 ~~hr~~ $\times$ $\dfrac{\text{750 mL solution}}{\text{12 hr}}$ $\times$ $\dfrac{\text{4 g amino acids}}{\text{100 mL solution}}$ = 60 g amino acids

　　　　 24 ~~hr~~ $\times$ $\dfrac{\text{750 mL solution}}{\text{12 hr}}$ $\times$ $\dfrac{\text{25 g glucose}}{\text{100 mL solution}}$ = 380 g glucose

　　　　 24 ~~hr~~ $\times$ $\dfrac{\text{500 mL solution}}{\text{12 hr}}$ $\times$ $\dfrac{\text{10 g lipid}}{\text{100 mL solution}}$ = 100 g lipid

　　　　 b. 60 ~~g amino acids (protein)~~ $\times$ $\dfrac{\text{4 kcal}}{\text{1 g protein}}$ = 200 kcal

　　　　 375 ~~g glucose (carbohydrate)~~ $\times$ $\dfrac{\text{4 kcal}}{\text{1 g carbohydrate}}$ = 1500 kcal

　　　　 100 ~~g lipid (fat)~~ $\times$ $\dfrac{\text{9 kcal}}{\text{1 g fat}}$ = 900 kcal

　　　　 For a total of: 200 kcal + 1500 kcal + 900 kcal = 2600 kcal per day

9.90 750 ~~mL brandy (solution)~~ $\times$ $\dfrac{\text{40.0 mL alcohol}}{\text{100 mL solution}}$ = 3.0×10^2 mL Alcohol

9.91 4.5 ~~mL propyl alcohol~~ $\times$ $\dfrac{\text{100 mL solution}}{\text{12 mL propyl alcohol}}$ = 38 mL of solution

9.92 75 ~~g glucose~~ $\times$ $\dfrac{\text{100 mL}}{\text{5.0 g glucose}}$ $\times$ $\dfrac{\text{1 L}}{\text{1000 mL}}$ = 1.5 L

9.93 250 ~~mL~~ $\times$ $\dfrac{\text{1 L}}{\text{1000 mL}}$ $\times$ $\dfrac{\text{2.0 mole KCl}}{\text{1 L}}$ $\times$ $\dfrac{\text{74.6 g KCl}}{\text{1 mole KCl}}$ = 37.3 g KCl

To make a 2.0 M KCl solution, weigh out 37.3 g KCl (0.500 mole) and place in a volumetric flask. Add enough water to dissolve the KCl and give a final volume of 0.250 L.

9.94 15.6 ~~g KCl~~ $\times$ $\dfrac{\text{1 mole KCl}}{\text{74.6 g KCl}}$ $\times$ $\dfrac{1}{\text{274 mL}}$ $\times$ $\dfrac{\text{1000 mL}}{\text{1 L}}$ = 0.763 mole/L = 0.763 M KCl

9.95 Mass of solution: 70.0 g solute + 130.0 g solvent = 200.0 g

    a. $\dfrac{70.0 \text{ g HNO}_3}{200.0 \text{ g solution}} \times 100 = 35.0\% \text{ (m/m) HNO}_3$

    b. $200.0 \text{ g solution} \times \dfrac{1 \text{ mL solution}}{1.21 \text{ g solution}} = 165 \text{ mL solution}$

    c. $\dfrac{70.0 \text{ g HNO}_3}{165 \text{ mL solution}} \times 100 = 42.4\% \text{ (m/v) HNO}_3$

    d. $\dfrac{70.0 \text{ g HNO}_3}{0.165 \text{ L solution}} \times \dfrac{1 \text{ mole HNO}_3}{63.0 \text{ g HNO}_3} = 6.73 \text{ M HNO}_3$

9.96 $\dfrac{15 \text{ g NaOH}}{100 \text{ mL}} \times \dfrac{1 \text{ mole NaOH}}{40.0 \text{ g NaOH}} \times \dfrac{1000 \text{ mL}}{1 \text{ L}} = 3.8 \text{ mole/L} = 3.8 \text{ M}$

9.97   **a.** $2.5 \text{ L} \times \dfrac{3.0 \text{ moles Al(NO}_3)_3}{1 \text{ L}} \times \dfrac{213 \text{ g Al(NO}_3)_3}{1 \text{ mole Al(NO}_3)_3} = 1600 \text{ g Al(NO}_3)_3$

    b. $75 \text{ mL} \times \dfrac{1 \text{ L}}{1000 \text{ mL}} \times \dfrac{0.50 \text{ mole C}_6\text{H}_{12}\text{O}_6}{1 \text{ L}} \times \dfrac{180 \text{ g C}_6\text{H}_{12}\text{O}_6}{1 \text{ mole C}_6\text{H}_{12}\text{O}_6} = 6.8 \text{ g of C}_6\text{H}_{12}\text{O}_6$

9.98 Isotonic concentrations of sodium chloride, potassium chloride, sodium bicarbonate, and glucose are used in the dialysate to maintain the concentrations of these various ions and glucose at normal levels in the blood.

9.99 A solution with a high salt (solute) concentration will dry flowers because water (solvent) flows out of the flowers' cells and into the salt solution to dilute the salt concentration.

9.100 A high potassium concentration in the dialyzing solution would allow potassium ions to enter the patient's blood to increase the K^+ level in the bloodstream back to a more normal range. The urea and sodium ion concentrations in the blood will be lowered to more normal ranges as these species flow into the dialyzing solution.

9.101 Drinking seawater, which is hypertonic, will cause water to flow out of the body cells and dehydrate the body's cells.

9.102 Pure water will be forced through a semipermeable membrane (separating the pure solvent from the salty solution) by the application of pressure to seawater. Because this process has the solvent flowing in the opposite direction than it would under normal osmotic pressure processes, it is referred to as "reverse osmosis."

9.103 1 Osm = Number of solute particles/L of solution

    a. $\dfrac{0.20 \text{ mole NaCl}}{1 \text{ L solution}} \times \dfrac{2 \text{ moles of ions}}{1 \text{ mole NaCl}} = 0.40 \text{ Osm}$

    b. $\dfrac{0.050 \text{ mole K}_2\text{CO}_3}{1 \text{ L solution}} \times \dfrac{3 \text{ moles of ions}}{1 \text{ mole K}_2\text{CO}_3} = 0.15 \text{ Osm}$

    c. $\dfrac{0.2 \text{ mole CaCl}_2}{1 \text{ L solution}} \times \dfrac{3 \text{ moles of ions}}{1 \text{ mole CaCl}_2} = 0.6 \text{ Osm}$

    d. $\dfrac{0.1 \text{ mole Na}_2\text{SO}_4}{1 \text{ L solution}} \times \dfrac{3 \text{ moles of ions}}{1 \text{ mole Na}_2\text{SO}_4} = 0.3 \text{ Osm}$

9.104 For "Ringer's solution" to be a physiological solution it must have an osmolarity of 0.3 Osm. In every Liter of solution there are 0.147 mole NaCl + 0.004 mole KCl + 0.004 mole $CaCl_2$

$$0.147 \text{ mole NaCl} \times \frac{2 \text{ moles of ions}}{1 \text{ mole NaCl}} = 0.294 \text{ Osmole}$$

$$0.004 \text{ mole KCl} \times \frac{2 \text{ moles of ions}}{1 \text{ mole KCl}} = 0.008 \text{ Osmole}$$

$$0.004 \text{ mole CaCl}_2 \times \frac{3 \text{ moles of ions}}{1 \text{ mole CaCl}_2} = 0.01 \text{ Osmole}$$

$$\frac{0.294 \text{ Osmole} + 0.008 \text{ Osmole} + 0.01 \text{ Osmole}}{1 \text{ L Ringer's solution}} = 0.31 \text{ Osm}$$

Ringer's solution is a physiological solution because it has the same osmotic pressure as blood.

9.105 Water will flow from the solution with the higher solvent concentration (lower solute concentration) into the solution with the higher solute concentration.
  a. B   **b.** B   **c.** stay the same
  d. stay the same   **e.** A

9.106 **a.** hemolysis   **b.** crenate
  c. stay the same (isotonic)   **d.** hemolysis

9.107 **a.** $50.0 \text{ mL} \times \dfrac{1 \text{ L}}{1000 \text{ mL}} \times \dfrac{1.5 \text{ mole KCl}}{1 \text{ L}} \times \dfrac{1 \text{ mole PbCl}_2}{2 \text{ mole KCl}} \times \dfrac{278 \text{ g PbCl}_2}{1 \text{ mole PbCl}_2} = 10. \text{ g PbCl}_2$

  b. $0.050 \text{ L} \times \dfrac{1.5 \text{ mole KCl}}{1 \text{ L}} \times \dfrac{1 \text{ mole PbCl}_2}{2 \text{ mole KCl}} \times \dfrac{1 \text{ L}}{2.0 \text{ mole PbCl}_2} \times \dfrac{1000 \text{ mL}}{1 \text{ L}} = 19 \text{ mL}$

9.108 **a.** $15.0 \text{ g Mg} \times \dfrac{1 \text{ mole Mg}}{24.3 \text{ g Mg}} \times \dfrac{2 \text{ moles HCl}}{1 \text{ mole Mg}} \times \dfrac{1000 \text{ mL}}{6.0 \text{ moles HCl}} = 206 \text{ mL HCl}$

  b. $0.50 \text{ L} \times \dfrac{2.0 \text{ mole HCl}}{1 \text{ L}} \times \dfrac{1 \text{ mole H}_2}{2 \text{ mole HCl}} \times \dfrac{22.4 \text{ L}}{1 \text{ mole H}_2} = 11 \text{ L H}_2$

  c. $\text{mole H}_2 = \dfrac{(735 \text{ mm Hg})(8.5 \text{ L})}{(62.4 \frac{\text{L} \cdot \text{mm Hg}}{\text{mole} \cdot \text{K}})(298 \text{ K})} = 0.34 \text{ moles H}_2$

  $0.34 \text{ mole H}_2 \times \dfrac{2 \text{ mole HCl}}{1 \text{ mole H}_2} = 0.68 \text{ mole HCl}$

  $250.0 \text{ mL} \times \dfrac{1 \text{ L}}{1000 \text{ mL}} = 0.2500 \text{ L HCl solution}$

  $\dfrac{0.68 \text{ mole HCl}}{0.2500 \text{ L}} = 2.7 \text{ M}$

  Using molar volume:

  $V(\text{at STP}) = 8.5 \text{ L} \times \dfrac{735 \text{ mm Hg}}{760 \text{ mm Hg}} \times \dfrac{273 \text{ K}}{298 \text{ K}} = 7.5 \text{ L (at STP)}$

  $7.5 \text{ L} \times \dfrac{1 \text{ mole}}{22.4 \text{ L}} = 0.34 \text{ moles}$

10
Acids and Bases

Study Goals

- Describe the characteristics of acids and bases.
- Identify conjugate acid-base pairs for Brønsted-Lowry acids and bases.
- Use the ion product of water to calculate $[H_3O^+]$, $[OH^-]$, and pH.
- Describe how to prepare a dilute solution of an acid or base.
- Write a balanced equation for reactions of acids and bases.
- Predict whether a salt will form an acidic, basic, or neutral solution
- Describe the function of a buffer.

Chapter Outline

10.1 Acid and Bases
Explore Your World: Acid and Bases in Products at Home
10.2 Conjugate Acid-Base Pairs
10.3 Strengths of Acids and Bases
10.4 Dissociation Constants
10.5 Ionization of Water
10.6 The pH Scale
Explore Your World: Using Vegetables and Flowers as pH Indicators
Health Note: Stomach Acid, HCl
Environmental Note: Acid Rain
10.7 Reactions of Acids and Bases
Explore Your World: Everyday Neutralization Reactions
Health Note: Antacids
10.8 Acidity of Salt Solutions
10.9 Buffers
Health Note: CO_2 and the Bicarbonate Buffer
10.10 Dilutions
10.11 Acid-Base Titration

Chapter Summary and Demonstrations

1. Acids and Bases

Acids and bases are defined using both the Arrhenius and Brønsted theories along with the names of common acids. The hydronium ion is shown as the component in acidic solutions. The strengths of acids and bases are compared and equations written for both weak and strong forms. In neutralization equations, an acid reacts with a base to produce a salt and water.

Demonstration: A clear spot plate (plastic or glass) is handy to use on the overhead projects. A blank transparency sheet beneath the spot plate protects against spills. Samples of acids and base with an indicator such as universal indicator show pH range. Mixing an acid and a base change the pH and the color of the indicator. The reactions can be described and equations for neutralization written as the reactions occur.

2. Ionization of Water and pH

The ionization of water leads to the ion product for water. Concentrations of hydronium ions and hydroxide ions are calculated using the K_w of water. Students observe the pH values of some common substances.

Demonstration: Some natural pigments form different colors with different hydrogen ion concentrations. Prepare an indicator by boiling some red cabbage leaves in water for 5 minutes. Cool the purple solution. Small amounts of household products such as vinegar, lemon juice, antacids, cleaners, shampoos, or detergents are placed in containers. Add cabbage juice to each and observe the color. A pink-orange color indicates a pH range of 1-4, a pink-lavender, 5-6, purple 7, green 8-11, and yellow 12-13. Classify the products as acidic, neutral or basic. Try other highly colored vegetables or fruits to determine their use as indicators.

3. Buffers

Changes in blood pH, causes and treatment are illustrated for respiratory and metabolic acidosis and alkalosis. Buffers are explained and the example of the carbonic acid-bicarbonate buffer system in the blood is used.

Demonstration: A clear spot plate (plastic or glass) is handy to use here as well. A blank transparency sheet beneath the spot plate protects against spills. To samples of water and buffers with an indicator, an acid or base is added. A change in pH occurs in water, while buffers show little change with a few drops of acid or base. The functions of a buffer can be explained as the reactions occur.

Laboratory Suggestions

Lab 19   Acids, Bases, pH, and Buffers

A natural dye is extracted from red cabbage for use as a pH indicator when testing standards with pH 1-12, and various common household substances. The effects of acids and bases on pH of water and buffers are observed.
A. pH Color Using Red Cabbage Indicator
B. Measurement of pH
C. Effect of Buffers on pH

Laboratory Skills to Demonstrate
   Standardization and measurement of pH using indicators
   Measuring pH using a pH meter

Lab 20   Acid-Base Titration

Students fill a buret with standardized NaOH and titrate a sample of vinegar using proper titration technique in reaching an endpoint. From the volume of NaOH, the molar concentration and percentage of acetic acid in vinegar is calculated. In another titration, the acid-absorbing capacity of a commercial antacid is determined. The neutralizing power of antacids is determined
A. Acetic Acid in Vinegar
B. Titration of an Antacid

Laboratory Skills to Demonstrate
   Proper use of a pipet and bulb
   Correct setup and procedure for acid-base titration
   Setting up a buret and proper technique of filling with NaOH
   Reaching an endpoint with an indicator
   Calculating the amount of acid or antacid in the sample tested

Answers and Solutions to Text Problems

10.1 According to the Arrhenius theory:
a. acids taste sour.
b. acids neutralize bases.
c. acids produce H_3O^+ ions in water.
d. potassium hydroxide is the name of a base.
e. a base is a proton acceptor.

10.2 a. base b. bases c. acid d. base e. acid

10.3 The names of nonoxy acids begin with *hydro-*, followed by the name of the anion. The names of oxyacids use the element root with *–ic acid*. Acids with one oxygen less than the common *–ic acid* name are named as *–ous acids*.
a. hydrochloric acid b. calcium hydroxide c. carbonic acid
d. nitric acid e. sulfurous acid

10.4 An acid that dissolves to give H^+ and a simple nonmetallic anion is naming by adding the prefix hydro- to the name of the anion and changing the anion ending to -ic acid. If an acid produces a polyatomic anion, the name of the acid is derived from the name of the polyatomic anion. Bases are named as ionic compounds containing hydroxide anions.
a. aluminum hydroxide b. hydrobromic acid c. sulfuric acid
d. potassium hydroxide e. nitrous acid

10.5 a. $Mg(OH)_2$ b. HF c. H_3PO_4
d. LiOH e. $Cu(OH)_2$

10.6 a. $Ba(OH)_2$ b. HI c. HNO_3 d. $Fe(OH)_3$ e. NaOH

10.7 The acid donates a proton (H^+), while the base accepts a proton.
a. Acid (proton donor) HI proton acceptor (base) H_2O
b. Acid (proton donor) H_2O proton acceptor (base) F^-

10.8 a. acid (proton donor) H_2O base (proton acceptor) CO_3^{2-}
b. acid (proton donor) H_2SO_4 base (proton acceptor) H_2O

10.9 To form the conjugate base, remove a proton (H^+) from the acid.
a. F^-, fluoride ion b. OH^-, hydroxide ion
c. HCO_3^-, bicarbonate ion d. SO_4^{2-}, sulfate ion

10.11 To form the conjugate acid, add a proton (H^+) to the base.
a. HCO_3^- bicarbonate ion b. H_3O^+ hydronium ion
c. H_3PO_4 phosphoric acid d. HBr hydrobromic acid

10.10 a. CO_3^{2-} carbonate ion b. H_2O water
c. PO_4^{3-} phosphate ion d. NO_2^- nitrite ion

10.11 To form the conjugate acid, add a proton (H^+) to the base.
a. HCO_3^- bicarbonate ion b. H_3O^+ hydronium ion
c. H_3PO_4 phosphoric acid d. HBr hydrobromic acid

10.12 a. HSO_4^- hydrogen sulfate ion b. HCN hydrogen cyanide
c. H_2O water d. $HClO_2$ chlorous acid

10.13 The conjugate acid is a proton donor and the conjugate base is a proton acceptor.
  a. acid $H_2CO_3^-$; conjugate base HCO_3^-; base H_2O; conjugate acid H_3O^+
  b. acid NH_4^+; conjugate base NH_3; base H_2O; conjugate acid H_3O^+
  c. acid HCN; conjugate base CN^-; base NO_2^- conjugate acid HNO_2

10.14 **a.** acid H_3PO_4 and base H_2O; conjugate base $H_2PO_4^-$ and conjugate acid H_3O^+
  b. acid H_2O and base CO_3^{2-}, conjugate base OH^- and conjugate acid HCO_3^-
  c. acid H_3PO_4 and base NH_3 conjugate base $H_2PO_4^-$ and conjugate acid NH_4^+

10.15 $NH_4^+ + H_2O \rightleftharpoons NH_3 + H_3O^+$

10.16 $CO_3^{2-} + H_2O \rightleftharpoons HCO_3^- + OH^-$

10.17 A strong acid is a good proton donor, whereas its conjugate base is a poor proton acceptor.

10.18 A weak acid dissociates only slightly; therefore its conjugate base has a strong attraction for protons.

10.19 Use Table 10.3 to answer.
  a. HBr   **b.** HSO_4^- **c.** H_2CO_3

10.20 **a.** H_3O^+ **b.** H_2SO_4 **c.** H_2CO_3

10.21 Use Table 10.3 to answer.
  a. HSO_4^- **b.** HF   **c.** HCO_3^-

10.22 **a.** HCO_3^- **b.** H_2O **c.** H_2CO_3

10.23 **a.** From Table 10.3, we see that H_2O is a weaker base than HCO_3^- and that H_2CO_3 is a weaker acid than H_3O^+. Thus the reactants are favored.
  b. From Table 10.3, we see that NH_4^+ is a weaker acid than H_3O^+ and H_2O is a weaker base than NH_3. Thus the reactants are favored.
  c. From Table 10.3, we see that NH_4^+ is a weaker acid than HCl and that Cl^- is a weaker base than NH_3. Thus the products are favored.

10.24 **a.** reactants; H_3O^+ is a stronger acid than H_3PO_4
  b. reactants; HCO_3^- is a stronger acid than H_2O
  c. reactants; H_3O^+ is a stronger acid than HS^-

10.25 The reactants are favored because NH_4^+ is a weaker acid than HSO_4^-.
  $NH_4^+ + SO_4^{2-} \rightleftharpoons NH_3 + HSO_4^-$

10.26 $HNO_2 + SO_4^{2-} \rightleftharpoons NO_2^- + HSO_4^-$

  This equilibrium favors the reactants because HSO_4^- is a stronger acid that HNO_2

10.27 The smaller the K_a, the weaker the acid. The weaker acid has the stronger conjugate base.
  a. H_2SO_3, which has a larger K_a than HS^-, is a stronger acid.
  b. The conjugate base forms by removing a proton from the acid, HSO_3^-.
  c. The stronger acid, H_2SO_3, has a weaker conjugate base.
  d. The weaker acid, HS^-, has a stronger conjugate base.
  e. H_2SO_3, the stronger acid, produces more ions.

10.28 **a.** HPO_4^{2-} is a weaker acid than formic acid HCOOH.   **b.** PO_4^{3-}
  c. HCOOH   **d.** HPO_4^-
  e. The stronger acid, which is formic acid HCOOH, ionizes more and produces more ions.

10.29 $H_3PO_4 + H_2O \rightleftharpoons H_3O^+ + H_2PO_4^-$
The K_a is the ratio of the [products] divided by the [reactants] with [H_2O] considered constant and part of the K_a

$$K_a = \frac{[H_3O^+][H_2PO_4^-]}{[H_3PO_4]}$$

10.30 $C_6H_5NH_2 + H_2O \xrightarrow{\longleftarrow} C_6H_5NH_3^+ + OH^-$

$$\frac{[C_6H_5NH_3^+][OH^-]}{[C_6H_5NH_2]} = 4.0 \times 10^{-10}$$

10.31 In pure water, a small fraction of the water molecules break apart to form H^+ and OH^-. The H^+ combines with H_2O to form H_3O^+. Every time a H^+ is formed a OH^- is also formed. Therefore, the concentration of the two must be equal in pure water.

10.32 The K_w is the product of the concentrations of the H_3O^+ and OH^- in water.

$$K_w = [H_3O^+][OH^-] = 1.0 \times 10^{-14}$$

10.33 In an acidic solution, [H_3O^+] is greater than [OH^-], which means that [H_3O^+] is greater than 1×10^{-7} M and the [OH^-] is less than 1×10^{-7} M.

10.34 The equilibrium for water shifts to reactants as OH^- is added, which decreases the [H_3O^+]. The [OH^-] is increased and the [H_3O^+] is decreased to maintain the K_w of 1.0×10^{-14}.
$H_2O + H_2O \xleftarrow{\hspace{1cm}} H_3O^+ + OH^-$

10.35 A neutral solution has [OH^-] = [H_3O^+] = 1.0×10^{-7} M. If [OH^-] is greater than 1×10^{-7}, the solution is basic; if [H_3O^+] is greater than 1×10^{-7} M, the solution is acidic.
 a. Acidic; [H_3O^+] is greater than 1×10^{-7} M.
 b. Basic, [H_3O^+] is less than 1×10^{-7} M.
 c. Basic; [OH^-] is greater than 1×10^{-7} M
 d. Acidic; [OH^-] is less than 1×10^{-7} M

10.36 a. basic; [H_3O^+] $< 1.0 \times 10^{-7}$ M, thus [OH^-]$> 1.0 \times 10^{-7}$ M
 b. acidic; [H_3O^+]$> 1.0 \times 10^{-7}$ M
 c. acidic; [OH^-] $< 1.0 \times 10^{-7}$ M thus [H_3O^+] $> 1.0 \times 10^{-7}$ M
 d. basic; [OH^-] $> 1.0 \times 10^{-7}$ M

10.37 The [H_3O^+] multiplied by the [OH^-] is equal to K_w, which is 1.0×10^{-14}. When [H_3O^+] is known, the [OH^-] can be calculated. Rearranging the K_w gives [OH^-] = $K_w/[H_3O^+]$
 a. 1.0×10^{-9} M   b. 1.0×10^{-6} M
 c. 2.0×10^{-5} M   d. 4.0×10^{-13} M

10.38 a. [OH^-] = 1.0×10^{-2} M   b. [OH^-] = 1.67×10^{-11} M
 c. .[OH^-] = 1.0×10^{-5} d. [OH^-] = 1.92×10^{-13}

10.39 The value of the [H_3O^+] multiplied by the value of the [OH^-] is always equal to K_w, which is 1×10^{-14}. When [H_3O^+] is known, the [OH^-] can be calculated.
Rearranging the K_w gives [OH^-] = $K_w /[H_3O^+]$
 a. 1.0×10^{-11} M   b. 2.0×10^{-9} M
 c. 5.6×10^{-3} M   d. 2.5×10^{-2} M

10.40 a. [OH^-] = 1.0×10^{-6} M   b. [OH^-] = 5.0×10^{-11} M
 c. .[OH^-] = 2.0×10^{-8} d. [OH^-] = 2.1×10^{-3}

10.41 In neutral solutions, $[H_3O^+] = 1.0 \times 10^{-7}$ M. pH $= -\log [1.0 \times 10^{-7}] = 7.00$. The pH value contains two *decimal places*, which represent the two significant figures in the coefficient 1.0.

10.42 The K_w product of $[H_3O^+] \times [OH^-] = 1.0 \times 10^{-14}$. If the $[OH^-]$ is given, the K_w is used to calculate $[H_3O^+]$; pH is determined using $-\log [H_3O^+]$.

10.43 An acidic solution has a pH less than 7. A neutral solution has a pH equal to 7. A basic solution has a pH greater than 7.
a. basic **b.** acidic **c.** basic **d.** acidic

10.44 **a.** acidic **b.** acidic **c.** basic **d.** acidic

10.45 An increase or decrease of 1 pH unit changes the $[H_3O^+]$ by a factor of 10. Thus a pH of 3 (10^{-3} M or 0.001 M) is 10 times more acid than a pH of 4 (10^{-4} M or 0.0001 M)

10.46 The pH is based on tens. A pH of 8 represents a $[H_3O^+]$ of 1×10^{-8}, which is 100 times greater than 1.0×10^{-10}, which is the $[H_3O^+]$ of pH 10.

10.47 The value of $[H_3O^+][OH^-]$ is equal to K_w, which is 1.0×10^{-14}. Rearranging the K_w gives $[H_3O^+] = K_w / [OH^-]$
a. 4.00 **b.** 8.52 **c.** 9.00 **d.** 3.40

10.48 **a.** 8.00 **b.** 5.30 **c.** 12.60 **d.** 11.90

10.49

$[H_3O^+]$	$[OH^-]$	pH	pOH	Acidic, Basic, or Neutral?
1.0×10^{-8} M	1.0×10^{-6} M	8.00	6.00	Basic
1.0×10^{-3} M	1.0×10^{-11} M	3.00	11.00	Acidic
2.8×10^{-5} M	3.6×10^{-10} M	4.55	9.45	Acidic
1.0×10^{-12} M	1.0×10^{-2} M	12.00	2.00	Basic

10.50

$[H_3O^+]$	$[OH^-]$	pH	pOH	Acidic, Basic, or Neutral?
1.0×10^{-10} M	1.0×10^{-4} M	10.00	4.00	Basic
1×10^{-7} M	1×10^{-7} M	7.0	7.0	Acidic
1.0×10^{-9} M	1.0×10^{-5} M	9.00	5.00	Acidic
6.4×10^{-12} M	1.6×10^{-3} M	11.19	2.81	Basic

10.51 Acids react with active metals to form H_2 and a salt of the metal. The reaction of acids with carbonates yields CO_2, H_2O, and a salt of the metal. In a neutralization, an acid and a base form a salt and H_2O.
a. $ZnCO_3 + 2HCl \longrightarrow ZnCl_2 + CO_2 + H_2O$
b. $Zn + 2HCl \longrightarrow ZnCl_2 + H_2$
c. $HCl + NaHCO_3 \longrightarrow NaCl + H_2O + CO_2$
d. $2 HNO_3 + Mg(OH)_2 \longrightarrow Mg(NO_3)_2 + 2 H_2O$

10.52 **a.** $KHCO_3 + HCl \longrightarrow CO_2 + H_2O + KCl$
b. $Ca + 2HNO_3 \longrightarrow Ca(NO_3)_2 + H_2$
c. $3H_2SO_4 + 2Al(OH)_3 \longrightarrow Al_2(SO_4)_3 + 6H_2O$
d. $Na_2CO_3 + H_2SO_4 \longrightarrow CO_2 + H_2O + Na_2SO_4$

10.53 In balancing a neutralization equation, the number of H^+ and OH^- must be equalized by placing coefficients in front of the formulas for the acid and base.

a. $2HCl + Mg(OH)_2 \longrightarrow MgCl_2 + 2 H_2O$ **b.** $H_3PO_4 + 3 LiOH \longrightarrow Li_3PO_4 + 3 H_2O$

10.54 **a.** $2HNO_3 + Ba(OH)_2 \longrightarrow Ba(NO_3)_2 + 2H_2O$
b. $3H_2SO_4 + 2Al(OH)_3 \longrightarrow Al_2(SO_4)_3 + 6H_2O$

10.55 In balancing a neutralization equation, the number of H^+ and OH^- must be equalized by placing coefficients in front of the formulas for the acid and base.

a. $H_2SO_4 + 2 NaOH \longrightarrow Na_2SO_4 + 2 H_2O$
b. $3 HCl + Fe(OH)_3 \longrightarrow FeCl_3 + 3 H_2O$
c. $H_2CO_3 + Mg(OH)_2 \longrightarrow MgCO_3 + 2 H_2O$

10.56 **a.** $H_3PO_4 + 3 NaOH \longrightarrow Na_3PO_4 + 3H_2O$
b. $HI + LiOH \longrightarrow LiI + H_2O$
c. $2HNO_3 + Ca(OH)_2 \longrightarrow Ca(NO_3)_2 + 2H_2O$

10.57 The anion of a weak acid removes a proton from H_2O to make a basic solution.

10.58 When a salt contains a cation such as NH_4^+ from a weak base (NH_3), the cation donates a proton to water. The resulting solution is acidic as long as the anion is from a strong acid, which does not interact with water.

10.59 A solution of a salt with an anion from a strong acid and a cation from a weak base will form an acidic solution. A salt with an anion from a weak acid and a cation from a strong base will form a basic solution. Solutions of salts with ions of strong acids and strong bases are neutral.

a. neutral
b. acidic: $NH_4^+ + H_2O \rightleftarrows NH_3 + H_3O^+$
c. basic: $CO_3^{2-} + H_2O \rightleftarrows HCO_3^- + OH^-$
d. basic: $S^{2-} + H_2O \rightleftarrows HS^- + OH^-$

10.60 **a.** basic; $SO_4^{2-} + H_2O \rightleftarrows HSO_4^- + OH^-$
b. neutral
c. neutral
d. acidic; $NH_4^+ + H_2O \rightleftarrows NH_3 + H_3O^+$

10.61 A buffer system contains a weak acid and its salt or a weak base and its salt.
a. This is not a buffer system, because it only contains a strong acid.
b. This is a buffer system; it contains the weak acid H_2CO_3 and its salt $NaHCO_3$.
c. This is a buffer system; it contains HF, a weak acid, and its salt KF.
d. This is not a buffer system because it contains the salts KCl and NaCl.

10.62 Answer c is a buffer solution of the weak acid CH_3COOH and its salt CH_3COONa

10.63 **a.** A buffer system keeps the pH of a solution constant.
b. The salt of the acid in a buffer is needed to neutralize any acid added.
c. In the buffer, the F^- (from salt of the weak acid) reacts with the H^+ to neutralize it.
d. In the buffer solution, HF (weak acid) reacts to neutralize the OH^-.

10.64 **a.** A buffer system keeps the pH of a solution constant.
b. The salt in a buffer is needed to neutralize any acid added.
c. When H^+ is added to the buffer, the NO_2^- reacts with the acid to neutralize it.
d. When OH^- is added to the buffer solution, the weak acid HNO_2 reacts with the base to neutralize it.

10.65 Rearrange the K_a for $[H_3O^+]$ and use to calculate pH.

$[H_3O^+] = 4.5 \times 10^{-4} \times \dfrac{[0.10 \text{ M}]}{[0.10 \text{ M}]} = 4.5 \times 10^{-4}$ $\text{pH} = -\log[4.5 \times 10^{-4}] = 3.35$

10.66 $CH_3COOH + H_2O \rightleftharpoons CH_3COO^- + H_3O^+$

$[H_3O^+] = K_a \times \dfrac{[CH_3COOH]}{[CH_3COO^-]} = 1.8 \times 10^{-5} \times \dfrac{[0.15 \text{ M}]}{[0.15 \text{ M}]} = 1.8 \times 10^{-5}$

$\text{pH} = -\log[1.8 \times 10^{-5}] = 4.74$

10.67 Rearrange the K_a for $[H_3O^+]$ and use to calculate pH.

$[H_3O^+] = 7.2 \times 10^{-4} \times \dfrac{[0.10 \text{ M}]}{[0.10 \text{ M}]} = 7.2 \times 10^{-4}$ $\text{pH} = -\log[7.2 \times 10^{-4}] = 3.14$

$[H_3O^+] = 7.2 \times 10^{-4} \times \dfrac{[0.060 \text{ M}]}{[0.120 \text{ M}]} = 3.6 \times 10^{-4}$ $\text{pH} = -\log[3.6 \times 10^{-4}] = 3.44$

10.68 $H_2CO_3 + H_2O \rightleftharpoons HCO_3^- + H_3O^+$

$[H_3O^+] = K_a \times \dfrac{[H_2CO_3]}{[HCO_3^-]} = 4.3 \times 10^{-7} \times \dfrac{[0.10 \text{ M}]}{[0.10 \text{ M}]} = 4.3 \times 10^{-7}$

$\text{pH} = -\log[4.3 \times 10^{-7}] = 6.37$

$[H_3O^+] = K_a \times \dfrac{[H_2CO_3]}{[HCO_3^-]} = 4.3 \times 10^{-7} \times \dfrac{[0.15 \text{ M}]}{[0.050 \text{ M}]} = 1.3 \times 10^{-6}$

$\text{pH} = -\log[1.3 \times 10^{-6}] = 5.89$

10.69 Dilution occurs when water added to the concentrate increases the volume of the soup.

10.70 When water is added to a concentrated solution (frozen lemonade) to make a less concentration solution, the process is called dilution.

10.71 **a.** $\dfrac{25.0 \text{ mL} \times 6.0 \text{ M}}{200 \text{ mL}} = 0.75 \text{ M}$

b. $\dfrac{25\% \times 10.0 \text{ mL}}{500 \text{ mL}} = 0.50 \%$

10.72 The final volume of a diluted solution can be found by using the relationship: $M_1V_1 = M_2V_2$. M_1 is the concentration of the initial solution and M_2 is the concentration of the final solution. V_1 is the initial volume of the solution and V_2 is the final volume.

$M_2 = \dfrac{M_1V_1}{V_2}$

a. $M_2 = \dfrac{(3.5 \text{ M})(5.0 \text{ mL})}{(250 \text{ mL})} = 0.070 \text{ M } H_2SO_4$

b. $M_2 = \dfrac{(50.0\%(5.0 \text{ mL})}{(100 \text{ mL})} = 2.5 \% \text{ } CH_3COOH$

10.73 **a.** $\dfrac{250 \text{ mL} \times 0.200 \text{ M}}{4.00 \text{ M}} = 13 \text{ mL}$

b. $\dfrac{750 \text{ mL} \times 0.100 \text{ M}}{6.0 \text{ M}} = 13 \text{ mL}$

10.74 $V_1 = \dfrac{M_2V_2}{M_1}$

a. $V_1 = \dfrac{(0.050 \text{ M})(10.0 \text{ mL})}{(0.20 \text{ M})} = 2.5 \text{ mL of } 0.10 \text{ M } Ba(OH)_2$

b. $V_1 = \dfrac{(0.20\,\%)(\,500\text{ mL})}{(10.0\%)} = 10$ mL of 10.0% NaOH

10.75 $\dfrac{25.0\text{ mL} \times 3.0\text{ M}}{0.15\text{ M}} = 500$ mL

Add 475 mL water to the 25 mL of 3.0 M solution to make 500 mL of solution.

10.76 $V_2 = \dfrac{M_1 V_1}{M_2}$

$V_2 = \dfrac{(40.0\text{ mL})(2.5\text{ M})}{(0.50\text{ M})} = 200$ mL

Add 160 mL water to 40.0 mL of 2.5 M HBr to make 200 mL of 0.50 M HBr.

10.77 To a known volume of formic acid, add a few drops of indicator. Place a NaOH solution of known molarity in a buret. Add NaOH to the acid solution until one drop changes the color of the solution. Use the volume and molarity of NaOH to calculate the moles of formic acid in the sample. Then calculate the concentration from the moles and volume of formic acid.

10.78 To a known volume of acetic acid, add a few drops of indicator. Place a NaOH solution of known molarity in a buret. Add NaOH to the acid solution until one drop changes the color of the solution. Use the volume and molarity of NaOH to calculate the concentrations of the acetic acid in the sample.

10.79 **a.** In the equation reaction, one mole of HCl reacts with one mole of NaOH.

22.0 ~~mL~~ NaOH $\times$ $\dfrac{1\text{ L}}{1000\text{ ~~mL~~}}$ $\times$ $\dfrac{2.0\text{ ~~moles NaOH~~}}{1\text{ L}}$ $\times$ $\dfrac{1\text{ mole HCl}}{1\text{ ~~mole NaOH~~}}$ = 0.044 moles HCl

The concentration of HCl is $\dfrac{0.044\text{ moles HCl}}{0.0050\text{ L}} = 8.8$ M HCl.

b. In the equation 1 mole of H_2SO_4 reacts with 2 moles of NaOH

15.0 ~~mL~~ NaOH $\times$ $\dfrac{1\text{ L}}{1000\text{ ~~mL~~}}$ $\times$ $\dfrac{1.0\text{ ~~moles NaOH~~}}{1\text{ L}}$ $\times$ $\dfrac{1\text{ mole }H_2SO_4}{2\text{ ~~moles NaOH~~}}$ = 0.0075 moles H_2SO_4

The concentration of H_2SO_4 is $\dfrac{0.0075\text{ moles }H_2SO_4}{0.010\text{ L}}$ = 0.75 M H_2SO_4.

c. 16.0 ~~mL~~ NaOH $\times$ $\dfrac{1\text{ L}}{1000\text{ ~~mL~~}}$ $\times$ $\dfrac{1.0\text{ ~~moles NaOH~~}}{1\text{ L}}$ $\times$ $\dfrac{1\text{ mole }H_3PO_4}{3\text{ ~~moles NaOH~~}}$ = 0.0053 moles H_3PO_4

The concentration of H_3PO_4 is $\dfrac{0.0053\text{ moles }H_3PO_4}{0.010\text{ L}}$ = 0.53 M H_3PO_4.

10.80 **a.** 0.0080 ~~L~~ $\times$ $\dfrac{6.0\text{ ~~moles NaOH~~}}{1\text{ ~~L~~}}$ $\times$ $\dfrac{1\text{ mole HCl}}{1\text{ ~~mole NaOH~~}}$ $\times$ $\dfrac{1}{0.0200\text{ L}}$ = 2.4 moles/L HCl = 2.4 M

sample volume in liters

b. 0.0250 ~~L~~ $\times$ $\dfrac{0.50\text{ ~~moles NaOH~~}}{1\text{ ~~L~~}}$ $\times$ $\dfrac{1\text{ mole }H_2SO_4}{2\text{ ~~mole NaOH~~}}$ $\times$ $\dfrac{1}{0.0100\text{ L}}$ = 0.63 M

sample volume in liters

c. 0.0180 ~~L~~ $\times$ $\dfrac{3.0\text{ ~~moles NaOH~~}}{1\text{ ~~L~~}}$ $\times$ $\dfrac{1\text{ mole }H_3PO_4}{3\text{ ~~mole NaOH~~}}$ $\times$ $\dfrac{1}{0.0300\text{ L }H_3PO_4}$ = 0.60 M

sample volume in liters

10.81 The name of an acid from a simple nonmetallic anion is formed by adding the prefix *hydro-* to the name of the anion and changing the anion ending to *-ic acid*. If the acid has polyatomic anion, the name of the acid uses the name of the polyatomic anion and ends in *-ic acid* or *-ous acid*. There is no prefix *hydro*. Bases are named as ionic compounds containing hydroxide anions.

    a. sulfuric acid, acid   **b.** potassium hydroxide, base

    c. calcium hydroxide, base   **d.** hydrochloric acid, acid   **e.** nitrous acid, acid

10.82   **a.** acidic   **b.** acidic   **c.** basic   **d.** basic   **e.** basic

10.83 Both strong and weak acids dissolve in water to give H_3O^+. They both neutralize bases, turn litmus red and phenolphthalein clear. Both taste sour and are electrolytes in solution. However, weak acids are only slightly dissociated in solution and are weak electrolytes. Strong acids, which are nearly completely dissociated in solution, are strong electrolytes.

10.84 Some ingredients found in antacids are $Al(OH)_3$, $Mg(OH)_2$, $CaCO_3$, $NaHCO_3$, and $KHCO_3$. Their function is to neutralize stomach acid.

10.85   **a.** $Mg(OH)_2$ is a strong base because all the base that dissolves is dissociated in aqueous solution.

    b. $Mg(OH)_2 + 2HCl \rightarrow 2H_2O + MgCl_2$

10.86 Acetic acid is only partially dissociated in solution and is thus a weak acid.

10.87   **a.** HF   **b.** H_3O^+ **c.** HNO_2 **d.** HCO_3^-

10.88   **a.** H_2O **b.** OH^- **c.** NO_2^- **d.** CO_3^{2-}

10.89 The pOH = $-\log[OH^-]$, which means that pH + pOH = 14.0.

    a. pH 7.70, pOH 6.30   **b.** pH 1.30, pOH 12.70

    c. pH 10.54, pOH 3.46   **d.** pH 11.7, pOH 2.3

10.90   **a.** basic   **b.** acidic   **c.** basic   **d.** basic

10.91 If the pH is given, the $[H_3O^+]$ can be found by using the relationship $[H_3O^+] = 1.0 \times 10^{-pH}$. The $[OH^-]$ can be found from $[H_3O^+][OH^-] = 1 \times 10^{-14}$.

    a. $[H_3O^+] = 1.0 \times 10^{-3}$ M $[OH^-] = 1.0 \times 10^{-11}$ M

    b. $[H_3O^+] = 1.0 \times 10^{-6}$ M $[OH^-] = 1.0 \times 10^{-8}$ M

    c. $[H_3O^+] = 1 \times 10^{-8}$ M $[OH^-] = 1 \times 10^{-6}$ M

    d. $[H_3O^+] = 1 \times 10^{-11}$ M $[OH^-] = 1 \times 10^{-3}$ M

10.92   **a.** Solution A, with a pH of 4.0 is more acidic.

    b. In A the $[H_3O^+] = 1 \times 10^{-4}$, in B the $[H_3O^+] = 1 \times 10^{-6}$

    c. In A the $[OH^-] = 1 \times 10^{-10}$, in B the $[OH^-] = 1 \times 10^{-8}$

10.93 The concentration of OH^- is calculated from the moles of NaOH and volume of the solution.

$$0.20 \text{ g NaOH} \times \frac{1 \text{ mole}}{40.0 \text{ g NaOH}} = 0.0050 \text{ mole NaOH}$$

$$\frac{0.0050 \text{ mole NaOH}}{0.25 \text{ L}} = 0.020 \text{ M NaOH}$$

10.94 $1.5 \text{ g HNO}_3 \times \dfrac{1 \text{ mole HNO}_3}{63.0 \text{ g HNO}_3} \times \dfrac{1}{0.50 \text{ L}} = 0.048 \text{ mole/L} = 0.048 \text{ M}$

10.95 $2.5 \text{ g HCl} \times \dfrac{1 \text{ mole HCl}}{36.5 \text{ g HCl}} \times \dfrac{1}{0.425 \text{ L}} \times \dfrac{1 \text{ mole H}_3\text{O}^+}{1 \text{ mole HCl}} = 0.16 \text{ M H}_3\text{O}^+ \ (1.6 \times 10^{-1} \text{ M H}_3\text{O}^+)$

$\text{pH} = -\log[1.6 \times 10^{-1} \text{ M}] = 0.79 \qquad \text{pOH} = 14.00 - 0.79 = 13.21$

10.96 $1.0 \text{ g Ca(OH)}_2 \times \dfrac{1 \text{ mole Ca(OH)}_2}{74.1 \text{ g Ca(OH)}_2} \times \dfrac{1}{0.875 \text{ L}} = 0.015 \text{ mole/L} = 0.015 \text{ M}$

$\dfrac{0.015 \text{ mole Ca(OH)}_2}{1 \text{ L}} \times \dfrac{2 \text{ moles OH}^-}{1 \text{ mole Ca(OH)}_2} = 0.030 \text{ mole OH}^-/\text{L} = 3.0 \times 10^{-2} \text{ M OH}^-$

$\text{pOH} = -\log[3.0 \times 10^{-2} \text{ M}] = 1.52 \quad \text{pH} = 14.00 - 1.52 = 12.48$

10.97 **a.** basic, contains an anion of a weak acid, HF
b. basic, contains an anion of a weak acid, HCN
c. acidic, contains a cation of a weak base, NH_4OH
d. neutral, contains ions of strong acid and base

10.98 **a.** basic; $SO_4^{2-} + H_2O \longrightarrow HSO_4^- + OH^-$
b. basic; $NO_2^- + H_2O \longrightarrow HNO_2 + OH^-$
c. neutral
d. acidic; $NH_4^+ + H_2O \longrightarrow NH_3 + H_3O^+$

10.99 In a buffer, the anion accepts H^+ and the cation provides H^+.
a. $H_2PO_4^- + H_3O^+ \longrightarrow H_3PO_4 + H_2O$
b. $H_3PO_4 + OH^- \longrightarrow H_2PO_4^- + H_2O$
c. $[H_3O^+] = 7.5 \times 10^{-3} = [0.10 \text{ M}]/[0.10 \text{ M}] = 7.5 \times 10^{-3} \quad \text{pH} = -\log(7.5 \times 10^{-3}) = 2.12$

10.100 **a.** $CH_3COO^- + H_3O^+ \longrightarrow CH_3COOH + H_2O$
b. $CH_3COOH + OH^- \longrightarrow CH_3COO^- + H_2O$

c. $[H_3O^+] = K_a \times \dfrac{[CH_3COOH]}{[CH_3COO^-]} = 1.8 \times 10^{-5} \times \dfrac{[0.10 \text{ M}]}{[0.10 \text{ M}]} = 1.8 \times 10^{-5}$
$\text{pH} = -\log[1.8 \times 10^{-5}] = 4.74$

10.101 **a.** When acidic compounds enter the blood, the body reacts by restore the blood pH. The pH of blood is controlled by the carbonic acid equilibrium.
$CO_2 + H_2O \longleftrightarrow H_2CO_3 \longleftrightarrow H^+ + HCO_3^-$

The body responds to excess H^+ by hyperventilating, which lowers the CO_2 and causes the equilibrium to shift to the left.
b. The underlying cause of the increased acidity should be treated. In the meanwhile, sodium bicarbonate is given.

10.102 **a.** $HCO_3^- + H_3O^+ \longrightarrow H_2CO_3 + H_2O$
b. $H_2CO_3 + OH^- \longrightarrow HCO_3^- + H_2O$

10.103 **a.** $0.025 \text{ L} \times \dfrac{0.10 \text{ mole HCl}}{1 \text{ L}} \times \dfrac{1 \text{ moles NaOH}}{1 \text{ mole HCl}} \times \dfrac{1000 \text{ mL NaOH}}{0.50 \text{ moles NaOH}} = 5.0 \text{ mL NaOH}$

b. $0.010 \text{ L} \times \dfrac{2.0 \text{ mole H}_2\text{SO}_4}{1 \text{ L}} \times \dfrac{2 \text{ mole NaOH}}{1 \text{ mole H}_2\text{SO}_4} \times \dfrac{1000 \text{ mL}}{0.50 \text{ moles NaOH}} = 80.0 \text{ mL NaOH}$

10.104 $H_2SO_4 + 2\,NaOH \longrightarrow Na_2SO_4 + 2H_2O$

$$0.025 \;\cancel{L} \times \frac{2.0 \;\cancel{\text{mole } H_2SO_4}}{1 \;\cancel{L}} \times \frac{2 \;\cancel{\text{moles NaOH}}}{1 \;\cancel{\text{mole } H_2SO_4}} \times \frac{1000 \;\text{mL NaOH}}{\cancel{1.0 \;\text{mole NaOH}}} = 100 \;\text{mL of NaOH}$$

10.105 $Ba(OH)_2 + 2\,HCl \longrightarrow BaCl_2 + 2H_2O$

a. $0.035 \;\cancel{L} \times \dfrac{0.15 \;\cancel{\text{mole Ba(OH)}_2}}{1\;\cancel{L}} \times \dfrac{2 \;\cancel{\text{moles HCl}}}{1 \;\cancel{\text{mole Ba(OH)}_2}} \times \dfrac{1000 \;\text{mL HCl}}{2.0 \;\cancel{\text{moles HCl}}} = 5.3 \;\text{mL}$

b. $0.0100 \;\cancel{L} \times \dfrac{2.0 \;\cancel{\text{mole KOH}}}{1\;\cancel{L}} \times \dfrac{1 \;\cancel{\text{mole HCl}}}{1 \;\cancel{\text{mole KOH}}} \times \dfrac{1000 \;\text{mL HCl}}{2.0 \;\cancel{\text{moles HCl}}} = 10 \;\text{mL HCl}$

10.106 $CH_3COOH + NaOH \longrightarrow CH_3COONa + H_2O$

$$0.0165 \;\cancel{L} \times \frac{0.500 \;\cancel{\text{mole NaOH}}}{1 \;\cancel{L}} \times \frac{1 \;\text{moles } CH_3COOH}{1 \;\cancel{\text{mole NaOH}}} \times \frac{1}{0.010 \;\text{L}} = 0.825 \;\text{M } CH_3COOH$$

Introduction to Organic Chemistry

Study Goals

- Identify the number of bonds for carbon and other atoms in organic compounds.
- Describe the tetrahedral shape of carbon with single bonds in organic compounds.
- Classify organic compounds as polar or nonpolar.
- Describe the properties that are characteristic of organic compounds.
- Identify the functional groups in organic compounds.
- Write condensed structural formulas for organic compounds.
- Write structural formulas for constitutional isomers.

Chapter Outline

Chapter Summary and Demonstrations

1. Organic Compounds

The bonding of carbon with hydrogen is reviewed and the tetrahedral structure of methane is introduced. Both expanded and condensed structural formulas are written for organic compounds

Demonstration: Models of Alkanes Model kits are very useful in the early instruction of organic compounds. In class, I pass out molecular model sets and ask students to work in groups and construct some of simple alkanes. We look at 3-dimensional structure and write wedge and dash structures for the molecules.

2. Properties of Organic Compounds

The chemical and physical properties of bonding, melting and boiling points, and the solubility in water of organic compounds are contrasted with those of inorganic compounds.

Demonstration: Physical Properties (lab or hood) Visual demonstrations of the differences in solubility of organic and inorganic compounds in water as compared to nonpolar solvents, in melting points and in their flammability can help students distinguish between the physical and chemical properties of organic and inorganic compounds.

3. Functional Groups

The classification of organic compounds according to their functional groups demonstrates the similarities among organic compounds.

Demonstration: Models of Alkanes Model kits are very useful in the early instruction of organic compounds. In class, I set out several models of organic compounds, which contain different functional groups. I ask students what is similar about the molecules and what is different. I have them describe those features that distinguish the molecules. Finally, I ask students to suggest ways to group the molecules by using those distinguishing features, which we finally call functional groups.

4. Constitutional Isomers

Many organic compounds have identical molecular formulas. When compounds with the same molecular formula have different arrangements of those atoms, they are constitutional isomers.

Demonstration: Models of Alkanes Model kits are very useful in explaining constitutional isomers. I give student a formula such as C_3H_8O and ask them to write different expanded structural formulas. This is a way for them to practice writing structures. Then I have them take three carbon atoms, eight hydrogen atoms, and one oxygen atom from the model kit to make as many models as they can. This hands on, visual approach helps students to understand the connections between atoms and the number of different arrangements.

Laboratory Suggestions

Lab 21   Properties of Organic Chemistry

The physical properties and bonds of organic compound are compared to those of inorganic compounds. Organic compounds are classified according to functional groups.
A. Color, Odor, and Physical State
B. Solubility
C. Combustion
D. Functional Groups

Laboratory Skills to Demonstrate
   Explain the colors and atoms represented by the organic model kits.
   Location of organic compounds in the Chemistry handbook
   Caution in the use of cyclohexane
   Caution when burning samples of organic compounds

Answers and Solutions to Text Problems

11.1 Carbon needs four bonds, nitrogen three bonds, and oxygen two bonds.

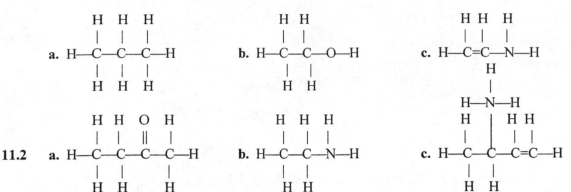

11.3 a. incorrect; carbon needs four bonds
b. incorrect; hydrogen can have only one bond
c. correct
d. correct

11.4 a. correct   b. incorrect   c. incorrect   d. correct

11.5 VSEPR theory predicts that the four bonds in CH_4 will be as far apart as possible, which means that the hydrogen atoms are at the corners of a tetrahedron.

11.6 Wedges indicate bonds that come forward from the page, and dashed lines show bonds going behind the plane of the page.

11.7 a. nonpolar
b. nonpolar; four polar bonds cancel in a tetrahedron
c. polar; dipoles do not cancel
d. polar; three nonpolar C—H bonds and one polar bond C—Br

11.8 a. polar   b. polar   c. polar   d. nonpolar

11.9 Organic compounds contain C and H and sometimes O, N, or a halogen atom. Inorganic compounds usually contain elements other than C and H.
a. inorganic   b. organic   c. organic
d. inorganic   e. inorganic   f. organic

11.10 a. organic   b. inorganic   c. inorganic
d. organic   e. organic   f. organic

11.11 a. Inorganic compounds are usually soluble in water.
b. Organic compounds have lower boiling points than most inorganic compounds.
c. Organic compounds often burn in air.
d. Inorganic compounds are more likely to be solids at room temperature.

11.12 a. inorganic   b. organic   c. organic   d. inorganic

11.13 **a.** Alcohols contain a hydroxyl group (—OH).
      b. Alkenes have carbon-carbon double bonds.
      c. Aldehydes contain a C=O bonded to at least one H atom.
      d. Esters contain a carboxyl group attached to an alkyl group.

11.14 **a.** amine   **b.** carboxylic acid; ester   **c.** ether   **d.** ketone

11.15 **a.** Ethers have an —O— group.
      b. Alcohols have a —OH group.
      c. Ketones have a C=O group between alkyl groups.
      d. Carboxylic acids have a —COOH group.
      e. Amines contain a N atom.

11.16 **a.** ester   **b.** amine   **c.** aldehyde   **d.** carboxylic acid   **e.** alkene

11.17 **a.** constitutional isomers; same molecular formula but different atom arrangement
      b. identical compounds; same order of atoms
      c. constitutional isomers; same molecular formula but different atom arrangement
      d. constitutional isomers; same molecular formula but different atom arrangement
      e. constitutional isomers; same molecular formula but different atom arrangement
      f. different compounds; different molecular formulas

11.18 **a.** constitutional isomers   **b.** identical   **c.** constitutional isomers
      d. constitutional isomers   **e.** constitutional isomers   **f.** different compounds

11.19

11.20

11.21 **a.** Organic compounds have covalent bonds; inorganic compounds have ionic as well as polar covalent and a few have nonpolar covalent bonds.
      b. Most organic compounds are insoluble in water; inorganic compounds are soluble in water.
      c. Most organic compounds have low melting points; inorganic compounds have high melting points.
      d. Most organic compounds are flammable; inorganic compounds are not flammable.

11.22 **a.** inorganic   **b.** organic   **c.** inorganic   **d.** organic

11.23 **a.** butane; organic compounds have low melting points
      b. butane; organic compounds burn vigorously in air
      c. potassium chloride; inorganic compounds have high melting points
      d. potassium chloride; inorganic compounds (ionic) produce ions in water
      e. butane; organic compounds are more likely to be gases at room temperature

11.24 **a.** cyclohexane   **b.** calcium nitrate   **c.** cyclohexane
      d. cyclohexane   **e.** calcium nitrate

11.25

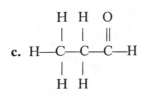 **a.**

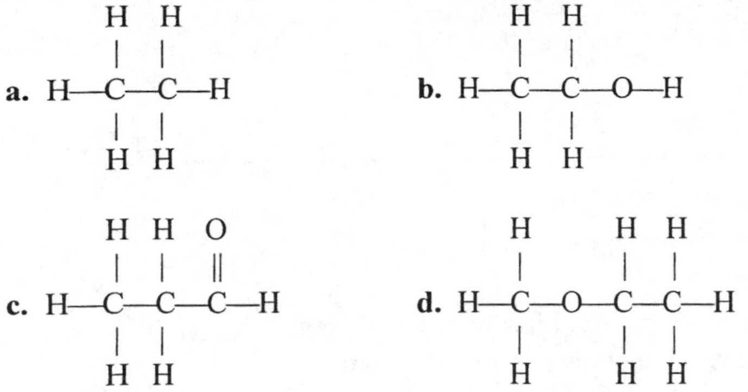

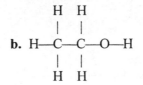 **b.**

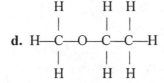 **c.**

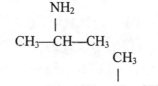 **d.**

11.26 **a.** C has 5 bonds; should be CH₃F

b. C in CH₂ only has 3 bonds; should be CH₃—CH₃

c. Cs have 6 bonds; should be HC CH

d. carbonyl C has five bonds; should be

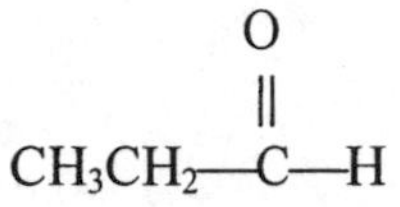

$$CH_3CH_2-\overset{\overset{\displaystyle O}{\|}}{C}-H$$

11.27 **a.** A hydroxyl group is —OH; a carbonyl group is C=O

b. An alcohol contains the hydroxyl (—OH) functional group; an ether contains a —C—O—C— functional group.

c. A carboxylic acid contains the COOH functional group; an ester contains a —COOC— functional group.

11.28 **a.** amine **b.** ketone **c.** alcohol
d. alkane **e.** alkyne **f.** ether

11.29 **a.** constitutional isomers **b.** different compounds **c.** constitutional isomers
d. different compounds **e.** constitutional isomers **f.** identical compounds
g. different compounds

11.30 **a.** CH₃—CH₂—CH₂—NH₂

$$CH_3-\overset{\overset{\displaystyle NH_2}{|}}{CH}-CH_3$$

b. CH₃—CH₂—NH—CH₂

c. $CH_3-\overset{\overset{\displaystyle CH_3}{|}}{N}-CH_3$

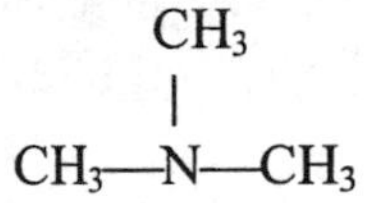

11.31 **a.** polar **b.** polar **c.** nonpolar
d. polar **e.** polar **f.** polar

11.32

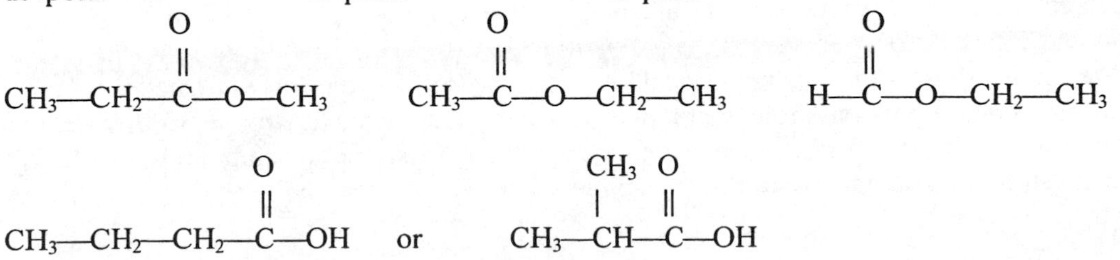

$$CH_3-CH_2-\overset{\overset{\displaystyle O}{\|}}{C}-O-CH_3 \qquad CH_3-\overset{\overset{\displaystyle O}{\|}}{C}-O-CH_2-CH_3 \qquad H-\overset{\overset{\displaystyle O}{\|}}{C}-O-CH_2-CH_3$$

$$CH_3-CH_2-CH_2-\overset{\overset{\displaystyle O}{\|}}{C}-OH \quad \text{or} \quad CH_3-\overset{\overset{\displaystyle CH_3}{|}}{CH}-\overset{\overset{\displaystyle O}{\|}}{C}-OH$$

11.33 **a.** alcohol **b.** unsaturated hydrocarbon **c.** aldehyde
d. saturated hydrocarbon **e.** carboxylic acid **f.** amine
g. tetrahedral **h.** constitutional isomers **i.** ester
j. hydrocarbon **k.** ether
l. unsaturated hydrocarbon **m.** functional group **n.** ketone

12
Alkanes

Study Goals

- Draw expanded, condensed, and line-bond structural formulas for alkanes.
- Draw the structural formulas of alkanes and their constitutional isomers.
- Write the IUPAC names for alkanes.
- Write the IUPAC and common names for haloalkanes; draw the condensed structural formulas.
- Write the IUPAC names, and draw the structural formulas for cycloalkanes.
- Describe the physical properties of alkanes and cycloalkanes.
- Write equations for the combustion and halogenation reactions of alkanes and cycloalkanes.

Chapter Outline

12.1 Alkanes
12.1 IUPAC Naming system for Alkanes
Environmental Note: Petroleum Products
12.3 Drawing Structural Formulas
12.4 Haloalkanes
Health Note: Common Uses of Halogenated Alkanes
Environmental Note: CFCs and Ozone Depletion
12.5 Cycloalkanes
12.6 Physical Properties of Alkanes and Cycloalkanes
12.7 Chemical Properties of Alkanes and Cycloalkanes
Health Note: Incomplete Combustion
Explore Your World: Combustion

Chapter Summary and Demonstrations

1. Organic Compounds and Their Names

The expanded and condensed structural formulas are written for alkanes. The alkanes are named using the IUPAC system of naming. Students learn the names of main chains, alkyl groups, and the numbering of the chain to indicate the location of those groups. The related families of the haloalkanes and cycloalkanes are also discussed along with the cis-trans isomers of cycloalkanes. The solubility, density, and uses of alkanes are described. Combustion and halogenation of alkanes are presented as chemical reactions of the alkane.

Demonstration: Models of Alkanes Model kits are very useful in the early instruction of organic compounds. In class, I pass out molecular model sets and ask students to work in groups and construct some of the simple alkanes as we begin the introduction to organic compounds. We look at 3-dimensional structure and name some of the smaller alkanes.

Laboratory Suggestions

Lab 22 Structures of Alkanes

From models of alkanes, students write structural formulas and names. Models of alkane isomers are observed and their complete structural formulas, condensed structural formulas, and names are written.
A. Structures of Alkanes
B. Constitutional Isomers
C. Cycloalkanes
D. Haloalkanes

Laboratory Skills to Demonstrate

The concept of constitutional isomers can be demonstrated with the model kits as a process of breaking a bond and attaching a group to a different part of the chain.
Writing condensed formulas from the complete structural formula.
Using a model kit to make a cycloalkane.

Answers and Solutions to Text Problems

12.1 **a.** The formula C_nH_{2n+2} indicates an alkane with a formula C_7H_{16}.
b. The formula C_nH_{2n+2} indicates $2(5)+2=12$ H atoms.
c. The formula C_nH_{2n+2} indicates H atoms $=(10-2)/2=4$ C atoms

12.2 **a.** C_9H_{20} **b.** $2 \times 8 + 2 = 18$ H atoms   **c.** $(26-2)+2=12$ C atoms

12.3 **a.** In expanded formulas, each C—H and each C—C bond is drawn separately.

$$\begin{array}{ccc} H & H & H \\ | & | & | \\ H-C-C-C-H \\ | & | & | \\ H & H & H \end{array}$$

b. A condensed formula groups hydrogen atoms with each carbon atom.
$CH_3-CH_2-CH_2-CH_2-CH_2-CH_3$

c. A line-bond formula shows only the bonds connecting the carbon atoms.

12.4 **a.**
$$\begin{array}{cccc} H & H & H & H \\ | & | & | & | \\ H-C-C-C-C-H \\ | & | & | & | \\ H & H & H & H \end{array}$$
b. $CH_3-CH_2-CH_2-CH_2-CH_2-CH_2-CH_2-CH_3$

c.

12.5 **a.** Pentane is a carbon chain of five (5) carbon atoms.
b. Heptane is a carbon chain of seven (7) carbon atoms.
c. Hexane is a carbon chain of six (6) carbon atoms.

12.6   **a.** methane   **b.** nonane   **c.** propane

12.7   Constitutional isomers have the same molecular formula, but different structural formulas. A different conformation of the same structure occurs when rotation about a single bond moves the attached groups into different positions, but does not change the arrangement of atoms.
      a. The same structure with two different conformations
      b. Same molecular formula, but different structures, which are constitutional isomers.
      c. Same molecular formula, but different structures, which are constitutional isomers.

12.8   **a.** constitutional isomers   **b.** constitutional isomers
      c. different conformations (same compound)

12.9   The alkyl name for a hydrocarbon substituent uses the name of the alkane, but changes the ending to –yl.
      a. propyl (from propane)   **b.** isopropyl
      c. butyl (from butane)   **d.** methyl (from methane)

12.10   **a.** ethyl   **b.** isobutyl   **c.** secondary (*sec-*) butyl   **d.** tertiary (*tert-*) butyl

12.11   **a.** 2-methylpropane has a chain of three carbon atoms with a methyl group on carbon 2.
      b. 2-methylpentane has a chain of five carbon atoms with a methyl group on carbon 2.
      c. 4-ethyl-2-methylhexane has a chain of six carbon atoms with a methyl group on carbon 2 closest to the end of the main chain, and an ethyl group on carbon 4. Ethyl is listed first alphabetically.
      d. 2,3,4-trimethylheptane is a main chain of seven carbon atoms with methyl groups on carbons 2, 3, and 4.
      e. 5-isopropyl-3-methyloctane is a main chain of eight carbons with a methyl group on carbon 3 and an isopropyl group (named first alphabetically) on carbon 5.

12.12   **a.** 2,3-dimethylbutane   **b.** 3-ethyl-3,4-dimethylhexane
      c. 2.4-dimethyl-5-propyloctane   **d.** 4-ethyl-3-methylheptane
      e. 3-ethyl-5-isopropyl-6-methylnonane

12.13   For line-bond formulas, carbon atoms are counted from the end of the chain and at each corner.
      a. 2,3-dimethylpentane   **b.** 3-ethyl-5-methylheptane
      c. 3-isopropyl-2,4-dimethylpentane

12.14   **a.** 3,4-diethylheptane   **b.** 2,3-dimethylhexane
      c. 2,3-dimethyl-4-*sec*-butylheptane

12.15   Draw the main chain with the number of carbon atoms in the ending. For example, butane has a main chain of 4 carbon atoms, and hexane has a main chain of 6 carbon atoms. Attach substituents on the carbon atoms indicated. For example, in 3-methylpentane, a CH_3— group is bonded to carbon 3 of a five-carbon chain.

$$\text{CH}_3$$
$$|$$
$$\text{CH}_3 \qquad \text{CH}-\text{CH}_3$$
$$| \qquad\qquad |$$
e. 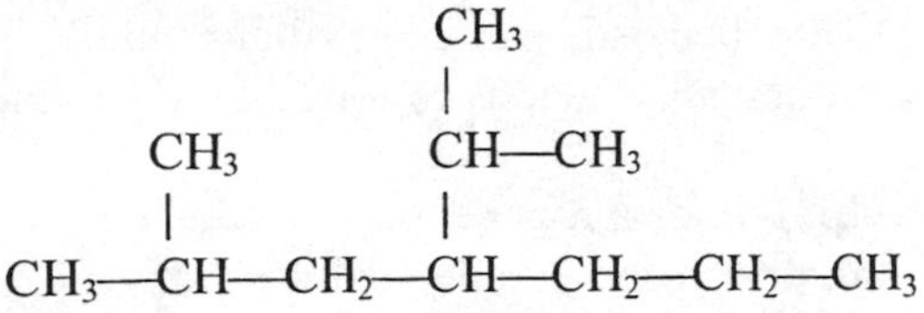 $\text{CH}_3-\text{CH}-\text{CH}_2-\text{CH}-\text{CH}_2-\text{CH}_2-\text{CH}_3$

$$\text{CH}_2-\text{CH}_2-\text{CH}_3$$
$$|$$
f. 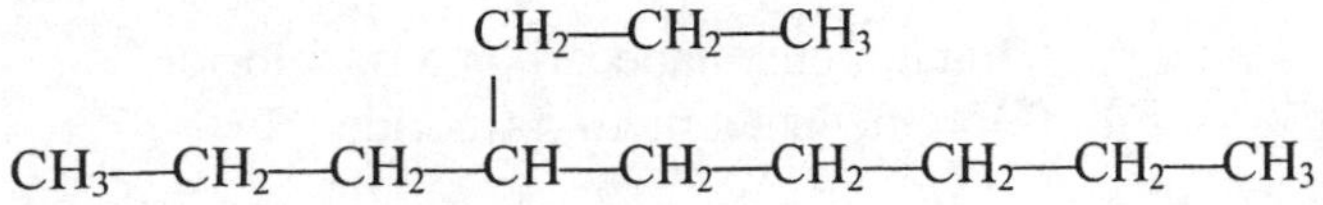 $\text{CH}_3-\text{CH}_2-\text{CH}_2-\text{CH}-\text{CH}_2-\text{CH}_2-\text{CH}_2-\text{CH}_2-\text{CH}_3$

12.16

$$\text{CH}_2\text{CH}_3$$
$$|$$
a. 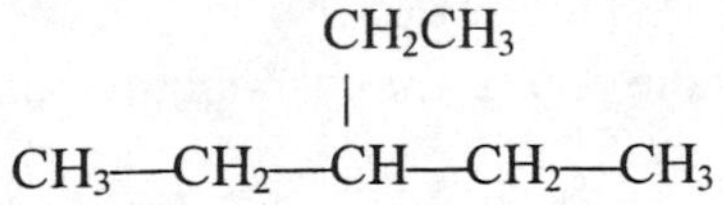 $\text{CH}_3-\text{CH}_2-\text{CH}-\text{CH}_2-\text{CH}_3$

$$\text{CH}_3 \quad \text{CH}_2\text{CH}_3$$
$$| \qquad |$$
b. 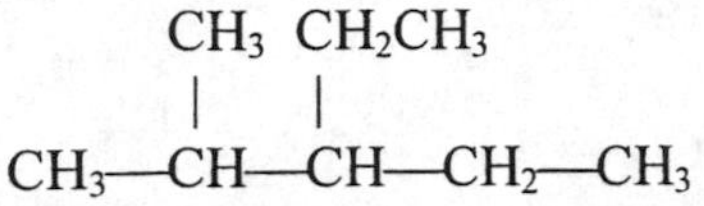 $\text{CH}_3-\text{CH}-\text{CH}-\text{CH}_2-\text{CH}_3$

$$\text{CH}_2\text{CH}_2\text{CH}_3$$
$$|$$
c. 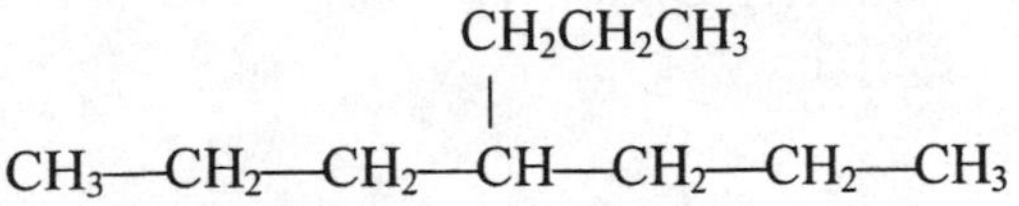 $\text{CH}_3-\text{CH}_2-\text{CH}_2-\text{CH}-\text{CH}_2-\text{CH}_2-\text{CH}_3$

$$\text{CH}_3 \quad \text{CH}_3 \qquad\quad \text{CH}_3$$
$$| \qquad | \qquad\qquad |$$
d. 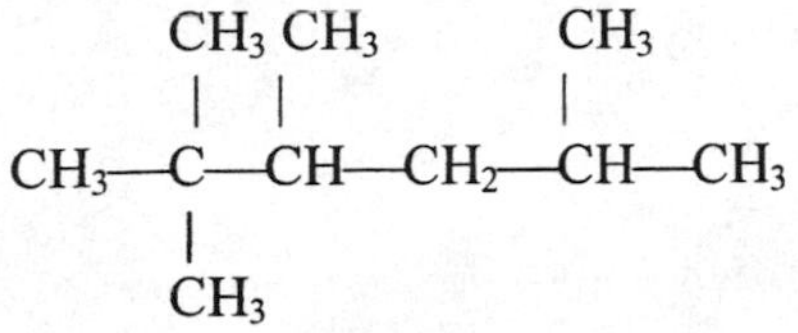 $\text{CH}_3-\text{C}-\text{CH}-\text{CH}_2-\text{CH}-\text{CH}_3$
$$|$$
$$\text{CH}_3$$

$$\text{CH}_3 \qquad\quad \text{CH}_2\text{CH}_3$$
$$| \qquad\qquad\quad |$$
e. 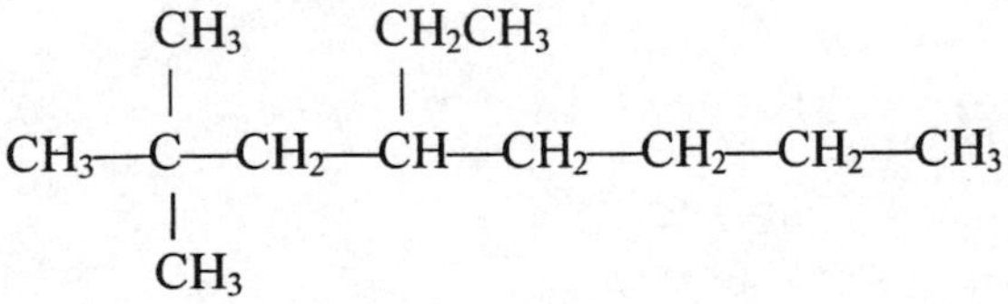 $\text{CH}_3-\text{C}-\text{CH}_2-\text{CH}-\text{CH}_2-\text{CH}_2-\text{CH}_2-\text{CH}_3$
$$|$$
$$\text{CH}_3$$

$$\text{CH}_3 \quad \text{CH}_2\text{CH}_3$$
$$| \qquad |$$
f. 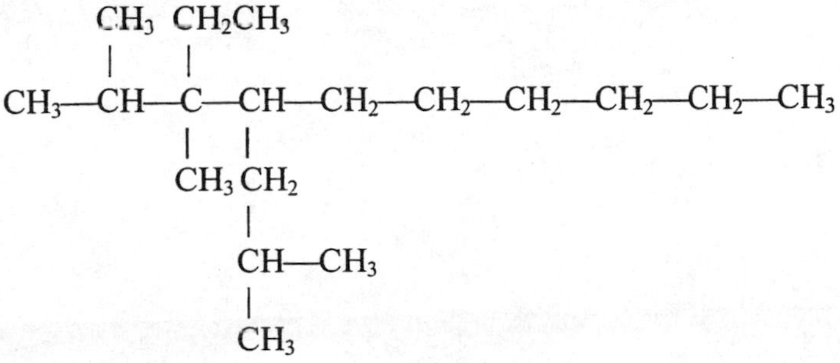 $\text{CH}_3-\text{CH}-\text{C}-\text{CH}-\text{CH}_2-\text{CH}_2-\text{CH}_2-\text{CH}_2-\text{CH}_2-\text{CH}_3$
$$| \quad |$$
$$\text{CH}_3 \ \text{CH}_2$$
$$|$$
$$\text{CH}-\text{CH}_3$$
$$|$$
$$\text{CH}_3$$

12.17 **a.** This problem wants the names of all the constitutional isomers that have a methyl group bonded to a seven-carbon chain: 2-methylheptane; 3-methylheptane; 4-methylheptane

b. This problem wants the names of all the constitutional isomers that have two methyl groups or an ethyl group bonded to a five-carbon chain;2,2-dimethylpentane; 3,3-dimethylpentane, 2,3-dimethylpentane; 2,4-dimethylpentane; 3-ethylpentane

12.18 **a.** The constitutional isomers that are octanes are 2-methyloctane, 3-methyloctane, 4-methyloctane.

b. The constitutional isomers that are dimethylhexanes are 2,2-dimethylhexane, 2,3-dimethylhexane, 2,4-dimethylhexane, 2,5-dimethylhexane, 3,3-dimethylhexane, 3,4-dimethylhexane

133

12.19 In the IUPAC system, the halogen substituent in haloalkanes is named as a halo- on the main chain of carbon atom; simple haloalkanes use common alkyl names followed by the name of the halogen.

    a. bromoethane, ethyl bromide   **b.** 1-fluoropropane, propyl fluoride

    c. 2-chloropropane, isopropyl chloride;   **d.** trichloromethane, chloroform
      sec-butylchloride

12.20 **a.** 2-chlorobutane   **b.** tetrachloromethanecarbon tetrachloride

    c. 2-iodo-2-methylpropane;   **d.** fluoromethane; methyl fluoride
      tert-butyliodide

12.21 **a.** 2-bromo-3-methylbutane   **b.** 3-bromo–2–chloropentane   **c.** 2-fluoro-2-methylbutane

12.22 **a.** 1,2,5-trichloropentane   **b.** 3,4-dibromoheptane   **c.** 4,4-dichloro-2,2-difluorohexane

12.23 **a.** $CH_3-\overset{\overset{\displaystyle Cl}{\displaystyle |}}{C}H-CH_3$ **b.** $CH_3-\overset{\overset{\displaystyle Br}{\displaystyle |}}{C}H-\overset{\overset{\displaystyle Cl}{\displaystyle |}}{C}H-CH_3$

    c. CH_3Br **d.** $CH_3-CH_2-CH_2-CH_2-Cl$

    e. $Br-\overset{\overset{\displaystyle Br}{\displaystyle |}}{C}H-\overset{\overset{\displaystyle Cl}{\displaystyle |}}{C}H-CH_2-\overset{\overset{\displaystyle F}{\displaystyle |}}{C}H-CH_3$ **f.** CBr_4

12.24 **a.** $Br-\overset{\overset{\displaystyle Br}{\displaystyle |}}{C}H-\underset{\underset{\displaystyle Br}{\displaystyle |}}{\overset{\overset{\displaystyle Br}{\displaystyle |}}{C}}-CH_3$ **b.** $CH_3-\underset{\underset{\displaystyle Br}{\displaystyle |}}{\overset{\overset{\displaystyle Br}{\displaystyle |}}{C}}-\overset{\overset{\displaystyle Cl}{\displaystyle |}}{C}H-\overset{\overset{\displaystyle Cl}{\displaystyle |}}{C}H-CH_3$

    c. $CH_3-\overset{\overset{\displaystyle CH_3}{\displaystyle |}}{C}H-Br$ **d.** CH_3-Cl

    e. $CH_3-\underset{\underset{\displaystyle CH_3}{\displaystyle |}}{\overset{\overset{\displaystyle Cl}{\displaystyle |}}{C}}-\overset{\overset{\displaystyle Cl}{\displaystyle |}}{C}H-CH_3$ **f.** $Cl-\underset{\underset{\displaystyle Br}{\displaystyle |}}{\overset{\overset{\displaystyle Cl}{\displaystyle |}}{C}}-Br$

12.25 Methyl chloride is CH_3Cl; ethyl chloride is CH_3-CH_2Cl.

12.26 $CH_3-\overset{\overset{\displaystyle Cl}{\displaystyle |}}{C}H-Cl$ $Cl-CH_2-CH_2-Cl$
      1,1-dichloroethane   1,2-dichloroethane

12.27 The isomers are written first using a four-carbon chain of butane and then with the three-carbon chain with a methyl group. To each carbon chain, a chlorine atom is attached to give different isomers.

    $Cl-CH_2-CH_2-CH_2-CH_3$ $CH_3-\overset{\overset{\displaystyle Cl}{\displaystyle |}}{C}H-CH_2-CH_3$
    1-chlorobutane   2-chlorobutane

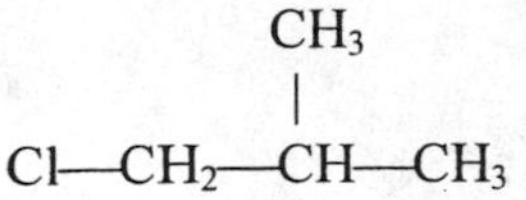

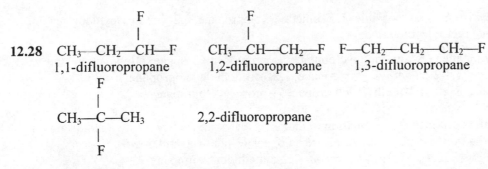

CH₃
|
Cl—CH₂—CH—CH₃

1-chloro-2-methylpropane

Cl
|
CH₂—C—CH₃
|
CH₃

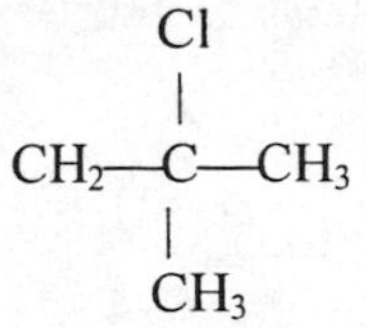

2-chloro-2-methylpropane

12.28
F
|
CH₃—CH₂—CH—F
1,1-difluoropropane

F
|
CH₃—CH—CH₂—F
1,2-difluoropropane

F—CH₂—CH₂—CH₂—F
1,3-difluoropropane

F
|
CH₃—C—CH₃
|
F

2,2-difluoropropane

12.29 The general formula for cycloalkanes is C_nH_{2n}.
 a. n = 5 C atoms; $2n$ = 10 H atoms; C_5H_{10}
 b. n = 4 C atoms; $2n$ = 8 H atoms; C_4H_8
 c. $2n$ = 12 H atoms; n = 6 C atoms; C_6H_{12}

12.30 C_nH_{2n}
 a. C_6H_{12} **b.** 5 × 2 = 10 H atoms **c.** 16 H atoms/2 = 8 C atoms

12.31 **a.** A ring of four carbon atoms is cyclobutane.
 b. A ring of five carbon atoms with one chlorine atom is chlorocyclopentane; no numbering is needed for a single substituent.
 c. A ring of six carbon atoms with one methyl group is methylcyclohexane; no numbering is needed for a single substituent.
 d. 1-bromo-3-methylcyclobutane
 e. 1-bromo-2-chlorocyclopentane
 f. 1,3-dibromo-5-methylcyclohexane

12.32 **a.** 1,2-dichlorocyclobutane **b.** 1-bromo-2-methylcyclopentane
 c. 1-ethyl-1-methylcyclohexane **d.** 1,1-dimethylcyclopropane
 e. 1-bromo-3-propylcyclobutane **f.** 1,3-dichlorocyclohexane

12.33 Draw the cyclic structure first, and then attach the substituents. When there are two or more substituents, start with the first on a carbon assigned number 1 and continue around the ring.

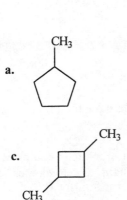

135

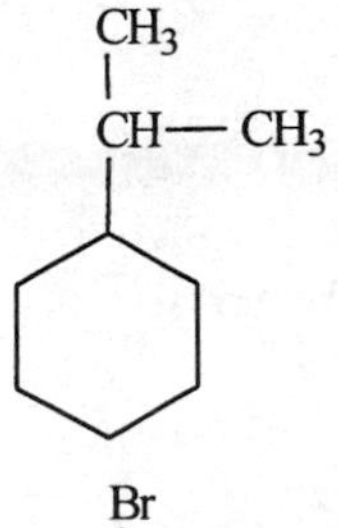

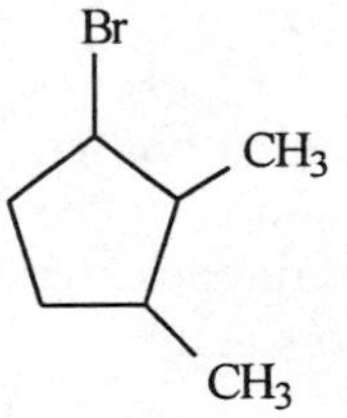

12.34

a.   b. 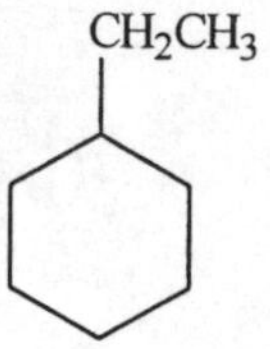   c. 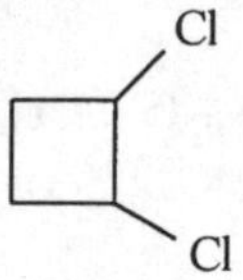   d.

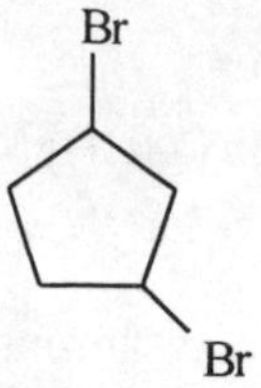

12.35 Four constitutional isomers are possible: 1,1-dimethylcyclopropane, 1,2-dimethylcyclopropane, ethylcyclopropane, methylcyclobutane.

12.36 1,1-dimethylcyclobutane; 1,2-dimethylcyclobutane; isopropylcyclopropane; ethylcyclobutane; methylcyclopentane; 1,1,2-trimethylcyclopropane, 1,2,3-trimethylcyclopropane; 1-ethyl-2-methylcyclopropane; 1-ethyl-1-methylcyclopropane; 1-propylcyclopropane

12.37 Cis and trans isomers differ in the orientation of atoms in space. In cis isomer, two atoms are on the same side; in the trans isomer, two atoms are on opposite sides (up and down).
a. Does not have *cis-, trans* isomers   **b.** *trans*-1,2-dimethylcyclopropane
c. *cis*-1,2-dichlorocyclobutane   **d.** *trans*-1,3-dimethylcyclopentane

12.38 **a.** *trans*-1,4-dichlorocyclohexane   **b.** *trans*-1-ethyl-3-methylcyclobutane
c. methylcyclohexane   **d.** *cis*-1,2-dimethylcyclohexane

12.39 In a cis isomer, two atoms or groups are written on the same side (both up or both down). In the trans isomer, two atoms or groups are written on opposite sides (up and down).

a.   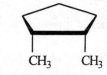   b.   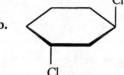   c.

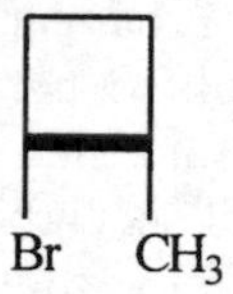

12.40

a.   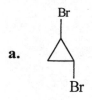   b.   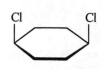   c.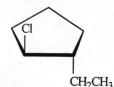

12.41 Alkanes are nonpolar and less dense than water.
a. CH₃—CH₂—CH₂—CH₂—CH₂—CH₂—CH₃   **b.** liquid
c. Insoluble in water   **d.** float
e. Lower

12.42 **a.** CH₃—CH₂—CH₂—CH₂—CH₂—CH₂—CH₂—CH₂—CH₃
b. liquid
c. No, nonane is insoluble in water.
d. Nonane floats in water.
e. Because nonane has more carbon atoms than heptane, nonane would have the higher boiling point of 151°C.

12.43 Longer carbon chains have higher boiling points. The boiling points of branched alkanes are usually lower than the same number of carbon atoms in a continuous chain. Cycloalkanes have higher boiling points than continuous-chain alkanes.
a. Heptane has a longer carbon chain.
b. Cyclopropane
c. The continuous chain hexane has a higher boiling point than its branched chain isomer.

12.44 **a.** butane; greater molar mass
b. cyclohexane; cycloalkanes have rigid structures that stack closely requiring higher boiling points than the corresponding alkane.
c. heptane ; the continuous chain alkanes are less compact, which allows more contact between molecules, and require higher boiling points.

12.45 In combustion, a hydrocarbon reacts with oxygen to yield CO_2 and H_2O.
a. $2C_2H_6 + 7O_2 \longrightarrow 4CO_2 + 6H_2O$ **b.** $2C_3H_6 + 9O_2 \longrightarrow 6CO_2 + 6H_2O$
c. $2C_8H_{18} + 25O_2 \longrightarrow 16CO_2 + 18H_2O$ **d.** $C_6H_{12} + 9O_2 \longrightarrow 6CO_2 + 6H_2O$

12.46 **a.** $2C_6H_{14} + 19O_2 \longrightarrow 12CO_2 + 14H_2O$ **b.** $2C_5H_{10} + 15O_2 \longrightarrow 10CO_2 + 10H_2O$
c. $C_9H_{20} + 14O_2 \longrightarrow 9CO_2 + 10H_2O$ **d.** $C_5H_{12} + 8O_2 \longrightarrow 5CO_2 + 6H_2O$

12.47 a. $CH_3—CH_2—Cl$ **b.**

c. $CH_3—\overset{\overset{\textstyle CH_3}{|}}{CH}—CH_2—Cl$ $CH_3—\overset{\overset{\textstyle CH_3}{|}}{\underset{\underset{\textstyle Cl}{|}}{C}}—CH_3$

12.48 **a.** $CH_3—CH_2—CH_2—CH_2 + Br_2 \longrightarrow CH_3—\overset{\overset{\textstyle Br}{|}}{CH}—CH_2—CH_3 + HBr$

b. $CH_3—CH_2—CH_2—CH_2—CH_2 + Br_2 \longrightarrow CH_3—\overset{\overset{\textstyle Br}{|}}{CH}—CH_2—CH_2—CH_3 + HBr$
and

$CH_3—CH_2—\overset{\overset{\textstyle Br}{|}}{CH}—CH_2—CH_3 + HBr$ and $Br—CH_3—CH_2—CH_2—CH_2—CH_3$

c. 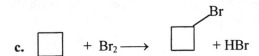 $+ Br_2 \longrightarrow$ $+ HBr$

12.49 Constitutional isomers have the same molecular formulas, but different arrangements of atoms.
a. constitutional isomers   **b.** constitutional isomers
c. same molecule   **d.** constitutional isomers

12.50 **a.** constitutional isomers   **b.** constitutional isomers
c. same molecule   **d.** constitutional isomers

12.51 The alkyl name for a hydrocarbon substituent uses the name of the alkane, but changes the ending to –yl.
a. methyl   **b.** propyl   **c.** isopropyl

12.52 **a.** ethyl   **b.** secondary (*sec-*) butyl   **c.** tertiary (*tert-*) butyl

12.53 Identify the longest carbon chain and number it from the end closest to the first substituent. Use the prefix di- when two substituents are identical.
a. 2,2-dimethylbutane   **b.** chloroethane
c. 2-bromo-4-ethylhexane   **d.** 1,1-dibromocyclohexane

12.54 **a.** 1-bromo-4-isopropylcyclohexane   **b.** 5-*sec*-butylnonane
  c. 3-methylhexane   **d.** 4-ethyl-3-methyloctane

12.55 Write the carbon atom in the main chain first. Attach the substituents listed in front of the alkane name or use the alkyl group indicated.

$$
\text{CH}_2\!-\!\text{CH}_3
$$

a. 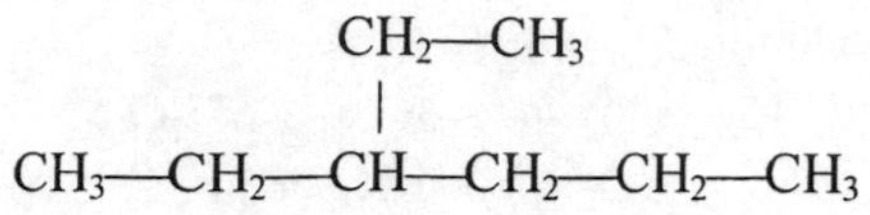 CH₃—CH₂—CH—CH₂—CH₂—CH₃

$$
\text{CH}_3 \quad \text{CH}_3
$$

b. 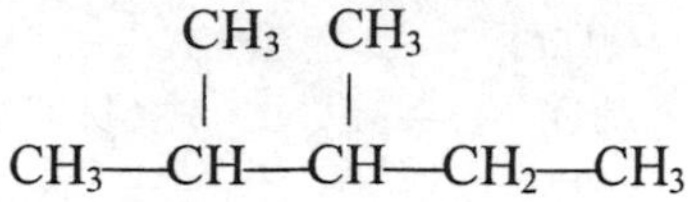 CH₃—CH—CH—CH₂—CH₃

$$
\text{Cl}
$$

c. 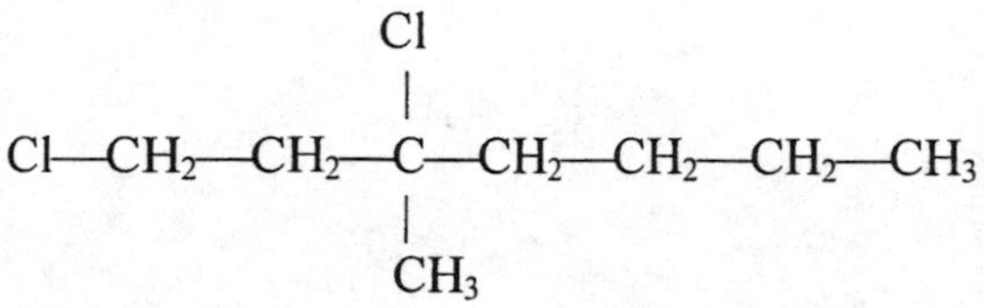 Cl—CH₂—CH₂—C—CH₂—CH₂—CH₂—CH₃

$$
\text{CH}_3
$$

d.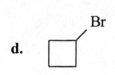

e. 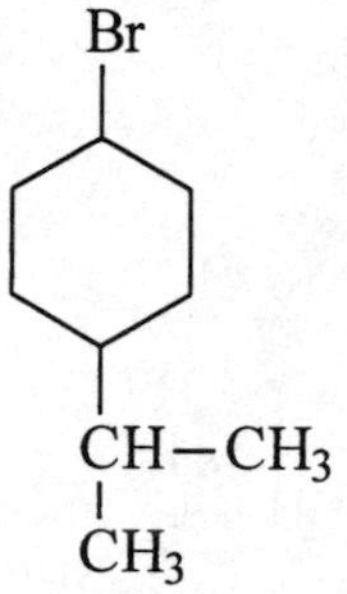
Br
(cyclohexane ring with Br at top and)
CH—CH₃
|
CH₃

$$
\text{CH}_3
$$

f. 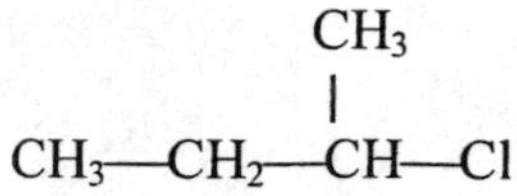 CH₃—CH₂—CH—Cl

12.56

a.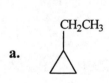
CH₂CH₃
(cyclopropane)

b. 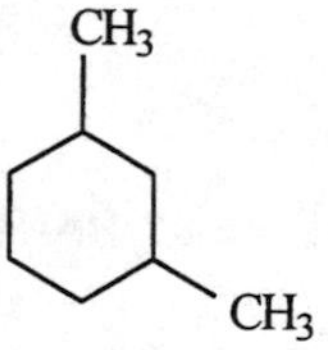
CH₃
(cyclohexane ring)
CH₃

c. 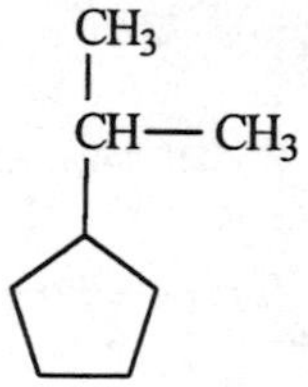
CH₃
|
CH—CH₃
(cyclopentane)

d. 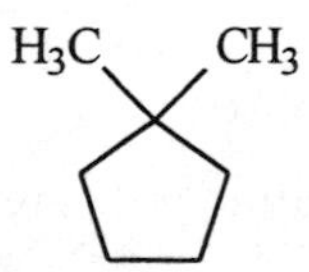
H₃C   CH₃
(cyclopentane)

e. 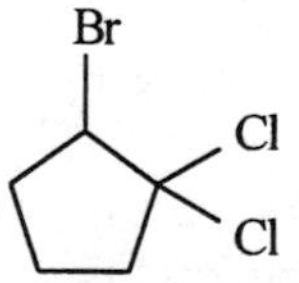
Br
Cl
Cl
(cyclopentane)

f. 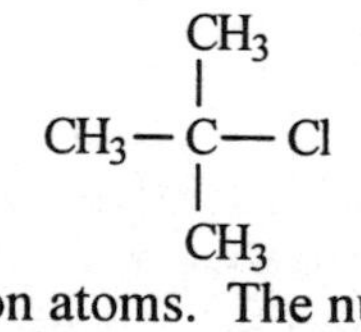
CH₃
|
CH₃—C—Cl
|
CH₃

12.57 A line-bond formula shows only the bonds connecting the carbon atoms. The number of bonds to hydrogen atoms is understood.

a.  (line structure)   **b.** 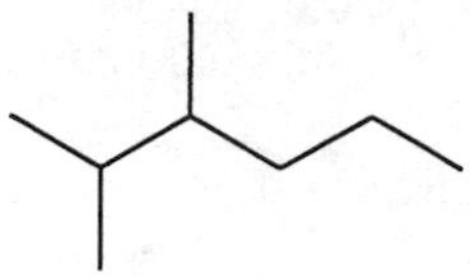 (line structure)   **c.** 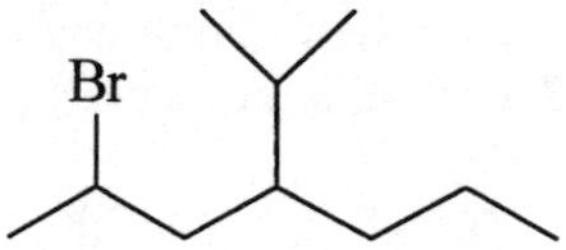 (line structure with Br)

12.58

a.  (line structure)   **b.** 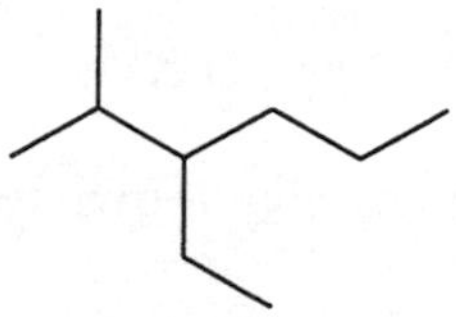 (line structure)   **c.** 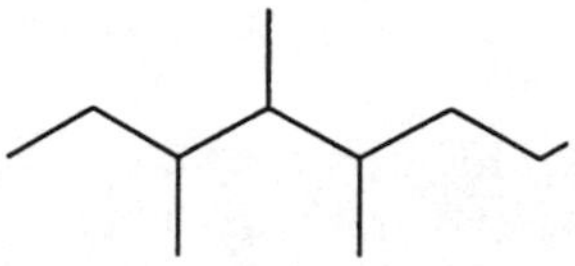 (line structure)

12.59 **a.** You should have two of the following possibilities.

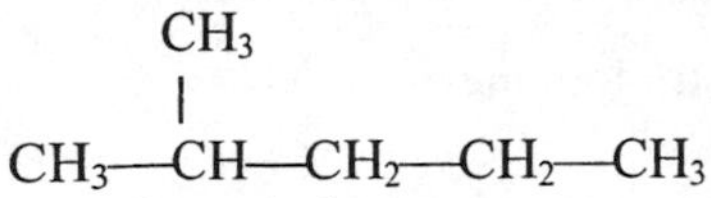

$$CH_3$$
$$|$$
$$CH_3—CH—CH_2—CH_2—CH_3$$
2-methylpentane

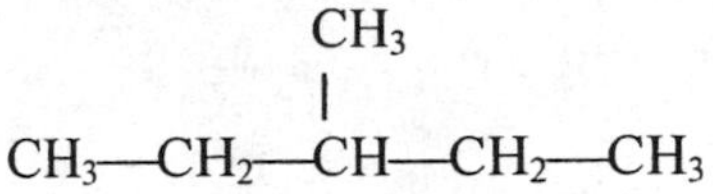

$$CH_3$$
$$|$$
$$CH_3—CH_2—CH—CH_2—CH_3$$
3-methylpentane

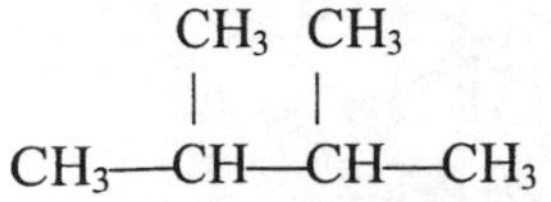

$$CH_3 \quad CH_3$$
$$| \qquad |$$
$$CH_3—CH—CH—CH_3$$
2,3-dimethylbutane

$$CH_3—CH_2—CH_2—CH_2—CH_2—CH_3$$
Hexane

b. The molecular formula C_7H_{16} has the following constitutional isomers:

$$CH_3—CH_2—CH_2—CH_2—CH_2—CH_2—CH_3 \quad \text{heptane}$$

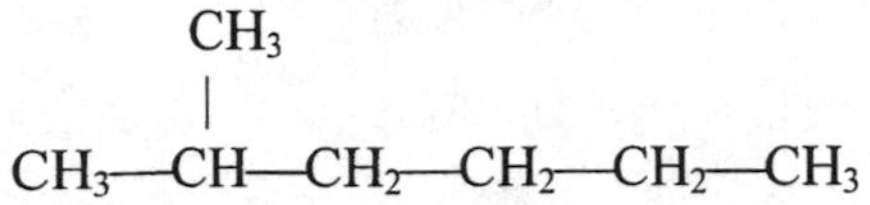

$$CH_3$$
$$|$$
$$CH_3—CH—CH_2—CH_2—CH_2—CH_3 \qquad \text{2-methylhexane}$$

$$CH_3$$
$$|$$
$$CH_3—CH_2—CH—CH_2—CH_2—CH_3 \qquad \text{3-methylhexane}$$

$$CH_3$$
$$|$$
$$CH_3—C—CH_2—CH_2—CH_3 \qquad \text{2,2-dimethylpentane}$$ 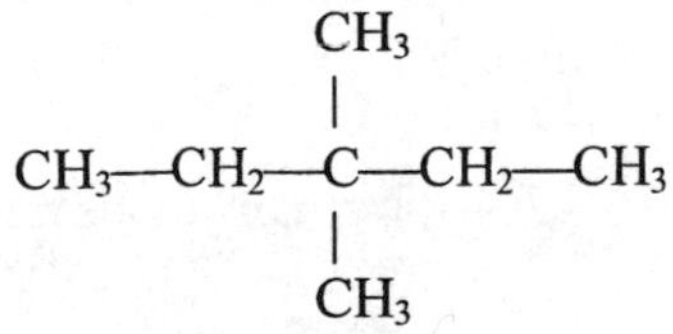
$$|$$
$$CH_3$$

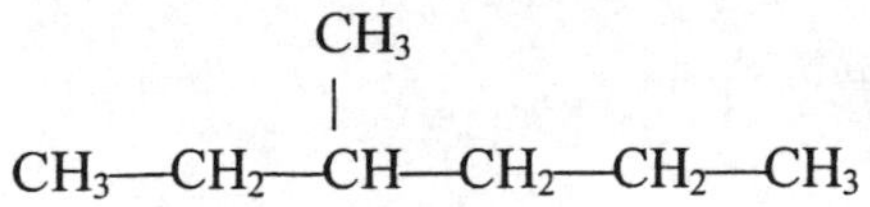

$$CH_3$$
$$|$$
$$CH_3—CH_2—C—CH_2—CH_3 \qquad \text{3,3-dimethylpentane}$$ 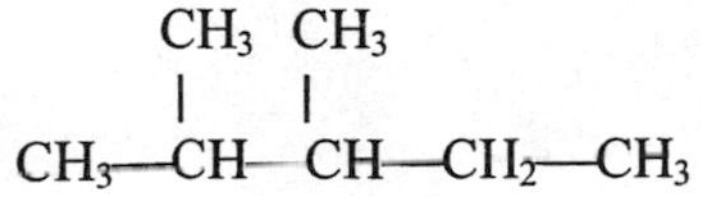
$$|$$
$$CH_3$$

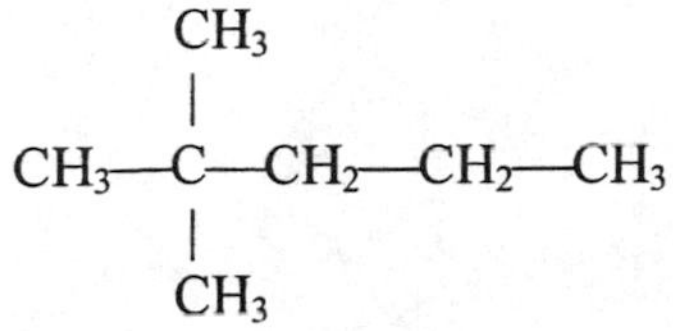

$$CH_3 \quad CH_3$$
$$| \qquad |$$
$$CH_3—CH—CH—CII_2—CH_3 \qquad \text{2,3-dimethylpentane}$$

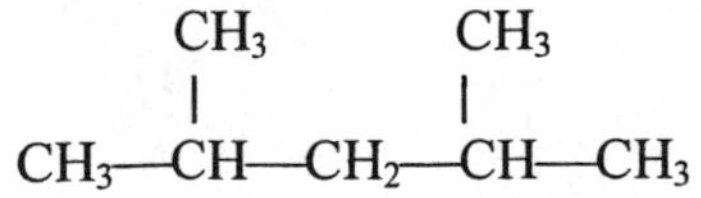

$$CH_3 \qquad\qquad CH_3$$
$$| \qquad\qquad\quad |$$
$$CH_3—CH—CH_2—CH—CH_3 \qquad \text{2,4-dimethylpentane}$$

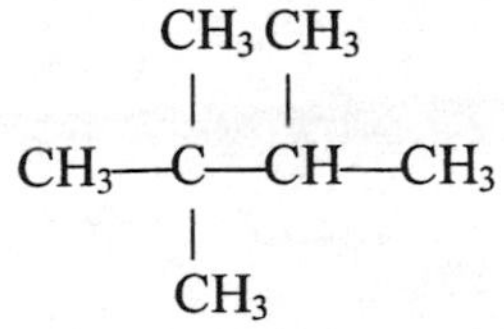

$$CH_3 \; CH_3$$
$$| \quad |$$
$$CH_3—C—CH—CH_3 \qquad \text{2,2,3-trimethylbutane}$$
$$|$$
$$CH_3$$

c. $CH_3—CH_2—CH_2—CH_2—CH_2—CH_3 \qquad \text{hexane}$

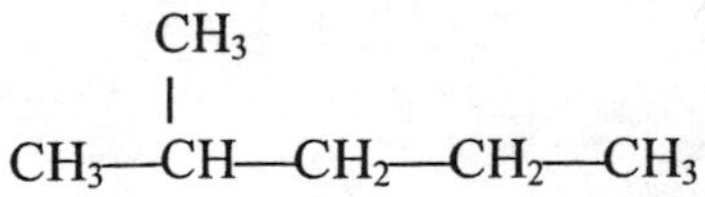

$$CH_3$$
$$|$$
$$CH_3—CH—CH_2—CH_2—CH_3 \qquad \text{2-methylpentane}$$

$$CH_3$$
$$|$$
$$CH_3—CH_2—CH—CH_2—CH_3 \qquad \text{3-methylpentane}$$

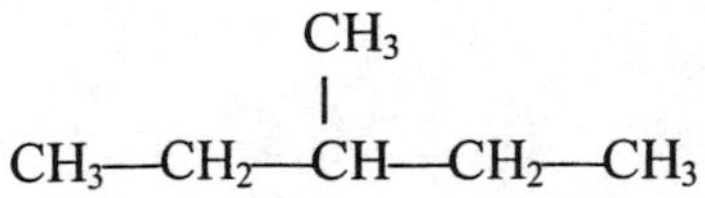

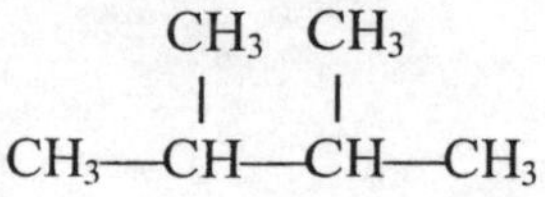

2,3-dimethylbutane

d.

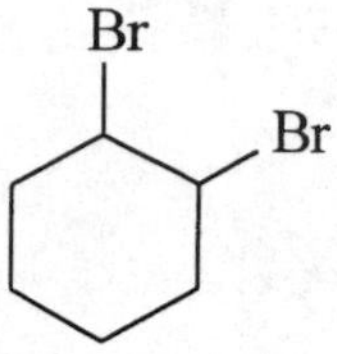

1,2-dibromocyclohexane

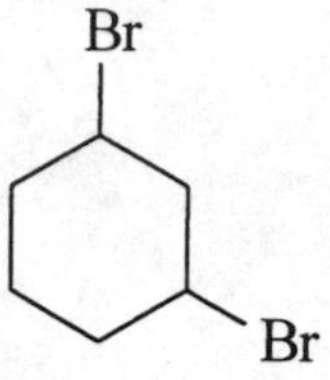

1,3-dibromocyclohexane

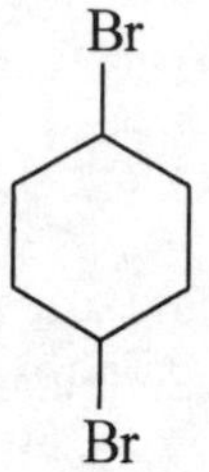

1,4-dibromocyclohexane

12.60 **a.** 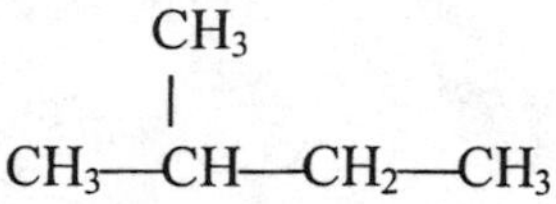

2-methylbutane

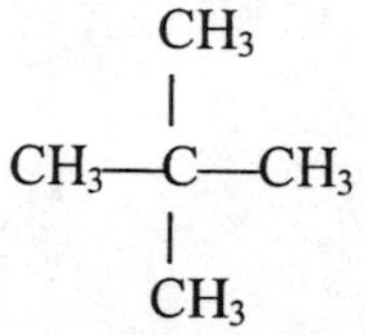

2,2-dimethylpropane

b.

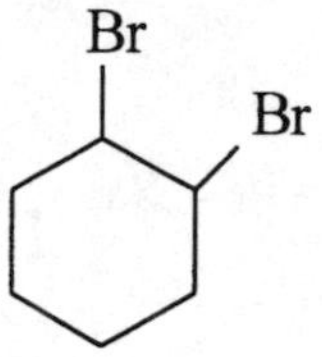

1,2-dibromocyclohexane

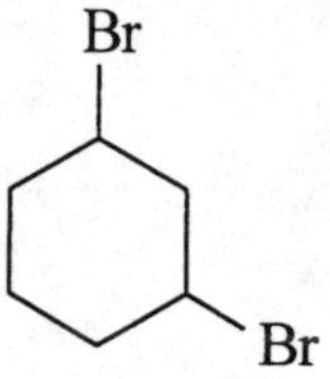

1,3-dibromocyclohexane

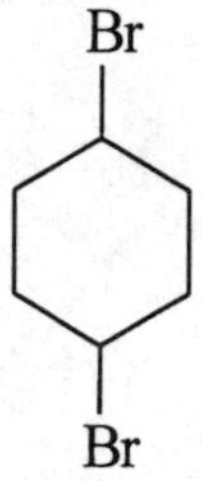

1,4-dibromocyclohexane

c. Only butanes shown

Cl—CH_2—CH_2—CH_2—CH_2—Cl 1,4-dichlorobutane

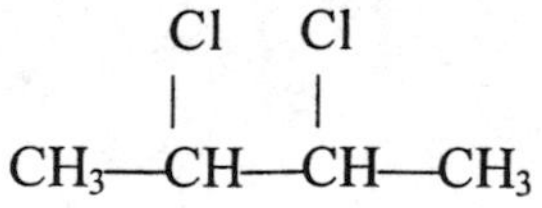

2,3-dichlorobutane

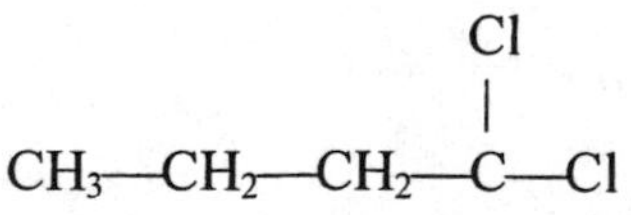

1,1-dichlorobutane

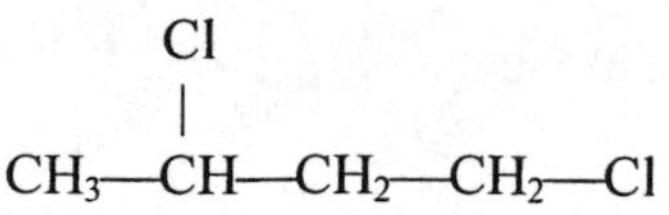

1,3-dichlorobutane

d.

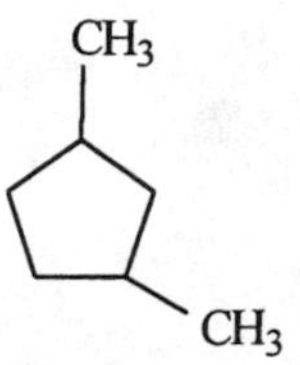

1,3-dimethylcyclopentane

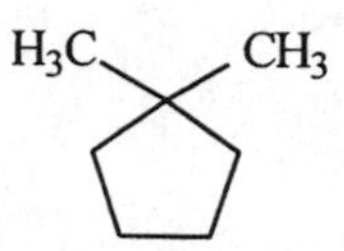

1,1-dimethylcyclopentane

12.61 Draw the structure and then write the correct name using IUPAC rules.
   a. 2-methylbutane   **b.** 2,3-dimethylpentane
   c. 1,3-dibromocyclohexane   **d.** hexane

12.62 **a.** hexane   **b.** 3-methylhexane
         c. 1,2-dichlorocyclopentane   **d.** 2,3-dimethylpentane

12.63 All of the following are constitutional isomers of $C_5H_{11}Cl$. You should have six.

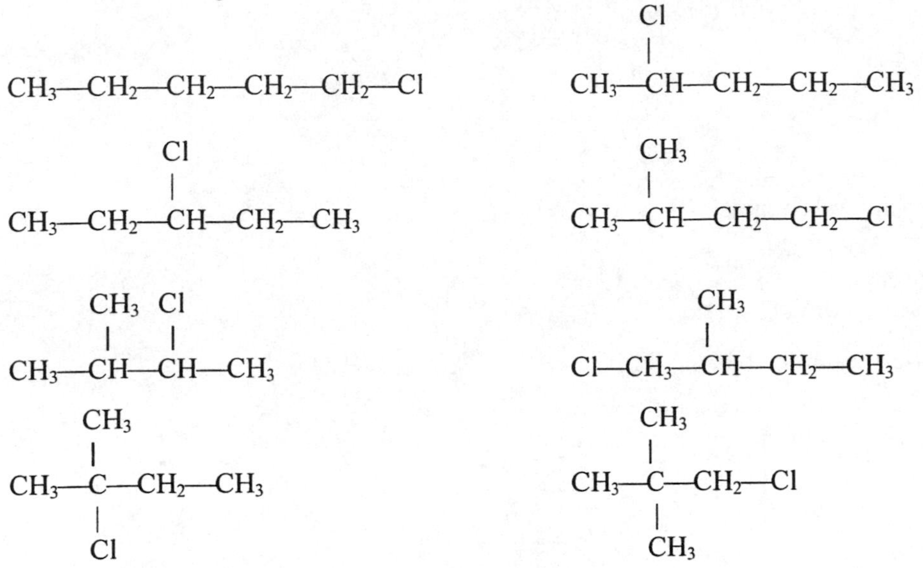

$$CH_3-CH_2-CH_2-CH_2-CH_2-Cl$$

$$\underset{\displaystyle CH_3-CH-CH_2-CH_2-CH_3}{\overset{\displaystyle Cl}{\vert}}$$

$$\underset{\displaystyle CH_3-CH_2-CH-CH_2-CH_3}{\overset{\displaystyle Cl}{\vert}}$$

$$\underset{\displaystyle CH_3-CH-CH_2-CH_2-Cl}{\overset{\displaystyle CH_3}{\vert}}$$

$$\underset{\displaystyle CH_3-CH-CH-CH_3}{\overset{\displaystyle CH_3\;\;\;\;Cl}{\vert\;\;\;\;\vert}}$$

$$\underset{\displaystyle Cl-CH_3-CH-CH_2-CH_3}{\overset{\displaystyle CH_3}{\vert}}$$

$$\overset{\displaystyle CH_3}{\underset{\displaystyle Cl}{\vert\atop CH_3-C-CH_2-CH_3\atop\vert}}$$

$$\overset{\displaystyle CH_3}{\underset{\displaystyle CH_3}{\vert\atop CH_3-C-CH_2-Cl\atop\vert}}$$

12.64 $\underset{\displaystyle CH_3-CH=CH-CH-Br}{\overset{\displaystyle Br}{\vert}}$ $\underset{\displaystyle CH_3-CH-C=CH_2}{\overset{\displaystyle Br\;\;\;\;Br}{\vert\;\;\;\;\vert}}$

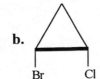

   and others

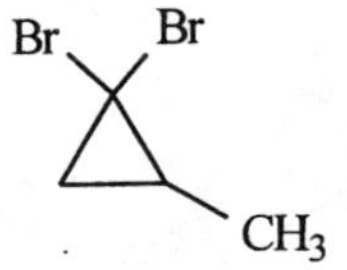

12.65 **a.** $\underset{\displaystyle CH_3-CH_2-CH-Br}{\overset{\displaystyle CH_3}{\vert}}$

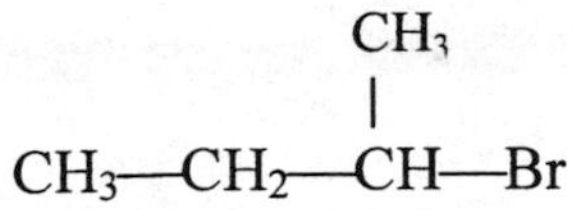

b. 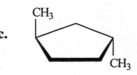   **c.** 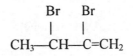   **d.**

12.66

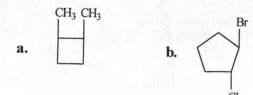

a.

b.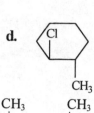

c. 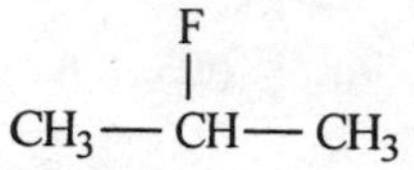
$$F$$
$$CH_3-CH-CH_3$$

d.

12.67 Condensed structural formula

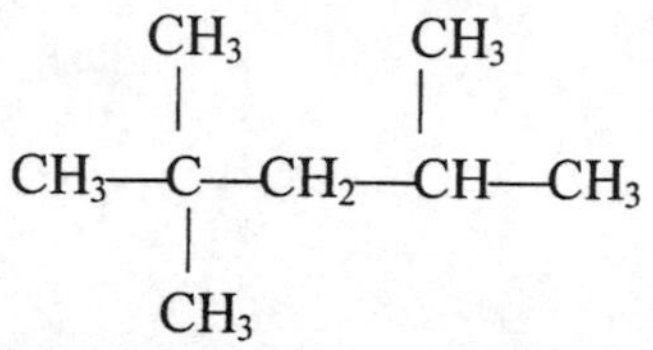

$$CH_3-C-CH_2-CH-CH_3$$

with CH_3 groups

molecular formula of C_8H_{18}

The combustion reaction: $2C_8H_{18} + 25O_2 \longrightarrow 16CO_2 + 18H_2O$

12.68

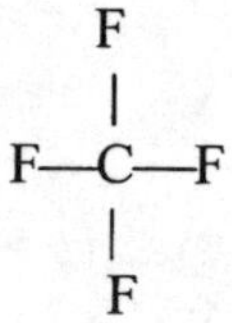

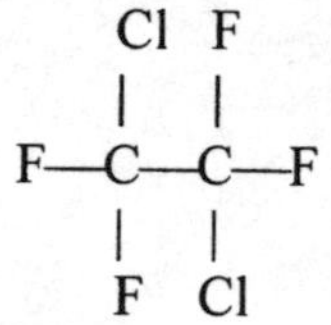

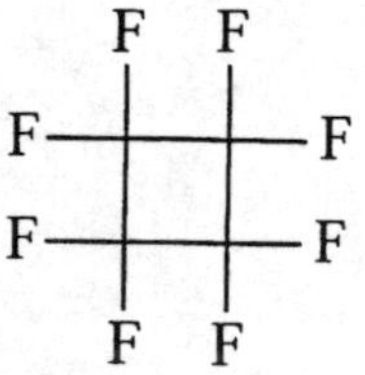

$$F-C-F$$ (with F above and below)

$$F-C-C-F$$ (with Cl, F above and F, Cl below)

(cyclobutane with F groups)

12.69 a. heptane b. cyclopentane
c. hexane d. cyclohexane

12.70 a. octane b. cyclopentane c. cyclohexane d. pentane

12.71 a. $C_3H_8 + 5O_2 \longrightarrow 3CO_2 + 4H_2O$
b. $C_5H_{12} + 8O_2 \longrightarrow 5CO_2 + 6H_2O$
c. $C_4H_8 + 6O_2 \longrightarrow 4CO_2 + 4H_2O$
d. $2C_8H_{18} + 25O_2 \longrightarrow 16CO_2 + 18H_2O$

12.72 a. $2C_6H_{14} + 19O_2 \longrightarrow 12CO_2 + 14H_2O$
b. $2C_7H_{14} + 21O_2 \longrightarrow 14CO_2 + 14H_2O$
c. $2C_5H_{10} + 15O_2 \longrightarrow 10CO_2 + 10H_2O$
d. $2C_4H_{10} + 13O_2 \longrightarrow 8CO_2 + 10H_2O$

12.73 a. CH_3-CH_2-Cl

b. $CH_3-CH_2-CH_2-Cl$ and $CH_3-CH-CH_3$ (with Cl above)

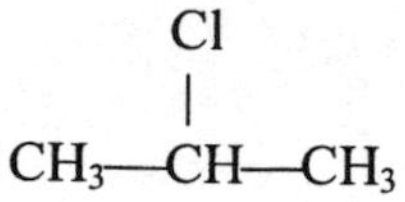

c. 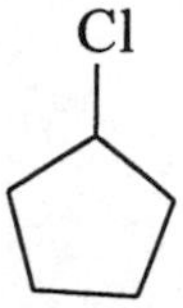 (cyclopentane with Cl substituent)

12.74 **a.**

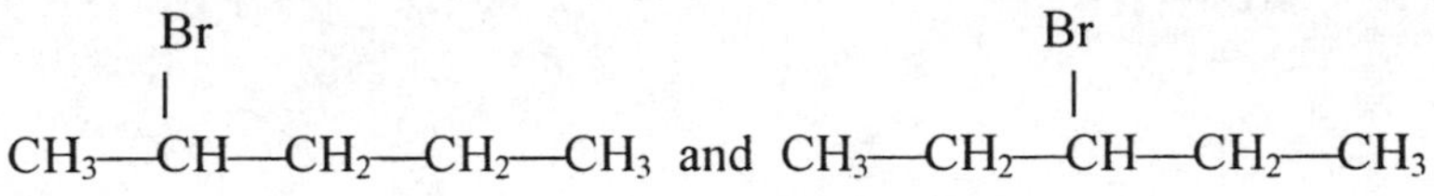

$$\overset{\overset{\displaystyle Br}{|}}{CH_3-CH-CH_2-CH_2-CH_3} \text{ and } \overset{\overset{\displaystyle Br}{|}}{CH_3-CH_2-CH-CH_2-CH_3}$$

and $Br-CH-CH_2-CH_2-CH_2-CH_3$

b.

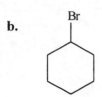

c.

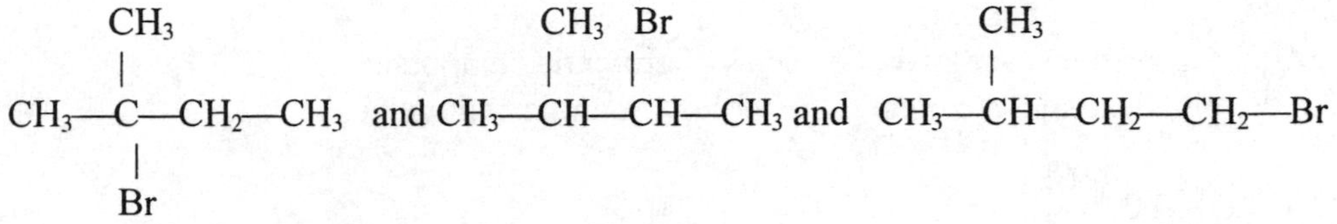

$$\overset{\overset{\displaystyle CH_3}{|}}{\underset{\underset{\displaystyle Br}{|}}{CH_3-C-CH_2-CH_3}} \text{ and } \overset{\overset{\displaystyle CH_3}{|}}{CH_3-CH-\overset{\overset{\displaystyle Br}{|}}{CH}-CH_3} \text{ and } \overset{\overset{\displaystyle CH_3}{|}}{CH_3-CH-CH_2-CH_2-Br}$$

And $\overset{\overset{\displaystyle CH_3}{|}}{Br-CH_2-CH-CH_2-CH_3}$

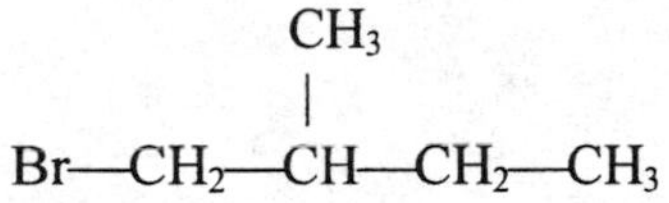

12.75 **a.** $C_5H_{12} + 8O_2 \longrightarrow 5CO_2 + 6H_2O$
b. 72.0 g/mole
c. $1 \text{ gal} \times \dfrac{3.78 \text{ L}}{1 \text{ gal}} \times \dfrac{1000 \text{ mL}}{1 \text{ L}} \times \dfrac{0.63 \text{ g}}{1 \text{ mL}} \times \dfrac{1 \text{ mole } C_5H_{12}}{72.0 \text{ g}} \times \dfrac{845 \text{ kcal}}{1 \text{ mole}} = 2.8 \times 10^4 \text{ kcal}$
d. $1 \text{ gal} \times \dfrac{3.78 \text{ L}}{1 \text{ gal}} \times \dfrac{1000 \text{ mL}}{1 \text{ L}} \times \dfrac{0.63 \text{ g}}{1 \text{ mL}} \times \dfrac{1 \text{ mole } C_5H_{12}}{72.0 \text{ g}} \times \dfrac{5 \text{ moles } CO_2}{1 \text{ mole } C_5H_{12}} \times \dfrac{22.4 \text{ L}}{1 \text{ mole}} = 3700 \text{ L}$

Study Goals

- Describe the physical and chemical properties of aromatic compounds.
- Write IUPAC and common names for alkenes and alkynes.
- Write structural formulas and names for cis-trans isomers of alkenes.
- Write equations for halogenation, hydration, and hydrogenation of alkenes and alkynes.
- Describe the formation of a polymer from alkene monomers.
- Describe the bonding in benzene.
- Write structural formulas and give the names of aromatic compounds.
- Describe the physical and chemical properties of aromatic compounds.

Chapter Outline

13.1   **Alkenes and Alkynes**
13.2   **Naming Alkenes and Alkynes**
        Explore Your World: Ripening Fruit
        Environmental Note: Fragrant Alkenes
13.3   **Cis-Trans Isomers of Alkenes**
        Explore Your World: Modeling Cis-Trans Isomers
        Health Note: Pheromones in Insect Communication
        Health Note: Cis-Trans Isomers for Night Vision
13.4   **Addition Reactions**
        Explore Your World: Unsaturation in Fats and Oils
        Health Note: Hydrogenation of Unsaturated Fats
13.5   **Polymerization**
        Explore Your World: Polymers and Recycling Plastics
13.6   **Aromatic Compounds**
        Health Note: Aromatic Compounds in Health and Medicine
        Health Note: Polycyclic Aromatic Hydrocarbons (PAHs)
13.7   **Properties of Aromatic Compounds**

Chapter Summary and Demonstrations

1. Functional Groups

The concept of functional groups is introduced. The IUPAC system and some common names are used to describe the nomenclature of alkenes and alkynes as unsaturated compounds. The cis-trans isomers and their name of alkenes are described.

2. Reactions of Alkenes

The reactive nature of unsaturated compounds is shown in the reactions, catalysts, and products of hydrogenation, hydrohalogenation, halogenation and hydration. Special interest topics include the chlorinated hydrocarbons used as pesticides, saturated and unsaturated fatty acids, and commercial uses of hydrogenation, polymers, and fused benzene rings in carcinogens.

Demonstration: Hold a spoon over the flame of a candle. What substance forms on the spoon that indicates a combustion process is occurring in the burning candle?

Laboratory Suggestions

Lab 23 Reactions of Hydrocarbons

The solubility of cycloalkanes, cycloalkenes, toluene, and an unknown hydrocarbon in water is observed. The reactions of these same compounds are also observed in combustion reactions, in reactions with bromine, and $KMnO_4$. Students use their test results to identify the unknown hydrocarbon tested.

A. Types of Hydrocarbons
B. Combustion
C. Bromine Test
D. Potassium Permanganate ($KmnO_4$) Test
E. Identification of Unknowns

Laboratory Skills to Demonstrate

Safety in the use of flammable organic substances and combustion reactions
Correlation of the disappearance of the orange bromine color to the presence of unsaturated sites in alkenes
Care in using bromine solution must be emphasized
Interpretation of color changes of $KMnO_4$ and the presence or absence of a double bond
How to apply test results to identify an unknown hydrocarbon

Answers and Solutions to Text Problems

13.1 **a.** An alkane has only sigma bonds.
  b. An alkyne has a sigma bond and two pi bonds.
  c. An alkene has the groups on the carbon atom arranged at 120°.

13.2 **a.** alkene **b.** alkane **c.** alkyne

13.3. **a.** An alkane has the general formula C_nH_{2n+2}
  b. An alkene has a double bond.
  c. An alkyne has a triple bond.
  d. An alkene has a double bond.
  e. A cycloalkene has a double bond in a ring.

13.4 **a.** cycloalkene **b.** alkyne **c.** alkene
  d. alkyne **e.** alkane

13.5. $CH_2=CH—CH_3$ Propene (propylene)

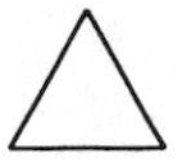

Cyclopropane

13.6 $CH_3—CH=CH—CH_3$ $CH_2=CH—CH_2—CH_3$

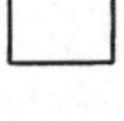

13.7 **a.** Propene contains three carbon atoms with a carbon-carbon double bond.
    Propyne contains three carbon atoms with a carbon-carbon triple bond.
  b. Cyclohexane is a six-carbon cyclic compound with all carbon-carbon single bonds.
    Cyclohexene is a six-carbon cyclic compound with a carbon-carbon double bond.

145

13.8   **a**. 1-butyne is a four-carbon compound with a triple bond between the first and second carbons. 2-butyne is a four-carbon compound with a triple bond between the second and third carbons.

     b. 1-methylcyclohexene is a six-carbon cyclic alkene with a methyl attached to one of the carbons in the double bond. 3-methylcyclohexene is a six carbon cyclic alkene with a methyl attached to one of the carbons next to the double bond.

13.9   **a**. The two-carbon compound with a double bond is ethene.

     b. 2-methyl-1-propene

     c. 4-bromo-2-pentyne

     d. This is a four-carbon cyclic structure with a double bond. The name is cyclobutene.

     e. This is a five-carbon cyclic structure with a double bond and an ethyl group. You must count the two carbons of the double bond as 1 and 2. The name is 4-ethylcyclopentene.

     f. Count the chain from the end nearest the double bond: 4-ethyl-2-hexene

13.10   **a**. 1-hexene   **b**. 6-methyl-2-heptyne   **c**. 1,4-dimethylcyclohexene

     d. 1,2-dimethylcyclobutene   **e**. 4,6-dichloro-1-heptene   **f**. 5,6-dichloro-2-heptyne

13.11   **a**. Propene is the three-carbon alkene. $H_2C=CH-CH_3$

     b. 1-pentene is the five-carbon compound with a double bond between carbon 1 and carbon 2. $H_2C=CH-CH_2-CH_2-CH_3$

     c. 2-methyl-1-butene has a four-carbon chain with a double bond between carbon 1 and carbon 2 and a methyl attached to carbon 2.

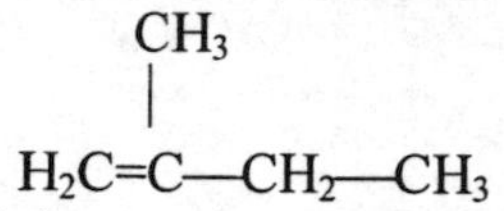

$$\begin{array}{c} CH_3 \\ | \\ H_2C=C-CH_2-CH_3 \end{array}$$

     d. 3-methylcyclohexene is a six-carbon cyclic compound with a double bond between carbon 1 and carbon 2 and a methyl group attached to carbon 3.

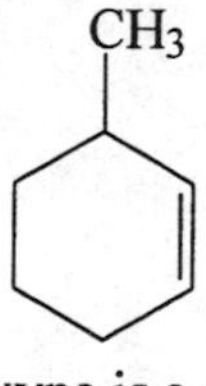

     e. 2-chloro-3-hexyne is a six-carbon compound with a triple bond between carbon 3 and 4 and a chlorine atom bonded to carbon 2.

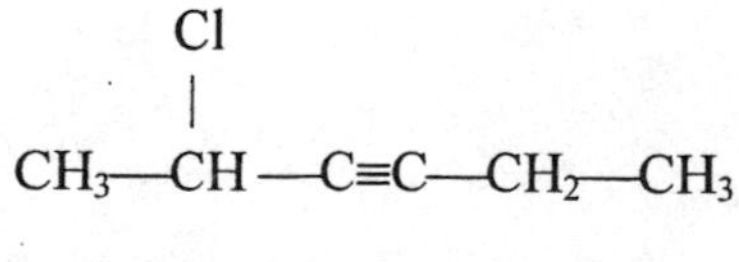

$$\begin{array}{c} Cl \\ | \\ CH_3-CH-C\equiv C-CH_2-CH_3 \end{array}$$

13.12   **a.** 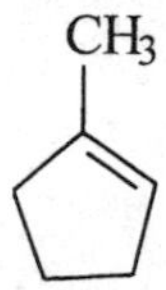   **b.** $H-C\equiv C-\overset{\overset{\textstyle CH_3}{|}}{C}H-CH_3$ **c.** $H_2C=CH-\overset{\overset{\textstyle CH_3}{|}}{C}H-\overset{\overset{\textstyle CH_3}{|}}{\underset{\underset{\textstyle CH_3}{|}}{C}}H-CH_3$

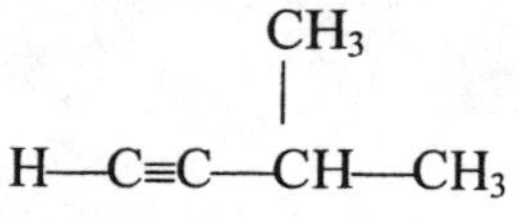

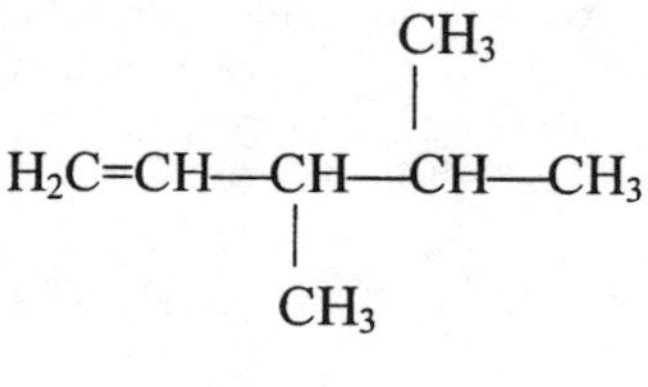

     d. 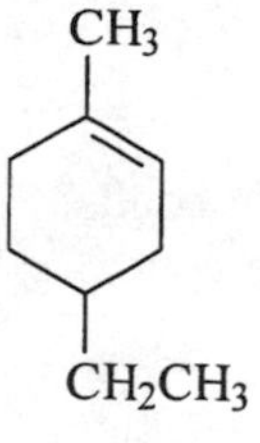   **e.**

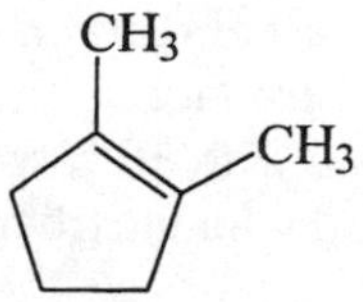

13.13 Constitutional isomers have the same number of each atom but the atoms are connected differently. Geometric isomers have different arrangements of the groups attached to a double bond.

13.14 In *cis*-2-butene, two methyl groups are on the same side of the double bond; in *trans*-2-butene, methyl groups are on opposite sides of the double bond.

13.15 There are four constitutional isomers with the molecular formula C_3H_5Cl, three are alkenes and one is a cycloalkane.

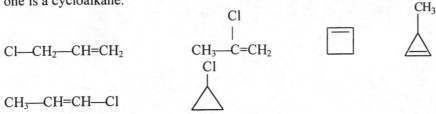

Cl—CH₂—CH=CH₂   CH₃—C=CH₂ (Cl)

CH₃—CH=CH—Cl

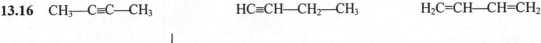

13.16 CH₃—C≡C—CH₃   HC≡CH—CH₂—CH₃   H₂C=CH—CH=CH₂

13.17 **a.** This compound cannot have cis-trans isomers since there are two identical hydrogen atoms attached to the first carbon.
b. This compound can have cis-trans isomers since there are different groups attached to each carbon atom in the double bond.
c. This compound cannot have cis-trans isomers since there are two of the same groups attached to each carbon.

13.18 **a.** This compound has cis-trans isomers.
b. This compound does not have cis-trans isomers.
c. This compound does not have cis-trans isomers.

13.19 **a.** *cis*-2-butene This is a four-carbon compound with a double bond between carbon 2 and carbon 3. Both methyl groups are on the same side of the double bond; it is cis.
b. *trans*-3-octene This compound has eight carbons with a double bond between carbon 3 and carbon 4. The alkyl groups are on opposite sides of the double bond; it is trans.
c. *cis*-3-heptene This is a seven-carbon compound with a double bond between carbon 3 and carbon 4. Both alkyl groups are on the same side of the double bond; it is cis.

13.20 **a.** *cis*-2-pentene   **b.** *trans*-2-heptene   **c.** *trans*-3-heptene

13.21 **a.** *trans*-2-butene has a four-carbon chain with a double bond between carbon 2 and carbon 3. The trans isomer has two methyl groups on opposite sides of the double bond.

CH₃   H
  \\   /
   C=C
  /   \\
H   CH₃

b. cis-2-pentene has a five-carbon chain with a double bond between carbon 2 and carbon 3. The cis isomer has alkyl groups on the same side of the double bond.

147

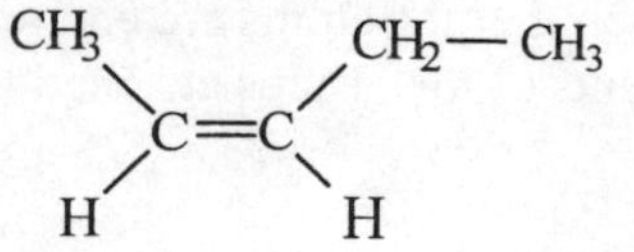

CH₃   CH₂—CH₃
   \\   /
    C=C
   /   \\
  H   H

c. *trans*-3-heptene has a seven carbon chain with a double bond between carbon 3 and carbon 4. The trans isomer has the alkyl groups on opposite sides of the double bond.

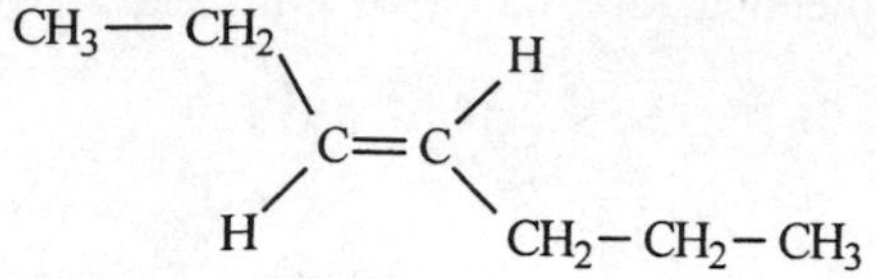

CH₃—CH₂   H
        \\   /
         C=C
        /   \\
       H   CH₂—CH₂—CH₃

13.22 a. CH₃CH₂   CH₂CH₃
                  \\   /
                   C=C
                  /   \\
                 H   H

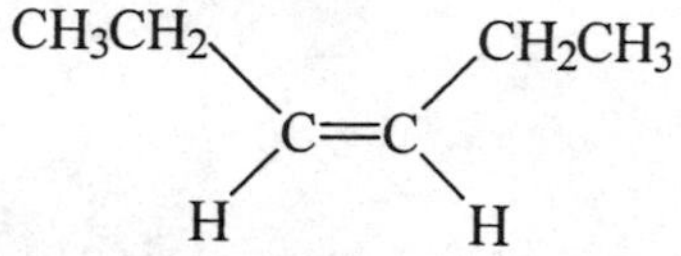

b. CH₃   H
           \\   /
            C=C
           /   \\
          H   CH₂CH₃

c. CH₃CH₂CH₂   CH₂CH₂CH₃
             \\   /
              C=C
             /   \\
            H   H

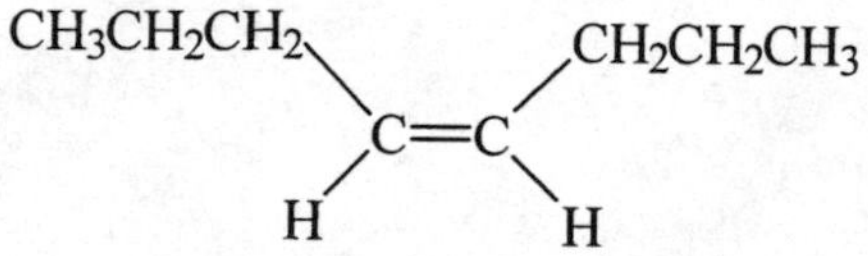

13.23 a. CH₃—CH₂—CH₂—CH₂—CH₃   pentane

b. 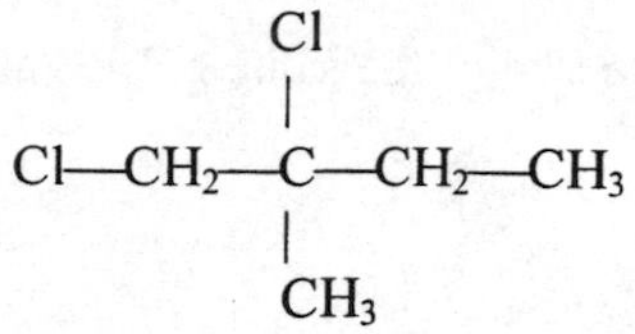
                Cl
                |
  Cl—CH₂—C—CH₂—CH₃   1,2-dichloro-2-methylbutane
                |
                CH₃

c. The product is a four-carbon cycloalkane with bromine atoms attached to carbon 1 and carbon 2. The name is 1,2-dibromocyclobutane.

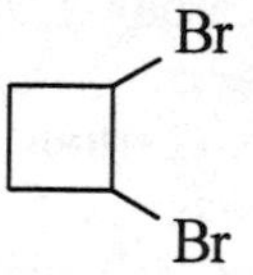

Br
□
Br

d. When H₂ is added to a cycloalkene, the product is a cycloalkane. Cyclopentene would form cyclopentane.

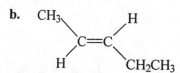

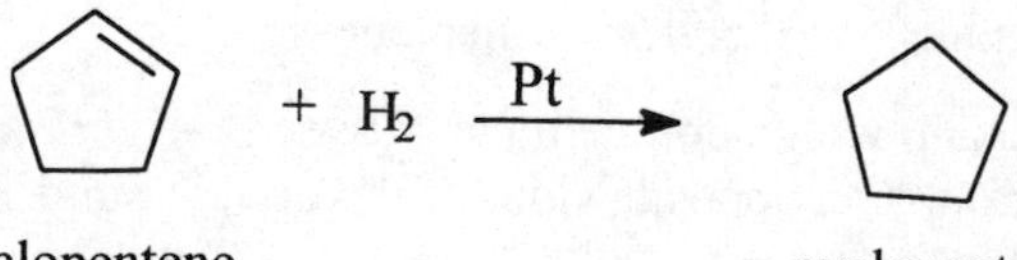

cyclopentene   + H₂ $\xrightarrow{\text{Pt}}$ cyclopentane

e. When Cl₂ is added to an alkene, the product is a dichloroalkane. The product is a four-carbon chain with chlorine atoms attached to carbon 2 and carbon 3 and a methyl group attached to carbon 2. The name of the product is: 2,3-dichloro-2-methylbutane

          CH₃   CH₃
          | |
CH₃—C=CH—CH₃   + Cl₂   ⟶   CH₃—C—CH—CH₃
                                           | |
                                           Cl Cl

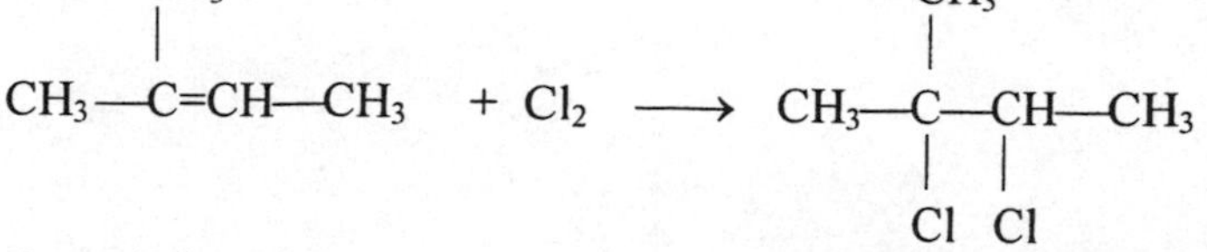

  2-methyl-2-butene   2,3-dichloro-2-methylbutane

f. CH$_3$—CH$_2$—CH$_2$—CH$_2$—CH$_3$ pentane

                        Br

                        |

13.24 **a.** 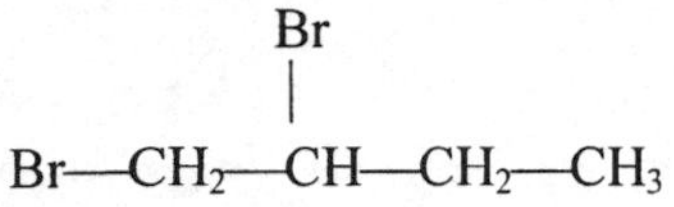 Br—CH$_2$—CH—CH$_2$—CH$_3$ 1,2-dibromobutane

b.    cyclohexane

c. CH$_3$—CH$_2$—CH$_2$—CH$_3$ butane

         CH$_3$

         |

d. 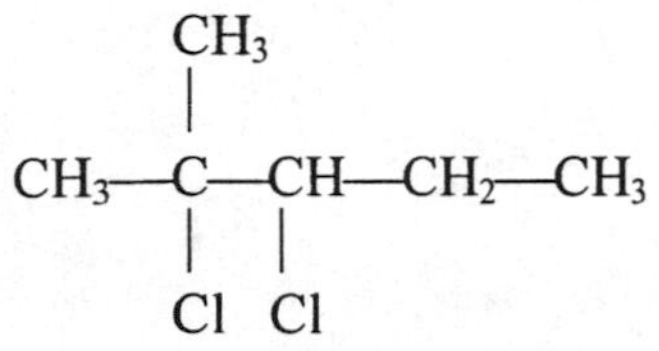 CH$_3$—C—CH—CH$_2$—CH$_3$ **e.**

         | |

         Cl Cl

2,3-dichloro-2-methylpentane   1,2-dibromo-3-methylcyclohexane

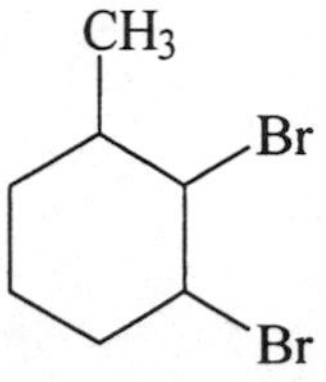

         CH$_3$ Cl Cl

         | | |

f. 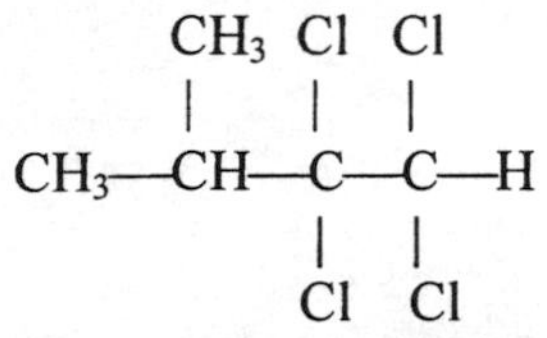 CH$_3$—CH—C—C—H   1,1,2,2-tetrachloro-3-methylbutane

              | |

              Cl Cl

13.25 **a.** When HBr is added to an alkene, the product is a bromoalkane. In this case, we do not need to use Markovnikov's rule.

                       Br

                       |

CH$_3$—CH$_2$—CH—CH$_3$

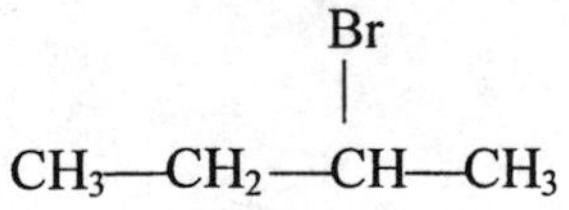

b. When H$_2$O is added to an alkene, the product is an alcohol. In this case, we do not need to use Markovnikov's rule.

        OH

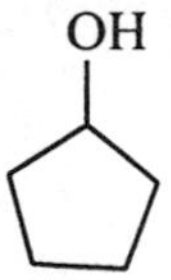

c. When HCl is added to an alkene, the product is a chloroalkane. We need to use Markovnikov's rule, which says that hydrogen adds to the carbon with the greatest number of hydrogens, in this case that is carbon 1.

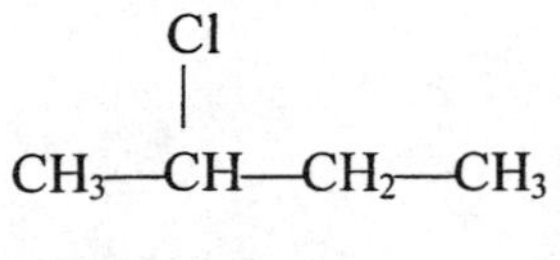

        Cl

        |

CH$_3$—CH—CH$_2$—CH$_3$

d. When HI is added to an alkene, the product is a iodoalkane. In this case, we do not need to use Markovnikov's rule.

        CH$_3$ I

        | |

CH$_3$—CH—CH—CH$_3$

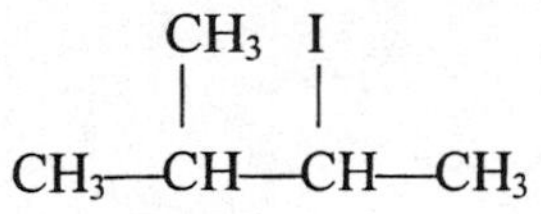

e. When HBr is added to an alkene, the product is a bromoalkane. We need to use Markovnikov's rule, which says that hydrogen adds to the carbon with the greatest number of hydrogens, in this case that is carbon 2.

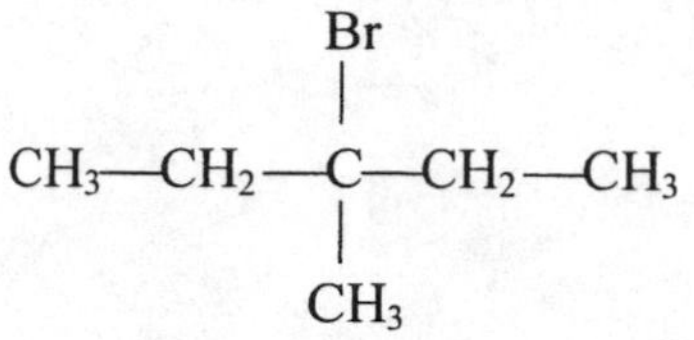

$$CH_3-CH_2-\underset{\underset{CH_3}{|}}{\overset{\overset{Br}{|}}{C}}-CH_2-CH_3$$

f. Using Markovnikov's rule, the H from HOH goes to the carbon 2 in the cyclohexane ring, which has more hydrogen atoms. The —OH then goes to carbon 1.

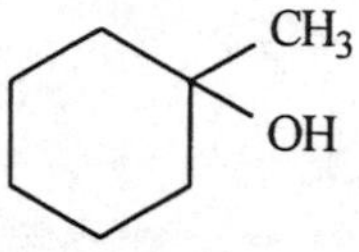

13.26 **a.** 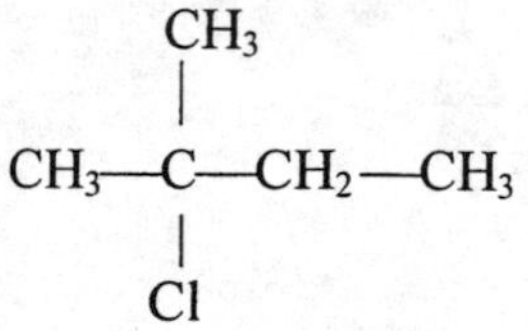 $CH_3-\underset{\underset{Cl}{|}}{\overset{\overset{CH_3}{|}}{C}}-CH_2-CH_3$ **b.** $CH_3-CH_2-CH_2-\underset{\underset{}{\overset{\overset{OH}{|}}{CH}}}-CH_2-CH_3$

c. $CH_3-\underset{\underset{Br}{|}}{\overset{\overset{CH_3}{|}}{C}}-CH_3$ **d.** 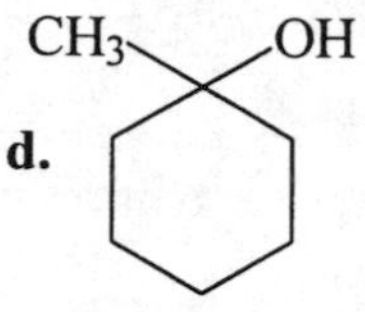 **e.**

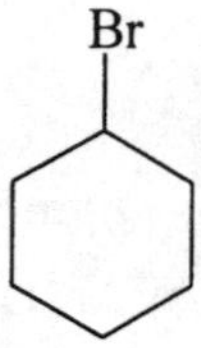

f. 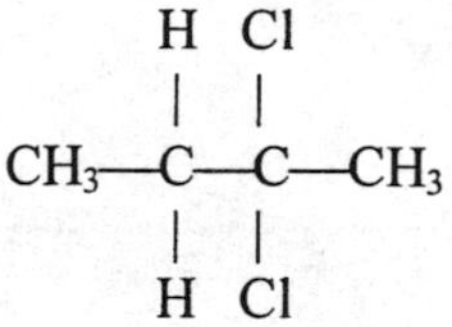 $CH_3-\underset{\underset{H}{|}}{\overset{\overset{H}{|}}{C}}-\underset{\underset{Cl}{|}}{\overset{\overset{Cl}{|}}{C}}-CH_3$

13.27 **a.** Hydrogenation of an alkene gives the saturated compound, the alkane.

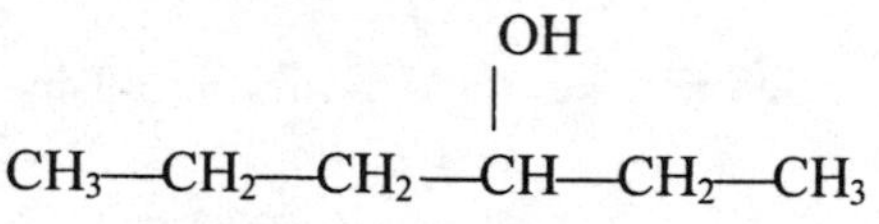

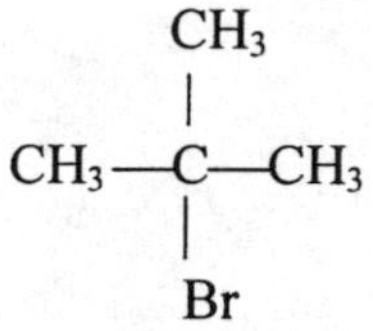

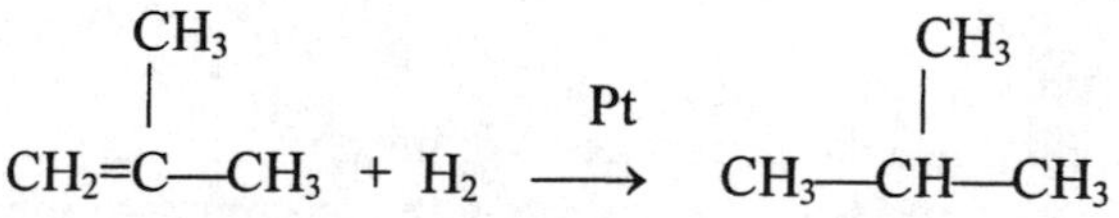

$$CH_2{=}\underset{\underset{}{\overset{\overset{CH_3}{|}}{C}}}-CH_3 + H_2 \xrightarrow{Pt} CH_3-\underset{\underset{}{\overset{\overset{CH_3}{|}}{CH}}}-CH_3$$

b. The addition of HCl to a cycloalkene gives a chlorocycloalkane.

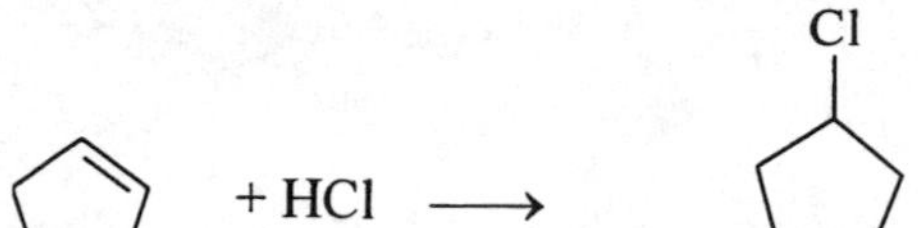

+ HCl ⟶

c. The addition of bromine (Br_2) to an alkene gives a dibromoalkane.

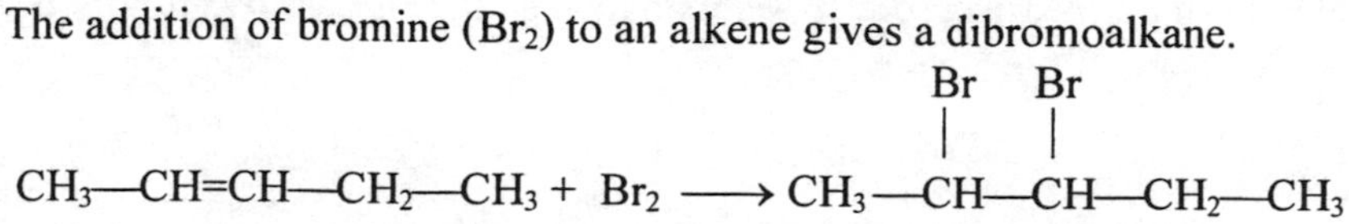

$$CH_3-CH{=}CH-CH_2-CH_3 + Br_2 \longrightarrow CH_3-\underset{\underset{}{\overset{\overset{Br}{|}}{CH}}}-\underset{\underset{}{\overset{\overset{Br}{|}}{CH}}}-CH_2-CH_3$$

d. Hydration (the addition of H_2O) to an alkene gives an alcohol. In this case, we use Markovnikov's rule and attach hydrogen to carbon 1.

$$CH_2=CH-CH_3 \ + \ H_2O \ \xrightarrow{H^+} \ CH_3\overset{\overset{\displaystyle OH}{|}}{-}CH-CH_3$$

e. $CH_3-C{\equiv}C-CH_3 \ + 2Cl_2 \longrightarrow \ CH_3\overset{\overset{\displaystyle Cl}{|}}{-}C\overset{\overset{\displaystyle Cl}{|}}{-}C-CH_3$ with Cl, Cl below

13.28 a. $+ \ H_2O \ \xrightarrow{H^+}$

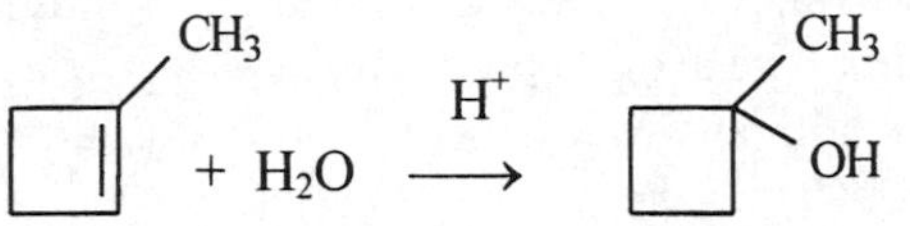

b. $CH_3-CH_2-CH=CH-CH_2-CH_3 \ + \ H_2 \ \xrightarrow{Pt} \ CH_3-CH_2-CH_2-CH_2-CH_2-CH_3$

c. $CH_3\overset{\overset{\displaystyle CH_3}{|}}{-}C=CH-CH_3 + HBr \longrightarrow \ CH_3\overset{\overset{\displaystyle CH_3}{|}}{\underset{\underset{\displaystyle Br}{|}}{-}}C-CH_2-CH_3$

d. $CH_3\overset{\overset{\displaystyle CH_3}{|}}{\underset{\underset{\displaystyle CH_3}{|}}{-}}C=C-CH_2-CH_3 + Cl_2 \longrightarrow \ CH_3\overset{\overset{\displaystyle CH_3\ Cl}{|\ \ |}}{\underset{\underset{\displaystyle Cl\ \ CH_3}{|\ \ |}}{-}}C-C-CH_2-CH_3$

e. $+ \ HCl \longrightarrow$

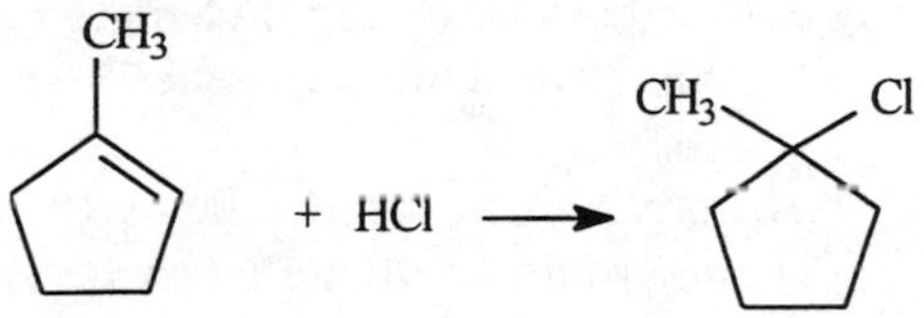

13.29 A polymer is a long-chain molecule consisting of many repeating smaller units. These smaller units are called monomers.

13.30 Monomers are the small carbon molecules which repeat to make polymers.

13.31 Teflon is a polymer of the monomer tetrafluoroethene.

13.32

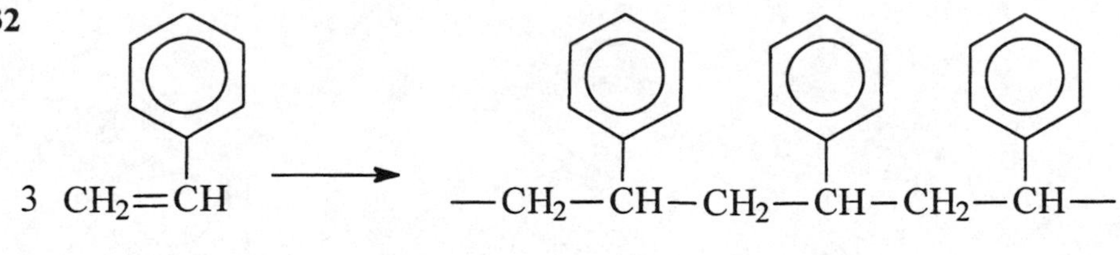

13.33 1,1-difluoroethene is the two carbon alkene with two fluorine atoms attached to carbon 1.

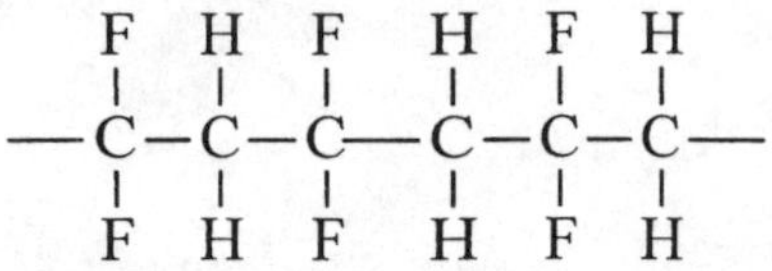

$$\begin{array}{cccccc}
F & H & F & H & F & H \\
| & | & | & | & | & | \\
-C- & C- & C- & C- & C- & C- \\
| & | & | & | & | & | \\
F & H & F & H & F & H
\end{array}$$

13.34

$$3\ CH_2=CH \longrightarrow \quad -CH_2-CH-CH_2-CH-CH_2-CH-$$

with CN groups on each CH carbon

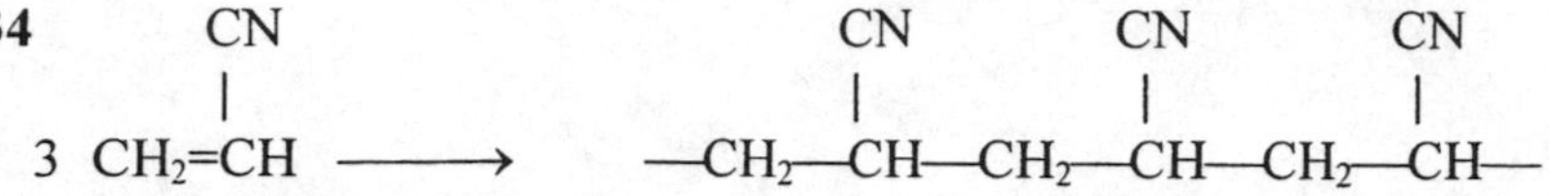

13.35 Cyclohexane, C_6H_{12}, is a cycloalkane in which six carbon atoms are linked by single bonds in a ring. In benzene, C_6H_6, an aromatic system links the six carbon atoms in a ring.

13.36 In the Health Note "Aromatic Compounds In health and Medicine, the aromatic portion of each molecule is the benzene ring.

13.37 The six carbon ring with alternating single and double bonds is benzene. If the groups are in the 1,2 position, this is ortho (*o*), 1,3 is meta (*m*) and 1,4 is para (*p*)
a. 1-chloro-2-methylbenzene; *o*-chlorotoluene
b. ethylbenzene
c. 1,3,5-trichlorobenzene
d. *m*-xylene; *m*-methyltoluene; 1,3-dimethylbenzene
e. 1-bromo-3-chloro-5-methylbenzene; 3-bromo-5-chlorotoluene
f. isopropyl benzene

13.38 **a.** benzene   **b.** methylbenzene; toluene
c. 1,3-dichlorobenzene; *m*-dichlorobenzene   **d.** 1,4-dimethylbenzene;*p*-xylene
e. benzyl bromide   **f.** 4-bromo-1,2-dichlorobenzene

13.39 **a.**   **b.**   The prefix *m* means that the two chloro groups are in the 1 and 3 position.

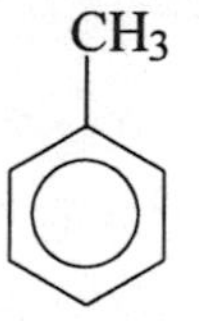

c.   **d.** 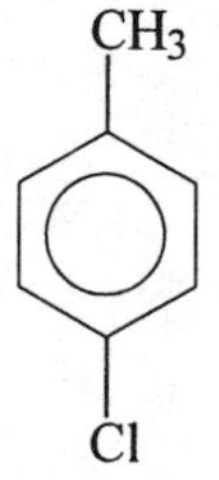   The prefix *p* means that the two groups are in the 1 and 4 position.

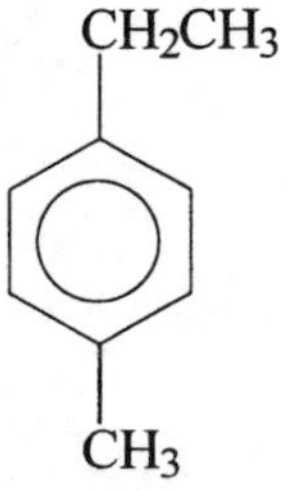

13.40

a.   **b.** 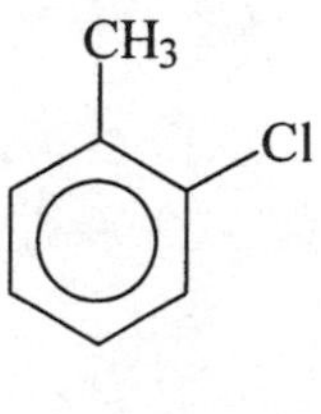   **c.** 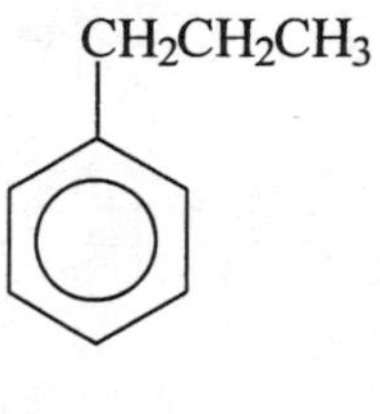   **d.**

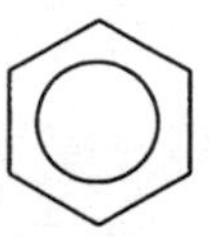

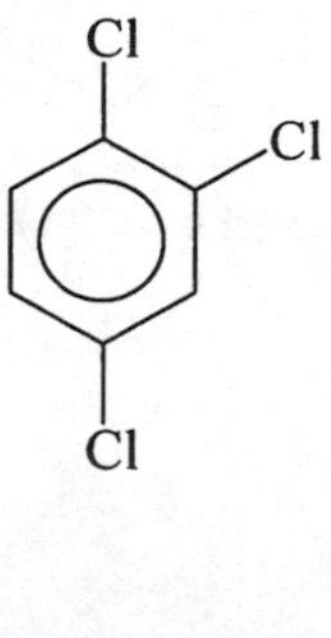

13.41   Benzene undergoes substitution reactions because a substitution reaction allows benzene to retain the stability of the aromatic system.

13.42   The aromatic ring in toluene is resistant to halogenation in the presence of light. However, the alkyl group does undergo halogenation as a substitution reaction in which a chlorine atom replaces a hydrogen atom when light is present.

13.43 a. No reaction

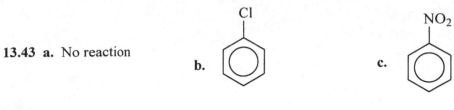

13.44

a. (structure) and (structure) and (structure)

b. (structure)   **c.** (structure)

13.45   Propane is the three-carbon alkane with the formula C_3H_8. All the carbon-carbon bonds in propane are single bonds. Cyclopropane is the three-carbon cycloalkane with the formula C_3H_6. All the carbon-carbon bonds in cyclopropane are single bonds. Propene is the three carbon compound which has a carbon-carbon double bond. The formula of propene is C_3H_6. Propyne is the three carbon compound with a carbon-carbon triple bond. The formula of propyne is C_3H_4.

13.46   Butane is the four-carbon alkane with the formula C_4H_{10}; the carbon-carbon bonds in butane are single bonds. Cyclobutane is a four-carbon cycloalkane with the formula C_4H_8. All the carbon-carbon bonds in cyclobutane are single bonds. Cyclopbutene is a four-carbon compound, which has a carbon-carbon double bond. The formula of butene is C_4H_6. 2-Butyne is a four-carbon compound with a carbon-carbon triple bond. The formula of propyne is C_4H_6.

13.47 a. This compound has a chlorine atom attached to a cyclopentane; the IUPAC name is chlorocyclopentane.

b. This compound has a five carbon chain with a chlorine atom attached to carbon 2 and a methyl group attached to carbon 4. The IUPAC name is: 2-chloro-4-methylpentane.

c. This compound contains a five-carbon chain with a double bond between carbon 1 and carbon 2 and a methyl group attached to carbon 2. The IUPAC name is: 2-methyl-1-pentene.

d. This compound contains a five-carbon chain with a triple bond between carbon 2 and carbon 3. The IUPAC name is: 2-pentyne

e. This compound contains a five-carbon cycloalkene with a chlorine atom attached to carbon 1. The IUPAC name is: 1-chlorocyclopentene

f. This compound contains a five carbon chain with a double bond between carbon 2 and carbon 3. The alkyl groups are on opposite sides of the double bond. The IUPAC name is: *trans*-2-pentene

g. This compound contains a six-carbon ring with a double bond and chlorine atoms attached to carbon 1 and carbon 3 The IUPAC name is: 1,3-dichlorocyclohexene

153

13.48 a.

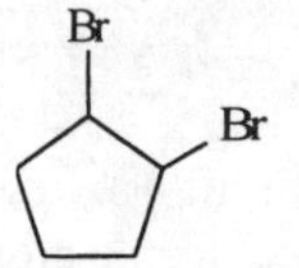

b. CH₃—C≡C—CH₂—CH₃

c.

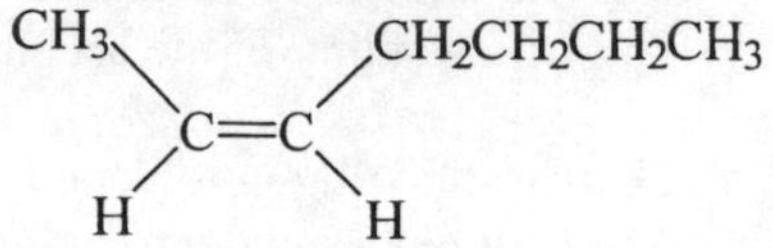

d. 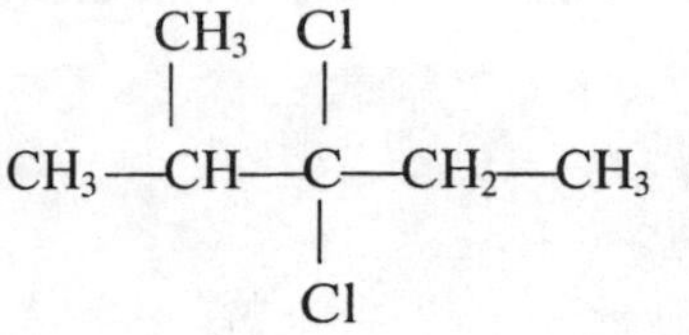 CH₃—CH—C—CH₂—CH₃   **e.** 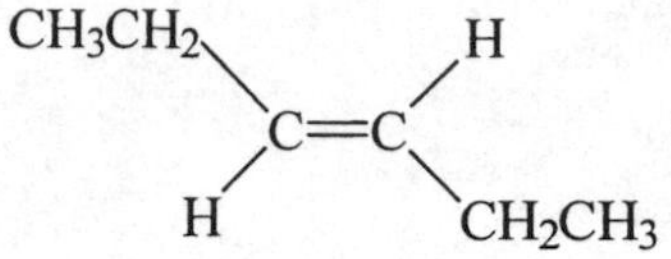   **f.**

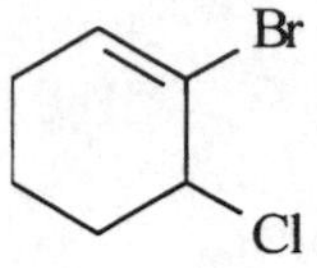

g. 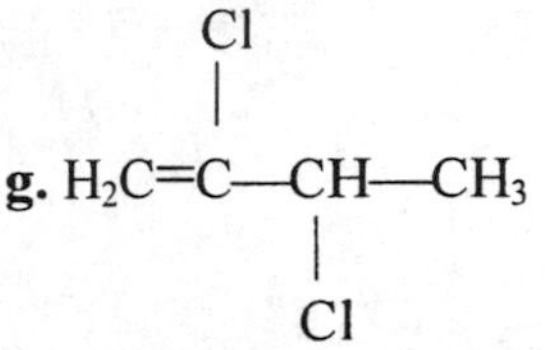 H₂C=C—CH—CH₃

13.49 a. These structures represent a pair of constitutional isomers. In one isomer, the chlorine is attached to one of the carbons in the double bond; in the other isomer the carbon bonded to the chlorine is not part of the double bond.

b. These structures are cis-trans isomers. In the cis isomer, the two methyl groups are on the same side of the double bond. In the trans isomer, the methyl groups are on opposite sides of the double bond.

c. These structures are identical and not isomers. Both have five carbon chains with a double bond between carbon 1 and carbon 2.

d. These structures represent a pair of constitutional isomers. Both have the molecular formula C₇H₁₆. One isomer is a six-carbon chain with a methyl group attached, whereas the other is a five-carbon chain with two methyl groups attached.

13.50

cyclobutane   methylcyclopropane   1-butene

H₂C=C–CH₃

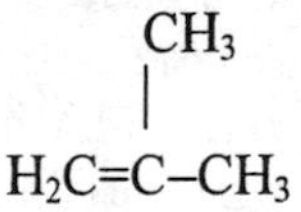

2-methyl-1-propene 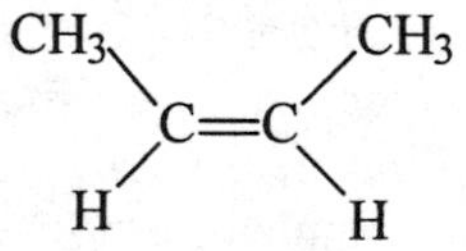   *cis*-2-butene 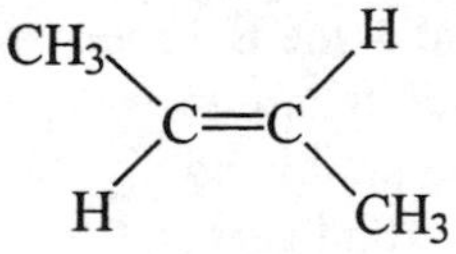   *trans*-2-butene

13.51 The structure of methylcyclopentane is

It can be formed by the hydrogenation of four cycloalkenes.

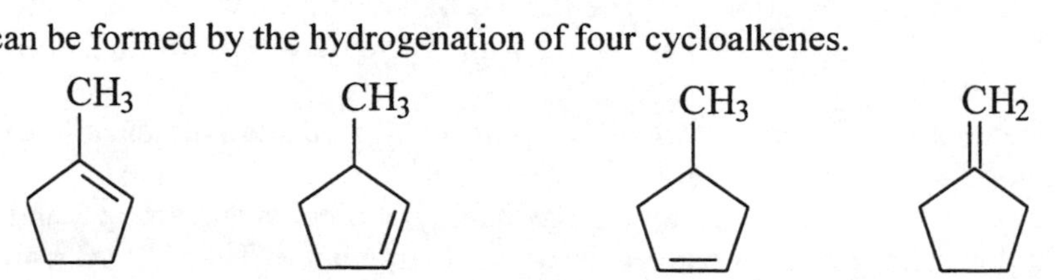

CH₃   CH₃   CH₃   CH₂

13.52 When light fall on a molecule of *cis*-2-retinal, which is attached to a protein, the cis isomer changes to trans. The trans isomer will not fit the protein and separation from the protein generates a signal, which the brain interprets as light.

13.53 **a.**

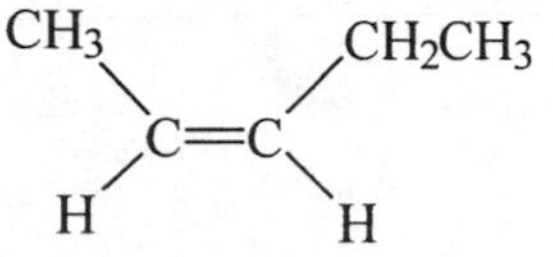

cis-2-pentene both alkyl groups are on the same side of the double bond

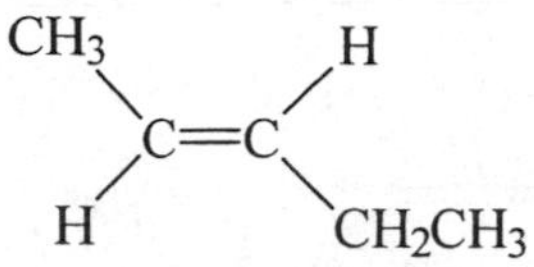

trans-2-pentene both alkyl groups are on opposite sides of the double bond

b.

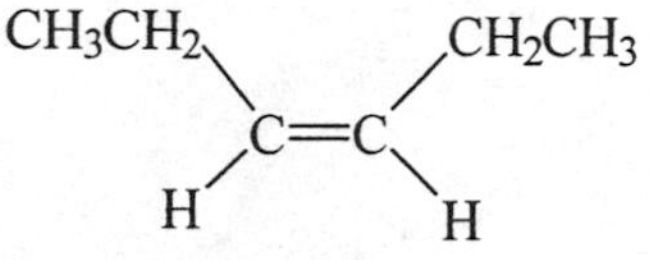

cis-3-hexene both alkyl groups are on the same side of the double bond

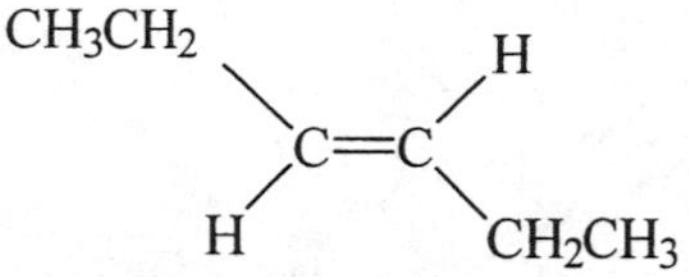

trans-3-hexene both alkyl groups are on opposite sides of the double bond

c.

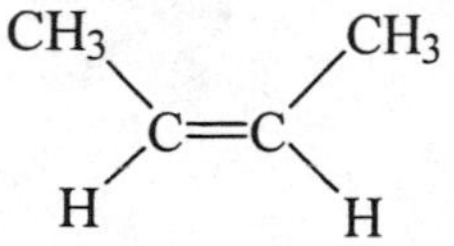

cis-2-butene both alkyl groups are on the same side of the double bond

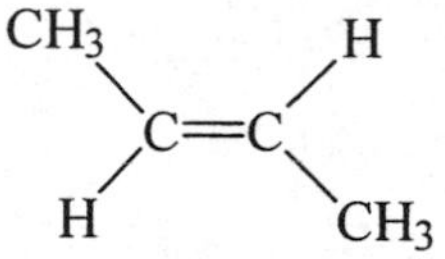

trans-2-butene both alkyl groups are on opposite sides of the double bond

d.

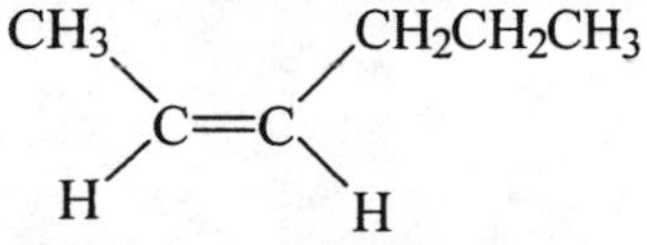

cis-2-hexene both alkyl groups are on the same side of the double bond

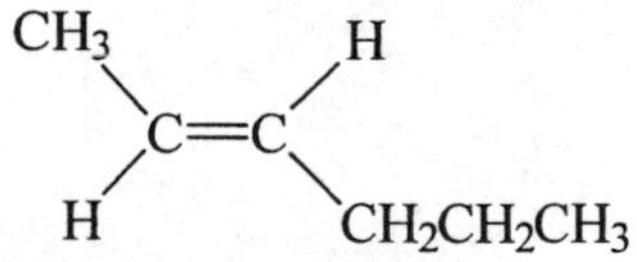

trans-2-hexene both alkyl groups are on opposite sides of the double bond

13.54 **a.** $CH_3-CH_2-CH_2-CH_3$ **b.** **c.** $CH_3-CH_2-\underset{\underset{\displaystyle Br}{|}}{CH}-CH_3$

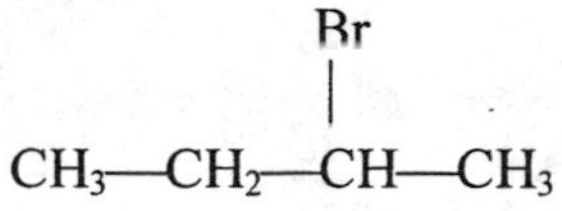

d. 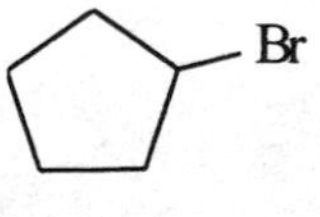 **e.** $CH_3-\underset{\underset{\displaystyle Cl}{|}}{CH}-\underset{\underset{\displaystyle Cl}{|}}{CH}-CH_3$ **f.** no reaction

g. $CH_3-CH_2-\underset{\underset{\displaystyle OH}{|}}{CH}-CH_3$ **h.** 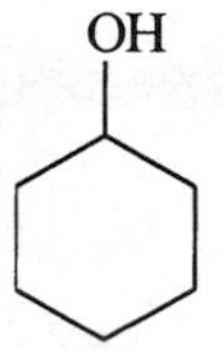 **i.** $CH_3-CH-\underset{\underset{\displaystyle CH_3}{|}}{\overset{\overset{\displaystyle CH_3}{|}}{C}}-CH_3$ with Cl

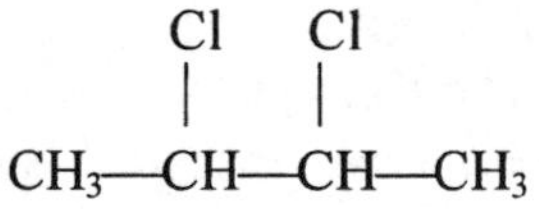

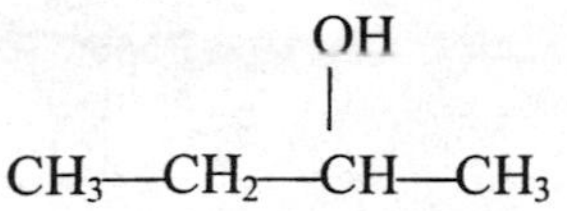

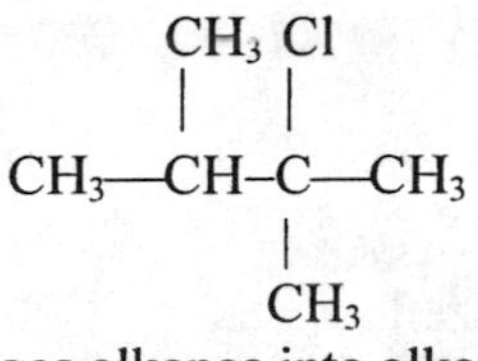

13.55 **a.** The reaction of H_2 in the presence of a Ni catalyst changes alkenes into alkanes. The reactant must be cyclohexene.

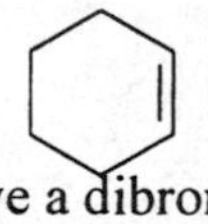

b. Br_2 adds to alkenes to give a dibromoalkane. Since there are bromine atoms on carbon 2 and carbon 3 the double bond in the reactant must have been between carbons 2 and 3.
$CH_3CH=CHCH_2CH_3$

c. HCl adds to alkenes to give a chloroalkane. The product has three carbons and the double bond must be between carbons 1 and 2.

$CH_2=CHCH_3$

d. An alcohol is formed when H_2O adds to an alkene in the presence of acid (H^+). The alkene which adds water to form

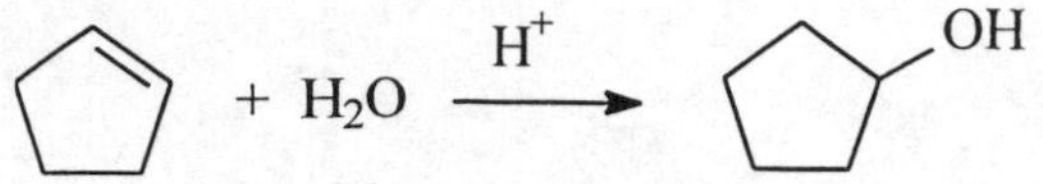

13.56 $2\ HC{\equiv}CH\ +5\ O_2 \longrightarrow 4\ CO_2\ +\ 2\ H_2O\ +\ heat$

13.57 Styrene is $H_2C{=}CH$ and acrylonitrile is $H_2C=CH$. A section copolymer of styrene and acrylonitrile would be:

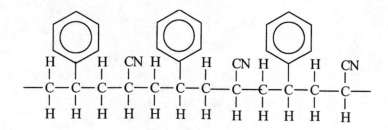

13.58

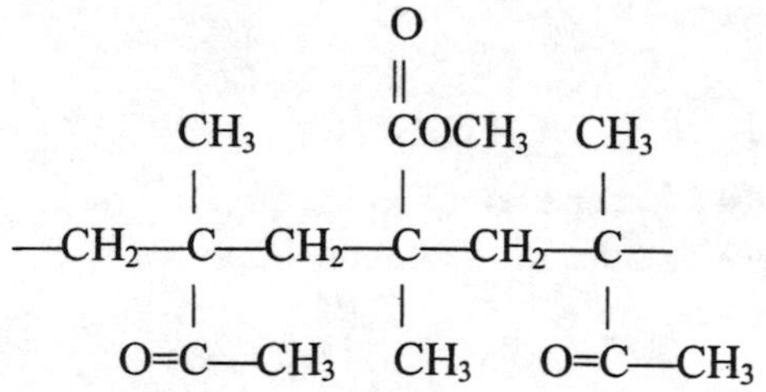

13.59 **a.** methylbenzene; toluene
b. 1-chloro-2-methylbenzene; *o*-chlorotoluene (1,2 position is *ortho, o*)
c. 1-ethyl-4-methylbenzene; *p*-ethyltoluene (1,4 position is *para,p*)
d. 1,3-diethylbenzene; *m*-diethylbenzene (1,3 position is *meta,m*)

13.60 a. b. 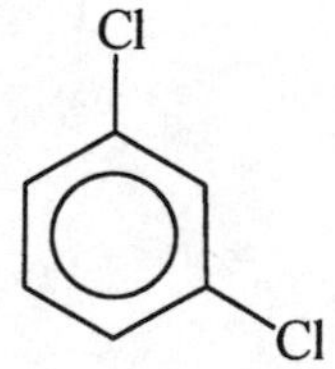 c. 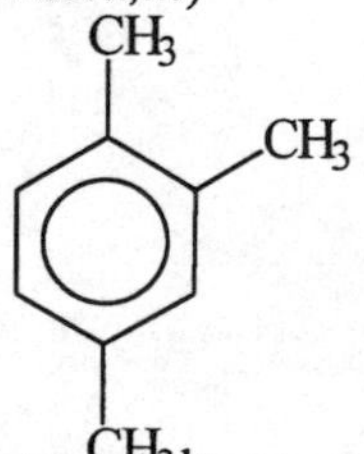 d.

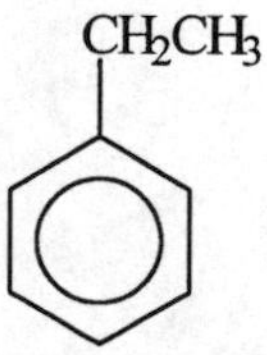

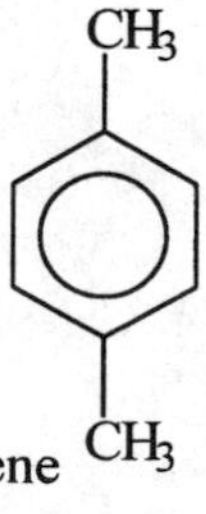

13.61 **a.** Chlorobenzene   **b.** *o*-bromotoluene, *m*-bromotoluene, *p*-bromotoluene
c. Benzenesulfonic acid   **d.** No products

13.62 **a.** Benzene and HNO_3 in the presence of sulfuric acid, H_2SO_4
b. Benzene and sulfur trioxide in the presence of sulfuric acid, H_2SO_4
c. Benzene and bromine in the presence of iron (III) bromide

14

Alcohols, Phenols, Ethers, and Thiols

Study Goals

- Classify alcohols as primary, secondary, or tertiary.
- Name and write the condensed structural formulas for alcohols, phenols, and thiols.
- Identify the uses of some alcohols and phenols.
- Name and write the condensed structural formulas for ethers.
- Describe the solubility in water, density, and boiling points of alcohols, phenols, and ethers.
- Write equations for combustion, dehydration, and oxidation of alcohols.

Chapter Outline

14.1 Structure and Classification of Alcohols
14.2 Naming Alcohols, Phenols, and Thiols
14.3 Some Important Alcohols and Phenols
14.4 Ethers
Health Note: Ethers as Anesthetics
14.5 Physical Properties of Alcohols, Phenols and Ethers
14.6 Reactions of Alcohols
Explore Your World: Combustion of Alcohol
Health Note: Oxidation of Alcohol in the Body

Chapter Summary and Demonstrations

1. Alcohols, Phenols, and Ethers

The study of organic functional groups continues with alcohols, phenols, and ethers. Thiols are introduced and related to the alcohols. The properties of alcohols and ethers are discussed including hydrogen bonding, boiling points and solubility in water. IUPAC naming is given for each family of oxygen- or sulfur-containing compounds. Where common names are still prevalent, they are given.

Demonstration: Look for names of alcohols, phenols, and thiols on the labels of products such as mouthwash, antifreeze, rubbing alcohol, food flavorings, cosmetics, and hair spray.

2. Oxidation and Dehydration

The reactions in this chapter include oxidation and dehydration of alcohols and sulfhydryl groups. A health topic discusses the oxidation of alcohol in the body.

Laboratory Suggestions

24 Alcohols and Phenols

Alcohols are classified as primary, secondary, or tertiary. Chemical testing with chromate allows students to distinguish between the classes of alcohols. Chemical and physical properties of alcohols and phenols are determined. Alcohols and phenol are oxidized with chromic acid and the structural formulas of the oxidation products written. Using the same chemical tests, an unknown alcohol is identified.

A. Structures of Alcohols and Phenol
B. Properties of Alcohols and Phenol
C. Oxidation of Alcohols
D. Ferric Chloride Test
E. Identification of Unknown

Laboratory Skills to Demonstrate

Proper technique for noting the odor of a substance in a test tube
Identification of a change in the orange color of chromic acid to green as an indication of the occurrence of an oxidation reaction

Answers and Solutions to Text Problems

14.1 In a primary (1°) alcohol the carbon bonded to the hydroxyl group (—OH) is attached to one alkyl group except for methanol; to two alkyl groups in a secondary alcohol (2°); and to three alkyl groups in a tertiary alcohol (3°).

    a. 1°   **b.** 1°   **c.** 3°   **d.** 2°   **e.** 3°

14.2   **a.** secondary   **b.** primary   **c.** primary
        d. tertiary   **e.** primary

14.3   **a.** This compound has a two-carbon chain (ethane). The final –e is dropped and –ol added to indicate an alcohol. The IUPAC name is ethanol.
    b. This compound has a four-carbon chain with a hydroxyl attached to carbon 2. The IUPAC name is 2-butanol.
    c. This compound has a six-carbon chain with a hydroxyl group attached to carbon 3. The IUPAC name is 3-hexanol.
    d. This compound has a four-carbon chain with a hydroxyl attached to carbon 1and a methyl attached to carbon 3. The IUPAC name is 3-methyl-1-butanol.
    e. This compound is a six-carbon cycloalkane with a hydroxyl attached to carbon 1 and two methyl groups, one attached to carbon 3 and the other to carbon 4. Since the hydroxyl is always attached to carbon 1 the number 1 is omitted in the name. The IUPAC name is 3,4-dimethylcyclohexanol.
    f. This compound has a seven-carbon chain with a hydroxyl attached to carbon 1 and three methyl groups, one attached to carbon 3 and two attached to carbon 5. The IUPAC name is 3,5,5-trimethyl-1-heptanol

14.4   **a.** 1-ethylcyclobutanol   **b.** 3-chloro-2-methyl-1-butanol
    c. 2,3-dimethyl-1-pentanol   **d.** 5,5-dichloro-2-pentanol
    e. 2,4-dimethylcyclopentanol   **f.** 3-ethyl-1-pentanol

14.5   **a.** 1-propanol has a three-carbon chain with a hydroxyl attached to carbon 1.

CH_3—CH_2—CH_2—OH

b. Methyl alcohol has a hydroxyl attached to a one-carbon alkane CH_3—OH.

c. 3-pentanol has a five-carbon chain with a hydroxyl attached to carbon 3.

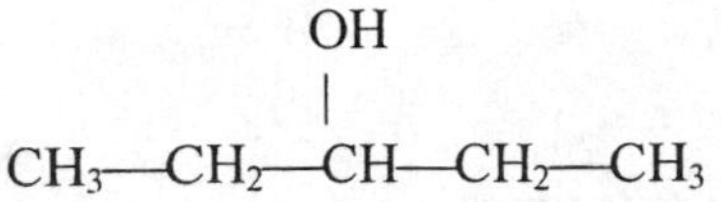

$$\overset{\displaystyle \text{OH}}{\overset{|}{CH_3-CH_2-CH-CH_2-CH_3}}$$

d. 2-methyl-2-butanol has a four-carbon chain with a methyl and hydroxyl attached to carbon 2.

$$CH_3-\overset{\overset{\displaystyle \text{OH}}{|}}{\underset{\underset{\displaystyle CH_3}{|}}{C}}-CH_2-CH_3$$

e. Cyclohexanol has a six-carbon cycloalkane with a hydroxyl attached.

f. 1,4-butanediol has a four-carbon chain (butane). The diol indicates that there are two hydroxyl groups, one attached to carbon 1 and one to carbon 4.

HO—CH_2—CH_2—CH_2—CH_2—OH

14.6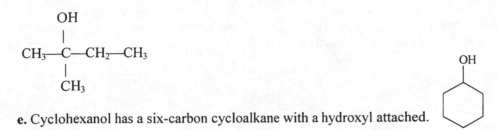

a. CH_3—CH_2—OH

b. 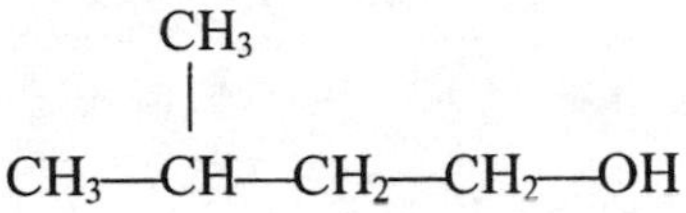 CH_3—$\overset{\overset{\displaystyle CH_3}{|}}{CH}$—$CH_2$—$CH_2$—OH

c.

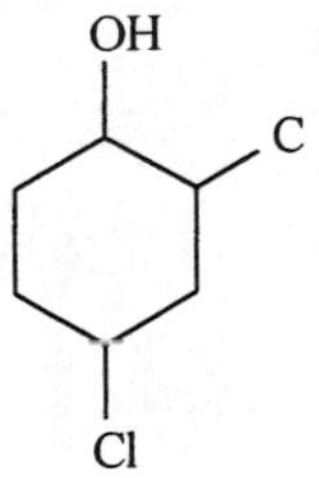

d. CH_3—CH_2—CH_2—OH

e.

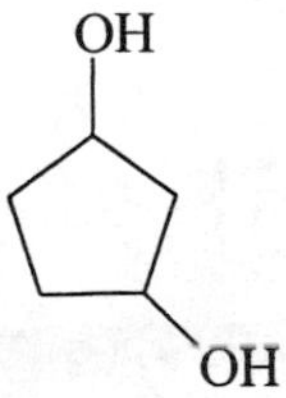

f. 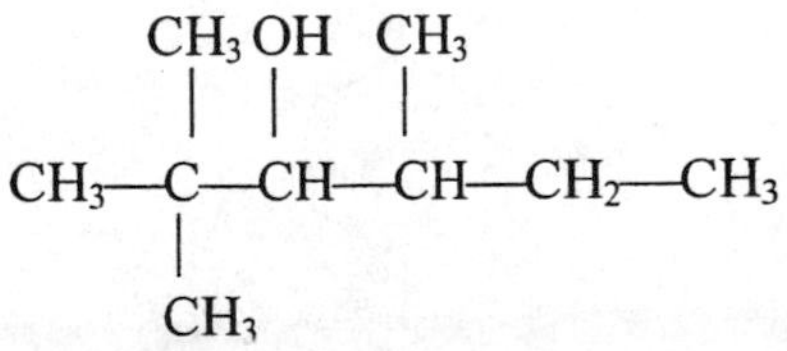 CH_3—$\overset{\overset{\displaystyle CH_3}{|}}{\underset{\underset{\displaystyle CH_3}{|}}{C}}$—$\overset{\overset{\displaystyle OH}{|}}{CH}$—$\overset{\overset{\displaystyle CH_3}{|}}{CH}$—$CH_2$—$CH_3$

14.7   A benzene ring with a hydroxyl group is called *phenol*. Substituents are numbered from the carbon bonded to the hydroxyl group as carbon 1. Common names use the prefixes *ortho, meta,* and *para.*
a. phenol
b. 2-bromophenol, *ortho*-bromophenol (Groups on the 1 and 2 positions are ortho)
c. 3,5-dichlorophenol
d. 3-bromophenol, *meta*-bromophenol (Groups on the 1 and 3 positions are meta)

14.8   **a.** 3-ethylphenol, *m*-ethylphenol   **b.** 2,5-dibromophenol
         c. 3-chlorophenol, *m*-chlorophenol   **d.** 2-chlorophenol, *o*-chlorophenol

14.9   **a.** The *m* (meta) indicates that the two groups are in the 1,3 arrangement.

b. The *p* (para) indicates that the two groups are in the 1,4 arrangement

c. Two chlorine atoms are attached to the aromatic system, one on carbon 2 and the other on carbon 5, with the hydroxyl attached to carbon 1.

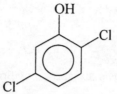

d. The *o* (ortho) indicates that the two groups are in the 1,2 arrangement

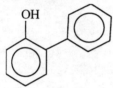

e. The name indicated that there is an ethyl group on carbon 4 with the hydroxyl on carbon 1.

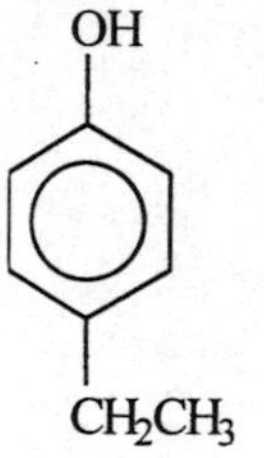

14.10   **a.**

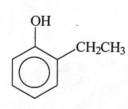

  b.

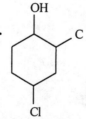

  c.

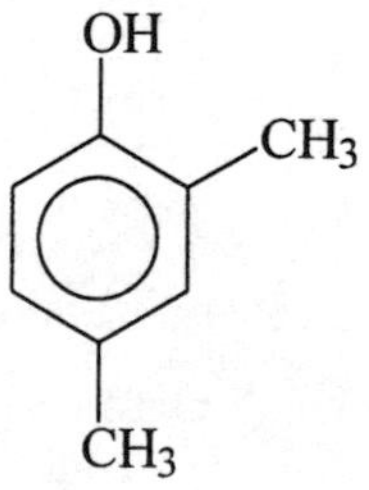

  d.

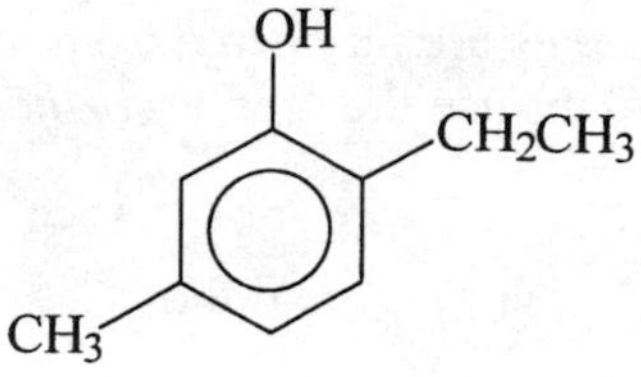

  e.

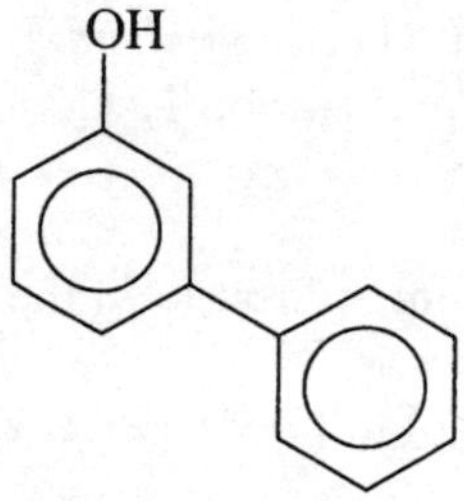

14.11 **a.** This is a one-carbon alkane with a thiol (–SH) group. The IUPAC name is methanethiol.
  b. This thiol has a three-carbon alkane with the thiol group attached to carbon 2. The IUPAC name is 2-propanethiol
  c. This compound has a four-carbon alkane with methyl groups attached to carbon 2 and carbon 3 and the thiol attached to carbon 1. The IUPAC name is 2,3-dimethyl-1-butanethiol.
  d. This compound has a thiol attached to a cyclobutane. The IUPAC name is cyclobutanethiol.

14.12 **a.** 1-propanethiol   **b.** 2-pentanethiol
  c. 2,2-dimethyl-1-propanethiol   **d.** cyclopentanethiol

14.13 **a.** ethanol   **b.** thymol   **c.** *ortho*-phenylphenol

14.14 **a.** 1,2-ethanediol; ethylene glycol forms oxalic acid
  b. BHA; butylated hydroxyanisole and BHT; butylated hydroxytoluene
  c. 1,2,3-propanetriol; glycerol

14.15 **a.** methoxyethane; ethyl methyl ether
  b. methoxycyclohexane, cyclohexyl methyl ether
  c. ethoxycyclobutane, cyclobutyl ethyl ether
  d. 1-methoxypropane, methyl propyl ether

14.16 **a.** 1-ethoxypropane, ethyl propyl ether   **b.** methoxybenzene, methyl phenyl ether; anisole
  c. ethoxycyclopentane, cyclopentyl ethyl ether **d.** methoxymethane, dimethyl ether

14.17 **a.** Ethyl propyl ether has a two-carbon group and a three-carbon group attached to oxygen by single bonds. CH_3—CH_2—O—CH_2—CH_2—CH_3

  b. Ethyl cyclopropyl ether has a two-carbon group and a three-carbon cyclo alkyl group attached to oxygen by single bonds.

  CH_3—CH_2—O—◁

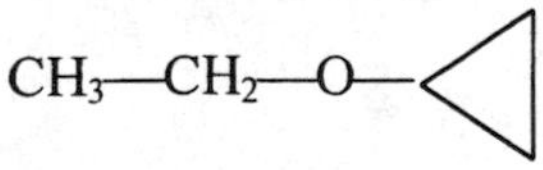

  c. Methoxycyclopentane has a one-carbon group and a five-carbon cycloalkyl group attached to oxygen by single bonds.

  OCH_3

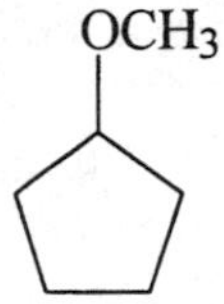

  d. 1-ethoxy-2-methylbutane has a four-carbon chain with a methyl attached to carbon 2 and an ethoxy attached to carbon 1.

  CH_3
   |
  CH_3—CH_2–O–CH_2—CH—CH_2—CH_3

  e. 2,3-dimethoxypentane has a five-carbon chain with two methoxy groups attached; one to carbon 2 and the other to carbon 3.

  OCH_3
   |
  CH_3—CH—CH—CH_2—CH_3
         |
        OCH_3

14.18   **a.** $CH_3CH_2-O-CH_2CH_3$ **b.**

c.

OCH₂CH₃ (OCH$_2$CH$_3$) attached to cyclohexane ring

d. $CH_3-\overset{\overset{\displaystyle CH_3}{|}}{\underset{\underset{\displaystyle OCH_3}{|}}{C}}-\overset{\overset{\displaystyle CH_3}{|}}{CH}-CH_3$ **e.**

OCH₃, OCH₃ on benzene ring

14.19   **a.** Constitutional isomers $(C_5H_{12}O)$ have the same formula, but different arrangements.
   b. Different compounds have different molecular formulas.
   c. Constitutional isomers $(C_5H_{12}O)$ have the same formula, but different arrangements.

14.20   **a.** constitutional isomers   **b.** constitutional isomers   **c.** constitutional isomers

14.21   The heterocyclic ethers with five atoms including one oxygen are named *furan*; six atoms including one oxygen are *pyrans*. A six-atom cyclic ether with two oxygen atoms is *dioxane*.
   a. tetrahydrofuran   **b.** 3-methylfuran   **c.** 5-methyl-1, 3-dioxane

14.22   **a.** furan   **b.** 2-methyl-1,4-dioxane   **c.** 4-methylpyran

14.23   **a.** methanol; hydrogen bonding of alcohols gives higher boiling points than alkanes.
   b. 1-butanol; alcohols hydrogen bond, but ethers cannot.
   c. 1-butanol; hydrogen bonding of alcohols gives higher boiling points than alkanes.

14.24   Glycerol can form more hydrogen bonds because it has three hydroxyl groups (—OH) compared to the hydrogen bond for one hydroxyl group in 1-pentanol.

14.25   **a.** yes, alcohols with 1-4 carbon atoms hydrogen bond with water
   b. yes; the water can hydrogen bond to the O in ether
   c. no; a carbon chain longer than 4 carbon atoms diminishes the effect of the —OH group.
   d. no; alkanes are nonpolar and do not hydrogen bond
   e. yes; the —OH in phenol ionizes in water, which makes it soluble

14.26   **a.** Ethanol contains a hydroxyl group (—OH)
   b. The oxygen in ethers can form hydrogen bonds with water.
   c. Alcohols with one to four carbon atoms are soluble in water. In alcohols with longer carbon chains, the effect of the —OH group is diminished.

14.27   Dehydration is the removal of an –OH and a –H from adjacent carbon atoms.

   a. $CH_3-CH_2-CH=CH_2$ **b.**

   c. In c, there are two possible products A and B. B will be the major product, since the hydrogen is removed from the carbon that has the smaller number of hydrogens.

A

B

d. In d, there are two possible products A and B. B will be the major product, since the hydrogen is removed from the carbon that has the smaller number of hydrogens.

$$CH_3—CH_2—CH_2—CH=CH_2 \qquad CH_3—CH_2—CH=CH—CH_3$$
$$A \qquad\qquad\qquad B$$

14.28   **a.** 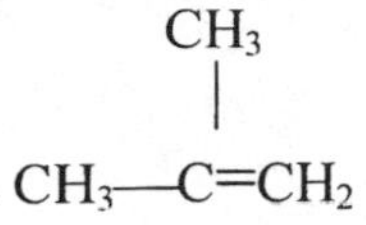 $\overset{\displaystyle CH_3}{\overset{|}{CH_3—C=CH_2}}$ **b.** 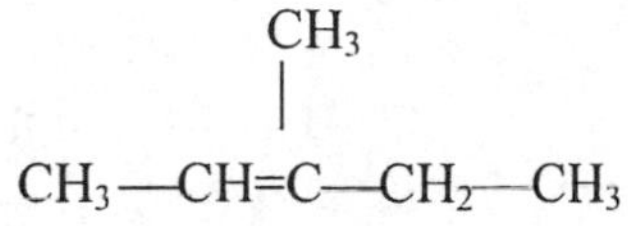 $\overset{\displaystyle CH_3}{\overset{|}{CH_3—CH=C—CH_2—CH_3}}$

c. 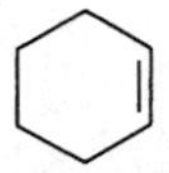   **d.** 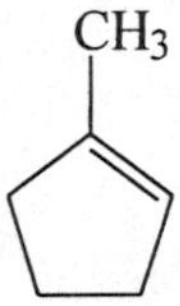 (structure with CH₃)

14.29 An ether is formed when H_2O is eliminated from two alcohols; the alkyl portion of one alcohol combines with the alkoxy portion of the other alcohol.

a. $CH_3—O—CH_3$ **b.** $CH_3—CH_2—CH_2—O—CH_2—CH_2—CH_3$

14.30 **a.** $CH_3CH_2—O—CH_2CH_3$ **b.** 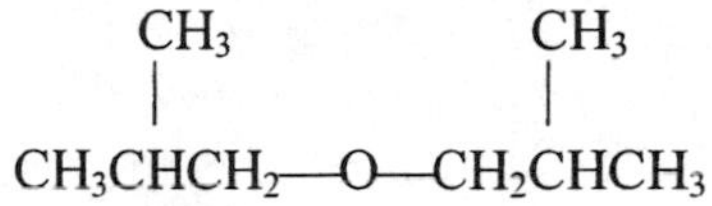 $\overset{\displaystyle CH_3}{\overset{|}{CH_3CHCH_2}}—O—\overset{\displaystyle CH_3}{\overset{|}{CH_2CHCH_3}}$

14.31 Alcohols can produce alkenes and ethers by the loss of water (dehydration).
a. $CH_3—CH_2—OH$

b. Since this ether has two different alkyl groups;,it must be formed from two alcohols.

    $CH_3—OH \; + \; CH_3—CH_2—OH$

c. OH (cyclohexanol structure)

14.32 **a.** $CH_3—CH_2—OH$ **b.** 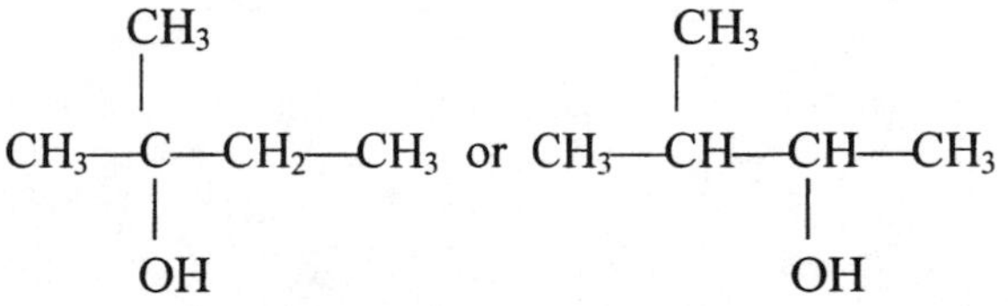 $\overset{\displaystyle CH_3}{\overset{|}{CH_3—C—CH_2—CH_3}}$ or $\overset{\displaystyle CH_3}{\overset{|}{CH_3—CH—CH—CH_3}}$ **c.** (cyclopentanol with OH)

with OH below the C and OH below the CH.

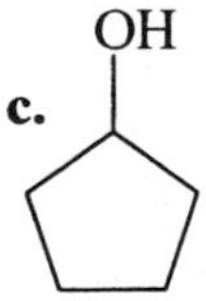

14.33 **a.** A primary alcohol oxidizes to an aldehyde and then to a carboxylic acid.

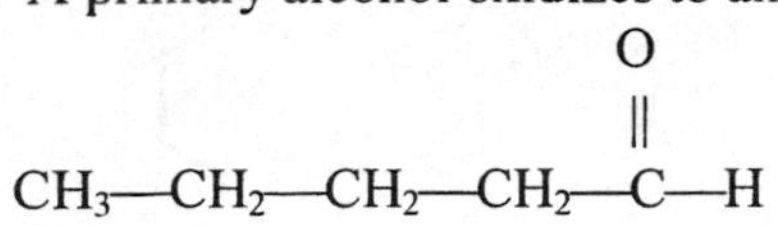

$$CH_3—CH_2—CH_2—CH_2—\overset{\displaystyle O}{\overset{||}{C}}—H \qquad \text{then} \qquad CH_3—CH_2—CH_2—CH_2—\overset{\displaystyle O}{\overset{||}{C}}—OH$$

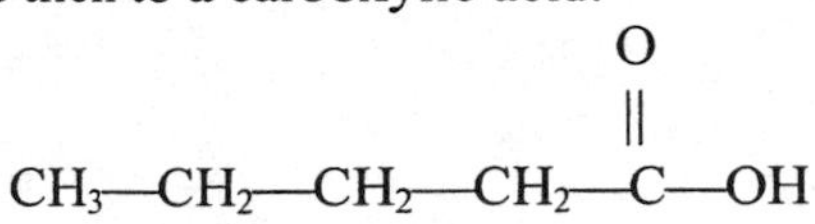

b. A secondary alcohol oxidizes to a ketone. $CH_3—CH_2—\overset{\displaystyle O}{\overset{||}{C}}—CH_3$

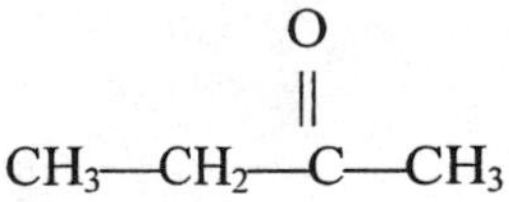

c. A secondary alcohol oxidizes to a ketone.

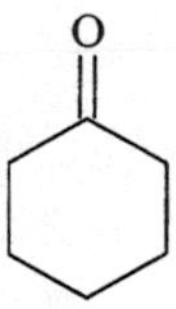

d. A secondary alcohol oxidizes to a ketone.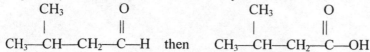

e. A primary alcohol oxidizes to an aldehyde and then to a carboxylic acid.

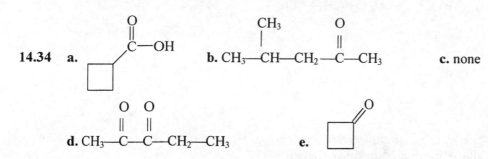

14.34 **a.** **b.** CH_3—CH—CH_2—$\overset{\overset{\textstyle O}{\|}}{C}$—$CH_3$ with CH_3 on the CH **c.** none

d. CH_3—$\overset{\overset{\textstyle O}{\|}}{C}$—$\overset{\overset{\textstyle O}{\|}}{C}$—$CH_2$—$CH_3$ **e.**

14.35 **a.** An aldehyde is the product of the oxidation of a primary alcohol CH_3—OH.
b. A ketone is the product of the oxidation of a secondary alcohol.

c. A ketone is the product of the oxidation of a secondary alcohol. CH_3—$\overset{\overset{\textstyle OH}{|}}{CH}$—$CH_2$—$CH_3$

d. An aldehyde is the product of the oxidation of a primary alcohol.

e. A ketone is the product of the oxidation of a secondary alcohol.

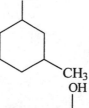

14.36 **a.** CH_3—CH_2—OH **b.** CH_3—$\overset{\overset{\textstyle OH}{|}}{CH}$—$\overset{\overset{\textstyle CH_3}{|}}{CH}$—$CH_3$ **c.**

d. CH_3—CH_2—CH_2—OH **e.** CH_3—$\overset{\overset{\textstyle CH_3}{|}}{CH}$—$CH_2$—$CH_2$—OH

14.37 **a.** 2° **b.** 1° **c.** 1° **d.** 2° **e.** 1° **f.** 3°

14.38 **a.** tertiary **b.** tertiary **c.** primary
d. tertiary **e.** primary **f.** secondary

14.39 **a.** alcohol **b.** ether **c.** thiol **d.** alcohol
e. ether **f.** cyclic ether **g.** alcohol **h.** phenol

14.40 **a.** phenol **b.** thiol **c.** ether **d.** alcochol
e. ether **f.** cyclic ether **g.** phenol **h.** phenol

14.41 **a.** 2-chloro-4-methylcyclohexanol **b.** methyoxy benzene; methyl phenyl ether
c. 2-propanethiol **d.** 2,4-dimethyl-2-pentanol
e. 1-methoxypropane; methyl propyl ether **f.** 3-methyl furan
g. 4-bromo-2-pentanol **h.** *meta*-cresol

14.42 **a.** 4-chlorophenol; *p*-chlorophenol **b.** 1-propanethiol
c. ethoxycyclopentane; cyclopentyl ethyl ether **d.** 2,4-dimethyl-2-pentanol
e. 3-methoxypentane **f.** 1.4-dioxane
g. 2,4-dichlorophenol **h.** 3,4-dimethylphenol

14.43

a.

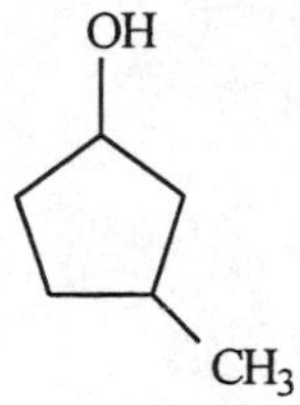

b.

c. 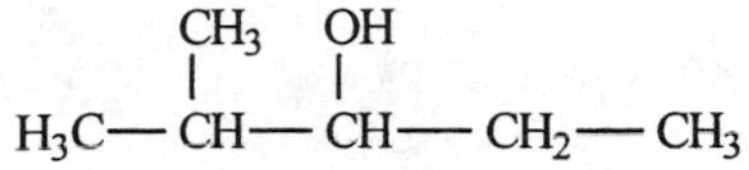 $H_3C-CH-CH-CH_2-CH_3$ with CH_3 and OH

d.

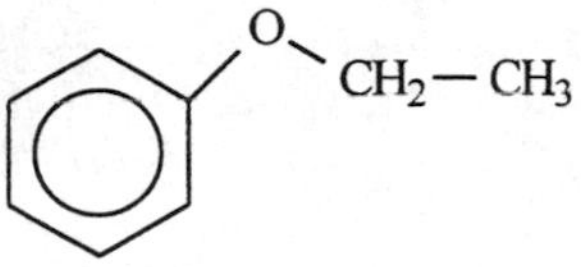

e. 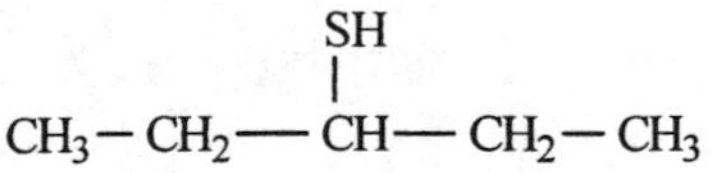 $CH_3-CH_2-CH-CH_2-CH_3$ with SH

f.

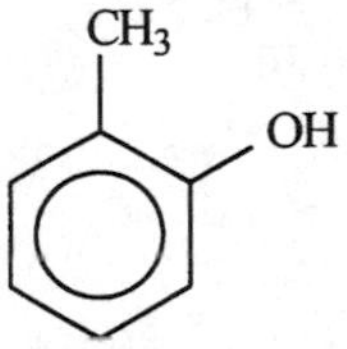

g.

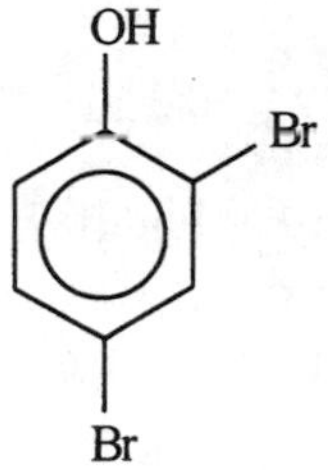

14.44 **a.** 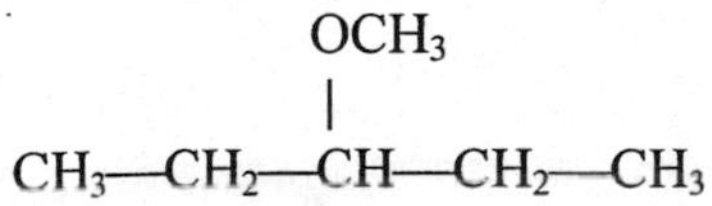 $CH_3-CH_2-CH-CH_2-CH_3$ with OCH_3

b.

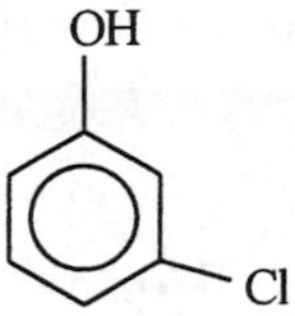

c. 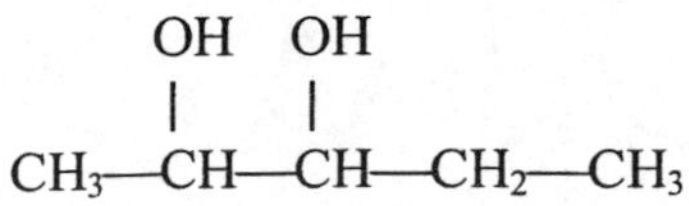 $CH_3-CH-CH-CH_2-CH_3$ with OH OH

d. $CH_3-CH_2-CH_2-O-CH_3$

e. CH_3-SH

f. 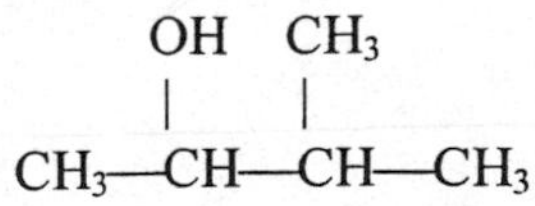 $CH_3-CH-CH-CH_3$ with OH CH_3

g.

165

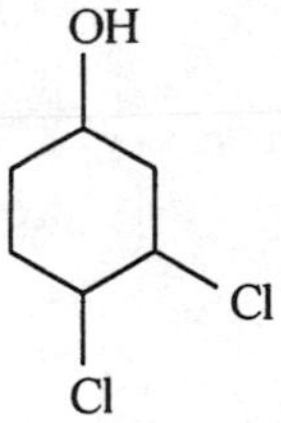

14.45 **a.** Glycerol is used in skin lotions. **b.** 1,2-ethanediol; ethylene glycol is used in antifreeze
c. Ethanol is produced by fermentation of grains and sugars.

14.46 **a.** methanol **b.** 2-propanol; isopropyl alcohol **c.** ethanol

14.47 Write the carbon chain first, and place the —OH on the carbon atoms in the chain to give
different structural formulas. Shorten the chain by one carbon, and attach a methyl group and
—OH group to give different compounds.

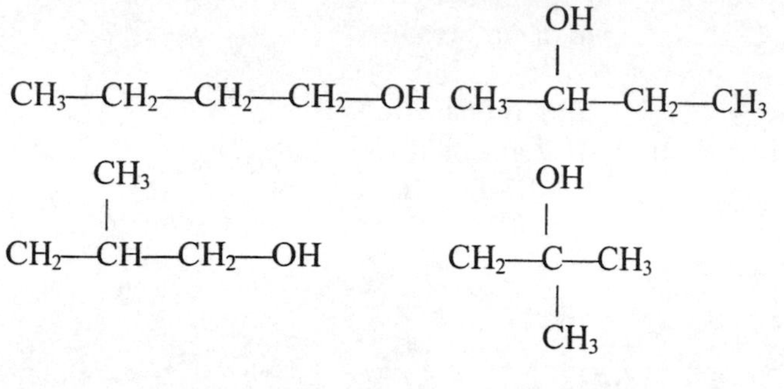

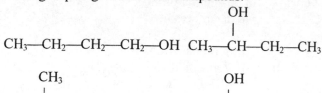

$$CH_3—CH_2—CH_2—CH_2—OH \qquad CH_3\overset{\overset{\displaystyle OH}{|}}{—CH—}CH_2—CH_3$$

$$CH_2\overset{\overset{\displaystyle CH_3}{|}}{—CH—}CH_2—OH \qquad CH_2\overset{\overset{\displaystyle OH}{|}}{\underset{\underset{\displaystyle CH_3}{|}}{—C—}}CH_3$$

14.48 $CH_3—O—CH_2—CH_2—CH_2—CH_3 \qquad CH_3—CH_2—O—CH_2—CH_2—CH_3$

$$CH_3—O—CH_2\overset{\overset{\displaystyle CH_3}{|}}{—CH—}CH_3 \qquad CH_3—CH_2—O\overset{\overset{\displaystyle CH_3}{|}}{—CH—}CH_3$$

$$CH_3—O\overset{\overset{\displaystyle CH_3}{|}}{—C—}CH_3 \qquad CH_3—O\overset{\overset{\displaystyle CH_3}{|}}{—CH—}CH_2—CH_3$$

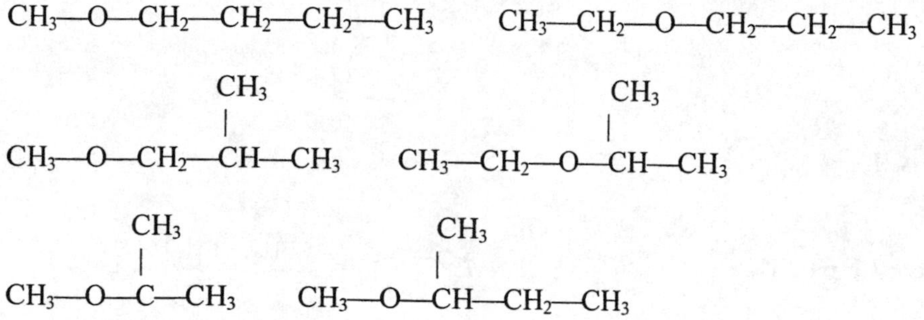

14.49 **a.** 1-propanol; hydrogen bonding **b.** 1-propanol; hydrogen bonding
c. 1-butanol; larger molar mass

14.50 **a.** ethyl alcohol **b.** 2-pentanol **c.** 1-butanol

14.51 **a.** soluble; hydrogen bonding **b.** soluble; hydrogen bonding
c. insoluble; long carbon chain diminishes effect of polar —OH on hydrogen bonding

14.52 **a.** soluble; three —OH groups **b.** insoluble; nonpolar hydrocarbon
c. soluble; two —OH groups makes longer hydrocarbon chain more soluble in water

14.53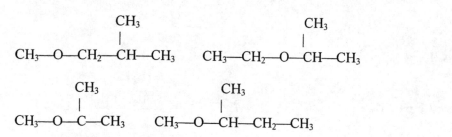

a. $CH_3—CH=CH_2$ **b.** 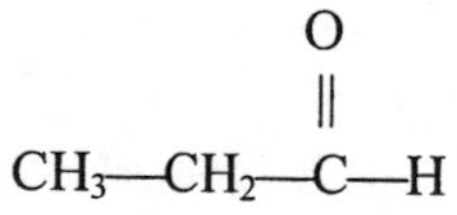 $CH_3—CH_2—\overset{\overset{\displaystyle O}{||}}{C}—H$

c. $CH_3—CH=CH—CH_3$ **d.** 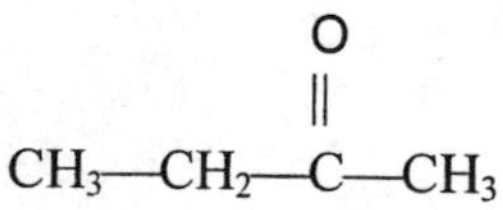 $CH_3—CH_2—\overset{\overset{\displaystyle O}{||}}{C}—CH_3$

e. $CH_3—CH_2—CH_2—O—CH_2—CH_2—CH_3$

f. 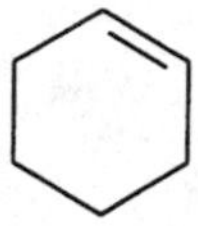   **g.**

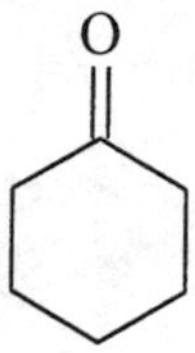

14.54 **a.** 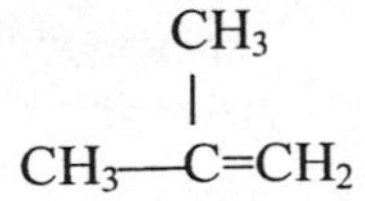 CH$_3$—C=CH$_2$ (with CH$_3$ on the C)

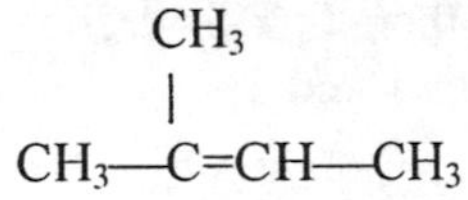

b. CH$_3$—C=CH—CH$_3$ (with CH$_3$ on the C)

c. CH$_3$—CH—C—CH$_3$ (with CH$_3$ and O)

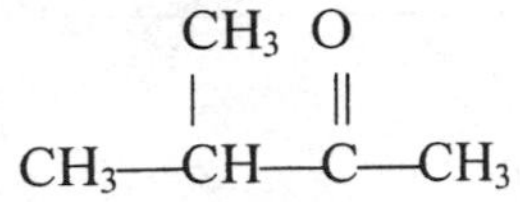

d. 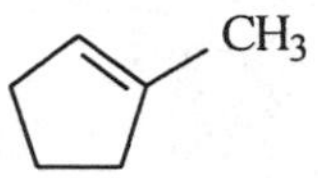 cyclopentene with CH$_3$

e. 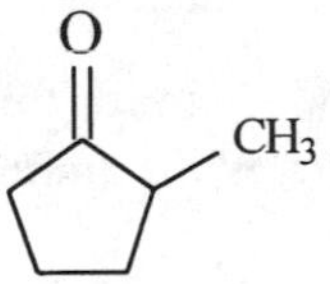 cyclopentanone with CH$_3$ (ketone, O)

f. CH$_3$—CH$_2$—O—CH$_2$—CH$_3$

g. CH$_3$—CH$_2$—CH=CH—CH$_3$

14.55 **a.** 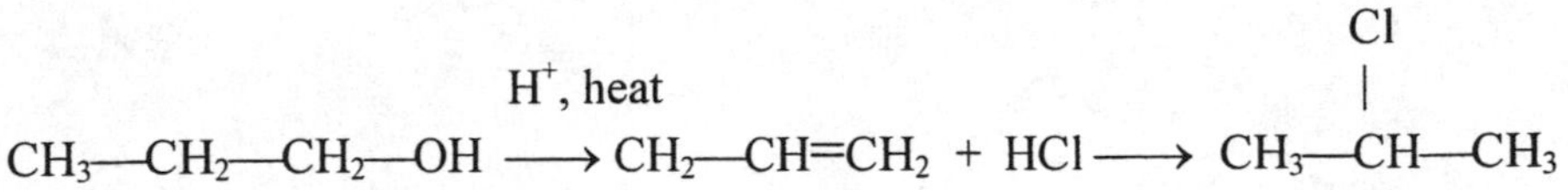 CH$_3$—CH$_2$—CH$_2$—OH $\xrightarrow{\text{H}^+, \text{ heat}}$ CH$_2$—CH=CH$_2$ + HCl $\longrightarrow$ CH$_3$—CH—CH$_3$ (with Cl)

b. 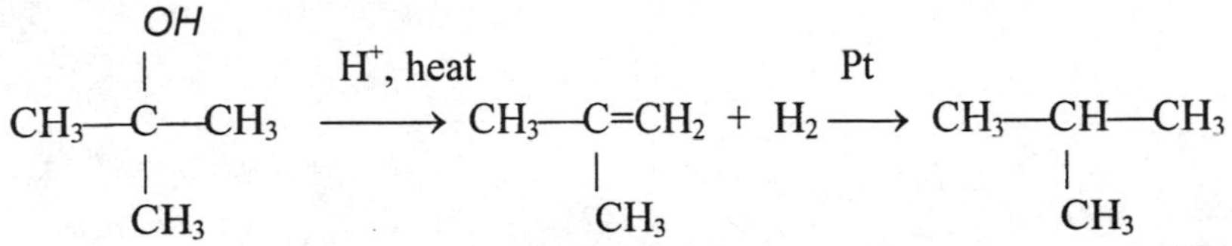 CH$_3$—C—CH$_3$ (with OH and CH$_3$) $\xrightarrow{\text{H}^+, \text{ heat}}$ CH$_3$—C=CH$_2$ (with CH$_3$) + H$_2$ $\xrightarrow{\text{Pt}}$ CH$_3$—CH—CH$_3$ (with CH$_3$)

c. CH$_3$—CH$_2$—CH$_2$—OH $\xrightarrow{\text{H}^+, \text{ heat}}$ CH$_3$—CH=CH$_2$ + H$_2$O $\xrightarrow{\text{H}^+}$ CH$_3$—CH—CH$_3$ (with OH)

$\xrightarrow{\text{[O]}}$ CH$_3$—C—CH$_3$ (with O)

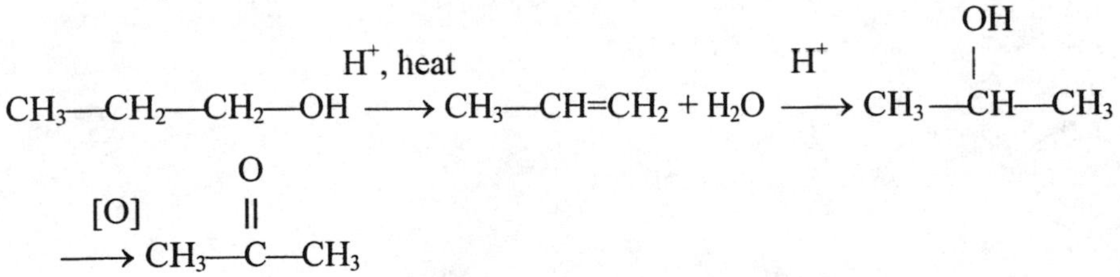

14.56 **a.** CH$_3$—CH$_2$—CH$_2$—CH$_2$—CH$_2$—OH $\xrightarrow{\text{H}^+, \text{ heat}}$ CH$_3$—CH$_2$—CH$_2$—CH=CH$_2$

b. 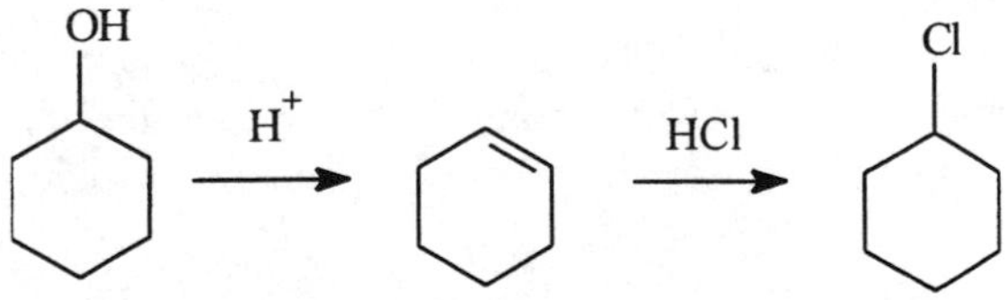 cyclohexanol (OH) $\xrightarrow{\text{H}^+}$ cyclohexene $\xrightarrow{\text{HCl}}$ chlorocyclohexane (Cl)

c. CH$_3$—CH$_2$—CH$_2$—CH$_2$—OH $\xrightarrow{\text{H}^+, \text{ heat}}$ CH$_3$—CH$_2$—CH=CH$_2$ + Cl$_2$ $\longrightarrow$

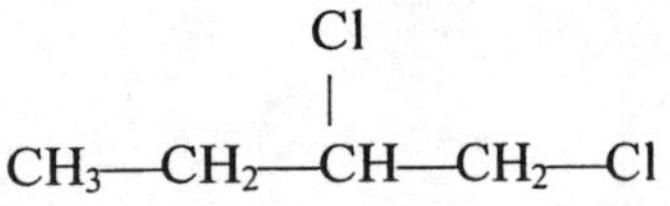

CH$_3$—CH$_2$—CH—CH$_2$—Cl (with Cl)

14.57 Testosterone contains cycloalkene, alcohol and ketone functional groups.

14.58 **a.** cycloalkene, phenol, ether   **b.** cycloalkene, ketone, alcohol, alkyne

14.59 4-hexyl-1, 3-benzenediol tells us that there is a six carbon group attached to carbon 4 of a benzene ring and hydroxyls attached to carbons 1 and 3.

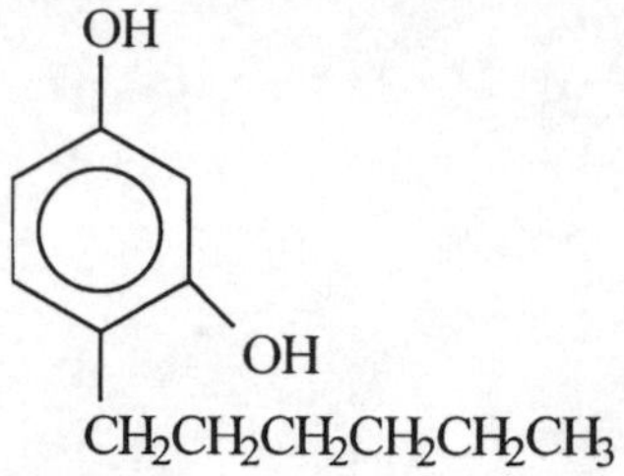

14.60 Menthol is 2–isopropyl–5–methylcyclohexanol. Thymol is 2–isopropyl–5–methylphenol. They have the same groups in the same position, but thymol is aromatic, while menthol is a cyclic alcohol.

14.61 **a.** 2,5-dichlorophenol is a benzene ring with a hydroxyl on carbon 1 and chlorine atoms on carbons 2 and 5.

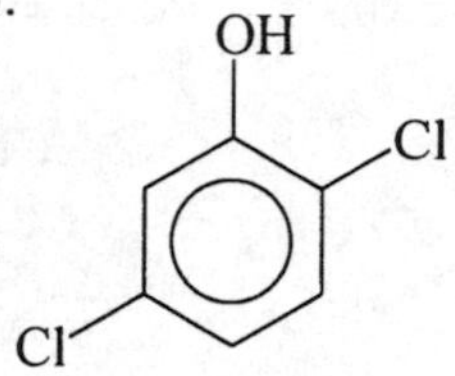

b.

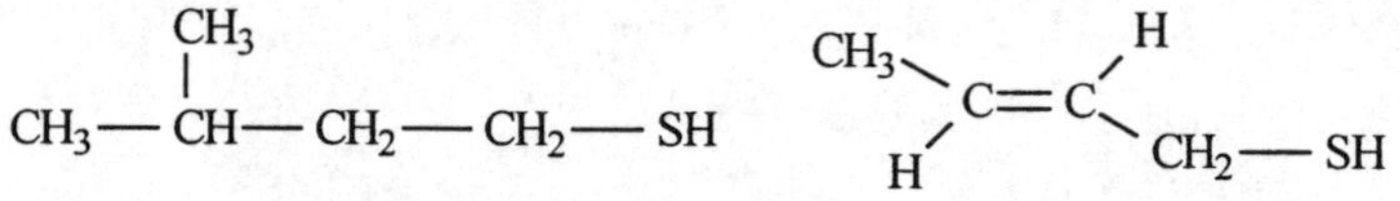

c.

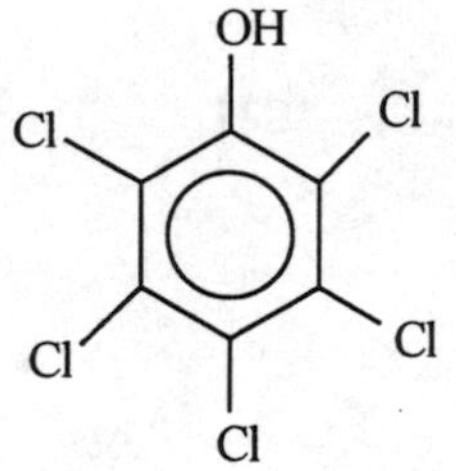

14.62 Dimethyl ether CH_3—O—CH_3 b.p. –24°C
Ethyl alcohol CH_3CH_2OH b.p. 79°C
The polar hydroxyl groups in ethyl alcohol form hydrogen bonds between the alcohol molecules, which requires a higher boiling point to separate them into gaseous molecule

15

Aldehydes, Ketones, and Chiral Molecules

Study Goals

- Name and write the condensed structural formulas for aldehydes and ketones.
- Describe some important aldehydes and ketones.
- Identify the chiral carbon atoms in organic molecules.
- Write equations for the oxidation of aldehydes and for the reduction of aldehydes and ketones.
- Draw the structural formulas of hemiacetals and acetals produced from the addition of alcohols to aldehydes and ketones.

Chapter Outline

15.1   **Structure and Bonding**
15.2   **Naming Aldehydes and Ketones**
15.3   **Some Important Aldehydes and Ketones**
         Environmental Note: Vanilla
15.4   **Physical Properties**
15.5   **Chiral Molecules**
         Health Note: Enantiomers in Biological Systems
15.6   **Oxidation and Reduction**
15.7   **Addition Reactions**

Chapter Summary and Demonstrations

1. Aldehydes and Ketones

The study of organic functional groups continues with the carbonyl group of aldehydes and ketones. The properties of ketones and aldehydes are discussed including hydrogen bonding, boiling points and solubility in water. IUPAC names and common names, if prevalent, are given for ketones and aldehydes.

Demonstration: Look for names of aldehydes, and/or ketones on the labels of products such as mouthwash, antifreeze, rubbing alcohol, food flavorings, cosmetics, and hair spray.

2. Chiral Molecules

Chiral molecules have one or more chiral carbons, which are bonded to four different atoms of groups of atoms. Chiral molecules known as stereoisomers have the same atoms bonded, but with different arrangements in space. Stereoisomers known as enantiomers have mirror images that cannot be superimposed.

Demonstration: Models of Chiral Molecules I start the discussion of chirality by having students compare their hands. Looking at their palms, we see that our thumbs go in opposite directions. We can match the direction of the thumbs only if we have one palm up and one palm down. If the hands face each other, they are mirror images. I use a mirror in class to provide the image of the other hand.

Model kits are very useful in building simple chiral molecules. I give students a formula such as CFClBrI and ask them to make the model. I try to find the mirror image among the models and compare the two. Or I ask students to now make a mirror image of the first model. Eventually, this hands on, visual approach helps students to understand the three-dimensional relationships between mirror images that is difficult to show in two dimensions. I make some larger models with an —OH group, aldehyde

169

group, —CH$_3$ group and —CH$_2$OH group. We make the mirror image as well. Then I present some ways to draw the structure using Fischer projections.

Laboratory Suggestions

Lab 25   Aldehydes and Ketones

Laboratory tests are used to identify the functional groups of aldehydes and ketones, chemical and physical properties. Aldehydes are oxidized and the structural formulas of the oxidation products are written.

A. Structures of Some Aldehydes and Ketones
B. Properties of Aldehydes and Ketones
C. Iodoform Test for Methyl Ketones
D. Oxidation of Aldehydes and Ketones
E. Identification of an Unknown

Laboratory Skills to Demonstrate

Proper technique for noting the odor of a substance in a test tube.
Identification of a change in the orange color of chromic acid to green as an indication of the occurrence of an oxidation reaction.
Identification of changes in the iodoform test.
Identification of a change from the blue color of Benedict's reagent to various shades of green to red-orange as a positive test for the oxidation of aldehydes to carboxylic acids.

Answers and Solutions to Selected Text Problems

15.1   **a.** ketone   **b.** aldehyde   **c.** ketone   **d.** aldehyde

15.2   **a.** aldehyde   **b.** aldehyde   **c.** ketone   **d.** ketone

15.3   **a.** 1   **b.** 1   **c.** 2

15.4   **a.** 2   **b.** 2   **c.** 1

15.5   **a.** propanal   **b.** 2-methyl-3-pentanone   **c.** 3-hydroxybutanal
         d. 2-pentanone   **e.** 3-methylcyclohexanone   **f.** 4-chlorobenzaldehyde

15.6   **a.** butanal   **b.** 4-hydroxy-2-pentanone   **c.** 5-methyl-3-hexanone
         d. cyclopentanone   **e.** 3,5-dichlorobenzaldehyde   **f.** 2-methyl-4-oxopentanal

15.7   **a.** acetaldehyde   **b.** methyl propyl ketone   **c.** formaldehyde

15.8   **a.** ethyl methyl ketone   **b.** diethyl ketone   **c.** propionaldehyde

15.9

a.
$$CH_3-\overset{\overset{\textstyle O}{\|}}{C}-H$$

b.
$$CH_3-\overset{\overset{\textstyle O}{\|}}{C}-CH_2-\overset{\overset{\textstyle OH}{|}}{CH}-CH_3$$

c.
$$CH_3-\overset{\overset{\textstyle Br}{|}}{CH}-\overset{\overset{\textstyle Br}{|}}{CH}-\overset{\overset{\textstyle O}{\|}}{C}-H$$

d.
$$CH_3-\overset{\overset{\textstyle O}{\|}}{C}-CH_2-CH_2-CH_2-CH_3$$

e.
$$CH_3-CH_2-\overset{\overset{\textstyle CH_3}{|}}{CH}-CH_2-\overset{\overset{\textstyle O}{\|}}{C}-H$$

f.
$$CH_3-\overset{\overset{\textstyle O}{\|}}{C}-\overset{\overset{\textstyle O}{\|}}{C}-H$$

170

5.10

a. 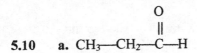 CH₃—CH₂—C(=O)—H

b. CH₃—CH₂—CH₂—C(=O)—H

c. CH₃—CH₂—CH(Br)—CH(OH)—CH₂—C(=O)—H

d. CH₂—C(=O)—CH₂—CH₂—Br

e. CH₃—CH₂—C(=O)—C(=O)—H

f. CH₃—C(=O)—CH₃

15.11

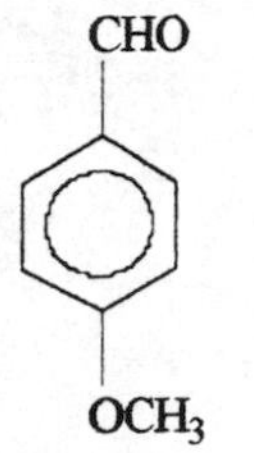

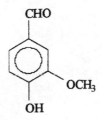

CHO—(ring)—OCH₃

15.12

CHO—(ring)—OCH₃, OH

15.13   a. benzaldehyde   b. acetone; propanone   c. formaldehyde

15.14   a. butanedione   b. acetone; propanone   c. formaldehyde

15.15   a. CH₃—CH₂—C(=O)—H has a polar carbonyl group.
b. pentanal has more carbons and thus a higher molar mass.
c. 1-butanol hydrogen bonds with other 1-butanol molecules.

15.16   a. 2-butanol molecules can hydrogen bond with each other;
b. The carbonyl group in butanone molecules provides dipole-dipole interactions.
c. Pentanone has a greater molar mass.

15.17   a. CH₃—C(=O)—C(=O)—CH₃: more hydrogen bonding
b. acetaldhyde; more hydrogen bonding
c. acetone; lower number of carbon atoms

15.18   a. Propanal; the carbonyl group hydrogen bonds with water.
b. Propanone has fewer carbon atoms.
c. Propanone; the carbonyl group hydrogen bonds with water.

15.19 No. The carbon chain diminishes the effect of the carbonyl group.

15.20 Yes. Carbonyl compounds with one to four carbon atoms are soluble in water. The alkyl group in aldehydes with five or more carbon atoms diminishes the polar effect of the carbonyl group.

15.21 **a.** achiral

b. chiral

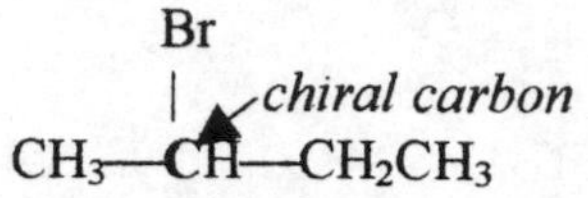

$$CH_3-\overset{\overset{\displaystyle Br}{|}}{CH}-CH_2CH_3 \quad \textit{chiral carbon}$$

c. chiral

$$CH_3-\overset{\overset{\displaystyle Br}{|}}{CH}-\overset{\overset{\displaystyle O}{||}}{C}-H \quad \textit{chiral carbon}$$

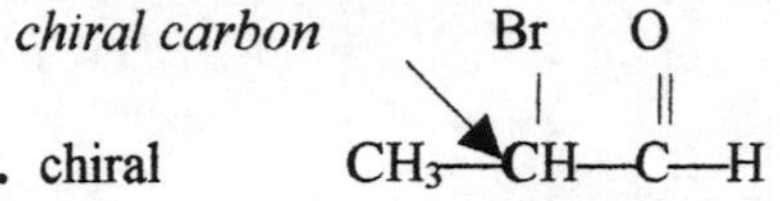

d. achiral

15.22 **a.** Yes. Carbon 2 is bonded to four different atoms or groups.
b. No. There are no carbon atoms attached to four different groups.
c. Yes. There are carbon atoms that are attached to four different groups.
d. Yes. Carbon 2 is bonded to a chlorine atom, hydrogen atom, methyl group and a —CH₂—Br group

15.23 **a.**

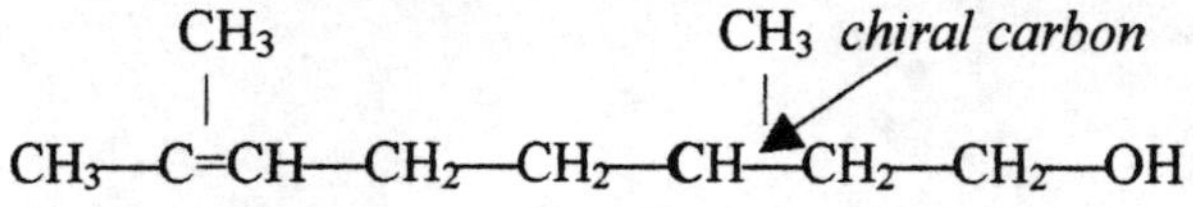

$$CH_3-\overset{\overset{\displaystyle CH_3}{|}}{C}=CH-CH_2-CH_2-\overset{\overset{\displaystyle CH_3}{|}}{CH}-CH_2-CH_2-OH \quad \textit{chiral carbon}$$

b.

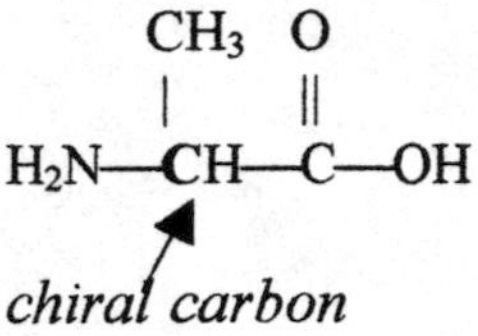

$$H_2N-\overset{\overset{\displaystyle CH_3}{|}}{CH}-\overset{\overset{\displaystyle O}{||}}{C}-OH$$

chiral carbon

15.24 **a.**

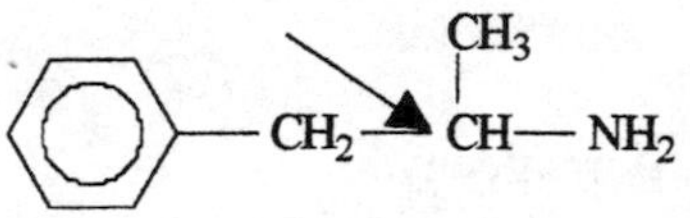

Benzene ring$-CH_2-\overset{\overset{\displaystyle CH_3}{|}}{CH}-NH_2$

b.

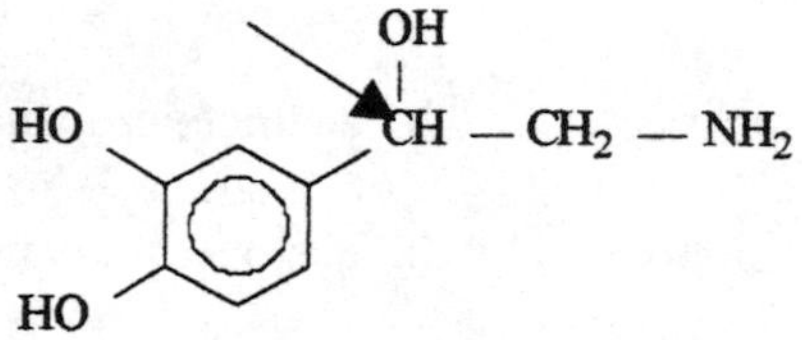

HO, HO-benzene ring$-\overset{\overset{\displaystyle OH}{|}}{CH}-CH_2-NH_2$

15.25 **a.**

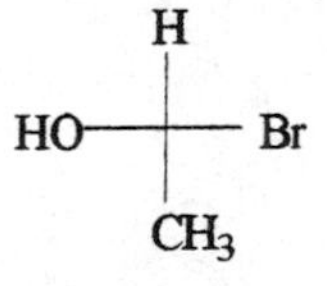

$HO\!-\!\!\overset{H}{\underset{CH_3}{|}}\!\!-\!Br$

b. $Cl\!-\!\!\overset{CH_3}{\underset{OH}{|}}\!\!-\!Br$

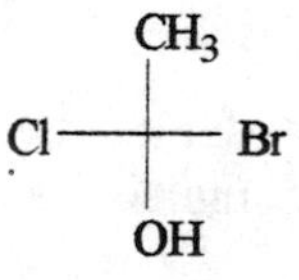

c. $HO\!-\!\!\overset{CHO}{\underset{CH_2CH_3}{|}}\!\!-\!H$

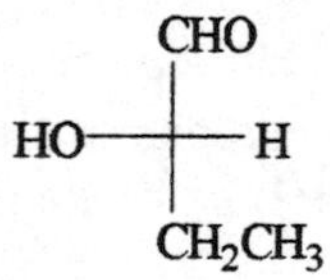

15.26 **a.** $HO\!-\!\!\overset{H}{\underset{CH_2OH}{|}}\!\!-\!Br$

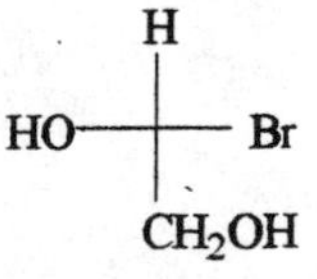

b. $H\!-\!\!\overset{CH_3}{\underset{CH_2OH}{|}}\!\!-\!OH$

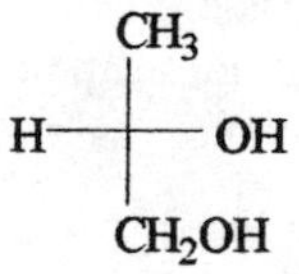

c. $HO\!-\!\!\overset{CHO}{\underset{CH_2OH}{|}}\!\!-\!H$

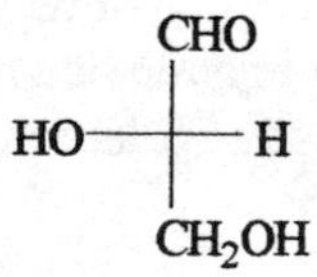

15.27 **a.** identical **b.** enantiomers **c.** identical **d.** enantiomers

15.28 **a.** enantiomers **b.** identical **c.** enantiomers **d.** enantiomers

15.29 **a.** An aldehyde is the product of the oxidation of a primary alcohol CH₃OH.
b. A ketone is the product of the oxidation of a secondary alcohol.

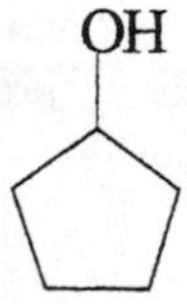

OH

(cyclopentane ring with OH)

c. A ketone is the product of the oxidation of a secondary alcohol.

$$CH_3-\underset{\underset{OH}{|}}{CH}-CH_2-CH_3$$

d. An aldehyde is the product of the oxidation of a primary alcohol.

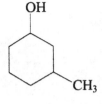

e. A ketone is the product of the oxidation of a secondary alcohol.

15.30 **a.** CH_3-CH_2-OH

b. $CH_3-\underset{\underset{CH_3}{|}}{CH_2}-\underset{\underset{OH}{|}}{CH}-CH_3$

c.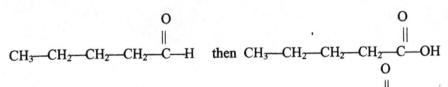

d. $CH_3-CH_2-CH_2-OH$

e. $CH_3-\underset{\underset{CH_3}{|}}{CH}-CH_2-CH_2-OH$

15.31 **a.** A primary alcohol will be oxidized to an aldehyde and then to a carboxylic acid.

$$CH_3-CH_2-CH_2-CH_2-\overset{\overset{O}{||}}{C}-H \quad \text{then} \quad CH_3-CH_2-CH_2-CH_2-\overset{\overset{O}{||}}{C}-OH$$

b. A secondary alcohol will be oxidized to a ketone. $\quad CH_3-CH_2-\overset{\overset{O}{||}}{C}-CH_3$

c. A secondary alcohol will be oxidized to a ketone.

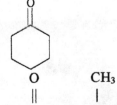

d. A secondary alcohol will be oxidized to a ketone. $\quad CH_3-\overset{\overset{O}{||}}{C}-CH_2-\underset{\underset{CH_3}{|}}{CH}-CH_3$

e. A primary alcohol will be oxidized to an aldehyde and then to a carboxylic acid.

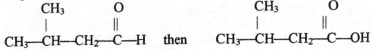

15.32 a.

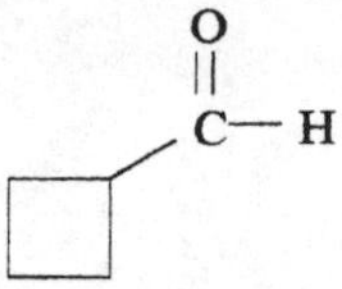

O
‖
C—H

(cyclobutyl group attached to C—H)

b.

CH₃   O
| ‖
CH₃—CH—CH₂—C—CH₃

c. *none*

d.

O O
‖ ‖
CH₃CCCH₂CH₃

e.

(cyclobutanone with =O)

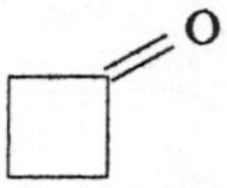

15.33 In reduction, an aldehyde will give a primary alcohol and a ketone will give a secondary alcohol.

a. Butyraldehyde is the four-carbon aldehyde; it will be reduced to a four carbon, primary alcohol.

CH₃—CH₂—CH₂—CH₂—OH

b. Acetone is a three-carbon ketone; it will be reduced to a three carbon secondary alcohol.

OH
|
CH₃—CH—CH₃

c. 3-bromohexanal is a six-carbon aldehyde with bromine attached to carbon 3. It reduces to a six-carbon primary alcohol with bromine on carbon 3.

Br
|
CH₃—CH₂—CH₂—CH—CH₂—CH₂–OH

d. 2-methyl-3-pentanone is a five-carbon ketone with a methyl group attached to carbon 2. It will be reduced to a five-carbon secondary alcohol with a methyl attached to carbon 2.

CH₃ OH
| |
CH₃—CH—CH–CH₂—CH₃

15.34 a.

OH
|
CH₃—CH₂—CH—CH₂—CH₂—CH₃

b. CH₃—OH

c.

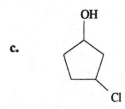

d.

OH
|
CH₃—CH—CH₂—CH₂—CH₃

15.35 a.

OH
|
CH₃—C—H
|
OH

b.

OH
|
H—C—H
|
OH

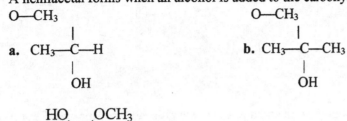

15.36 **a.** 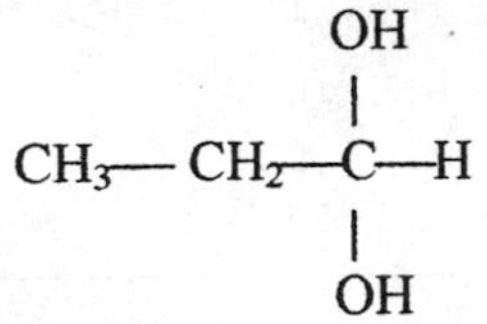 CH₃—CH₂—C—H (with OH above and OH below the C) **b.** 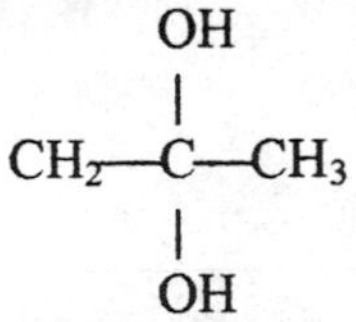 CH₂—C—CH₃ (with OH above and OH below)

15.37 **a.** hemiacetal (ethanol and formaldehyde) **b.** hemiacetal **c.** acetal
d. hemiacetal **e.** acetal

15.38 **a.** neither **b.** neither **c.** hemiacetal
d. acetal **e.** neither

15.39 A hemiacetal forms when an alcohol is added to the carbonyl of an aldehyde or ketone.

a. CH₃—C—H (with O—CH₃ above and OH below)   **b.** CH₃—C—CH₃ (with O—CH₃ above and OH below)

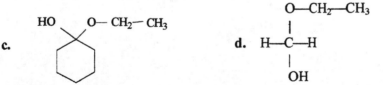

c.

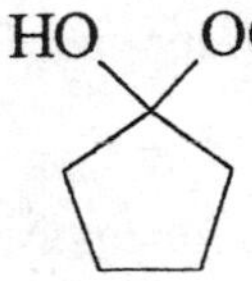

d. 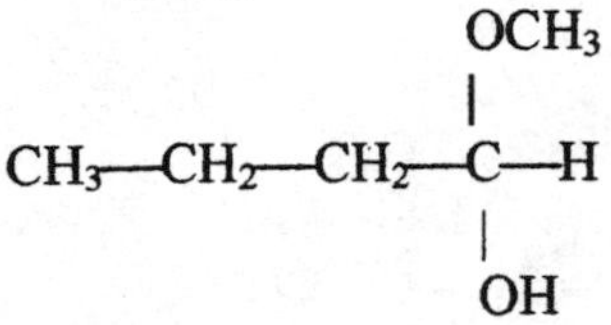 CH₃—CH₂—CH₂—C—H (with OCH₃ above and OH below)

15.40

a. 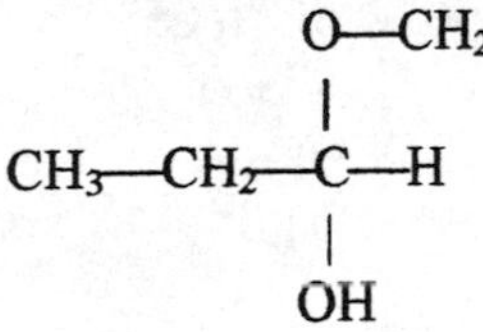 CH₃—CH₂—C—H (with O—CH₂—CH₃ above and OH below)   **b.** 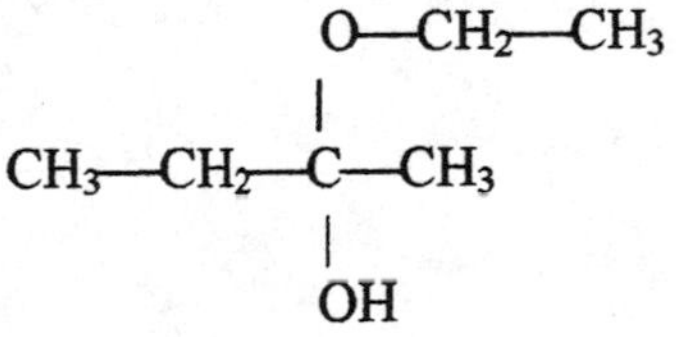 CH₃—CH₂—C—CH₃ (with O—CH₂—CH₃ above and OH below)

c.

d. H—C—H (with O—CH₂—CH₃ above and OH below)

15.41 An acetal forms when a second molecule of alcohol reacts with a hemiacetal.

a. CH₃—C—H (with OCH₃ above and OCH₃ below)   **b.** CH₃—C—CH₃ (with OCH₃ above and OCH₃ below)

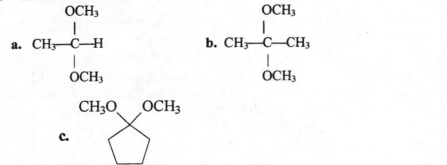

c.

$$\text{d.} \quad CH_3-CH_2-CH_2-\overset{\overset{\displaystyle OCH_3}{|}}{\underset{\underset{\displaystyle OCH_3}{|}}{C}}-H$$

15.42

$$\text{a.} \quad CH_3-CH_2-\overset{\overset{\displaystyle O-CH_2-CH_3}{|}}{\underset{\underset{\displaystyle O-CH_2-CH_3}{|}}{C}}-H$$

$$\text{b.} \quad CH_3-CH_2-\overset{\overset{\displaystyle O-CH_2-CH_3}{|}}{\underset{\underset{\displaystyle O-CH_2-CH_3}{|}}{C}}-CH_3$$

$$\text{c.} \quad CH_3-CH_2-O \quad O-CH_2-CH$$

$$\text{d.} \quad H-\overset{\overset{\displaystyle O-CH_2-CH_3}{|}}{\underset{\underset{\displaystyle O-CH_2-CH_3}{|}}{C}}-H$$

15.43 The carbonyl group consists of a sigma bond and a pi bond, which is an overlapping of the *p* orbitals of the carbon and oxygen atom.

15.44 The C=O double bond has a dipole because the oxygen atom is strongly electronegative compared to the carbon atom.

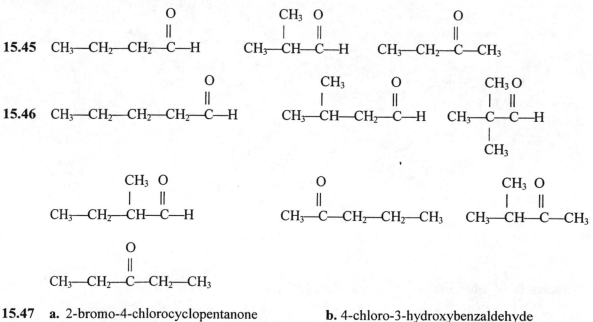

15.45

$$CH_3-CH_2-CH_2-\overset{\overset{\displaystyle O}{||}}{C}-H \qquad CH_3-\overset{\overset{\displaystyle CH_3}{|}}{CH}-\overset{\overset{\displaystyle O}{||}}{C}-H \qquad CH_3-CH_2-\overset{\overset{\displaystyle O}{||}}{C}-CH_3$$

15.46

$$CH_3-CH_2-CH_2-CH_2-\overset{\overset{\displaystyle O}{||}}{C}-H \qquad CH_3-\overset{\overset{\displaystyle CH_3}{|}}{CH}-CH_2-\overset{\overset{\displaystyle O}{||}}{C}-H \qquad CH_3-\overset{\overset{\displaystyle CH_3}{|}}{\underset{\underset{\displaystyle CH_3}{|}}{C}}-\overset{\overset{\displaystyle O}{||}}{C}-H$$

$$CH_3-CH_2-\overset{\overset{\displaystyle CH_3}{|}}{CH}-\overset{\overset{\displaystyle O}{||}}{C}-H \qquad CH_3-\overset{\overset{\displaystyle O}{||}}{C}-CH_2-CH_2-CH_3 \qquad CH_3-\overset{\overset{\displaystyle CH_3}{|}}{CH}-\overset{\overset{\displaystyle O}{||}}{C}-CH_3$$

$$CH_3-CH_2-\overset{\overset{\displaystyle O}{||}}{C}-CH_2-CH_3$$

15.47 a. 2-bromo-4-chlorocyclopentanone   b. 4-chloro-3-hydroxybenzaldehyde
c. 3-chloropropanal; β-chloropropionaldehyde d. 5-hydroxy-3-hexanone
e. 2-chloro-3-pentanone   f. 3-methylcyclohexanone

15.48 a. butanone; ethyl methyl ketone   b. 3,5-dichlorobenzaldehyde
c. 1-chlorocyclopentanone   d. 3-hydroxy-4-methylpentanal
e. methyl phenyl ketone   f. 3-oxobutanal; β-oxobutyraldehyde

15.49 a. 3-methylcyclopentanone is a five-carbon cyclic structure with a methyl group located two carbons from the carbonyl group.

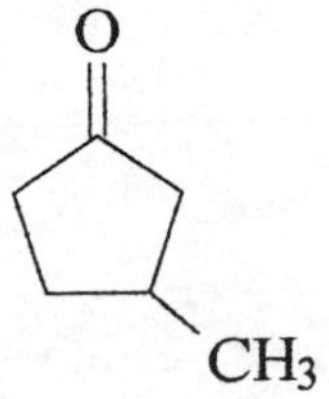

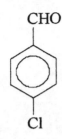

b. *p*-chlorobenzaldehyde is a benzene with an aldehyde group and a chlorine on carbon 4.

CHO

Cl

c. *β*-chloropropionaldehyde is a three-carbon aldehyde with a chlorine located two carbons from the carbonyl group.

$$\overset{\displaystyle O}{\overset{\displaystyle \|}{Cl-CH_2-CH_2-C-H}}$$

d. Butanone is a four-carbon ketone.

$$\overset{\displaystyle O}{\overset{\displaystyle \|}{CH_3-C-CH_2-CH_3}}$$

e. This is a six-carbon aldehyde with a methyl group on carbon 3.

$$\overset{\displaystyle CH_3}{\overset{\displaystyle |}{CH_3-CH_2-CH_2-CH}} \ \ \overset{\displaystyle O}{\overset{\displaystyle \|}{-CH_2-C-H}}$$

f. This has a seven-carbon chain with a carbonyl group on carbon 2.

$$\overset{\displaystyle O}{\overset{\displaystyle \|}{CH_3-C-CH_2-CH_2-CH_2-CH_2-CH_3}}$$

15.50 a. $\overset{\displaystyle O}{\overset{\displaystyle \|}{CH_3-CH_2-C-H}}$

b. $\overset{\displaystyle Cl \ \ \ O}{\overset{\displaystyle | \ \ \ \ \|}{CH_3-CH_2-CH-C-H}}$

c.

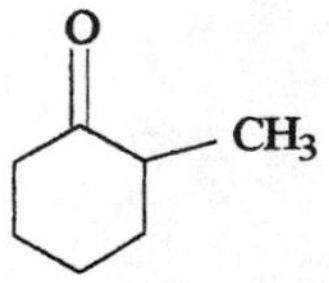

O

CH₃

d. $\overset{\displaystyle CH_3 \ \ \ \ \ \ CH_3 \ \ \ \ \ \ O}{\overset{\displaystyle | \ \ \ \ \ \ \ \ \ | \ \ \ \ \ \ \ \|}{CH_3-CH-CH_2-CH-CH_2-C-H}}$

e. 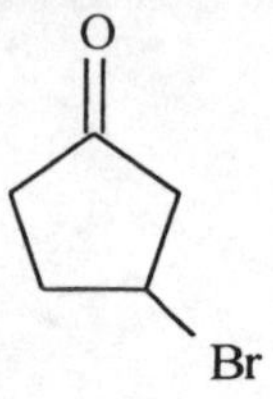 (cyclopentanone with Br substituent)

f. 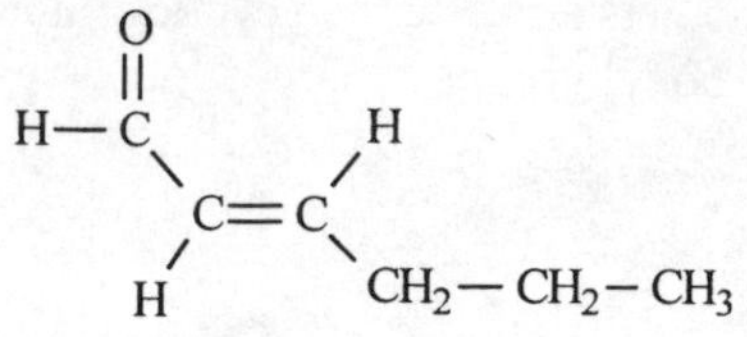 (structure: H—C(=O)—C=C with H and CH₂—CH₂—CH₃ groups)

15.51 Compounds b, c, and d are soluble in water because they have polar groups with oxygen atoms that hydrogen bond with water and less than five carbon atoms.

15.52 Compounds a, b, and c are soluble in water because they have polar groups with oxygen atoms that hydrogen bond with water and less than five carbon atoms.

15.53 **a.** CH_3-CH_2-OH; polar —OH group can hydrogen bond

b. $CH_3-CH_2-\overset{\displaystyle O}{\overset{\|}{C}}-H$; polar carbonyl group can hydrogen bond

c. $CH_3-CH_2-CH_2-OH$; polar —OH group can hydrogen bond

15.54 **a.** $CH_3-CH_2-CH_2-CH_2-\overset{\displaystyle O}{\overset{\|}{C}}-H$; greater molar mass of the two carbonyl compounds

b. $CH_3-\overset{\displaystyle O}{\overset{\|}{C}}-CH_3$; dipole-dipole interactions increased boiling point compared to an alkane

c. $CH_3-\overset{\displaystyle O}{\overset{\|}{C}}-CH_3$; a symmetrical molecule has more dipole-dipole interactions

15.55 A chiral carbon is bonded to four different groups.

a. 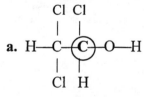   **b.** None.   **c.** None.

d. 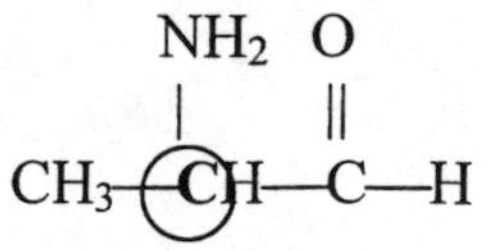 $CH_3-\overset{\displaystyle NH_2}{\underset{}{C}}H-\overset{\displaystyle O}{\overset{\|}{C}}-H$ **e.** 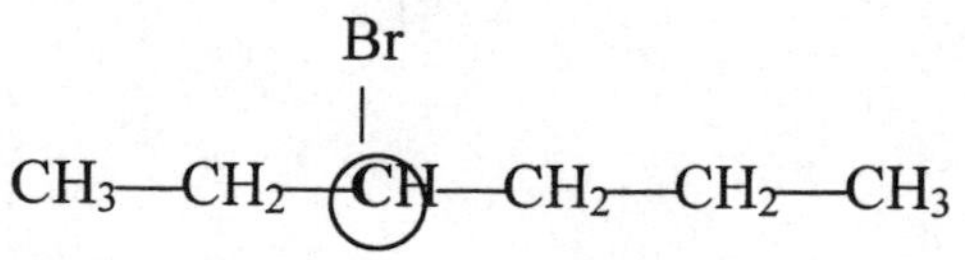 $CH_3-CH_2-CH-CH_2-CH_2-CH_3$ (with Br on circled C)

f. None

15.56 **a.** None

b. 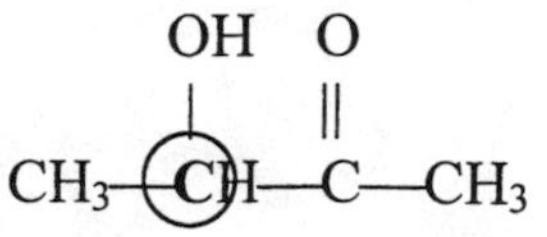 $CH_3-\overset{\displaystyle OH}{\underset{}{C}}H-\overset{\displaystyle O}{\overset{\|}{C}}-CH_3$

c. None

d. None

e. 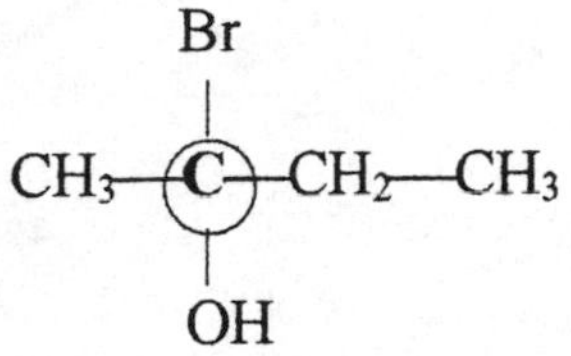 CH₃—C—CH₂—CH₃ with Br above the C and OH below the C

$$CH_3-\overset{Br}{\underset{OH}{C}}-CH_2-CH_3$$

f. None

15.57 Enantiomers are mirror images
 a. identical
 b. enantiomers
 c. enantiomers (turn 180°)
 d. enantiomers

15.58 **a.** enantiomers
 b. identical
 c. identical
 d. enantiomers

15.59 Primary alcohols oxidize to aldehydes and then to carboxylic acids. Secondary alcohols oxidize to ketones.

a. 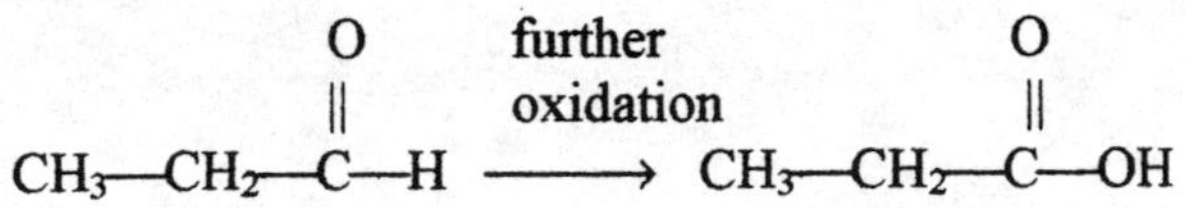 $CH_3-CH_2-\overset{O}{\overset{\|}{C}}-H \xrightarrow{\text{further oxidation}} CH_3-CH_2-\overset{O}{\overset{\|}{C}}-OH$

b. $CH_3-\overset{O}{\overset{\|}{C}}-CH_2-CH_2-CH_3$

c. $CH_3-CH_2-CH_2-\overset{O}{\overset{\|}{C}}-OH$

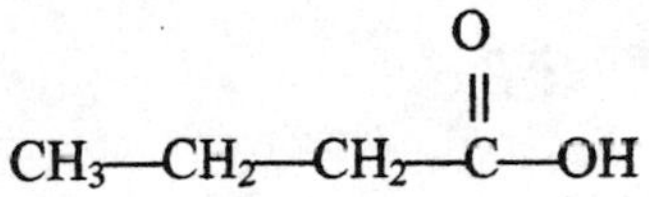

d.

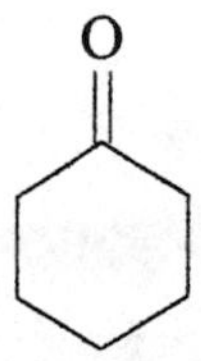

15.60

a. 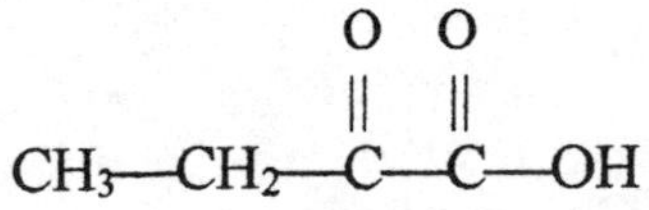 $CH_3-CH_2-\overset{O}{\overset{\|}{C}}-\overset{O}{\overset{\|}{C}}-OH$

b. 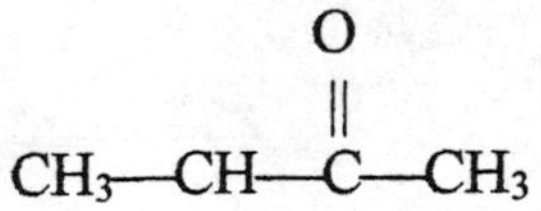 $CH_3-CH-\overset{O}{\overset{\|}{C}}-CH_3$

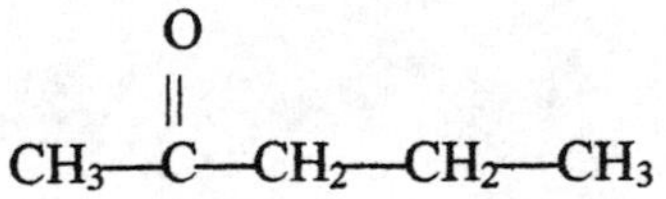

179

c. CH_3—$\underset{\underset{\displaystyle CH_3}{|}}{CH}$—$CH_2$—$\underset{\displaystyle \overset{O}{\|}}{C}$—OH

d.

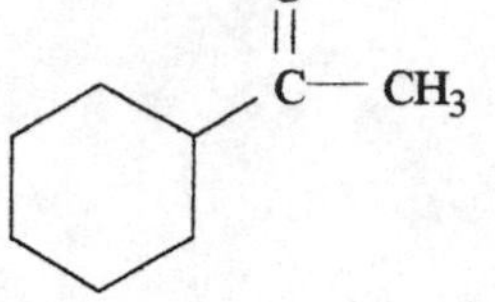

15.61 a. CH_3—$\underset{\underset{\displaystyle OH}{|}}{CH}$—$CH_3$

b.

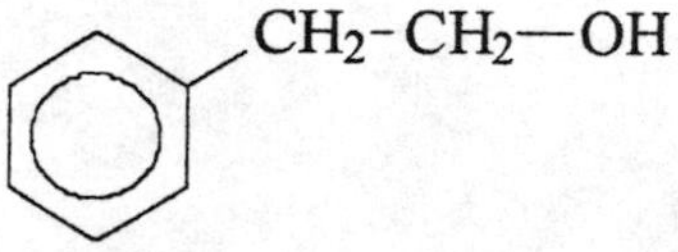

CH_2-CH_2—OH

c. CH_3—$\underset{\underset{\displaystyle CH_3}{|}}{CH}$—$CH_2$—$\underset{\underset{\displaystyle OH}{|}}{CH}$—$CH_3$

15.62 a. CH_3—CH_2—OH   **b.**

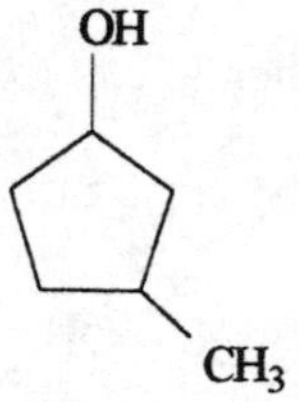

c. CH_3—OH

15.63 a. CH_3—CH=CH_2 + H_2O $\xrightarrow{\;H^+\;}$ CH_3—$\underset{\underset{\displaystyle OH}{|}}{CH}$—$CH_3$ $\longrightarrow$ CH_3—$\underset{\displaystyle \overset{O}{\|}}{C}$—$CH_3$
  Propene   propanone

b. CH_3—CH_2—CH_2—$\underset{\displaystyle \overset{O}{\|}}{C}$—H + H_2 $\xrightarrow{\;Ni\;}$ CH_3—CH_2—CH_2—CH_2—OH $\xrightarrow{\;H^+,\ heat\;}$

CH_3—CH_2—CH=CH_2 + Br_2 $\longrightarrow$ CH_3—CH_2—$\underset{\underset{\displaystyle Br}{|}}{CH}$—$CH_2$—Br

c. CH_3—CH_2—CH_2—$\underset{\displaystyle \overset{O}{\|}}{C}$—H + H_2 $\xrightarrow{\;Ni\;}$ CH_3—CH_2—CH_2—CH_2—OH $\xrightarrow{\;H^+,\ heat\;}$
  Butanal

CH_3—CH_2—CH=CH_2 + H_2O $\longrightarrow$ CH_3—CH_2—$\underset{\underset{\displaystyle OH}{|}}{CH}$—$CH_3$ $\xrightarrow{\;[O]\;}$

15.64 **a.** CH_3—CH_2—CH_2—CH_2—$\overset{\overset{\displaystyle O}{\displaystyle \|}}{C}$—H + H_2 $\xrightarrow{\text{Ni}}$ CH_3—CH_2—CH_2—CH_2—CH_2—OH

$\xrightarrow{\text{H}^+, \text{ heat}}$ CH_3—CH_2—CH_2—$CH=CH_2$

b. CH_3—CH_2—CH_2—CH_2—OH $\xrightarrow{\text{H}^+, \text{ heat}}$ CH_3—CH_2—$CH=CH_2$ + H_2O $\xrightarrow{\text{H}^+}$

CH_3—CH_2—$\overset{\overset{\displaystyle OH}{\displaystyle |}}{CH}$—$CH_3$ $\xrightarrow{[O]}$ CH_3—CH_2—$\overset{\overset{\displaystyle O}{\displaystyle \|}}{C}$—$CH_3$

c.   + H_2O $\xrightarrow{\text{H}^+}$ $\xrightarrow{\text{oxidation}}$

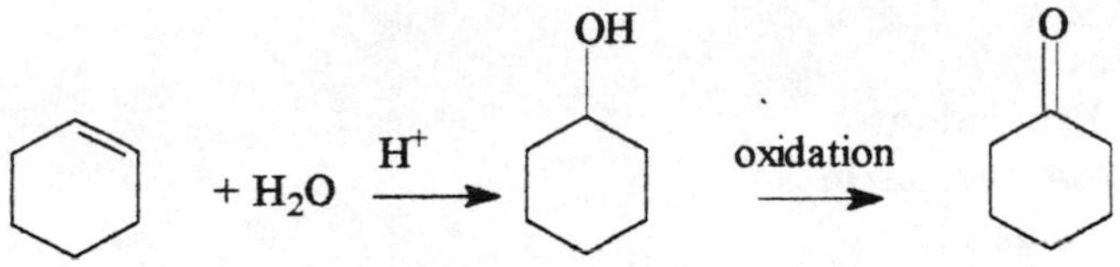

15.65 **a.** acetal; propanal and methanol
b. hemiacetal; butanone and ethanol
c. acetal; cyclohexanone and ethanol

15.66 **a.** hemiacetal; propanal and methanol
b. hemiacetal; cyclohexanone and 2-propanol
c. acetal; ethanal (acetaldehyde) and 1-propanol

Study Goals

- Identify the common carbohydrates in the diet.
- Distinguish between monosaccharides, disaccharides, and polysaccharides.
- Identify the chiral carbons in a carbohydrate.
- Label the Fischer projection for a monosaccharide as the D- or L-enantiomer.
- Write Haworth structures for monosaccharides.
- Describe the structural units and bonds in disaccharides and polysaccharides.

Chapter Outline

Chapter Summary and Demonstrations

1. Monosaccharides, Chiral Molecules, and Fischer Projections

The monosaccharides are classified as aldo- or ketopentoses and aldo- or ketohexoses. The structures of chiral and achiral molecules are compared. Fischer projections and Haworth structures for the anomers of the monosaccharides are drawn. The oxidation of saccharides and the formation of glycosidic bonds is emphasized in types of reactions.

2. Types of Carbohydrates

The major monosaccharides and disaccharides in the diet are discussed along with some medical problems with utilization of glucose including blood glucose levels in normal, hyper-, and hypoglycemic conditions are described. The polysaccharides are described along with the type of bonding between monomer units. Identification tests for carbohydrates complete the chapter.

Demonstration: Types of Carbohydrates I have students compare the nutritional labeling on breakfast cereal boxes with emphasis on the types of carbohydrates listed. Then discuss the role of sucroses, complex carbohydrates, and fiber in the diet.

Demonstration: Have students chew on a cracker for 4-5 minutes. Identify the taste of starch in the cracker. As an enzyme in saliva breaks apart the bonds in the starch, smaller sugars and monosaccharides form. After a few minutes, ask students how the taste of the cracker changes. Why?

Laboratory Suggestions

Lab 26 Types of Carbohydrates

Students identify the characteristic functional groups of carbohydrates and observe some physical and chemical properties of some common carbohydrates.
A. Monosaccharides
B. Disaccharides
C. Polysaccharides

Lab 27 Tests for Carbohydrates

Physical and chemical tests are used to distinguish between monosaccharides, disaccharides, and polysaccharides.
A. Benedict's Test for Reducing Sugars
B. Seliwanoff's Test for Ketoses
C. Fermentation Test
D. Iodine Test for Polysaccharides
E. Hydrolysis of Disaccharides and Polysaccharides
F. Testing Foods for Carbohydrates

Laboratory Skills to Demonstrate

Observation of positive results for carbohydrate tests.
Identification of a change from the blue color of Benedict's reagent to various shades of green to red-orange as a positive test for the oxidation of aldehydes to carboxylic acids.
Preparation of fermentation tubes.
Use of pipets and bulbs.

Answers and Solutions to Text Problems

16.1 Photosynthesis requires CO_2, H_2O, and the energy from the sun. Respiration requires O_2 from the air and glucose from our foods.

16.2 In photosynthesis, plants use the energy from sunlight to synthesize carbohydrates from carbon dioxide and water. In respiration, carbohydrates (mainly glucose) are oxidized to carbon dioxide and water and provide energy to do work in the cells of our body.

16.3 A monosaccharide is a simple sugar composed of three to six carbon atoms. A disaccharide is composed of two monosaccharide units.

16.4 A polysaccharide is a complex carbohydrate made of thousands of monosaccharide units.

16.5 Hydroxyl groups and a carbonyl are found in all monosaccharides.

16.6 An aldose is a monosaccharide with an aldehyde group; a ketose is a monosaccharide with a ketone group.

16.7 The name ketopentose tells us that the compound contains a ketone functional group and has five carbon atoms. In addition, all monosaccharides contain hydroxyl groups.

16.8 An aldohexose has six carbon atoms, several hydroxyl groups, and an aldehyde group.

16.9 **a.** This monosaccharide is a ketose; it has a carbonyl between two carbon atoms.
b. This monosaccharide is an aldose; it has a CHO, an aldehyde group.
c. This monosaccharide is a ketose; it has a carbonyl between two carbon atoms.
d. This monosaccharide is an aldose; it has a CHO, an aldehyde group.
e. This monosaccharide is an aldose; it has a CHO, an aldehyde group.

16.10 **a.** hexose   **b.** pentose   **c.** triose   **d.** pentose   **e.** hexose

16.11 A Fischer projection is a two-dimensional representation of the three dimensional structure of a molecule.

16.12

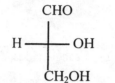

D-glyceraldehyde 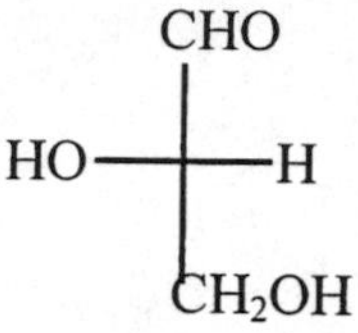   L-glyceraldehyde

16.13 **a.** This structure is a D isomer since the hydroxyl group on the chiral carbon farthest from the carbonyl is on the right.
b. This structure is a D isomer since the hydroxyl group on the chiral carbon farthest from the carbonyl is on the right.
c. This structure is an L isomer since the hydroxyl group on the chiral carbon farthest from the carbonyl is on the left.
d. This structure is a D isomer since the hydroxyl group on the chiral carbon farthest from the carbonyl is on the right.

16.14 **a.** D isomer   **b.** L isomer   **c.** D isomer   **d.** L isomer

16.15

a.

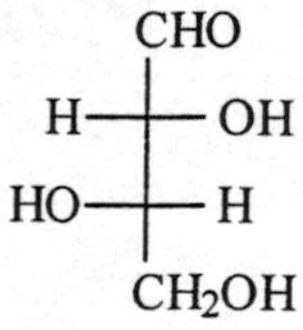

b..

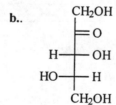

c.

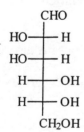

d.

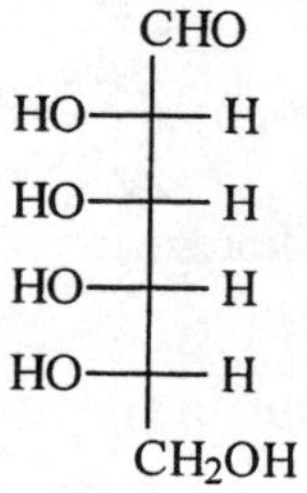

16.16

a.

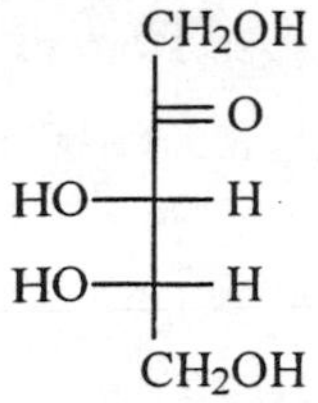

```
      CH₂OH
       |
       C=O
       |
  HO———H
       |
  HO———H
       |
      CH₂OH
```

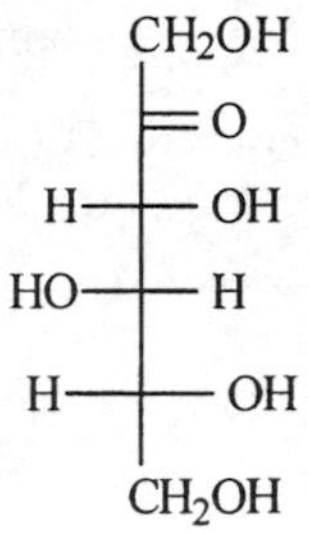

b.

```
      CH₂OH
       |
       C=O
       |
   H———OH
       |
  HO———H
       |
   H———OH
       |
      CH₂OH
```

c.

```
       CHO
        |
  HO————H
        |
   H————OH
        |
  HO————H
        |
  HO————H
        |
      CH₂OH
```

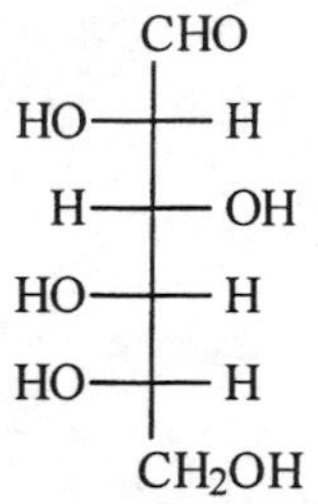

d.

```
       CHO
        |
   H————OH
        |
   H————OH
        |
   H————OH
        |
      CH₂OH
```

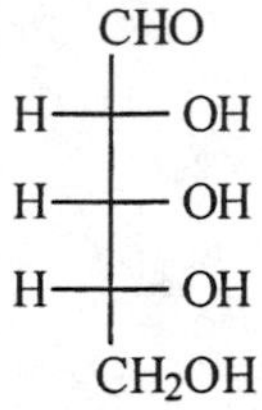

16.17 L-glucose is the mirror image of D-glucose.

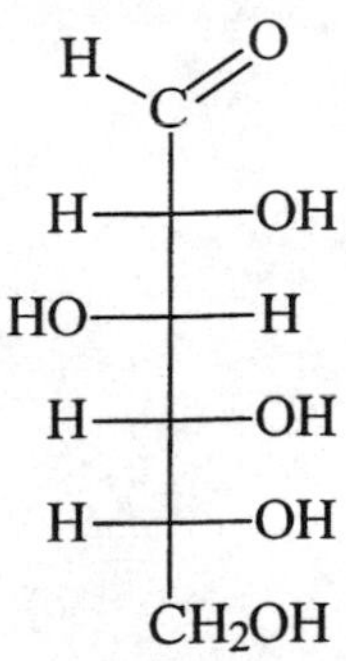

```
     H   O
      \ //
       C
       |
   H———OH
       |
  HO———H
       |
   H———OH
       |
   H———OH
       |
     CH₂OH
   D-glucose
```

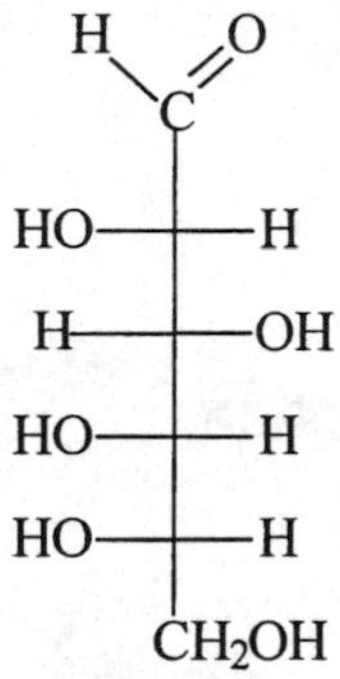

```
     H   O
      \ //
       C
       |
  HO———H
       |
   H———OH
       |
  HO———H
       |
  HO———H
       |
     CH₂OH
   L-glucose
```

16.18

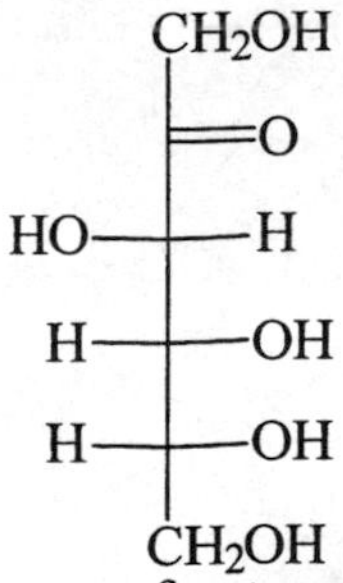

```
     CH₂OH
       |
       C=O
       |
  HO———H
       |
   H———OH
       |
   H———OH
       |
     CH₂OH
   D-fructose
```

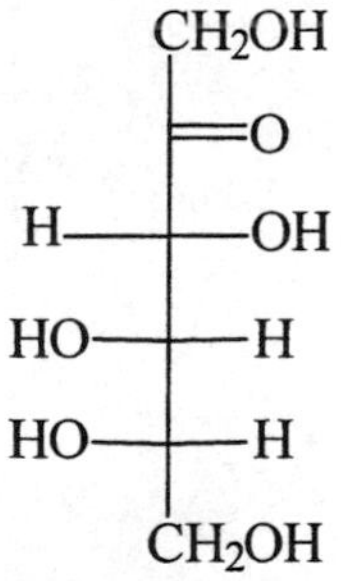

```
     CH₂OH
       |
       C=O
       |
   H———OH
       |
  HO———H
       |
  HO———H
       |
     CH₂OH
   L-fructose
```

16.19 In D-galactose the hydroxyl on carbon four extends to the left, in glucose this hydroxyl group goes to the right.

16.20 D-Glucose is an aldehyde with the carbonyl group on carbon 1; D-fructose is a ketone with the carbonyl group on carbon 2.

16.21 **a.** Glucose is also called blood sugar.
b. Galactose is not metabolized in the condition called galactosemia.
c. Another name for fructose is fruit sugar.

16.22 **a.** glucose   **b.** galactose, glucose   **c.** fructose

16.23 In the cyclic structure of glucose, there are five carbon atoms and an oxygen atom in the ring.

16.24 The cyclic structure of fructose is a five-atom ring of four carbon atoms and an oxygen atom. The five-atom ring is a result of the formation of the hemiacetal when the hydroxyl group on carbon 5 reacts with the ketone group on carbon 2.

16.25 In the α anomer, the hydroxyl (–OH) on carbon 1 is down; in the β anomer the hydroxyl (–OH) on carbon 1 is up.

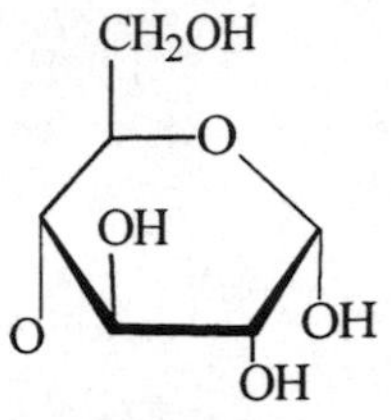

α-D-Glucose 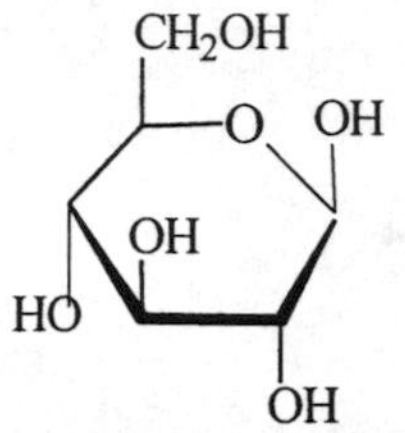   β-D-Glucose

16.26

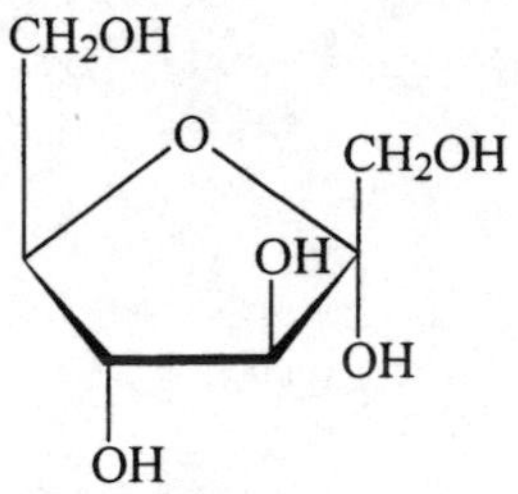

α-D-Fructose 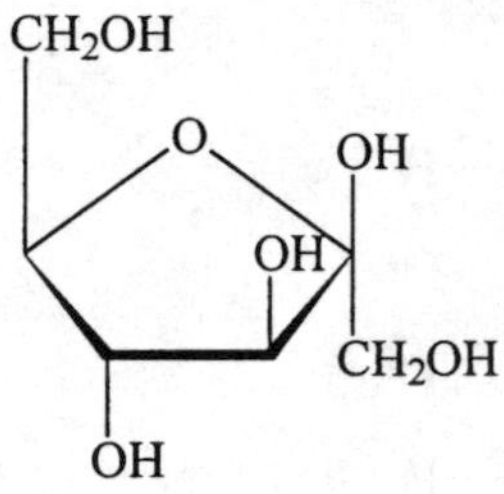   β-D-Fructose

16.27 **a.** This is the *α*-anomer because the —OH on carbon 1 is down.
b. This is the *α*-anomer because the —OH on carbon 1 is down.

16.28 **a.** This is the β anomer.

b. This is the α anomer.

16.29

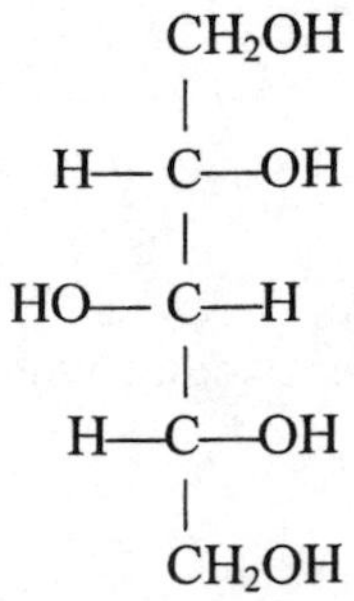

$$
\begin{array}{c}
CH_2OH \\
| \\
H-C-OH \\
| \\
HO-C-H \\
| \\
H-C-OH \\
| \\
CH_2OH
\end{array}
$$

Xylitol

16.30

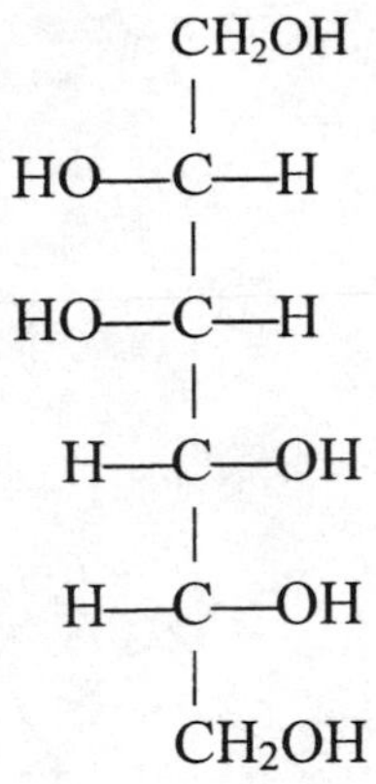

```
        CH₂OH
         |
  HO—C—H
         |
  HO—C—H
         |
   H—C—OH
         |
   H—C—OH
         |
        CH₂OH
```

Mannitol

16.31   Oxidation product:

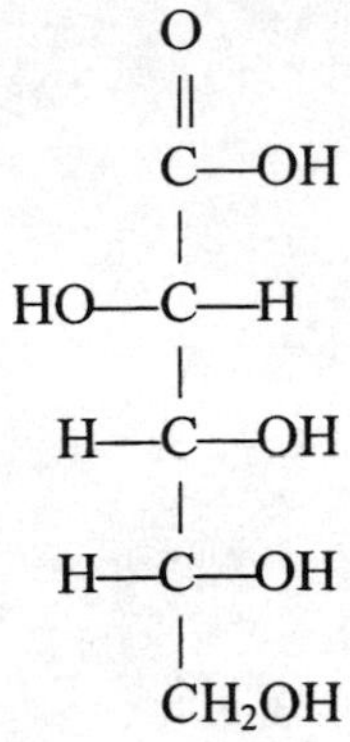

```
         O
         ‖
         C—OH
         |
  HO—C—H
         |
   H—C—OH
         |
   H—C—OH
         |
        CH₂OH
```

Reduction product:

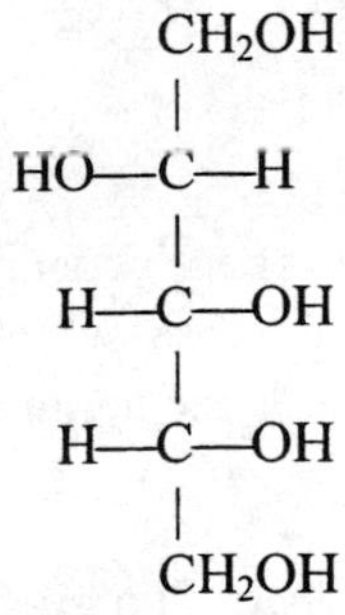

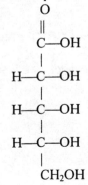

```
        CH₂OH
         |
  HO—C—H
         |
   H—C—OH              D -arabitol
         |
   H—C—OH
         |
        CH₂OH
```

16.32 Oxidation product:

```
         O
         ‖
         C—OH
         |
   H—C—OH
         |
   H—C—OH
         |
   H—C—OH
         |
        CH₂OH
```

Reduction product:

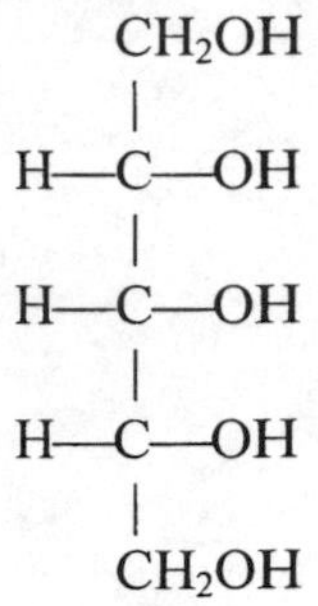
CH2OH
H—C—OH
H—C—OH
H—C—OH
CH2OH

D-ribitol

16.33

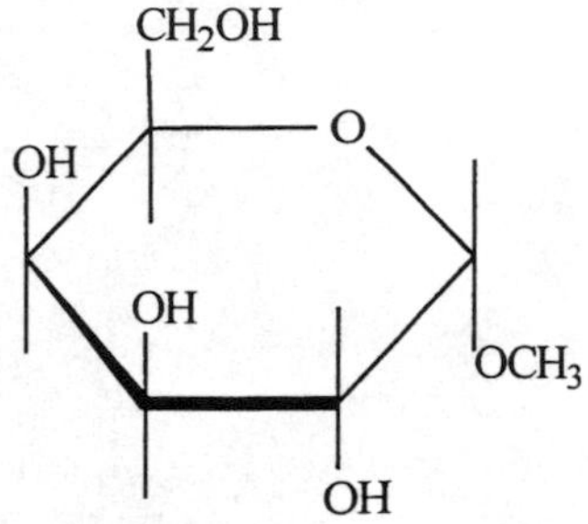
CH2OH
O
OH
OH
OCH3
OH

α-anomer

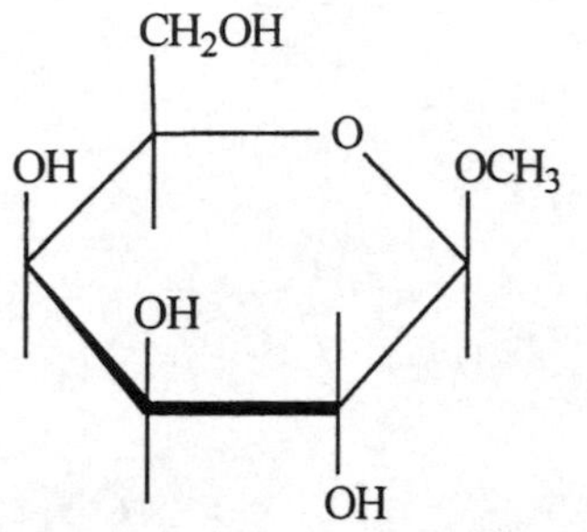
CH2OH
O
OH
OCH3
OH
OH

β-anomer

16.34

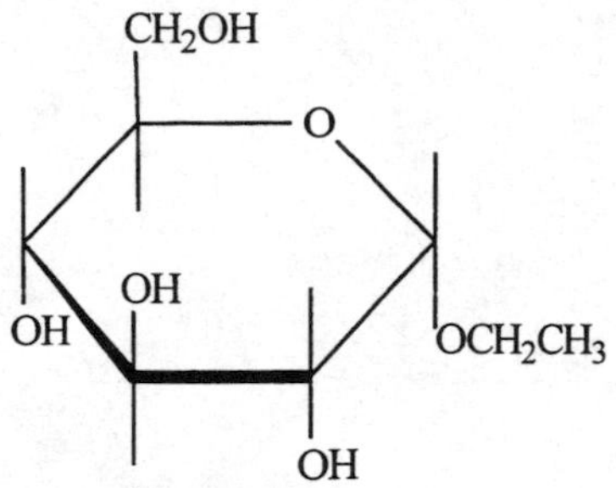
CH2OH
O
OH
OH
OCH2CH3
OH

α-anomer

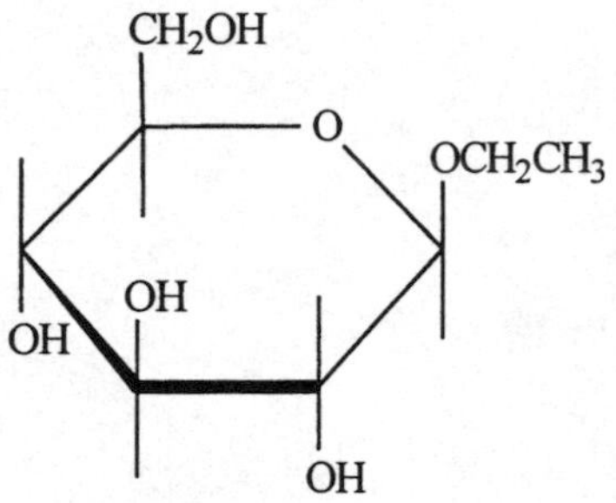
CH2OH
O
OCH2CH3
OH
OH
OH

β-anomer

16.35 **a.** When this disaccharide is hydrolyzed galactose and glucose are produced. The glycosidic bond is a β-1,4 bond since the ether bond is up from the 1 carbon of the galactose, which is on the left in the drawing to the 4 carbon of the glucose on the right. β-lactose is the name of this disaccharide since the free hydroxyl is up.

b. When this disaccharide is hydrolyzed, two molecules of glucose are produced. The glycosidic bond is an α-1,4 bond since the ether bond is down from the 1 carbon of the glucose on the left to the 4 carbon of the glucose on the right. α-maltose is the name of this disaccharide since the free hydroxyl is down.

16.36 **a.** The disaccharide is β-maltose, which has an α-1,4-glycosidic bond between two D -glucose monosaccharide units.

b. The disaccharide is sucrose, which has an α-1, β-2-glycosidic bond between an α- D -glucose and a β- D -fructose monosaccharide units.

16.37 **a.** Will undergo mutarotation; can be oxidized

b. Will undergo mutarotation; can be oxidized

16.38 **a.** Maltose undergoes mutarotation.

b. Sucrose does not undergo mutarotation.

16.39 **a.** Another name for table sugar is sucrose.
 b. Lactose is the disaccharide found in milk and milk products.
 c. Maltose is also called malt sugar.
 d. When lactose is hydrolyzed, the products are the monosaccharides galactose and glucose.

16.40 **a.** sucrose **b.** maltose **c.** lactose **d.** sucrose

16.41 **a.** Amylose is an unbranched polymer of glucose units joined by α-1,4 bonds; amylopectin is a branched polymer of glucose joined by α-1,4 and α-1,6 bonds.
 b. Amylopectin, produced by plants, is a branched polymer of glucose joined by α-1,4 and α-1,6 bonds. Glycogen, which is made by animals, is a highly branched polymer of glucose joined by α-1,4 and α-1,6 bonds.

16.42 **a.** Amylose is an unbranched chain of D-glucose units connected by α-1,4-glycosidic bonds. Cellulose, the structural material of plants, is an unbranched chain of D-glucose units connected by β-1,4-glycosidic bonds.
 b. Cellulose, the structural material of plants, is an unbranched chain of D-glucose units connected by β-1,4-glycosidic bonds. Glycogen, the storage form of glucose in the human body, is a brancher polymer of D-glucose joined by α-1,4 and α-1,6 bonds.

16.43 **a.** Cellulose is not digestible by humans since we do not have the enzymes necessary to break the β-1,4-glycosidic bonds in cellulose.
 b. Amylose and amylopectin are the storage forms of carbohydrates in plants.
 c. Amylose is the polysaccharide, which contains only α-1,4 glycosidic bonds.
 d. Glycogen contains many α-1,4 and α-1,6 bonds and is the most highly branched polysaccharide.

16.44 **a.** glycogen **b.** cellulose **c.** amylopectin, glycogen **d.** amylose, amylopectin

16.45 They differ only at carbon 4; the —OH in D-glucose is on the right side and in D-galactose it is on the left side.

16.46 The carbonyl carbon in D-glucose is carbon 1 (aldehyde), whereas in D-fructose, the carbonyl group is on carbon 2 (ketone).

16.47 D-galactose is the mirror image of L-galactose. In D-galactose, the —OH group on carbon 5 is on the right side whereas in L-galactose, the —OH group on carbon 5 is on the left side.

16.48 In α-D-glucose, the —OH on carbon 1 is written down, whereas in β-D-glucose, the —OH is written up.

16.49 a.

L-Gulose

b.

α-D-gulose

β-D-gulose

16.50 a.

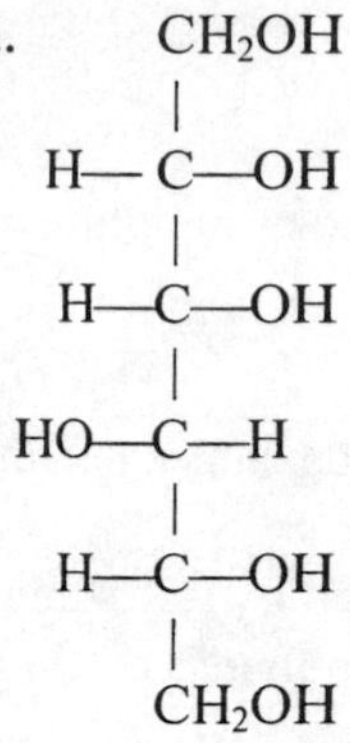

$$CH_2OH$$
$$|$$
$$H—C—OH$$
$$|$$
$$H—C—OH$$
$$|$$
$$HO—C—H$$
$$|$$
$$H—C—OH$$
$$|$$
$$CH_2OH$$

D-Gulitol

b.

$$CH_2OH$$
$$|$$
$$H—C—OH$$
$$|$$
$$H—C—OH$$
$$|$$
$$HO—C—H$$
$$|$$
$$H—C—OH$$
$$|$$
$$CH_2OH$$

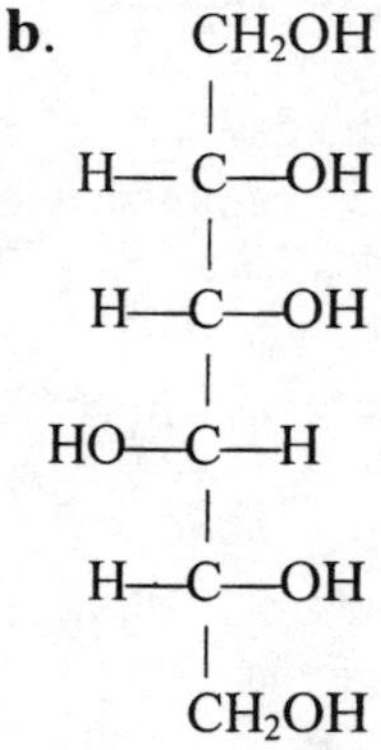

D-Gulonic acid

16.51 Since sorbitol can be oxidized to D-glucose, it must contain the same number of carbons with the same groups attached as glucose. The difference is that sorbitol has only hydroxyls while glucose has an aldehyde group. In sorbitol, the aldehyde group is changed to a hydroxyl.

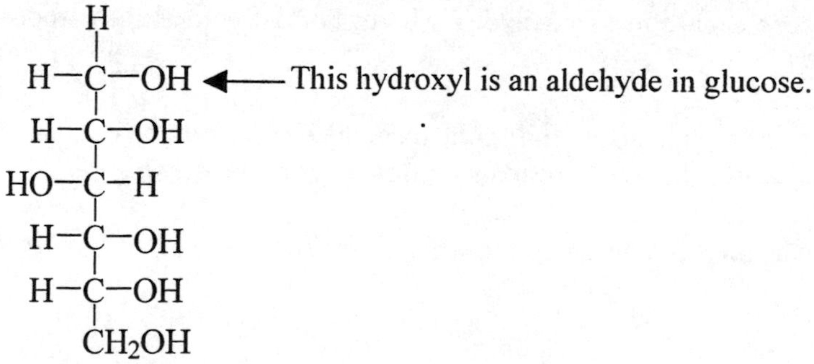

$$H$$
$$|$$
$$H—C—OH \longleftarrow \text{This hydroxyl is an aldehyde in glucose.}$$
$$H—C—OH$$
$$HO—C—H$$
$$H—C—OH$$
$$H—C—OH$$
$$CH_2OH$$

16.52 Galactose, glucose, and fructose

16.53 The α-galactose forms an open chain structure and when the chain closes, it can form both α- and β-galactose.

16.54 Lactose and maltose have free anomeric carbons that can open up to make an aldehyde group available for oxidation. In sucrose, the anomeric carbon is tied up and not free to provide an aldehyde group.

16.55

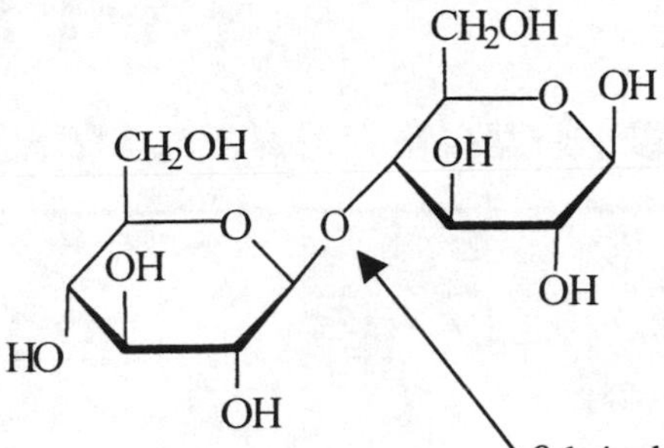

β-1,4-glycosidic bond. The bond from the glucose on the left is up (β).

16.56

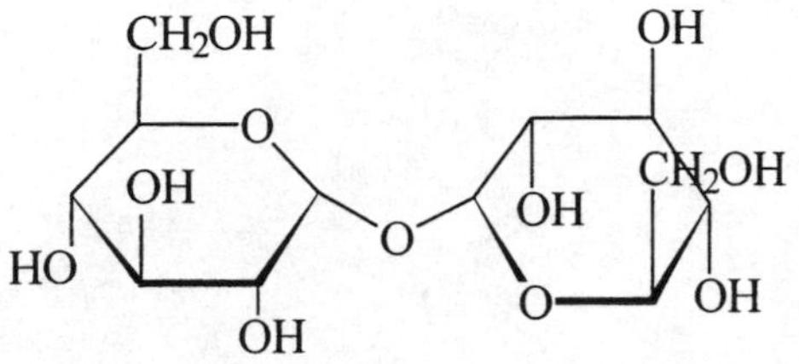

16.57 a.

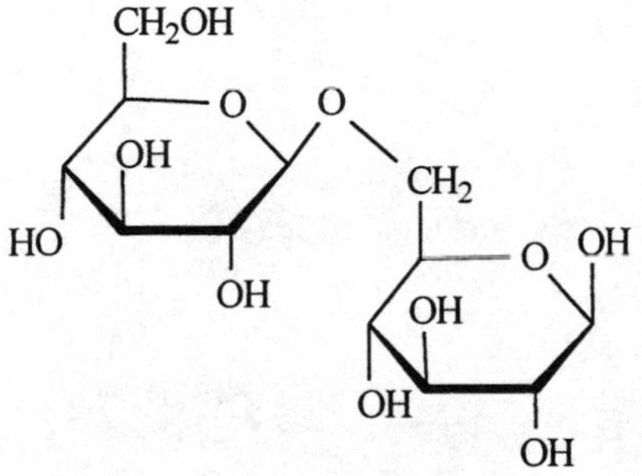

b. Yes. The hemiacetal on the right side can open up to form the open chain with an aldehyde.

16.58 a. B **b.** C **c.** A **d.** D

Carboxylic Acids and Esters

Study Goals

- Name and write structural formulas of carboxylic acids and esters.
- Describe the boiling points and solubility of carboxylic acids.
- Write equations for the ionization of carboxylic acids in water.
- Write equations for the esterification, hydrolysis, and saponification of esters.

Chapter Outline

Chapter Summary and Demonstrations

1.   Carboxylic acids and Esters

This chapter on organic chemistry discusses carboxylic acids and their ester derivatives. Carboxylic acids and esters are named according to IUPAC and common naming systems. The physical properties of carboxylic acids including their boiling points and solubility as well as the pleasant aromas and flavors of esters are discussed.

Demonstration: Acids and Esters Carboxylic acids are introduced by a discussion of commonly occurring acids in substances that may be found in the home or grocery store such as aspirin, fruits, wines, and vinegar. To introduce esters, I pass around examples of pleasant smelling compounds that are esters such as oranges and bananas. This may include both the chemical substance and the natural product. In addition, I may also bring to class examples of fats and oils, which are the esters of glycerol and long-chain carboxylic acids.

Laboratory Suggestions

Lab 28 Carboxylic Acids and Esters

Students determine the solubility and acidity of carboxylic acids and their salts. Equations are written for the neutralization and esterification of carboxylic acids. Esters are prepared and their characteristic odors identified. Equations are written for the hydrolysis and saponification of esters.
A. Carboxylic Acids and Their Salts
B. Preparation of Esters
C. Hydrolysis of Esters

Laboratory Skills to Demonstrate
Caution in the use of acid.
Proper technique in noting the odor of a compound.

Lab 29 Synthesis of Aspirin

Aspirin is synthesized using the esterification of salicyclic acid with acetic anhydride. Crude aspirin and commercial tablets are tested for purity using color they produce with $FeCl_3$. Some physical and chemical properties of aspirin are determined. A variety of analgesics are analyzed using thin-layer chromatography.
A. Preparation of Aspirin
B. Testing Aspirin Products
C. Analysis of Analgesics

Laboratory Skills to Demonstrate
Caution in the handling of acetic anhydride and the addition of water to the product.
Proper use of the Büchner funnel and filtration apparatus.
Proper use of pipets and bulbs.
Calculating a percent yield.

Answers and Solutions to Text Problems

17.1 Methanoic acid (formic acid) is the carboxylic acid that is responsible for the pain associated with ant stings.

17.2 Ethanoic acid (acetic acid) is the acid found in vinegar.

17.3 Each compound contains three carbon atoms. They differ because propanal, an aldehyde, contains a carbonyl group bonded to a hydrogen. In propanoic acid, the carbonyl group connects to a hydroxyl group.

17.4 Benzaldehyde is an aromatic aldehyde with a carbonyl group attached to hydrogen. Benzoic acid is an aromatic acid with a hydroxyl group attached to a carbonyl.

17.5 a. Ethanoic acid (acetic acid) is the carboxylic acid with two carbons.
b. Butanoic acid (butyric acid) is the carboxylic acid with four carbons.
c. 2-chloropropanoic acid (α-chloropropionic acid) is a three-carbon carboxylic acid with a chlorine on the carbon next to the carbonyl.
d. 3-methylhexanoic acid is a six-carbon carboxylic acid with a methyl on carbon 3.
e. 3,4-dihydroxybenzoic acid has a carboxylic acid group on benzene and two hydroxyl groups on carbons 3, and 4.
f. 4-bromopentanoic acid is a five-carbon carboxylic acid with a —Br atom on carbon 4.

17.6   **a.** methanoic acid (formic acid)
     b. 2-bromopentanoic acid
     c. benzoic acid
     d. 4-chlorobenzoic acid (*para*- chlorobenzoic acid)
     e. 3-methylbutanoic acid; β-methylbutyric acid
     f. 2-chloroethanoic acid; α-chloroacetic acid

17.7

                       O
                       ‖
a. CH₃—CH₂—C—OH   Propionic acid has three carbons.

b.
   O
   ‖
   C—OH

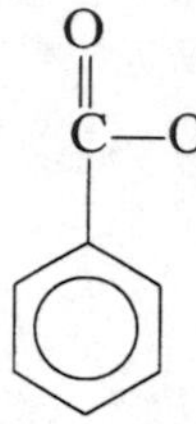

                             Benzoic acid is the carboxylic acid of benzene.

               O
               ‖
c. Cl—CH₂—C—OH 2-chloroethanoic acid is a carboxylic acid that has a two-carbon chain with a chlorine atom on carbon 2.

                    O
                    ‖
d. HO—CH₂—CH₂—C—OH 3-hydroxypropanoic acid is a carboxylic acid that has a three-carbon chain with a hydroxyl on carbon 3.

               CH₃ O
                | ‖
e. CH₃—CH₂—CH—C—OH α-methylbutyric acid is a carboxylic acid that has a four-carbon chain with a methyl on the second (α) carbon.

               Br   Br   O
               | | ‖
f. CH₃—CH₂—CH—CH₂—CH—CH₂—C—OH 3,5-dibromoheptanoic acid is a carboxylic acid that has a seven-carbon chain with two bromine atoms, one on carbon 3 and the other on carbon 5.

17.8 **a.** CH₃CH₂CH₂COH   **b.** 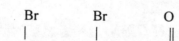   **c.** HOCH₂COH

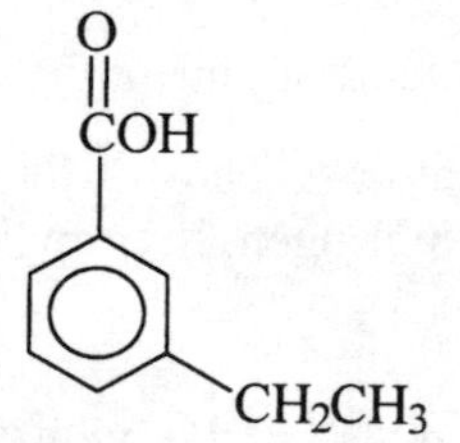

               Br O
               | ‖
  d. BrCH₂CH₂CHCOH   **e.**   **f.** CH₃CH₂CCH₂CH₂COH

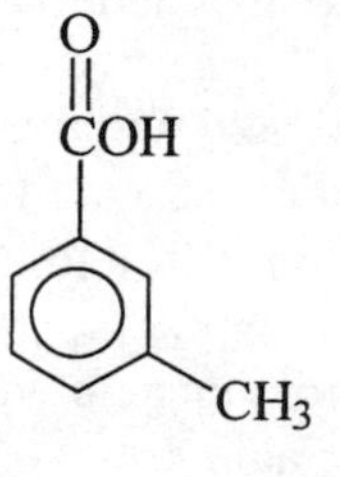

17.9 Aldehydes and primary alcohols oxidize to produce the corresponding carboxylic acid.

a. $H-\overset{\overset{\displaystyle O}{||}}{C}-OH$

b. $CH_3-\overset{\overset{\displaystyle O}{||}}{C}-OH$

c. $CH_3-\overset{\overset{\displaystyle CH_3}{|}}{C}H-CH_2-\overset{\overset{\displaystyle O}{||}}{C}-OH$

d. cyclopentane ring with $CH_2-\overset{\overset{\displaystyle O}{||}}{C}-OH$

17.10 a. $CH_3-CH_2-CH_2-CH_2-CH_2-\overset{\overset{\displaystyle O}{||}}{C}-OH$ b. $CH_3-CH_2-CH_2-CH_2-\overset{\overset{\displaystyle O}{||}}{C}-OH$

c. $CH_3-\overset{\overset{\displaystyle CH_3}{|}}{C}H-CH_2-\overset{\overset{\displaystyle O}{||}}{C}-OH$

d. benzene ring with $CH_2-\overset{\overset{\displaystyle O}{||}}{C}-OH$

17.11 a. Butanoic acid has a higher molar mass and would have a higher boiling point.
b. Propanoic acid can form more hydrogen bonds and would have a higher boiling point.
c. Butanoic acid can form more hydrogen bonds and would have a higher boiling point.

17.12 a. Propanoic acid has the higher boiling point because it can form dimers that effectively double the molar mass.
b. Hexanoic acid has the higher boiling because it has the greater molar mass.
c. Acetic acid has the higher boiling point because it can form dimers that effectively double the molar mass.

17.13 a. acetone, propanol, propanoic acid Propanoic acid forms the most hydrogen bonds of the three compounds.
b. butanoic acid, propanoic acid, acetic acid. Acetic acid has only two carbon atoms and the lowest molar mass of the group.
c. propane, ethanol, acetic acid. Acetic acid forms the most hydrogen bonds of the three compounds.

17.14 a. diethyl ether, butanone, butanoic acid
b. formic acid, acetic acid, propanoic acid
c. butanone, 1-butanol, butanoic acid

17.15 a. $H-\overset{\overset{\displaystyle O}{||}}{C}-OH + H_2O \rightleftharpoons H-\overset{\overset{\displaystyle O}{||}}{C}-O^- + H_3O^+$

b. $CH_3-CH_2-\overset{\overset{\displaystyle O}{||}}{C}-OH + H_2O \rightleftharpoons CH_3-CH_2-\overset{\overset{\displaystyle O}{||}}{C}-O^- + H_3O^+$

c. $CH_3-\overset{\overset{\displaystyle O}{||}}{C}-OH + H_2O \rightleftharpoons CH_3-\overset{\overset{\displaystyle O}{||}}{C}-O^- + H_3O^+$

195

17.16 **a.**

$$CH_3-\overset{\overset{\displaystyle CH_3}{|}}{CH}-\overset{\overset{\displaystyle O}{\|}}{C}-OH + H_2O \rightleftharpoons CH_3-\overset{\overset{\displaystyle CH_3}{|}}{CH}-\overset{\overset{\displaystyle O}{\|}}{C}-O^- + H_3O^+$$

b.

$$HO-CH_2-\overset{\overset{\displaystyle O}{\|}}{C}-OH + H_2O \rightleftharpoons HO-CH_2-\overset{\overset{\displaystyle O}{\|}}{C}-O^- + H_3O^+$$

c.

$$CH_3-CH_2-CH_2-\overset{\overset{\displaystyle O}{\|}}{C}-OH + H_2O \rightleftharpoons CH_3-CH_2-CH_2-\overset{\overset{\displaystyle O}{\|}}{C}-O^- + H_3O^+$$

17.17 **a.**

$$H-\overset{\overset{\displaystyle O}{\|}}{C}-OH + NaOH \longrightarrow H-\overset{\overset{\displaystyle O}{\|}}{C}-O^- Na^+ + H_2O$$

b.

$$CH_3-CH_2-\overset{\overset{\displaystyle O}{\|}}{C}-OH + NaOH \longrightarrow CH_3-CH_2-\overset{\overset{\displaystyle O}{\|}}{C}-O^- Na^+ + H_2O$$

c.

$$C_6H_5-\overset{\overset{\displaystyle O}{\|}}{C}-OH + NaOH \longrightarrow C_6H_5-\overset{\overset{\displaystyle O}{\|}}{C}-O^- + H_2O$$

7.18 **a.**

$$CH_3-\overset{\overset{\displaystyle O}{\|}}{C}-OH + KOH \longrightarrow CH_3-\overset{\overset{\displaystyle O}{\|}}{C}-O^- K^+ + H_2O$$

b.

$$CH_3-CH_2-\overset{\overset{\displaystyle CH_3}{|}}{CH}-\overset{\overset{\displaystyle O}{\|}}{C}-OH + KOH \longrightarrow CH_3-CH_2-\overset{\overset{\displaystyle CH_3}{|}}{CH}-\overset{\overset{\displaystyle O}{\|}}{C}-O^- K^+ + H_2O$$

c.

$$Cl-C_6H_4-\overset{\overset{\displaystyle O}{\|}}{C}OH + KOH \longrightarrow Cl-C_6H_4-\overset{\overset{\displaystyle O}{\|}}{C}O^- K^+ + H_2O$$

17.19 A carboxylic acid salt is named by replacing the *-oic ic* ending of the acid name with *ate*.

   a. The acid is methanoic acid (formic acid). The carboxylic acid salt is sodium methanoate, (sodium formate).

   b. The acid is propanoic acid (propionic acid). The carboxylic acid salt is sodium propanoate (sodium propionate).

   c. The acid is benzoic acid. The carboxylic acid salt is sodium benzoate.

17.20 **a.** potassium ethanoate; potassium acetate

   b. potassium 2-methylbutanoate; potassium α-methylbutyrate

   c. potassium *para*-chlorobenzoate

17.21 **a.** This is an *aldehyde* since it has a carbonyl bonded to carbon and hydrogen.

   b. This is an *ester* since it has a carbonyl bonded to oxygen that is also bonded to a carbon.

   c. This is a *ketone* since it has a carbonyl bonded to two carbon atoms.

   d. This is a *carboxylic acid* since it has a carboxylic group; a carbonyl bonded to a hydroxyl.

17.22 **a.** carboxylic acid   **b.** ester   **c.** aldehyde   **d.** ester

17.23

a. CH₃—C(=O)—O—CH₃   The carbonyl portion of the ester has two carbons bonded to a methyl group.

b. CH₃—CH₂—CH₂—C(=O)—OCH₃   The carbonyl portion of the ester is a four-carbon chain bonded to a one carbon methyl group.

c.

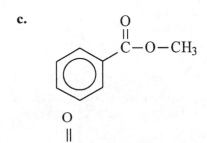

17.24 **a.** H—C(=O)—O—CH₃   **b.** CH₃—CH₂—C(=O)—O—CH₃

c. CH₃—CH₂—CH₂—CH(CH₃)—C(=O)—O—CH₃

17.25 A carboxylic acid and an alcohol react to give an ester with the elimination of water.

a. CH₃—CH₂—C(=O)—O—CH₂—CH₂—CH₃

b. CH₃—CH₂—CH₂—CH₂—C(=O)—O—CH(CH₃)—CH₃

17.26 **a.** CH₃—CH₂—C(=O)—O—CH₃

b.

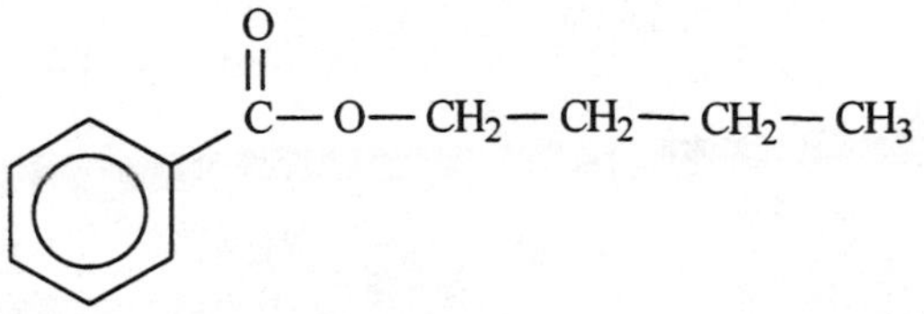

Benzene ring—C(=O)—O—CH₂—CH₂—CH₂—CH₃

17.27 **a.** The carbonyl portion of the ester is derived from methanoic acid (formic acid). The alcohol is methanol (methyl alcohol).
b. The carbonyl portion of the ester is derived from ethanoic acid (acetic acid). The alcohol is methanol (methyl alcohol).
c. The carbonyl portion of the ester is derived from butanoic acid (butyric acid). The alcohol is methanol (methyl alcohol).
d. The carbonyl portion of the ester is derived from 3-methylbutanoic acid (β-methylbutyric acid). The alcohol is ethanol (ethyl alcohol).

17.28 **a.** Propanoic acid (propionic acid) and ethanol (ethyl alcohol)
      b. Hexanoic acid and methanol (methyl alcohol)
      c. 2-methylbutanoic acid (α-methylbutyric acid) and methanol (methyl alcohol)
      d. Propanoic acid (propionic acid) butanol (butyl alcohol)

17.29 **a.** The name of this ester is methyl methanoate (methyl formate). The carbonyl portion of the ester contains one carbon; the name is derived from methanoic (formic) acid. The alkyl portion has one carbon; it is methyl.

      b. The name of this ester is methyl ethanoate (methyl acetate). The carbonyl portion of the ester contains two carbons. The name is derived from ethanoic (acetic) acid. The alkyl portion has one carbon, which is methyl.

      c. The name of this ester is methyl butanoate (methyl butyrate). The carbonyl portion of the ester contains four carbons; the name is derived from butanoic (butyric) acid. The alkyl portion has one carbon, which is methyl.

      d. The name of this ester is ethyl-3-methyl butanoate (ethyl-β-methyl butyrate). The carbonyl portion of the ester has a four-carbon chain with a methyl group attached to the third (β) carbon, counting the carboxyl carbon as 1. The alkyl portion with two carbons is an ethyl.

17.30 **a.** ethyl butanoate; ethyl butyrate   **b.** methyl hexanoate
      c. methyl-3-methylbutanoate   **d.** butyl propanote; butyl propionate

17.31

             O
             ‖
    a. CH_3—C—O—CH_3 Acetic acid is the two carbon carboxylic acid. Methanol gives a one-carbon alkyl group.

           O
           ‖
    b. H—C—O—CH_2—CH_2—CH_2—CH_3 Formic acid is the carboxylic acid bonded to the four-carbon 1-butanol.

                          O
                          ‖
    c. CH_3—CH_2—CH_2—CH_2—C—O—CH_2—CH_3 Pentanoic acid is the carboxylic acid bonded to ethanol.

               O   Br
               ‖ |
    d. CH_3—CH_2—C—O—CH_2—CH—CH_3 Propanoic acid is the carboxylic acid bonded to 2-bromo-1-propanol.

             O
             ‖
17.32 **a.** CH_3—C—O—CH_2—CH_2— CH_2—CH_2—CH_2—CH_3

                    O
                    ‖
    b. CH_3—CH_2—C—O—CH_2—CH_2—CH_3

                  OH O
                  | ‖
    c. CH_3—CH_2—CH—C—O—CH_2 — CH_3 **d.**

17.33 **a.** The flavor and odor of bananas is pentyl ethanoate (pentyl acetate).
b. The flavor and odor of oranges is octyl ethanoate (octyl acetate).
c. The flavor and odor of apricots is pentyl butanoate (pentyl butyrate).
d. The flavor and odor of raspberries is isobutyl methanoate (isobutyl formate).

17.34 **a.** pineapple   **b.** pear   **c.** strawberry   **d.** rum

17.35 **a.**

$$CH_3-\overset{\overset{\displaystyle O}{\|}}{C}-OH$$

b. $CH_3-CH_2-CH_2-CH_2-OH$

c.

$$CH_3-O-\overset{\overset{\displaystyle O}{\|}}{C}-CH_3$$

17.36 **a.** $CH_3-CH_2-CH_2-OH$ hydrogen bonds

b.

$$CH_3-\overset{\overset{\displaystyle O}{\|}}{C}-O-CH_3 \qquad \text{dipole-dipole attractions}$$

c.

$$CH_3-O-\overset{\overset{\displaystyle O}{\|}}{C}-H \qquad \text{dipole-dipole attractions}$$

17.37 Acid hydrolysis of an ester adds water in the presence of acid and gives a carboxylic acid and an alcohol.

17.38 The products of the base hydrolysis of an ester are an alcohol and the salt of a carboxylic acid.

17.39 Acid hydrolysis of an ester gives the carboxylic acid and the alcohol, which were combined to form the ester; basic hydrolysis of an ester gives the salt of carboxylic acid and the alcohol, which combine to form the ester.

a.

$$CH_3-CH_2-\overset{\overset{\displaystyle O}{\|}}{C}-O^-\quad Na^+ \text{ and } CH_3-OH$$

b.

$$CH_3-\overset{\overset{\displaystyle O}{\|}}{C}-OH \text{ and } CH_3-CH_2-CH_2-OH$$

c.

$$CH_3-CH_2-CH_2-\overset{\overset{\displaystyle O}{\|}}{C}-OH \text{ and } CH_3-CH_2-OH$$

d.

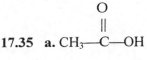 —COOH and CH_3CH_2OH

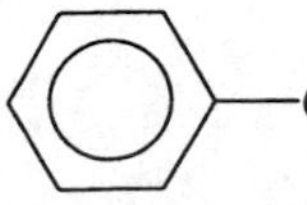

e.

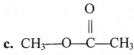 —COO$^-$ Na$^+$ and CH_3CH_2OH

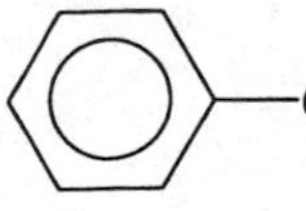

17.40

a. $CH_3CH_2-\overset{\overset{\displaystyle O}{\|}}{C}-OH$ and $CH_3CH_2CH_2CH_2-OH$

b. $H-\overset{\overset{\displaystyle O}{\|}}{C}-O^- \ Na^+$ and CH_3CH_2-OH

c. $CH_3CH_2-\overset{\overset{\displaystyle O}{\|}}{C}-OH$ and CH_3-OH

d. $CH_3CH_2-\overset{\overset{\displaystyle O}{\|}}{C}-OH$ and ⬡—OH

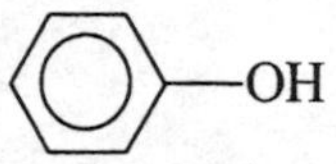

e. 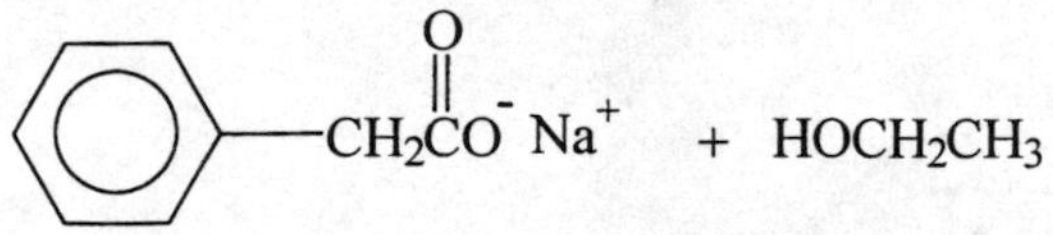 ⬡—$CH_2\overset{\overset{\displaystyle O}{\|}}{C}O^- \ Na^+$ + $HOCH_2CH_3$

17.41 **a.** 3-methylbutanoic acid; β-methylbuyric acid
  b. ethylbenzoate
  c. ethyl propanoate; ethylpropionate
  d. 2-chlorobenzoic acid; *ortho*chlorobenzoic acid
  e. 4-hydroxypentanoic acid
  f. 2-propyl ethanoate; isopropyl acetate

17.42 **a.** 4-methylpentanoic acid
  b. 3,5-dichlorobenzoic acid
  c. methylbenzoate
  d. methylbutanoate; methybutyrate
  e. ethyl 3-methylbutanoate
  f. 2-hydroxy-4-methylpentanoic acid

17.43 $CH_3-CH_2-CH_2-CH_2-\overset{\overset{\displaystyle O}{\|}}{C}-OH$ $CH_3-CH_2-\overset{\overset{\displaystyle CH_3}{|}}{CH}-\overset{\overset{\displaystyle O}{\|}}{C}-OH$

  $CH_3-\overset{\overset{\displaystyle CH_3}{|}}{CH}-CH_2-\overset{\overset{\displaystyle O}{\|}}{C}-OH$ $CH_3-\underset{\underset{\displaystyle CH_3}{|}}{\overset{\overset{\displaystyle CH_3}{|}}{C}}-\overset{\overset{\displaystyle O}{\|}}{C}-OH$

17.44 $CH_3-\overset{\overset{\displaystyle O}{\|}}{C}-O-CH_2-CH_3$ $H-\overset{\overset{\displaystyle O}{\|}}{C}-O-CH_2-CH_2-CH_3$

  $CH_3-CH_2-\overset{\overset{\displaystyle O}{\|}}{C}-O-CH_3$ $H-\overset{\overset{\displaystyle O}{\|}}{C}-\overset{\overset{\displaystyle CH_3}{|}}{CH}-CH_3$

17.45 **a.** $CH_3-O-\overset{\overset{\displaystyle O}{\|}}{C}-CH_3$

b.

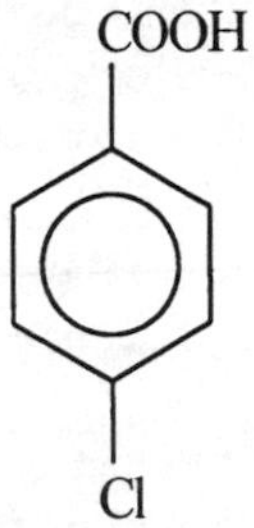

4-chlorobenzoic acid structure (COOH on top, Cl on bottom of benzene ring)

c. $Cl-CH_2-CH_2-\overset{\overset{\displaystyle O}{\|}}{C}-OH$

d. $CH_3-CH_2-O-\overset{\overset{\displaystyle O}{\|}}{C}-CH_2-CH_2-CH_3$

e. $CH_3-CH_2-\overset{\overset{\displaystyle CH_3}{|}}{CH}-CH_2-\overset{\overset{\displaystyle O}{\|}}{C}-OH$

f. 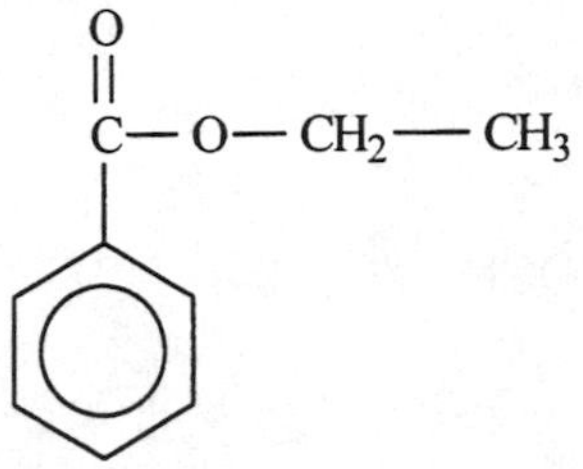 $\overset{\overset{\displaystyle O}{\|}}{C}-O-CH_2-CH_3$ (benzene ring attached)

17.46 **a.** $CH_3-CH_2-\overset{\overset{\displaystyle Br}{|}}{CH}-\overset{\overset{\displaystyle O}{\|}}{C}-OH$

b. $CH_3-CH_2-CH_2-\overset{\overset{\displaystyle O}{\|}}{C}-O-CH_2-CH_3$

c. 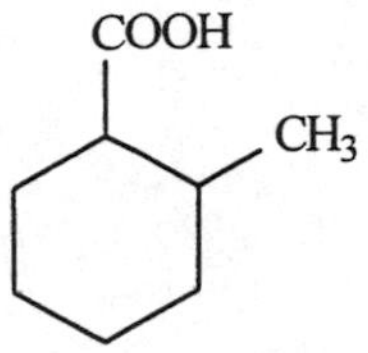 cyclohexane ring with COOH and CH_3 substituents

d. $CH_3-\overset{\overset{\displaystyle CH_3}{|}}{CH}-CH_2-\overset{\overset{\displaystyle CH_3}{|}}{CH}-CH_2-\overset{\overset{\displaystyle O}{\|}}{C}-OH$

e. $CH_3-\overset{\overset{\displaystyle O}{\|}}{C}-O-CH_2-CH_2-CH_3$

f. 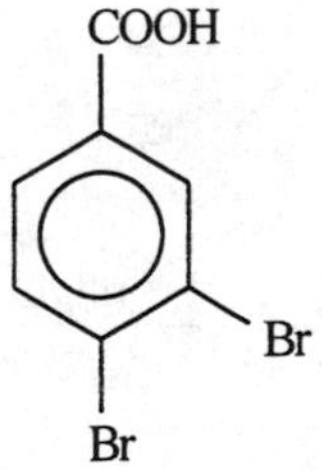 benzene ring with COOH on top, Br, Br on bottom

17.47

a. $CH_3-\overset{\overset{\displaystyle O}{\|}}{C}-OH$

b. $CH_3-CH_2-\overset{\overset{\displaystyle O}{\|}}{C}-OH$

c. $CH_3-CH_2-CH_2-\overset{\overset{\displaystyle O}{\|}}{C}-OH$

17.48 **a.** $CH_3-CH_2-CH_2-OH$

b. $CH_3-CH_2-\overset{\overset{\displaystyle O}{\|}}{C}-OH$

c. $CH_3-\overset{\overset{\displaystyle O}{\|}}{C}-O-CH_3$

17.49   The presence of two polar groups in the carboxyl group allows hydrogen bonding, including the formation of a dimer that doubles the effective molar mass and requires a higher temperature to form gas.

17.50   Of these three compounds, butanal would have the lowest boiling point, then 1-butanol, and propionic acid would have the highest because it forms dimers: butanal 76°C, 1-butanol 118°C, and propionic acid 141°C.

17.51   Compounds b, c, d, and e are all soluble in water

17.52   Compounds a, d, and e are soluble in water.

17.53

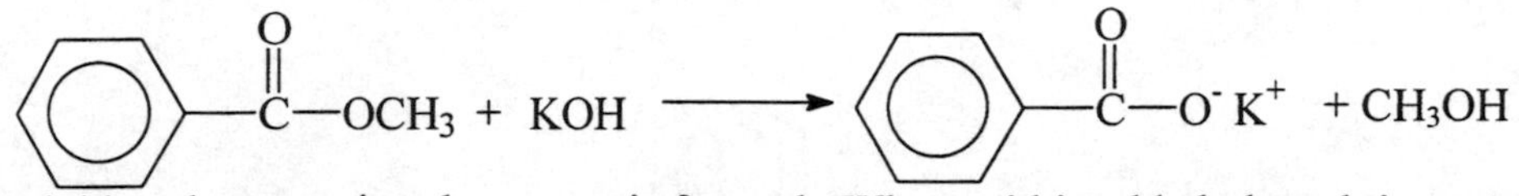

A soluble salt, potassium benzoate, is formed. When acid is added, the salt is converted to insoluble benzoic acid.

17.54   Hexanoic acid can form a salt with NaOH and the salt (sodium hexanoate) is soluble.

17.55   **a.** hydroxyl and carboxylic acid

b.

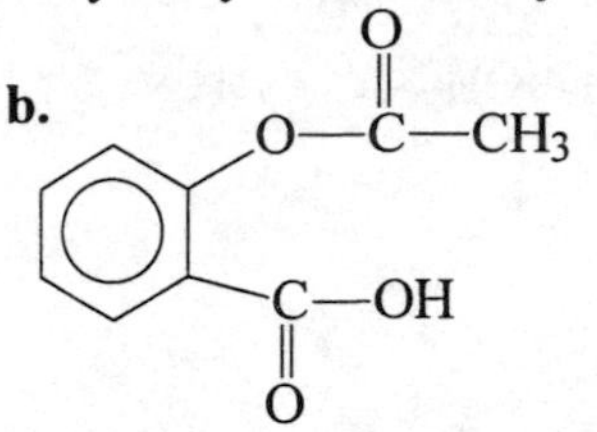

c.

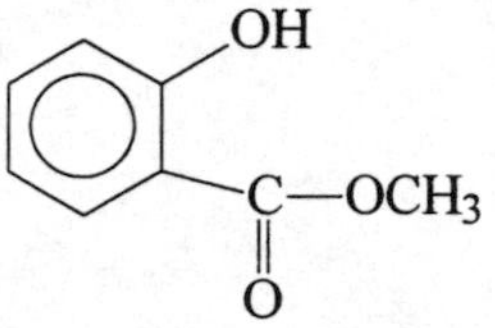

17.56 $3.00 \text{ g } C_7H_6O_2 \times \dfrac{1 \text{ mole}}{122 \text{ g}} \times \dfrac{1 \text{ L NaOH}}{0.100 \text{ mole NaOH}} \times \dfrac{1000 \text{ mL}}{1 \text{ L}} = 246 \text{ mL NaOH}$

17.57

a. $CH_3-CH_2-\overset{\overset{\displaystyle O}{\|}}{C}-O^- + H_3O^+$

b. $CH_3-CH_2-\overset{\overset{\displaystyle O}{\|}}{C}-O^-\ K^+ + H_2O$

c. $CH_3-CH_2-\overset{\overset{\displaystyle O}{\|}}{C}-O-CH_3 + H_2O$

d.

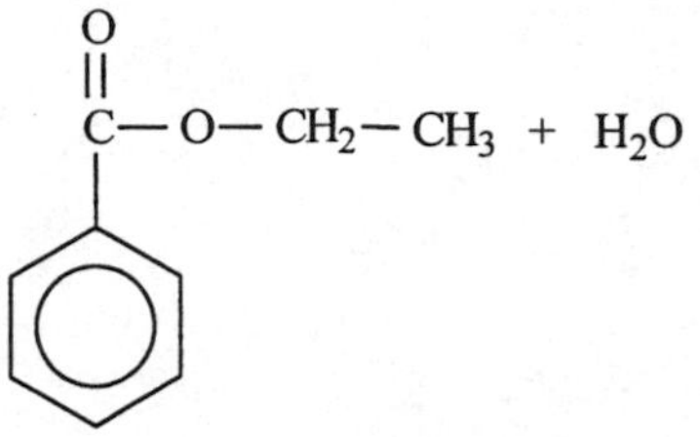

17.58

a. $CH_3-\overset{\overset{\displaystyle O}{\|}}{C}-O^-\ Na^+$

b. $CH_3-\overset{\overset{\displaystyle O}{\|}}{C}-O^-\ +\ H_3O^+$

c. $CH_3-\overset{\overset{\displaystyle CH_3}{|}}{CH}-\overset{\overset{\displaystyle O}{\|}}{C}-O^-\ K^+$

d. $CH_3-\overset{\overset{\displaystyle CH_3}{|}}{CH}-\overset{\overset{\displaystyle O}{\|}}{C}-O-CH_3$

17.59 a. 3-Methylbutanoic acid is needed to react with methanol (CH_3-OH).
b. 3-Chlorobenzoic acid is needed to react with ethanol (CH_3-CH_2-OH).
c. Hexanoic acid is needed to react with methanol (CH_3-OH).

17.60 a. butanoic (butyric) acid and ethanol
b. propanoic (propionic) acid and 2-chlorophenol
c. 2,3-butanoic acid and methanol

17.61

a. $CH_3-CH_2-\overset{\overset{\displaystyle O}{\|}}{C}-OH$ and $HO-\overset{\overset{\displaystyle CH_3}{|}}{CH}-CH_3$

b. $CH_3-\overset{\overset{\displaystyle CH_3}{|}}{CH}-\overset{\overset{\displaystyle O}{\|}}{C}-O^-\ Na^+$ and $HO-CH_2-CH_2-CH_3$

17.63 a. $CH_2=CH_2\ +\ H_2O\ \overset{H^+}{\longrightarrow}\ CH_3-CH_2-OH\ \overset{[O]}{\longrightarrow}\ CH_3-\overset{\overset{\displaystyle O}{\|}}{C}-OH$

b. $CH_3-CH_2-CH_2-CH_2-OH\ \overset{[O]}{\longrightarrow}\ CH_3-CH_2-CH_2-\overset{\overset{\displaystyle O}{\|}}{C}-OH$

17.64 a. $CH_3-CH_2-CH_2-CH_2-CH_2-OH\ \overset{[O]}{\longrightarrow}\ CH_3-CH_2-CH_2-CH_2-\overset{\overset{\displaystyle O}{\|}}{C}-OH$

b. $CH_3-CH_2-OH\ \overset{[O]}{\longrightarrow}\ CH_3-\overset{\overset{\displaystyle O}{\|}}{C}-OH\ +\ CH_3-CH_2-OH\ \overset{H^+}{\longrightarrow}\ CH_3-\overset{\overset{\displaystyle O}{\|}}{C}-O-CH_2-CH_3$

18
Lipids

Study Goals

- Describe the properties and types of lipids.
- Write the structures of triacylglycerols obtained from glycerol and fatty acids.
- Draw the structure of the product from hydrogenation, hydrolysis, and saponification of triacylglycerols.
- Distinguish between phospholipids, glycolipids, and sphingolipids.
- Describe steroids and their role in bile salts, vitamins, and hormones.
- Describe the lipid bilayer in a cell.

Chapter Outline

Chapter Summary and Demonstrations

1. Types of Lipids

Lipids are discussed in terms of their components and solubility in various solvents. Saturated and unsaturated fatty acids are described along with a comparison of their melting points.

Demonstration: I introduce this chapter with examples of lipids such as margarine, butter, lard, cooking oils (corn, olive, safflower), gallstones, and vitamin A and oil of lemon.

Demonstration: Read the labels on some vegetable oils, margarines, or peanut butter. Ask students what they know about saturated fat, unsaturated fats, and polyunsaturated fats. What process occurred if the label states that the product is partially hydrogenated?

2. Fatty Acids and Triglycerides

The formation of the ester linkage between alcohols and fatty acids in waxes or glycerol and fatty acids in triglycerides is shown. Several reactions of the triglycerides including hydrogenation, acid and enzyme hydrolysis, saponification and oxidation are described.

Demonstration: A discussion of hydrogenation of vegetable oils in the production of margarine is an eye opener for many students. I place bottles of oil on the table along with a tub and cube of margarine, and perhaps some Crisco. I ask the students how the oils in the bottles become the solid products in front of them. This leads into a practical discussion of hydrogenation and the terms associated with lipids such as unsaturated and saturated fats.

3. Phospholipids

The phospholipids are discussed along with their dual polarity and function in cell membranes. Students are asked to look at the difference in properties for each of the components in cell membranes. The chapter concludes with the coverage of steroids and steroid hormones with a discussion of high- and low-density lipoproteins.

Demonstration: Bring in samples of lecithin, a phospholipid, and perhaps some cholesterol (if you have gallstones). A discussion of anabolic steroids (see health note) is interesting to students who are athletes or lift weights.

Laboratory Suggestions

Lab 30 Lipids

Students observe the physical and chemical properties of some common lipids and draw the structure of a typical triacylglycerol. Chemical tests are used to distinguish between saturated and unsaturated fats. A sample of hand lotion is prepared, which illustrates the physical properties of various types of lipids.
A. Triacylglycerols
B. Physical Properties of Some Lipids and Fatty Acids
C. Bromine Test for Unsaturation
D. Preparation of Hand Lotion

Laboratory Skills to Demonstrate
   Remind students of the change in color with bromine adds to a double bond.

Lab 31 Glycerophospholipids and Steroids

Students isolate cholesterol and lecithin from egg yolk using extraction techniques. The differences in solubility of cholesterol and lecithin in acetone and ether is used to separate the steroid from the glycerophospholipid.
   A. Isolating Cholesterol in Egg Yolk
   B. Isolating Lecithin in Egg Yolk

Laboratory Skills to Demonstrate
   Caution in use of flammable solvents
   Proper disposal techniques for organic compounds

Lab 32 Saponification and Soaps

Soap is prepared by the saponification of a triglyceride and collected. The behavior of soap with soft water, oil and $CaCl_2$ is observed.
A. Saponification: Preparation of Soap
B Properties of Soap and Detergents

Laboratory Skills to Demonstrate
   Caution in the saponification procedure using NaOH to form soap.
   Use of the Büchner filtration apparatus.

Answers and Solutions to Text Problems

18.1   Lipids provide energy, protection, and insulation for the organs in the body.

18.2   Some of the different kinds of lipids are oils, fats, waxes, glycerophospholipids, sphingolipids, and steroids.

18.3   Since lipids are not soluble in water, they are nonpolar molecules.

18.4 CCl_4, diethyl ether and benzene might dissolve an oil stain.

18.5   All fatty acids contain a long chain of carbon atoms with a carboxylic acid group.
Saturated fats contain only carbon-to-carbon single bonds; unsaturated fats contain one or more double bonds. More saturated fats are from animal sources, while vegetable oils contain more unsaturated fatty acids.

18.6   Because the molecules of a saturated fatty acid (like stearic acid) fit closer together than the molecules of polyunsaturated fatty acid, there are stronger attractions between saturated fatty acid molecules requiring more energy (higher melting points) to break them apart and form liquid

18.7   **a.** palmitic acid

b. oleic aicd

18.8   **a.** stearic acid

b. linolenic acid

18.9   **a.** Lauric acid has only carbon-carbon single bonds; it is saturated.
b. Linolenic has three carbon-carbon double bonds; it is unsaturated.
c. Palmitoleic has one carbon-carbon double bond: it is unsaturated.
d. Stearic acid has only carbon-carbon single bonds; it is saturated.

18.10   **a.** unsaturated   **b.** saturated   **c.** saturated   **d.** unsaturated

18.11   In a cis double bonds, the alkyl groups are on the same side of the double bond, whereas in trans fatty acids, the alkyl groups are on opposite sides.

18.12   **a.** Both myristic and stearic acid are saturated; myristic acid has 14 carbons and stearic acid has 18 carbons. The fatty acid with the smaller number of carbon atoms would have the lower melting point.
b. Stearic acid and linoleic acid both have 18 carbon atoms. Linoleic acid is unsaturated and the presence of a double bond means that the molecules cannot fit closely; linoleic acid would have a lower melting point.
c. Oleic acid and linolenic acid both have 18 carbon atoms. Oleic acid is monounsaturated and linolenic acid is polyunsaturated. The presence of many double bonds means that the molecules of linolenic acid cannot fit closely and linolenic acid will have a lower melting point.

18.13 In an omega-3 fatty acid, the first double bond occurs at carbon 3 counting from the methyl. In an omega-6 fatty acid, the first double bond occurs at carbon 6.

18.14 **a.** Omega-3 fatty acids are found in fish oils; omega-6 fatty acids are found in vegetable oils.
b. Omega-3 fatty acids lower the tendency for blood platelets to stick together and decrease the possibility of blood clots and subsequent heart attacks.

18.15 Arachidonic acid contains four double bonds and no side groups. In PGE$_2$, a part of the chain forms cyclopentane and there are hydroxyl and ketone functional groups.

18.16 PGE is a prostaglandin with a ketone group at carbon 9, whereas PGF has a hydroxyl group at carbon 9.

18.17 Prostaglandins affect blood pressure, stimulate contraction and relaxation of smooth muscle.

18.18 Anti-inflammatory drugs such as aspirin block the production of prostaglandins, which cause pain and inflammation when they are released during tissue injury.

18.19 Palmitic acid is the 16-carbon saturated fatty acid.
$$CH_3-(CH_2)_{14}-\overset{\overset{\displaystyle O}{\|}}{C}-O-(CH_2)_{29}-CH_3$$

18.20 $CH_3(CH_2)_{18}\overset{\overset{\displaystyle O}{\|}}{C}O(CH_2)_{21}CH_3$

18.21 Fats are composed of fatty acids and glycerol. In this case, the fatty acid is stearic acid, an 18-carbon saturated fatty acid.

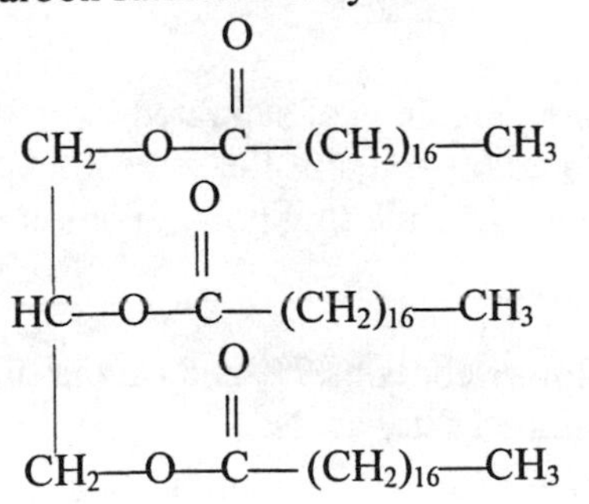

$$
\begin{array}{l}
CH_2-O-\overset{\overset{\displaystyle O}{\|}}{C}-(CH_2)_{16}-CH_3\\[4pt]
\;\;|\\
HC-O-\overset{\overset{\displaystyle O}{\|}}{C}-(CH_2)_{16}-CH_3\\[4pt]
\;\;|\\
CH_2-O-\overset{\overset{\displaystyle O}{\|}}{C}-(CH_2)_{16}-CH_3
\end{array}
$$

18.22

$$
\begin{array}{l}
CH_2-O-\overset{\overset{\displaystyle O}{\|}}{C}-(CH_2)_{14}-CH_3\\[4pt]
\;\;|\\
CH-O-\overset{\overset{\displaystyle O}{\|}}{C}-(CH_2)_{14}-CH_3\\[4pt]
\;\;|\\
CH_2-O-\overset{\overset{\displaystyle O}{\|}}{C}-(CH_2)_7-CH=CH-(CH_2)_7CH_3
\end{array}
$$

$$
\begin{array}{l}
CH_2-O-\overset{\overset{\displaystyle O}{\|}}{C}-(CH_2)_{14}-CH_3\\[4pt]
\;\;|\\
CH-O-\overset{\overset{\displaystyle O}{\|}}{C}-(CH_2)_7CH=CH(CH_2)_7CH_3\\[4pt]
\;\;|\\
CH_2-O-\overset{\overset{\displaystyle O}{\|}}{C}-(CH_2)_{14}-CH_3
\end{array}
$$

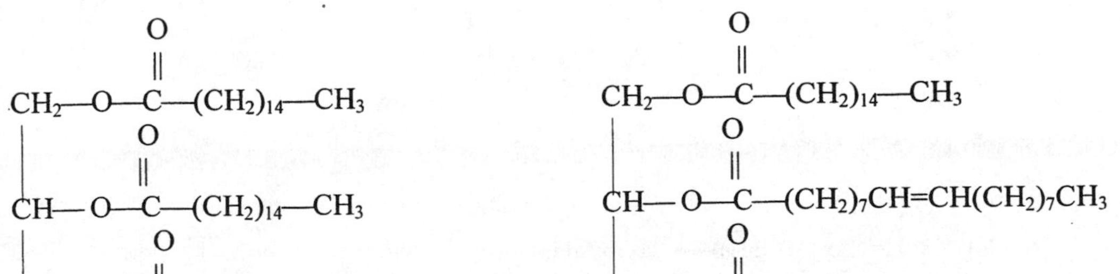

18.23 Tripalmitin has three palmitic acids (16 carbon saturated fatty acid) forming ester bonds with glycerol.

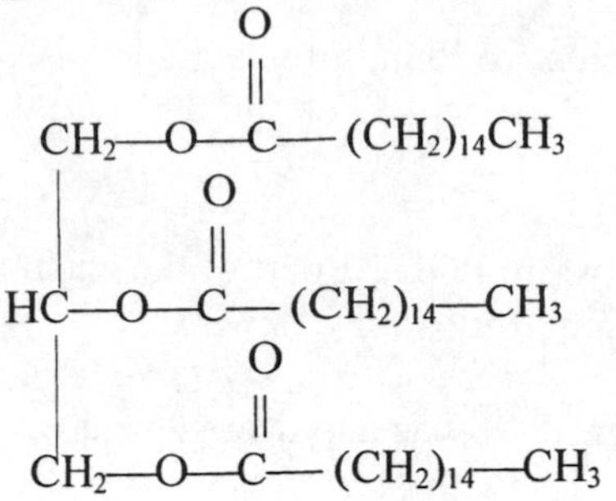

$$
\begin{array}{l}
\text{CH}_2\text{—O—C—(CH}_2)_{14}\text{CH}_3 \\
\qquad\qquad\overset{\displaystyle O}{\overset{\|}{}} \\
\text{HC—O—C—(CH}_2)_{14}\text{—CH}_3 \\
\text{CH}_2\text{—O—C—(CH}_2)_{14}\text{—CH}_3
\end{array}
$$

18.24

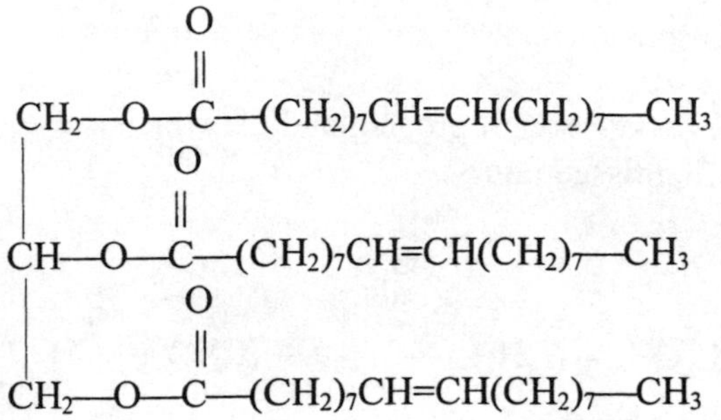

$$
\begin{array}{l}
\text{CH}_2\text{—O—C—(CH}_2)_7\text{CH=CH(CH}_2)_7\text{—CH}_3 \\
\text{CH—O—C—(CH}_2)_7\text{CH=CH(CH}_2)_7\text{—CH}_3 \qquad\text{Triolein} \\
\text{CH}_2\text{—O—C—(CH}_2)_7\text{CH=CH(CH}_2)_7\text{—CH}_3
\end{array}
$$

18.25 Safflower oil contains fatty acids with two or three double bonds; olive oil contains a large amount of oleic acid, which has a single (monounsaturated) double bond.

18.26 Olive oil contains more unsaturated fatty acids than butter fat.

18.27 Although coconut oil comes from a vegetable source, it has large amounts of saturated fatty acids and small amounts of unsaturated fatty acids. Since coconut oil contains the same kinds of fatty acids as animal fat, coconut oil has a melting point similar to the melting point of animal fats.

18.28 **a.** Sunflower oil contains about 8% saturated fatty acids; safflower contains 7% and canola oil is about 2% saturated fatty acids; corn oil is about 15% unsaturated fatty acids.
b. It does not appear that the claim is valid if the other oils are considered leading oils.

18.29

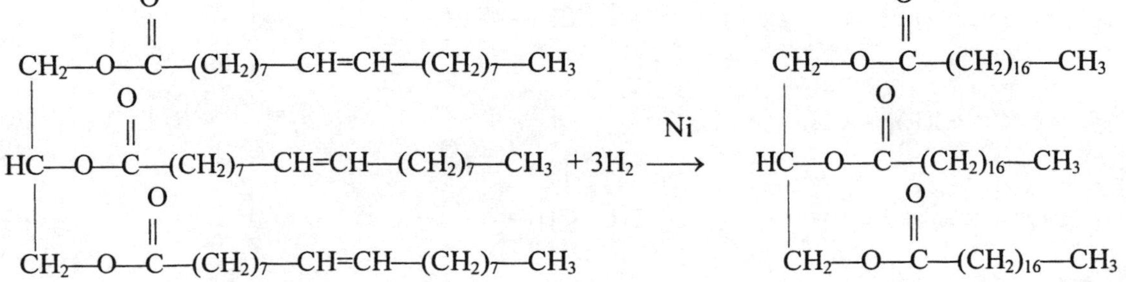

$$
\begin{array}{l}
\text{CH}_2\text{—O—C—(CH}_2)_7\text{—CH=CH—(CH}_2)_7\text{—CH}_3 \\
\text{HC—O—C—(CH}_2)_7\text{—CH=CH—(CH}_2)_7\text{—CH}_3 \;+\; 3\text{H}_2 \;\xrightarrow{\text{Ni}} \\
\text{CH}_2\text{—O—C—(CH}_2)_7\text{—CH=CH—(CH}_2)_7\text{—CH}_3
\end{array}
$$

$$
\begin{array}{l}
\text{CH}_2\text{—O—C—(CH}_2)_{16}\text{—CH}_3 \\
\text{HC—O—C—(CH}_2)_{16}\text{—CH}_3 \\
\text{CH}_2\text{—O—C—(CH}_2)_{16}\text{—CH}_3
\end{array}
$$

18.30

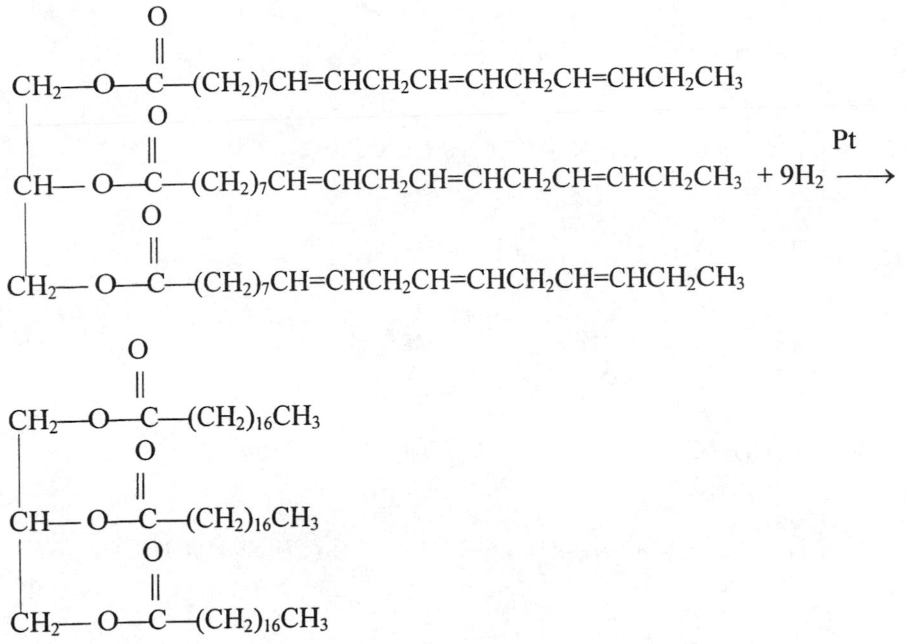

$$CH_2-O-\overset{\overset{\textstyle O}{\|}}{C}-(CH_2)_7CH=CHCH_2CH=CHCH_2CH=CHCH_2CH_3$$

$$CH-O-\overset{\overset{\textstyle O}{\|}}{C}-(CH_2)_7CH=CHCH_2CH=CHCH_2CH=CHCH_2CH_3 + 9H_2 \xrightarrow{\text{Pt}}$$

$$CH_2-O-\overset{\overset{\textstyle O}{\|}}{C}-(CH_2)_7CH=CHCH_2CH=CHCH_2CH=CHCH_2CH_3$$

$$CH_2-O-\overset{\overset{\textstyle O}{\|}}{C}-(CH_2)_{16}CH_3$$

$$CH-O-\overset{\overset{\textstyle O}{\|}}{C}-(CH_2)_{16}CH_3$$

$$CH_2-O-\overset{\overset{\textstyle O}{\|}}{C}-(CH_2)_{16}CH_3$$

18.31 **a.** Partial hydrogenation means that some of the double bonds in the unsaturated fatty acids have been converted to single bonds.
  b. Since the margarine has more saturated fatty acids than the original vegetable oil, the fatty acid interact more strongly and remain solid at higher temperatures.

18.32 To prevent the reaction with oxygen in the air with the unsaturated bonds in the vegetable oil an oil without preservatives is kept tightly closed and in a refrigerator. The oxidation reaction that turns oil rancid is accelerated at room temperature.

18.33 Acid hydrolysis of a fat gives glycerol and the fatty acids. Basic hydrolysis (saponification) of fat gives glycerol and the salts of the fatty acids.

a.

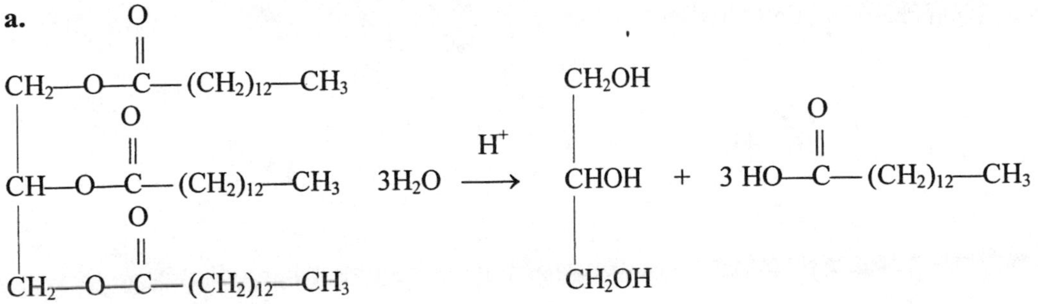

$$CH_2-O-\overset{\overset{\textstyle O}{\|}}{C}-(CH_2)_{12}-CH_3$$

$$CH-O-\overset{\overset{\textstyle O}{\|}}{C}-(CH_2)_{12}-CH_3 \quad 3H_2O \xrightarrow{H^+} \quad \begin{matrix} CH_2OH \\ | \\ CHOH \\ | \\ CH_2OH \end{matrix} + 3\;HO-\overset{\overset{\textstyle O}{\|}}{C}-(CH_2)_{12}-CH_3$$

$$CH_2-O-\overset{\overset{\textstyle O}{\|}}{C}-(CH_2)_{12}-CH_3$$

b.

$$CH_2-O-\overset{\overset{\textstyle O}{\|}}{C}-(CH_2)_{12}-CH_3$$

$$CH-O-\overset{\overset{\textstyle O}{\|}}{C}-(CH_2)_{12}-CH_3 \quad 3NaOH \longrightarrow \quad \begin{matrix} CH_2OH \\ | \\ CHOH \\ | \\ CH_2OH \end{matrix} + 3Na^{+\;-}O-\overset{\overset{\textstyle O}{\|}}{C}-(CH_2)_{12}-CH_3$$

$$CH_2-O-\overset{\overset{\textstyle O}{\|}}{C}-(CH_2)_{12}-CH_3$$

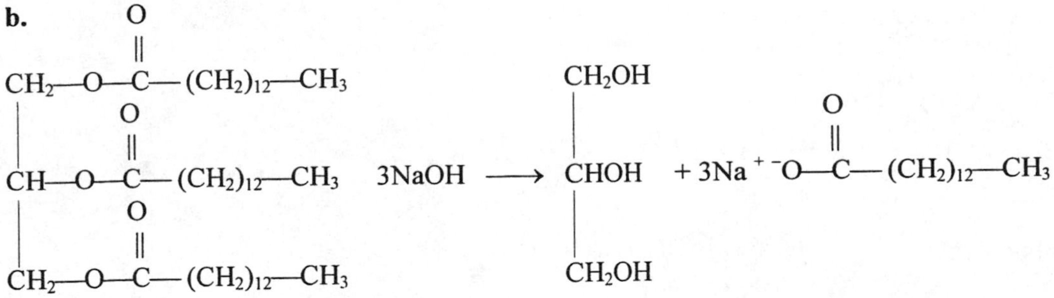

18.34 **a.**

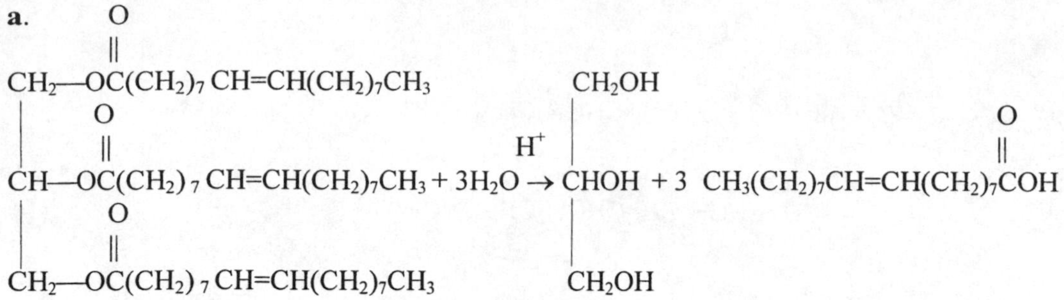

$$\text{CH}_2\text{—OC(CH}_2)_7\text{ CH=CH(CH}_2)_7\text{CH}_3$$

Triolein + 3H₂O $\xrightarrow{\text{H}^+}$ Glycerol + 3 Oleic acid

CH₂—OC(CH₂)₇ CH=CH(CH₂)₇CH₃
| O
| ‖
CH—OC(CH₂)₇ CH=CH(CH₂)₇CH₃ + 3H₂O → CHOH + 3 CH₃(CH₂)₇CH=CH(CH₂)₇COH
| O
| ‖
CH₂—OC(CH₂)₇ CH=CH(CH₂)₇CH₃   CH₂OH

Triolein   Glycerol   +   3 Oleic acid

b.

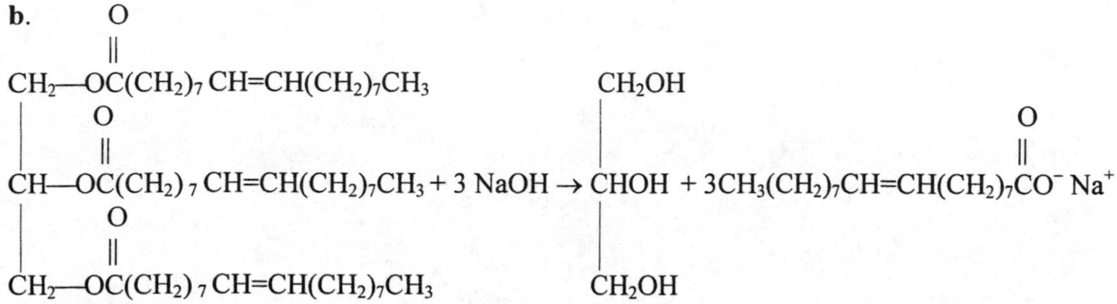

CH₂—OC(CH₂)₇ CH=CH(CH₂)₇CH₃
| O
| ‖
CH—OC(CH₂)₇ CH=CH(CH₂)₇CH₃ + 3 NaOH → CHOH + 3CH₃(CH₂)₇CH=CH(CH₂)₇CO⁻ Na⁺
| O
| ‖
CH₂—OC(CH₂)₇ CH=CH(CH₂)₇CH₃   CH₂OH
Triolein   Glycerol   +   3 Sodium oleate

18.35 A triacylglycerol is a combination of three fatty acids bonded to glycerol by ester bonds. Olestra is sucrose bonded to six to eight fatty acids by ester bonds. Olestra cannot be digested because digestive enzymes cannot break down the molecule.

18.36 **a.** When an oil is partially hydrogenated, that means that only some of the double bonds in the oil have been converted to single bonds.
   b. During hydrogenation, some cis double bonds open, but close again reforming double bonds that are trans rather than cis. The trans arrangement is the more stable configuration because it places the bulky groups on opposite sides of the double bond.
   c. You can minimize the trans fatty acids in your diet by not eating large amounts of hydrogenated or partially hydrogenated fats.

18.37

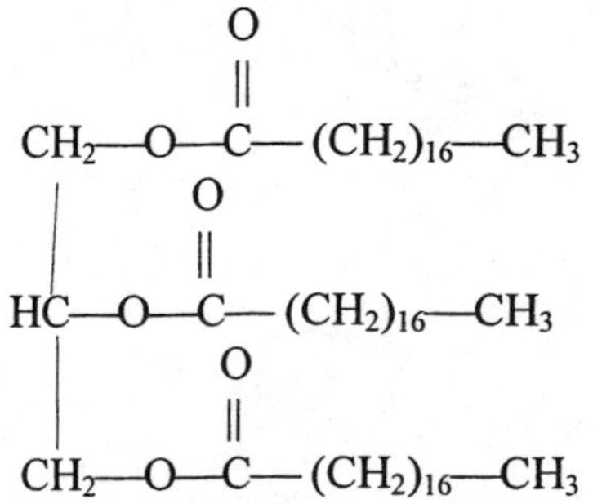

CH₂—O—C—(CH₂)₁₆—CH₃
| O
| ‖
HC—O—C—(CH₂)₁₆—CH₃
| O
| ‖
CH₂—O—C—(CH₂)₁₆—CH₃

18.38 **a.**

CH₂—OH   + 2 HO—C—(CH₂)₁₆—CH₃
| O
| ‖
CH—OH   +   HO—C—(CH₂)₇ CH=CH(CH₂)₇CH₃
|
|
CH₂—OH

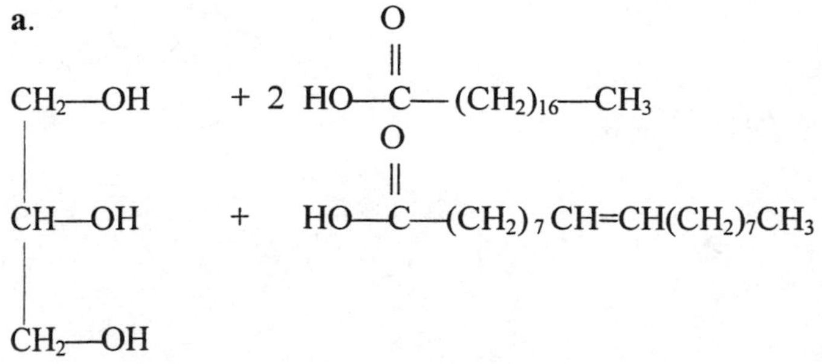

18.39 A triacylglycerol consists of glycerol and three fatty acids. A glycerophospholipid consists of glycerol, two fatty acids, a phosphate group, and an amino alcohol.

18.40 In lecithins, the amino alcohol is choline; in cephalins, the amino alcohol is ethanolamine.

18.41

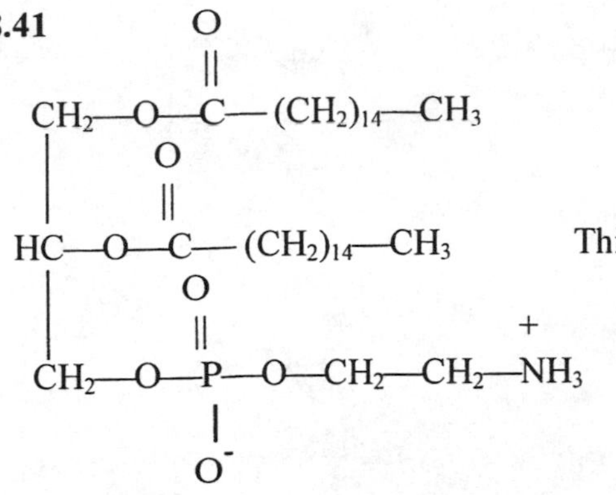

$$
\begin{array}{l}
CH_2-O-\overset{\overset{\displaystyle O}{\|}}{C}-(CH_2)_{14}-CH_3 \\
\quad | \qquad \overset{\overset{\displaystyle O}{\|}}{} \\
HC-O-\overset{\overset{\displaystyle O}{\|}}{C}-(CH_2)_{14}-CH_3 \\
\quad | \qquad \overset{\overset{\displaystyle O}{\|}}{} \\
CH_2-O-\overset{\overset{\displaystyle O}{\|}}{\underset{\underset{\displaystyle O^-}{|}}{P}}-O-CH_2-CH_2-\overset{+}{N}H_3
\end{array}
$$

This is a cephalin.

18.42

$$
\begin{array}{l}
CH_2-O-\overset{\overset{\displaystyle O}{\|}}{C}-(CH_2)_{14}-CH_3 \\
\quad | \\
CH-O-\overset{\overset{\displaystyle O}{\|}}{C}-(CH_2)_{14}-CH_3 \\
\quad | \\
CH_2-O-\overset{\overset{\displaystyle O}{\|}}{\underset{\underset{\displaystyle O^-}{|}}{P}}-O-CH_2CH_2-\overset{\overset{\displaystyle CH_3}{|}}{\underset{\underset{\displaystyle CH_3}{|}}{\overset{+}{N}}}-CH_3
\end{array}
$$

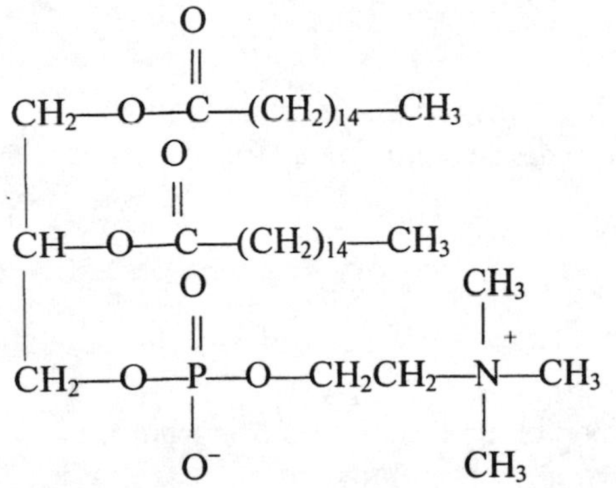

18.43 This phospholipid is a cephalin. It contains glycerol, oleic acid, stearic acid, phosphate, and ethanolamine.

18.44 This phospholipid is a lecithin with stearic and palmitic acid, phosphate and choline.

18.45 A glycerophospholipid consists of glycerol, two fatty acids, a phosphate group, and an amino alcohol. A sphingolipid contains the amino alcohol sphingosine instead of glycerol.

18.46 A cerebroside is a glycosphingolipid containing sphingosine, a fatty acid and a monosaccharide, which is using galactose. A ganglioside also contains sphingosine and a fatty acid, but differs in the number of monosaccharides, which is two or more such as glucose and galactose.

18.47 $CH_3-(CH_2)_{12}-CH=CH-CH-OH$

$CH-NH-\overset{\overset{\displaystyle O}{\|}}{C}-(CH_2)_{14}-CH_3$

Palmitic acid

galactose

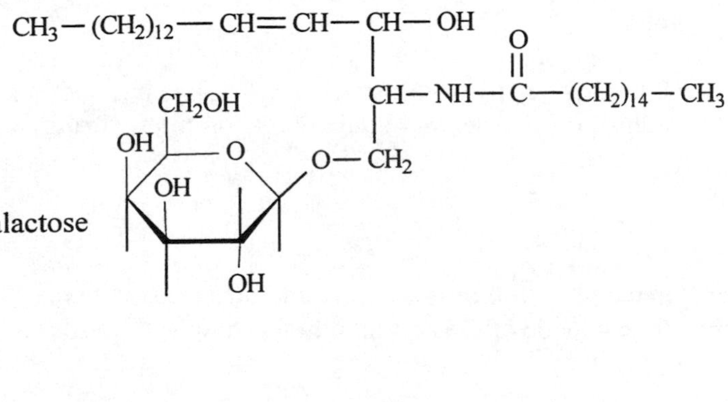

18.48 In sphingomyelin, the amino alcohol is choline.

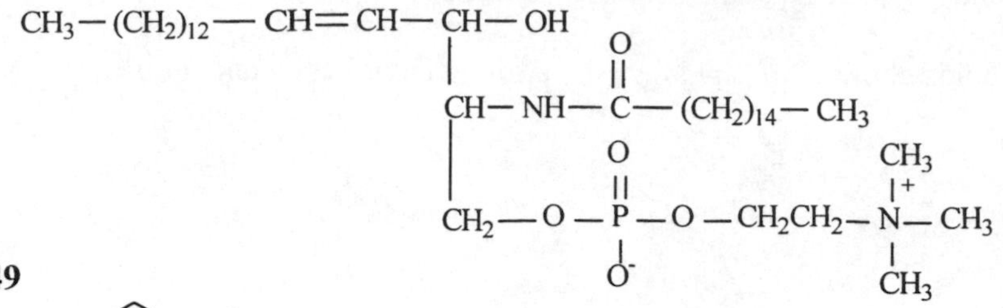

$$CH_3-(CH_2)_{12}-CH=CH-CH-OH$$

$$CH-NH-\overset{\overset{\displaystyle O}{\|}}{C}-(CH_2)_{14}-CH_3$$

$$CH_2-O-\overset{\overset{\displaystyle O}{\|}}{\underset{\underset{\displaystyle O^-}{|}}{P}}-O-CH_2CH_2-\overset{\overset{\displaystyle CH_3}{|}}{\underset{\underset{\displaystyle CH_3}{|}}{N}}{}^+-CH_3$$

18.49

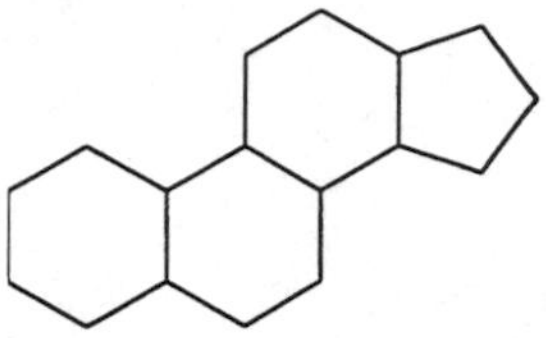

18.50 b, c, d, e

18.51 Bile salts emulsify fat globules, which makes the fat easier to digest by lipases.

18.52 When the cholesterol level in the bile stored in the gallbladder exceeds saturation level, a solid called a gallstone is produced.

18.53 Lipoproteins are large, spherically shaped molecules that transport lipids in the bloodstream. They consist of an outer layer of phospholipids and proteins surrounding an inner core of hundreds of nonpolar lipids and cholesterol esters.

18.54 Lipoproteins form water-soluble complexes for transport through the bloodstream by combining nonpolar lipids with polar phospholipids and proteins.

18.55 Chylomicrons have a lower density than VLDLs. They pick up triacylglycerols from the intestine, whereas VLDLs transport triacylglycerols synthesized in the liver.

18.56 LDLs are low-density lipoproteins that deposit excess cholesterol in the arteries, which can restrict blood and increase the risk of heart disease. The HDLs, high-density lipoproteins, remove excess cholesterol from tissues and carry it to the liver where it is converted to bile salts for elimination.

18.57 "Bad" cholesterol is the cholesterol carried by LDLs to the tissues where it can form deposits called plaque, which can narrow the arteries.

18.58 HDLs are called "good" cholesterol because they carry excess cholesterol from tissues to the liver where it is converted to bile salts for elimination.

18.59 Both estradiol and testosterone contain the steroid nucleus and a hydroxyl group, but testosterone has a ketone group, a double bond, and an extra methyl group. Estradiol has a benzene ring and a second hydroxyl group.

18.60 Both have a steroid nucleus, 3 ketone, 2 methyl and hydroxyl groups. Cortisone has another hydroxyl group on the last ring, and prednisone has a second double bond on the first ring.

18.61 Testosterone is a male sex hormone.

18.62 b

18.63 Cell membranes contain a number of lipids: phospholipids that contain fatty acids with cis double bonds, glycolipids which are on the outside of the cell membrane and in animal membranes, cholesterol.

18.64 The lipid bilayer consists of two rows of phospholipids, with the hydrophobic tails forming the center of the bilayer. The polar hydrophilic parts are situated along the outside of the bilayer. This bilayer creates a separation between the contents of a cell and its surroundings.

18.65 The function of the lipid bilayer in the plasma membrane is to keep the cell contents separated from the outside environment and to allow the cell to regulate the movement of substances into and out of the cell.

18.66 The unsaturated fatty acids have kinks in their carbon chains that provide a flexible, not fixed, structure that is dynamic and fluid-like.

18.67 The peripheral proteins in the membrane emerge on the inner or outer surface only, whereas the integral proteins extend through the membrane to both surfaces.

18.68 Carbohydrates are part of glycolipid structures and also attached to proteins (glycoproteins) on the outer surface of the cell membranes.

18.69 The carbohydrates glycoproteins and glycolipids on the surface of cells act as receptors for cell recognition and chemical messengers such as neurotransmitters.

18.70 A semipermeable cell membrane retains certain components within the membrane, while nutrients can enter and waste products can leave the cell. This semipermeable function is obtained by a lipid bilayer of glycerophospholipids and sphingolipids along with proteins and carbohydrates. Some molecules flow by simple diffusion through the membrane, while others flow by facilitated transport via integral proteins that extend through the membrane.

18.71 Substances move through cell membrane by simple transport, facilitated transport, and active transport.

18.72 **a.** facilitated transport **b.** simple (passive) transport **c.** active transport

18.73 Beeswax and carnauba are waxes. Vegetable oil and capric triacylglycerol are triacylglycerols.

$$CH_2-O-\overset{\overset{\displaystyle O}{\displaystyle \|}}{C}-(CH_2)_8-CH_3$$
$$CH-O-\overset{\overset{\displaystyle O}{\displaystyle \|}}{C}-(CH_2)_8-CH_3 \qquad \text{Capric triacylglycerol}$$
$$CH_2-O-\overset{\overset{\displaystyle O}{\displaystyle \|}}{C}-(CH_2)_8-CH_3$$

18.74 Hydrogenation converts the unsaturated 18-carbon oleic and linoleic acids to saturated 18-carbon stearic acid. The final product is a saturated fat with one palmitic acid and two stearic acids.

18.75 **a.** A typical monounsaturated fatty acid has a cis double bond.
b. A trans fatty acid has a trans double bond with the alkyl groups on opposite sides of the double bond.
c.

18.76

$$CH_2-O-\overset{\overset{\textstyle O}{\|}}{C}-(CH_2)_7\,CH=CH(CH_2)_7CH_3$$

$$CH-O-\overset{\overset{\textstyle O}{\|}}{C}-(CH_2)_7\,CH=CH(CH_2)_7CH_3 + 3H_2 \xrightarrow{\ \ Pt\ \ }$$

$$CH_2-O-\overset{\overset{\textstyle O}{\|}}{C}(CH_2)_7\,CH=CH(CH_2)_7CH_3$$

Triolein

$$CH_2-O-\overset{\overset{\textstyle O}{\|}}{C}-(CH_2)_{16}CH_3$$

$$CH-O-\overset{\overset{\textstyle O}{\|}}{C}-(CH_2)_{16}CH_3$$

$$CH_2-O-\overset{\overset{\textstyle O}{\|}}{C}-(CH_2)_{16}CH_3$$

Tristearin

The hydrogenation of the oleic acids converts them into stearic acids, which makes the product tristearin. One mole of triolein requires 3 mole H_2 or 6.0 g H_2 to completely hydrogenate the fat. At STP, 3 moles $\times$ 22.4 L/mole or 67.2 liters of hydrogen are needed for the reaction.

18.77

$$CH_2-O-\overset{\overset{\textstyle O}{\|}}{C}-(CH_2)_{16}-CH_3$$

$$CH-O-\overset{\overset{\textstyle O}{\|}}{C}-(CH_2)_{16}-CH_3 \qquad \text{glyceryl tristearate}$$

$$CH_2-O-\overset{\overset{\textstyle O}{\|}}{C}-(CH_2)_{16}-CH_3$$

$$CH_2-O-\overset{\overset{\textstyle O}{\|}}{C}-(CH_2)_{14}-CH_3$$

$$CH-O-\overset{\overset{\textstyle O}{\|}}{C}-(CH_2)_{14}-CH_3 \qquad \text{lecithin}$$

$$CH_2-O-\overset{\overset{\textstyle O}{\|}}{P}-O-CH_2-CH_2-\overset{+}{N}-CH_3$$

with pendant CH_3 groups on the N and O^- on the P.

18.78 **a.** 46 g $\times$ 9 kcal/g   = 410 kcal from fat; (410/830) $\times$ 100   = 49 % fat
       b. 29 g $\times$ 9 kcal/g   = 260 kcal from fat; (260/518) $\times$ 100   = 50.% fat
       c. 18 g $\times$ 9 kcal/g   = 160 kcal from fat; (160/560) $\times$ 100   = 29% fat
       d. 21 g $\times$ 9 kcal/g   = 190 kcal from fat; (190/470) $\times$ 100   = 40 % fat
       e. 28 g $\times$ 9 kcal/g   = 250 kcal from fat; (250/480) $\times$ 100   = 52% fat
The fats in these foods are from animal sources and would be expected to be mostly saturated fats.

18.79 Stearic acid is a fatty acid. Sodium stearate is soap. Glyceryl tripalmitate, safflower oil, whale blubber and adipose tissue are triacylglycerols. Beeswax is a wax. Lecithin is a glycerophospholipid. Sphingomyelin is a sphingolipid. Cholesterol, progesterone, and cortisone are steroids.

18.80 Hibernating animals in cold climates have more unsaturated triacylglycerols because unsaturated triacylglycerols will not solidify at cold temperatures.

18.81 **a.** 5   **b.** 1, 2, 3, 4   **c.** 2
          d. 1, 2   **e.** 1, 2, 3, 4   **f.** 2, 3, 4, 6

18.82 Cell membranes contain the following components:
          a. cholesterol   **b.** triacylglycerols   **c.** carbohydrates
          d. proteins   **f.** glycerophospholipids   **g.** sphingolipids

18.83 **a.** 4   **b.** 3   **c.** 1
          d. 4   **e.** 4   **f.** 3
          g. 2   **h.** 1

Study Goals

- Name and write structural formulas of amines and amides.
- Describe the ionization of amines in water.
- Describe the boiling points of amines and amides compared to alkanes and alcohols.
- Describe the solubility of amines and amides in water.
- Write equations for the neutralization and amidation of amines.
- Describe acid and base hydrolysis of amides.

Chapter Outline

19.1   **Amines**
         Health Note: Amines in Health and Medicine
19.2   **Naming Amines**
19.3   **Physical Properties of Amines**
19.4   **Amines React as Bases**
19.5   **Heterocycli Amines and Alkaloids**
         Health Note: Synthesizing Drugs
19.6   **Structure and Names of Amides**
         Health Note: Amides in Health and Medicine
19.7   **Hydrolysis of Amides**

Chapter Summary and Demonstrations

1. Amines and amides

The final chapter on organic chemistry discusses nitrogen-containing compounds along with their amide derivatives. Amines are classified as primary, secondary and tertiary and named according to IUPAC and common naming systems. Heterocyclic amines are introduced and their role in alkaloids and other physiological amines is described.

Demonstration: Amines and Amides Amines and amides are introduced by a discussion of commonly occurring nitrogen-containing compounds such as fish, window-cleaners, and certain drugs. At this time, I hand out pharmacy leaflets that come with prescription drugs. Students identify,the functional groups as well as the amine and amide bonds that give physiological activity. As extra credit, they can write a paper about the drug, its functions, and side effects.

Laboratory Suggestions

Lab 33 Amines and Amides

Amines are classified as primary, secondary or tertiary, their structural formulas drawn, and their names written. Some physical properties of amines are observed and an equation is written for the formation of amine salt, amidation and hydrolysis reactions.

A. Structure and Classification of Amines
B. Solubility of Amines in Water
C. Neutralization of Amines with Acids
D. Amides

Laboratory Skills to Demonstrate

Proper technique in noting the odor of a compound.
Care in the use of concentrated ammonia.
Caution in the use of conc. H_3PO_4
Proper use of the Büchner funnel and filtration apparatus

Lab 34 Synthesis of Acetaminophen

The analgesic acetaminophen is synthesized from *p*-aminophenol and acetic anhydride. The product may be purified and the percent yield calculated. Acetanilide is isolated from an impure sample and the percent yield is determined.

A. Synthesis of Acetaminophen
B. Isolating Acetanilide from an Impure Sample

Laboratory Skills to Demonstrate

Care in working with *p*-aminophenol and acetic anhydride.
Proper use of the Büchner funnel and filtration apparatus

Lab 35 Plastics and Polymerization

Synthetic polymers found in common household products are sorted using density, combustion, and solubility in acetone. Gluep and Slime® are from polyvinyl alcohol or Elmer's glue and a saturated borax (NaB_4O_7) solution. Polystyrene is synthesized from styrene monomers as an example of plastics used to make plastic glasses and coffee cups. Nylon, which is a group polyamides made by the condensation of diamines and dicarboxylic acids, is synthesized and pulled from an interface as a thread.

A. Classification of Plastics
B. Gluep and Slime
C. Polystyrene
D. Nylon

Laboratory Skills to Demonstrate

Formation of aluminum boat for polystyrene
Care in the use of hexamethylenediamine and sebacic chloride and respiratory
Process of forming an interface and removal of nylon polymers

Answers and Solutions to Text Problems

19.1 In a primary amine, there is one alkyl group (and two hydrogen atoms) attached to a nitrogen atom.

19.2 In a tertiary (3°) amine, three alkyl or aromatic groups are bonded to the nitrogen atom.

19.3 **a.** This is a primary (1°) amine; there is only one alkyl group attached to the nitrogen atom.
b. This is a secondary (2°) amine; there are two alkyl groups attached to the nitrogen atom.
c. This is a primary (1°) amine; there is only one alkyl group attached to the nitrogen atom.
d. This is a tertiary (3°) amine; there are three alkyl groups attached to the nitrogen atom.
e. This is a tertiary (3°) amine; there are three alkyl groups attached to the nitrogen atom.

19.4 **a.** primary (1°)   **b.** tertiary (3°)   **c.** secondary (2°)
d. primary (1°)   **e.** secondary (2°)

19.5 The common name of an amine consists of naming the alkyl groups bonding to the nitrogen atom in alphabetical order. In the IUPAC name, the *e* in the alkane chain is replaced with *amine*.
a. An ethyl group attached to —NH_2 is ethylamine. In the IUPAC name, the *e* in ethane is replaced by *amine*: ethanamine

b. Two alkyl groups attach to nitrogen as methyl and propyl for methylpropylamine. The IUPAC name based on the longer chain of propane with a methyl group attached to the nitrogen atoms is *N*-methyl-1-propanamine.

c. Diethylmethylamine; *N*-methyl-*N*-ethylethanamine

d. Isopropylamine; 2-propanamine

19.6 **a.** propylamine; 1-propanamine   **b.** methylpropylamine; *N*-methyl-1-propanamine
c. butylamine; 1-butanamine   **d.** triethylamine; *N,N*-diethylethanamine

19.7 The amine of benzene is called aniline. In amines where a more oxidized functional group takes priority, the —NH_2 group is named as an *amino* group and numbered.
a. 2-butanamine   **b.** 2-chloroaniline
c. 3-aminopropanal   **d.** *N*-ethylaniline

19.8 **a.** 3-aminobutanone   **b.** 1,4-pentanediamine
c. 4-bromo-*N*-methylaniline   **d.** *N*-ethyl-*N*-methylaniline

19.9 **a.** CH_3—CH_2—NH_2
b.

NHCH$_3$

c. CH_3—CH_2—CH_2—CH_2—$\overset{\overset{\displaystyle H}{|}}{N}$—$CH_2$—$CH_2$—$CH_3$

d. CH_3—$\overset{\overset{\displaystyle NH_2}{|}}{CH}$—$CH_2$—$CH_2$—$CH_3$

19.10 **a.**
$$CH_3-\overset{\overset{\displaystyle H}{|}}{N}-CH_3$$

b. 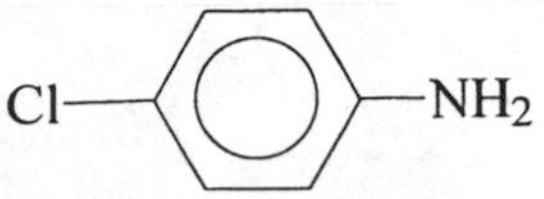 $Cl-\!\!\!\bigcirc\!\!\!-NH_2$

c. 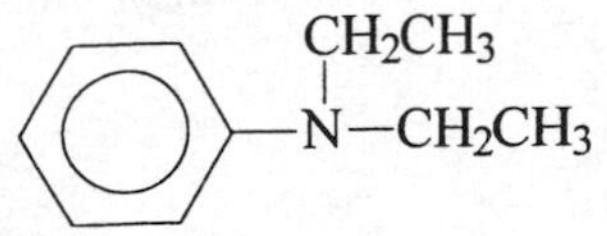 $\bigcirc\!\!\!-\overset{\overset{\displaystyle CH_2CH_3}{|}}{N}-CH_2CH_3$

d. $CH_3-CH_2-\overset{\overset{\displaystyle O}{||}}{C}-CH_2-CH_2-NH_2$

19.11 Amines have higher boiling points than hydrocarbons, but lower than alcohols of similar mass.
  a. CH_3-CH_2-OH **b.** $CH_3-CH_2-CH_2-NH_2$ **c.** $CH_3-CH_2-CH_2-NH_2$

19.12 **a.** $CH_3-CH_2-CH_2-NH_2$ **b.** $CH_3-CH_2-CH_2-NH_2$
  c. $CH_3-CH_2-CH_2-OH$

19.13 Propylamine is a primary amine and forms two hydrogen bonds, which gives it the highest boiling point. Ethylmethylamine, a secondary amine, forms one hydrogen bond, and butane cannot form hydrogen bonds. Thus butane has the lowest boiling point of the three compounds.

19.14 The linear amine has a higher boiling point that the branched amine, but the alcohol has a higher boiling than the amines: trimethylamine 3°C, propylamine 48°C, and 1-propanol 97°C.

19.15 Amines with one to five carbon atoms are soluble. The solubility in water of amines with longer carbon chains decreases.
  a. yes; soluble   **b.** yes; soluble   **c.** no   **d.** yes; soluble

19.16 Amines with one to five carbon atoms are soluble in water. In larger amines, the hydrocarbon chain diminishes the effect of hydrogen bonding.
  a. yes; soluble   **b.** yes; soluble (borderline)   **c.** yes; soluble **d.** no

19.17 Amines, which are weak bases, bond with a proton from water to give a hydroxide ion and an ammonium ion.

  a. $CH_3-NH_2 + H_2O \rightleftarrows CH_3-NH_3^+ + OH^-$

  b. $CH_3-\overset{\overset{\displaystyle CH_3}{|}}{N}H + H_2O \rightleftarrows CH_3-\overset{\overset{\displaystyle CH_3}{|}}{N}H_2^+ + OH^-$

  c. $\overset{\overset{\displaystyle NH_2}{|}}{\bigcirc} + H_2O \rightleftharpoons \overset{\overset{\displaystyle NH_3^+}{|}}{\bigcirc} + OH^-$

219

19.18 **a.** $CH_3-CH_2-NH_2 + H_2O \longrightarrow CH_3-CH_2-NH_3^+ + OH^-$

b. $CH_3-CH_2-CH_2-NH_2 + H_2O \longrightarrow CH_3-CH_2-CH_2-NH_3^+ + OH^-$

c.

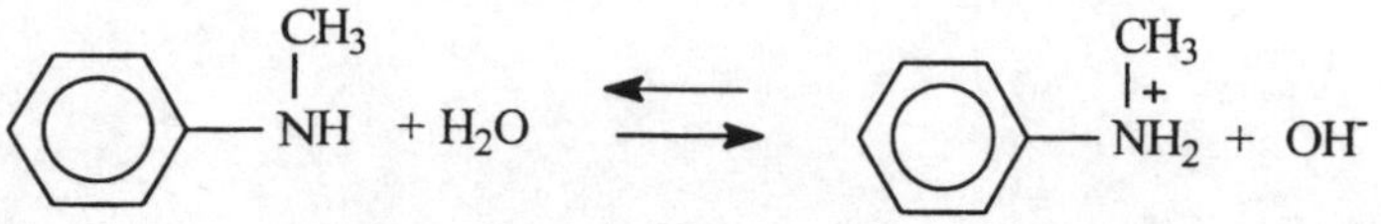

$$\bigcirc-\underset{\underset{CH_3}{|}}{N}H + H_2O \rightleftarrows \bigcirc-\underset{\underset{CH_3}{|}}{\overset{+}{N}}H_2 + OH^-$$

19.19 Amines, which are weak bases, combine with the proton from HCl to yield the ammonium chloride salt.

a. $CH_3-NH_2 + HCl \longrightarrow CH_3-NH_3^+ \; Cl^-$

b. $CH_3-\underset{\underset{CH_3}{|}}{N}H + HCl \longrightarrow CH_3-\underset{\underset{CH_3}{|}}{\overset{+}{N}}H_2 \; Cl^-$

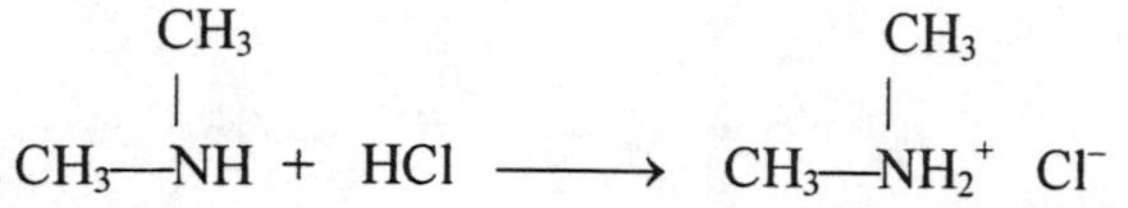

c.

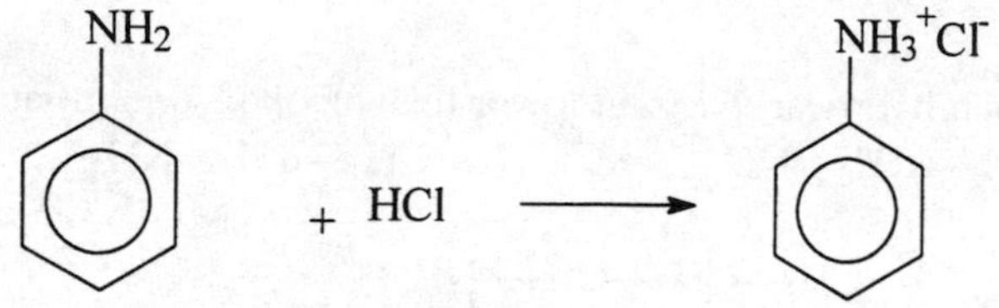

$$\underset{NH_2}{\bigcirc} + HCl \longrightarrow \underset{NH_3^+Cl^-}{\bigcirc}$$

19.20 **a.** $CH_3-CH_2-NH_2 + HCl \longrightarrow CH_3-CH_2-NH_3^+ \; Cl^-$

b. $CH_3-CH_2-CH_2-NH_2 + HCl \longrightarrow CH_3-CH_2-CH_2-NH_3^+ \; Cl^-$

c.

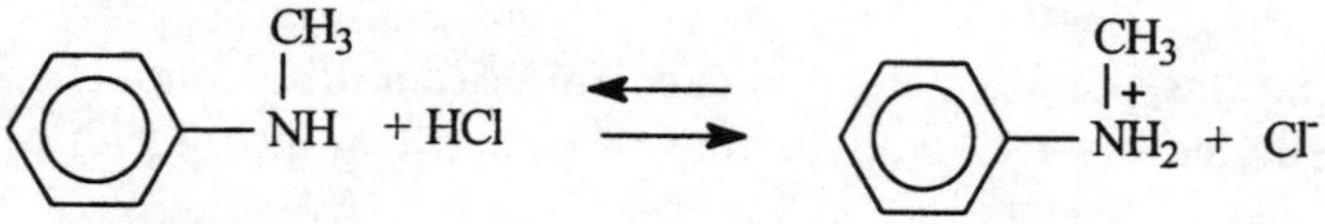

$$\bigcirc-\underset{\underset{CH_3}{|}}{N}H + HCl \rightleftarrows \bigcirc-\underset{\underset{CH_3}{|}}{\overset{+}{N}}H_2 + Cl^-$$

19.21 **a.** $H_2N-\bigcirc-\overset{\overset{O}{\|}}{C}-O-CH_2-CH_2-\underset{\underset{CH_2CH_3}{|}}{\overset{\overset{CH_2CH_3}{|}}{\overset{+}{N}}}-H \quad Cl^-$

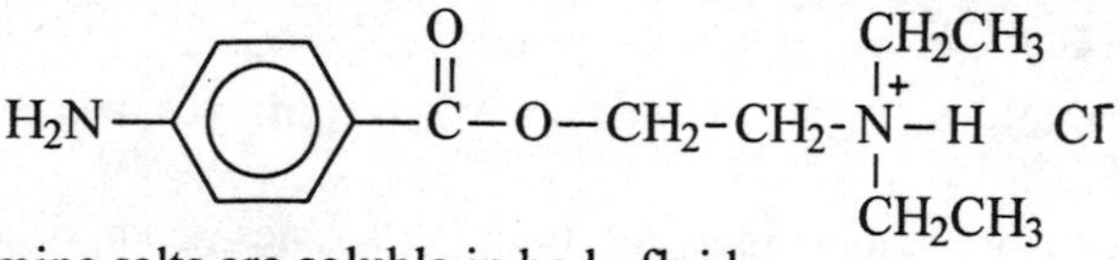

b. Amine salts are soluble in body fluids.

19.22 **a.**

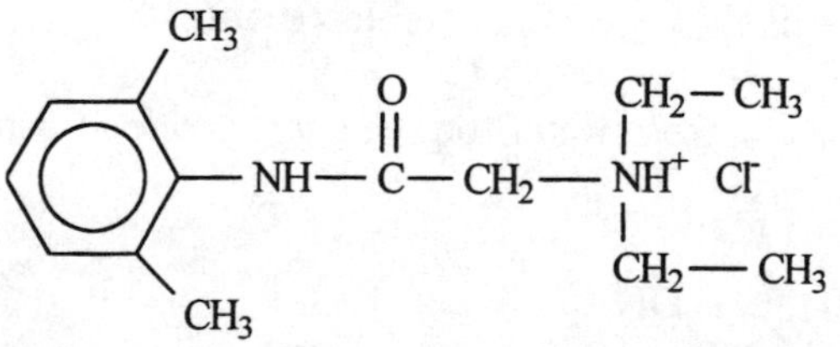

$$\underset{\underset{CH_3}{|}}{\overset{\overset{CH_3}{|}}{\bigcirc}}-NH-\overset{\overset{O}{\|}}{C}-CH_2-\underset{\underset{CH_2-CH_3}{|}}{\overset{\overset{CH_2-CH_3}{|}}{\overset{+}{N}}}H \quad Cl^-$$

b. The amine salt is more soluble in water and body fluids than the amine.

19.23 **a.** Aniline is an amine.
b. An amine with three alkyl groups attached to the nitrogen atom
c. A nitrogen atom in a ring is a heterocyclic amine.
d. A nitrogen atom in a ring is a heterocyclic amine.

19.24 **a.** amine   **b.** heterocyclic amine   **c.** heterocyclic amine   **d.** heterocyclic amine

19.25 **c.** Pyrimidine has two nitrogen atoms in a ring of six atoms.
d. Pyrrole has one nitrogen atom in a ring of five atoms

220

19.26　**b.** In a purine, a pyrimidine ring is bonded to imidazole.

　　　c. Imidazole is a five-atom ring with two nitrogen atoms and two double bonds.

　　　d. Pyrrolidine is a saturated five-atom ring with one nitrogen atom.

19.27　The five-atom ring with one nitrogen atom and two double bonds is pyrrole.

19.28　Pyrrole and piperidine

19.29　Carboxylic acids react with amines to eliminate water and form amides

$$\text{a.} \quad CH_3-\overset{\displaystyle O}{\overset{\displaystyle \|}{C}}-NH_2$$

$$\text{b.} \quad CH_3-\overset{\displaystyle O}{\overset{\displaystyle \|}{C}}-NH-CH_2-CH_3$$

c.

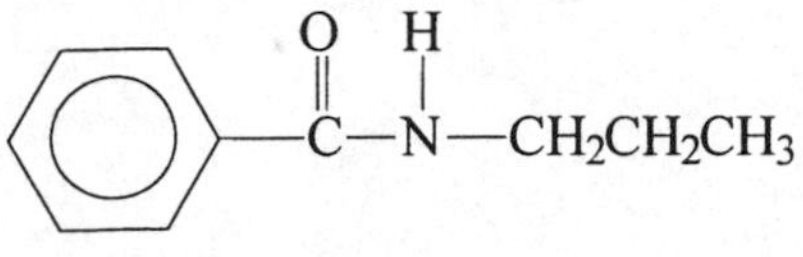

19.30　a.
$$CH_3CH_2CH_2CH_2\overset{\displaystyle O}{\overset{\displaystyle \|}{C}}-NH_2$$

　　　b.
$$CH_3\overset{\displaystyle CH_3}{\overset{\displaystyle |}{C}}HCH_2\overset{\displaystyle O}{\overset{\displaystyle \|}{C}}-\overset{\displaystyle H}{\overset{\displaystyle |}{N}}-CH_2CH_2CH_3$$

　　　c.

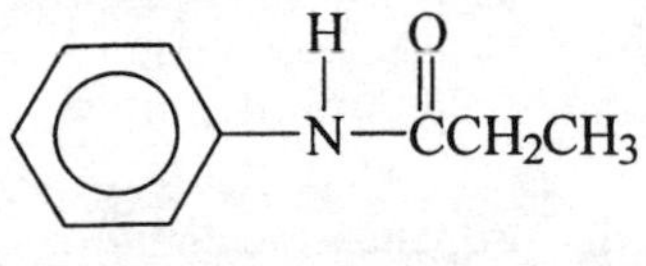

19.31　**a.** *N*-methylethanamide (*N*-methylacetamide). The N-methyl means that there is a one-carbon alkyl group attached to the nitrogen. Ethanamide tells us that the carbonyl portion has two carbon atoms.

　　　b. Butanamide (butyramide) is a chain of four carbon atoms bonded to an amino group.

　　　c. Methanamide (formamide)

　　　d. *N*-methylbenzamide. The *N*-methyl means that there is a one-carbon alkyl group attached to the nitrogen. Benzamide tells us that this is the amide of benzoic acid.

19.32　**a.** N-ethylpropanamide; N-ethylpropionamide

　　　b. hexanamide

　　　c. N-methyl–N–propylethanamide; N–methyl–N–propylacetamide

　　　d. N, N–diethylbenzamide

19.33　**a.** This is an amide of propionic acid, which has three carbon atoms.

$$CH_3-CH_2-\overset{\displaystyle O}{\overset{\displaystyle \|}{C}}-NH_2$$

　　　b. 2-methyl indicates that a methyl is bonded to carbon 2 in an amide chain of five carbon atoms.

$$CH_3-CH_2-CH_2-\overset{\displaystyle CH_3}{\overset{\displaystyle |}{C}}H-\overset{\displaystyle O}{\overset{\displaystyle \|}{C}}-NH_2$$

$$\text{c. } H-\overset{\displaystyle O}{\overset{\displaystyle \|}{C}}-NH_2$$

d. The nitrogen atom in *N*-ethylbenzamide is bonded to an ethyl group.

$$\bigcirc\!\!\!\!\!\!\!\bigcirc-\overset{O}{\overset{\|}{C}}-\overset{H}{\overset{|}{N}}-CH_2\text{-}CH_3$$

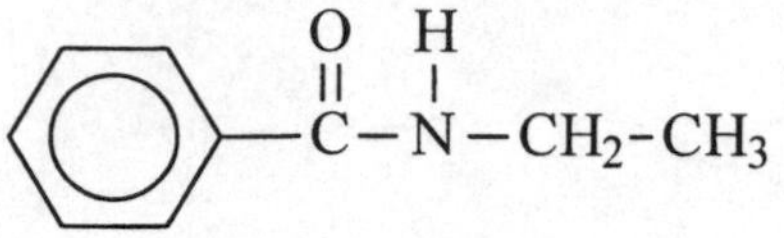

e. The nitrogen atom is bonded to an ethyl group in *N*-ethylbutyramide.

$$CH_3-CH_2-CH_2-\overset{O}{\overset{\|}{C}}-\overset{H}{\overset{|}{N}}-CH_2-CH_3$$

19.34 $\text{a. } H-\overset{\displaystyle O}{\overset{\displaystyle \|}{C}}-NH_2$ **b.** 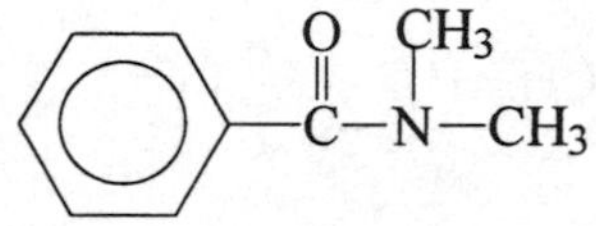 $\bigcirc\!\!\!\!\!\!\!\bigcirc-\overset{O}{\overset{\|}{C}}-\overset{CH_3}{\overset{|}{N}}-CH_3$

$\text{c. } CH_3-\overset{CH_3}{\overset{|}{CH}}-CH_2-\overset{O}{\overset{\|}{C}}-NH_2$ $\text{d. } CH_3-CH_2-CH_2-CH_2-\overset{Cl}{\overset{|}{C}}-\overset{O}{\overset{\|}{C}}-NH_2$

$\text{e. } CH_3-CH_2-\overset{Cl}{\overset{|}{CH}}-CH_2-\overset{O}{\overset{\|}{C}}-\overset{H}{\overset{|}{N}}-CH_2-CH_2-CH_3$

19.35 **a.** Acetamide; primary amines have more hydrogen bonds and higher boiling points.
  b. Propionamide can hydrogen bond, but butane cannot.
  c. *N*-methylpropanamide can hydrogen bond, but *N,N*-dimethylpropanamide cannot.

19.36 **a.** acetamide   **b.** propanamide (forms two hydrogen bonds)
  c. *N*-methylpropanamide (tertiary amides cannot form hydrogen bonds)

19.37 Acid hydrolysis of amides gives the carboxylic acid and the amine salt.
  $\text{a. } CH_3-COOH \;+\; NH_4^+\,Cl^-$ $\text{b. } CH_3-CH_2-COOH + NH_4^+\,Cl^-$

  $\text{c. } CH_3-CH_2-CH_2-COOH + \cdot CH_3-NH_3^+\,Cl^-$ **d.**  $\bigcirc\!\!\!\!\!\!\!\bigcirc-COOH \;+\; NH_4^+\,Cl^-$

  $\text{e. } CH_3-CH_2-CH_2-CH_2-COOH \;+\; CH_3-CH_2-NH_3^+\,Cl^-$

19.38 $\text{a. } CH_3CH_2\overset{CH_3}{\overset{|}{CH}}-\overset{O}{\overset{\|}{C}}-O^-\,Na^+ + NH_3$

  $\text{b. } CH_3CH_2CH_2CH_2-\overset{O}{\overset{\|}{C}}-O^-\,Na^+ \;+\; NH(CH_2CH_3)_2$

  c. 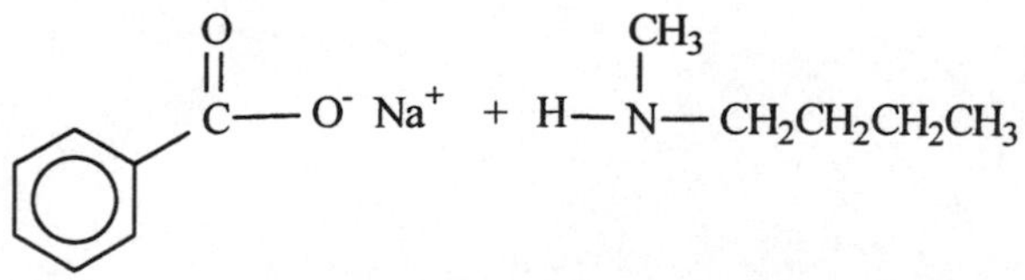 $\bigcirc\!\!\!\!\!\!\!\bigcirc-\overset{O}{\overset{\|}{C}}-O^-\,Na^+ \;+\; H-\overset{CH_3}{\overset{|}{N}}-CH_2CH_2CH_2CH_3$

$$\underset{\text{d.}}{} \overset{\text{CH}_3 \quad \text{O}}{\underset{|}{\text{CH}_3\text{CH}}} \overset{||}{\underset{}{\text{C}}} \text{O}^- \text{Na}^+ \; + \; \overset{\text{CH}_3}{\underset{|}{\text{NH}}} \text{CH}_2\text{CH}_3$$

e.

$$\overset{\text{O} \quad \text{H}}{\underset{||}{\text{C}}} \overset{|}{\underset{}{\text{N}}} \text{CH}_2 - \text{CH}_2 - \text{CH}_3$$

19.39 $\text{CH}_3-\text{CH}_2-\text{CH}_2-\text{NH}_2$ $\text{CH}_3-\text{CH}_2-\text{NH}-\text{CH}_3$ $\overset{\text{CH}_3}{\underset{|}{\text{CH}_3-\text{N}-\text{CH}_3}}$
Propanamine 1°   *N*-methylmethanamine 2°   trimethylamine 3°

$\overset{\text{CH}_3}{\underset{|}{\text{CH}_3-\text{CH}-\text{NH}_2}}$ 2-propanamine 1°

19.40 **a.** methyldiethylamine; *N*-ethyl-*N*-methylethanamine 3°   **b.** butylamine; 1-butanamine 1°
c. ethylpropylamine; *N*-ethyl-1-propanamine 2°   **d.** pyrrolidine 2°
e. *N*-methylaniline
f. ethylmethylisobutyl amine; *N*-ethyl-*n*-methyl-2-methylpropamine
g. diethyldimethyl ammonium chloride

19.41 **a.** $\overset{\text{NH}_2}{\underset{|}{\text{CH}_3-\text{CH}_2-\text{CH}-\text{CH}_2-\text{CH}_3}}$

b.
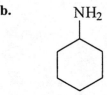

c. This is an ammonium salt with two methyl groups bonded to the nitrogen atom.

$\overset{\text{CH}_3}{\underset{|}{\text{CH}_3-\text{NH}_2^+ \; \text{Cl}^-}}$

d. Three ethyl groups are bonded to a nitrogen atom

$\overset{\text{CH}_2-\text{CH}_3}{\underset{|}{\text{CH}_3-\text{CH}_2-\text{N}-\text{CH}_2-\text{CH}_3}}$

e. This six-carbon chain has a —NH_2 group on carbon 3 and an —OH on carbon 2.

$\overset{\text{OH} \quad \text{NH}_2}{\underset{|\qquad|}{\text{CH}_3-\text{CH}-\text{CH}-\text{CH}_2-\text{CH}_2-\text{CH}_3}}$

f. $\overset{\text{CH}_3}{\underset{\text{CH}_3}{\text{CH}_3-\overset{|+}{\text{N}}-\text{CH}_3 \; \text{Br}^-}}$

g. Two methyl groups are bonded to the nitrogen of aniline.

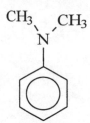

19.42   **a.** 1-butanol   **b.** propylamine   **c.** butylamine   **d.** propylamine

19.43   The smaller amines are more soluble in water.
    a. ethylamine   **b.** trimethylamine
    c. butylamine   **d.** $NH_2\text{—}CH_2\text{—}CH_2\text{—}CH_2\text{—}CH_2\text{—}CH_2\text{—}NH_2$

19.44   **a.** methanmide   **b.** propanamide   **c.** *N*-methyethanamide
    d. *N*-ethylbutanamide   **e.** *N*-butyl-*N*-methylethanamide

19.45   **a.** Quinine obtained from the bark of the cinchona tree is used in the treatment of malaria.
    b. Nicotine is a stimulant found in cigarettes and cigars.
    c. Caffeine is an alkaloid in coffee, tea, soft drinks, and chocolate.
    d. Morphine and codeine are painkillers obtained from the oriental poppy plant.

19.46   **a.** imidazole   **b.** pyrrole   **c.** pyrrolidine
    d. piperidine   **e.** pyrrole

19.47   **a.** An amine in water accepts a proton from water, which produces an ammonium ion and OH⁻.

    $CH_3\text{—}CH_2\text{—}NH_3^+\ OH^-$

    b. The amine accepts a proton to give an ammonium salt: $CH_3\text{—}CH_2\text{—}NH_3^+\ Cl^-$

    c. $CH_3\text{—}CH_2\overset{+}{\text{—}NH_2}\text{—}CH_3\ OH^-$

    d. $CH_3\text{—}CH_2\overset{+}{\text{—}NH_2}\text{—}CH_3\ Cl^-$

    e. An ammonium salt and a strong base produce the amine, a salt, and water.

    $CH_3\text{—}CH_2\text{—}CH_2\text{—}NH_2\ +NaCl+H_2O$

              CH_3
              |
    f. $CH_3\text{—}CH_2\text{—}NH\ +NaCl+H_2O$

19.48   aromatic ring, ketone, heterocyclic amines, carboxylic acid

19.49   carboxylic acid salt, aromatic, amine, haloaromatic

19.50   The salt form is more soluble in water and body fluids than the amine.

19.51   **a.** aromatic, amine, amide, carboxylic acid, cycloalkene
    b. aromatic, ether, alcohol, amine
    c. aromatic, carboxylic acid
    d. phenol, amine, carboxylic acid
    e. aromatic, ether, alcohol, amine, ketone
    f. aromatic, amine

Study Goals

- Classify proteins by their functions in the cells.
- Draw the structures of amino acids.
- Draw the zwitterion forms of amino acids at the isoelectric point, and at pH levels above and below the isoelectric point.
- Write the structural formulas of di- and tripeptides.
- Identify the structural levels of proteins as primary, secondary, tertiary, and quaternary.
- Describe the effects of denaturation on the structure of proteins.

Chapter Outline

20.1 **Functions of Proteins**
20.2 **Amino Acids**
20.3 **Amino Acids as Acids and Bases**
20.4 **Formation of Peptides**
  Career Focus: Rehabilitation Specialist
20.5 **Protein Structure: Primary and Secondary Levels**
  Health Note: Natural Opiates in the Body
20.6 **Protein Structure: Tertiary and Quaternary Levels**
  Health Note: Essential Amino Acids
  Health Note: Protein Structure and Mad Cow Disease
  Health Note: Sickle-Cell Anemia
20.7 **Protein Hydrolysis and Denaturation**
  Explore Your World: Denaturation of Milk Protein

Chapter Summary and Demonstrations

1. Amino Acids

Amino acids are described as the building blocks of proteins. Structures, names, R groups, and polarity in water are discussed. The amphoteric properties of amino acids are described in terms of isoelectric points, zwitterion forms and changes in acid and base. Amino acids are categorized as essential or nonessential.

2. Peptide Bonds and Protein Structure

The peptide bond is described as the amide bond between amino acids in the primary structure of a protein. The structural formulas of di- and tripeptides are written. The secondary forms of protein structure include the alpha helix, pleated sheet and collagen. The interaction of side groups to form the cross-links of tertiary structure is discussed. The breakdown in the secondary and tertiary structural levels is described as part of a discussion on denaturation of proteins. The discussion includes agents that bring about denaturation such as high temperatures, acidic or basic conditions, and organic solvents.

Laboratory Suggestions

36 Amino Acids

The side (R) groups in amino acids are identified and used to determine if an amino acid will be acidic, basic, or neutral; hydrophobic or hydrophilic. Paper chromatography separates amino acids and an unknown amino acid in a mixture. R_f values for amino acids and unknown are calculated and the unknown identified.

A. Amino Acids
B. Chromatography of Amino Acids

Laboratory Skills to Demonstrate

Preparation of paper for amino acid chromatography
Use of ninhydrin spray

37 Peptide and Proteins

Students identify the structural patterns of proteins and observe denaturation. Milk is acidified to the isoelectric point to coagulate the milk protein casein. Chemical tests are used to identify proteins and amino acids.

A. Peptide Bonds
B. Structure of Proteins
C. Denaturation of Proteins
D. Isolation of Casein (Milk Protein)
E. Color Tests for Proteins

Answers and Solutions to Text Problems

20.1   **a.** Hemoglobin, which carries oxygen in the blood, is a transport protein.
b. Collagen, which is a major component of tendon and cartilage, is a structural protein.
c. Keratin, which is found in hair, is a structural protein.
d. Amylase, which catalyzes the breakdown of starch, is an enzyme.

20.2   **a.** hormonal   **b.** protection   **c.** storage   **d.** enzyme

20.3   All amino acids contain a carboxylic acid group and an amino group on the alpha carbon.

20.4   The side chain in leucine is a hydrocarbon group that is nonpolar. In serine, the side group contains an —OH group, which makes it polar.

20.5

20.6

a. 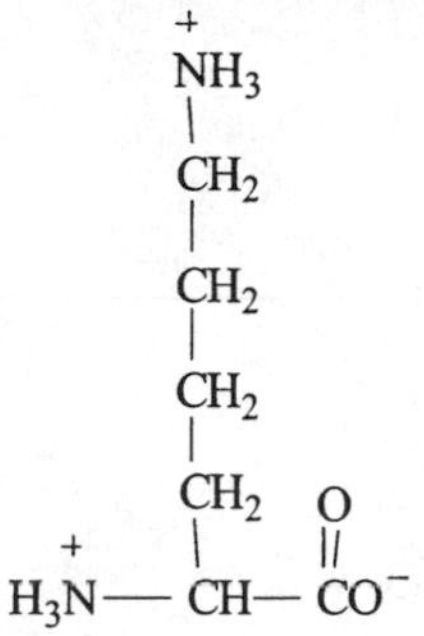
$$H_3\overset{+}{N}—CH—CO^- $$
with side chain $CH_2—CH_2—CH_2—CH_2—\overset{+}{N}H_3$

b. 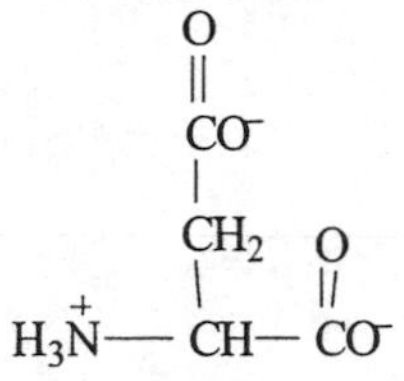
$$H_3\overset{+}{N}—CH—CO^-$$
with side chain $CH_2—CO^-$ (C=O)

c.
$$H_3\overset{+}{N}—CH—CO^-$$
with side chain $CH_2—CH(CH_3)(CH_3)$

d. 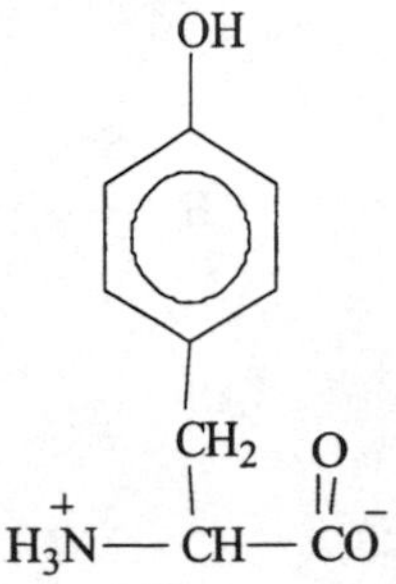
$$H_3\overset{+}{N}—CH—CO^-$$
with side chain CH_2—benzene ring—OH

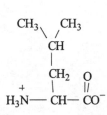

20.7   **a.** Alanine, which has a methyl (hydrocarbon) side group, is nonpolar
b. Threonine has a side group that contains the polar –OH. Threonine is polar.
c. Glutamic acid has a side group containing a polar carboxylic acid. Glutamic acid is acidic.
d. Phenylalanine has a side group with a nonpolar benzene ring. Phenylalanine is nonpolar.

20.8   **a.** basic   **b.** acidic   **c.** nonpolar   **d.** polar

20.9   The abbreviations of most amino acids is derived from the first three letters in the name.
a. alanine   **b.** valine   **c.** lysine   **d.** cysteine

20.10   **a.** tryptophan   **b.** methionine   **c.** proline   **d.** glycine

20.11   In the L isomer, the —NH_2 is on the left side of the horizontal line of the Fischer projection; in D isomer, the —NH_2 group is on the right.

a. 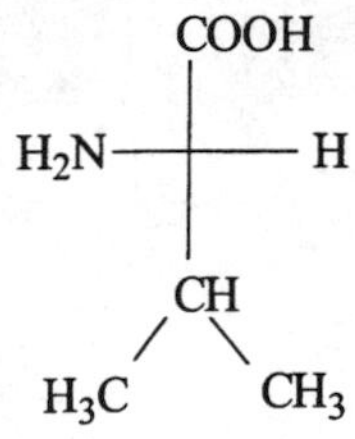
$$COOH$$
$$H_2N—|—H$$
$$CH$$
$$H_3C \quad CH_3$$

b. 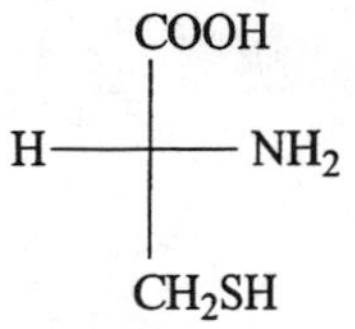
$$COOH$$
$$H—|—NH_2$$
$$CH_2SH$$

20.12   **a.** 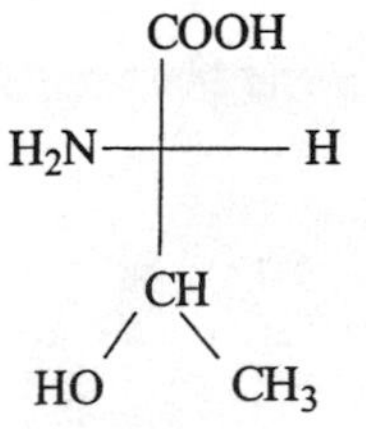
$$COOH$$
$$H_2N—|—H$$
$$CH$$
$$HO \quad CH_3$$

b. 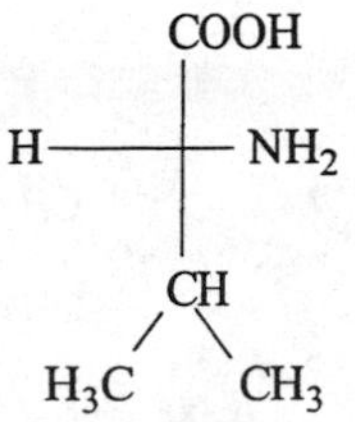
$$COOH$$
$$H—|—NH_2$$
$$CH$$
$$H_3C \quad CH_3$$

20.13   A zwitterion is formed when the H from the acid part of the amino acid is transferred to the amine portion of the amino acid. The resulting dipolar ion has an overall zero charge.

a. 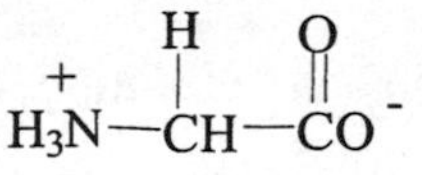
$$H_3\overset{+}{N}—CH—CO^-$$
with H and O on the CH and CO

b. 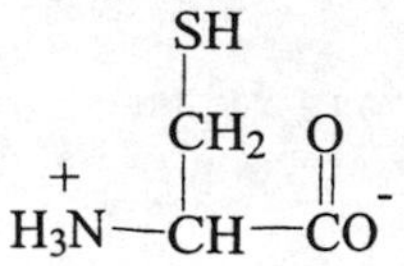
$$H_3\overset{+}{N}—CH—CO^-$$
with side chain $CH_2—SH$

c. 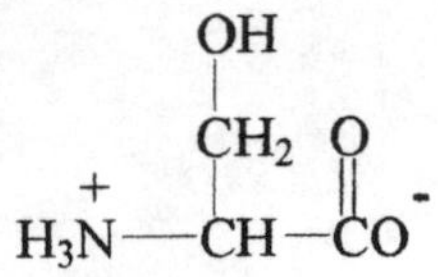
$$\overset{OH}{\underset{\overset{|}{\underset{CH_2}{|}}}{}} \quad H_3\overset{+}{N}-CH-\overset{O}{\overset{||}{C}}O^-$$

d. 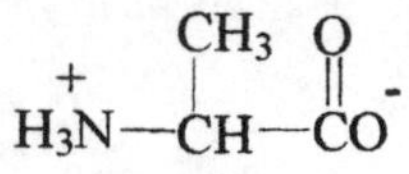
$$\overset{CH_3}{\underset{|}{}} \quad H_3\overset{+}{N}-CH-\overset{O}{\overset{||}{C}}O^-$$

20.14 a.

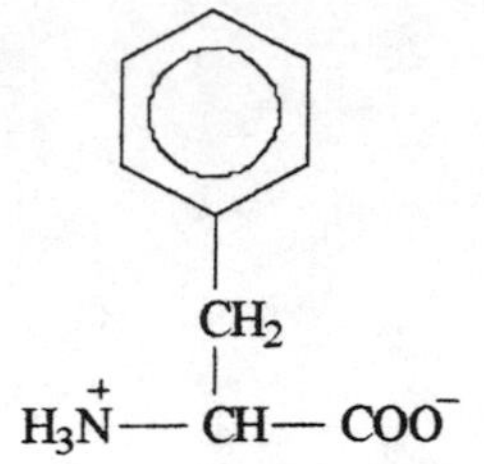

$$H_3\overset{+}{N}-CH-COO^-$$
with CH_2 and benzene ring

b. 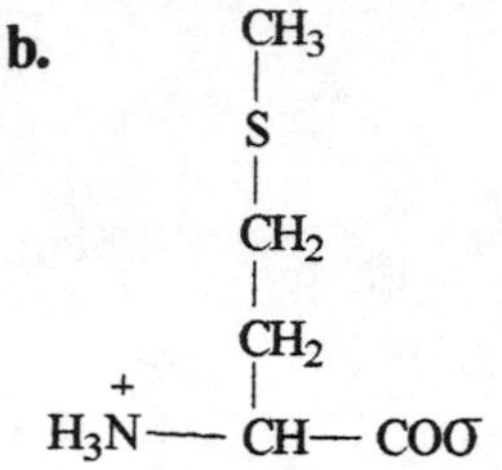
$$\overset{CH_3}{\underset{\overset{|}{S}}{}} \quad \overset{|}{CH_2} \quad \overset{|}{CH_2} \quad H_3\overset{+}{N}-CH-COO^-$$

c. 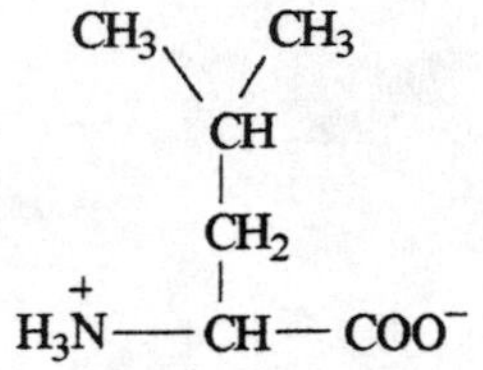
$$\overset{CH_3 \diagdown \diagup CH_3}{\underset{\overset{|}{CH}}{}} \quad \overset{|}{CH_2} \quad H_3\overset{+}{N}-CH-COO^-$$

d. 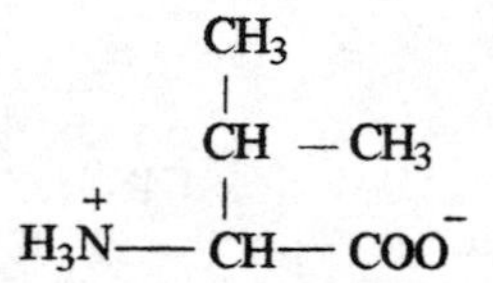
$$\overset{CH_3}{\underset{\overset{|}{CH}-CH_3}{}} \quad H_3\overset{+}{N}-CH-COO^-$$

20.15 At low pH (highly acidic), the –COO⁻ of the zwitterion accepts a proton and the amino acid has a positive charge overall.

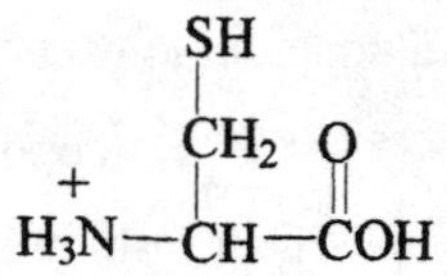

a. 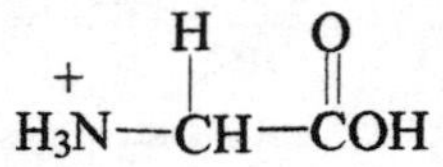
$$\overset{H}{\underset{|}{}} \quad H_3\overset{+}{N}-CH-\overset{O}{\overset{||}{C}}OH$$

b.
$$\overset{SH}{\underset{\overset{|}{CH_2}}{}} \quad H_3\overset{+}{N}-CH-\overset{O}{\overset{||}{C}}OH$$

c.
$$\overset{OH}{\underset{\overset{|}{CH_2}}{}} \quad H_3\overset{+}{N}-CH-\overset{O}{\overset{||}{C}}OH$$

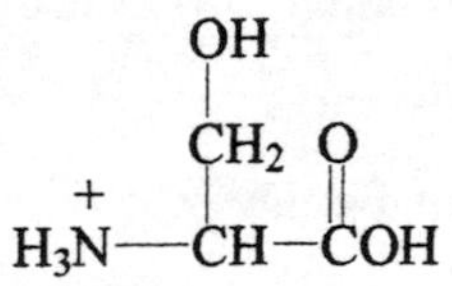

d. 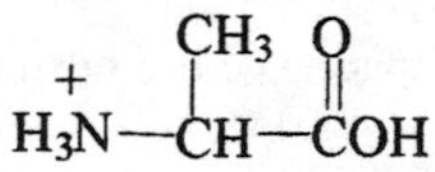
$$\overset{CH_3}{\underset{|}{}} \quad H_3\overset{+}{N}-CH-\overset{O}{\overset{||}{C}}OH$$

20.16 a.

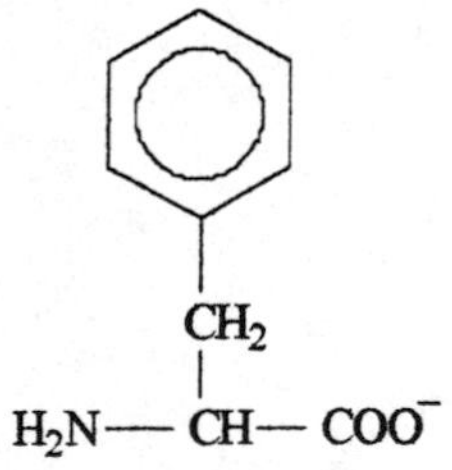

$$H_2N-CH-COO^-$$
with CH_2 and benzene ring

b. 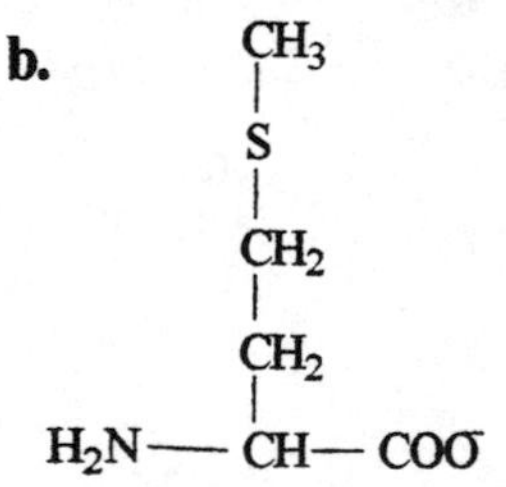
$$\overset{CH_3}{\underset{\overset{|}{S}}{}} \quad \overset{|}{CH_2} \quad \overset{|}{CH_2} \quad H_2N-CH-COO^-$$

c. 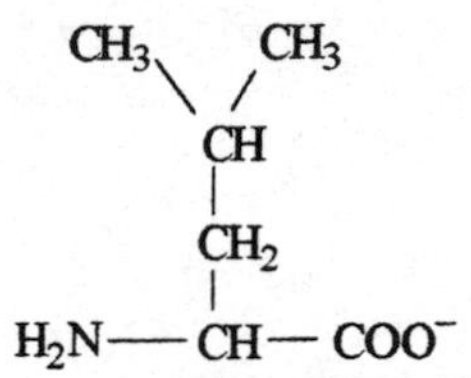
$$\overset{CH_3 \diagdown \diagup CH_3}{\underset{\overset{|}{CH}}{}} \quad \overset{|}{CH_2} \quad H_2N-CH-COO^-$$

d. 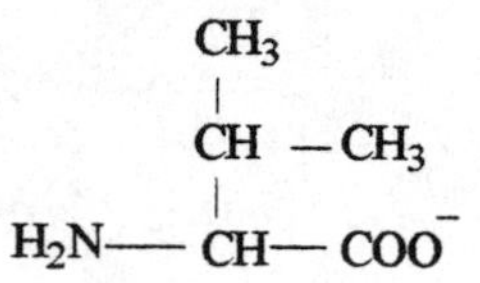
$$\overset{CH_3}{\underset{\overset{|}{CH}-CH_3}{}} \quad H_2N-CH-COO^-$$

20.17 a. A negative charge means the zwitterion donated a proton from —NH₃⁺, which occurs at pH levels above the isoelectric point
b. A positive charge means the zwitterion accepted a proton (H⁺) from an acidic solution, which occurs at a pH level below the isoelectric point.

c. A zwitterion with a net charge of zero means that the pH level is equal to the isoelectric point.

20.18   **a.** at the pI   **b.** below the pI   **c.** above the pI

20.19   In a peptide, the amino acids are joined by peptide bonds (amide bonds). The first amino acid has a free amine group, and the last one has a free carboxyl group.

a. 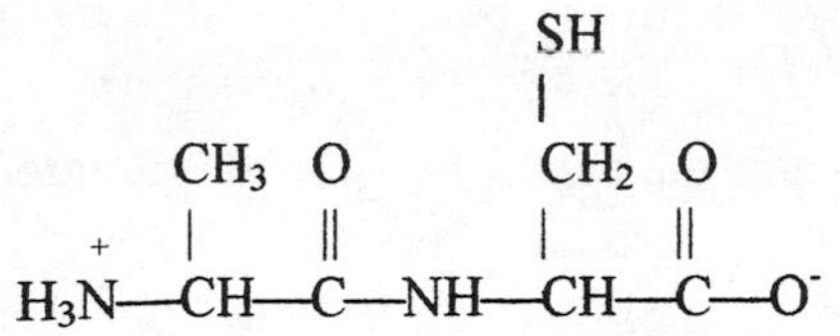
$$H_3N^+—CH—C—NH—CH—C—O^-$$
Ala-Cys

b. 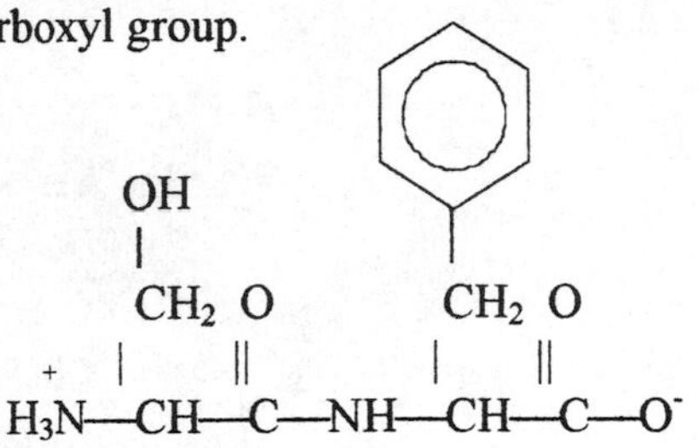
$$H_3N^+—CH—C—NH—CH—C—O^-$$
Ser-Phe

c. 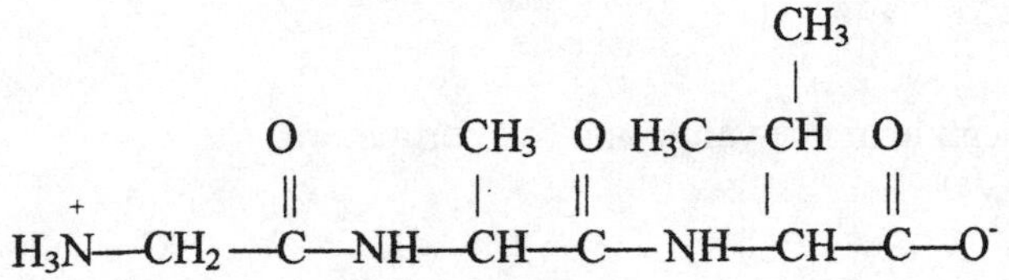
$$H_3N^+—CH_2—C—NH—CH—C—NH—CH—C—O^-$$
Gly-Ala-Val

d. 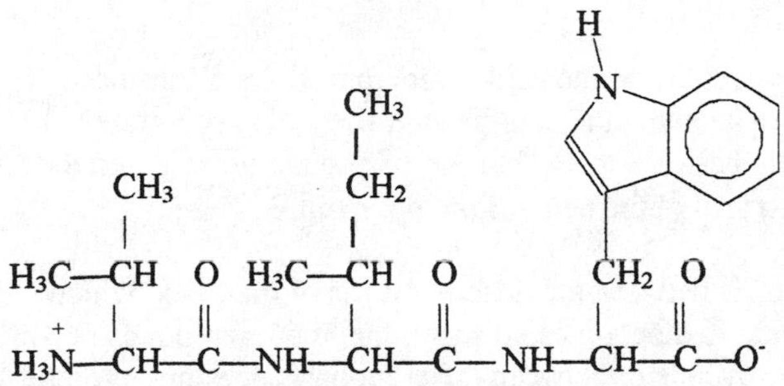
$$H_3N^+—CH—C—NH—CH—C—NH—CH—C—O^-$$
Val-Ile-Trp

20.20   **a.** 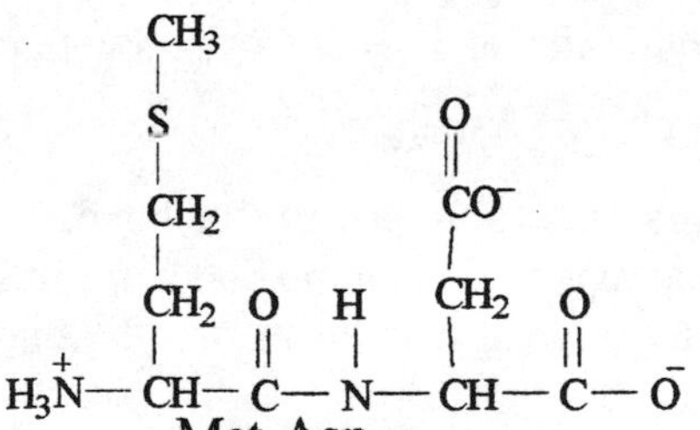
$$H_3N^+—CH—C—N—CH—C—O^-$$
Met-Asp

b. 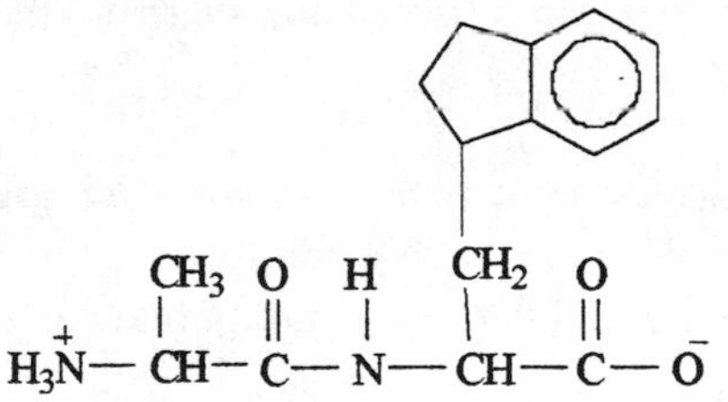
$$H_3N^+—CH—C—N—CH—C—O^-$$
Ala-Trp

c. 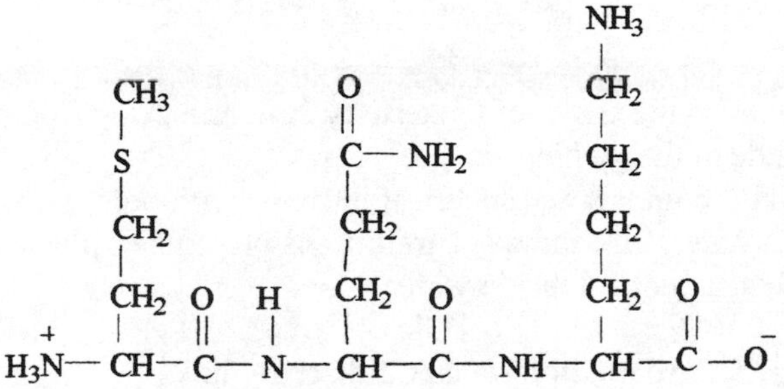
$$H_3N^+—CH—C—N—CH—C—NH—CH—C—O^-$$
Met-Gln-Lys

d.

```
                                    O
                                    ‖
                                    CO⁻
                                    |
                                    CH₂
                                    |
      HN   ⁺NH                      |
        \ /                         |
                                    |
       CH₂    O   H  H    O   H   CH₂   O   H   CH₃   O
        |     ‖   |  |    ‖   |    |    ‖   |    |    ‖
  H₃N⁺—CH —  C — N—CH —  C — N— CH — C — N— CH — C — O⁻
```

His-Gly-Glu-Ala

20.21 The primary structure of a protein is the order of amino acids; the bonds that hold the amino acids together in a protein are amide or peptide bonds.

20.22 Proteins may have the same number and type of amino acids but the sequence of one may differ from the sequence of the other.

20.23 The possible primary structure of a tripeptide of one valine and two serines are: Val-Ser-Ser, Ser-Val-Ser, and Ser-Ser-Val

20.24 The three types of secondary structure are α helix, β-pleated sheet and the triple helix.

20.25 When a protein forms a secondary structure, the amino acid chain arranges itself in space. The common secondary structures are: the alpha helix, the beta-pleated sheet, and the triple helix.

20.26 In the α helix, there is hydrogen bonding between the NH group of one amino acid and the C=O group of another amino acids in the next turn of the helix of the polypeptide chain.

20.27 In an alpha helix, there are hydrogen bonds between the different turns of the helix, which preserves the helical shape of the protein. In a beta-pleated sheet, the hydrogen bonds occur between two protein chains that are side by side or between different parts of a long protein.

20.28 In a β-pleated sheet there are hydrogen bonds between the polypeptide chains that lie side by side in a sheet. In a triple helix there are three polypeptide chains that are woven together like a rope.

20.29 **a.** The two cysteine residues have —SH groups, which react to form a disulfide bond.
b. Glutamic acid is acidic and lysine is basic; the two groups form an ionic bond, or salt bridge.
c. Serine has a polar —OH group that can form a hydrogen bond with the carboxyl group of aspartic acid.
d. Two leucine residues are hydrocarbon and nonpolar. They would have a hydrophobic interaction.

20.30 **a.** Nonpolar side groups would be found in the center of the tertiary structure away from water.
b. Polar groups would be on the outside of the globular shape.
c. Myoglobin is a globular protein that is compact and spherical in shape with polar side groups on the surface to make it soluble in water. Silk and wool are fibrous proteins of pleated sheets with many nonpolar side groups that are not soluble in water.

20.31 **a.** The R group of cysteine with the —SH group can form disulfide cross-links.
b. Leucine and valine are found on the inside of the protein since they have nonpolar side groups and are hydrophobic.
c. The cysteine and aspartic acid are on the outside of the protein since they are polar.
d. The order of the amino acid (the primary structure) provides the R groups, whose interactions determine the tertiary structure of the protein.

20.32 **a.** Disulfide bonds join different sections of the protein chain to give a 3-dimensional shape. Disulfide bonds are important in the tertiary and quaternary structures.

   b. Peptide bonds join the amino acids building blocks in the primary structure.

   c. Hydrogen bonds that hold protein chains together are found in the secondary structures of β-pleated sheets of fibrous proteins and in the triple helices of collagen.

   d. In the secondary structure of α–helices, hydrogen bonding occur between the carbonyl oxygen and nitrogen atom in the amide bonds.

   e. The hydrophobic side chains pull a protein chain into a tertiary structure.

   f. A triple-helix is a secondary structure.

   g. The combination of two or more protein units is a quaternary structure

20.33 The complete hydrolysis of the tripeptide Gly-Ala-Ser will give the amino acids glycine (Gly), alanine (Ala), and serine (Ser).

20.34 The hydrolysis products would be the same, the three amino acids alanine, serine and glycine. The order of the amino acids has no effect on the amino acids that are formed.

20.35 Partial hydrolysis of the tetrapeptide His-Met-Gly-Val could give the following dipeptides: Met-Gly, His-Met, and Gly-Val

20.36 When the pentapeptide Ser-Leu-Gly-Gly-Ala is hydrolyzed the following tripeptides could be formed: Ser-Leu-Gly ; Leu-Gly-Gly; Gly-Gly-Ala

20.37 The primary level, the sequence of amino acids in the protein, is affected by hydrolysis.

20.38 Denaturation affects the secondary, tertiary and quaternary structural levels of a protein.

20.39 **a.** Placing an egg in boiling water coagulates the protein of the egg by breaking the hydrogen bonds and disrupting the hydrophobic interactions.

   b. Using an alcohol swab coagulates the protein of any bacteria present by forming new hydrogen bonds and disrupting hydrophobic interactions.

   c. The heat from an autoclave will coagulate the protein of any bacteria on the surgical instruments by breaking the hydrogen bonds and disrupting the hydrophobic interactions.

   d. Cauterization (heating) of a wound leads to coagulation of the protein and helps to close the wound by breaking hydrogen bonds and disrupting hydrophobic interactions.

20.40 **a.** Acids cause a disruption of ionic bonds and tertiary structure.

   b. Heat above optimum temperature disrupts hydrogen bonds and side group attractions.

   c. Heavy metals disrupt disulfide bonds and tertiary structure.

   d. High temperatures will coagulate the protein in the E. coli bacteria and destroy it.

20.41 **a.** A combination of rice and garbanzo beans contains all the three essential amino acids.

   b. A combination of lima beans and cornmeal beans contains all the three essential amino acids.

   c. A salad of garbanzo beans and lima beans does not contain all the three essential amino acids; it is deficient in tryptophan.

   d. A combination of rice and lima beans contains all the three essential amino acids.

   e. A combination of rice and oatmeal does not contain all the essential amino acids; it is deficient in lysine.

   f. A combination of oatmeal and lima beans contains the three essential amino acids.

20.42 Denaturation is the disruption of the bonds that produce the biologically active structure of a protein. Hydrolysis is the breaking of peptide bonds by water.

20.43 **a.** The secondary structure of a protein depends on hydrogen bonds to form a helix or a pleated sheet. The tertiary structure is determined by the interaction of R groups and determines the three dimensional structure of the protein.

b. Nonessential amino acids are synthesized by the body, but essential amino acids must be supplied by the diet.

c. Polar amino acids have hydrophilic side groups while nonpolar amino acids have hydrophobic side groups.

d. Dipeptides contain two amino acids, while tripeptides contain three.

e. An ionic bond is an interaction between a basic and acidic side group, a disulfide bond links the sulfides of two cysteines.

f. Fibrous proteins consist of three to seven alpha helixes coiled like a rope. Globular proteins form a compact spherical shape.

g. The alpha helix is the secondary shape like a spiral staircase or corkscrew. The beta-pleated sheet is a secondary structure that is formed by many proteins side by side.

h. The tertiary structure of a protein is its three dimensional structure. In the quaternary structure, two or more peptide subunits are grouped.

20.44 **a.** Albumin, which is negative since the buffer pH is above the isoelectric pH.

b. Lysozyme. Since the buffer pH is below the isoelectric pH of lysozyme, the protein will have a positive charge.

c. Hemoglobin, the isoelectric pH is the same as the buffer pH.

20.45 **a.** _-keratins are fibrous proteins that provide structure to hair, wool, skin, and nails.

b. _-keratins have a high content of cysteine.

20.46 **a.** Collagen makes up about one-third of protein in vertebrates. It is found in connective tissue, blood vessels, skin, tendons, ligaments, the cornea of the eye, and cartilage.

b. Collagen consists of three polypeptides woven together like a braid called a triple helix.

20.47 **a.**

$$H_3\overset{+}{N}-CH-\overset{O}{\overset{\|}{C}}-\overset{H}{\overset{|}{N}}-CH-\overset{O}{\overset{\|}{C}}-\overset{H}{\overset{|}{N}}-CH-\overset{O}{\overset{\|}{C}}-O^-$$

with side chains CH_2OH, $(CH_2)_4$—NH_2, and CH_2—$COOH$

b. This segment contains polar R groups, which would be found on the surface of a globular proteins where they can hydrogen bond with water.

20.48 **a.**

$$H_3\overset{+}{N}-CH-\overset{O}{\overset{\|}{C}}-\overset{H}{\overset{|}{N}}-CH-\overset{O}{\overset{\|}{C}}-\overset{H}{\overset{|}{N}}-CH-\overset{O}{\overset{\|}{C}}-O^-$$

with side chains CH_3—CH—CH_3 (isopropyl), CH_3, and CH_2—$CH(CH_3)$—CH_3

b. The side chains in this peptide segments are nonpolar, which would place it at the nonpolar center of a globular protein.

20.49 **a.** The _-pleated sheet is a secondary structure that contains high amount of Val, Pro, and Ser, which have small side groups.

b. His, Met, and Leu are found predominantly in an _-helix secondary structure.

232

20.50 **a.** hydrogen bonding **b.** hydrophobic **c.** salt bridges (ionic)

20.51 Serine is a polar amino acid, whereas valine is nonpolar. Valine would be in the center of the tertiary structure. However, serine would pull that part of the chain to the outside surface of the protein where valine forms hydrogen bonds with water.

20.52 The protein in rice is lacking in the essential amino acid lysine. Thus, a protein containing lysine such as beans, peas, or soy will complement rice.

20.53 **a.** 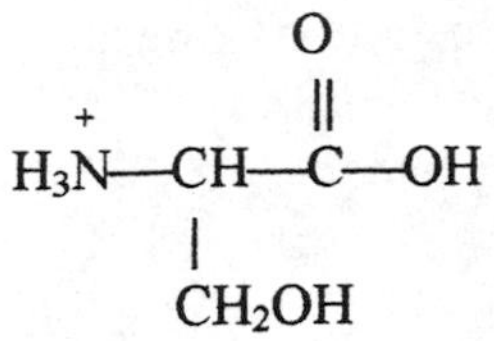 **b.** 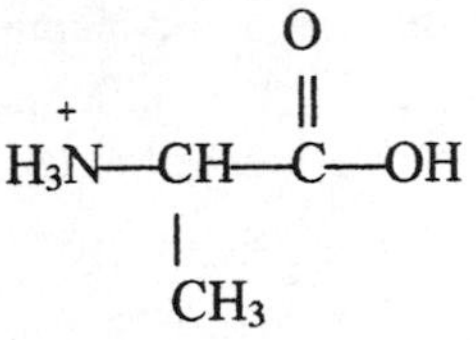

c. 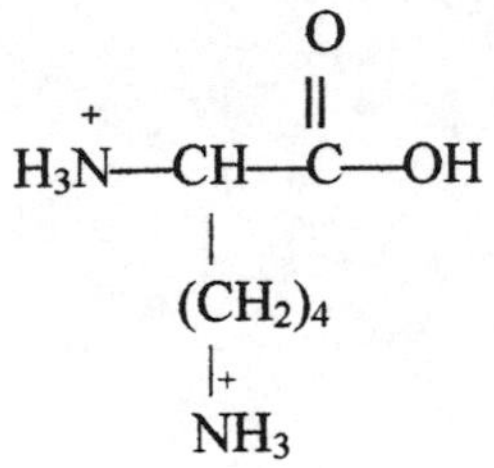

20.54 **a.** 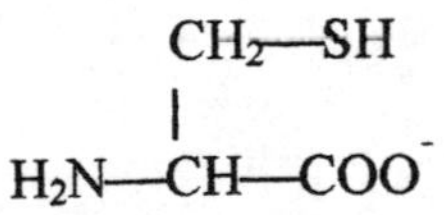 **b.** 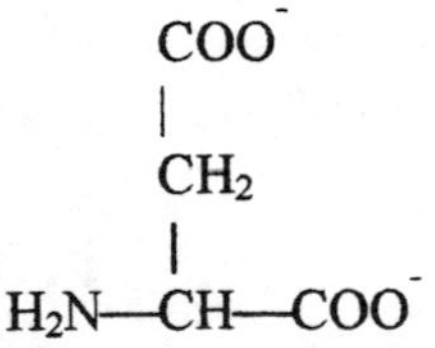 **c.** 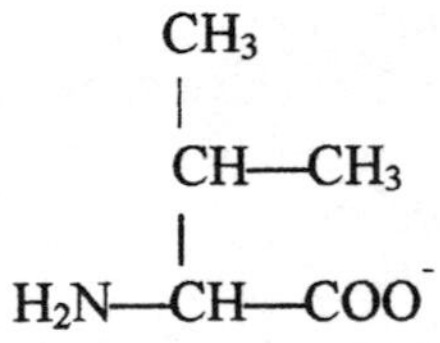

21
Enzymes

Study Goals

- Classify enzymes according to the type of reaction they catalyze.
- Describe the lock and key and induced fit models of enzyme action.
- Discuss the effect of changes in temperature, pH, and concentration of substrate on enzyme action.
- Describe the competitive, noncompetitive, and irreversible inhibition of enzymes.
- Discuss feedback control and regulation of enzyme action by allosteric enzymes.
- Identify the types of cofactors that are necessary for enzyme action.
- Describe the functions of vitamins and coenzymes.

Chapter Outline

Chapter Summary and Demonstrations

1. Enzymes

Catalysts and their effects upon the rate of a reaction and upon the energy of activation help to explain the role of enzymes as biological catalysts. The specificity of enzymes is explained with an emphasis upon the total shape and structure of the protein. The lock-and-key theory and the induced-fit theory provide a model for the catalytic action of enzymes.

2. Enzyme Activity

The effect on enzyme activity of substrate concentration, enzyme concentration, optimum temperature and pH are discussed and illustrated with diagrams of enzyme activity. Competitive inhibition, noncompetitive, and irreversible inhibition of enzymes is discussed. Antibiotics are used as an illustration of inhibitory effects of medicines.

Laboratory Suggestions

Lab 38 Enzymes

A solution of amylase is prepared. Chemical tests are conducted with time that indicate that rate of an enzyme-catalyzed reaction. Students observe the effects of enzyme concentration, temperature, pH, and inhibitors upon enzyme activity.
A. Effect of Enzyme Concentration
B. Effect of Temperature
C. Effect of pH
D. Inhibition of Enzyme Activity 348

Laboratory Skills to Demonstrate
Procedure for observing results in timed experiments.
Preparation of constant temperature baths.

Lab 39 Vitamins

Various vitamins are identified water-soluble or fat-soluble. The vitamin C content in a variety of citrus juices are determined and compared to the daily nutritional requirement. The effect of heat upon vitamin C is determined.
A. Solubility of Vitamins
B. Standardization of Vitamin C
C. Analysis of Vitamin C in Fruit Juices and Fruit Drinks
D. Heat Destruction of Vitamin C

Laboratory Skills to Demonstrate
Setting up a buret.
Reaction with starch indicator.

Answers and Solutions to Text Problems

21.1   The chemical reactions can occur without enzymes, but the rates are too slow. Catalyzed reactions, which are many times faster, provide the amounts of products needed by the cell at a particular time.

21.2   Enzymes lower the energy of activation for a reaction, which allows more reacting molecules to form product.

21.3   a. Oxidoreductases catalyze oxidation and reduction.
       b. Transferases move groups such as amino or phosphate groups from one substance to another.
       c. Hydrolases use water to split bonds in molecules such as carbohydrates, peptides, and lipids.

21.4   a. addition or removal of a group to or from a double bond without hydrolysis or oxidation
       b. rearrangement of atoms to form isomers
       c. bonding of molecules using ATP energy.

21.5   a. A hydrolase enzyme would catalyze the hydrolysis of sucrose.
       b. An oxidoreductase enzyme would catalyze the addition of oxygen (oxidation).
       c. An isomerase enzyme would catalyze converting glucose to fructose.
       d. A transferase enzyme would catalyze moving an amino group.

21.6   **a.** lyase   **b.** oxidoreductase   **c.** hydrolase   **d.** lyase

21.7   **a.** A lyase such as a decarboxylase removes CO_2 from a molecule.
        b. The transfer of an amino group to another molecule would be catalyzed by a transferase.

21.8   **a.** ligase   **b.** oxidoreductase

21.9   **a.** Succinate oxidase catalyzes the oxidation of succinate.
        b. Fumarate hydrase catalyzes the addition of water to fumarate.
        c. Alcohol dehydrogenase removes 2H from an alcohol.

21.10   **a.** sucrase   **b.** aspartate transferase (transaminase)
        c. pyruvate decarboxylase

21.11   **a.** An enzyme has a tertiary structure that recognized the substrate.
        b. The combination of the enzyme and substrate is the enzyme-substrate complex.
        c. The substrate has a structure that complements the structure of the enzyme.

21.12   **a.** The active site (1) on an enzyme is where catalytic activity occurs.
        b. In the induced-fit model (3), the active site adjusts to the substrate shape.
        c. In the lock-and-key model (2), the active site is considered to have a rigid shape that only fits
            a substrate with that geometry.

21.13   **a.** The equation for an enzyme-catalyzed reaction is:
        E + S $\rightleftarrows$ ES $\longrightarrow$ E + P
        E = enzyme, S = substrate, ES = enzyme-substrate complex, P = products
        b. The active site is a region or pocket within the tertiary structure of an enzyme
            that accepts the substrate, aligns the substrate for reaction, and catalyzes the reaction.

21.14   **a.** An enzyme speeds up the reaction of substrate because an enzyme lowers the activation
            energy for the reaction of that substrate.
        b. As soon as the enzyme releases product, the enzyme is available to catalyze the reaction of
            more substrate

21.15   Isoenzymes are slightly different forms of an enzyme that catalyze the same reaction in different
        organs and tissues of the body.

21.16   The LDH isoenzyme in the heart consists of four H polypeptide subunits, whereas the LDH
        isoenzyme in the liver consists of four M polypeptide subunits.

21.17   A doctor might run tests for the enzymes CK, LDH, and AST to determine if the patient had a
        heart attack.

21.18   LDH could indicate liver damage, and AST could indicate cirrhosis or hepatitis.

21.19   **a.** Decreasing the substrate concentration decreases the rate of reaction.
        b. Running the reaction at a pH below optimum pH will decrease the rate of reaction.
        c. Temperature above 37°C (optimum pH) will denature the enzymes and decrease the rate
            of reaction.
        d. Increasing the enzyme concentration would increase the rate of reaction.

21.20   **a.** increases rate   **b.** decreases rate   **c.** decreases rate   **d.** decreases rate

21.21   pepsin, pH 2; urease, pH 5; trypsin; pH 8

21.22 **a.** Trypsin has an optimum pH at about pH 9; pH 5 is not the optimum pH.
  b. Yes, urease is at its optimum pH of 5
  c. Pepsin has an optimum pH at about pH 1.5; pH 4 is not the optimum pH.
  d. Trypsin has an optimum pH at about pH 8; pH 8 is the optimum pH.
  e. Pepsin has an optimum pH of about pH 2; pH 2 is optimum pH

21.23 **a.** If the inhibitor has a structure similar to the structure of the substrate, the inhibitor is competitive
  b. If adding more substrate cannot reverse the effect of the inhibitor, the inhibitor is noncompetitive.
  c. If the inhibitor competes with the substrate for the active site, it is a competitive inhibitor.
  d. If the structure of the inhibitor is not similar to the structure of the substrate, the inhibitor is noncompetitive.
  e. If adding more substrate reverses inhibition, the inhibitor is competitive.

21.24 **a.** It would be a reversible competitive inhibitor because the structure of oxaloacetate is similar to the structure of succinate, the substrate.
  b. As a competitive inhibitor, oxaloacetate would fit into the active site.
  c. Increasing the concentration can reverse the effect of the competitive inhibitor succinate, the substrate for the reaction.

21.25 **a.** Methanol has the structural formula CH_3—OH whereas ethanol is CH_3—CH_2—OH.
  b. Ethanol has a structure similar to methanol and could compete for the active site.
  c. Ethanol is a competitive inhibitor of methanol oxidation.

21.26 **a.** No; the antibiotic only inhibits enzymes in bacteria.
  b. It inhibits an enzyme required to build cell walls in bacteria, but not in human cells.
  c. Antibiotics are irreversible inhibitors.

21.27 Digestive enzymes are proteases and would digest the proteins of the organ where they are produced if they were active immediately upon synthesis.

21.28 If the zymogen trypsinogen is converted to active trypsin in the pancreas, the active enzyme can digest the proteins of the pancreas, which causes inflammation.

21.29 In feedback inhibition, the product binds to the first enzyme in a series changing the shape of the active site. If the active site can no longer bind the substrate effectively, the reaction stops.

21.30 If the first enzyme in a sequence is inhibited, no intermediate compounds are produced for any of the other enzymes in the pathway. The second or third enzyme in a sequence are not needed for feedback regulatory control

21.31 When a regulator molecule binds to an allosteric site, the shape of the enzyme is altered, which makes the active site more or less reactive and thereby increases or decreases the rate of the reaction.

21.32 A negative inhibitor binds to an enzyme in such a way that the catalysis of the substrate is slowed or stopped. A positive inhibitor binds to an enzyme to increase the rate of the reaction.

21.33 **a.** 3; A negative regulator binds to the allosteric site and slows down the reaction.
  b. 4; Typically the first enzyme in a reaction sequence is an allosteric enzyme, which regulates the flow of substrates through the sequence to yield end product.
  c. 1; A zymogen is an inactive form of an enzyme.

21.34 **a.** 1; zymogen   **b.** 2; a positive regulator   **c.** 4; allosteric enzyme

21.35 **a.** The active form of this enzyme requires a cofactor.
          b. The active form of this enzyme requires a cofactor.
          c. A simple enzyme is active as a protein.

21.36 **a.** requires a cofactor   **b.** simple   **c.** requires a cofactor

21.37 **a.** THF   **b.** NAD$^+$

21.38 **a.** FAD   **b.** TPP

21.39 **a.** Pantothenic acid (vitamin B$_5$) is part of coenzyme A.
          b. Tetrahydrofolate (THF) is a reduced form of folic acid.
          c. Niacin (vitamin B$_3$) is a component of NAD$^+$.

21.40 **a.** thiamine (vitamin B$_1$)   **b.** riboflavin (vitamin B$_2$)   **c.** pyridoxine (vitamine B$_6$)

21.41 **a.** A deficiency of vitamin D or cholecalciferol can lead to rickets.
          b. A deficiency of ascorbic acid or vitamin C can lead to scurvy.
          c. A deficiency of niacin or vitamin B$_3$ can lead to pellagra.

21.42 **a.** vitamin A (retinol)   **b.** vitamin B$_{12}$ (cobalamin)   **c.** vitamin B$_2$ (thiamine)

21.43 Vitamin B$_6$ is a water-soluble vitamin, which means that each day any excess of vitamin B$_6$ is eliminated from the body.

21.44 Vitamin A is a fat-soluble vitamin that is stored in the body in fat deposits and cell membranes. Because it is not eliminated on a daily basis, it can accumulate to high levels (hypervitaminosis).

21.45 The side chain —CH$_2$OH on the ring is oxidized to —CHO, and the other —CH$_2$OH forms a phosphate ester.

21.46 Folic acid undergoes reduction to form THF by adding four hydrogen atoms to two double bonds in pyrimidine.

21.47 The many different reactions that take place in cells require different enzymes because enzymes react with only a certain type of substrate.

21.48 No. Enzymes are synthesized when needed in the cell and broken down when not needed. It would be inefficient for a cell to tie up atoms in enzymes that are not needed for catalysis.

21.49 When exposed to conditions of strong acids or bases, or high temperatures, enzymatic proteins are denatured rapidly causing a loss of tertiary structure and catalytic activity.

21.50 Enzymes are proteins, which are denatured in acidic or basic conditions and by high temperatures.

21.51 **a.** The reactant is lactose and the products are glucose and galactose.

b.

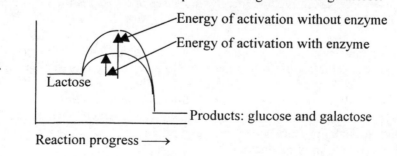

c. By lowering the energy of activation, the enzyme furnishes a lower energy pathway by which the reaction can take place.

21.52 **a.** maltose ⟶ 2 glucose
   b.

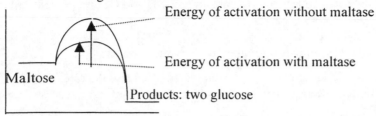

Energy of activation without maltase

Energy of activation with maltase

Maltose

Products: two glucose

Reaction progress ⟶

c. Maltase lowers the activation energy for the hydrolysis of maltose.

21.53 **a.** The disaccharide lactose is a substrate.
   b. The –*ase* in lactase indicates that it is an enzyme.
   c. The –*ase* in urease indicates that it is an enzyme.
   d. Trypsin is an enzyme, which hydrolyzes polypeptides.
   e. Pyruvate is a substrate.
   f. The –*ase* in transaminase indicates that it is an enzyme.

21.54 **a.** substrate (S)   **b.** enzyme (E)   **c.** enzyme (E)
   d. substrate (S)   **e.** substrate (S)   **f.** enzyme (E)

21.55 **a.** Urea is the substrate of urease.
   b. Lactose is the substrate of lactase.
   c. Aspartate is the substrate of aspartate transaminase.
   d. Tyrosine is the substrate of tyrosine synthetase.

21.56 **a.** maltose   **b.** fructose   **c.** phenol   **d.** sucrose

21.57 **a.** The transfer of an acyl group is catalyzed by a transferase.
   b. Oxidases are classified as oxidoreductases.
   c. A lipase, which splits esters bonds in lipids with water, is a hydrolase.
   d. A decarboxylase is classified as a lyase.

21.58 **a.** isomerase   **b.** oxidoreductase   **c.** ligase   **d.** hydrolase

21.59 **a.** In this reaction, oxygen is added to an aldehyde. The enzyme that catalyzes this reaction would be an oxidoreductase.
   b. In this reaction, a dipeptide is hydrolyzed. The enzyme that catalyzes this reaction would be a hydrolase.
   c. In this reaction, water is added to a double bond. The enzyme that catalyzes this reaction would be a lyase.

21.60 **a** An enzyme that catalyzes removal of a group and involves a double bond is a lyase.
   b In this reaction, carbon dioxide is added to a ketoacid using ATP. The enzyme that catalyzes this reaction would be a ligase.
   c The conversion of glucose-6-phosphate to fructose-6-phosphate is an isomerization and an isomerase would be the enzyme that catalyzes the reaction.

21.61 Sucrose fits the shape of the active site in sucrase, but lactose does not.

21.62 In the induced-fit model, the active site adjusts to fit the shape of the substrate; the substrate adjusts it shape to better fit the active site. Thus, one enzyme can catalyze a group of substrates.

21.63 A heart attack may be the cause. Normally the enzymes LDH and CK are present only in low levels in the blood.

21.64 An elevated ALT (alanine transaminase) level could indicate hepatitis.

21.65 **a.** An enzyme is saturated if adding more substrate does not increase the rate.
b. An enzyme is unsaturated when increasing the substrate increases the rate.

21.66 **a.** Pepsin is functional at pH 2, which is its optimal pH.
b. This enzyme is not functional at 37°C because it has an optimum temperature of 100°C.

21.67 In a reversible inhibition, the inhibitor can dissociate from the enzyme, whereas in irreversible inhibition, the inhibitor forms a strong covalent bond with the enzyme and does not dissociate. Irreversible inhibitors act as poisons to enzymes.

21.68 The inhibitor in competitive reversible inhibition competes for the active site because it has a structure similar to the substrate. Increasing the substrate concentration reverses the inhibition. The inhibitor in noncompetitive inhibition is not similar to the substrate and does not compete for the active site. Increasing the substrate concentration does not reverse the inhibition. To re-establish enzyme activity, the concentration of the inhibitor must decrease.

21.69 **a.** The oxidation of glycol to an aldehyde and carboxylic acid is catalyzed by an oxidoreductase.
b. At high concentration, ethanol, which acts as a competitive inhibitor of ethylene glycol, would saturate the enzyme to allow ethylene glycol to be removed from the body without producing oxalic acid.

21.70 **a.** Lactase is the enzyme that hydrolyzes milk; it is a hydrolase.
b. Enzymes such as lactase are denatured at high temperatures.

21.71 **a.** Antibiotics such as amoxicillin are irreversible inhibitors.
b. Antibiotics inhibit enzymes needed to form cell walls in bacteria, not humans.

21.72 **a.** The insecticide may be inhibiting acetyl cholinesterase, which blocks the transmission of nerve impulses.
b. Insecticides may contain compounds that are irreversible inhibitors that block nerve conduction and cause paralysis.

21.73 **a.** When pepsinogen enters the stomach, the low pH cleaves a peptide from its protein chain to form pepsin.
b. An active protease would digest the proteins of the pancreas rather than the proteins in the foods entering the stomach.

21.74 **a.** prothrombin
b. Thrombin is needed to coagulate blood to stop bleeding. If it were active in the blood stream, blood clots would form and blood flow would be diminished. The active form is produced only where injury and bleeding occurs.

21.75 An allosteric enzyme contains sites for regulators that alter the enzyme and speed up or slow down the rate of the catalyzed reaction.

21.76 A positive regulator speeds up a reaction by changing the structure of an enzyme to bind substrate more effectively. A negative regulator slows a reaction by changing the structure of an enzyme that prevents the proper binding of a substrate. Both types are needed to regulate the rate of an enzyme-catalyzed reaction to meet the requirements for end product.

21.77 The end product of the reaction pathway is a negative regulator that binds to the enzyme to decrease or stop the first reaction in the reaction pathway.

21.78 If the first enzyme in a sequence is inhibited, no intermediate compounds are produced for any of the other enzymes in the pathway. If a second or third enzyme were the allosteric enzyme, the first enzyme would produce a product that would accumulate, which is inefficient. The enzymes following the first enzyme in a sequence are not needed for feedback regulatory control unless they would be control points for other pathways.

21.79 **a.** The Mg^{2+} is a cofactor, which is required by this enzyme.
b. A protein that is catalytically active is a simple enzyme.
c. Folic acid is a coenzyme, which is required by this enzyme.

21.80 **a.** contains a cofactor   **b.** simple enzyme   **c.** contains a cofactor

21.81 **a.** Coenzyme A requires pantothenic acid (B_5).
b. NAD^+ requires niacin (B_3).
c. Biocytin requires biotin.

21.82 **a.** folate and THF
b. riboflavin (B_2) and FAD
c. pyridoxine and pyridoxal phosphate

21.83 A vitamin combines with an enzyme only when the enzyme and coenzyme are needed to catalyze a reaction. When the enzyme is not needed, the vitamin dissociates for use by other enzymes in the cell.

21.84 There is a daily requirement for water-soluble vitamins because many are used by enzymes as cofactors to carry out enzyme-catalyzed reactions. Because the water-soluble vitamins are not stored in the body, they must be replenished each day.

21.85 **a.** A deficiency of niacin can lead to pellagra.
b. A deficiency of vitamin A can lead to night blindness.
c. A deficiency of vitamin D can weaken bone structure.

21.86 **a.** A deficiency of cobalamin is associated with anemia.
b. A deficiency of vitamin C can lead to scurvy.
c. A deficiency of vitamin K can lead to increased bleeding.

Study Goals

- Draw the structures of the nitrogen bases, sugars, and nucleotides in DNA and RNA
- Describe the structures of DNA and RNA.
- Explain the process of DNA replication.
- Describe the preparation of recombinant DNA
- Describe the transcription process during the synthesis of mRNA.
- Use the codons in the genetic code to describe protein synthesis.
- Explain how an alteration in the DNA sequence can lead to mutations in proteins.
- Describe the regulation of protein synthesis in the cells.

Chapter Outline

22.1 **Components of Nucleic Acids**
22.2 **Nucleosides and Nucleotides**
22.3 **Primary Structure of Nucleic Acids**
22.4 **DNA Double Helix: A Secondary Structure**
22.5 **DNA Replication**
22.6 **Types of RNA**
22.7 **Transcription: Synthesis of mRNA**
22.8 **The Genetic Code**
22.9 **Protein Synthesis: Translation**
        Health Note: Many Antibiotics Inhibit Protein Synthesis
22.10 **Genetic Mutations**
        Explore Your World: A Model for DNA Replication and Mutation
22.11 **Recombinant DNA**
        Health Note: Cancer
22.12 **Viruses**
        Health Note: Cancer

Chapter Summary and Demonstrations

1. DNA and RNA

The components and structures of the nucleic acids, DNA and RNA, are described. The concept of complementary base pairing is emphasized for an understanding of the process by which DNA is replicated and its synthesis of mRNA for protein synthesis in the ribosomes. The control of protein synthesis through induction and repression is discussed. The concept of recombinant DNA is introduced as a method of placing a foreign DNA into a gene for the production of a particular protein. The changes in DNA structure as a result of a mutation and the consequent effects upon the amino acid order and structure of the resulting protein are discussed along with examples of genetic diseases. Additional topics include the role of DNA in cancer and viruses.

Demonstration Large-scale models of DNA are useful to show the double helix of DNA.

Laboratory Suggestions

Lab 40 DNA Components and Extraction

Students write the structures of the components of DNA. In plant cells, DNA strands are combined with protein and RNA molecules. Students extract and isolate DNA from a variety of plant and animal cells. Three processes are required: (1) breaking down the cellular membranes, (2) heating the mixture and denaturing the proteins, and (3) precipitating the DNA as a white, stringy, fibrous material.

A. Components of DNA
B. Extraction of DNA

Laboratory Skills to Demonstrate
Preparation of plant or animal cells for extraction of DNA
Removing DNA strands from a solution of DNA

Answers and Solutions to Text Problems

22.1   DNA contains two purines, adenine (A) and guanine (G) and two pyrimidines, cytosine (C) and thymine (T). RNA contains the same bases, except thymine (T) is replaced by the pyrimidine uracil (U).
  a. pyrimidine   **b.** pyrimidine

22.2   **a.** purine   **b.** purine

22.3   DNA contains two purines, adenine (A) and guanine (G) and two pyrimidines, cytosine (C) and thymine (T). RNA contains the same bases, except thymine (T) is replaced by the pyrimidine uracil (U).
  a. DNA   **b.** Both DNA and RNA

22.4   **a.** present in both DNA and RNA   **b.** Adenine is present in both DNA and RNA

22.5   Nucleotides contain a base, a sugar and a phosphate group. The nucleotides found in DNA would all contain the sugar deoxyribose. The four nucleotides are: deoxyadenosine-5'-monophosphate (dAMP), deoxythymidine-5'-monophosphate (dTMP), deoxycytidine-5'-monophosphate (dCMP), and deoxyguanosine-5'-monophosphate (dGMP)

22.6   Adenosine monophosphate (AMP), guanosine monophosphate (GMP), cytidine monophosphate (CMP), and uridine monophosphate (UMP).

22.7   **a.** Adenosine is a nucleoside found in RNA.
  b. Deoxycytidine is a nucleoside found in DNA.
  c. Uridine is a nucleoside found in RNA.
  d. Cytidine-5'-monophosphate is a nucleotide found in RNA.

22.8   **a.** nucleoside (DNA)   **b.** nucleoside (RNA)
  c. nucleoside (RNA)   **d.** nucleotide (RNA)

243

22.9

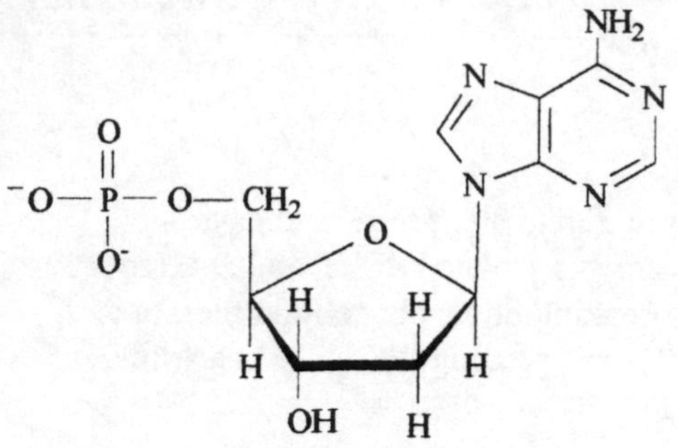

22.10

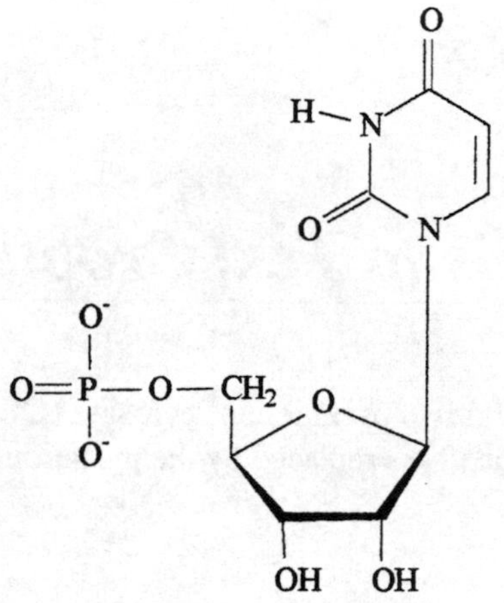

22.11 The nucleotides in nucleic acids are held together by phosphodiester bonds between the 3'—OH of a sugar (ribose or deoxyribose), a phosphate group, and the 5'—OH of another sugar.

22.12 One end of a polymer of nucleic acid consists of a sugar with a free 5'-phosphate group and the other end consists of a sugar with a free 3'-hydroxyl group.

22.13

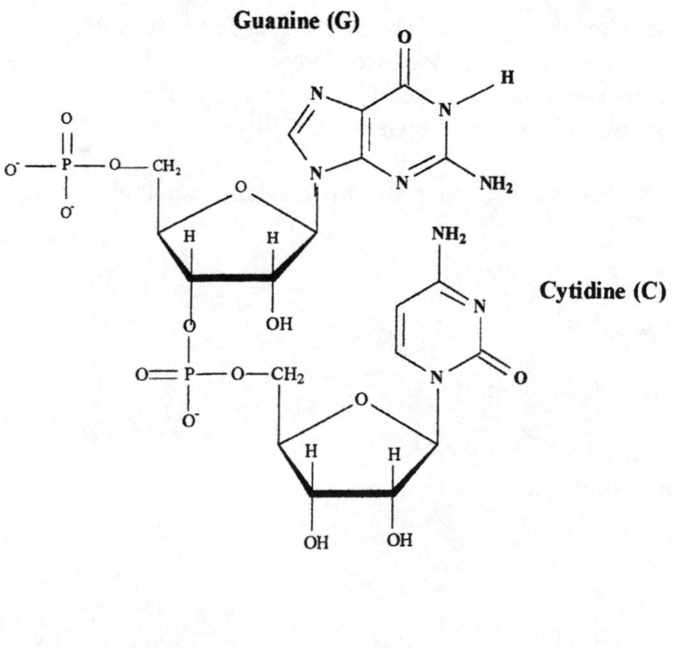

12.14

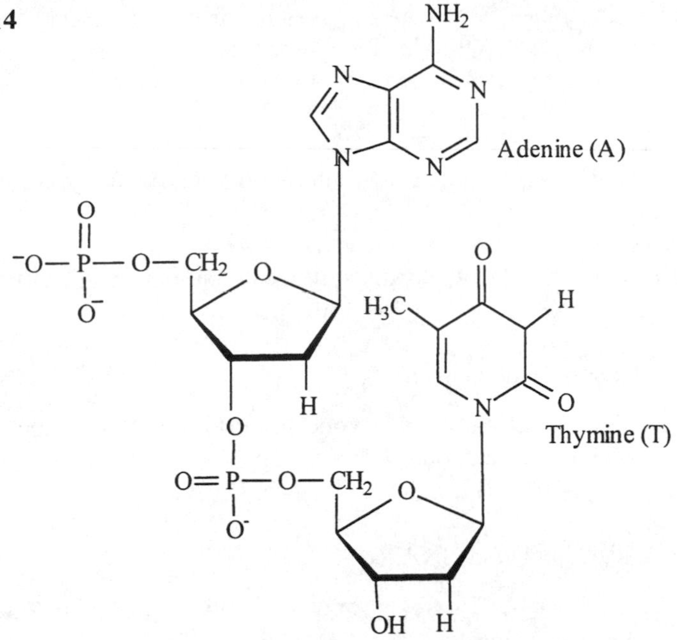

22.15   The two DNA strands are held together by hydrogen bonds between the bases in each strand.

22.16   In complementary base pairing, there are three hydrogen bonds between G and C (or C—G), and two hydrogen bonds between A and T (or T—A). There are no other combinations of bases.

22.17   **a.** Since T pairs with A, if one strand of DNA has the sequence 5'—AAAAAA—3', the second strand would be: 3'—TTTTTT—5'.
   b. Since C pairs with G, if one strand of DNA has the sequence 5'—GGGGGG—3', the second strand would be: 3'—CCCCCC—5'.
   c. Since T pairs with A, and C pairs with G, if one strand of DNA has the sequence 5'—AGTCCAGGT—3', the second strand would be 3'—TCAGGTCCA—5'.
   d. Since T pairs with A, and C pairs with G, if one strand of DNA has the sequence 5'—CTGTATACGTTA, the second strand would be: 3'—GACATATGCAAT—5'.

22.18   **a.** 3'—AAAAAA—5'   **b.** 3'—GGGGGGGGG—5'
   c. 3'—TACCGT—5'   **d.** 3'—TATACGCGATTT—5'

22.19   The enzyme helicase unwinds the DNA helix to prepare the parent DNA strand for the synthesis of daughter DNA strands.

22.20   DNA polymerase catalyzes the formation of phosphodiester bonds between the nucleotides. At a replication form, DNA polymerase forms bonds between 5'-phosphate of one nucleotide and the 3'-hydroxyl of the next. On the lagging strand, short sections of DNA are synthesized by several DNA polymerases and connected by DNA ligase to give the 3'-5' DNA strand.

22.21   First, the two DNA strands separate in a way that is similar to the unzipping of a zipper. Then the enzyme DNA polymerase begins to copy each strand by pairing each of the bases in the strands with its complementary base: A pairs with T and C with G. Finally, a phosphodiester bond joins the base to the new, growing strand.

22.22   DNA polymerase synthesizes a continuous DNA strand on only one strand called the leading strand. On the other strand, which is the lagging strand, short sections of DNA are synthesized in the opposite direction. This requires the synthesis of short sections called Okazaki fragment by several DNA polymerases, which are connected by DNA ligase to give the 3'-5' DNA strand.

2.23 Ribosomal RNA (rRNA) is found in the ribosomes, which are the sites for protein synthesis. Transfer RNA (tRNA) brings specific amino acids to the ribosomes for protein synthesis. Messenger RNA (mRNA) carries the information needed for protein synthesis from the DNA in the nucleus to the ribosomes.

22.24 The three types of RNA are the messenger RNA (mRNA), ribosomal RNA (rRNA), and transfer RNA (tRNA).

22.25 A ribosome, which is about 65% rRNA and 35% protein, consists of a small subunit and a large subunit.

22.26 The transfer RNA molecule (tRNA) is the smallest type of RNA.

22.27 In transcription, the sequence of nucleotides on a DNA template (one strand) is used to produce the base sequences of a messenger RNA. The DNA unwinds and one strand is copied as complementary bases are placed in the mRNA molecule. In RNA, U (uracil) is paired with A in DNA.

22.28 In RNA, U, A, C, and G complement A, T, C, and G in DNA.

22.29 In mRNA, C, G and A pair with G, C and T in DNA. However, in mRNA U will pair with A in DNA. The strand of mRNA would have the following sequence: 5'—GGC—UUC—CAA—GUG—3'.

22.30 5'—AUGCCGUUCGAU—3'

22.31 In eukaryotic cells, genes contain sections called exons that code for protein and sections called introns that do not code for protein.

22.32 A newly formed mRNA in eukaryotes or pre-RNA produced by DNA in the nucleus contains sections known as exons that code for proteins along with section called introns that do not code for protein. Before the pre-RNA leaves the nucleus, it is processed to remove the introns and produce a functional mRNA that leaves the nucleus and takes the genetic information to the ribosomes.

22.33 An operon is a section of DNA that regulates the synthesis of one or more proteins.

22.34 The operon model operates at the transcription level where the absence or presence of an end product speeds up or slows down the synthesis of mRNAs for a specific enzyme.

22.35 When the lactose level is low in *E. coli*, a repressor produced by the mRNA from the regulatory gene binds to the operator blocking the synthesis of mRNA from the genes and preventing the synthesis of protein.

22.36 In the lactose operon, the presence of lactose induces the synthesis of the enzymes such as galactosidase, which is needed for the metabolism of lactose. The lactose inactivates a repressor that has blocked the production of galactosidase mRNA. With the repressor removed, RNA polymerase can transcribe the genes in the operon that code for the lactose enzymes.

22.37 A codon is the three-base sequence (triplet) in mRNA that codes for a specific amino acid in a protein.

22.38 The genetic code is the three-base codons that specify particular amino acids for protein synthesis. There are one to six different codons for each of the 20 amino acids; there are other codons for the initiation and termination of synthesis

22.39   **a.** The codon CUU in mRNA codes for the amino acid leucine.
b. The codon UCA in mRNA codes for the amino acid serine.
c. The codon GGU in mRNA codes for the amino acid glycine.
d. The codon AGG in mRNA codes for the amino acid arginine.

22.40   **a.** lysine (Lys)   **b.** valine (Val)   **c.** arginine (Arg)   **d.** alanine (Ala)

22.41   When AUG is the first codon, it signals the start of protein synthesis and incorporates methionine as the first amino acid in the peptide. Eventually the initial methionine is removed as the protein forms its secondary and tertiary protein structure. In the middle of an mRNA sequence AUG codes for methionine.

22.42   The codons UGA, UAA, and UAG indicate the end of the synthesis of a particular protein.

22.43   A codon is a base triplet in the mRNA template. An anticodon is the complementary triplet on a tRNA for a specific amino acid.

22.44   There must be at least one tRNA for each of the amino acids used to synthesize proteins.

22.45   The three steps in translation are: initiation, translocation, and termination.

22.46   Protein synthesis takes place at the ribosomes in the cytoplasm.

22.47   The mRNA must be divided into triplets and the amino acid coded for by each triplet read from the table.
a. The codon AAA in mRNA codes for lysine: —Lys—Lys—Lys—
b. The codon UUU codes for phenylalanine and CCC for proline: —Phe—Pro—Phe—Pro—
c. —Tyr—Gly—Arg—Cys—

22.48   **a.** —Lys—Pro—Leu—Ala—   **b.** —Pro—Arg—Ser—Pro—STOP
c. —Met—His—Lys—Glu—Val—Leu—

22.49   After a tRNA attaches to the first binding site on the ribosome, its amino acid forms a peptide bond with the amino acid on the tRNA attached to the second binding site. The ribosome moves along the mRNA and a new tRNA with its amino acid occupies the open binding site.

22.50   Translocation is the movement of the ribosome along the mRNA to read another codon and place the next amino acid in the growing peptide chain.

22.51   **a.** By using the pairing: DNA bases   C G T A
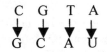
mRNA bases   G C A U
The mRNA sequence can be determined: 5'—CGA—AAA—GUU—UUU—3'.
b. The tRNA triplet anticodons would be as follows: GCU, UUU, CAA, AAA.
c. The mRNA is divided into triplets and the amino acid coded for by each triplet read from the table. Using codons in mRNA: Arg—Lys—Val—Phe.

22.52   **a.** 5'—ACA—CCC—CAA—UAA—3'
b.   —UGU—GGG—GUU—AUU—
c.   —Thr—Pro—Gln—STOP

22.53   In a substitution mutation an incorrect base replaces a base in DNA.

22.54   If the substitution of a base in DNA changes the amino acid coded for by the mRNA codon, then the order of amino acids will differ at that point.

22.55   If the resulting codon still codes for the same amino acid, there is no effect. If the new codon codes for a different amino acid, there is a change in the order of amino acids in the polypeptide.

22.56   If the mutation replaces one or more amino acids that do not form the same types of cross-links as in the functional protein, then the structure of the resulting protein can be altered so much that it has little or no functional activity.

22.57   The normal triplet TTT in DNA transcribes to AAA in mRNA. AAA codes for lysine. The mutation TTC in DNA transcribes to AAG in mRNA, which also codes for lysine. Thus, there is no effect on protein synthesis.

22.58   A DNA base sequence of CCC produces a mRNA codon of GGG that codes for glycine, a nonpolar amino acid. The mutation ACC produces a mRNA codon of UGG that codes for tryptophan that is also a nonpolar amino acid that will replace the glycine.

22.59   **a.** —Thr—Ser—Arg—Val— is the amino acid sequence produced by normal DNA.
b. —Thr—Thr—Arg—Val— is the amino acid sequence produced by a mutation.
c. —Thr—Ser—Gly—Val— is the amino acid sequence produced by a mutation.
d. —Thr—STOP   Protein synthesis would terminate early. If this mutation occurs early in the formation of the polypeptide, the resulting protein will probably be nonfunctional.
e. The new protein will contain the sequence —Asp—Ile—Thr—Gly—.
f. The new protein will contain the sequence —His—His—Gly—.

22.60   **a.** Leu-Lys-Arg-Val   **b.** Pro-Lys-Arg-Val
c. Leu-Lys-Arg-Val   **d.** Leu-STOP   synthesis of the protein stops

22.61   **a.** Both codons GCC and GCA code for alanine.
b. A vital ionic cross-link in the tertiary structure of hemoglobin cannot be formed when the polar glutamine is replaced by valine, which is nonpolar. The resulting hemoglobin is malformed and less capable of carrying oxygen.

22.62   **a.** Alanine is also a nonpolar amino acid and would have similar cross-linking behavior to the leucine. Thus enzyme activity will be maintained because the protein structure will not undergo major change.
b. UCA codes for serine, while UAA codes for STOP and the protein would be terminated at this point.

22.63   *E. coli* are used in recombinant DNA work because they are easy, fast and inexpensive to grow. They contain plasmids, the portion of the cell into which the foreign DNA can be inserted. Then the plasmids are replicated to make copies of the foreign DNA.

22.64   Plasmids are small, circular pieces of DNA found within certain bacterial cells like E. coli.

22.65   The cells of the *E. coli* are soaked in a detergent solution, which dissolves the plasma membrane and frees the plasmids, which can then be collected.

22.66   The restriction enzymes are used to cut the DNA of the plasmids at specific locations. When foreign DNA is cut with the same restriction enzyme and mixed with the plasmid DNA, the two pieces will combine.

22.67   A gene for a specific protein is inserted into plasmids by using a restriction enzyme that cuts the DNA in the plasmids in specific places. The same enzyme is used to cut a piece from the DNA to be inserted. The cut-out genes and the cut plasmids are mixed, and DNA ligase, an enzyme that catalyzes the joining of DNA, is added. After the foreign gene is inserted into the plasmids, *E. coli* take up the plasmids and replication begins.

22.68 DNA polymerase amplifies the amount of DNA, so that a small initial sample can be increased to an amount that can be studied.

22.69 A DNA fingerprint is the unique set of fragments that are formed from an individual's DNA. Each individual possesses unique DNA and each DNA gives a unique set of fragments and a unique fingerprint.

22.70 Many beneficial proteins such as human insulin, human growth factor, interferon and blood clotting factor are produced through recombinant DNA.

22.71 A virus contains either DNA or RNA, but not both, inside a protein coating.

22.72 A virus does not have the material necessary for growth and reproduction, so the virus invades other cells and takes these materials from the host cell.

22.73 **a.** An RNA-containing virus must make viral DNA from the RNA, a process called reverse transcription.
b. A virus that uses reverse transcription is a retrovirus.

22.74 Vaccines are inactive forms of a virus. The vaccine boosts the immune response of the body and causes the body to produce antibodies to the virus.

22.75 Nucleoside analogs like AZT or ddI mimic the structures of nucleosides that the HIV virus uses for DNA synthesis. These analogs are incorporated into the new viral DNA chain, but the lack of a hydroxyl group in position 3' of the sugar stops the chain from growing any longer and prevents replication of the virus.

22.76 Protease inhibitors stop the production of proteins needed for viral replication. Without the necessary proteins, the virus cannot make copies of itself.

22.77 **a.** pyrimidine   **b.** purine   **c.** pyrimidine
d. pyrimidine   **e.** purine

22.78 **a.** both   **b.** both   **c.** RNA only   **d.** DNA only   **e.** both

22.79 **a.** thymine and deoxyribose   **b.** adenine and ribose
c. cytosine and ribose   **d.** guanine and deoxyribose

22.80 **a.** cytosine, ribose   **b.** adenine, deoxyribose
c. guanine, deoxyribose   **d.** uracil, ribose

22.81 They are both pyrimidines, but thymine has a methyl group.

22.82 In cytosine, there is an —NH_2 whereas uracil has a keto group.

22.83

22.84

22.85 They are both polymers of nucleotides connected through phosphodiester bonds between alternating sugar and phosphate groups with bases extending out from each sugar. What is similar about the primary structure of RNA and DNA?

22.86 In the primary structure, the bases attached to each of the sugars extend out from the backbone. In RNA, the sugar is ribose, were as in DNA, the sugar is deoxyribose. Most of the nitrogen bases are the same except that uracil replaces thymine in RNA.

22.87 28% T, 22% G, and 22% C

22.88 A DNA with 20% cytosine also has 20% guanine, which means that adenine and thymine are each 30%.

22.89 **a.** There are two hydrogen bonds between A and T in DNA.
b. There are three hydrogen bonds between G and C in DNA.

22.90 Adenine and thymine can only form two hydrogen bonds, whereas guanine and cytosine form three hydrogen bonds. Because each base pair contains a purine and a pyrimidine, the distance between the two DNA strands is equal. Other combinations of base pairs would not maintain an equal distance along the DNA polymer.

22.91 **a.** 3'—CTGAATCCG—5'
b. 5'—ACGTTTGATCGT—3'
c. 3'—TAGCTAGCTAGC—5'

22.92 **a.** 3'—AATGCCTGGCG—5'
b. 3'—TATCGGGAATGACC—5'
c. 5'—CCGGATGGAATTGCTGC—3'

22.93 DNA polymerase synthesizes the leading strand continuously in the 5' to 3' direction. The lagging strand is synthesized in small segments called Okazaki fragments because it must grow in the 3' to 5' direction.

22.94 The short Okazaki fragment are joined by DNA ligase to give the 3'-5' DNA strand.

22.95 One strand of the parent DNA is found in each of the two copies of the daughter DNA molecule.

22.96 During replication, several open sections (replication forks) along the DNA polymer are available simultaneously to several DNA polymerases that synthesize the complementary DNA strands.

22.97 **a.** tRNA   **b.** rRNA   **c.** mRNA

22.98 **a.** ribosomal RNA (rRNA)   **b.** transfer RNA (tRNA)   **c.** messenger RNA (mRNA)

22.99 a. ACU, ACC, ACA, and ACG   **b.** UAU, UCC, UCA, and UCG
c. UGU and UGC

22.100 a. GUU, GUC, GUA, GUG   **b.** CCU, CCC, CCA, CCG   **c.** CAU, CAC

22.101 a. AAG codes for lysine   **b.** AUU codes for isoleucine   **c.** CGG codes for arginine

22.102 a. glutamine   **b.** glycine   **c.** asparagine

22.103 Using the genetic code the codons indicate the following:
start(methionine) —Tyr—Gly—Gly—Phe—Leu—stop

22.104 Met (start)—Try—Gly—Gly—Phe—Met—stop

22.105 The anticodon consists of the three complementary bases to the codon.
a. UCG   **b.** AUA   **c.** GGU

22.106 a. CAC   **b.** GGG   **c.** CUU

22.107 Three nucleotides are needed for each amino acid plus a start and stop triplet, which makes a minimum total of 33 nucleotides.

22.108 Each codon contains three nucleotides. Therefore, $35 \times 3 = 105$. If we count the start codon for methionine and the codon for stop, the total is 111 nucleotides.

22.109 A DNA virus attaches to a cell and injects viral DNA that uses the host cell to produce copies of DNA to make viral RNA. A retrovirus injects viral RNA from which complementary DNA is produced by reverse transcription.

23

Metabolic Pathways for Carbohydrates

Study Goals

- Explain the role of ATP in anabolic and catabolic reactions.
- Compare the structures and function of the coenzymes NAD^+, FAD, and coenzyme A.
- Give the sites, enzymes, and products for the digestion of carbohydrates.
- Describe the key reactions in the degradation of glucose in glycolysis.
- Describe the three possible pathways for pyruvate.
- Discuss the impact of ATP levels on glycogen metabolism.
- Describe gluconeogenesis and the Cori cycle.

Chapter Outline

23.1   **Metabolism and Cell Structure**
23.2   **ATP and Energy**
         Health Note: ATP Energy and Ca^{2+} Needed to Contract Muscles
23.3   **Important Coenzymes in Metabolic Pathways**
23.4   **Digestion of Carbohydrates**
         Explore Your World: Carbohydrate Digestion
         Health Note: Lactose Intolerance
23.5   **Glycolysis: Oxidation of Glucose**
23.6   **Pathways for Pyruvate**
23.7   **Glycogen Metabolism**
23.8   **Gluconeogenesis: Glucose Synthesis**

Chapter Summary and Demonstrations

The production of energy via metabolic pathways is discussed as essential to the survival of the cell. ATP production in the respiratory chain is related to the oxidative steps of the citric acid cycle. The central role of acetyl CoA is emphasized. Energy production for aerobic and anaerobic pathways is compared. While glucose oxidation is considered as the major source of energy, the energy-producing pathways of fatty acids, glycerol and amino acids are discussed.

Laboratory Suggestions

Lab 41   Digestion of Foodstuffs

Students use chemical tests to identify the hydrolysis products of carbohydrates, fats, and proteins.
A. Digestion of Carbohydrates
B. Digestion of Fats
C. Protein Digestion

Laboratory Skills to Demonstrate
    Review hydrolysis of carbohydrates, fats, and proteins.

Answers and Solutions to Text Problems

23.1 The digestion of polysaccharides takes place in stage 1.

23.2 In stage 3, small molecules are converted to CO_2, H_2O, and energy for ATP synthesis.

23.3 A catabolic reaction breaks down larger molecules to smaller molecules accompanied by the release of energy.

23.4 An anabolic reaction uses energy in the cell to build large molecules needed by the cell.

23.5 **a.** (3) Smooth endoplasmic reticulum is the site for the synthesis of fats and steroids.
b. (1) Lysosomes contain hydrolytic enzymes.
c. (2) The Golgi complex modifies products from the rough endoplasmic reticulum.

23.6 **a.** (3) The plasma membrane separates cell contents from surroundings.
b. (1) The mitochondria are the sites of energy production.
c. (2) The rough endoplasmic reticulum synthesizes proteins for secretion.

23.7 The phosphoric anhydride bonds (P—O—P) in ATP release energy that is sufficient for energy-requiring processes in the cell.

23.8 The energy released by the hydrolysis of ATP is linked with an energy-requiring reaction (anabolic) and used to "drive" that reaction.

23.9 **a.** PEP $+ H_2O \longrightarrow$ pyruvate $+ P_i + 14.8$ kcal /mole
b. ADP $+ P_i + 7.3$ kcal/mole $\longrightarrow$ ATP $+ H_2O$
c. Coupled: PEP $+$ ADP $\longrightarrow$ ATP $+$ pyruvate $+ 7.5$ kcal /mole

23.10 **a.** ATP $+ H_2O \longrightarrow$ ADP $+ P_i + 7.3$ kcal/mole
b. glycerol $+ P_i + 2.2$ kcal /mole $\longrightarrow$ glycerol-3-phosphate
c. Coupled: glycerol $+$ ATP $\longrightarrow$ glycerol-3-phosphate $+$ ADP $+ 5.1$ kcal /mole

23.11 **a.** Pantothenic acid is a component in coenzyme A.
b. Niacin is the vitamin component of NAD^+.
c. Ribitol is the alcohol sugar that makes up riboflavin in FAD.

23.12 **a.** FAD   **b.** NAD^+ **c.** Coenzyme A

23.13 In biochemical systems, oxidation is usually accompanied by gain of oxygen or loss of hydrogen. Loss of oxygen or gain of hydrogen usually accompanies reduction.
a. The reduced form of NAD^+ is abbreviated NADH.
b. The oxidized form of $FADH_2$ is abbreviated FAD.

23.14 **a.** $FADH_2$ **b.** NAD^+

23.15 The coenzyme FAD accepts hydrogen when a dehydrogenase forms a carbon-carbon double bond.

24.16 When a carbon-oxygen bond is formed, the coenzyme is NAD^+.

23.17 Digestion breaks down the large molecules in food into smaller compounds that can be absorbed by the body. Hydrolysis is the main reaction involved in the digestion of carbohydrates.

23.18 The _-amylase is produced by the salivary glands to begin the hydrolysis of the _-glycosidic bonds in the polysaccharide amylose. The hydrolysis of the smaller sections of amylose (dextrins) continues in the small intestine with _-amylase produced by the pancreas.

23.19 **a.** The disaccharide lactose is digested in the small intestine to yield galactose and glucose.
b. The disaccharide sucrose is digested in the small intestine to yield glucose and fructose.
c. The disaccharide maltose is digested in the small intestine to yield two glucose molecules.

23.20 **a.** small intestine; lactase   **b.** small intestine; sucrase

c. small intestine; maltase

23.21 Glucose is the starting reactant for glycolysis.

23.22 The end product of glycolysis is two molecules of pyruvate.

23.23 In the initial reactions of glycolysis, ATP molecules are required to add phosphate groups to glucose.

23.24 Two ATP molecules are used for the initial steps in gylcolysis.

23.25 When fructose-1, 6-bisphosphate splits, glyceraldehyde-3-phosphate and dihydroxyacetone phosphate are formed. The dihydroxyacetone phosphate is converted to glyceraldehyde-3-phosphate for subsequent reactions.

23.26 One of the triose molecules is a ketose that cannot be oxidized further. The isomerization of the ketose to a second molecule of glyceraldehyde-3-phosphate provides a compound that can be oxidized later in the glycolysis pathway.

23.27 ATP is produced directly in glycolysis in two places. In reaction 7, phosphate from 1,3-bisphosphoglycerate is transferred to ADP and yield ATP. In reaction 10, phosphate from phosphoenolpyruvate is transferred directly to ADP.

23.28 The oxidation of a glucose molecule utilizes two ATP molecules. Later the two triose products of glycolysis produce four ATP by direct phosphorylation to give a net yield of two ATP.

23.29 **a.** In glycolysis, phosphorylation is catalyzed by the enzyme hexokinase.
b. In glycolysis, direct transfer of a phosphate group is catalyzed by the enzyme phosphokinase.

23.30 **a.** isomerase   **b.** aldolase

23.31 **a.** In the phosphorylation of glucose to glucose-6-phosphate 1 ATP is required.
b. One ATP is required for the conversion of glyceraldehyde-3-phosphate to 1,3-bisphosphoglycerate.
c. When glucose is converted to pyruvate, two ATP and two NADH are produced.

23.32 **a.** One ATP is produced for each triose molecule.
b. One ATP is required.
c. One ATP is produced for each phosphoenolpyruvate.

23.33 **a.** The first ATP is hydrolyzed in the first reaction in glycolysis; the change of glucose to glucose-6-phosphate.
b. Direct substrate phosphorylation occurs in reaction 7 of glycolysis when the transfer of phosphate from 1,3-bisphosphoglycerate to ADP generates ATP. In reaction 10 of glycolysis, phosphate is transferred from phosphoenolpyruvate directly to ADP.

    c. In reaction 4 of glycolysis, the six-carbon fructose-1, 6-bisphosphate is converted to two three-carbon molecules.

23.34   **a.** Step 2, conversion of glucose-6-phosphate to fructose-6-phosphate and step 5, conversion of diydroxyacetone phosphate to glyceraldehyde-3-phosphate, both involve isomerization.

    b. NAD^+ is reduced in step 6, when two glyceraldehyde-3-phosphate are converted to 1,3-diphosphoglycerate.

    c. The second ATP is synthesized in step 10, when phosphoenolpyruvate is changed to pyruvate

23.35   Galactose reacts with ATP to yield galactose-1-phosphate, which is converted to glucose phosphate, an intermediate in glycolysis. Fructose reacts with ATP to yield fructose-1-phosphate, which is cleaved to give dihydroxyacetone phosphate and glyceraldehyde. Dihydroxyacetone phosphate isomerizes to glyceraldehyde-3-phosphate, and glyceraldehyde is phosphorylated to glyceraldehyde-3-phosphate, which is an intermediate in glycolysis.

23.37   **a.** Low levels of ATP activate phosphofructokinase to increase the rate of glycolysis.

    b. When ATP levels are high, ATP inhibits phosphofructokinase and slows or prevents glycolysis.

23.38   **a.** Low levels of ATP will activate pyruvate kinase and increase the rate of glycolysis.

    b. High levels of fructose-1,6-bisphosphate will inhibit pyruvate kinase and slow or stop glycolysis.

23.39   A cell converts pyruvate to acetyl CoA only under aerobic conditions; there must be sufficient oxygen available.

23.40   The change of pyruvate to acetyl CoA is catalyzed by the enzyme pyruvate dehydrogenase; the coenzyme NAD^+ is required as well. .

23.41   The overall reaction for the conversion of pyruvate to acetyl CoA is:

$$CH_3-\overset{\overset{\displaystyle O}{\|}}{C}-COO^- + NAD^+ + HS-CoA \longrightarrow CH_3-\overset{\overset{\displaystyle O}{\|}}{C}-S-CoA + CO_2 + NADH + H^+$$

      pyruvate   *acetyl CoA*

23.42   Under anaerobic conditions, pyruvate maybe converted to lactate or ethanol.

23.43   The reduction of pyruvate to lactate regenerates NAD^+, which allows glycolysis to proceed and produce two ATP.

23.44   After strenuous exercise, the oxygen in the cells is rapidly depleted and lactate accumulates. The presence of the lactate causes the muscles to tire and become sore.

23.45   During fermentation the three-carbon compound pyruvate is reduced to ethanol while decarboxylation removes one carbon as CO_2.

23.46   When fermentation takes place, the products are ethanol and carbon dioxide gas. The production of the carbon dioxide gas could cause the pressure to build up and the container may explode.

23.47   In glycogenesis, glycogen is synthesized from glucose molecules.

23.48   Glycogenolysis is the breakdown of glycogen to produce glucose.

23.49   Muscle cells break down glycogen to glucose 6-phosphate, which enters glycolysis.

23.50 Glucagon activates the breakdown of glycogen in the liver.

23.51 Glycogen phosphorylase cleaves the glycosidic bonds at the ends of glycogen chains to remove glucose monomers as glucose 1-phosphate.

23.52 Phosphoglucomutase catalyzes the reversible reactions of glucose-1-phosphate to glucose-6-phosphate in glycogenolysis and glucose-6-phosphate to glucose-1-phosphate in glycogenesis.

23.53 When there are no glycogen stores remaining in the liver, gluconeogenesis synthesizes glucose from noncarbohydrate compounds such as pyruvate and lactate.

23.54 The three enzymes in glycolysis that are not used in gluconeogenesis are pyruvate kinase, phosphofructokinase, and hexokinase.

23.55 The enzymes in glycolysis that are also used in their reverse directions for gluconeogenesis are phosphoglucoisomerase, aldolase, triosephosphate isomerase, glyceraldehyde 3-phosphate dehydrogenase, phosphoglycerokinase, phosphoglyceromutase, and enolase.

23.56 In gluconeogenesis, two lactate units in the skeletal muscle are converted to two pyruvate and used to produce glucose.

23.57 **a.** Low glucose levels activate glucose synthesis.
b. Glucagon produced when glucose levels are low activates gluconeogenesis.
c. Insulin produced when glucose levels are high inhibits gluconeogenesis.

23.58 **a.** Low glucose levels inhibit glycolysis.
b. Insulin activates glycolysis
c. Glucagon inhibits glycolysis

23.59 Metabolism includes all the reactions in cells that provide energy and material for cell growth.

23.60 Catabolic reactions break down complex molecules and anabolic reactions build large molecules from simple ones. Catabolic reactions provide energy, whereas anabolic reactions are energy requiring.

23.61 Stage 1 involves the degradation of large molecules such as polysaccharides.

23.62 State 2 degrades monomers such as glucose to two- and three-carbon molecules.

23.63 A eukaryotic cell has a nucleus, whereas a prokaryotic cell does not.

23.64 The organelles are specialized structures that perform the specific functions in the cell.

23.65 ATP is the abbreviation for adenosine triphosphate.

23.66 Adenosine diphosphate

23.67 $\text{ATP} + H_2O \longrightarrow \text{ADP} + P_i + 7.3 \text{ kcal } (31\text{kJ})/\text{mole}$

23.68 $300 \text{ kcal} \times 1 \text{ mole ATP}/7.3 \text{ kcal} = 41 \text{ moles ATP required}$

23.69 FAD is the abbreviation for flavin adenine dinucleotide.

23.70 FAD is used in oxidation reactions that produce a carbon-carbon (C=C) double bond.

23.71 NAD^+ is the abbreviation for nicotinamide adenine dinucleotide.

23.72 NAD^+ is used in oxidation reactions that produce a carbon-oxygen (C=O) double bond.

23.73 The reduced forms of these coenzymes include hydrogen obtained from an oxidation reaction.
a. $FADH_2$ **b.** $\text{NADH} + H^+$

256

23.74   **a.** riboflavin (vitamin B$_2$)   **b.** niacin   **c.** pantothenic acid (vitamin B$_3$)

23.75   Lactose undergoes digestion in the mucosal cells of the small intestine to yield galactose and glucose.

23.76   When sucrose is digested in the small intestine, the products are glucose and fructose.

23.77   Galactose and fructose are converted in the liver to glucose phosphate compounds that can enter the glycolysis pathway.

23.78   Hydrolysis

23.79   Glucose is the reactant and pyruvate is the product of glycolysis.

23.80   NAD$^+$

23.81   Reactions 1 and 3 involve phosphorylation of hexoses with ATP, and reactions 7 and 10 involve direct substrate phosphorylation that generates ATP.

23.82   When ATP levels are high, enzymes such as phosphofructokinase and pyruvate kinase are inhibited. When ATP levels are low (ADP is high), the enzymes are activated.

23.83   Reaction 4 catalyzed by aldolase converts fructose 1,6-bisphosphate into two triose phosphates.

23.84   In reactions 1-5 of glycolysis 2 ATP are utilized, whereas reaction 6-10 produce 4 ATP. Thus a net of 2 ATP are produced for every glucose molecule that undergoes glycolysis.

23.85   Phosphoglucoisomerase converts glucose-6-phosphate to the isomer fructose-6-phosphate.

23.86   1,3-bisphophoglycerate

23.87   Pyruvate is converted to lactate when oxygen is not present in the cell (anaerobic) to regenerate NAD$^+$ for glycolysis.

23.88   One carbon atom of pyruvate is removed as CO$_2$.

23.89   Phosphofructokinase is an allosteric enzyme that is activated by high levels of AMP and ADP because the cell needs to produce more ATP. When ATP levels are high, ATP inhibits phosphofructokinase, which reduces its catalysis of fructose-6-phosphate.

23.90   Pyruvate kinase is inhibited at ATP, which causes glucose-6-phosphate to accumulate and inhibit the phosphorylation of glucose. Thus, when ATP levels are high, glucose cannot enter the glycolysis pathway.

23.91   The rate of glycogenolysis increases when blood glucose levels are low and glucagon has been secreted, which accelerate the breakdown of glycogen.

23.92   Glucose-1-phosphate from glycogenolysis is converted to glucose-6-phosphate, which can then enter glycolysis.

23.93   The breakdown of glycogen in the liver produces glucose.

23.94   glucose-6-phosphate

23.95 The cells in the liver, but not skeletal muscle, contain a phosphatase enzyme needed to convert glucose--phosphate to free glucose that can diffuse through cell membranes into the blood stream. Glucose-6-phosphate, which is the end product of glycogenolysis in muscle cells, cannot diffuse easily across cell membranes.

23.96 The rate of glycogenesis increases when glucose levels are high. Insulin produced in the pancreas enters the bloodstream and accelerates the synthesis of glycogen.

23.97 Insulin increases the rate of glycogenolysis and glycolysis, and decreases the rate of glycogenesis. Glucagon decreases the rate of glycogenolysis and glycolysis, and increases the rate of glycogenesis.

23.98 When glycogen stores are depleted, glucose is synthesized from noncarbohydrate compounds such as lactate, amino acids, and glycerol.

23.99 The Cori cycle is a cyclic process that involves the transfer of lactate from muscle to the liver where glucose is synthesized, which can be used again by the muscle.

23.100 **a.** glycogenolysis   **b.** gluconeogenesis
         c. glycolysis   **d.** glycogenesis

23.101 **a.** Low glucose increases the breakdown of glycogen.
      b. Insulin produced when glucose levels are high decreases the rate of glycogenolysis in the liver.
      c. Glucagon secreted when glucose levels are low increases the breakdown of glycogen.
      d. High levels of ATP decrease the breakdown of glycogen.

23.102 **a.** decrease   **b.** increase   **c.** decrease   **d.** increase

23.103 **a.** High glucose levels decrease the synthesis of glucose (gluconeogenesis).
      b. Insulin produced when glucose levels are high decreases glucose synthesis.
      c. Glucagon secreted when glucose levels are low increases glucose synthesis.
      d. High levels of ATP decrease glucose synthesis (gluconeogenesis).

23.104 **a.** increase   **b.** increase   **c.** decrease   **d.** decrease

Metabolism and Energy Production

Study Goals

- Describe the reactions in the citric acid cycle that oxidize acetyl CoA.
- Explain how electrons from NADH and H^+ and FAD move along the electron transport chain to form H_2O.
- Describe the role of oxidative phosphorylation in ATP synthesis.
- Calculate the ATP produced by the complete combustion of glucose.

Chapter Outline

Chapter Summary and Demonstrations

The production of energy via metabolic pathways is discussed as essential to the survival of the cell. ATP production in the respiratory chain is related to the oxidative steps of the citric acid cycle. The central role of acetyl CoA is emphasized. Energy production for aerobic and anaerobic pathways is compared. The ATP energy from glucose is calculated.

Laboratory Suggestions

42   Analysis of Urine

Chemical tests are used to determine pH, specific gravity, and the presence of electrolytes and organic compounds in urine-like specimens. Chemical tests or commercial test strips are used to analyze the presence of proteins, glucose, and ketone bodies in urine-like specimens.
   A. Color, pH and Specific Gravity
   B. Electrolytes
   C. Glucose
   D. Ketone Bodies
   E. Protein
   F. Urobilinogen

   Laboratory Skills to Demonstrate
      Procedure for using a urine hydrometer
      Matching a test strip to the code on the container.

Answers and Solutions to Text Problems

24.1   Other names for the citric acid cycle are the Krebs cycle and tricarboxlyic acid cycle.

24.2   The citric acid cycle begins by combining acetyl CoA and oxaloacetate.

24.3   One turn of the citric acid cycle converts 1 acetyl CoA to $2CO_2$, $3NADH + 3H^+$, $FADH_2$, GTP (ATP), and HS—CoA.

24.4   Oxaloacetate is regenerated at the end of the citric acid cycle?

24.5   The reactions in steps 3 and 4 involve oxidative decarboxylation, which reduces the length of the carbon chain by one carbon in each reaction.

24.6   There is a dehydration in reaction 2,

24.7 NAD^+ is reduced by the oxidation reactions 3, 4, and 8 of the citric acid cycle.

24.8   FAD is reduced in reaction 6 when succinate is converted to fumarate.

24.9   In reaction 5, GDP undergoes a direct substrate phosphorylation to yield GTP, which converts ADP to ATP and regenerates GDP for the citric acid cycle.

24.10   3 NADH and 1 $FADH_2$ are produced in one turn of the citric acid cycle.

24.11   **a.** The six-carbon compounds in the citric acid cycle are citrate and isocitrate.
      b. Decarboxylation reactions remove carbon atoms as CO_2, which reduces the number of carbon atoms in a chain (reactions 3 and 4).
      c. The one five-carbon compound is _-ketoglutarate.
      d. Several reactions are oxidation reactions; isocitrate ⟶ _-ketoglutarate; _-ketoglutarate ⟶ succinyl CoA; succinate⟶ fumarate; malate ⟶ oxaloacetate
      e. Secondary alcohols are oxidized in reactions 3 and 8.

24.12   **a.** Two CO_2 per citric acid cycle
      b. Succinyl CoA, succinate, fumarate, malate, oxaloacetate
      c. One GTP
      d. Oxidations of isocitrate (reaction 3) and α-ketoglutarate (reaction 4)
      e. Hydration of aconitate (reaction 1) and fumarate (reaction 6)

24.13   **a.** Citrate synthase combines oxaloacetate with acetyl CoA.
      b. Succinate dehydrogenase and aconitase converts a carbon-carbon single bond to a double bond.
      c. Fumarase adds water to the double bond in fumarate; aconitase adds water to the double bond in iconitate from citrate.

24.14   **a.** aconitase   **b.** α-ketoglutarate dehydrogenase   **c.** nucleotide phosphokinase

24.15   **a.** NAD^+ accepts 2H from the oxidative decarboxylation of isocitrate.
      b. GDP is phosphorylated in the formation of succinate.
      c. FAD accepts 2H when the carbon-carbon single bond in succinate is oxidized to a carbon-carbon double bond in fumarate.

24.16   **a.** NAD^+ **b.** NAD^+ **c.** NAD^+

24.17 Isocitrate dehydrogenase and α-ketoglutarate dehydrogenase are allosteric enzymes, which increase or decrease the flow of materials through the citric acid cycle.

24.18 Low levels of NADH activate the citric acid cycle and high levels of NADH inhibit the cycle.

24.19 High levels of ADP means there are low levels of ATP. To provide more ATP for the cell, the reaction rate of the citric acid cycle increases.

24.20 When NADH and ATP levels are high, there is a decrease in the production of acetyl CoA from pyruvate, which slows the rate of the citric acid cycle. Low levels of ATP stimulate the conversion of pyruvate to acetyl CoA providing fuel for the citric acid cycle and increasing the rate.

24.21 The Fe^{3+} is the oxidized form of the iron in cytochrome *c*.

22.22 $FMNH_2$ is the reduced form.

24.23 **a.** The loss of $2H^+$ and $2e^-$ is oxidation.   **b.** The gain of $2H^+ + 2e^-$ is reduction.

24.24 **a.** reduction   **b.** oxidation

24.25 NADH and $FADH_2$ produced in glycolysis, oxidation of pyruvate, and the citric acid cycle provide the electrons for electron transport.

24.26 As electrons move along the electron transport chain, the energy level drops.

24.27 FAD is reduced to $FADH_2$, which provides $2H^+$ and $2e^-$ for coenzyme Q, then cytochrome *b*, and then cytochrome *c*.

24.28 NAD^+, FMN, cytochrome a_3, O_2

24.29 The mobile carrier coenzyme Q (or Q) transfers electrons from complex I to III. It also transfers electrons from complex II to complex III.

24.30 Cytochrome *c* is the mobile carrier that carries an electron from complex III to complex IV>

24.31 When NADH transfers electrons to FMN in complex I, NAD^+ is produced.

24.32 The electrons from $FADH_2$ are transferred to coenzyme Q to give QH_2 and oxidized FAD.

24.33 **a.** $NADH + H^+ + \underline{FMN} \longrightarrow \underline{NAD^+} + FMNH_2$
    b. $QH_2 + 2 Fe^{3+} cyt\ b \longrightarrow Q + \underline{2\ Fe^{2+}\ cyt\ b} + 2H^+$

24.34 **a.** $Q + \underline{FADH_2} \longrightarrow \underline{QH_2} + FAD$
    b. $2\ cyt\ a\ (Fe^{3+}) + 2\ cyt\ a_3\ (Fe^{2+}) \longrightarrow \underline{2\ cyt\ a\ (Fe^{2+})} + \underline{2\ cyt\ a_3\ (Fe^{3+})}$

24.35 In oxidative phosphorylation, the energy from the oxidation reactions in the electron transport chain is used to drive ATP synthesis.

24.36 As energy is released from oxidations along the transport chain, it is used to move protons into the intermembrane space. The accumulation of high-energy protons creates a proton gradient.

24.37 Protons must pass through F_0 channel of ATP synthase to return to the matrix. During the process, energy is released to drive the synthesis of ATP in F_1.

24.38 When high-energy protons move through ATP synthetase, energy is provided to combine a phosphate with ADP, a process called oxidative phosphorylation.

24.39 The oxidation of the reduced coenzymes NADH and $FADH_2$ by the electron transport chain generates energy to drive the synthesis of ATP.

24.40 The electrons from NADH enter the electron chain at a higher energy level than the electrons from $FADH_2$. Thus, the greater energy difference for electrons from NADH provides energy that drives the synthesis of three ATP.

24.41 ATP synthase consists of two protein complexes known as F_0 and F_1.

24.42 Electrons flowing through F_0 provide energy that turns the center unit in F_1. In F_1, ADP and P_i combine to form ATP, which is released as the shape of the sites in F_1 change.

24.43 The loose (L) site in ATP synthase begins the synthesis of ATP by binding ADP and P_i.

24.44 Energy is required to convert the tight site of ATP synthase to an open(O) site, which releases the ATP.

24.45 Glycolysis takes place in the cytoplasm, not in the mitochondria. Because NADH cannot cross the mitochondrial membrane, one ATP is hydrolyzed to transport the electrons from NADH to FAD. The resulting $FADH_2$ produces only 2 ATP for each NADH produced in glycolysis.

24.46 Under anaerobic conditions, the maximum yield is 36 ATP per glucose molecule.

24.47 **a.** 3 ATP are produced by the oxidation of NADH in electron transport.
b. 2 ATP are produced in glycolysis when glucose degrades to 2 pyruvate.
c. 6 ATP are produced when 2 pyruvate are oxidized to 2 acetyl CoA and 2 CO_2.
d. 12 ATP are produced in one turn of the citric acid cycle as acetyl CoA is converted to 2 CO_2.

24.48 **a.** 2 ATP   **b.** 36 ATP   **c.** 2 ATP   **d.** 2 ATP

24.49 The oxidation reactions of the citric acid cycle produce a source of reduced coenzymes for the electron transport chain and ATP synthesis.

24.50 In the citric acid cycle, oxaloacetate is regenerated, which is available to pick up acetyl CoA and start the cycle again.

24.51 The electron transport chain regenerates the oxidized forms of the coenzymes NAD^+ and FAD for use again by the citric acid cycle.

24.52 The reduced coenzymes $NADH/H^+$ and $FADH_2$ are needed for the electron transport chain.

24.53 **a.** Citrate and isocitrate are six-carbon compounds in the citric acid cycle.
b. α-Ketoglutarate is a five-carbon compound.
c. The compounds α-ketoglutarate, succinyl-CoA, and oxaloacetate have keto groups.

24.54 **a.** succinyl CoA, succinate, fumarate, malate, and oxaloacetate
b. Citrate, isocitrate, and malate have hydroxyl groups.
c. There are carbon-carbon double bonds in aconitate and fumarate. There are carbon-oxygen double bonds in many of the compounds in the citric acid cycle.

24.55 **a.** In Reaction 4, α-ketoglutarate, a five-carbon keto acid, is decarboxylated.
     b. In Reaction 1 and 7, double bonds in aconitate and fumarate are hydrated.
     c. NAD^+ is reduced in Reactions 3, 4, and 8.
     d. In Reactions 3 and 8, a secondary hydroxyl group in isocitrate and malate is oxidized.

24.56 **a.** FAD is reduced in reaction 6.
     b. In reaction 3, isocitrate is decarboxylated to give _-ketoglutarate.
     c. In reaction 6, a carbon-carbon double bond forms when fumarate undergoes dehydrogenation with FAD.
     d. In reaction 5, GDP undergoes direct phosphorylation to give GTP.

24.57 **a.** NAD^+ is the coenzyme for the oxidation of a secondary hydroxyl group in isocitrate to a keto group in α-ketoglutarate.
     b. NAD^+ and CoA are needed in the oxidative decarboxylation of α-ketoglutarate to succinyl CoA.

24.58 **a.** succinate dehydrogenase   **b.** malate dehydrogenase

24.59 **a.** High levels of NADH inhibit isocitrate dehydrogenase and α-ketoglutarate dehydrogenase to slow the rate of the citric acid cycle.
     b. High levels of ATP inhibit the citric acid cycle.

24.60 **a.** increase the rate of the citric acid cycle to provide more ATP
     b. increase the rate of the citric acid cycle to provide more ATP

24.61 **a.** A heme group is found in all the cytochromes (4).
     b. FMN (1) contains a ribitol group.

24.62 **a.** (1) FMN   **b.** (3) CoQ

24.63 **a.** CoQ is a mobile carrier.
     b. Fe-S clusters are found in complexes I, III, and IV.
     c. cyt a_3 is part of complex IV

24.64 **a.** cyt b is part of complex II   **b.** cyt c is a mobile carrier
     c. FMN is part of complex I

24.65 **a.** $FADH_2$ is oxidized in complex II: $FADH_2 + Q \longrightarrow FAD + QH_2$
     b. Cyt a (Fe^{2+}) is oxidized in complex IV:
     Cyt a (Fe^{2+}) + Cyt a_3 (Fe^{3+}) $\longrightarrow$ Cyt a (Fe^{3+}) + Cyt a_3 (Fe^{2+})

24.66 **a.** cyt c (Fe^{3+}) + cyt a (Fe^{2+})
     b. NAD^+ + $FMNH_2$

24.67 Complete the following by adding the substances that are missing:

a.

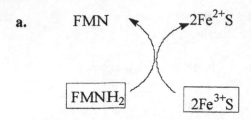

b.

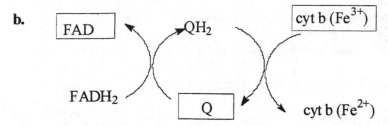

24.68 **a.** NADH + H$^+$; FMN
b. 2 cyt a (Fe^{2+}); 2 cyt $a3$ (Fe^{2+}); H$_2$O

24.69 The transfer of electrons by complexes I, III, and IV generate energy to pump protons out of the matrix into the inner membrane space.

24.70 The accumulation of protons decreases pH in the intermembrane space and creates a proton gradient.

24.71 In the chemiosmotic model, energy released by the flow of protons through the ATP synthase is utilized for the synthesis ATP.

24.72 The synthesis of ATP occurs in the ATP synthase part of the electron transport chain.

24.73 In the inner membrane space, there is a higher concentration of protons, which reduces the pH and forms an electrochemical gradient. As a result protons flow into the matrix where the proton concentration is lower and the pH is higher.

24.74 The protons obtained from the oxidations reactions must be pumped from the end in the matrix to be released at the other end, which is in the intermembrane space.

24.75 Two ATP molecules are produced from the energy generated by the electrons from FADH$_2$ moving through electron transport to oxygen.

24.76 3 ATP are produced from each NADH + H$^+$.

24.77 **a.** Amytal and rotenone inhibit the transfer of electrons in NADH dehydrogenase (complex I).
b. Antimycin inhibits electron flow from cyt b to cyt c_1 in complex III.
c. Cyanide and carbon monoxide inhibit the flow of electron through cytochrome c oxidase (complex IV).

24.78 **a.** The coenzymes that precede the blocked site remain in their reduced forms.
b. The coenzymes that follow the blocked site remain in their oxidized forms.

24.79   The oxidation of glucose to pyruvate by glycolysis produces 6 ATP. 2 ATP are formed by direct phosphorylation along with 2 NADH. Because the 2 NADH are produced in the cytosol, the electrons are transferred to form 2 $FADH_2$, which produces an additional 4 ATP. The oxidation of glucose to CO_2 and H_2O produces 36 ATP.

24.80   The NADH produced from glycolysis cannot pass through the mitochondrial membrane. Therefore, the hydrogen ions and electrons from the NADH in the cytoplasm are transferred to dihydroxyacetone phosphate, which is reduced to glycerol-3-phosphate to regenerate NAD^+. After glycerol-3-phosphate moves into the mitochondria, the hydrogen ions and electrons reduced FAD to give $FADH_2$ and $FADH_2$ produces two ATP in the electron transport chain.

24.81   a. 4 ATP $\times$ 7.3 kcal/mole = 29 kcal (actual ATP produced from glycolysis because the protons from the NADH in the cytoplasm are shuttled to FAD in the mitochondria).
b. 6 ATP $\times$ 7.3 kcal/mole = 44 kcal (2 pyruvate to 2 acetyl CoA)
c. 24 ATP $\times$ 7.3 kcal/ mole = 175 kcal (2 acetyl CoA citric acid cycle)
d. 36 $\times$ 7.3 kcal/mol = 263 kcal (complete oxidation of glucose to CO_2 and H_2O)

24.82   a. 29 kcal/ 687 kcal $\times$ 100 = 4.2%
b. 44 kcal/687 $\times$ 100 = 6.4%
c. 175 kcal/687 $\times$ 100 = 35%

24.83   In a calorimeter, the complete combustion of glucose gives 687 kcal. The efficiency of ATP synthesis is determined by comparing the total kcal in 36 ATP (283 kcal in problem 24.81) to the energy obtained from glucose in a calorimeter.
    283 /687 x 100 = 38.0% efficient

24.84   4 moles glucose $\times$ 283 moles ATP/1 mole glucose $\times$ 7.3 kcal/1 mole ATP = 8260 kcal
When 4 moles of glucose are completely oxidized at 38% efficiency, 8260 kcal of energy would be conserved.

24.85   The ATP synthase extends through the inner mitochondrial membrane with the F_0 part in contact with the proton gradient in the intermembrane space, while the F_1 complex is in the matrix.

24.86   Protons from the matrix where oxidation reactions take place are pumped through complexes I, IIII, and IV into the intermembrane space where they accumulate and form a proton gradient.

24.87   As protons from the proton gradient move through the ATP synthase to return to the matrix, energy is released and used to drive ATP synthesis at F_1.

24.88   ADP and P_i enter the loose (L) site on ATP synthase. When the shape of the site changes to tight (T), ATP is formed. The site then changes to open (O), and ATP is released.

24.89   A hibernating bear has stored fat as brown fat, which can be used during the winter for heat rather than ATP energy.

24.90   A diet medication that is an uncoupler may transport protons through the inner membrane or block the changed in the F_0 part of ATP synthase. Because ATP synthesis is bypassed, the energy of electron transport is released as heat, which will cause an increase in body temperature.

Metabolic Pathways for Lipids and Amino Acids

Study Goals

- Describe the sites, enzymes, and products for the digestion of triacylglycerols.
- Describe the oxidation of fatty acids via β-oxidation.
- Calculate the ATP produced by the complete oxidation of a fatty acid.
- Explain ketogenesis and the conditions in the cell that form ketone bodies.
- Describe the biosynthesis of fatty acids from acetyl CoA.
- Describe the sites, enzymes, and products of the digestion of dietary proteins.
- Explain the role of transamination and oxidative deamination in the degradation of amino acids.
- Describe the formation of urea from ammonium ion.
- Explain how carbon atoms from amino acids are prepared to enter the citric acid cycle or other pathways.
- Show how nonessential amino acids are synthesized from substances used in the citric acid cycle and other pathways.

Chapter Outline

Chapter Summary

The oxidation of fatty acids to acetyl CoA is described along with the ATP energy from fats and the formation of ketone bodies. Fatty acid synthesis from acetyl CoA describes the way in which carbohydrates contribute to fat stores. The digestion of proteins and the degradation of amino acids discuss how carbon atoms from amino acids can enter the citric acid cycle. We also see how components of the citric acid cycle are converted to nonessential amino acids for protein synthesis. The urea cycle discusses how ammonium ion from amino acid degradation is detoxified in the body.

Answers and Solutions to Text Problems

25.1   The bile salts emulsify fat to give small fat globules for lipase hydrolysis.

25.2   The triacylglycerols in the intestinal lining are coated with proteins to form lipoproteins called chylomicrons, which are polar and can be transported through the lymph system and into the bloodstream.

25.3   Fats are mobilized when blood glucose and glycogen stores are depleted.

25.4   Glycerol is phosphorylated using ATP to give glycerol-3-phosphate, which is oxidized to dihydroxyacetone phosphate. This product can now enter glycolysis or gluconeogenesis.

25.5   Glycerol is converted to glycerol-3-phosphate and then to dihydroxyacetone phosphate, which is an intermediate of glycolysis.

25.6   Glycerol is converted to glycerol-3-phosphate and then to dihydroxyacetone phosphate, which can enter gluconeogenesis to produce glucose.

25.7   Fatty acids are activated in the cytosol of the mitochondria.

25.8   Carnitine is a charged carrier that transports fatty acids across the inner mitochondrial into the matrix.

25.9   The coenzymes FAD and NAD^+ are required for _-oxidation.

25.10 Isomerization occurs in _ oxidation when the fatty acid has an unsaturated site. The typical cis double bond must be converted to a trans double bond for the hydration step of beta oxidation.

25.11 The designation beta (_) carbon is based on the common names of carboxylic acids whereby the alpha _ carbon and the beta (_) carbons are adjacent to the carboxyl group.

a. CH_3—CH_2—CH_2—CH_2—CH_2—$\overline{C}H_2$—CH_2—$\overset{\overset{\displaystyle O}{\|}}{C}$—S—CoA

b. CH_3—$(CH_2)_{14}$—$\overline{C}H_2$—CH_2—$\overset{\overset{\displaystyle O}{\|}}{C}$—S—CoA

c. CH_3—CH_2—CH=CH—CH_2—CH_2—CH_2—$\overline{C}H_2$—CH_2—$\overset{\overset{\displaystyle O}{\|}}{C}$—S—CoA

25.12

a. CH_3—$(CH_2)_{12}$—$\overset{\overset{\displaystyle OH}{|}}{C}H$—$CH_2$—$\overset{\overset{\displaystyle O}{\|}}{C}$—S—CoA

b. CH_3—$(CH_2)_6$—$\overset{\overset{\displaystyle H}{|}}{C}$=$\overset{\underset{\displaystyle H}{|}}{C}$—$\overset{\overset{\displaystyle O}{\|}}{C}$—S—CoA

c. CH_3—$(CH_2)_4$—$\overset{\overset{\displaystyle O}{\|}}{C}$—S—CoA   + CH_3—$\overset{\overset{\displaystyle O}{\|}}{C}$—S—CoA

25.13

$$\text{a., b. } CH_3-(CH_2)_6-CH_2-CH_2-\overset{\displaystyle O}{\overset{\|}{C}}-S-CoA$$

c.

$$CH_3-(CH_2)_8-\overset{\displaystyle O}{\overset{\|}{C}}-S-CoA \ + \ NAD^+ \ + \ FAD + H_2O + SH-CoA \longrightarrow$$

$$CH_3-(CH_2)_6-\overset{\displaystyle O}{\overset{\|}{C}}-S-CoA \ + \ CH_3-\overset{\displaystyle O}{\overset{\|}{C}}-S-CoA \ + \ NADH + H^+ + FADH_2$$

d. $CH_3-(CH_2)_8-COOH + 5CoA + 4FAD + 4NAD^+ + 4H_2O \longrightarrow$
   $5\text{Acetyl CoA} + 4FADH_2 + 4NADH + 4H^+$

25.14

$$\text{a., b. } CH_3-(CH_2)_{18}-CH_2-CH_2-\overset{\displaystyle O}{\overset{\|}{C}}-S-CoA$$

c.

$$CH_3-(CH_2)_{18}-\overset{\displaystyle O}{\overset{\|}{C}}-S-CoA \ + \ NAD^+ \ + \ FAD + H_2O + SH-CoA \longrightarrow$$

$$CH_3-(CH_2)_{16}-\overset{\displaystyle O}{\overset{\|}{C}}-S-CoA \ + \ CH_3-\overset{\displaystyle O}{\overset{\|}{C}}-S-CoA \ + \ NADH + H^+ + FADH_2$$

d. $CH_3-(CH_2)_{18}-COOH + 10\ CoA + 9FAD + 9NAD^+ + 9H_2O \longrightarrow$
   $10\text{Acetyl CoA} + 9FADH_2 + 9NADH + 9H^+$

25.15 The hydrolysis of ATP to AMP hydrolyzes ATP to ADP, and ADP to AMP, which provides the same amount of energy as the hydrolysis of 2 ATP to 2 ADP.

25.16 12 ATP are obtained when one acetyl CoA goes through the citric acid cycle

25.17 **a.** The _-oxidation of a chain of 10 carbon atoms produces 5 acetyl CoA units.
  b. A C_{10} fatty acid will go through 4 _-oxidation cycles.
  c. 60 ATP from 5 acetyl CoA (citric acid cycle) + 12 ATP from 4 NADH + 8 ATP from 4 $FADH_2$ −2 ATP (activation) = 80 −2 = 78 ATP

25.18 **a.** 10 acetyl CoA units   **b.** 9 cycles   **c.** 163 ATPs

25.19 Ketogenesis is the synthesis of ketone bodies from excess acetyl CoA from fatty acid oxidation, which occurs when glucose is not available for energy. This occurs in starvation, fasting, and diabetes.

25.20 Without carbohydrates, the body breaks down body fat, which results in the production of many acetyl CoA molecules.

25.21 Acetoacetate undergoes reduction using $NADH + H^+$ to yield _-hydroxybutyrate.

25.22 Acetoacetate undergoes decarboxylation to form acetone.

25.23 High levels of ketone bodies lead to ketosis, a condition characterized by acidosis (a drop in blood pH values), and characterized by excessive urination and strong thirst.

25.24 Diabetics are unable to metabolize glucose and break down large amount of fats, which give high levels of acetyl CoA resulting in the formation of ketone bodies.

25.25 Fatty acid synthesis takes place in the cytosol of cells in liver and adipose tissue.

25.26 ACP, which is an acyl carrier protein, is used to activate acetyl and acyl groups.

25.27 Fatty acid synthesis starts when acetyl CoA, HCO_3^-, and ATP produce malonyl CoA.

25.28 In fatty acid synthesis, malonyl-ACP adds another acetyl group to a growing acyl-ACP chain.

25.29   **a.** (3) malonyl CoA transacylase converts malonyl CoA to malonyl ACP.
       b. (1) acetyl CoA carboxylase combines acetyl CoA with bicarbonate to yield malonyl CoA.
       c. (2) acetyl CoA transacylase converts acetyl CoA to acetyl ACP.

25.30   **a.** (3) 3-hydroxy-ACP dehydrase   **b.** (4) enoyl-ACP reductase
       c. (1) _-ketoacyl-ACP synthase   **d.** (2) _-ketoacyl-ACP reductase

25.31   **a.** A C_{10} fatty acid requires the formation of 4 malonyl ACP, which uses 4 HCO_3^-.
       b. 4 ATP are required to produce 4 malonyl CoA.
       c. 5 acetyl CoA are needed to make 1 acetyl ACP and 4 malonyl ACP.
       d. A C_{10} fatty acid requires 4 malonyl ACP and 1 acetyl ACP.
       e. A C_{10} fatty acid chain requires 4 cycles with 2 NADPH/cycle or a total of 8 NADPH.
       f. The four cycles remove a total of 4 CO_2.

25.32   **a.** A C_{14} fatty acid requires the formation of 6 malonyl ACP, which requires $6HCO_3^-$.
       b. 6 ATP are required to produce 6 malonyl CoA.
       c. 7 acetyl CoA are needed to make 1 acetyl ACP and 6 malonyl ACP.
       d. A C_{14} fatty acid requires 6 malonyl ACP and 1 acetyl ACP.
       e. A C_{14} fatty acid chain requires 6 cycles with 2 NADPH/cycle or a total of 12 NADPH.
       f. The six cycles remove a total of 6 CO_2.

25.33 The digestion of proteins begins in the stomach and is completed in the small intestine.

25.34 Protein turnover is the process of synthesizing proteins and breaking them down.

25.35 Nitrogen-containing compounds in the cells include hormones, heme, purines and pyrimidines for nucleotides, proteins, nonessential amino acids, amino alcohols, and neurotransmitters.

25.36 If they are not used to build protein, amino acids are excreted because they cannot be stored.

25.37 The reactants are an amino acid and an _-keto acid, and the products are a new amino acid and a new _-keto acid.

25.38 transaminases (aminotransferases)

25.39 In transamination, an amino group replaces a keto group in the corresponding _-keto acid.

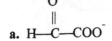
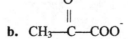
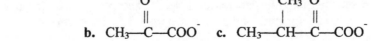

25.40

a. $^-OOC-CH_2-\overset{\overset{\displaystyle O}{\|}}{C}-COO^-$

b. $CH_3-CH_2-\overset{\overset{\displaystyle CH_3}{|}}{CH}-\overset{\overset{\displaystyle O}{\|}}{C}-COO^-$

c. $HO-CH_2-\overset{\overset{\displaystyle O}{\|}}{C}-COO^-$

25.41 In an oxidative deamination, the amino group in an amino acid such as glutamate is removed as an ammonium ion. The reaction requires NAD^+ or $NADP^+$.

$$^-OOC-\overset{\overset{\displaystyle \overset{+}{N}H_3}{|}}{CH}-CH_2-CH_2-COO^- + H_2O + NAD^+ (NADP^+) \xrightarrow{\text{\textit{Glutamate dehydrogenase}}}$$
Glutamate

$$^-OOC-\overset{\overset{\displaystyle O}{\|}}{C}-CH_2-CH_2-COO^- + NH_4^+ + NADH \ (NADPH) + H^+$$
$\_$-Ketoglutarate

25.42 Glutamate forms when the amino group from any of the amino acids is transferred to $\_$-ketoglutarate. In the process of oxidation deamination, glutamate converts that amino group to ammonium ion.

25.43 NH_4^+ is toxic if allowed to accumulate in the liver.

25.44 Urea formation requires two ATP.

25.45 $H_2N-\overset{\overset{\displaystyle O}{\|}}{C}-NH_2$

25.46 $H_2N-\overset{\overset{\displaystyle O}{\|}}{C}-O-\overset{\overset{\displaystyle O}{\|}}{\underset{\underset{\displaystyle O^-}{|}}{P}}-O^-$

25.47 The carbon atom in urea is obtained from the CO_2 produced by the citric acid cycle.

25.48 One ATP is used in each turn of the urea cycle.

25.49 Glucogenic amino acids can be used to produce intermediates for glucogenesis, which is glucose synthesis.

25.50 A ketogenic amino acid generates acetoacetyl CoA or acetyl CoA, which can enter the ketogenesis pathway and form ketone bodies or lipogenesis and form fatty acids.

25.51 a. The three-carbon atom structure of alanine is converted to pyruvate.
b. The four-carbon structure of aspartate is converted to fumarate or oxaloacetate.

    c. Valine is converted to succinyl CoA.

    d. The five-carbon structure from glutamine can be converted to _-ketoglutarate.

25.52   **a.** Acetoacetyl CoA; acetyl CoA   **b.** oxaloacetate

        c. pyruvate   **d.** _-ketoglutarate

25.53   Humans can synthesize only nonessential amino acids.

25.54   The essential amino acids must be obtained from the diet.

25.55   Glutamine synthetase catalyzes the addition of an amino group to glutamate using energy from the hydrolysis of ATP.

25.56   The synthesis of tyrosine requires phenylalanine.

25.57   **Phenylketonurnia**

25.58   PKU is treated with a diet that is low in phenylalanine and high in tyrosine.

25.59   Triacylglycerols are hydrolyzed to monoacylglycerols and fatty acids in the small intestine, which are reformed into triacylglycerols in the intestinal lining for transport as lipoproteins to the tissues.

25.60   Chylomicrons are lipoproteins in which triacylglycerols are coated with proteins.

25.61   Fats can be stored in unlimited amounts in adipose tissue compared to the limited storage of carbohydrates as glycogen.

25.62   Stored fats are mobilized when triacylglycerols in the adipose tissue are converted to fatty acids and glycerol.

25.63   The fatty acids cannot diffuse across the blood-brain barrier.

25.64   Red blood cells do not have mitochondria, which are required for the oxidation of fatty acids.

25.65   **a.** Glycerol is converted to glycerol- 3-phosphate and to dihydroxyacetone phosphate, which can enter glycolysis or gluconeogenesis.

        b. Activation of fatty acids occurs on the outer mitochondrial membrane.

        c. The energy cost is equal to 2 ATP.

        d. Only fatty acyl CoA can move into the intermembrane space for transport by carnitine into the matrix.

25.66   **a.** Activation of a fatty acid involves the reaction of ATP and coenzyme A.

        b. The oxidation of a fatty acid occurs at the _ carbon.

        c. Reaction 1 requires FAD and reaction 3 requires NAD^+.

        d. One cycle produces 5 ATP

25.67   Lauric acid, CH_3—$(CH_2)_{10}$—COOH, is a C_{12} fatty acid. ($C_{12}H_{24}O_2$)

                                              O

                                              ‖

        a. and b. CH_3—$(CH_2)_8$—CH_2—CH_2—C——CoA

                            —   —

        c. Lauryl-CoA + 5 CoA + 5 FAD + 5 NAD^+ + 5 H_2O ⟶

                              6 Acetyl CoA + 5 $FADH_2$ + 5 NADH + 5H^+

   d. Six acetyl CoA units are produced.
   e. Five cycles of _ oxidation are needed.
   f.

activation	$\longrightarrow$	-2 ATP
6 acetyl CoA $\times$ 12	$\longrightarrow$	72 ATP
5 FADH$_2$ $\times$ 2	$\longrightarrow$	10 ATP
5 NADH $\times$ 3	$\longrightarrow$	15ATP
Total		95 ATP

25.68 Caproic acid with 6 carbon atoms will produce 3 acetyl CoA and go through the _ oxidation cycle two times.

activation	$\longrightarrow$	-2 ATP
3 acetyl CoA $\times$ 12	$\longrightarrow$	36 ATP
2 FADH$_2$ $\times$ 2	$\longrightarrow$	4 ATP
2 NADH $\times$ 3	$\longrightarrow$	6 ATP
Total		44 ATP

   When glucose undergoes complete oxidation, a total of 36 ATP are produced.

25.69 **a.** _ oxidation   **b.** _ oxidation
       c. Fatty acid synthesis   **d.** _ oxidation
       e. Fatty acid synthesis   **f.** Fatty acid synthesis

25.70 **a.** fatty acid synthesis   **b.** _ oxidation
       c. _ oxidation   **d.** _ oxidation
       e. _ oxidation   **f.** _ oxidation

25.71 **a.** (1) fatty acid oxidation   **b.** (2) the synthesis of fatty acids

25.72 **a.** (2) the synthesis of fatty acids
       b. (1) _ oxidation

25.73 Ammonium ion is toxic if allowed to accumulate in the liver.

25.74 Ornithine is regenerated.

25.75 **a.** Citrulline   **b.** Carbamoyl phosphate

25.76 **a.** Urea and aspartate are produced from arginine.
       b. Arginine and fumarate are produced from argininosuccinate.

25.77 **a.** The carbon atom structure of valine is converted to pyruvate.
       b. Lysine, a ketogenic amino acid, is converted to acetoacetyl CoA.
       c. The degradation of methionine produces succinyl-CoA.
       d. Glutamate can be converted to five-carbon _-ketoglutarate.

25.78 **a.** acetyl CoA, acetoacetyl CoA   **b.** acetyl CoA
       c. pyruvate   **d.** fumarate, acetoacetyl CoA

25.79 Serine is degraded to pyruvate, which is oxidized to acetyl CoA. The oxidation produces NADH + H$^+$, which provides 3 ATP. In one turn of the citric acid cycle, the acetyl CoA provides 12 ATP. Thus, serine can provide a total of 15 ATP.

25.80 14 kg fat $\times$ 1000 g/kg $\times$ 0.49 moles ATP/g fat = 6900 moles ATP